A HORIZON Guide

# GREAT HISTORIC
# PLACES OF EUROPE

A HORIZON Guide

# GREAT HISTORIC PLACES OF EUROPE

BY THE EDITORS OF
HORIZON MAGAZINE

EDITOR IN CHARGE
BEVERLEY HILOWITZ

INTRODUCTION BY
MARSHALL B. DAVIDSON

PUBLISHED BY American Heritage Publishing Co., Inc., New York
BOOK TRADE DISTRIBUTION BY McGraw-Hill Book Company

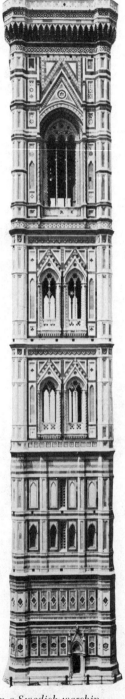

Staff for this Book

**EDITOR**
Beverley Hilowitz

**ASSOCIATE EDITOR**
Margot Brill Higgins

**CONTRIBUTING EDITORS**
Bruce Bohle
Barbara Leish
Alfred Mayor
Wendy Buehr Murphy
Angela Weldon

**COPY EDITOR**
Helen C. Dunn

**DESIGNER**
Sara Krizmanich

**PICTURE EDITOR**
Ellen F. Zeifer

**RESEARCHERS**
Linda K. Johnsen
Donna F. Whiteman

---

American Heritage
Publishing Co., Inc.

**PRESIDENT AND PUBLISHER**
Paul Gottlieb

**GENERAL MANAGER, BOOK DIVISION**
Kenneth W. Leish

**EDITORIAL ART DIRECTOR**
Murray Belsky

Library of Congress Cataloging in Publication Data

Main entry under title:

A Horizon guide: great historic places of Europe.

    Companion vol. to M. B. Davidson's The Horizon book
of great historic places of Europe.
    1. Europe—Description and travel—1971-
— Guide-books.    2. Historic sites—Europe—Guide-books.
I. Hilowitz, Beverley, ed.    II. Horizon (New York,
1958-    )
D909.H73            914'.03'55            74-10941
ISBN  0-07-028915-8

---

HALF-TITLE PAGE: *a 17th-century carved lion from a Swedish warship*
TITLE PAGE: *the Alcazar in Segovia, Spain*
COPYRIGHT PAGE: *the Campanile in Florence, Italy*

# TABLE OF CONTENTS

# INTRODUCTION

Western Europe is virtually a solid mass of historic places. After all, the record has been laid down by several millenniums of civilized activity. Since the last Ice Age peoples of various origins have swarmed across the face of the land, clambering over the mountains, trundling across the plains, pushing up or drifting down the rivers. They came as migrants and conquerors, as plunderers and settlers, and as merchants and adventurers. Hordes came down from the north and east, hungry for the sun and the warmth, the glamour and the treasure, of the early civilized Mediterranean world. Others moved up from the south along ancient trade routes to traffic in commodities from the north, and to linger and settle in fertile valleys. They warred for advantages they could not otherwise gain, and at major crossroads of their interminable traffic they founded cities. Gradually nationalities formed about kindred people or were given shape by strong rulers. And century after century, successive cultural deposits were laid down that testified in material form to human accomplishment and aspiration. There is all too much evidence of human conflicts as well—crumbled fortifications, hilltop keeps with their moats and dungeons and towers, once-scarred battlefields grown green again with time. No comparable area on this globe has such a multiplicity of tangible reminders of a rich and varied past. Greek temples of pure classic strain are neighbor to vast Roman arenas, and these in turn can be seen from towering Gothic cathedrals that after five or six centuries still perform their original purpose, within the confines of cities that in other ways have become up-to-date world centers. Americans have ancestors whose lives were once firmly rooted amid these old and varied works of man. America is indeed heir to the human experience they so picturesquely represent and recall. And every year Americans by the hundreds of thousands find their way to one or another part of Europe to satisfy their natural curiosity about the historic places that await their visit, as well as to profit from a familiarity with ways of life and scenes that hold boundless interest for the appreciative tourist.

The entries in this book have been selected to guide the tourist toward a wide variety of experience. He who chooses the road to Santiago de Compostela in northwest Spain is almost surely following some route that for centuries was thronged with devout pilgrims trudging to that shrine of Saint James from every corner of Europe. (Dante likened their numbers to the myriad stars that form the Milky Way.) If a pilgrimage is the goal, the way to Canterbury Cathedral is haunted by the presence of Chaucer's merry company heading for that sacred spot before the altar where the saintly Thomas à Becket was cut down in cold blood in 1170. The greatest of all Christian shrines is, of course, Saint Peter's Basilica in Rome, a monument of such impressive splendor, so many hallowed associations, and such rich history that it stands apart in the world as a pilgrimage center—and as a tourist attraction.

The tides of European history have often been turned by the blood of warriors. It is impossible to visit the site of the Battle of Hastings and not speculate on how vastly different English history would have been these past many centuries had Harold not fallen in that narrow defeat before the invading Normans. If William had fallen instead, as was quite as likely, he would now be remembered simply as William the Bastard, rather than as William the Conqueror

—if remembered at all. It is hard to recognize the quiet, green countryside at Waterloo as a crossroads of destiny where in the autumn
of 1815 hundreds of thousands of troops hurled shot at one another
until Napoleon's dwindling ranks broke and fled, leaving the little
emperor's shattered dreams of glory on the battlefield along with a
host of bleeding corpses. On the picturesque coast of Normandy,
at Omaha Beach, within sight of lush fields and peacefully brooding
cows, half-sunken hulls and twisted metal debris have been delib-
erately left as grim memorials to the Allies of World War II who
breached the German defenses there and thus signaled the end of
Hitler's extravagant claims to power.

The studied, formal elegance of European architecture at its best
is a revelation to most Americans, unused to such display at home.
In Paris the Place de la Concorde, with its statuary, fountains, esplanade, and handsome flanking buildings that cover one hundred
thousand square yards, is possibly the most celebrated urban space
in the world—which is not to mention its tree-lined vistas that look
up the Champs-Élysées to the Arc de Triomphe in one direction,
and through the gardens of the Tuileries to the Louvre in the other.
On a more intimate scale, the late medieval structures that enclose
the Grand-Place at Brussels provide a gemlike setting for urban
affairs that in its separate way is also unrivaled as a public place.
At Bath, England, the noble Royal Crescent, conjoined dwellings
that present a uniform façade for more than a thousand yards,
marked a somewhat controversial innovation in eighteenth-cen-
tury town planning. Close to Beau Nash's fashionable spa (once a
Roman watering place) and to a popular museum of American decorative art, the crescent remains a prospect that delights the eye and
recalls a particular phase of English history.

The diversity of cultural attractions in Europe is virtually endless.
Of the scores upon scores of museums, three of the largest—the
British Museum, the Louvre, and the Uffizi—alone house many of
the greatest masterpieces ever created throughout the world at
large. To draw closer to the creative spirit one can visit the home of
El Greco at Toledo, of Rembrandt in Amsterdam, of Beethoven in
Bonn, of Mozart in Salzburg, or, considering artists in another me-
dium, the home of Shakespeare at Stratford-on-Avon, of Hans
Christian Andersen in Odense, or of Goethe in Frankfurt, among
many others. Europe has always been entertaining, of course. From
the ancient Greek theater at Epidaurus to the famous and resplen-
dent opera houses at Milan, Paris, and Vienna, a stage has ever been
set for dramatic and musical performances—performances that in
season continue to draw international audiences. In the end, Europe presents a kaleidoscopic pageant of human imagination and
of human enterprise in all directions, set in an infinitely varied
countryside.

How the tourist can best find his way to one site or another, and
how he can best understand what he will witness when he gets
there, are problems to which this guide is addressed. More than
a thousand historic sites are alphabetically listed in the following
pages. Many more could be added, but not without making the
guide cumbersome and more complicated than is desirable. (It has
been designed to travel with you.) The sites here represent a highly
selective list, based on their relative interest and importance.
There are enough entries, however, to keep an earnest tourist busy
for many seasons, and to provide him with a representative picture
of the land and its people, of its past and its present.

M.B.D.

GREECE

**AEGINA,** *in the Saronic Gulf of the Aegean Sea, 15 nautical miles from Piraeus*
About 1000 B.C. the Dorians minted the first Greek coins on this
island. The most impressive ancient monument on Aegina is the
well-preserved **Temple of Aphaia.** Situated on a terrace in the
northeast of Aegina and surrounded by pine trees, the temple was
built by Greeks to commemorate their victory over the Persians at
Salamis (*see*) in 480 B.C. Twenty-five columns remain standing.
Other classical ruins include the fifth-century B.C. **Temple of
Aphrodite,** and an **Oros,** an open-air altar to Zeus on a mountaintop.
Aegina also contains the ruins of the medieval town of **Palaiokhora,**
where residents of the island took refuge from pirates. Some 40
Byzantine churches survive. During the Greek war of independence
Aegina served briefly (1828–29) as the capital of the Greek nation.

## ATHENS AND VICINITY

ACROPOLIS, *accessible from the western slope*
The ancient ruins atop this 512-foot hill comprise Athens' most
impressive landmark. The city of Athens is said to have been
founded on these heights long before the days of recorded history
by the mythological serpent-god Cecrops, who was succeeded by
the serpent-man Erechtheus. Over the centuries, from the Mycenaean period (1400–1200 B.C.) onward, as the city gradually
expanded beyond the rocky plateau down around the foot of the
hill, the Acropolis remained the citadel of Athens, the seat of temples and sanctuaries where people came to pray and seek refuge in
time of war. During the Persian Wars, at the beginning of the
fifth century B.C., the temples of the Acropolis were destroyed by
Xerxes' armies. For nearly half a century the Acropolis lay in ruins,
until Pericles, whose victories over the Persians gave Athens
hegemony over the other Greek city-states, ushered in the Golden
Age of Athens. In a vast rebuilding program he lavished enormous
sums to adorn the Acropolis with masterpieces of architecture and
art—many of which remain standing in various stages of preserva-
tion today. Upon ascending the Acropolis, the visitor passes through
the porticoes of the **Propylaea,** the imposing gateway to the sacred
precincts of the summit. Built by the architect Mnesicles between
437 and 432 B.C., it was not completed because of the outbreak of
the Peloponnesian War. To the right of the Propylaea on a high
platform stands the diminutive **Temple of Niké Apteros** (Wingless
Victory), constructed to commemorate Greece's victory over Persia.
Subsequently destroyed by the Turks during their occupation of
Greece between the 15th and 19th centuries, the building has been
reconstructed. A path, or **Sacred Way,** formerly lined with statues
and now littered with slabs of marble and broken columns, leads
to the **Parthenon,** erected by architects Ictinus and Callicrates between 447 and 432 B.C. The Parthenon's simplicity, grandeur, and
harmonious proportions make the temple the most perfect example
of Doric architecture in existence. Dedicated to the goddess
Athena, guardian of Athens, this Pentelic marble structure, also
known as the Virgin's Chamber, was adorned by the sculptor
Phidias, who created the surviving portion of the interior frieze,
which represents the Panathenaic procession in honor of the goddess Athena. The chambers of the Parthenon were filled with
bullion and priceless ornaments, and the building served as a
public treasury. During the early Christian era the Parthenon was
converted into a church and later, under the Turks, was turned into
a mosque with a minaret. In 1687, during the Venetian siege of
Athens, much of the Parthenon, being used at the time as a Turkish

*Page 9. Top: the Parthenon on the Acropolis in Athens. Left: Doric Tholos at
Delphi. Center right, top: Venetian fortress at Methone. Center right, bottom:
Lion Gate at Mycenae. Below: the theater at Epidaurus*

gunpowder magazine, was reduced to ruins when it was struck by a shell. Fragments of the metopes, friezes, and other sculptures were salvaged in 1801 by Lord Elgin, who removed them to England; they are now displayed in the British Museum. North of the Parthenon stands the **Erechtheum,** the most important religious shrine on the Acropolis and the site of the legendary contest between Athena and Poseidon for the patronage of the city. Athena won by causing an olive tree to spring from the ground at this spot. The southern portico of this elegant example of Ionic architecture is supported not by columns, but by six maidens known as caryatids. During the Ottoman period a Turkish governor housed his harem here. The **Acropolis Museum,** near the east end of the Parthenon, houses rare treasures of Attic art uncovered here.

### AGORA, *under the north side of the Acropolis*

Encompassing six acres, the Agora served as the commercial, political, and social center of Athens from early in the sixth century B.C. until the city was sacked by barbarians in A.D. 267. Surrounded by public buildings and traversed by major urban roads, the open market square not only was thronged with citizens conducting day-to-day business, but was a favorite forum of philosophers, poets, and entertainers as well. The Panathenaic procession crossed the Agora annually on its way to the Acropolis (*see*). Excavations here have uncovered the foundations of such important municipal structures as the **Tholos,** Athens' administrative headquarters, the **Bouleuterion,** where the 400 senators convened, the **Metroon,** which housed the city archives, and the **Stoa of Zeus,** where Socrates discoursed. The **Stoa of Attalus,** donated in the second century B.C. by the king of Pergamum in Asia Minor as a memorial to Greek culture, has been reconstructed. The two-story shedlike edifice originally contained a 382-foot-long colonnade that offered businessmen protection from the elements; each floor had 21 rooms, which were used for shops and offices and which currently house an archaeological museum.

### ARCH OF HADRIAN, *east of the Acropolis off Amalias Avenue*

In the second century A.D. Emperor Hadrian erected this landmark to demarcate ancient Athens from the newly built "City of Hadrian" beyond it. The monument consists of a Roman arch surmounted by Corinthian pilasters, an architrave, and pediment.

### AREOPAGUS (HILL OF ARES), *100 yards west of the Acropolis*

According to ancient myth, the council of gods sat on this eminence and tried Ares, the god of war, for murdering one of Poseidon's sons. In the first judgment ever to be handed down at a public trial, Ares was acquitted. Beginning in the fifth century B.C., criminal court sessions for homicide cases were held on the Areopagus, by which name Greece's highest court is still known. A chasm at the site is also associated with the legendary Eumenides, or Furies, who pursued Orestes from Mycenae to Athens after he murdered his mother, Clytemnestra. In A.D. 54 Saint Paul preached to the Athenians from this slope and converted the senator Dionysus— later canonized as Saint Denis, patron saint of Athens.

### CHORAGIC MONUMENT OF LYSICRATES, *below eastern walls of the Acropolis on Lysikratou Street*

This small circular marble building was raised in the fourth century B.C. in honor of a group of musicians who won a contest in the nearby Theater of Dionysus (*see*). During the 17th century the edifice was converted into a library on the premises of a French Capuchin monastery, where Lord Byron later resided during his first visit to Athens. Theresa Makris, who lived in a house overlooking the monastery, inspired the "maid of Athens" in Byron's poem.

### DIPYLON GATE, *off Apostolou Pavlou Street*

This rectangular court with its twin gates, constructed under Lycurgus between 338 and 326 B.C., served as the principal portal of Athens. Travelers taking the road to Piraeus or the Sacred Way to Eleusis left the city through the Dipylon. The gateway was also a popular haunt of prostitutes of the period, who offered their charms to weary travelers entering the city. On either side of the Dipylon is situated the **Ceramicos,** a cemetery that served Athens from early in the Bronze Age until the fourth century B.C. and still contains interesting sepulchral monuments.

### MONASTERY OF DAPHNI, *8 kilometers west on the road to Corinth*

Enclosed within tall battlemented walls, this 11th-century monastery is an outstanding example of Byzantine architecture and contains the finest mosaics in Greece. In 1205 Daphni was occupied by Frankish crusaders, who were finally expelled by the Turks in 1458. The monastery was subsequently returned to the Greeks. During the Greek war of independence (1821–29) Daphni served as a fortress. Standing today are the church of the convent with its partially restored mosaics and a portion of the monks' cells.

### PNYX, *northwest of Philopapus Hill, opposite the entrance to the Acropolis*

In ancient times the Athenian citizen body assembled on a semicircular terrace at the summit of this low rocky hill. Such orators as Solon, Themistocles, Pericles, and Demosthenes addressed their audiences from a platform consisting of a solid rectangular block projecting from a wall of rock. Today the Pnyx is the site of Sound and Light shows, presented in three languages during the summer.

### PRISON OF SOCRATES, *Philopapus Hill facing the entrance to the Acropolis*

Tradition has it that this cave served as the prison where the philosopher Socrates (470?–399 B.C.) was confined for corrupting Athenian youth with his advanced ideas on religion. The philosopher is believed to have quaffed the fatal goblet of hemlock here.

### STADIUM, *Queen Olga Avenue*

This modern stadium of white Pentelic marble is a replica of the ancient Panathenaic stadium designed by Lycurgus in the fourth century B.C. and completed by Herodes Atticus, a public-spirited Roman of the second century A.D. The stadium contains a tunnel believed to have been used for animals during Roman gladiatorial bouts. Since 1896 the stadium has been the scene of the revived Olympic games in Greece.

### TEMPLE OF OLYMPIAN ZEUS, *off Amalias Avenue*

Begun in 530 B.C. under the tyrant Pisistratus and completed seven centuries later in A.D. 130 by the Roman emperor Hadrian, this edifice—354 feet long, 135 feet wide, and 90 feet high—was the largest temple in Greece, and perhaps in the world. In the fourth century B.C. Aristotle designated the unfinished structure a wonder, comparable to the pyramids of Egypt. Alaric's Goths destroyed the temple in the fourth century A.D., and its masonry was used as building material during the Middle Ages. Today only the ruins of 16 columns, 56 feet high, survive.

THEATER OF DIONYSUS, *southern slope of the Acropolis*
Begun about 400 B.C. on the site of two earlier theaters and altered over the years, this semicircular stone theater was once the center of dramatic activity in Athens. Here the tragedies of Aeschylus, Sophocles, and Euripides were performed. During the Roman period the lower row of seats was built for priests and distinguished persons. Emperor Nero added the sculptures at the face of the stage. The theater could accommodate 30,000 spectators.

THESEUM, *west of the Agora off Apostolou Pavlou Street*
Erected about 460–50 B.C., this Doric temple is one of the best-preserved structures of ancient Greece. Erroneously called the Theseum because the frieze depicts the exploits of Theseus, the temple was actually dedicated to Hephaestus, the god of artisans and blacksmiths. In the fifth century A.D. the edifice was converted into the Greek Orthodox church of Saint George.

TOWER OF THE WINDS, *western slope of the Acropolis*
Constructed in the first century B.C., this 40-foot-tall octagonal tower, also known as the Water Clock of Andronicos, was equipped with a hydraulic clock, sundial, and weather vane. Its eight sides, sculpted with figures representing the winds, face the direction of the eight winds into which the compass was divided. During the Turkish occupation the structure served as an Islamic school.

VAVRONA (BRAURON), *along the Marathon coast of Attica near Markopoulon*
The remains of the **Shrine of Artemis,** virgin goddess of birth and fertility, have been uncovered and partially restored at this site. According to myth, Iphigenia, daughter of Agamemnon, was rescued by her brother, Orestes, from the land of Taurus on the Black Sea and was taken to this spot, where she became a high priestess of Artemis. Iphigenia's tomb has been identified here. During the fifth century B.C. daughters from the best Athenian families were taught complicated ritual dances in a stoa (colonnaded portico) on the premises, of which only the foundations remain.

BASSAE, *near Phigalia in the central Peloponnesus*
Dedicated to Apollo by the Phigalians in 418 B.C. in gratitude for saving them from a pestilence, the temple at Bassae is one of the best-preserved of ancient Greece. This impressive monument by the architect of the Parthenon (*see Acropolis*) stands in solitude against a backdrop of wild mountains.

CAPE SOUNION, *64 kilometers from Athens via Laurion*
High on a rocky promontory at the southernmost tip of Attica stands an ancient walled acropolis crowned by the ruins of the **Temple of Poseidon,** which was built by Pericles in the fifth century B.C. to replace an earlier structure destroyed by the Persians. In the 19th century Lord Byron carved his name on one of the twelve remaining Doric columns of the temple. The panorama of sea and islands from this platform, especially at sunset, is one of the most spectacular in Greece.

**CHAERONEA,** *109 kilometers from Athens on the way to Delphi in Boeotia*
This was the scene of the famous battle of 338 B.C. in which Philip II of Macedon and his son Alexander defeated the armies of Athens and Thebes. Two later battles occurred at this site—in 86 B.C. the Roman general Sulla defeated the generals of Mithridates VI of Pontus (Asia Minor), and in A.D. 1311 Franks under the duke of Athens were conquered by Catalans. Today a colossal stone lion commemorates the Thebans slain in battle, and a mound marks the spot where Macedonian soldiers are buried.

**CORFU,** *in the Ionian Sea, accessible by boat from Piraeus and Egoumenitsa*
Colonized by the Corinthians in 734 B.C., this island, known in ancient times as Corcyra, preserves many monuments erected by the successive nations that occupied it. In 432 B.C. Corfu declared war on Corinth and became an ally of Athens, thus precipitating the Peloponnesian War. Alexander the Great seized the island in the fourth century B.C. Corfu was ruled in turn by the Romans, Byzantines, Normans, Venetians, French, and British before it was ceded to Greece in 1864. Reminders of Corfu's past include the ancient **Temple of Artemis,** on the peninsula of Paleopolis; the **Church of Hagios Spyridon,** containing the body of the island's patron saint; the **Old Venetian Fort** (built during the Venetian occupation, 1386–1797), to the north of the harbor of Corfu; and the **Achilleum Palace,** the residence of Elizabeth, empress of Austria, who moved to Corfu after the suicide of her son, Crown Prince Rudolf, in 1889; the palace was subsequently purchased by Kaiser Wilhelm II.

**CORINTH.** *See* OLD CORINTH

**CRETE**
KNOSSOS PALACE, *about 6 kilometers southeast of Herakleion*
Built about the 16th century B.C. on the site of a smaller palace that had been erected 400 years earlier and destroyed by an earthquake, this structure is the most impressive of the Minoan palaces. It represents the climax of one of the most brilliant and sophisticated civilizations the world had yet known. Dating back to the third millennium B.C., the history of the Minoan kingdom is inextricably associated with the legendary saga of King Minos (son of Zeus and Europa), Ariadne, Theseus, and the Minotaur, a ferocious half-beast, half-man. The successive Minoan ruler-priests adopted the title of Minos and practiced a form of religion in which bulls had a prominent part. About 1800 B.C. one King Minos united Crete politically and established a vast maritime empire that included the Cyclades, the Peloponnesus, and parts of Sicily and mainland Greece. The golden days of Minoan civilization came to an abrupt end in the 15th century B.C., either as a result of an invasion by subject peoples or destruction by an earthquake, or a combination of both. The palace of Knossos was reduced to charred ruins in a devastating fire about 1400 B.C. By 1200 B.C. Crete was again divided into warring, primitive city-states. In 1899 the English archaeologist Sir Arthur Evans discovered the remains of Knossos, and he subsequently reconstructed much of the palace. Possessing a labyrinthine floor plan, the palace contains a complex of royal chambers grouped around a central quadrangle; many of the rooms display restored wall frescoes. A grand staircase leads to a throne room, which contains the oldest throne in Europe. In the vicinity are the **Royal Villa, Theater** area, **Little Palace, viaduct,** ancient **Hostel, House of the High Priest, Royal Temple Tomb,** and the 15th-cen-

*The entrance to the Minoan Palace of Knossos on Crete, which is adorned with frescoes of vase bearers*

tury B.C. **Tomb of Isopata.** Other remains of Knossos are exhibited at the **Archaeological Museum** in Herakleion.

GORTYNA, *45 kilometers southwest of Herakleion*
The most important city of Dorian Crete (from the 12th century B.C.), Gortyna became the capital of Roman Crete after the Romans occupied the island in 66 B.C. It was finally destroyed by the Saracens in the eighth century A.D. The site contains many ruins, and the famous inscription known as the Code of Gortyn, a code of family law, was found here.

HERAKLEION, *accessible by daily plane and boat from Athens*
Known in the Middle Ages as Candia—derived from the Greek word for "moat"—Herakleion was occupied in 1204 by the Venetians, who for nearly 500 years used the town as their principal stronghold and port in the east Mediterranean. In 1669, after a prolonged 24-year siege, the Venetians under Francesco Morosini finally surrendered Crete to the Turkish vizier Ahmed Kuprili. The Turks ruled Crete for the next 200 years, until the island was granted home rule; Crete was incorporated into Greece in 1913. Among the Venetian monuments preserved at Herakleion are a baroque **fountain** in the center of town, decorated with the lions of Saint Mark, and the old **ramparts,** constructed in 1206 around Herakleion's perimeter and among the longest walls in the world. There are also a few Turkish remains.

PHAESTOS, *55 kilometers southwest of Herakleion*
Situated on a hill commanding a splendid view of the plain of Mesara, the conglomeration of Minoan buildings that stood here resembled Knossos Palace (*see*). Phaestos was destroyed by the rival city of Gortyna (*see*). Today only foundations remain. At nearby **Hagia Triada** by the sea are the remains of still another Minoan structure, probably a baronial villa.

**DELOS,** *in the Cyclades Islands, accessible by boat from Mykonos*

Situated in the center of the Aegean Sea, Delos was the most important island of antiquity. It was the legendary birthplace of the god Apollo, and about 800 B.C. it became his holy sanctuary for Ionian Greeks. In 540 B.C. Delos came under Athenian influence when the tyrant Pisistratus purified the island by removing the remains of all people buried here. During the period of Athenian hegemony after the defeat of the Persians in the fifth century B.C., Delos became the treasury of the Delian League, a confederacy of Greek city-states organized for mutual defense against further Persian invasions. In 423 B.C. the Athenians repurified Delos and deported all living residents to Asia to prevent the sanctuary from becoming defiled. In Hellenistic times, from 315 to 166 B.C., when Delos was independent, and after 166 B.C., when Athens again dominated the island, Delos became an important commercial port for vessels passing between Greece, Italy, and the Levant. Delos was destroyed by Mithridates VI of Pontus in 88 B.C. and never fully rebuilt. Today the **Sanctuary of Apollo** contains remains of the **Temple of the Athenians,** a sixth-century B.C. archaic temple, a group of treasuries, and the **Portico of Antigonus,** a Macedonian king. On a terrace are five archaic stone lions, symbolic guardians of the sanctuary. At the summit of Mount Kynthos are the **Sanctuaries of Zeus and Athena.** On the west slope of the mountain are the ruins of the late Hellenistic residential city, which include a **Theater** and several residences—the **Houses of Dionysus,** the **Trident,** and the **Masks**—which contain exceptionally fine frescoes.

**DELPHI,** *161 kilometers from Athens on a spur of Mount Parnassus in Boeotia*

Situated upon what the ancients called the navel of the earth, Delphi was the site of the sanctuary of Apollo and the most renowned oracle of all time. At a sacred spot in the Temple of Apollo there would emanate from a fissure in the earth mysterious exhalations, which were received by a priestess who would go into a trance or frenzy and make incoherent utterances; these were then interpreted by a priest. From remotest antiquity until A.D. 381, when the Christian emperor Theodosius I proscribed paganism, suppliants would consult the oracle on matters of religion, politics, and individual morality. Although the keynote of the prophesies was their ambiguity, their influence on men's destinies through their interpretation was enormous. Today an ancient wall around the sanctuary of Apollo encloses ruins of monuments dedicated to various Greek states and some 20 treasuries, where the wealth and archives of the city-states were housed; the **Treasury of the Athenians** has been reconstructed from its original marble blocks. Only the podium and peristyle remain of the **Temple of Apollo.** Above the temple stands a **Theater** built in the fourth century B.C. where dramatic performances are still held, and a **Stadium** where the athletic contests known as the Pythian games took place every four years. East of the sanctuary is the **Castalian Spring,** where pilgrims purified themselves before visiting the oracle. Opposite the precincts of Apollo are a group of ruins called the **Marmaria,** consisting of two **Temples of Athena,** a Doric **Tholos,** and traces of a **Gymnasium.** The **Museum** at Delphi displays the world-renowned bronze statue of a charioteer and exhibits of archaic sculpture.

**DODONA,** *19 kilometers southwest of Ioannina in Epirus*

The seat of an ancient oracle dating from as early as 2000 B.C.—even older than the oracle at Delphi (*see*)—Dodona has been considered the cradle of Greek civilization. Dodona became the earliest sanctuary dedicated to the cult of Zeus in the 13th century B.C.; by interpreting the rustling of leaves on a sacred oak, priests supposedly divined the god's will. In the *Iliad* Homer described Achilles praying to the Dodona Zeus. Alaric's Goths destroyed the **Temple of Zeus** in the sixth century A.D., and today only the foundations and a few Doric columns remain. A **Theater**, built in the third century B.C. by the king of Epirus, Pyrrhus—who won a costly "pyrrhic" victory over the Romans (279 B.C.) at Asculum—has been restored.

**ELEUSIS,** *20 kilometers northwest of Athens on the road to Corinth*
The famous Eleusinian Mysteries, or secret religious rites in honor of Demeter, the goddess of fertility, and her daughter Persephone, were celebrated at this site throughout antiquity. According to legend, Eleusis was where all agriculture originated; Demeter taught the Eleusinian king Triptolemos her rites and sent his son to teach the rest of mankind the secrets of tilling the soil. The annual performance of the Mysteries probably included an enactment of the story of Demeter, orgiastic dances, songs, and spectacular torchlight processions. Among the ruins of the sanctuary today are the foundations of a **Temple of Demeter** and the great inner chamber of the recently excavated **Telesterion**, or Hall of the Mysteries.

**EPIDAURUS,** *32 kilometers northeast of Nauplia in the Peloponnesus*
Epidaurus was the most famous shrine of Asclepius, the god of medicine (*see also Kos*). The sick from all over ancient Greece came to the sanctuary to consult the god, who, it was believed, effected cures or remedies through dreams. However, the healing of various illnesses was not entrusted to faith alone; medical treatment was also prescribed here. The remarkable curative powers of the god are attested to by the numerous votive tablets left by the healed. In the **Sacred Precinct of Epidaurus or Hieron** are the foundations and ruins of such buildings as the Doric **Temple of Asclepius,** built about 460 B.C., the **Abaton,** an early version of a hospital ward, and the round **Tholos.** Designed at the end of the fourth century B.C. by the architect Polyclitus, the **Theater** is the best preserved in Greece. Containing 55 tiers of seats and accommodating 14,000 spectators, the theater boasts such perfect acoustics that it is the scene of the Festival of Epidaurus, held here every summer, in which ancient dramas are revived. A **Museum** contains reconstructions of the Tholos, temple, and gateway to the Temple of Artemis.

**HYDRA,** *in the western Aegean Sea, 36 nautical miles from Piraeus*
The tall, stately houses in the town of Hydra were built about 1800 by one-time mountaineers who had amassed great wealth by running the British blockade during the Napoleonic Wars. Each structure was a self-contained establishment with its own bakery, storeroom, and cistern—ready, if need be, to resist a siege. Hydra's seafarers later distinguished themselves during the Greek war of independence. Today some of Hydra's historical mansions may be visited during the summer.

**IOANNINA (JANINA, YANNINA),** *446 kilometers northwest of Athens in Epirus*
Founded by the Byzantine emperor Justinian in A.D. 527–528, Ioannina became an important town after the 11th century, when the walls of the **Citadel** were repaired by a Norman prince who seized the city in 1082. In 1430 the Turks took Ioannina. An abortive rebellion in 1612 by the Greeks led to their expulsion from the

citadel and their replacement by Jews. Late in the 18th century the Albanian despot Ali Pasha established his rule at Ioannina—then becoming a center of Hellenic culture—and for a time governed independently of the Turkish sultan. Later Ali Pasha relied on his Greeks subjects in his rebellion against the Turks; from December, 1820, until January, 1822, the so-called Lion of Ioannina withstood a siege by the Turks in the citadel until he was captured and executed. Today **Ali Pasha's Tomb,** near the 15th-century **Fethié Mosque,** as well as the 17th-century **Mosque of Aslan Pasha** and the citadel, with its old Jewish quarter, may be visited.

**IOS,** *in the southern Aegean Sea, Cyclades Islands*
Homer, the great epic poet who flourished about 850 B.C., is believed to be buried in a mound on the side of this island opposite the town of Ios.

**KOS,** *in the southeastern Aegean Sea, Dodecanese Islands*
This island was the birthplace (about 460 B.C.) of Hippocrates, the "father of medicine." According to legend, an ancient plane tree in the town of Kos is a descendant of the tree under which Hippocrates ministered to his patients. In the third century B.C. Berenice, wife of Ptolemy I, gave birth to Ptolemy II, king of Egypt 285–246 B.C., on Kos. Preserved here today are the **Asclepieion,** the Hellenistic sanctuary of Asclepius, god of medicine, the medieval **Castle of the Knights of Rhodes,** guarding the harbor, and the 18th-century **Mosque of the Loggia,** made of marble from a Byzantine basilica, which in turn had been constructed from the remains of a Hellenistic arcade.

**LECHAINA VICINITY**
CASTEL TORNESE, *on the plain of Elis west of Lechaina in the Peloponnesus*
Erected by Geoffroi de Villehardouin in 1222 to defend the important Frankish port of Clarenza, this hexagonal castle is an impressive example of French medieval architecture. Castel Tornese derives its name from the Tournois coins that were minted there by the Franks. Clarenza was eventually taken from the Franks and destroyed by Constantine XI Palaeologus, the last Byzantine emperor (1448–53). The bailey, keep, and vaulted gallery of the Castel Tornese are still intact.

**MARATHON BATTLEFIELD,** *40 kilometers northeast of Athens in Attica*
This site between the Gulf of Marathon and Mount Pentelikon was the scene of the famous battle in 490 B.C. between the Athenians under Miltiades and the invading Persian armies of Darius I. The Greek hoplites (infantry soldiers) defeated a much larger force of heavily armored Persians. The runner who raced the long distance back to the Acropolis (*see*) of Athens to bring news of the victory and expired upon reaching his destination gave birth to the term "marathon," a test of endurance. The site of the most ferocious fighting is marked by a mound, or soros, where the Athenians killed in battle were buried.

**MEGALOPOLIS,** *24 kilometers south of Tripolis in the central Peloponnesus*
This city was founded by the great Theban general Epaminondas in 370 B.C., the year after he conquered the Spartans at the Battle of Leuctra. Boasting walls 5½ miles long and the largest theater in Greece, Megalopolis served as the center of the Arcadian League.

It was finally razed by Spartan King Cleomenes III (235–219 B.C.); today only ruins remain.

**METEORA MONASTERIES,** *at the northwest corner of the Thessalian plain near Kalambaka*

On rocky formations resembling gigantic pillars that rise 500 to 600 feet above the valley floor stand the ruins of the renowned monasteries of Meteora, which were erected during the troubled and warlike years of the 14th century as a refuge for hermits and other pious people. Originally there were more than 20 monasteries, and today several remain, including **Saint Stephen, Hagia Trias, Saint Baarlaam,** and the **Great Meteoron,** on whose premises is the beautiful **Church of the Metamorphosis.**

**METHONE,** *on the coast of Messenia in the southwest Peloponnesus*

Situated at a strategic site along the coast, this medieval fortress was built early in the 1200s by Crusaders and Venetians. Methone, and nearby Korone on the other side of the western prong of the Peloponnesus, represented the first Venetian footholds on the Greek mainland and were known as the eyes of the republic.

**MISSOLONGHI,** *via Highway E19 on the Gulf of Patras in Acarnania*

Situated on the edge of a lagoon, Missolonghi became famous throughout Europe because of the long siege—May, 1825, to April, 1826—it heroically sustained against Turko-Egyptian armies during the Greek war of independence. The inhabitants, on the verge of starvation, made a last effort to break through enemy lines on April 22, 1826, but most perished in the attempt. The incident aroused sympathy in Europe and America for the Greek cause. Today the **Tabia,** a memorial cemetery, contains a monument to the philhellenes from all nations who died fighting for Greek liberty. Preserved here are the **house** where Lord Byron, who was serving as commander of the Greek forces, died of fever, and two **forts** that played an important role in the siege.

**MISTRA,** *8 kilometers southwest of Sparta in the Peloponnesus*

Founded in 1249 by the Frankish lord Guillaume de Villehardouin, this medieval town was seized in 1263 by the Byzantine emperor Michael Palaeologus. For the next century Mistra remained the capital of a Byzantine despotat and the center of resistance against the Franks in the surrounding region. The Byzantine rulers succeeded in reconquering most of the Peloponnesus; by the 15th century Mistra boasted a population of 40,000 and was one of the liveliest cultural and intellectual centers of the Byzantine Empire. Mistra fell to the Ottoman Turks in 1460. The stronghold was abandoned after an earthquake in 1850 and today is known as the dead town. Mistra's ruins include the **Frankish Castle,** the Byzantine churches of **Pantanassa** and **Saint Demetrius,** both of which contain superb frescoes, and the monastery of **Peribleptos.**

**MONEMVASIA,** *on the Aegean Sea, about 96 kilometers southeast of Sparta in the Peloponnesus*

Built upon a massive rock and known as the Gibraltar of Medieval Greece, this impregnable Byzantine and Venetian fortress served as a refuge for the Greeks in their wars with the Franks. For centuries the town of Monemvasia—called Malvoisie by the Franks and Malmsey by the English—was celebrated for its vineyards, until the arrival of the Turks in the 15th century. According to tradition, when the duke of Clarence was condemned to death by Edward IV, he asked "to be drowned in a cask of Malmsey."

## MOUNT ATHOS, *on the Chalcidice Peninsula in Macedonia*

Founded by Basilian monks in the tenth century, this monastic community on the Hagion Oros (Holy Mountain) has maintained its autonomy under Byzantine emperors, Ottoman sultans, and the modern Greek government. At Mount Athos today are 20 monasteries administered from the center of Karyai by a representative committee under the direct rule of the patriarch at Constantinople. Many medieval Byzantine manuscripts are preserved here. Females of any species are not permitted on the premises.

## MOUNT OLYMPUS, *about 25 kilometers southwest of Katerine in Thessaly*

The cloud-capped summit of this rugged 9,570-foot-high mountain was the legendary home of the pantheon of Greek deities. In historic times the mountain was of strategic importance, barring access from Macedonia to Thessaly and being by-passed only at the **Petra Pass** and **Vale of Tempe**. Today Mount Olympus, with its **Chapel of Elias**, is a sacred Christian shrine and place of pilgrimage.

## MYCENAE, *about 10 kilometers northeast of Argos in the Peloponnesus*

Serving as a fortified royal residence from as early as 3000 B.C., the citadel of Mycenae was the home of the ill-fated family of Atreus —made famous in the tragedies of Aeschylus and Sophocles—who occupied the premises at the time of the Trojan War in about 1200 B.C. Excavations here have corroborated the general reliability of tradition and legend. Homer's "Golden Mycenae" became a reality when archaeologists uncovered art treasures of gold and ivory, which are now in the Archaeological Museum in Athens. The remains of the royal city include the beehive-shaped **Tombs of Agamemnon** (also known as the Treasury of Atreus) **and Clytemnestra**, outside the reconstructed walls of the citadel, the **Lion Gate** entrance to the citadel, and six shaft graves, or **Royal Tombs**, inside the walls of Mycenae.

## NAUPAKTOS, *on north shore of the Gulf of Corinth in Acarnania*

Known as Lepanto during the Middle Ages, Naupaktos was the port from which the Turkish fleet, in 1571, sailed to meet the navies of Venice and Spain under Don John of Austria in the famous Battle of Lepanto at the entrance to the Gulf of Corinth. The Turks were soundly defeated, and their naval supremacy in the Mediterranean ended. Today **Venetian fortifications** and a **castle** have been preserved.

## NAUPLIA, *near the head of the Gulf of Argolis in the Peloponnesus*

Founded by the legendary Nauplius, father of Palamedes—who served with Agamemnon during the Trojan War and who reputedly invented dice, mathematics, and the alphabet—this town was important during the medieval and modern periods of Greek history. The Venetians occupied Nauplia from 1388 until 1540, during which time they enlarged the fortress known as the **Palamidi**, begun earlier by Crusaders. After the liberation of Greece from the Turks, Nauplia became the first capital of Greece. The first governor of Greece was assassinated outside the **Church of Saint Spyridon** in 1831, and from 1832 to 1834 Otto, first king of the Hellenes, resided in the Palamidi. Another **Venetian fort** on the island of **Bourtzi** at the entrance to the harbor is now a hotel.

**NICOPOLIS,** *on the Ionian Sea near Preveza in Epirus*

This town was established in 31 B.C. by the Roman emperor Augustus to commemorate his victory over Mark Antony and Cleopatra at Actium. Today Roman ruins and several Byzantine churches survive.

**OLD CORINTH,** *about 8 kilometers from New Corinth in the Peloponnesus*

Advantageously situated at the key point of communications between northern Greece and the Peloponnesus and the Ionian and Aegean seas, ancient Corinth was for many centuries the leading commercial city-state in Greece. Founded in prehistoric times, Corinth attained unparalleled splendor and prestige under the tyrants Cypselus and his son Periander in the latter half of the seventh century B.C. Although the rise of Athens, and subsequently Sparta, in the fifth century B.C. temporarily eclipsed Corinth, the city regained its supremacy after the Corinthian War (395–387 B.C.) and again became the largest and most prosperous city in Greece. The Romans wrought total destruction on Corinth in 146 B.C., but in 44 B.C. Julius Caesar refounded Corinth on its former site as a Roman colony. It was to the pleasure-seeking Corinthians that Saint Paul preached in A.D. 51, but the Apostle failed to make them mend their dissolute ways. Corinth was burned by the Goths in A.D. 395 and destroyed by an earthquake in 521. Rising from a huge rock atop the ancient city, the citadel, or **Acrocorinthus**—formerly surmounted by a temple to Aphrodite with 1,000 priestess-prostitutes in attendance—was converted into a fortress during the Middle Ages and periodically enlarged by Byzantines, Crusaders, Venetians, and Turks. Today the crenelated walls at the summit of the Acrocorinthus are among the most imposing monuments of medieval Greece. Ruins of ancient Corinth include the **Temple of Apollo,** built about 550 B.C. and the city's only extant Greek remain; the **Lechaion Road,** faced by the public and private buildings of Roman Greece; the **Fountain of Peirene,** which supplied Corinth with water; and the **Bema,** or **Rostra,** a tribunal on which Roman high officials appeared before the public.

**OLYMPIA,** *16 kilometers east of Pyrgos in the western Peloponnesus*

This important sanctuary to Zeus is where the famous Olympic games originated. From 776 B.C.—the year of the First Olympiad, from which the ancient Greeks reckoned their dates—until Emperor Theodosius I abolished the games about A.D. 393, athletes from all over the Greek world came here every fourth year to compete for the title of "Olympic victor." Contests were held in running, boxing, horse racing, and the pancratium, a brutal sport combining wrestling and boxing. The ruins of the **Altis,** or grove, consist of the great Doric **Temple of Zeus,** erected between 468 and 457 B.C., in which victors received their laurel wreaths; the **Hereum,** the oldest extant Greek temple, built about 900 B.C.; 12 **Treasure Houses** erected by various Greek cities in homage to Zeus; the **Philippeum,** which contained statues of the family of Philip of Macedon; and the **Stadium,** which accommodated 30,000 spectators.

**PATMOS,** *in the eastern Aegean Sea off the southwest coast of Asia Minor*

Saint John the Divine wrote the Book of Revelation on this island. Deported from Ephesus to Patmos by the emperor Domitian in A.D. 95, Saint John received his revelation on the summit of a hill, south of the port, in the Cave of Saint Anne, now enshrined by the

*A scene on Patmos, the island of pilgrimage where Saint John the Divine wrote the Apocalypse in a cave*

**Church of the Apocalypse.** God reputedly spoke through a crack in a rock, and the saint dictated the message to his disciple Prochorus, who used a sloping rock as his desk. Here also is the stone, embellished with silver halos, that Saint John used as a pillow. Legend has it that a rock in the harbor was originally the sorcerer Kypnos, whom Saint John transformed into his present shape. Also on Patmos is a **Monastery,** near the village of Chora, founded late in the 11th century B.C. by Alexius I. Among the many historical manuscripts in the library is the famous fifth-century **Codex Porphyrius,** written in silver, which contains most of the Gospel of Saint Mark.

**PATRAS,** *outside the narrows of the Gulf of Corinth in the Peloponnesus*

During the Byzantine era this city was an important port where travelers from Western Europe debarked. Saint Andrew, Patras' patron saint, was crucified here earlier, and his head is among the city's sacred relics. In 1205 Guillaume de Champlite and Geoffroi de Villehardouin undertook the Frankish conquest of the Peloponnesus from Patras, which subsequently became the seat of a Latin archbishop. The city finally fell to the Turks in the 15th century. Today a **Roman Theater** and **Frankish Castle** are preserved in Greece's third largest city.

**PELLA,** *about 32 kilometers northwest of Salonika in Macedonia*

In 356 B.C. Alexander the Great was born at this one-time capital of Macedonia, and here he received his education from Aristotle. Alexander's father, King Philip II, had made Pella the capital of a united Greece, and the city subsequently rose in importance until it was destroyed by the Romans in 168 B.C. Today the recently excavated remains of Pella include the **Palace of King Archelaus,** built about 400 B.C., buildings with well-preserved mosaic floors, ancient water supply lines, and a sewer; and the nearby reservoir known as **Alexander's Bath.**

**PHILIPPI,** *about 16 kilometers northwest of Kavalla in Macedonia*

Philip II of Macedon founded this city in 358 B.C. It was here in 42 B.C. that Brutus and Cassius were defeated in battle by Mark

Antony and Octavian. Subsequently Saint Paul preached his first sermon in Europe at Philippi and baptized Lydia the cloth merchant, his first convert to Christianity. Excavations here have uncovered the remains of a fifth-century **basilica**, a **Roman agora, fortress, theater, and temples.** On rocky ledges above the road is the **prison** where Saint Paul and Saint Silas were detained with their feet "made fast in the stocks."

**POROS,** *in the Saronic Gulf opposite the Peloponnesus, 32 nautical miles from Piraeus*

Situated on this offshore island are the remains of the **Sanctuary of Poseidon,** center of the Amphictyonic League, a group of city-states sharing a common religious center, and the site where the Athenian orator and statesman Demosthenes killed himself in 322 B.C. Near the village of Troizen are the ruins of ancient **Troezen,** scene of the tragedy of Phaedra.

**PYLOS,** *at the north end of Pylos Bay in the southwest Peloponnesus*

Just off this rocky peninsula occurred in 1827 a great naval battle in which the allied fleets of Russia, Great Britain, and France defeated Turko-Egyptian forces, signaling an important victory in the Greek struggle for independence. In ancient times Pylos prospered during the Mycenaean era—approximately 1400–1200 B.C.—and in 425 B.C., during the Peloponnesian War, was the scene of a 72-day siege in which the Athenians forced the Spartans to surrender a garrison on the offshore island of **Sphakteria.** Today Pylos is dominated by a **Venetian Castle.** Four miles to the north is the recently excavated **Palace of Nestor,** reputedly the home of the venerable king of Homeric legend.

**RHODES,** *in the Dodecanese Islands, about 12 miles off Turkish coast*

The various civilizations that have flourished on Rhodes during its long and eventful history have left behind a wealth of monuments. During antiquity the towns of Lindos, Camirus, and Ialysus formed part of a religious and political confederacy known as the Dorian Hexapolis. The prosperous island was occupied by Romans in 76 B.C. The maritime law that was formulated here during the pre-Christian era became known to seafaring peoples throughout the civilized world. After the fall of the Roman Empire Rhodes was governed by the Byzantines. In 1306 Rhodes was sold to the military order of the Knights of Saint John of Jerusalem, who fortified the town of Rhodes and successfully resisted the onslaughts of the Turks for more than 200 years. In 1522, after a six-month siege, the island fell to Suleiman the Magnificent. The Turks ceded Rhodes to Italy in 1912; Rhodes became part of Greece in 1945. Today important ancient remains are preserved at **Lindos,** whose scenic **Acropolis,** situated on a headland jutting high above the sea, is crowned by the **Temple of Athena Lindia.** Here also are a **Byzantine Church** and a **Medieval Castle.** In the village below is the **Church of Our Lady of Lindos,** built by the knights. Surrounded by a long and well-preserved medieval wall and entered through **Saint Catherine's Gate** and other portals, the old town of **Rhodes** contains such Gothic structures as the **Castellania** (knights' market building), the **Knights' Hospital,** now a museum, the reconstructed **Castella,** or Grand Master's Palace, and the inns of the various nationalities. There are many Turkish vestiges in the walled town, including the **Mosque of Rezip** and the **Hammam of Suleiman** (baths). The port of Mandraki in the modern town of Rhodes was once guarded by the Colossus of Rhodes, one of the Seven Wonders of the World, which has long since disappeared.

**SALAMIS,** *in the Saronic Gulf, accessible by boat from Piraeus and other mainland ports*

The great naval battle of 480 B.C. between the Greeks and the Persians under Xerxes took place in the narrow strait between this island and Attica. Some 380 Greek ships decimated the Asiatic fleet and forced the main body of the Persian army to retreat to Asia Minor.

**SALONIKA (THESSALONICA),** *at the head of the Gulf of Salonika in Macedonia*

Situated by the sea, Salonika was a flourishing center of commerce during the Macedonian, Roman, and Byzantine periods. The city was founded in 315 B.C. by the general Cassander, who named it in honor of his wife, the sister of Alexander the Great. As capital of Macedonia under the Romans, Salonika, on the Via Egnatia connecting Rome and Constantinople, was visited by Saint Paul and soon became an early center of Christianity. In A.D. 306 the emperor Galerius caused the martyrdom of Saint Demetrius, who became Salonika's patron saint and protector. The city was second only to Constantinople in the Byzantine Empire. Its stout walls, however, were not impermeable to attack by the Saracens in 904, the Normans in 1185, and by Boniface III, count of Montferrat, who seized the town in 1204; after 1246 Salonika was sold to the Venetians. In 1430 the Turk Murad II captured the city in the worst siege of its history and thus initiated 500 years of Ottoman domination, ending only in 1912–13 when the Greeks took Salonika and immediately destroyed most of the minarets and other vestiges of Turkish rule. Preserved today are the remains of the Hellenistic walls, enlarged by the Romans, the **Triumphal Arch of Galerius,** erected in A.D. 303, and the Byzantine **Churches of Saint George, Saint Panteleimon, Saint Demetrius, Saint Catherine,** the **Twelve Apostles, Panaghia Chalkeon,** and the **Cathedral of Saint Sophia;** most of these were constructed between the 4th and 14th centuries and many contain splendid mosaics and frescoes. Other notable sights are the medieval ramparts of the **Citadel of the Seven Towers** and the **White Tower,** the city's most striking landmark, built by the Venetians in the 15th century. An archaeological museum is housed in the old **Mosque of Yeni Djami.**

**SAMOTHRACE,** *in the northern Aegean Sea, accessible from Alexandroupolis*

Samothrace was the site of the Panhellenic **Sanctuary of the Great Gods,** originally Thracian deities whom the Greeks adapted to their own mythology. The sanctuary was the scene of a public summer festival to which representatives of the Greek city-states would come and pay obeisance. Various mystery cults also flourished here; initiates included the historian Herodotus and Philip of Macedon. Ruins of sixth-century B.C. temples, the third-century B.C. **Rotunda of Arsinoe,** a reception hall, and the **Hieron,** or sanctuary proper, have been excavated. At a fountain near the temples the famous Winged Victory of Samothrace was found in 1863; the statue is now in the Louvre museum in Paris.

**SPARTA,** *on the Eurotas River in the southern Peloponnesus*

The militaristic and totalitarian city-state of ancient Sparta dominated the political and cultural history of the Peloponnesus.

After the defeat of Athens in the Peloponnesian War (431–404 B.C.), Sparta attained hegemony over all Greece. According to tradition, the knight Lycurgus presented Sparta with a code of laws, under which the city was organized on a warlike basis between 900 and 600 B.C. Sons of Spartan citizens were taken from their parents at an early age and subjected to rigorous and austere military training unparalleled for oppressiveness. As a result Sparta created the most formidable fighting force in Greece. Remains of ancient Sparta include ruins of the **Sanctuary of Athena** on the acropolis overlooking a **Hellenistic Theater,** the foundations of **Artemis' Sanctuary,** where Spartan youths were flogged in so-called contests of the whips, fragments of **Apollo's Shrine** at Amyclae, and the site of the **Agora.**

**THEBES,** *about 48 kilometers northwest of Athens in Boeotia*

Tradition has it that the Phoenician Cadmus founded Thebes. The town was subsequently ruled by the house of the Labdacidae, whose most illustrious member was the ill-fated Oedipus, the protagonist of Greek epic and tragedy. After 371 B.C., when the Theban general Epaminondas defeated Sparta, Thebes briefly dominated the other Greek city-states. Alexander the Great razed Thebes in the fourth century B.C., sparing only the home of the poet Pindar. The city regained some prosperity during the Middle Ages. Today ancient gateways of the **Palace of Cadmus,** remains of the **Temple of the Ismenian Apollo,** and a **Frankish Tower,** built by the de la Roche family in the 13th century, survive.

**THERMOPYLAE,** *north of Delphi in Boeotia*

This 50-foot-wide pass between a precipitous mountain and the sea was the scene of a bloody battle between the Greeks and the Persians in 480 B.C. Invading from the north, the Persian army under the great King Xerxes planned to enter central Greece through this pass. Leonidas, king of Sparta, took personal command of a small force of 300 to defend Thermopylae. The Greeks, greatly outnumbered, repulsed the Persians, until the invaders crossed the mountain by a secret path and trapped the defenders. The Spartans and Leonidas fought gallantly until they died. "Thermopylae" subsequently became a Greek rallying cry.

**TIRYNS,** *halfway between Argos and Nauplia in the eastern Peloponnesus*

This legendary birthplace of Hercules is the site of a Mycenaean palace that stood on the foundations of a palace built as early as 3000 B.C. Between 2000 and 1600 B.C. the huge **Cyclopean Walls**—containing stones weighing 60 tons each—were constructed, and a vaulted gallery was added a few centuries later.

**VEROIA,** *60 kilometers southwest of Salonika via the Salonika road*

Saint Paul preached to the Jewish community of this provincial Roman capital (at a site near the present mosque) after he was expelled from Salonika (*see*). Later, under the Turks, the Greek inhabitants of Veroia built unobtrusive Byzantine churches in outbuildings around their courtyards; they include the **Churches of Saint Nicholas, Saint Christos, Saint George,** and the **Prophet Elias.**

# ITALY
## & MALTA

### VATICAN CITY
### SAN MARINO

**ALBANO LAZIALE,** *25 kilometers southeast of Rome in Latium*
Legend has it that the oldest town in Latium, originally known as Alba Longa, was established in 1150 B.C. by Ascanius, son of Aeneas. Its long-time rivalry with Rome culminated during the early years of the republic in the legendary combat of the Horatii, who represented Rome and have been immortalized in Jacques Louis David's painting *The Oath of the Horatii,* and the Curiatii, who represented Alba Longa. Although two of the three Horatii brothers were killed, the third brother killed his three Curiatii adversaries, and the supremacy of Rome was established. Preserved today are the foundations of a Roman **villa** owned by Pompey, the remains of a second-century A.D. **cistern** that held 81,500 gallons of water, and the curious **Tomb of the Horatii and Curiatii** at the exit from town on the road to Ariccia.

**ALBEROBELLO,** *60 kilometers southeast of Bari via N-16 in Apulia*
This town is the center of a district renowned for its groups of curious white domed structures built without the use of mortar and known as trulli. Trulli are thought to have originated several centuries before Christ and were carried to Italy by prehistoric peoples coming from Asia Minor. The oldest extant trulli in Alberobello date from the 16th century, when the counts of Acquaviva established a small community here and prohibited the use of binding materials in their architecture in order to avoid royal building permits and their consequent taxation. Just south of town is the **Monumental Zone,** with the greatest concentration of trulli. Many of the whitewashed structures are decorated with crosses and painted signs of cryptic meaning, which perhaps are survivals of the period (17th and early 18th centuries) when the mystical brotherhood of the Rosicrucians, whose secret learning dealt with occult symbols, spread throughout the Mediterranean area.

**AMALFI,** *via N-163 on the Gulf of Salerno in Campania*
The existence of this maritime town was first recorded in the sixth century A.D. During the ninth century Amalfi became the first of the Italian maritime republics and along with Gaeta and Venice monopolized trade with Constantinople and the Levant; in 848 its fleet was sent to assist Pope Leo IV in the struggle against the Saracens. The maritime republic of Amalfi reached the zenith of its prosperity and sea power in the 11th century, when the *Tavole Amalfitane* (*Amalfi Navigation Tables*) regulated trade throughout the Mediterranean; this famous code was used until 1570 and today is preserved in the **Town Hall.** During the early Middle Ages the Amalfi fleet transported many crusaders to Palestine, where Amalfians erected several churches and a hospital in Jerusalem, whence the origin of the famous order of Saint John of Jerusalem, or Knights Hospitalers. Amalfi's importance began to decline after the 12th century, when it was taken over by the Normans. Reflecting Amalfi's former splendor today is the 11th-century Lombard-Norman–style **Cathedral of Saint Andrew,** containing the relics of Saint Andrew, which are believed to exude a miraculous oil. Begun in 1103, the adjoining **Cloisters of Paradise,** which for two centuries housed the tombs of Amalfi's aristocrats, reveal a combination of Romanesque austerity and oriental fantasy. Surviving also are remains of the **Arsenal,** where the gigantic galleys—boasting 120 oars each—were built that carried traders to distant parts of Africa and Asia, and an old **Watch Tower,** erected to guard the harbor against Saracen invaders.

*Page 27. Top: panorama of Florence. Center: the Grand Canal in Venice. Below left: the Colosseum in Rome. Right: the Tyrolese countryside near the Brenner Pass. Bottom: Mount Vesuvius seen from the forum in Pompeii*

**ANAGNI,** *67 kilometers southeast of Rome via A-2 in Latium*

Perched on a rocky spur, this medieval town was a papal summer residence as well as the birthplace of four popes, including Boniface VIII (1235?–1303). In 1303 Boniface excommunicated King Philip the Fair of France, who unsuccessfully sought papal funds. Enraged, the monarch sent his partisans led by Chancellor Guillaume de Nogaret and Sciarra Colonna, a Roman whose family was an enemy of the pope, into Anagni on September 7, 1303. At the papal palace they dragged Boniface off his throne and struck him, whereupon the pope said, "Here is my head. Here is my neck." After being kept prisoner three days, the pope was freed by the citizens of Anagni. Boniface returned to Rome, where he died within the month. Today the only remains of the former papal palace where Boniface was mistreated are **arches** in the Alley of Saint Michel. Erected from 1072 until 1104 and later remodeled in the Gothic style, the **Cathedral,** where Philip the Fair, as well as Frederick Barbarossa (1123?–90), Holy Roman Emperor, were excommunicated, contains a beautiful mosaic pavement, frescoes, and a 14th-century statue of Pope Boniface VIII.

**ANCONA,** *via N-16 overlooking the Adriatic Sea in The Marches*

This town was colonized in the fourth century B.C. by Greeks from Syracuse (*see*) in Sicily and in the second century A.D. was made into a port by Emperor Trajan. **Trajan's Arch** was raised in A.D. 115 by the Roman senate and people in honor of that emperor's activities here. During the Middle Ages and Renaissance Ancona was an independent maritime republic; the town was incorporated into the Papal States in 1532. Important monuments include the **Cathedral of San Ciriaco,** originally erected on the site of a temple of Venus about the sixth century, when it was the seat of Cyriac, first bishop of Ancona and subsequently the ecumenical patriarch of Constantinople, and remodeled in the Romanesque style about 1150; and the **Loggia dei Mercanti,** a Gothic edifice of 1443 used for merchants' meetings. The important archaeological collection of the **National Museum of The Marches** is housed in the 16th-century Palazzo Feretti.

**ANDRIA**

CASTEL DEL MONTE, *about 53 kilometers west of Bari via A-17 in Apulia*

Situated on a bluff dominating the plain below, this proud solitary castle was erected in 1240 by Emperor Frederick II of Hohenstaufen. Octagonal in plan with eight octagonal towers and boasting walls 100 feet high and 8 feet thick, the magnificently preserved structure was the emperor's favorite residence and was used also as a fortress. The lavishly decorated interior suggests almost Oriental comfort and was perhaps built to emulate the crusaders' castles in Syria that Frederick had seen on a journey to the Levant. In the 14th century members of the Spanish house of Aragon used the castle as a prison and subsequently as a hunting lodge.

**ANZIO,** *southeast of Rome via N-148 in Latium*

Known as Antium in ancient times, this seaport served as a pirate stronghold of the Volscian tribe. In 490 Coriolanus, the exiled Roman hero and subject of Shakespeare's tragedy, took refuge here and campaigned against Rome. The town was taken by the Romans in 341 B.C. and subsequently became a popular seaside resort and the birthplace of Emperors Caligula (A.D. 12–41) and Nero (A.D. 37–

68). The modern **harbor** was constructed in 1698 under Pope Innocent XII. During World War II Anzio was the scene of the January 22, 1944, amphibious landing of Anglo-American troops, who took the Germans by surprise behind their lines and established a bridgehead. It was not until May 25, four months later, that the United States Fifth Army reduced the Monte Cassino (*see Cassino*) strong point and linked up with the Anzio force. The Allies then advanced on Rome, which fell on June 4.

**AOSTA,** *via A-5, N-26, and N-27 in Piedmont*

This Alpine town was founded as a Roman military post by Emperor Augustus in 24 B.C. to commemorate the victory of Terentius Varro Mureno over the Salassi tribe the previous year. Roman ruins here include the **Pretoria Gateway,** constructed of huge blocks of stone at the time of Augustus, the honorary **Arch of Augustus,** erected in 23 B.C., and a **theater, road,** and **amphitheater.** The **Collegiate Church of Sant' Orso** was placed under the invocation of an archdeacon in the sixth century and added to over the centuries. During the Middle Ages Aosta was an important religious center and the birthplace of the scholastic philosopher Saint Anselm (1033–1109), who became archbishop of Canterbury in 1093. Begun in the 12th century, the **Cathedral** contains the 14th-century tomb of Count Thomas II of Savoy, a member of the great dynasty that ruled Piedmont from the 11th century. The town was later the setting of the *Leper of Aosta,* a novel written by the Frenchman Xavier de Maistre, who took refuge there in 1793 during the Reign of Terror; the **Torre del Lebbroso,** where the leper was confined for 20 years, still stands among the **ramparts.**

**AQUILA,** *via N-17 in the Abruzzi*

According to tradition this town sprang up miraculously with 99 quarters surrounding 99 castles, 99 squares, 99 fountains, and 99 churches. Aquila was actually founded in 1240 by Emperor Frederick II of Hohenstaufen, who incorporated it into the kingdom of Naples and made the imperial eagle its emblem. Charles I of Anjou subsequently erected this town's ramparts. The chief monument is **Saint Bernardino's Basilica,** built between 1454 and 1472, which contains the mausoleum of Saint Bernardino of Siena *(see),* who died here in 1444; the saint's motto, "Jesus Hominum Salvator" (Jesus Saviour of Mankind), appears in the form of the initials IHS on many of Aquila's old houses. Other sights include the fortress-like **Castle,** built by the Spaniards in the 1500s, the **Santa Maria di Collemaggio Basilica,** begun in 1287 by Pietro di Murrone, a hermit who later became Pope Celestine V, and the **Fountain of the 99 Conduits,** with 99 masks spouting water, designed in 1272 and remodeled in the 1400s.

**AQUILEIA,** *10 kilometers inland from the head of the Adriatic via N-14 and A-4 in Venetia*

Tradition has it that in 181 B.C., while this town was being laid out as a Roman stronghold against Illyrian tribes, an eagle (*aquila*) hovered overhead, whence its name. Under the Roman Empire Aquileia was a prosperous commercial city—ruins of the old Roman **port** are at the end of the Via Sacra—and Augustus made it his base of operations in his war against the Germans. The town was ravaged by Attila and his Huns in A.D. 452, and its inhabitants fled to the lagoon-locked islands that were to become the town of Venice. In the sixth century Aquileia became the capital of a patriarchate governed by bishops who refused to pay allegiance to the Roman see. The town later became a fief of the Holy Roman Empire, and in the 15th century it came under the rule of Venice. Preserved here is the **Basilica**, raised in the 11th century on the remains of a fourth-century structure; behind it are the **graves** of 910 unknown soldiers of World War I.

**AREZZO,** *via N-71 in Tuscany*

Settled by the Etruscans, this town flourished under the Romans. During the Middle Ages Arezzo was a free commune that produced such illustrious natives as Guido d'Arezzo, inventor of the musical scale in the 11th century, and the poet Petrarch in the 14th century; in 1384 it was annexed to Florence. Principal sights include the 14th-century Gothic **Church of San Francesco** (Saint Francis), containing Piero della Francesca's masterful frescoes entitled *Legend of the Cross;* the **Cathedral,** erected from 1286 to 1510, boasting fine stained-glass windows by the celebrated Guillaume de Marcillat, who worked at the Vatican with Raphael and Michelangelo; the Renaissance **Church of Santa Maria della Grazie,** with an altar by Andrea della Robbia; the **Piazza Grande,** surrounded by medieval palaces with battlemented towers; the **Loggia Palace,** designed by Giorgio Vasari between 1573 and 1581; and the Romanesque **Church of Santa Maria della Pieve,** whose bell tower of 1330 is known as the campanile "of the 100 holes," because it is pierced by many windows. An art gallery and museum of medieval art are housed in the 15th-century **Palazzo della Dogana** (Customs' Palace).

**ARQUÀ PETRARCA,** *24 kilometers southwest of Padua via N-16d in the Euganean Hills in Venetia*

This medieval village was where the poet Petrarch, the leading humanist of the Renaissance, retired in 1370 and spent the last four years of his life. Petrarch's former **residence** contains the library chair where the poet was found dead with his head in an open book on his 70th birthday on July 20, 1374, as well as other mementos. **Petrarch's Tomb** is near the church door in the village square.

**ASCOLI PICENO,** *via N-4 or N-8 at the confluence of the Castellano and Tronto rivers in The Marches*

This ancient town was captured by the Romans in 268 B.C. and made into a provincial capital. Ascoli's Roman inhabitants were massacred during the Social War in 90 B.C., but the town was retaken by the Romans the next year. After crossing the Rubicon in 49 B.C., Julius Caesar occupied Ascoli. The town was ruled by bishops from the eighth century, became an independent republic in the 1100s, and was made a papal domain in the 15th century. The medieval aspect of Ascoli is preserved in the **Piazza del Popolo,** the historic center of the city, lined with edifices that include the austere 13th-century **Palazzo del Popolo,** dominated by a tower, which contains the **Archaeological Museum;** and the Gothic **Church of San Francesco,** abutted by the elegant 16th-century **Loggia dei Mercanti,** where merchants assembled. In the **Old Quarter** are the **Ercolani Tower** —the tallest of the town's feudal towers—the **Casa Longobarda,** a Lombard-Romanesque mansion, the **Ponte di Solestà,** a single-arched Roman bridge built in the early years of the empire, and the **Church of Saints Vincent and Anastasius,** dating from the fourth century and rebuilt in the Romanesque style. Dedicated to Saint Emidio of Treveri, the **Cathedral** was begun in 1000; the adjoining **Baptistery** was built in the 1100s from Roman ruins.

**ASSISI,** *via N-75B on the slopes of Mount Subasio in Umbria*

Established by the Romans, this medieval town is associated with the legends of Saint Francis and Saint Clare. Born here in 1182, Saint Francis, while a prisoner of war at Perugia (*see*) in 1201, renounced his worldly ways and decided to devote himself to God and a life of poverty and self-denial. He thereafter became a mystic who experienced visions of the Virgin and Christ, composed the first poems in the Italian language about the beauties of nature, preached kindness to animals, and in 1210 founded the famous order of mendicant friars known as the Franciscans. Saint Clare (1194–1253), under the influence of Saint Francis, entered a nunnery in 1212 and later established the order of Poor Clares. Assisi abounds in mementos of the two saints. The celebrated **Basilica of San Francesco** and its monastery were completed in 1253 by Brother Elias, a disciple of Saint Francis's; the lower church was decorated by the best artists of the Florentine, Sienese, and Umbrian schools and houses in its crypt the **Tomb of Saint Francis**; the upper church contains frescoes by Giovanni Cimabue and Giotto's famous scenes—28 in all—from the life of Saint Francis, executed from 1296 to 1304. The **Church of Santa Chiara** (Saint Clare), built from 1257 to 1265, contains Saint Clare's coffin. The **Cathedral of San Ruffino,** erected in 1140, contains the font where the two saints and Holy Roman Emperor Frederick II (1194–1250) were baptized. Occupying the site of the old Roman forum, the **Piazza del Commune** is faced by the **Temple of Minerva,** which was converted into a church. About four kilometers east of Assisi is the **Carcieri Hermitage,** which originally consisted of isolated cells in caves in the rock and was used as a retreat by Saint Francis; later in the 15th century it was rebuilt by Saint Bernardino of Siena (*see*). Just south of town is the **Convent di San Damiano** (Saint Damian), in whose church Saint Francis was called to his vocation, and Saint Clare drove away the Saracens; Saint Clare died in the sparse dormitory. The vast **Basilica of Santa Maria degli Angeli** (Saint Mary of the Angels) was raised in 1569 on the site where Saint Francis and his brotherhood built huts and restored an oratory known as the **Porziuncula** (small portion) **Chapel;** in the chapel Saint Francis heard Saint Clare take her vows and had a vision of the future greatness of the Franciscans; behind the chapel is the cell where Saint Francis died in 1226.

**BAIA,** *via N-7Q on the Bay of Naples in Campania*

Founded by the Greeks and named after Baios, Ulysses' companion in the *Odyssey,* who died and was buried here, this port town became the most popular resort of the Roman Empire. Augustus, Nero, other emperors, and patricians competed with one another in erecting sumptuous villas; and the thermal spa was provided with the most complete hydrotherapy equipment in antiquity. The fall of the empire contributed to the fall of Baia, which was later sacked by the Saracens and nearly abandoned. Recently excavated thermal ruins include the **Bath of Sosendra,** the **Springs of Mercury,** the **Bath of Venus,** and the **Temple of Diana.** Preserved also is a **Castle** built on the site of one of Caesar's villas in the 16th century A.D. to defend Baia against pirates.

**BARI,** *via N-16 on the Adriatic coast in Apulia*

Legend has it that Bari was first settled by Illyrians and later colonized by the Greeks. Bari became the seat of Byzantine rule in southern Italy between the 9th and 11th centuries. During the Middle Ages the town prospered under the Normans and subsequently the Hohenstaufens. In the 16th century Bari declined under the Sforzas of Milan and the Spanish. Clustered on its promontory, the **Old Town** today still recalls the medieval and Byzantine periods in spite of heavy bombing sustained in World War II. The Romanesque **Basilica of San Nicola** (Saint Nicholas) was begun in 1087 at the behest of the Norman prince Roger Guiscard after sailors had absconded with the saint's relics from Myra in Asia Minor and brought them back to Bari. The church was erected on the site of the former **Court of Catapan,** the residence of the Byzantine governors, and two truncated towers from the earlier building frame the basilica's façade. Saint Nicholas's remains are housed in the crypt. Preserved at Bari also are the **Cathedral,** originally erected in the Byzantine style between 1034 and 1062 and reconstructed in the next century in the Romanesque style, and the **Castle,** built by the Norman king Roger in 1137 and reconstructed by Frederick II of Hohenstaufen between 1233 and 1240.

### BERGAMO, *via A-4 and N-42 in Lombardy*

This ancient Roman town was, during the Renaissance, the birthplace of General Bartolommeo Colleoni (1400–1475), commander of the Venetian Republic, and later of the composer Gaetano Donizetti (1797–1848). The magnificent Renaissance **Colleoni Chapel** of the **Church of Santa Maria Maggiore** was erected from 1470 to 1476 by Giovanni Antonio Amadeo, architect of the Carthusian monastery at Pavia (*see*), as a mausoleum for Colleoni, who is interred in a tomb surmounted by an equestrian statue. Sights in the upper town, or **Old Town,** include the **Palazzo della Ragione,** begun in 1199 and one of the oldest communal palaces in Italy, and the **Palazzo Scamozziano** (1610), on the **Piazza Vecchia,** the historic center of Bergamo. Begun in the 1300s, the **Rocca,** or citadel, was remodeled by the Venetians, who annexed Bergamo in 1428.

### BOLOGNA, *via N-64 in Emilia*

Colonized by the Etruscans, this city in later years was successively overrun by Gauls, Romans, and barbarians. Bologna revived in the 12th century and flourished under an independent communal government from the 13th to the 16th centuries, during which time towers, churches, and palaces arose and the arts thrived. As in other Italian towns the political factions of Guelphs and Ghibellines fought one another in the 13th century, and in 1249 the Guelphs prevailed over the imperial army of Frederick II; the emperor's son Enzio was captured and imprisoned in the **Palazzo di Re Enzio** until his death in 1272. The celebrated university—Europe's oldest—was established here between 1060 and 1100, and by the 13th century it boasted 10,000 students; anatomy lessons were given as early as the 1300s, and centuries later the inventor Guglielmo Marconi (1874–1937) studied wireless telegraphy here. The 16th-century **Palazzo Archiquinassio** was the seat of the university until 1803; today the edifice contains the university library, which includes 10,000 manuscripts. Among the principal sights today are the Gothic **Palazzo Communale,** in front of which is a colossal **Statue of Pope Gregory XII,** a native of Bologna, who invented the present Gregorian calendar in 1582, the **Palazzo del Podestà,** or governor's palace, rebuilt in 1492, and the famous Renaissance **Fontana del Nettuno** (fountain of Neptune), created in 1566. The **Piazza di Porta Ravegnana** is renowned for its two 12th-century leaning towers, built by noble families as places of refuge, and its **Mercanzia** (merchants' house), erected about 1382, from whose balcony sentences

*In Bologna, the university (left) and the fountain of Neptune (right)*

were passed and bankruptcies proclaimed. The late-14th-century **Palazzo Bevilacqua** was the scene of the 1647 Council of Trent, ending the Thirty Years' War. Recalling the town's former ecclesiastical importance are the huge **Basilica of San Petronio**, begun in honor of Bologna's patron saint in 1390, whose nave was the scene of the coronation of Emperor Charles V in 1530. The **Church of Santo Stefano** comprises eight different churches, the oldest dating from the fourth century (the courtyard contains the bowl in which Pilate washed after turning Christ over to the Jews). The **Church of San Giacomo Maggiore**, established in 1267, houses the mausoleum of the Bentivoglio family, who ruled Bologna in the 15th century; and the **Church of San Domenico** was completed in 1233 to shelter the tomb of Saint Dominic, who died at Bologna in 1221.

**BRENNER PASS,** *on A22 in Trentino-Alto Adige*
Situated at 4,500 feet in the Alps, this historic pass connects Innsbruck, Austria, and Bolzano, Italy. The Romans used it as a route into central Europe, and it was traversed in turn by the Teutonic invaders of Italy. In 1772 a carriage road was built over the pass, and in 1867 a railroad with 22 tunnels was completed. In 1940–41 Hitler and Mussolini met here several times.

**BRESCIA,** *via A-4 near Lake Garda in Lombardy*
This ancient Celtic settlement developed under the Romans into a flourishing town. Brescia later became a Lombard duchy and was a free commune during the Middle Ages, when it became wealthy as a manufacturer of weapons and armor, supplying all of Europe until the 18th century. The city became a Venetian domain from 1426 to 1797. In 1512 Brescia was besieged and pillaged by French troops under Gaston de Foix. Brescia later resisted Austrian rule in a ten-day rebellion in 1849 and earned the nickname "Lioness." Standing on the **Piazza della Loggia** are the **Loggia,** built between 1492 and 1574 and now used as the town hall, the **Palazzo dell' Orlogio** (palace of the clock), surmounted by Venetian Moorish figures, and the **Palazzos Monte Vecchio** (1484) and **Monte Nuovo**

(1497), pawnbroking establishments. On the **Piazza del Duomo** are the white marble **New Cathedral,** begun in 1604, the **Old Cathedral,** raised in the 1100s on the site of a seventh-century basilica, and the **Broletto,** the former town hall, begun in 1187 and completed in, the 16th century; from its balcony public proclamations were made. Other sights include the **Museum of Roman Antiquities,** built on the remains of the Capitoline Temple, erected by Emperor Vespasian in A.D. 78, the **Museum of Christian Art,** housed in the classical **Church of the Monastery of Santa Giulia,** and the **Basilica of San Salvatore,** begun in the eighth century and incorporating Roman columns. Heavy bombing in World War II destroyed many other monuments.

**BRINDISI,** *via N-16 on the Adriatic coast in Apulia*

Serving as a gateway for trade between Europe and the East, Brindisi was a principal port of the Romans. A 66-foot-tall marble **column** near the harbor is the surviving one of a pair erected by the Romans to mark the terminus of the Appian Way *(see Rome).* The Roman poet Virgil died suddenly near the port in 19 B.C. on his way home from a visit to Greece. During the Middle Ages the crusaders embarked for the Holy Land at Brindisi; the **Fountain of Tancredi,** where crusaders watered their horses, was constructed in 1192 by the Norman king Tancred to commemorate the marriage of his son here; and in 1227 Frederick II of Hohenstaufen erected a **Swabian Castle** at the site of the old Roman walls on the western creek of the harbor, which was enlarged in the 1400s by Ferdinand I of Aragon. In the mid-15th century the Aragonese also erected the **Red Castle** in the Middle Port after the evacuation of the ancient town of Otranto in southeast Apulia by the Turks.

**CAPRI,** *18 miles off the coast in the Bay of Naples*

Reputed to be the most beautiful island in the world, Capri, with its fairy grottoes, magnificent panoramas, and subtropical vegetation, was a favorite resort of the ancient Romans. Emperors Augustus and Tiberius built 12 villas here, and Tiberius spent the last years of his life (27–37 A.D.) on Capri. Preserved today is the **Villa Iovis,** the former palace of Tiberius, standing like a solitary fortress on top of Mount Tiberio. **Capri,** the principal town on the island, is the site of the 14th-century Carthusian **Monastery of Saint James.** An earlier church, that of **Saint Costanzo,** erected from the 10th to the 11th centuries, houses the body of Saint Costanzo, patriarch of Constantinople and patron saint of Capri. At the town of **Anacapri** is the **Villa San Michele,** erected late in the 1800s for the Swedish doctor-author Axel Munthe.

**CAPUA,** *via N-7B on the Volturno River in Campania*

Ancient Capua, near the present town of Santa Maria Capua Vetere, was where Hannibal and his troops, after the Battle of Cannae in 216 B.C., basked in luxury and thus grew soft and came to be defeated by the Roman general Scipio Africanus. Preserved here is a Roman **triumphal arch** and a first-century A.D. **amphitheater,** which is the second largest in Italy after the Colosseum *(see Rome).* A **Norman Palace** was built from the stones of the amphitheater at the present site of Capua in the 11th century. During the Renaissance, in 1501, Cesare Borgia, with papal support, besieged the town and massacred 5,000 inhabitants; the bells of the **Cathedral**—which sustained great damage in World War II—still toll a death knell on the anniversary of this bloody occasion.

**CASSINO,** *via A-2 on the Rapido River in Campania*

Founded in Roman times, this town is famous for the **Monastery of Monte Cassino,** the mother house of the Benedictine order, established on the site of a temple of Apollo by Saint Benedict in 529. Tradition has it that the saint performed many miracles and composed his complete set of rules requiring chastity, obedience, poverty, study, and manual labor here. Over the centuries the abbey was destroyed by Lombards, Saracens, and other invaders. Throughout the darkest period of the Middle Ages the abbey influenced monastic life throughout Europe, served as a haven for the arts and sciences, and received students; the once world-famous library still contains 10,000 volumes and manuscripts. By 1060 Monte Cassino, under Abbot Didier, was esteemed the richest in the world. During World War II, from October, 1943, to May, 1944, the abbey was held by the Germans as the center post on the **Gustav Line,** a fortified system of defenses guarding the approaches to Rome, and was destroyed by the Allies in bitter fighting before the final German retreat (*see also Anzio and Salerno*). Today the monastery has been reconstructed. A **Lighthouse** commemorates the 1,100 members of the Polish Corps who were killed here.

**CASTEL GONDOLFO.** *See* CASTELLI ROMANI

**CASTELLI ROMANI,** *45 kilometers southeast of Rome via Route 5 in Latium*

This region in the Alban Hills overlooking the Roman Campagna was named for the 13 *castelli* (castles) built here during the Middle Ages. In ancient Roman times patricians built expensive villas in the vicinity. On the **Tusculum Estate,** where Cato was born in 234 B.C., Cicero wrote his treatise *Disputationes Tusculanae.* Castle sites include the nearby towns of **Frascati; Grottaferrata,** famous for its abbey established by Greek Basilian monks in 1004; **Castel Gondolfo,** the papal summer residence built between 1598 and 1603 by Carlo Maderna; **Nemi,** dominated by the **Castle of Ruspoli;** and **Ariccia,** with its mansions of the Chigi family; as well as **Marino, Albano, Genzano di Roma, Rocca di Papa, Rocca Priora, Monte Compatri, Monte Porzio, Catone,** and **Colonna.**

**CERTALDO,** *40 kilometers southwest of Florence via A-1 in Tuscany*

Giovanni Boccaccio (1313–75), friend of Petrarch and author of the renowned collection of tales known as the *Decameron,* spent the last years of his life in this town. In the rampart-encircled **Upper Town** are the storyteller's **house** and the **Boccaccio Museum,** which were damaged during World War II but have since been restored. A stone marker in the 13th-century **Church of San Jacopo** designates where the writer was buried.

**CERVETERI,** *35 kilometers southeast of Civitavecchia via A-16 in Latium*

This town stands near the site of the former Etruscan town of Caere, which was founded in the eighth century B.C. and over the centuries developed into a prosperous maritime center. With the aid of the Carthaginians the Etruscans waged successful warfare against the Greek colonies in the Mediterranean, expanded overseas, and became the seat of a refined culture. Tradition has it that the vestal virgins took refuge here when the Gauls sacked Rome in 390 B.C. Caere began to decline during the fourth century B.C.; the tyrant Denys of Syracuse (*see*) pillaged her ports, and the town was taken by Romans in 350 B.C. Caere was subsequently decimated by epidemics of malaria and Saracen invasions and was eventually abandoned in favor of the present Cerveteri in the 13th century A.D. The most interesting vestige of the vanished city is the **Banditaccia Necropolis,** whose huge extent reveals the importance of the cult of death to the Etruscans. This monumental area contains tumuli, or burial chambers, dating from the seventh to the third centuries B.C.; the most remarkable is the **Tomba dei Rilievi,** whose subterranean walls are decorated with painted reliefs depicting everyday Etruscan life.

**CORTONA,** *32 kilometers south of Arezzo via N-71 in Tuscany*
This ancient Etruscan town became an important art center in the 1300s, when the Sienese primitive painters, and later Fra Angelico, came here to work. Cortona was the birthplace of the famous Luca Signorelli (1441–1523)—a precursor of Michelangelo, and later of the baroque artist Pietro da Cortona (1596–1669). On the **Piazza del Duomo** near the ramparts stands the **Cathedral,** an 11th-century Romanesque structure remodeled during the Renaissance, and the **Diocesan Museum,** with its masterpieces by Fra Angelico and Luca Signorelli. Other sights include the **Piazza della Repubblica,** with its 13th-century **Palace of the Commune,** the Gothic **Church of San Francesco,** built in 1245 by Brother Elias, a disciple of Saint Francis's, who is buried here, and the 13th-century **Palazzo Pretorio,** containing exhibits of local antiquities.

**COSENZA,** *via A-3 or N-19 in Calabria*
This town was the scene of the death of Alaric, king of the Visigoths, in A.D. 410; after sacking Rome, the chieftain and his army were en route to conquer Sicily when he died here. His warriors reputedly buried him, with all his treasures, beneath the bed of the Busento River. Begun in 1185 and completed in 1222, the **Cathedral** houses the tomb of Isabella of Hainaut, the wife of King Philip Augustus of France. The pregnant queen fell from her horse at Cosenza and died giving birth to her child, the future Louis VIII, in 1190. Dominating the town is a Norman **Castle,** which in 1434 was the site of the marriage of Louis III of Anjou, brother of King Charles V of France, to Margaret of Savoy.

**CREMONA,** *via N-234, N-10, and N-45bis in Lombardy*
This ancient town was colonized by the Romans in 218 B.C. as an outpost against Gallic tribes. In A.D. 69 Cremona was destroyed and subsequently rebuilt by Emperor Vespasian. During the fifth century Cremona was again destroyed by the Huns, and in the sixth century it was rebuilt by the Lombard king Agilulf. The city was pillaged by Henry VIII of Luxembourg early in the 1300s and came under the domination of Milan (*see*) in 1334. Cremona became famous in the 17th and 18th centuries for the manufacture of stringed instruments; a celebrated native was Antonio Stradivari (1644–1737), the world's greatest violinmaker. Historic monuments include the imposing Lombard-Romanesque **Cathedral,** consecrated in 1190, with its late-13th-century, 387-foot-high **Torrazzo**— the tallest campanile in Italy; the early-16th-century **Palazzo Fodri,** the municipal palace, and the Renaissance **Palazzo Affaitati,** erected in 1561 and housing the **Municipal Museum.** About 2½ kilometers from town is the **Church of San Sigismondo.**

**CUMAE,** *via N-7Q on the Bay of Naples in Campania*
Situated on a hill overlooking the volcanic Campi Flegrei region, this ancient town was founded as a Greek colony between the

seventh and sixth centuries B.C. The Greeks defeated the Etruscans in a naval battle off the coast here in 474 B.C. Romans captured Cumae in 334 B.C., after which it began a course of decline that continued until it was looted by the Saracens in A.D. 915. Preserved at Cumae is the **Cave of the Sibyl,** hollowed out of rocks by the Greeks, where, according to popular belief, the sibyl rendered her oracles. Other ruins in the vicinity include the **Temples of Apollo** and **Zeus** on the **Acropolis, Cocceio's Cave,** an underground gallery linking Cumae with **Lake Averno,** made during the reign of Agrippa, and the **Arco Felice,** a 65-foot-high triumphal arch erected during Domitian's reign, between A.D. 81 and 96. Situated within a crater, the celebrated **Lake Averno,** believed by the ancients to be the entrance to the underworld, was mentioned in the *Odyssey* and *Aeneid* and during the empire was used by the Romans as a naval base, linked by a tunnel and canal to the sea.

**DONGO,** *via N-35 on Lake Como in Lombardy*

Toward the end of World War II, on April 27, 1945, Benito Mussolini and his mistress Clara Petacci were captured at this village by anti-Fascist partisans. They were executed the following day near Messegra, south of Tremezzo.

**ELBA,** *in the Tyrrhenian Sea in the Tuscan Archipelago*

As early as the sixth century B.C. the Etruscans were working iron mines on this island. Later, from May 3, 1814, to February 26, 1815, Elba and its neighbor Pianosa served as home for the fallen Emperor Napoleon. Napoleon presided over his tiny principality with a court of about a thousand soldiers under the control of Bertrand, grand marshal of the palace. During his brief stay Napoleon constructed roads, improved farming methods, and waxed nostalgic for his native Corsica on the horizon. Napoleon used a **Villa at San Martino** as his summer residence; he also stayed at the unpretentious **Villa dei Mulini** (mill villa) at **Portoferraio,** a town guarded by ruined ramparts.

**FERRARA,** *via A-13, N-16, or N-64 in Emilia*

Originally an independent commune, this city was ruled by the house of Este from 1208 until 1598. Ferrara experienced its golden age during the Renaissance, when it boasted a population of 100,000 and was the center of a society renowned for its gaiety and feudal splendor. Ferrara developed its own school of painting and was the home of the poet Ludovico Ariosto (1474–1533), who wrote the popular bestseller *Orlando Furioso,* and Torquato Tasso (1544–95), author of the epic poem *Jerusalem Delivered.* After 1598 Ferrara became a papal possession, and in the 1800s Napoleon made the town the departmental capital of the lower Po. Ferrara's principal remaining monument after heavy bombing in 1943–44 is the 14th-century fortresslike **Castello Estense;** its great halls recall the brilliance of its social gatherings, and its grim dungeons attest to the tyranny of the Estes. Other sights include the **Cathedral,** begun in 1135; the **Palazzo Schifanoia** (carefree palace), completed in 1469 as a summer residence for the Estes; the **Palazzo Diamanti,** built in the 15th and 16th centuries with a façade cut in facets like diamonds, which contains a picture gallery; the 15th-century **Church of Corpus Domini,** where Alfonso I, Lucrezia Borgia, and other Estes are buried; the **House of Ariosto,** where the poet died; and the **Hospital of Sant'Anna,** where the poet Tasso was confined for insanity for nearly seven years.

## FLORENCE AND VICINITY

BAPTISTERY, *on the Piazza del Duomo*
Dedicated to Saint John the Baptist, patron and protector of Florence, this octagonal structure was originally erected in the seventh or eighth century, possibly on the site of a former Roman temple, and served as the principal church of the city until the erection of the cathedral (*see*). In 1200 the wool merchants' guild had the building remodeled in its present form. The signory, or governing body of magistrates, sponsored a competition early in the 1400s for the decoration of the baptistery's bronze doors, which was won handily by Lorenzo Ghiberti. Executed between 1425 and 1452 with scenes from the Bible, the doors were a century later deemed by Michelangelo to be "worthy of the gates of Paradise." Inside the magnificently decorated interior, the poet Dante (1265–1321) and others were baptized. Opposite the baptistery, the 14th-century **Loggia del Bigallo** was where lost or abandoned children were exhibited to the charitable public.

BARGELLO PALACE, *on the Via del Proconsolo*
Begun in 1255 and completed in 1258, this forbidding-looking palace, built around a majestic courtyard, was originally the home of the *podestà*, Florence's chief magistrate, who according to the city statutes was always a foreigner. Throughout its history the structure was the scene of much violence and bloodshed. During the 14th century the palace suffered from fire and riots. In 1574 the building was converted into a prison and place of execution for criminals under the direction of the police chief, or *bargello*—whence its name. The vaulted hall was used as a torture chamber. Instruments of torture were burned in 1782, and from 1867 to 1875 the palace was restored to its present appearance and converted into the National Museum of Arts and Crafts. Today the museum houses a magnificent Renaissance sculpture collection, including the famous *David* of Donatello, the first nude statue executed since antiquity, and several of Michelangelo's youthful works.

CAMPANILE (BELL TOWER), *on the Piazza del Duomo*
In 1334 the artist-architect Giotto presented to the signory, the city magistrates, a plan for a bell tower adjoining the cathedral (*see*), which was duly approved. A decree was issued that "the Campanile ... exceed in magnificence, height and excellence of workmanship everything of the kind that had been previously achieved by Greeks and Romans when at the zenith of their greatness," and the foundations were laid. After Giotto's death in 1337, the work was continued by his successors in accordance with the original plans. Today the 276-foot-high structure, with its graceful lines and multicolored marble facing, remains unsurpassed in beauty.

CASA BUONARROTI, *70 Via Ghibellina*
The great sculptor, painter, and architect Michelangelo (1475–1564) resided here. His descendants transformed the dwelling into a museum, which they bequeathed to the city. The building houses youthful sculptures of the artist, including two marble reliefs executed under the patronage of Lorenzo the Magnificent, as well as manuscripts, drawings, and models.

CATHEDRAL OF SANTA MARIA DEL FIORE (SAINT MARY OF THE FLOWER), *on the Piazza del Duomo*
Named in allusion to the lily on the city crest, which marks the tra-

dition that Florence was founded in a field of flowers, this cathedral was commissioned by the Florentine republic and clothmakers' guild and was begun in 1296 by Arnolfo di Cambio. The multicolored marble-faced structure was completed in 1434 with the installation of Filippo Brunelleschi's great 350-foot-high dome. Among the many historic events that took place here was a dramatic episode in the conspiracy of the Pazzi banking family, abetted by Pope Sixtus IV, against their rivals the Medici, who ruled Florence. During mass on April 26, 1478, the choir was the scene of the attempted murder of Lorenzo the Magnificent, who was stabbed but escaped to safety; his brother, Giuliano, was killed by the hired assassins. Later, in 1493, Girolamo Savonarola, the fanatical Dominican prior of the monastery of San Marco (*see*), fulminated from the pulpit here against worldly vanities before terrified audiences. The axial chapel contains the bronze sarcophagus of Saint Zenobius, first bishop of Florence, sculpted by Ghiberti. In the first chapel of the north transept is the unfinished *Pietà* executed by Michelangelo at the age of 80. The artist Giotto was buried in the corner of the cathedral nearest his campanile (*see*). Beneath the building are the remains of the basilica of Saint Repartata, Florence's first cathedral.

**CHURCH OF SAN LORENZO (SAINT LAWRENCE),** *off the Via Canto de' Nelli*

Built on the site of a church consecrated by Saint Ambrose in 393, this Renaissance edifice was begun in 1419 by Brunelleschi and his pupils and paid for by the Medici. The façade was never completed. As the parish church and family vault of the Medici dynasty, San Lorenzo witnessed baptisms, the splendid marriage of Lorenzo the Magnificent to Clarice Orsini, when the entire population of Florence was feted for three days and nights, and funerals; the church was also the scene in 1564 of the solemn funeral ceremony for Michelangelo, whose body was buried in the church of Santa Croce (*see*). This church is renowned for its two Medici chapels. The **New Sacristy,** a quadrangular structure, was designed between 1520 and 1524 to contain the tombs of Giuliano de' Medici, duke of Nemours, and Lorenzo de' Medici, duke of Urbino. Surmounted with colossal statues representing the former as a man of action and the latter as a thinker, the tombs occupied Michelangelo for ten years and are among the world's sculptural masterpieces. Erected in 1604, the octagonal **Princes' Chapel** houses the sarcophagi of the six grand dukes of Tuscany. Adjoining the church is the famous **Laurentian Library**—Europe's first public library—designed by Michelangelo in 1523 and containing 10,000 books.

**CHURCH OF SANTA CROCE (HOLY CROSS),** *on the Piazza Santa Croce*

This Franciscan church was begun in 1294 by Arnolfo di Cambio and soon became the favorite Florentine place of burial. Within the single spacious nave are the elaborate tombstones of such illustrious Italians as the poet Dante (d. 1321), who was actually buried at Ravenna (*see*) since he had been banished from Florence for political reasons, the sculptor Ghiberti (d. 1455), the political theorist Niccolò Machiavelli (d. 1527), the painter and sculptor Michelangelo (d. 1564), and the scientist Galileo (d. 1642). Built for the great Florentine banking families, the **Bardi** and **Peruzzi Chapels** were adorned with frescoes by Giotto about 1310. At the end of the 13th-century cloisters to the right of the façade is the **Pazzi Chapel,** designed by Brunelleschi between 1429 and 1446.

**FIESOLE,** *on a hill to the north overlooking the valley of the Arno*
When Rome was a mere village this hilltop town was a flourishing Etruscan city; groups of its inhabitants are believed to have migrated to the valley below and founded a settlement that later became Florence. Fiesole subsequently became a Roman colony. Preserved today are the remains of the cyclopean **Etruscan Walls,** a well-preserved **Roman Theater** constructed about 80 B.C., the Tuscan-Romanesque **Cathedral,** with its battlemented bell tower, founded in 1028, and the **Monastery of San Francesco** (Saint Francis) on top of the hill. At the foot of the hill is the **Villa Palmieri,** where the company of ladies and gentlemen in Giovanni Boccaccio's *Decameron* spent ten days telling stories after they fled from plague-stricken Florence in 1348. The nearby **Villa of Careggi,** the most famous of the Medici villas, was built by Cosimo the Elder in the 1400s and subsequently became the favorite residence of Lorenzo the Magnificent.

**HOUSE AND TOWER OF DANTE,** *on the Via Dante Alighieri*
This medieval house and tower was the birthplace in 1265 of the great poet Dante Alighieri. The fortresslike structure was built at a time of civic unrest when members of the Florentine nobility possessed towers to which they could retire in the event of danger.

**MEDICI-RICCARDI PALACE,** *on the Via de Ginori*
This massive Renaissance palace was built by the architect Michelozzo di Bartolommeo between 1444 and 1452 for Cosimo Medici the Elder. The Medici family subsequently resided here for the next hundred years. Lorenzo the Magnificent (1449–92) made this establishment a brilliant center of the arts, which was visited by the most eminent personalities of the period; his son Giovanni, the future Pope Leo X, spent his childhood here; and Catherine de Médicis, who became queen of France, was born at the palace in 1519. The Riccardi family later acquired the structure. Principal features include the tiny private **Chapel,** decorated in 1469 with exquisite frescoes by Benozzo Gozzoli for Piero de' Medici (the Gouty), the **Medici Museum,** containing the death mask of Lorenzo the Magnificent, and the **Gallery,** with its immense ceiling fresco created in 1683 by Luca Giordano.

**MONASTERY OF SAN MARCO (SAINT MARK),** *off the Via Ricasoli*
Originally erected for Sylvestrian monks in 1430, this monastery was transferred to the Dominicans at the behest of Cosimo de' Medici in the mid-1400s. The architect Michelozzo refurbished the buildings, and the artist Fra Angelico adorned the walls with frescoes. In the cells of distinguished monks, Fra Angelico and his assistants executed edifying scenes intended to encourage meditation. Later in the century, from 1490 to 1498, the monastery was the seat of the great Dominican prior and preacher Savonarola, who believed that his divine mission was to make Italian urbanites repent of their profligate ways and abstain from luxurious living. Although his impassioned oratory from the pulpit at San Marco and later the cathedral (*see*) initially swayed the people, and he briefly became their political and spiritual leader, Savonarola antagonized Lorenzo the Magnificent and Pope Alexander VI, was excommunicated, and was eventually burned at the stake in 1498.

**PIAZZA DELLA SIGNORIA,** *off the Via Condotta*
Serving as the political and social center of the Florentine repub-

Florence's Piazza della Signoria, with the Palazzo Vecchio at left

lic, this square has witnessed many great historic events. Here unfolded the fierce struggle between Guelphs and Ghibellines—rival political factions—that divided Florence for centuries. The piazza was also a battleground of the 1478 conspiracy of the Pazzi banking family against the Medici. In 1497 the fanatical Dominican friar Savonarola had a huge pyramid of "vanities"—costumes, masks, cosmetics, musical instruments, books of poetry, and works of art —burned on the square; a year later, on May 23, 1498, Savonarola was himself burned at the stake at a spot now marked by a **bronze medallion.** During the 15th and 16th centuries the piazza was also the scene of public festivals, tournaments, and bullfights. So many statues of prominent Florentines—as well as such works of art as Donatello's sculpture *Judith and Holofernes,* symbolizing liberty —were placed on the piazza during this period that it became virtually an open-air museum. A replica of Michelangelo's *David,* the original of which is in the **Galleria dell' Accademia,** is also here. Dominating the piazza is the battlemented **Palazzo Vecchio** (old palace), begun in 1298 to serve as a residence for the members of the signory, the city's ruling council, and as a place for public deliberation. Savonarola was confined in its lofty tower for six weeks in 1498 before his execution. In 1550 Cosimo I de' Medici, grand duke of Tuscany, occupied the premises. Since 1881 the edifice has been used as the town hall. The **Loggia dei Lanzi** on the piazza—raised between 1376 and 1383—was used as a public meeting place in rainy weather and in the mid-1500s served as a guardroom for the Lanzi, foot soldiers of Cosimo I. Other buildings on the piazza include the **Mercanzia,** the former chamber of commerce built in 1559, and the **Palazzo della Condotta,** the domicile of officials entrusted to pay *condottieri,* the captains of mercenary armies.

PITTI PALACE, *on the Piazza dei Pitti on the left bank of the Arno River*
Intended to surpass all other Florentine palaces, this monumental Renaissance structure, faced with unhewn blocks of stone, was begun after plans by Brunelleschi in the mid-1400s for Luca Pitti, a rich merchant and one of the principal rivals of the Medici. After Luca's attempt to assassinate Piero de' Medici in 1466 failed, he lost his power and the building was left unfinished until 1549, when it was purchased by the Medici grand duke, Cosimo I, and completed as his residence. Later that century the Grand Ducal Palace, as it was called, was the home of Cosimo I's granddaughter, Marie de' Médicis, the future wife of King Henry IV of France. From 1865 to 1871 the Pitti Palace was occupied by the king of Italy when Florence was capital of the kingdom. Today the left wing of the

palace contains the **Palatine Gallery,** with its priceless paintings collected by the Medici that include masterpieces by the greatest artists of every age—Filippo Lippi, Titian, Tintoretto, and Rubens. Other sights at the Pitti Palace are the **Royal Apartments,** the **Silver Museum,** and the **Gallery of Modern Art.**

PONTE VECCHIO (OLD BRIDGE), *on the Arno River*
Florence's oldest bridge has commanded the crossing of the Arno at this site since Etruscan times. About 200 B.C. the Via Flamina, the great road connecting Rome with northern Italy and Germany, passed over the bridge, and the Roman camp of Florentia on the banks of the Arno subsequently developed into a rapidly growing town. The Ponte Vecchio was given its present appearance by Taddeo Gaddi in the 14th century A.D., and in 1345 butchers installed themselves in the 40 shops flanking the bridge. In the 16th century silversmiths and goldsmiths occupied the lateral shops, above which a corridor linking the Uffizi and Pitti palaces (*see both*) on either side of the river was built by Vasari. During World War II the Germans destroyed all bridges on the Arno except this one.

SAN MINIATO AL MONTE, *in the hills above town off the Viale Galileo*
Begun in 1013 and completed in the 13th century, this fine example of Tuscan-Romanesque architecture was dedicated to Saint Miniato, who introduced Christianity to Florence, was martyred in 250, and was buried on this hill. The church and surrounding monastery are enclosed by **ramparts** erected by Michelangelo in 1529; it was at these fortifications the following year that the artist distinguished himself in the defense of Florence against the troops of the Holy Roman Emperor, who were besieging the city. Nearby is the **Torre de Gallo** (Galileo's tower), where the famous scientist invented the telescope in 1609 and made his astronomical observations.

UFFIZI PALACE, *on the Piazzale degli Uffizi*
This Renaissance palace was commissioned by Grand Duke Cosimo I, founder of the junior branch of the Medici dynasty, to house the *uffizi,* or government offices. The imposing edifice was designed and erected by the architect Vasari between 1560 and 1574. The world-renowned Uffizi Gallery was established by Cosimo's son Francesco I, a devoted patron of the arts, who appointed Bernardo Buontalenti to arrange the art and sculpture collections of the Medici. Additions to the gallery were made over the years, and with the death of the last Medici in 1737 the gallery was donated to the Tuscan state on the condition that the collection always remain in Florence. Today the remarkable painting collection on the second floor—showing the development of Italian painting as well as other European schools and culminating in the **Sandro Botticelli Room,** which contains such masterpieces as *The Birth of Venus* and *Primavera*—is considered to be the richest and most varied in the world.

GENOA, *via A-12, N-1, and N-45 on the Tyrrhenian Sea in Liguria*
Established about 700 B.C. by Ligurian tribesmen, Genoa was later part of the Roman Empire and was occupied by the Lombards in A.D. 641. During the Middle Ages Genoa became an important maritime republic renowned for its strong fleet; as a result of its participation in the Crusades, Genoa founded trading posts in the eastern Mediterranean run by the famous Banco di San Georgio, the world's oldest bank, which administered the republic's revenues. In 1284 Genoa established its naval supremacy in the Tyrrhe-

nian Sea by defeating the Pisans at the Battle of Meloria. In 1380 Genoa was defeated by Venice at Choggia and lost control of the Levant, and throughout the 15th century it was dominated by foreign powers. Genoese independence was reasserted in 1528, when the great seaman and father of his country Andrea Doria (1468–1560) transferred his allegiance from France to Emperor Charles V of Spain on the condition that his city be a sovereign republic under a new oligarchic constitution. The 16th and 17th centuries saw intense artistic activity along with a general decline of commercial prosperity; from 1600 until 1684 Genoa gradually lost her Oriental possessions to the Turks, and her trade with North America was diverted to Atlantic ports. Occupation by the Austrians in 1746 led to a popular insurrection, which expelled the imperial troops. Genoa ceded Corsica to France in 1768, was later part of the French Empire, and by the 1815 Treaty of Vienna was joined to Sardinia. During World War II Genoa suffered damage from Allied bombings between 1942 and 1944. Chief sights include the immense **port**—today Italy's largest—with the city's oldest **lighthouse**, erected in 1544, rising 520 feet above the sea; the **Monument to Christopher Columbus** (1451–1506), the discoverer of America, who was born at Genoa; the Gothic **Palazzo San Georgio**, raised in 1260 and used from 1408 as the headquarters of the Banco di San Georgio, which contains in its **Grand Council Hall** 35 statues of Genoa's benefactors; and the **Cathedral of San Lorenzo,** begun in 985 and remodeled several times over the centuries, which preserves the ashes of Saint John the Baptist and the Sacro Catino (sacred cup) from which Christ reputedly drank at the Last Supper. In the heart of the **Old City** are the **Piazza Bianchi**, with the **Old Exchange**, and the **Torre degli Embriachi,** the surviving remnant of a 12th-century castle of the Genoese captain Guglielmo Embriacho, who during the Crusades led the Genoese in the capture of Jerusalem in 1099 and of Caesarea two years later. Possessing more palaces than any other town in Italy, Genoa boasts the **Palazzo Doria Tursi,** built in 1564 and now the town hall, the **Palazzos Bianco** and **Rosso,** erected for the Brignole Sale family and now housing art galleries, the **Palazzo Reale,** constructed about 1650 and subsequently purchased by the house of Savoy, the **Palazzo dell' Universita,** founded as a Jesuit College in 1623 and converted into a university in 1812, the 13th-century **Palazzo Ducale,** the former residence of the doges, and the Renaissance **Palazzo Doria del "Principe,"** presented in 1522 by the community to Andrea Doria, whose tomb and sword are in the nearby Gothic **Church of San Matteo.** About 1½ kilometers from town is the **Campo Santo,** or cemetery of Staglieno, laid out in 1850 and containing the tomb of the great Italian patriot and revolutionary Giuseppe Mazzini (1805–72).

**GREAT SAINT BERNARD PASS.** *See* SWITZERLAND

**GUBBIO,** *via N-219 or N-29B in Umbria*
Situated on the slopes of Monte Ingino and girdled by ramparts, this old Roman town was a prosperous free commune in the 11th and 12th centuries A.D. In 1151 the fiercely Ghibelline (a political faction opposed by the rival Guelphs) citizens of Gubbio under Bishop Ubaldi (later canonized) won a miraculous victory over a league of 11 other towns. Legend has it that Saint Francis visited the town early in the 1200s and pacified a ferocious wolf that was ravaging the countryside. The wolf was subsequently adopted by the people, and after its death its tomb became an object of pil-

grimage. The **Chapel of the Vittoria,** outside the ramparts, commemorates this miracle. From 1384 to 1508 Gubbio was governed by the Montefeltro family, dukes of Urbino; during his reign from 1444 until 1482 Federigo da Montefeltro enriched his native town with noble works of art. Gubbio became a papal possession from 1624 until 1680. Principal sights include the **Old Town,** the severe-looking Gothic **Palazzo dei Consoli** (consuls' palace), one of the finest public palaces in Italy, the **Palazzo Ducale,** erected in 1476 for Federigo da Montefeltro, and the well-preserved **Roman Theater,** dating from the time of Augustus.

**HERCULANEUM,** *via N-7Q on the Bay of Naples in Campania*
Legend has it that this seashore town was founded by Hercules, whence its name. Herculaneum was occupied by the Oscans, an aboriginal tribe, in the sixth century B.C. and successively by the Greeks, Etruscans, and Samnites, an ancient people descended from the Sabines. In the fourth century B.C. the Romans took the settlement. Like nearby Pompeii (*see*), Herculaneum met its tragic destiny in A.D. 79, when an eruption of Mount Vesuvius buried it under an immense torrent of mud and lava from 50 to 100 feet deep. Early in the 1700s Emmanuel de Lorraine, prince of Elbeuf, discovered the ancient theater while digging a well. Later in the 18th century the systematic excavation of Herculaneum was begun by Charles de Bourbon. Principal sights today, which give an intimate view of life 2,000 years ago, include the **Casa dell' Albergo,** a villa later converted into an apartment house, the **House with the Mosaic Atrium,** the **Casa Samnitica,** with its fine frescoes, the **Baths,** constructed at the time of Augustus and containing in the cloakroom skeletons of the attendants who sought refuge there during the eruption of Vesuvius, the **House of the Stags,** a patrician mansion, the **Palestra,** used for sports, and the **Pistrinum,** or bakery. Many of the objects found at Herculaneum are now in the National Archaeological Museum (*see*) at Naples.

**LAKE TRASIMENO,** *28 kilometers west of Perugia via N-75b in Umbria*
The shores of this lake were the scene of Hannibal's victory over the Romans on June 24, 217 B.C. Fought in torrid heat on the plain extending from Cortona (*see*) to the lake, the battle resulted in the slaughter of 16,000 Roman troops that included their leader, Consul Gaius Flaminius, by the Carthaginians; afterward the lake was red with blood. During World War II fierce fighting between the German and British armies took place at the site between June 28 and July 3, 1944.

**LORETO,** *via N-16 near the Adriatic coast in The Marches*
Containing the famous **Casa Santa** (holy house) of the Virgin Mary, this town is one of the world's most celebrated Christian places of pilgrimage. Legend has it that the Virgin was born at the House of Nazareth and subsequently resided there with her family upon their return from Egypt. Later Empress Helena, mother of Constantine, worshiped at the house and erected a church over it. By the 13th century the church was in ruins and threatened with desecration by Saracens. In 1291 two angels miraculously transplanted the Casa Santa to Dalmatia; still endangered, the structure was again removed by angels across the Adriatic to its present site on December 9, 1294, and deposited in a laurel grove—the Latin *lauretum*— whence the name Loreto. The shrine became a popular pilgrimage site, and the present church, known as the **Santuario della Santa**

Casa, was erected over it between 1465 and 1587, when it was completed by Pope Sixtus V, who also fortified the city with massive brick ramparts against possible Saracen attack; a **Statue of Sixtus V** stands in front of the church. Situated beneath the dome, the 36-by-17-foot Casa Santa—originally of rude stone—has been encased with marble reliefs and statues.

### LUCCA, *via A-11 in Tuscany*

This ancient Etruscan town became under the Romans an important city laid out on the plan of a military camp. After the fall of the empire, Lucca was ruled successively by Ostrogoths, Lombards, and Franks and in the 11th century became an independent commune. In 1314 the town fell to Uguccione della Faggiuola, lord of Pisa (*see*), who resided here with the poet Dante. After being passed back and forth between the Pisans and Florentines, Lucca purchased its freedom in 1369 from Holy Roman Emperor Charles IV for 100,000 florins and remained a republic until the French invasion of 1799. In 1805 Napoleon gave Lucca as a duchy to his sister Elisa Baciocchi, who laid out the **Piazza Napoleone** and was responsible for many civic improvements. In 1814 Lucca was taken by the Bourbon dukes of Parma, who ceded the city to Tuscany in 1847. Preserved here are the sixth-century **Cathedral of San Martino** (Saint Martin), remodeled in its present Romanesque style in the 11th century, which contains the **Volto Santo** (Holy Visage), a crucifix believed to be miraculous, the 12th-century Romanesque **Church of San Michele** (Saint Michael), and the **Old Town**, with its picturesque squares, palaces, towers, and ramparts.

### MANTUA, *via N-10 and N-62 in Lombardy*

Settled by the Etruscans, Mantua developed into a flourishing town under the Romans. Born here in 70 B.C., the poet Virgil made Mantua the scene of his *Georgics*. Under the princely Gonzaga family, which governed the city from 1328 to 1708, Mantua attained great prosperity and had a magnificent court. Austria annexed the duchy in 1708 and retained it, except for the Napoleonic period (1797–1814) until 1866, when it passed to Italy. Mantua's principal monument is the 450-room **Palazzo Ducale**, facing the Piazza Sordello and comprising the 16th-century palace proper, the 14th-century **Castello San Georgio**, a fortress, and the Renaissance ducal **Chapel of Santa Barbara**; the sumptuously decorated apartments contain many masterpieces of art, and the **Camera degli Sposi** (spouses' room) is painted with frescoes by Mantegna. Nearby the tall **Torre Gabbia** was where wrongdoers were exhibited. Other sights include the 13th-15th century **Palazzo Broletto**, the municipal building; the **Piazza delle Erbe** (square of herbs), faced by the 13th-century **Palazzo della Ragione** (law courts); the 15th-century **Clock Tower**; the **Church of San Lorenzo**; and a Romanesque rotunda. Also in Mantua are the Renaissance **Church of Sant' Andrea**, containing the preserved blood of Christ in its crypt, and the **Palazzo del Te'**, erected between 1525 and 1535 as a summer residence of the Gonzagas and decorated with huge frescoes.

### MILAN AND VICINITY, *via A-1, A-4, A-7, or A-8 in Lombardy*

Originally settled by Celtic tribes, this town was conquered by the Romans in 222 B.C. and subsequently developed into a large and wealthy city. From A.D. 305 to 402 Milan served as the seat of the western Roman emperors; here in 312 Constantine promulgated his Edict of Milan, making Christianity the official state religion; and in 375 Saint Ambrose, a doctor of the church, became the city's first bishop. Between the fifth and sixth centuries Milan was successively overrun by Attila's hordes, Franks, Burgundians, and the Lombards, who established a kingdom, which in 756 was taken by Pepin, king of the Franks, whose son Charlemagne donned the iron crown of the kings of Lombardy in 774. During the latter Middle Ages Lombard money changers and lenders from Milan were renowned throughout Europe. In 1277 the Visconti family became lords of Milan; the best-known Visconti, the tyrannical Gian Galeazzo (1351–1402), assumed the title of duke in 1395 and married Isabelle of Valois, whose great-grandson became King Louis XII of France, whence the origin of French claims to Italy. The Sforza family seized power in 1447, and under their patronage Milan became the capital of the richest state in Italy; Lodovico Sforza, Il Moro (1451–1508), transformed the city into virtually a new Athens, visited by the most eminent scholars, poets, artists—including Leonardo da Vinci—architects, musicians, and engineers of the period; Louis XII invaded Milan in 1500 and captured Lodovico, who ended his days in a French prison. The duchy became a Spanish possession in 1535 and was ceded to Austria in 1713. In 1797 the French army under Napoleon captured Milan, which then became the capital of the Cisalpine Republic and in 1805 the capital of the kingdom of Italy. The city suffered heavy bombardment during World War II and was taken by the Allies on April 29, 1945. The most celebrated structure in Milan today is the Flamboyant Gothic **Cathedral** of white marble, begun in 1386 by Gian Galeazzo Visconti and worked on for centuries, its façade being completed by order of Napoleon in 1809. Adorned with belfries, gables, pinnacles, and some 2,000 statues, the immense edifice accommodates 40,000 people. In the monastery refectory adjoining the Renaissance **Church of Santa Maria della Grazie** is Leonardo da Vinci's great masterpiece *The Last Supper,* executed for Lodovico Il Moro between 1495 and 1497. Founded in 386 by Bishop Ambrose, who baptized Saint Augustine here and whose remains are in its crypt, and rebuilt in the 11th and 12th centuries, the **Basilica of Sant' Ambrogio** was the church where Lombard kings and German em-

*The celebrated Flamboyant Gothic Cathedral of Milan*

perors were crowned. Also established in the fourth century, the **Basilica of Sant' Eustorgio,** in the 13th century, was the scene of the first tribunal against heresy; from an open-air pulpit in front of the church, Saint Peter Martyr, the inquisitor general, denounced heretics; his inhumane persecution of suspects led to his assassination in 1252, and his body is now entombed in a magnificent 14th-century sarcophagus in the **Portinari Chapel.** Other sights include the **Loggia degli Osii,** erected in 1316, from whose balcony sentences were meted out to criminals; the **Teatro alla Scala,** the world's most famous opera house, opened in 1779; the huge **Castello Sforzesco,** erected in the 1400s for Francesco Sforza on the site of the former Visconti Castle, which now contains a museum; the 17th-century **Palazzo e Pinacoteca de Brera,** housing a picture gallery; and the **Ospedale Maggiore,** a hospital founded by Francesco Sforza in 1456. Sixteen kilometers southeast of Milan is **Melegnano,** the scene of the famous 1515 battle in which the French under King Francis I defeated the Swiss troops of the duke of Milan; a monument marks the spot where Francis was dubbed a knight.

**MODENA,** *via A-1 or N-12 in Emilia*

Established by the Romans, this town in A.D. 1289 fell under the domination of the Este family, who governed from Ferrara (*see*). In 1540 Modena was elevated from a marquisate to duchy status. When they were expelled from Ferrara by the pope in 1598, the Estes moved to Modena, where, under Francesco I and Francesco II, the town reached the zenith of its prosperity. The city rebelled twice— in 1830 and 1848—against the Austrian rule to which it was subjected after 1814. Modena won its freedom in 1859 and became part of the kingdom of Italy in 1860. The town's principal monument is the 12th-century Romanesque **Cathedral,** dedicated to its patron saint, Geminiano, whose body is in the crypt; its 315-foot-tall **Campanile,** or bell tower, known as La Ghirlandina (symbol of the city), houses the famous "stolen pail"—an apple of discord for centuries— which was spirited away from Bologna in 1325. Other sights include the 18th-century **Palazzo dei Musei,** with the 600,000-volume Este library, the Este gallery of Emilian painting, the Cabinet of Medals, and the City Museum of Antiquities; and the baroque **Palazzo Ducale,** erected in 1634 under Francesco I d'Este.

**MONT CENIS PASS AND TUNNEL,** *via N-25 in the Graian Alps linking Modane, France, with Susa in Piedmont*

In 218 B.C. the Carthaginian general Hannibal possibly crossed the Alps into Italy by way of this 46-mile-long pass. Since the fourth century A.D. many invading armies have used the pass to enter Italy. Napoleon had a carriage road constructed here between 1803 and 1813. About 26 kilometers southwest of the pass is the Mont Cenis Tunnel, built between 1857 and 1870 and the first of the great tunnels through the Alps.

**MONTE CASSINO.** *See* CASSINO

**MONTE GRAPPA,** *via Strada Cadorna overlooking the Brenta River valley in Venetia*

During World War I, from the winter of 1917 until June, 1918, Italian troops bravely defended this mountain stronghold from the Austrians, who began their offensive drive at Caporetto. Today a huge ossuary contains the remains of 25,000 Italians and Austrians killed in action here.

**MONZA,** *via A-4 in Lombardy*

This town is dominated by its **Cathedral,** which was founded in 595 by Queen Theodolinda of the Lombards and was rebuilt in the Lombard-Gothic style in the 14th century. German emperors, including Henry II in 1014 and Frederick Barbarossa in the 12th century, received the iron crown of the kings of Lombardy here; the crown, whose iron rim is believed to have been made from a nail of the Holy Cross, is now placed over the altar. At Monza also is the **Villa Reale,** a Neoclassical structure inhabited by Eugene de Beauharnais, the French viceroy to Italy early in the 1800s, and later occupied by Humbert I, second king of Italy, who was assassinated by an anarchist here in 1900.

**NAPLES**

CASTEL NUOVO (NEW CASTLE), *on the Piazza del Municipio*

Originally constructed between 1279 and 1282 by Charles I of Anjou in a style reminiscent of the French fortresses of the period, this imposing castle, with its battlemented tower, was the royal residence of the Angevin rulers of Naples (1268–1442), and subsequently of the Spanish house of Aragon (1442–1503) and the Spanish viceroys (1504–1707). The castle's entrance, a grand triumphal arch of white marble, was built between 1455 and 1468 upon the order of Alfonso I of Aragon to commemorate his capture of Naples from the Angevins in 1442. Bas-reliefs on the bronze door beneath the arch illustrate the struggles of Ferdinand of Aragon against the forces of René of Anjou. The **Palatine Chapel,** or church of Saint Barbara, at the end of the courtyard was originally embellished with Giotto's frescoes, which have now been lost. During the reign of the viceroys the castle was the scene of brutal torture.

CERTOSA DI SAN MARTINO (CARTHUSIAN MONASTERY OF SAINT MARTIN), *on the Vomero Hill*

This famous charterhouse was originally constructed during the period of Angevin rule (1268–1442) at Naples by Charles, duke of Calabria, in 1325 and completed by Giovanni d'Anjou in 1368. The structure was remodeled in the Neapolitan baroque style in the 1600s. Today the former monastery contains the **National Museum of San Martino,** which features Neapolitan history, costume, and art. Overlooking the charterhouse is the bastioned 14th-century **Castel Sant' Elmo,** rebuilt by the Spanish in the 1500s.

CHURCH OF SANTA CHIARA (SAINT CLARE), *on the Via Mariano Semmola*

Erected in the Provençal Gothic style by King Robert the Wise of Anjou and his wife, Sancia of Majorca, this edifice is one of the most important churches in Naples. Although Giotto decorated its walls with frescoes, the paintings were whitewashed away when the interior was redecorated in the baroque style in the 1700s. During the 18th century the Neapolitan nobility and the royal family attended this church. The structure suffered heavy bombardment from air raids in 1943 and was subsequently restored. Today the chancel contains many sepulchral monuments, including the richly sculpted tomb of Robert the Wise, created in 1345, two years after his death.

CHURCH OF SANTA MARIA DEL CARMINE, *adjoining the Piazza del Mercato Nuovo*

This 12th-century church contains the remains of the German prince Conradin of Hohenstaufen, who in 1267–68 led an abortive attempt to overthrow the tyrannical rule in southern Italy of Charles of Anjou, who was abetted by the pope. Crossing the Alps in 1267, Conradin went to Rome, where by popular acclaim he was pronounced emperor. However, Conradin's force lost the battle at Tagliacozzo, outside Rome, and the 16-year-old prince was captured and delivered to the cruel Charles at Naples. Executed on the **Piazza del Mercato** on October 29, 1268, Conradin's last words were "Ah, my mother, what sorrow I have caused thee." A statue created by Bertel Thorvaldsen in 1847 now stands over Conradin's tomb. The church also contains the pulpit where Masaniello, leader of a popular uprising against the Spanish viceroy, spoke to the people in 1647 before he was murdered; although the insurrectionists were briefly successful, Spanish authority was reimposed in 1648.

### DUOMO SAN GENNARO (CATHEDRAL OF SAINT JANUARIUS), *on the Via Duomo*

Begun in 1272 on the site of the former temple of Apollo and Neptune—whence the antique granite columns of its interior—this cathedral was dedicated to San Gennaro, patron saint of Naples, who was the bishop of Benevento and was martyred in 305. The 17th-century baroque chapel of San Gennaro houses a silver reliquary with the skull of the saint, made in 1306, and an ampulla (flask) containing the saint's blood, which, according to tradition, miraculously liquifies three times a year. The cathedral also contains over its central portal the monument of Charles I of Anjou, built in 1559 to replace one destroyed earlier, and the tomb of Andrew of Hungary, who was strangled in 1345 by order of his wife, Queen Jeanne I of Naples. The cathedral has been restored several times.

### NATIONAL ARCHAEOLOGICAL MUSEUM, *on the Piazza del Museo*

This palace was originally constructed by the architect Domenico Fontana in 1586 to contain the royal stable and subsequently served as the seat of the university until 1777. In that year Charles III de Bourbon brought together in this building the works of art, constituting the famous Farnese collection, that he had inherited from his mother, Elisabetta Farnese. Later other collections were installed, including many of the antiquities uncovered at Pompeii and Herculaneum (*see both*), and the palace is now one of the most important public museums in the world.

### PALAZZO REALE (ROYAL PALACE), *on the Piazza del Plebiscito*

Although this grandiose palace was begun by order of the Spanish viceroy count de Lemos in 1600, after designs by Domenico Fontana, it was occupied by kings of Naples only after 1734. Niches on the long façade contain eight marble statues representing the various dynasties that ruled Naples from 1140 onward: Roger of Normandy, Frederick II of Hohenstaufen, Charles I of Anjou, Alfonso I of Aragon, Holy Roman Emperor Charles V, Charles III de Bourbon, Joachim Murat of imperial France, and Victor Emanuel II. Rebuilt after a fire of 1837, the palace now contains an important collection of tapestries and paintings.

### ORVIETO, *via A-1 in Umbria*

Built on a pedestal of volcanic rock, this town stands on the site of the former Volsinii, one of the 12 ancient Etruscan strongholds, which was destroyed by the Romans in 280 B.C. During the Middle Ages Orvieto was a center of the political faction of Guelphs, partisans of the pope; many a pontiff found refuge here during times of civil strife and foreign invasion. The town is dominated by its magnificently adorned **Cathedral,** begun in 1285, which contains a chapel with frescoes by Fra Angelico and Luca Signorelli (*see also Cortona*). Other sights include the **Well of San Patrizio,** completed in 1540—a marvelous feat of engineering consisting of a hollow tower 200 feet deep—the 12th-century **Palazzo del Popolo,** the 13th-century **Papal Palace,** constructed of volcanic rock, and numerous Etruscan tombs.

**OSTIA ANTICA,** *24 kilometers southwest of Rome via N-7 in Latium*
Founded in the seventh century B.C., this town at the mouth of the Tiber River flourished as Rome's principal trading port, where food supplies were sent to the city. At the height of the Roman Empire, Ostia boasted a population of 100,000 persons, and from the third century A.D. it also served as a naval base. About the time of Constantine, in the fourth century, the town began to decline, its population decimated by malaria and its harbor silting up. Centuries later, in 846, Ostia was the scene of a naval victory for the allied fleets of Pope Leo IV, and the towns of Naples and Amalfi (*see*), against the Saracens. Papal prayers were said to have brought on a storm that demolished the Moslem fleet. Ancient ruins preserved in the **Old Town** today include the **Caserma dei Vigili,** a firemen's barracks, the **Augusteum,** a temple for the worship of emperors, the **Piazzale delle Corporazioni,** where 70 commercial offices were situated, the **Thermopolium,** a bar with a marble counter and painted decorations of the items for sale, the **Insula dei Diptini,** three houses with wall frescoes, the **Baths,** the **Forum,** and the **Horrea Epagathiana,** a great warehouse. On the outskirts of Ostia is the late-15th-century **Castle** built by Cardinal d'Estouteville to defend Rome from pirates.

**PADUA,** *via N-11, N-47, and N-16 in Venetia*
A prosperous Roman city, Padua was in subsequent centuries overrun by the Huns and Goths and was restored under Charlemagne. During the Middle Ages the town was an important center of religious, cultural, and commercial life. Padua's university—the second oldest in Italy—was established in 1222 by Holy Roman Emperor Frederick II, and over the centuries it became famous for its faculties of law and medicine; students here included the poets Dante, Petrarch, and Tasso, and Galileo served as a professor; the university is currently situated in a palace known as the **Bo,** with a 16th-century court and a perfectly preserved anatomy theater of 1594. Dominating the **Piazza del Santo**—the monumental center of Padua—is the Romanesque-Gothic **Church of Sant' Antonio,** a colossal basilica known to the Paduans as Il Santo, which was erected from 1232 to 1307; the edifice was dedicated to Saint Anthony, who was born in 1195 at Lisbon, earned renown during his lifetime for his remarkable eloquence and for his performance of miracles, and died at Padua in 1231. Also on the piazza are the **Oratory of San Georgio,** erected about 1377 and containing fine Giottesque frescoes, the **School of Saint Anthony,** housing the Municipal Museum, and the celebrated equestrian **Statue of General Erasmo Gattamelata,** created in 1447 by Donatello in honor of the great hero of the Venetian Republic. Civic buildings preserved at Padua include the 14th-century **Palazzo del Capitano,** which was the former seat of the Venetian governor (Venice conquered Padua in 1414), and the **Palazzo della Ragione** (law courts), erected from 1172 to 1219 and famous for its **Salone,** a 260-foot-long room containing the

*In Pisa, the Campanile, or Leaning Tower (left) and the Cathedral (right)*

**Stone of Dishonor,** on which wrongdoers were exhibited. The **Chapel of the Madonna dell' Arena,** also called the **Scrovegni Chapel,** is decorated with a cycle of 38 frescoes painted by Giotto between 1304 and 1306; during the execution of these works the artist played host to the exiled poet Dante. The **Chapel of the Eremitani** (hermits), raised between 1264 and 1306 and embellished with frescoes painted by Mantegna in 1455, was damaged by bombing during World War II, in March, 1944, and has since been restored. Padua was liberated by the Allies in April, 1945.

**PAESTUM,** *41 kilometers southeast of Salerno via N-18 in Campania*

This city was founded and named Poseidonia by Greek colonists from Sybaris in the sixth century B.C. Later, under the Romans, Paestum became an important political and commercial center. Paestum began its decline with the downfall of the Roman Empire; a malaria epidemic and Saracen depredations early in the tenth century succeeded in driving out the inhabitants. Today ruins of the ancient city testify to its former greatness; they include the Doric-style **Basilica,** raised in the fifth century B.C., the **Temple of Neptune** (actually dedicated to Hera), and the **Temple of Ceres,** originally erected in honor of Athena.

**PARMA,** *via A-1 or N-62 in Emilia*

Situated on the ancient **Via Emiliana,** which still passes through it, this Roman colony declined after the fall of the empire, revived in the sixth century under the Ostrogoth monarch Theodoric, was a free city during the Middle Ages, and became a papal domain in 1513. Pope Paul III Farnese gave Parma to his debauched and tyrannical son, Pier Luigi, in 1545, and the Farnese family, patrons of the arts and letters, subsequently ruled Parma until 1727. In 1731 the city came under French Bourbon control; Don Philip, who reigned from 1749 to 1765, married King Louis XV's favorite daughter, Babette; his son, Ferdinand of Parma, established the academy of fine arts and patronized Giambattista Bodoni, the famous typographer. In the 19th century Napoleon's widow, the former empress Marie-Louise, became duchess of Parma, and the author Stendhal resided here, making the city the setting for his novel *The Charterhouse of Parma*. The principal historic site of Parma is the **Centro Episcopale** (Episcopal center), around which are grouped the Lombard-Romanesque **Cathedral**, whose dome is decorated with famous frescoes by Correggio, a native of Parma; the **Baptistery**, of Veronese marble, erected from 1196 to 1322; the baroque **Church of San Giovanni**, also decorated by Correggio; and the **Palazzo "della Pilotta**," completed in 1622 and named after the games of fives played in its court; it houses the **Museum of Antiquities**, the **National Gallery**, the **Palatine Library**, and the **Farnese Theater** (1619).

**PAVIA AND VICINITY,** *via A-1, A-7, N-35, N-234, and N-235 in Lombardy*
Founded by the Romans, this town later rivaled Milan (*see*) as a capital of the Lombard kings until its conquest by Charlemagne in the eighth century. Known as the City of a Hundred Towers—symbolizing the power of the patricians—during the Middle Ages, Pavia prospered under the domination of the Visconti family of Milan. In the 14th century it became the seat of a famous university, which was attended by Petrarch and later by Christopher Columbus. The Battle of Pavia was fought on the outskirts of town in 1525 between the armies of Holy Roman Emperor Charles V and Francis I, king of France, who was defeated and taken prisoner. Of historic interest is the **Basilica of San Michele**, originally raised by Lombard kings and later rebuilt in the Romanesque style, which was where Charlemagne, in 774, and succeeding German emperors were crowned "kings of Italy." Remodeled about 1100 in the Lombard-Romanesque style, the **Church of San Pietro in Cielo d'Oro** contains in its chancel the sumptuous white marble tomb of Saint Augustine (354–430), whose relics were brought to Pavia in 723. Other sights include the **Cathedral**, begun in 1488, to which Bramante and Leonardo da Vinci contributed plans, an 11th-century **Municipal Tower** to its left, and the **Castello Visconteo**, begun in the 1300s by Galeazzo II Visconti of Milan, which now houses the Municipal Collection and the Museum of Archaeology and Romanesque Sculpture. One mile west of Pavia is the **Church of San Lanfranco**, which contains the tomb of Lanfranc (1005?–89), a native of Pavia who served as archbishop of Canterbury under William the Conqueror. About 10 kilometers from town is the celebrated **Certosa** (charterhouse) **di Pavia**, or **Carthusian Monastery**, a magnificent example of Lombard art, which was established in 1396 by Gian Galeazzo Visconti in fulfillment of a vow made to his wife and was worked on by legions of artists for centuries; covered with sculpture, the renowned façade was begun in 1473 by the brothers Mantegazza and Amadeo; the monastic buildings were completed early in the 1400s, and the richly decorated cloisters after 1450; the church contains the tombs of the Viscontis and Sforzas.

**PERUGIA AND VICINITY,** *via N-75B overlooking the valley of the Tiber in Umbria*

One of the 12 federated city-states of ancient Etruria, this town, despite its massive Etruscan ramparts, fell to the Romans in 310 B.C. During the Middle Ages Perugia was an independent commune, and in the Renaissance the town produced an important school of Umbrian painters, the most famous of whom was Perugino, teacher of Raphael. Today Perugia's medieval character is reflected in the buildings on the **Piazza 4 Novembre**: the grandiose 13th-century Gothic **Palazzo Communale** or **Dei Priori** houses the National Gallery of Umbria with its collection of Perugian painters

of the 15th and 16th centuries; the **Fontana Maggiore** (great fountain), constructed in 1275, is covered with decorative sculptures; the unfinished 15th-century Gothic **Cathedral of San Lorenzo** houses the Virgin's wedding ring; and the **Collegio del Cambio,** the 15th-century chamber of commerce and exchange, contains fine frescoes by Perugino. Other sights include the **Etruscan Arch,** built of massive stone blocks, and the **Church of San Domenico,** containing the tomb of Pope Benedict XI, who ruled only eight months and is believed to have been poisoned in 1304 during the conspiracy of Anagni (*see*). About 6 kilometers southeast of Perugia is the **Hypogeum,** an Etruscan cemetery hewn in rock containing the tomb of the Volumni family of about 300 B.C.

**PIACENZA,** *via A-1, N-9, or N-10 in Emilia*
This town at the end of the **Via Emiliana** was settled by the Romans to guard an approach to the Po River. An independent republic during the 12th century, Piacenza was subsequently placed under the overlordship of the Visconti, the Sforzas, and the popes. When Pope Paul III Farnese gave the town in 1545 to his debauched son, Pier Luigi, who was assassinated there two years later, Piacenza came under the influence of the Farnese family, its destiny linked to that of Parma (*see*). In 1848, during the Italian independence movement, Piacenza was the first town to join Piedmont in establishing the Italian union. Today principal sights consist of the **Old Town,** girded by brick ramparts, the Lombard-Gothic **Palazzo Municipale** (town hall), erected in 1281, and the Romanesque **Cathedral,** raised in 1122; on its 300-foot-tall **Campanile,** or bell tower, is the *gabbia,* an iron cage in which criminals were exposed naked to public mockery.

**PISA,** *via N-1 at the mouth of the Arno River in Tuscany*
This ancient town was founded by the Etruscans and became a Roman colony in 180 B.C. During the 11th century A.D. Pisa prospered as one of the chief commercial ports in the Mediterranean, rivaling Genoa and Venice, and waged victorious wars against the Saracens, capturing Sardinia in 1025, and later the Balearic Islands. Pisans took part in the First Crusade in 1099, helping to capture Jerusalem and establishing a profitable trade with the East. Pisa reached the zenith of its power and wealth in the late 12th and early 13th centuries, a period marked by the development of the arts and the erection of splendid buildings. Late in the 1200s Pisa, aligned with the political faction of Ghibellines, involved itself in terrible struggles with surrounding Guelph republics; Pisa's power was broken in 1284 at the Battle of Meloria, when its navy was destroyed by the Genoese. A succession of lordships ruled the city until 1405, when it fell to the Florentines. Noble buildings that recall the grandeur of the Pisan republic include the round marble **Baptistery,** built between 1153 to 1278, and the **Cathedral,** begun in 1263 to commemorate the great naval victory over the Saracens at Palermo, Sicily (*see*), completed in 1118, which served as a model for other cathedrals in Tuscany; the interior contains a famous marble pulpit created by Nicola Pisano, and the bronze lamp whose motion inspired Galileo (1564–1642)—who was born here—to conceive his theory of the pendulum. Pisa's most famous structure is the **Campanile,** which owing to its oblique position is known as the Leaning Tower, begun in 1174 by Bonnano Pisano. The belfry began to incline before the third story was built, either due to a defect in the foundations or the settling of the subsoil, and the upper portion was

built with an incline in the opposite direction; from its summit Galileo worked out the laws of gravity. Sights remaining after heavy air bombardments in 1943–44 include the **Campo Santo** (sacred field), a cemetery, begun in 1270 and consisting of covered galleries containing tombstones, sculptures, frescoes, and a large domed chapel. The **Piazza dei Cavalieri**, the former center of town, is faced by the **Palazzo dell' Orlogio**, restored by Vasari in 1560, which originally comprised the ill-famed "Tower of Hunger," in which Count Ugolino della Gherardesca and his sons and grandsons were starved to death in 1288, and the National Museum of Pisan Sculpture and Painting, housed in the 15th-century **Monastery of San Matteo** (Saint Matthew).

### POMPEII, *via A-3 on the Bay of Naples in Campania*

Established by the Oscans in the fifth century B.C., Pompeii was initially under Greek influence and after the Samnite wars (343–290 B.C.) came under Roman domination. By the days of the late republic, Pompeii boasted a population of about 30,000, flourished as a popular resort city for wealthy patricians, and later was visited by emperors. In A.D. 63 nearby Mount Vesuvius, an active volcano, caused an earthquake that nearly razed the town. The inhabitants subsequently rebuilt the structures in the style of imperial Rome, but on August 24, A.D. 79, one of the most disastrous volcanic eruptions in history completely destroyed Pompeii—killing 2,000 people—as well as other towns in the region such as Stabiae and Herculaneum (*see*). Buried under a crust of volcanic rock, Pompeii was rediscovered in the 17th century, and in 1748, under Charles III de Bourbon, systematic excavations began. Today nearly an entire antique city has been uncovered, providing a precious fund of knowledge about the everyday domestic life of the ancient Romans. Most of the buildings that have been excavated are of brick with marble or plastic facing. The streets are lined with high pavements and steppingstone crosswalks for pedestrians. The **Forum,** the central part of town where religious festivals were held, was also a public meeting place. Buildings here included the **Basilica,** Pompeii's largest, most magnificent edifice, which was used for business transactions and the administration of justice, the **Temple of Apollo,** created before the Romans arrived, the **Temple of Jupiter,** and the **Macellum,** or market. Other ruins include the **Great Theater,** which seated 5,000, the **Odeon,** a small covered theater used for concerts, mimes, and ballets, accommodating 800 spectators, the **Amphitheater,** one of the oldest in Italy, constructed in 80 B.C., the **Stabian Baths,** with separate compartments for men and women, the **Fullonica Stephani,** a laundry and dyeworks, the **Porta Marina,** a gateway through which passed the road to the sea, and the **Herculanean Gate,** the main entrance into Pompeii. Of the many elegant villas formerly inhabited by aristocrats, the best known are the **Casa di Menandro,** decorated with fine paintings and mosaics, the excellently preserved **Casa dei Vettii,** with its remarkable frescoes, the **Villa of the Mysteries,** with its representations of initiation rites for the cult of Dionysus, and the **Casa del Poetica Tragico,** with its watchdog mosaic in the vestibule bearing the inscription "Cave Canem" (beware of the dog).

### POZZUOLI, *via N-7Q on the Bay of Naples in Campania*

Founded by the Greeks, this town, known as Puteoli to the Romans, became the principal port of Italy for trade with the East and Egypt before the opening of Ostia (*see Ostia Antica*). Saint Paul the

Apostle spent a week at Pozzuoli before proceeding to Rome in A.D. 62. The fall of the Roman Empire, volcanic eruptions from the nearby crater of Solfatara, and barbarian invasions combined to reduce the prosperous city to a humble fishing village. Pozzuoli's principal ruin is the imposing **Amphitheater,** which was completed under Emperor Vespasian (A.D. 69–79), and which, with a seating capacity of 40,000, was the fourth largest arena in Italy; here during the reign of Diocletian (284–305), Saint Januarius, patron saint of Naples (*see Duomo San Gennaro*), and his companions were martyred by being thrown to wild beasts. Preserved also are remains of the **Macellium,** or **Temple of Serapis,** the protecting goddess of trade, which was formerly a market lined with shops.

**RAVENNA AND VICINITY,** *via N-16 and N-309 in Emilia*
Strategically situated near the port of Classis, which was founded by the Roman emperor Augustus and could accommodate 250 war galleys, this town became the capital of the Western Roman Empire in A.D. 402, when Honorius abandoned Milan (*see*). The emperor's sister Galla Palcidia ruled Ravenna in place of her son Valentinian III during the fifth century. Subsequently the town fell to the Ostrogoths under Kings Odoacer (476–493) and Theodoric the Great (493–526), a Christian convert, who began to embellish it. In 540 Byzantine potentates conquered Ravenna, and the town—favored by Eastern Roman Emperor Justinian and Empress Theodora—developed into an important center of Christianity, governed by viceroys known as exarchs, and virtually became the Byzantium of the West. The bloody Battle of Ravenna was fought here in 1512, in which the young French warrior Gaston de Foix defeated the Spaniards and army of Pope Julius II; Gaston was killed, however, on the outskirts of town, a spot marked by the **French Column,** constructed in 1557. Today Ravenna contains rich and magnificent examples of early Christian art; its brilliant mosaics, described by Dante as a "symphony of color," are the finest in Europe. Sumptuous mosaics may be seen in the **Mausoleum of Galla Placidia,** erected about A.D. 450 and the oldest edifice in Ravenna; in the octagonal domed **Church of San Vitale,** begun in 525 on the spot

*Left: Theodoric's Tomb in Ravenna. Right: the Appian Way approaching Rome*

where Saint Vitalis was martyred and consecrated in 547 by Archbishop Maximian; in the **Baptistery of the Orthodox,** converted from a bathhouse in the fifth century; and in the **Basilica of Sant' Apollinare Nuovo,** erected about 500 by Theodoric. Other sights are **Dante's Tomb,** created in 1483—after his banishment from Florence, the poet resided in exile at Verona and then at Ravenna, where he died in 1321; and **Theodoric's Tomb,** a rough stone-domed monument constructed in 526. About 5 kilometers south of Ravenna is the **Basilica of Sant' Apollinare in Classe,** begun in 534 on the burial site of Saint Apollinaris, Ravenna's first martyr and bishop; consecrated in 549 and adorned with sixth- and seventh-century mosaics, the church is all that survives of the ancient town of Classis.

**RIMINI,** *via A-14 or N-16 on the Adriatic coast in Emilia*

Settled by the Umbrians, this town was taken by the Romans in 268 B.C. and became an outpost against the Gauls at the junction of the **Via Emilia** and the **Via Flaminia.** Julius Caesar occupied the town in 49 B.C. after crossing the Rubicon. Beginning in the 13th century A.D., Rimini rose to the pinnacle of its prosperity under the Malatesta family, who came to power in 1239 and ruled like tyrants for several centuries. The worst of the Malatestas was the military leader Sigismondo I, who in the 15th century murdered three wives, tortured his children, and yet was a cultivated patron of the arts and literature. In 1508 Rimini became a papal possession. During World War II it suffered severely from aerial bombardment. Preserved today is the Renaissance-style **Tempio Malatestiano,** a former Gothic cathedral remodeled after designs by Leon Battista Alberti in 1447 to shelter the remains of Isotta, Sigismondo I's mistress, which contains the tombs of the Malatestas. Other sights include the **Bridge of Tiberius,** completed under that emperor in A.D. 21, and the **Arch of Augustus,** raised in 27 B.C.

## ROME AND VICINITY

APPIAN WAY (VIA APPIA ANTICA), *approaching Rome from the southeast*

Begun by Censor Appius Claudius Caecus in 312 B.C., the most celebrated road of antiquity served as the principal communications link between Rome and southern Italy, Greece, and the eastern territories of the empire. Monuments along this picturesque thoroughfare include (leaving Rome at the gate of Saint Sebastian) the **Church of Domine Quo Vadis?,** built on the site where, legend has it, Saint Peter received a vision from Christ counseling him to return to Rome and martyrdom; the **Catacombs** *(see)*; the fourth-century **Church of San Sebastiano,** honoring the martyred saint, situated next to the cemetery where the Apostles Peter and Paul were originally buried; the **Circus of Maxentius,** raised in A.D. 309 by the emperor in honor of his son Romulus, whose tomb is nearby; and the **Tomb of Cecilia Metella,** a cylindrical tower erected in the last years of the republic, which in A.D. 1302 was transformed into a battlemented stronghold of the Caetani family. Although a modern highway (Route 7) is built alongside much of the Appian Way, out in the Roman Campagna the **Ancient Zone of the Appian Way** is still covered with the original Roman pavement; flanking the road are the ruins of many small tombs, including the **Tomb of the Horatii and Curiatii** *(see Albano Laziale),* and the remains of the **Villa Quintilii,** the former residence of two brothers who were assassinated in A.D. 182 by Emperor Commodus, who appropriated their property.

## ARCH OF CONSTANTINE, *on the Via di San Gregorio facing the Colosseum*

The largest and best-preserved arch in Rome was erected in A.D. 315 by the Roman senate and people to commemorate Emperor Constantine's victory over his rival Maxentius at the bridge of Milvio three years earlier. Bas-reliefs on the arch depict scenes from the life of Constantine as well as from the lives of his predecessors, Trajan, Hadrian, and Marcus Aurelius.

## BASILICA OF SAN GIOVANNI IN LATERANO (SAINT JOHN LATERAN), *on the Piazza di Porta San Giovanni*

Rome's cathedral and oldest church is situated on the site of the ancient palace of Plautinus Lateranus, a Roman of noble birth who plotted against Nero in the first century A.D. and as a result had his family property confiscated. The palace was subsequently restored to the Laterans and eventually became part of the dowry of Fausta, daughter of Maximus Erculeum, who married the emperor Constantine. After his conversion, Constantine presented the buildings to the pope to be used as an episcopal residence; a great church was erected at the site between 311 and 314 and consecrated by Pope Miltiades. Over the following centuries the church was destroyed and rebuilt many times. The basilica was abandoned by the popes when the Holy See was transferred to Avignon in 1307, and it suffered a disastrous fire the following year. Restored by Urban V in the 14th century and decorated by Francesco Borromini in the 17th century, the church houses in its vestibule an ancient marble statue of Constantine. The piazza on which the basilica stands has in its center a red granite **Egyptian Obelisk,** which was raised for a fourth-century-B.C. temple at Thebes, Egypt, and which was brought to Rome by Constantine. The basilica is surrounded by a 16th-century structure in which are preserved the **Scala Santa,** or holy staircase, of 28 steps, which, according to tradition, Jesus ascended when he was presented before Pontius Pilate for judgment; the octagonal **Baptistery of Saint John,** constructed by Constantine; and the stately **Lateran Palace** of 1586, which houses a fabulous collection of art in three different sections.

## BASILICA OF SAN PAOLO FUORI LE MURA (SAINT PAUL WITHOUT THE WALLS), *on the Via Ostiense*

The largest church in Rome after Saint Peter's Basilica (*see*), this basilica was established on the site of the tomb of Saint Paul the Apostle by Emperor Constantine in 314. The structure was enlarged by Emperor Valentian II in 386 and completed in the fifth century under Emperor Honorius, whose sister, Galla Placida, had the fabulous mosaic decorations installed in the nave. Nearly destroyed by fire in 1823, the basilica was restored and consecrated by Pope Pius IX in 1854.

## BASILICA OF SANTA MARIA MAGGIORE (SAINT MARY MAJOR), *on the Via Cavour*

According to local legend, the Virgin appeared in a vision to Pope Liberius and John, the Roman patrician, on August 5, A.D. 352, and ordered the men to erect a church on the site where snow would fall the following day. Evidence indicates that this church was actually begun by Pope Sixtus III in 431; the structure was remodeled in the 13th and 18th centuries, and it is presently the largest church in Rome dedicated to the Madonna. Raised in 1277, the Romanesque campanile, or bell tower, is the tallest in Rome.

**BATHS OF CARACALLA,** *off the Via delle Termi di Caracalla*
Accommodating up to 1,600 bathers, these enormous brick baths were built in A.D. 217 by the emperor Caracalla, one of late Rome's most dissolute rulers. The high degree of refinement of the Romans of that epoch is reflected in these opulent structures adorned with statues, stuccoes, and marbles. The baths consisted of the Frigidarium, the first great hall near the entrance, which contained the cold-water swimming pool, the Tepidarium, a tepid bath in a center hall adjoining the gymnasium, and the Calidarium, a hot vapor bath in a circular hall. Used until the sixth century, when they were damaged by Gothic invaders, the baths are now used for operatic performances. The Baths of Caracalla were exceeded in size only by the **Baths of Diocletian** (located on the Piazza della Repubblica), which were constructed between A.D. 298 and 306, accommodated more than 3,000 bathers, and were converted into the **Church of Santa Maria degli Angeli** in 1561 by Michelangelo. Today the former Baths of Diocletian also contain the **National Museum of Rome,** with its collection of Greek, Roman, and Christian art.

**CASTEL SANT' ANGELO,** *on the Piazza Adriana*
Erected between A.D. 135 and 139 to serve as a mausoleum for the emperor Hadrian and his successors, this imposing edifice in the form of a circular tower upon a square foundation was a funerary monument for 80 years, until the reign of Septimius Severus. Dominating the Tiber, the structure subsequently served as a fortress, a palace for popes and princes, a prison, and a military barracks. The castle received its present name after 590 when, legend has it, Gregory the Great, while trying to arrest a plague that was devastating Rome, received a vision of the Destroying Angel, who appeared atop this fortress sheathing his sword; the plague thereupon subsided. In honor of this event a bronze angel sculpted by Pierre Antoine Verschaffelt was placed on the building's summit by Pope Benedict XIV in 1753. The castle served as the prison of Pope Gregory VII in 1084, during his quarrel with Emperor Henry IV over investiture, and later, during the Renaissance, was where the victims of the powerful Borgia family were incarcerated and often murdered. Connected by a tunnel to the Vatican Palace (*see*), the edifice served as a sanctuary for the popes, especially in 1527, when Rome was sacked by the troops of Charles V. Today the Castel Sant' Angelo houses a museum that contains, in addition to its masterpieces of art, sculpture, and historical weapons, the prison cell of the famous Renaissance sculptor Benvenuto Cellini.

**THE CATACOMBS,** *extending from the exit from Rome on either side of the Appian Way*
These ancient tunnels hollowed out of volcanic rock were where the early Christians worshiped and were buried. Constructed on the site of a Roman necropolis, the most important catacombs are those of **Saint Callistus,** which second-century Christians used as a meeting place and sanctuary from persecution; these catacombs contain the **Crypt of the Popes** and the venerated tomb of the martyred Saint Cecilia, discovered by Pope Paschal I in 812. The **Catacombs of San Sebastiano,** containing the tomb of Saint Sebastian as well as many early Christian inscriptions, are situated beneath the **Church of San Sebastiano** (*see Appian Way*). Built at the end of the first century by Saint Domitilla, niece of Emperor Domitian, the **Catacombs of Domitilla** are the most extensive in Rome and contain the tombs of Saints Nereus and Achilleus, which are now housed

under a fourth-century church; the subterranean chamber of the Flavians; and the cell of Saint Petronilla. Constructed between the second and fourth centuries, the well-preserved **Catacombs of Saint Agnes,** a saint martyred in 104, lie beneath the **Church of Sant' Agnese** and contain many interesting epigraphic monuments.

### CHURCH OF GESÙ, *on the Via del Plebiscito*

The mother church of the Jesuit order was constructed by the architect Giacomo da Vignola in 1568. The structure itself, with its numerous chapels, altars, tribunes, and wide bays, and its single nave to facilitate preaching, expresses the aim of the Counter Reformation, which was to make Catholicism more accessible and appealing to the people. Saint Ignatius of Loyola, founder of the Jesuits, is buried beneath the elaborate altar in a chapel in the left transept. A solid silver statue of the saint originally stood in the chapel, but Pope Pius VI melted it down to pay a war debt to Napoleon.

### COLOSSEUM, *off the Via dei Fori Imperiali*

Also known as the Flavian Amphitheater, this immense structure is the most important monument of ancient Rome. Begun in A.D. 72 on the site of a lake near the Domus Aurea (*see*), or Nero's House, the edifice was dedicated by Titus in A.D. 80 in a three-month-long celebration during which 500 wild beasts and many gladiators were slain. Gladitorial combats, venations (the slaying of wild beasts), and the persecution of early Christians took place in the arena—which had a seating capacity of more than 50,000 spectators—until such amusements were abolished by Emperor Honorius in A.D. 405. Damaged by an earthquake in the mid-fifth century, the Colosseum was converted into a fortress, and during the Middle Ages it was used by the popes as a marble quarry. Today the Colosseum still reflects its former splendor; it consists of three superimposed stories composed of arches supported by piers. The emperor's box was situated on a podium that surrounded the arena, and separate thrones were provided for senators, government officials, and vestal virgins; knights and tribunes sat in the first tier of seats; citizens sat in the second, and the third tier and gallery were reserved for the lower classes and slaves.

### COLUMN OF MARCUS AURELIUS, *on the Piazza Colonna*

Erected between A.D. 176 and 193, this 98-foot-high shaft commemorates the victories of Emperor Marcus Aurelius over the Germans and Sarmatians. Bas-reliefs depict episodes in the emperor's

*From left to right in Rome: equestrian statue of Marcus Aurelius in the Piazza dei Campidoglio; the Roman Forum; a view of the Tiber River showing the*

wars, and the column is surmounted by a statue of Saint Paul, placed there in the 16th century by Pope Sixtus V.

**DOMUS AUREA,** *on the Via Labicano opposite the Colosseum*
This fabulous "golden house" was raised by Emperor Nero after the devastating fire that swept Rome in A.D. 64. The rooms of the palace were lavishly decorated with frescoes and stucco in the Pompeian style, which later inspired painters during the Renaissance. The structure is now in ruins.

**IMPERIAL FORUMS,** *off the Via dei Fori Imperiali to the north of the Roman Forum*
In the last days of the republic, from the time of Julius Caesar on, the Roman Forum (*see*) became inadequate to accommodate a growing population, and these forums were built to supplement the original. The **Forum of Julius Caesar,** the earliest, was begun in 54 B.C. Consisting of a porticoed piazza enclosing religious and secular structures, the forum was dominated by the **Temple of Venus Genetrix,** constructed in 46 B.C. in honor of the goddess who aided Caesar in his victory over his rival Pompey at the Battle of Pharsalus, Greece, in 48 B.C. Three Corinthian columns of the structure survive. The **Augustan Forum,** begun in 32 B.C. to commemorate Brutus and Cassius, two of the conspirators who murdered Caesar and were then killed themselves at the Battle of Philippi in 42 B.C., is highlighted by the ruins of the **Temple of Mars** the **Avenger.** Constructed in A.D. 114, the **Forum of Trajan** was the largest and latest forum of the imperial age. The 100-foot-high **Trajan's Column** is ornamented with spiral reliefs depicting the emperor's military exploits against the Dacians; below are Trajan's sepulchral vault and **Trajan's Market,** an impressive suite of buildings used for offices and shops. Adjoining the Imperial Forums and facing the Colosseum (*see*) are the ruins of the imposing **Basilica of Maxentius and Constantine,** which was begun in A.D. 306 and used as law courts and an exchange.

**KING VICTOR EMMANUEL II MONUMENT,** *on the Capitoline Hill facing the Corso*
Erected from 1885 to 1911 by Count Giuseppe Sacconi, this colossal marble memorial, 500 feet long and 200 feet high—the largest in the world—was dedicated to Victor Emmanuel II, father of his country and first king of a united Italy, who reigned from 1861 to 1878. The monument is embellished with statues, sculptural works, foun-

*Castel Sant' Angelo on the right and Saint Peter's Basilica on the left; the monumental Spanish Steps leading up from the Piazza di Spagna*

tains, and a huge equestrian statue in gilded bronze of the king, mounted on what is known as the **Altar of the Fatherland.** Beneath the altar is the **Tomb of the Unknown Soldier** of World War I.

### MAUSOLEUM OF AUGUSTUS, *off the Via di Ripetta*
This monument was raised by Emperor Augustus in 27 B.C. to serve as a mausoleum for himself and the imperial family. Funeral urns were placed in a crypt inside. During the Middle Ages the structure was used as a fortress. Nearby is the **Ara Pacis Augustus,** an altar built in 13 B.C. to honor the era of peace the emperor had inaugurated. Both structures have been reconstructed.

### PALATINE HILL, *off the Via di San Teodoro near the Roman Forum*
One of the celebrated seven hills of Rome, the Palatine was where Romulus in 754 B.C. traced the boundary of the original city of Rome. Noble families, including those of Cicero, Catiline, and Mark Antony, resided here during the republic. When Augustus became emperor in 27 B.C., he erected his palace on the hill, as did subsequent emperors of the imperial period. During the Renaissance, in the 1500s, the ancient structures that had previously fallen into ruin were incorporated into the magnificent Villa Farnese, of which the **Farnese Gardens** survive today. Ancient remains include the **Temple of Cybele,** constructed in 204 B.C. and restored by Augustus, the **House of Livia,** which really belonged to Augustus, and the subterranean **Crypto Porticus,** built in the time of Nero to link the palaces of Augustus and Tiberius. Nearby are the late-first-century **Flavian Palace,** where the emperors held their audiences, the **House of Augustus,** a private imperial residence, and below it is a **Hippodrome,** or stadium, built by Domitian. At the end of the terraced garden are ruins of the **Baths of Septimius Severus,** which were supplied with water from the aqueducts of Claudius, and the **Palace of Septimius Severus.**

### PANTHEON, *off the Via Seminario*
Dedicated to the seven planetary divinities, this edifice, with its majestic dome, was built by Agrippa in 27 B.C., restored by Domitian after the fire of A.D. 80, and given its present appearance by Emperor Hadrian between 117 and 125. Pope Boniface IV converted the building into a Christian church in 609, and during the Middle Ages the Pantheon was used as a fortress. Subsequent popes despoiled the building, especially Pope Urban VIII, who in the 17th century melted down the bronze roof for 80 cannon in the Castel Sant' Angelo (*see*) and for Bernini's baldaquin in Saint Peter's Basilica (*see*). Seven kings of Italy and the painter Raphael are buried here.

### PIAZZA DEI CAMPIDOGLIO, *on the Capitoline Hill*
Situated on one of the original seven hills of Rome that served as an acropolis and religious center in the early days of Roman history, this piazza was laid out by Michelangelo in 1536 upon the occasion of Holy Roman Emperor Charles V's visit to Rome. The Campidoglio is approached by the monumental **stairs,** or "cardonate," designed by Michelangelo; about midway up is a **statue** commemorating Tribune Cola di Rienzi, who in 1354 led a victorious revolt against the papacy. The stately palaces flanking the square are the **Senatorial Palace,** with its remarkable double staircase, which is built on the site of the ancient Roman senate and is currently used as the town hall of Rome; the **Capitoline Museum,** established by

Pope Sixtus IV in the 15th century, which contains a collection of classical sculpture; and the **Palace of the Conservatori,** which houses a museum of ancient statues, including the colossal marble head of the emperor Constantine. In the center of the Campidoglio stands the enormous **Equestrian Statue of Marcus Aurelius,** created in the second century A.D. and the only imperial equestrian statue ever discovered.

### PIAZZA NAVONA, *off the Via dei Coronari*

This baroque square was the site of the stadium built by Domitian in the first century A.D. and used for horse racing, whence its elliptical shape. During the Middle Ages the popes flooded the piazza and floated small boats on it for aquatic festivals. Today the sculptor Giovanni Lorenzo Bernini's famous **Fountain of the Four Rivers,** completed in 1651, is situated in the center of the piazza. The **Church of Sant' Agnese,** on the west side of the square, is, according to legend, built on the site where Saint Agnes was publicly exposed before her martyrdom; her long hair veiled her from the gaze of the multitude. Bounding the piazza also is the early Renaissance **Palazzo della Cancelleria,** built from 1483 to 1510, which is currently the residence of the pontifical chancellor.

### PIAZZA DI SPAGNA

This celebrated square stands on the site of the old Spanish embassy to the Holy See. A boat-shaped fountain in the center was built in 1598 to commemorate the great flood of that year. Facing the piazza are the **Palace of the Propaganda Fide,** erected in 1627 and the world headquarters of Catholic missions, the **Church of Trinità dei Monti,** constructed between 1495 and 1585 for the French residents of Rome, and a colossal flight of 137 steps completed in 1725. A tablet at the foot of the **Spanish Steps** designates the **house** where Keats died in 1821; on the **Via Sistina,** nearby, many artists and intellectuals resided during the 19th century.

### ROMAN FORUM, *between the Capitoline (Piazza Campidoglio) and the Palatine hills*

During the republican era, between 502 and 27 B.C., this forum was the hub of religious, civil, and commercial activity in Rome. The forum was abandoned after the barbarian invasions of the fifth century A.D. and was known as the Campo Vaccino—field of cows—at the time of the Renaissance. Excavations took place here during the 19th and 20th centuries. Outside the forum wall is the **Portico of the Dei Consentes,** an elegant colonnade of A.D. 367 dedicated to the cult of the 12 Roman gods. Nearby are ruins of the **Temple of Vespasian,** built in A.D. 81, and the **Temple of Concord,** erected in 370 B.C. to commemorate the reconciliation of the patricians and the plebeians. Beneath the **Church of San Giuseppe** is the famous subterranean **Mamertine Prison;** the upper cell served as the state prison of ancient Rome and confined, among others, Jugurtha, king of Numidia, and Vercingetorix, chief of the Gauls; the lower chamber, constructed in 300 B.C., was where Saint Peter baptized his jailers with water from a spring that miraculously burst forth there. Just inside the forum entrance on the **Via dei Fori Imperiali** are the remains of the **Basilica Emilia,** constructed in 179 B.C., which was used for business transactions. The adjacent **Curia** was rebuilt by Julius Caesar and in the fourth century by Diocletian; its great meeting hall housed the senate during the late empire. Opposite the Curia is the **Lapis Niger,** a black marble platform that according to tradition covered the grave of Romulus, founder of Rome. A fragment of a pyramid nearby contains what is believed to be the oldest extant inscription in the Latin language, carved in the sixth or fifth century B.C. The imposing **Triumphal Arch of Septimius Severus**, consisting of three archways, was raised in A.D. 203 to commemorate the tenth anniversary of the emperor's reign, as well as his defeat of the Parthians. The **Rostrum**, to the left of the arch, served as a tribune for orators and was decorated with the prows of ships captured by Roman galleys at Antium in 338 B.C. On the main square of the forum are the **Column of Phocas**, the latest monument on the forum, erected in A.D. 608, and the ruins of the **Temple of Saturn**, built in 497 B.C. and restored in 42 B.C. and in the third century A.D., in which was celebrated the Saturnalia, whence our modern carnivals derive, and whose basement formerly held the state treasury. Adorning the **Via Sacra**, where triumphal processions marched, is the **Basilica Julia**, erected by Julius Caesar in 54 B.C. and used as a law court and exchange. Nearby are the remains of the **Temple of Castor and Pollux**, erected in 484 B.C. to commemorate the heavenly twins, known as the Dioscuri, children of Zeus, who aided the Romans in defeating the Tarquins and Latins at the Battle of Lake Regillus. To the left, the **Pool of Juturna** was where the Dioscuri watered their horses upon bringing news of their victory to the forum. The most important Christian structure on the forum, the venerable **Church of Santa Maria Antiqua**, was the first pagan temple in Rome to be converted into a church; it contains frescoes created from the sixth to eighth centuries. The circular **Temple of Vesta** contained a sacred flame tended by maidens who resided in the **House of the Vestal Virgins**, raised in the early years of the republic. Also in the vicinity are the **Temple of Julius Caesar**, constructed by Octavian in 42 B.C. on the site where Julius Caesar had been cremated two years earlier, the ruins of the **Arch of Augustus**, erected in 19 B.C., the second-century A.D. **Temple of Antoninus and Faustina**, and the **Arch of Titus**, built in A.D. 81, whose famous bas-reliefs commemorate the victories of Vespasian and Titus, conquerors of Jerusalem.

### VILLA ADRIANA, *27 kilometers from Rome via N-3 in Latium*
Begun in A.D. 120 outside the ancient resort town of Tivoli, which according to tradition was established four centuries before the foundation of Rome by the Siculi, this imperial villa, with its fountains, statues, cypresses, and lakes, was the favorite residence of the emperor Hadrian. Here were built reproductions in miniature of the monuments that Hadrian had been impressed by on his travels around the empire, especially in Greece and Egypt, and they were filled with statues that he brought back. Hadrian's successors further embellished the villa, and it was later sacked by barbarians. During the Renaissance, popes began excavating the villa. Chief sights today include the four-faced gateway known as the **Pecile of Athens**, the **Canopus**, a copy of an Egyptian canal, the **Maritime** and **Greek Theaters**, the **Terrace of Tempe**, and the **Imperial Palace**.

### VILLA MEDICI, *on the Viale Trinita dei Monti*
Raised in the mid-1500s for Cardinal Ricci, this villa was acquired by the Medici family as a residence for their cardinals in the 1600s. In 1803 Napoleon made the villa into the Roman headquarters of the French Academy, founded by Louis XIV in 1660, where winners of the Prix de Rome would attend a 3½-year course.

*A vista of the beautiful medieval towers of San Gimignano*

**SALERNO,** *via A-3 on the Gulf of Salerno in Campania*

Established by the Greeks and subsequently ruled by the Romans, this town became a principality of the Lombards, who invaded Italy in 568. During the Middle Ages the town prospered and became renowned for its school of medicine, the oldest in the Western world, which from the tenth century was run by the Benedictines. In 1076 the Norman leader Robert Guiscard captured Salerno from his brother-in-law Gisolf, who ceded a precious relic, the tooth of Saint Matthew, along with the town, and made Salerno the capital of the kingdom of Naples. In 1084 the **Cathedral of Saint Matthew,** whose crypt houses the tooth of Saint Matthew, was erected in the Sicilian-Norman style by Guiscard and consecrated by Pope Gregory VII, who was buried there the following year. Pope Gregory had been responsible for the significant reform of making the investiture of popes a duty vested solely in the College of Cardinals, rather than a privilege of the Holy Roman Emperor; and aided by Guiscard, he had duly humbled Emperor Henry IV in a costly war that reduced Rome's monuments to ruins and forced him to retire to Salerno. During World War II **Salerno Beach** was the site of Allied landings during the campaign to liberate Italy from the German army (*see also Taranto*). General Mark Clark's United States Fifth Army landed on September 9, 1943, one day after Italy had officially surrendered. Hopes of a quick campaign vanished as panzer counterattacks nearly pushed the invaders into the sea. American paratroopers reinforced the beachhead, and the Allies drove on to Naples by October 1.

**SAN GIMIGNANO,** *via A-11 in Tuscany*

Girdled by ramparts pierced by three gates, San Gimignano is known as the town of the beautiful towers. During the Middle Ages families of noble birth competed with one another in erecting tall towers, which they used as places of refuge during the civil disturbances caused by the Guelphs and Ghibellines, rival political

65

ITALY

factions. In 1300 the poet Dante, an envoy of Florence, spoke in the new **Palazzo del Popolo,** or **del Podestà** (of the governor), which had been begun in 1288 and boasted a 117-foot-tall tower, and urged the commune to send representatives to an assembly of Guelphs; however, he failed to placate the feuding families. In addition to 14 extant towers—there were originally 72—medieval remains include the 11th-century **Cathedral,** with its **Chapel of Santa Fina,** dedicated to the local saint of the wallflowers (flowers allegedly grew on Saint Fina's coffin and on the town towers on the day of her death); the old **Palazzo del Podestà,** with its two towers and municipal loggia, erected in 1239; the **Piazza del Cisterno,** with its 13th-century cistern in the center; and the 13th-century **Churches of Sant' Agostino** and **San Jacobo,** which belonged to the Templars.

**SAN REMO,** *via N-1 on the Italian Riviera in Liguria*

The famous Canary palms lining the main promenade—the **Corso dell' Imperatrice**—of this resort town supply palm branches to Saint Peter's Basilica (*see*) in Rome every Palm Sunday. This privilege was granted to the Bresca family of San Remo in 1586 by Pope Sixtus V, after the sailor Bresca provided valuable assistance in raising the enormous granite obelisk in front of Saint Peter's. After World War I, in April, 1920, San Remo was the scene of an international conference of countries that had participated in the war. Sights include the 12th-century **Romanesque Cathedral** and the **Old Town.**

**SARDINIA**

**CAGLIARI,** *via N-31 at the southern tip of the island*

This port town was founded by the Phoenicians and later colonized by the Carthaginians, who occupied Sardinia in the seventh century B.C. Cagliari came under Roman domination after 238 B.C. When the Pisans established their supremacy on Sardinia in A.D. 1200, after 200 years of sporadic warfare with Genoa, they fortified the town and erected a Romanesque-Gothic **Cathedral.** Preserved today are the **Roman Amphitheater,** the fifth-century **Saint Saturninus's Basilica**—one of the oldest Christian churches in the Mediterranean—and the **Tower of Saint Pancrus,** a vestige of the Pisan fortifications. An important military base, the town was bombed for two years (1941–43) during World War II.

**NURAGHI DI SERRA ORRIOS,** *22 kilometers east of Nuoro near the Dorgali road*

Consisting of huge blocks of stone laid without mortar, these curious dwellings, known as nuraghi, were constructed by Sardinia's prehistoric inhabitants during the Bronze and early Iron ages. More than 6,000 nuraghi are scattered, singly or in groups, throughout the island; many were built along coasts and valleys as defenses against invaders. Shaped like truncated cones, the nuraghi contained rooms that served as the chieftain's home and offered shelter and protection to local tribesmen.

**SICILY**

**AGRIGENTO,** *via N-118, N-189, and N-115*

Situated 1,000 feet above the sea, this ancient town was the wealthiest and second largest community in Sicily during the Greek period. The Greek philosopher and statesman Empedocles was born here in the fifth century B.C.; in modern times Agrigento was the birthplace of the dramatist Luigi Pirandello (1867–1936). Today there are many remains of Agrigento's former grandeur. Although a number of the majestic Doric temples that stood in the **Valley of the Temples** were destroyed by earthquakes and the antipagan zeal of the early Christians, the **Temple of Concord,** erected between 450 and 440 B.C. and later used as a church, is the best extant specimen of Doric architecture in the Hellenic world. Preserved also are ruins of the **Temple of Hercules,** the oldest temple at Agrigento, dating from the sixth century B.C., and the fifth-century-B.C. **Temples of Jupiter** and of **Juno Lacina.** Other sights include the first-century-B.C. **Oratory of Phalaris,** dedicated to the first "tyrant" of Agrigento, the **Amphitheater,** and the **Roman Town.**

### MESSINA, *via N-114 at the entrance to the Strait of Messina*

This is the legendary home of the female monsters Scylla and Charybdis, which challenged sailors in Homer's *Odyssey*. Established in the fifth century, Messina was involved in the Punic War against Carthage in 264 B.C. and subsequently became an influential Roman town. The chief sight today is the **Cathedral,** built in 1092, damaged by the great earthquake of 1908, and since restored. In World War II, during the Allied conquest of Sicily—which was achieved in 39 days—General George Patton's United States Seventh Army and General Sir Bernard Montgomery's British Eighth Army converged on Messina on August 17, 1943. But the Germans had evaded them and escaped to Italy with three crack divisions. (*See also Palermo.*)

### MONREALE, *via N-186 overlooking Palermo*

This famous Benedictine abbey was constructed from 1174 to 1189 by order of the Norman king William II, "the Good." A masterpiece of ecclesiastical architecture, the **Cathedral** reflects a remarkable combination of Norman architecture and Sicilian-Arab decoration; the interior is encrusted with 70,000 square feet of splendid Byzantine mosaics, and the right transept contains the tombs of William I and William II, whose wife was Joan, daughter of King Henry II of England. The **Cloisters** of the adjoining monastery consist of pointed arches resting on paired columns grouped around a court, in the center of which is a Saracen fountain reminiscent of the Alhambra in Spain.

### PALERMO, *via N-113*

Settled by the Phoenicians in 700 B.C., Panormus, as it was called, was taken over in 350 B.C. by the Cathaginians, under whom it became a powerful stronghold. The Romans captured the town in 274 B.C. Palermo passed successively to the Goths, who invaded Sicily in A.D. 440, the Byzantine emperors, who conquered the city in 535, and to the Saracens in 831. Under the Arabs Palermo flourished as the capital of an emirate, and its buildings and luxuriant gardens rivaled those of Córdoba and Cairo in oriental splendor. In 1072 the Norman descendants of the Hautevilles and the Guiscards occupied Palermo and made it their capital in Sicily. Count Roger II took the title "king of the Two Sicilies," which he ruled from 1130 to 1154. Splendid Norman churches, palaces, monasteries, and villas arose in this golden age to make Palermo one of the most beautiful cities of southern Italy and a center of trade between Europe and Asia. In the first half of the 13th century, under Emperor Frederick II of Hohenstaufen, Palermo became a center of Italian poetry and scientific studies. Charles I of Anjou, with papal support, took Palermo in 1066 and initiated a period of unpopular French rule. An insurrection known as the Sicilian Vespers occurred on Easter Day, 1282, when, as the bells of the Norman **Church of Santo Spirito** were ringing, a Sicilian maiden on her way to her wedding at the church was insulted by French soldiers. An uprising broke out and every Frenchman who could not pronounce the word *cicero* (chickpea) was massacred. The rebellion spread throughout Palermo, a republic was proclaimed, and the Angevins were expelled from Sicily in a few weeks. The Spanish Aragonese dominated the town from 1300 until 1647, when there was a successful revolt against their tyrannical rule. The Neapolitan Bourbons governed Palermo from 1718 until 1860, when the patriot Giuseppe Garibaldi entered Palermo triumphantly and annexed Sicily to the kingdom of Italy. Surviving structures characteristic of the Norman era include the **Cathedral of the Assunta** (Assumption), erected from 1169 to 1185, which contains the magnificent sarcophagi of King Roger II and Emperor Frederick II; the **Church of San Giovanni degli Eremiti** (Saint John of the Hermits), established in 1132 by King Roger II, who employed Moslem architects to work on the building—whence the red domes—which became a favorite Norman burial place; the **Church of La Martorana**, founded in 1143 by George of Antioch, admiral of the fleet under King Roger II; and the **Palace of the Normans**, erected from 1130 to 1140 and currently used to house the Sicilian parliament. Other sights include the Gothic **Palazzo Chiarmonte**, built in 1307, which served as a model for many edifices in Italy, the **Capuchin Catacombs,** containing 8,000 well-preserved corpses, and the square known as the **Quattro Conti** (four corners), bounded by Spanish baroque buildings. During World War II Palermo was taken on July 22, 1943, by the United States Seventh Army under General Patton, who had landed on the southern coast of the island only twelve days earlier. (*See also Messina.*)

### SEGESTA, *via N-113*

Tradition has it that Segesta was established by Trojan fugitives in the 12th century B.C. The town waged continual warfare with its rival, nearby Selinus, until the latter was destroyed in 409 B.C. During the first Punic War, in 264 B.C., Segesta switched her allegiance from Carthage to Rome. The city was abandoned after it was ravaged by Saracens in the tenth century A.D. Surviving today are a Doric **Temple,** erected and never completed at the time of Augustus, and a fifth-century B.C. **Theater** hewn in rock.

### SYRACUSE AND VICINITY, *via N-115 and N-162*

This rival city to Athens was colonized by Greeks from Corinth who settled on the island of **Ortygia** (site of the old city) and drove out the Phoenicians in 734 B.C. Situated in a fertile region, the colony thrived and soon sent out daughter colonies throughout Sicily. At the height of its splendor in the fifth and fourth centuries B.C., when it was the largest and most important town of Sicily, Syracuse boasted a population of nearly 500,000, two ports, and several limestone quarries, where prisoners were interned. In 413 B.C. Syracuse destroyed the Athenian land and naval forces besieging it. Of the many despotic tyrants who governed Syracuse, the most famous was Dionysius the Elder (430–367 B.C.), who, constantly afraid of being overthrown, kept a sword suspended by a horsehair over the head of Damocles, one of the courtiers envious of his position. An ally of Carthage during the Punic Wars, Syracuse fell to the Romans in 211 after a three-year siege, during which the renowned geometrician Archimedes, a native of Syracuse, helped defend his town by inventing weapons and setting fire to the Roman fleet by focusing the sun's rays through mirrors and lenses. Syracuse subsequently became a provincial Roman town and was converted to Christianity by Saint Paul. In 535 it was captured by the Byzantines and was plundered and destroyed by Saracens in 878; in 1085 it was taken by Normans and became part of the kingdom of the Two Sicilies. Ancient remains include the well-preserved fifth-century B.C. **Greek Theater,** where Aeschylus's *Persians* was first performed, the **Altar of Hiero II,** erected by that tyrant for public sacrifices, the **Paradise** and **Capuchins Quarries,** where 7,000 Athenians were imprisoned in 413 B.C., the **Ear of Dionysius,** a lobe-shaped grotto which permitted the tyrant to overhear prisoners confined below, and the **Cordmakers' Cave,** where hemp was spun. The **Old Town** on Ortygia, erected by the Normans, includes the seventh-century **Cathedral** and the **Arethusa Fountain,** the legendary birthplace of the city, where the nymph Arethusa, pursued by the river god Alpheus, changed herself into a spring. Eleven miles northwest of town is the **Castle of Euryelus,** a fortress erected by Dionysius, where Archimedes set fire to the Roman fleet.

**TAORMINA,** *via N-114 on the northeast coast of Sicily*

Inhabited since the eighth century B.C., this town overlooking the sea was re-established by the Carthaginians in 397 B.C. Taormina became a Roman ally after the death of Hiero II in 215 B.C. and was burned by Saracens in A.D. 902. Sights include the **Greek Theater,** erected in the third century B.C. and later reconstructed by the Romans for use as an amphitheater, and the medieval **Castle,** built on Monte Tauro on the site of the former acropolis.

**SIENA,** *via A-1 or N-2 in Tuscany*

Legend has it that this town was established in the eighth century B.C. by Senus, son of Remus, founder of Rome—whence its name and the she-wolf on the city crest. Siena was converted to Christianity by the Roman noble Ansanus, who was martyred in A.D. 303. Siena became an independent republic in 1125. By early in the 13th century Siena was flourishing as the banking center and trade capital of Italy. From 1230 on Siena's commercial rivalry with Florence resulted in a series of futile and hopeless wars, which, along with internal dissension and factionalism, eventually led to its decline; in 1257 the Sienese Ghibellines defeated the Florentine Guelphs at the Battle of Montaperti, one of the fiercest, bloodiest encounters in the history of Tuscany. For the next 80 years victorious Siena distinguished itself in the arts and architecture and reached its pinnacle of power and prosperity. After the Black Plague of 1348, in which 80,000 perished in Siena and the vicinity, the city began to decay. In 1531 Siena lost its independence and became a vassal of the Holy Roman Emperor. The Sienese revolt against the besieging troops of Charles V in 1555 has become famous in the annals of warfare for the heroic resistance of its citizenry, especially its women; nearly half the population perished. Siena ceased to be a city-state in 1559, when it was annexed by Cosimo I de' Medici, first grand duke of Tuscany. During the Italian independence movement in 1859, Siena became the first Tuscan city to vote for the monarchy of King Victor Emmanuel II. Today Siena is one of the richest towns in Italy in historic monuments. Mentioned in Dante's *Purgatorio,* the **Piazza del Campo** was the center of Siena where people assembled for councils of good and evil and where festivals were held—the Palio, a horse race held since medieval times, is still run around this square. On one side is the Gothic **Palazzo Pubblico,** or town hall, erected from 1289 to 1309 to house the city magistrates and governor; below its slender **Mangia Tower,** a brick belfry completed in 1349, is the **Cappella di Piazza,** a loggia where in 1425 the eloquent preacher Fra Bernardino (later sainted) urged the Sienese to mend their evil ways. The **Loggia di Mercanzia,** a 15th-century guild for merchants, also faces the piazza. The polychrome marble Gothic **Cathedral** was begun in 1265 and completed in 1380 on the site of an ancient temple to Minerva; the interior contains a remarkable octagonal pulpit by Nicola Pisano executed 1266–68, a marble pavement inlaid with pictures known as *graffiti,* the **Cathedral Museum,** celebrated for its paintings by Duccio, and the **Libreria Piccolomini,** built in 1495 by Cardinal Francesco Piccolomini, the future Pope Pius III; the **Baptistery of San Giovanni** (Saint John), behind the cathedral, forms its crypt. Other churches include the 13th-century Gothic **Church of San Domenico,** where Saint Catherine (1347–80) had her many visions and trances and whose reliquary contains her head, and the late-13th-century **Church of San Francesco** (Saint Francis), outside the city wall. Rich in secular architecture, Siena boasts such fine palaces as the **Palazzo Tolomei,** begun in 1203, which in 1310 served as the residence of Robert of Anjou, king of Naples; the early-14th-century **Palazzo del Capitano,** where the captains of war and justice resided; the **Palazzo Saracini,** raised late in the 1200s, which at one time was the seat of the republic; the Renaissance-style **Palazzo Piccolomini,** raised in 1470 for the father of Pope Pius III; and the elegant 14th-century **Palazzo Buonsignori,** which houses the Pinacoteca, or picture gallery, with its collection of paintings by such masters of the Sienese primitive school as Duccio, Simone Martini, and Ambrogio Lorenzetti.

**SORRENTO,** *via N-145 on the Bay of Naples in Campania*

According to legend, this beautiful town stands on the site where Ulysses resisted the lure of the sirens by plugging his sailors' ears with wax and having himself lashed to the mast of his ship. During the days of imperial Rome, Surrentum, with its sunny climate, enchanting gardens, and magnificent vistas, was a retreat where wealthy Romans built luxurious villas. Sorrento was still appreciated as a resort in the 19th century, when Shelley, Byron, Stendhal, Longfellow, Nietzsche, and Ibsen vacationed here. Sights today include the baroque **Church of San Francesco,** with its 14th-century cloisters. Torquato Tasso (1544–95), author of the renowned epic poem *Jerusalem Delivered,* was born here.

**SPOLETO,** *via N-3 in Umbria*

Dating from Etruscan and Roman times, this town was the capital of an important Lombard duchy from the sixth to the eighth centuries A.D. During the Middle Ages Saint Francis frequented the city. A notable sight is the **Piazza del Duomo,** faced by **palaces,** the **Baptistery,** and the 12th-century **Cathedral,** which was frescoed between 1467 and 1469 by Fra Filippo Lippi and houses the artist's mausoleum. Other features of Spoleto include the 755–foot-long **Bridge of Towers,** constructed in the 14th century over a Roman aqueduct and terminated by a **Fort** used to guard the approaches, and the venerable fourth-century **Basilica of San Salvatore** (Saint Saviour), which, erected by Byzantine monks and incorporating a former Roman temple, is one of the earliest Christian churches in Italy. In the 1950s composer Gian Carlo Menotti instituted the

Spoleto Festival of Two Worlds, a cultural event of art, music, and film held every June.

**TARANTO,** *via N-106 and N-7 in Apulia*

Founded in the eighth century B.C. by Spartans, Tarentum, as it was known in ancient times, subsequently became a flourishing city of Magna Graecia. The Romans took Tarentum in 272 B.C. and established a colony there in 123 B.C. The town subsequently declined and was captured successively by Ostrogoths in 494, Byzantines in 540, Lombards in 675, Arabs in 856, Saracens in 929, and Normans in 1063. Taranto became part of the kingdom of Naples and was joined to the kingdom of Italy in 1860, after which time it became an important naval base. During World War II, in November, 1940, aerial bombardments by the British caused heavy damage to the Italian fleet. The British seized Taranto in September, 1943 (*see also Salerno*). Sights include the **Naval Base,** the **Old Quarter,** protected by its 16th-century **Castle,** and the **National Museum,** with its collection of Greek antiquities.

**TARQUINIA,** *20 kilometers northwest of Civitavecchia via N-1 in Latium*

Founded in the 12th or 13th century B.C., this Etruscan city on the Marta River became a thriving port. By the sixth century B.C. Tarquinia was the leader of the 12 Etruscan city-states and ruled the entire coast of Etruria and Latium. The town came under Roman domination sometime late in the fourth century B.C., received Roman citizenship in 90 B.C., and subsequently declined. Lombards pillaged Tarquinia in the seventh century, after which the population moved to the town's present site, about 2 kilometers from its original position. Today Tarquinia is guarded by medieval fortifications that include 25 **towers** and a **citadel.** Constructed in 1439, the Renaissance **Palazzo Vitelleschi** houses the **National Museum,** containing Etruscan antiquities. About 4 kilometers southeast of town is the famous **Necropolis,** a vast burial ground containing thousands of tombs from the sixth through the first centuries B.C., many of which are decorated with paintings illustrating the customs and religion of the Etruscans.

**TODI AND VICINITY,** *via N-3A in Umbria*

Founded by the Etruscans and later occupied by the Romans, this town was a flourishing commercial center during the Middle Ages. Facing the **Piazza del Popolo,** the old heart of Todi, are the Gothic **Priors' Palace,** one-time seat of the governor, boasting Guelph battlements, and the 13th-century **Palazzo del Capitano Popolo** (palace of the captain of the people), with its Ghibelline battlements. Other monuments include the **Church of San Fortunato,** erected from 1292 to 1460 and housing the tomb of the Franciscan monk, poet, and author Jacopone da Todi (1230–1306), the ruins of the 14th-century **Rocca** (castle), and the **Church of Santa Maria della Consolazione,** erected from 1508 to 1524 after designs by Bramante and located about a kilometer west of town.

**TRENT,** *via N-12, N45bis, and N-47 in Venetia*

This ancient Alpine town served as a Roman military base and in later centuries was overrun by Ostrogoths, Lombards, and Franks. Trento prospered under the rule of prince-bishops of the Holy Roman Empire from 1027 until 1803, when it was taken by Napoleon. From 1545 to 1563 the town was the scene of the Council of Trent, which had been called by Pope Paul III to combat Protestantism and signaled the beginning of the Counter Reformation; sessions of the council were held at the Romanesque marble **Cathedral**, built from the 11th century to 1515 and containing the tombs of many of Trent's bishops, and at the Renaissance **Church of Santa Maria Maggiore**. Trent was an Austrian possession from 1814 until 1918, when it was liberated by the Italian army during World War I; the Treaty of Versailles at the conclusion of hostilities incorporated the town and its surrounding province into Italy. Other sights include the **Castello del Buon Consiglio** (castle of good counsel), a medieval stronghold remodeled in the 15th century where the prince-bishops resided. Here Italy's greatest World War I martyr, Cesare Battisti, was executed by the Austrians in 1916. The castle now houses the national museum.

**TRIESTE AND VICINITY,** *via A-4, N-14, and N-15 at the head of the Adriatic in Venetia*

This ancient town was a battleground of Celtic and Illyrian tribes until it was conquered about 177 B.C. by the Romans, under whom it developed into a prosperous seaport and center of trade, its citadel protecting the frontiers of the empire. During the Middle Ages, from 948 to 1202, Trieste flourished under the rule of the patriarchs of Aquileia (*see*) and subsequently came under the domination of Venice in the 13th century, paying a yearly tribute of ships and swearing allegiance to the republic. Austria ruled Trieste from 1382 until 1719, when the city became a free port. Trieste was held by the French from 1809 to 1814 and became an Austrian crown land in 1867. After World War I the town was incorporated into Italy by the 1919 Treaty of Saint Germain. During World War II Yugoslavs occupied Trieste. From 1947 until 1954 the city was administered by an allied military government and then was returned to Italy. Chief sights include the enormous **harbor**, with its canal-port of 1756, the hilltop **Cathedral of San Giusto**, founded in the fifth century on the ruins of a Roman temple, the nearby **Arco di Riccardo**, where King Richard "Coeur de Lion" of England was imprisoned on his return from the Crusades in 1192, and the 15th-16th–century **Castle**, housing a museum of weapons and furniture. About 6 kilometers northwest of town is the **Castle of Miramar**, erected from 1854 to 1856 for the ill-fated Archduke Maximilian of Austria, who became emperor of Mexico and was executed in 1867.

**TURIN AND VICINITY,** *via N-25, N-11, and N-4 in Piedmont*

Founded by the Taurini tribe, this town was destroyed by the Carthaginian general Hannibal in 218 B.C. and became a Roman colony under Emperor Augustus. From A.D. 590 until 636 Turin was the seat of a Lombard duchy, and in the ninth century it became a capital of the Holy Roman Emperor. In 1045 the town passed to Humbert the White-Handed, founder of the house of Savoy, Europe's oldest reigning dynasty, which ruled Savoy and Piedmont for nearly nine centuries; Humbert's descendants ruled as counts, beginning in 1106, and dukes, beginning with Amadeus VIII in the 15th century. After being occupied by the French from 1536 to 1562, Turin became capital of the duchy in 1563. Turin was besieged and taken by the French in 1640, but it successfully withstood a siege by the armies of Louis XIV in 1706. In 1720 Turin became capital of the kingdom of Sardinia and residence of the royal family; under the enlightened rule of King Charles Emmanuel III (1730–73) Turin grew into the "finest village in the world," with neatly laid out roads and squares. Under Napoleon from 1800 to 1814, Turin served as the capital of the department of the Po. During the 19th century Turin was a center of the Risorgimento (independence movement), and from 1861 to 1865 it was the first capital of a united Italy under King Victor Emmanuel II. Turin suffered damage from Allied air raids during World War II and was taken by American troops in April, 1945. A masterpiece of town planning, the **Piazza San Carlo** is faced by the **Churches of San Carlo** and **Santa Christina** and the 17th-century **Palazzo of the Marquesses of Caraglio e Senantes,** which served as the residence of French ambassadors from 1771 to 1789; in the center is a **Statue of Philibert Emmanuel,** the hero of the 1557 Battle of San Quentin, in which the French were defeated. The Renaissance **Cathedral of San Giovanni Battista,** erected in 1498, houses the Holy Shroud, in which Christ's body was supposedly wrapped after his descent from the cross. Nearby are Roman ruins that include the **Palatine Gate** and the **Old Theater.** One of Turin's splendid palaces is the **Palazzo Madama** on the **Piazza Castello,** which incorporates part of the old Augustinian ramparts and boasts Renaissance and medieval façades; here late in the 1600s resided Marie-Christine of France, the widow of Charles Emmanuel II. Others are the 17th-century **Palazzo Reale,** built from 1646 to 1658, the residence of the princes of Savoy, which now contains the **Royal Armory,** one of the most important collections of arms in Europe, including Napoleon's sword; and the 17th-century **Palazzo Carignano,** where King Victor **E**mmanuel II was born in 1820. About 17 kilometers from town is the **Superga Basilica,** constructed from 1717 to 1731, which contains the tombs of the kings of Sardinia.

**UDINE AND VICINITY,** *via N-13, A-4, and N-54 in Venetia*

From 1238 to 1420 this hillside town was the seat of the patriarchs of Aquileia (*see*) and was subsequently governed by the Venetians. During World War I, from 1915 to 1917, Udine was the headquarters of the Italian supreme command. Facing the Piazza della Liberta are the Gothic **Loggia del Lionello,** or town hall, raised in 1457, and the 16th-century Renaissance **Loggia di San Giovanni.** On an eminence overlooking the town is the impressive **Castello,** erected in the 1500s on the site of the former castle of the patriarchs of Aquileia as the seat of representatives of the Venetian Republic, who held council in a magnificent chamber embellished with frescoes; the castle now houses a museum. Below the castle stands the Gothic **Cathedral,** decorated with 18th-century frescoes by Tiepolo. Six kilometers from town is the village of **Campo Formio,** where France and Austria concluded a 1797 treaty marking the end of Napoleon's first campaign in Italy.

**URBINO,** *via N-73bis on a hill between the Apennines and the Adriatic in The Marches*

This town rose to prominence and prosperity under the benevolent rule of the Montefeltro family, who governed from the 13th century to the 16th. The patriarch of the dynasty, Guido il Vecchio, count of Montefeltro and a staunch Ghibelline partisan, made himself master of Urbino in 1292. Urbino reached the zenith of its fortunes under Federigo da Montefeltro, who ruled from 1444 to 1482 and became duke of Urbino in 1475. The most able general of his time, Federigo was also an accomplished ruler beloved by his subjects and a generous patron of the arts; his **Ducal Palace,** completed in 1472, was celebrated for its beauty and was a center of cultivated society. Federigo's son Guido Ubaldo, with his distinguished wife, Elizabeth Gonzaga, continued his father's example; his court was used as a model by Baldassare Castiglione in writing *Il Cortegiano* (The Courtier), which became the gentleman's code. The della Rovere family acquired Urbino in 1508, and the principality passed to the church in 1526. Today the ducal palace houses the **National Gallery** of The Marches. Also in Urbino is **Raphael's House,** where the artist was born in 1483 and where he resided until the age of 14; his first fresco, a Madonna, hangs here, and in the courtyard is the stone on which he ground his colors.

## VENICE AND VICINITY

ACCADEMIA DI BELLE ARTI (ACADEMY OF FINE ARTS), *on the Grand Canal at the Ponte dell' Accademia*
Established on the premises of the former convent, school, and church of Santa Maria della Carità by order of Napoleon in 1807, this gallery displays an important group of paintings by Venetian masters created between the 14th and 18th centuries. The collections, representing such artists as Il Giorgione, Giovanni Bellini, Tintoretto, Titian, and Paolo Veronese, are composed chiefly of works coming from churches, convents, and monasteries that had been suppressed by Napoleon in 1798, as well as of donations from noble families.

ARSENAL, *on the Rio dell' Arsenale and the Rio delle Gorne*
Established in 1104 and remodeled in the 15th and 16th centuries, this arsenal was celebrated throughout Europe; at its peak of activity it could construct and furnish a small galley in a single day. Two towers guarding the entrance to the basin were erected in 1574. Housing a **Naval Museum** today, the arsenal contains a model of one of the doges' famous bucentaurs, or state barges.

BASILICA OF SAN MARCO, *on the east end of the Piazza di San Marco*
This celebrated church was founded in 830 on the site of an earlier chapel to enshrine the precious relics, carried here from Alexandria, of Saint Mark the Evangelist, who became Venice's protector and patron saint and whose symbol is the winged lion. The basilica subsequently became the state church of the Venetian Republic, where newly elected doges were presented to the public. From 1065 to 1094 the basilica was reconstructed and enlarged in the Byzantine style with a cruciform plan, a domed roof, and profuse and lavish Oriental adornment. Many works of art enriching the church were brought back by Venetian expeditions to the Levant; the central doorway is surmounted by four bronze horses dating from antiquity, which were carried to Venice in 1204 by Doge Enrico Dandolo, who had ransacked Constantinople while on a Crusade; Napoleon removed the horses to Paris in 1797, but they were returned upon the fall of the French Empire. Features of the interior include more than 40,000 square feet of **mosaics,** the renowned **Pala d'Oro,** or golden altarpiece, created in Constantinople in 976, the **pulpit** where the Venetian people were addressed in times of national crisis, and **Tombs of the Doges** in the atrium and baptistery. The **Zeno Chapel** was where Saint Mark's remains first rested upon arriving in Venice. In front of the basilica is the 324-foot-tall **Campanile,** originally raised in the 14th century and rebuilt after its collapse in 1902. At its base, the small marble building known as the **Loggetta,** built in 1540, was formerly a meeting place of nobles and the seat of military procurators during sessions of the senate. On the corner of the basilica's southern façade is the **Pietra del Bando,** where laws were promulgated to the people.

## CHURCH OF SAN ZANIPOLO (SAINT JOHN AND SAINT PAUL), *on the Campo San Zanipolo*

Begun by Dominicans in 1234 and consecrated in 1430, this Gothic church is the second most important church in Venice after the basilica of San Marco (*see*). Many of the city's doges, patricians, admirals, artists, and other notables are buried and glorified in sumptuous tombs adorning the walls of the interior. The spacious square on which the church faces is dominated by the famous equestrian **Statue of Bartolommeo Colleoni**, the *condottiere* (mercenary military leader) who was a native of Bergamo (*see*) and served the Venetian Republic; upon his death in 1475, Colleoni bequeathed his vast fortune to the republic on the condition that his statue be built on the Piazza di San Marco (*see*); since a law forbade the erection of monuments there, the senate ingeniously evaded the condition by having Colleoni's statue raised on the piazza of the **Scuola di San Marco**, a charitable guild adjoining the church, which now houses the city hospital; designed by the Florentine artist Andrea del Verrocchio and completed by Alessandro Leopardi, the lifelike statue was unveiled to the public in 1496.

## CHURCH OF SANTA MARIA GLORIOSA DE' FRARI, *on the Campo dei Frari*

Erected between 1330 and 1417, this immense Franciscan Gothic church houses the splendid sepulchral monuments of such famous Venetians as the unfortunate Doge Francesco Foscari (*see Grand Canal*), who died in 1457, the painter Titian, who perished from the plague in 1576, and the sculptor Antonio Canova, who died in 1822. The "Frari" also contains magnificent altarpieces painted by Giovanni Bellini and Titian and donated by wealthy patrician families.

## CORTE DEL MILIONE, *near the church of San Giovanni Grisostomo*

This was the family residence of the celebrated explorer Marco Polo. In 1271 Marco, his father, and his uncle departed for the East;

*In Venice, the Campanile and Cathedral domes rising above the Piazza di San Marco (left) and the Bridge of Sighs (right)*

they crossed Asia and arrived at the court of the Great Khan, the Tartar emperor of China, where they were cordially received. The men returned to Venice in 1295 laden with the fabulous wealth of the Orient. Marco Polo's account of his travels fired the European imagination with tales of the wonderful cities and millions of treasures of the East and thus earned him the nickname Marco Milione.

### GRAND CANAL, *traversing the city*

This nearly 2-mile-long canal is the largest of Venice's 150 intersecting waterways and its principal thoroughfare. Here took place the annual ceremony, instituted in 1173, known as the Sposalizio del Mare (Nuptials of the Sea), in which the doge would proclaim Venice's authority on the Adriatic; from a bucentaur, or state barge, the doge would cast a wedding ring into the sea with the words "We espouse thee, Sea, in sign of true and lasting dominion." At the canal's entrance is the **Church of Santa Maria della Salute**, raised from 1632 to 1656 by order of the republic as a votive offering for being spared from the plague that ravaged the city in 1630. The **Dogana di Mare** (customhouse) stands nearby. Situated in the original nucleus of town is the majestic **Rialto Bridge**—the largest of the city's 400 bridges—consisting of a single marble arch 90 feet in span and designed between 1580 and 1592 with a pronounced hump in order to allow an armed galley to pass beneath. The Grand Canal is lined with approximately 200 magnificent marble palaces, erected from the 12th to the 18th centuries, which belonged to patrician families whose names were inscribed in the *Golden Book of the Republic*. Celebrated edifices on the east bank include the Gothic **Ca' d'Oro** (golden house), Venice's most elegant palace, built in 1440 with a gilded façade and now housing the **Franchetti Gallery** of tapestries, sculptures, and paintings; and the **Palazzo Vendramin-Calergi**, where the composer Richard Wagner died in 1883. On the west bank are the imposing baroque **Palazzo Rezzonico**, built in 1680, where the poet Robert Browning died in 1889, which now houses the **Settecento** (17th-century) **Museum** of furniture and paintings, and the 15th-century **Palazzo Foscari**, the residence of Doge Francesco Foscari, who reigned from 1423 until 1457, when he was deposed after falling under the suspicion of the ruling Council of Ten; later King Henry III of France stayed here upon his return from Poland in 1574.

### LIBRERIA VECCHIA (OLD LIBRARY), *on the Piazzetta di San Marco opposite the Palazzo Ducale*

Erected from 1536 to 1553 by Andrea Sansovino to house the **Marciana Library**, this striking edifice is considered to be the most magnificent civic structure of 16th-century Italy. The library itself was established by the poet Petrarch (1304–74), who 12 years before his death bequeathed his valuable collection of ancient manuscripts to the Venetian senate. The collection was added to and enriched over the centuries, and the Marciana Library now contains 750,000 volumes and pamphlets. Exhibited in the **Golden Room** are the codices, incunabula, and Flemish miniatures. Adjacent to the library along the Grand Canal (*see*) is the 16th-century **Zecco Mint**.

### MURANO, *about 1 kilometer north on the lagoon in Venetia*

Occupying a cluster of five islets intersected by canals, this town has been the seat of the famous Venetian glassmaking industry since 1292. Chief sights include the Byzantine-Romanesque **Church of Santissimi Maria e Donato**, erected in the 11th century and boasting a slim campanile and fine mosaics, and the 16th-century Renaissance **Palazzo Giustiniani,** which houses a **Glasswork Museum,** with unique examples of glass from ancient to modern times.

PALAZZO DUCALE, *facing the Piazzetta di San Marco*

Reflecting the power and glory of the Venetian Republic, this magnificent palace, begun in 820 for the first doge of Venice and reconstructed and enlarged in the 12th and later centuries, was the official residence of the doges and the seat of government where all councils of state were held. The main entrance, known as the **Porta della Carta,** built in 1443, was where public decrees were posted. The inner courtyard, with its richly sculpted well beds, was the scene of the 1355 beheading of Doge Marino Falieri, who had conspired against the republic. The landing on top of the **Scala dei Giganti** (giants' staircase), leading into the palace, was where every doge, surrounded by electors, was crowned. Features of the interior include the **Scala d'Oro** (golden stairway), created by Sansovino in 1556, whose use was allotted only to nobles named in the elite *Golden Book;* the **Doges' Apartments,** now containing the **Archaeological Museum;** the **Collegio** (college hall), where the doge and privy council granted audiences to foreign ambassadors; the **Senate Chamber;** and the **Grand Council Chamber**—the finest room of the palace, decorated with masterpieces by Tintoretto and Veronese—where the ruling body of nobles made decisions for war and peace. Joining the **Criminal Courts** in the palace to the **Carceri,** or prisons (from which Giovanni Jacopo Casanova escaped in 1756), on the other side of the canal is the **Ponte Sospiri** (Bridge of Sighs), so called because criminals were led across its covered passageway to hear their sentences and afterward be executed.

PIAZZA DI SAN MARCO, *via the Grand Canal*

This piazza, which Napoleon termed "the most beautiful salon in Europe," is the historic heart of Venice, where the inhabitants of the republic assembled for government ceremonies as well as for other festivities and enjoyment. Three **flagpoles** in front of the **Basilica of San Marco** (*see*) on the east side of the square originally carried the banners of Cyprus, Candia (Crete), and Morea (Peloponnesus), kingdoms which Venice ruled at the zenith of her power in the 15th century. The piazza is bounded on its other three sides by a harmonious group of buildings that include the **Procuratie Vecchio** (old law courts), with its adjoining **Torre dell' Orlogio** (clock tower) of the late 1400s, the **Procuratie Nuove** (new law courts), which Napoleon later converted into his royal palace, and the **Nuovo Fabbrica** (new factory), erected by order of Napoleon in 1810 and containing the **Correr Museum,** with its historic and artistic collections. The square opens on to the **Piazzetta,** providing access to the Grand Canal (*see*) and serving as Venice's principal entrance to the sea, where expeditions to the east embarked and where fleets returned laden with booty. Flanked by the **Libreria Vecchia** and the **Palazzo Ducale** (*see both*), the piazzetta was also known as Il Broglio (intrigue) because from 10:00 A.M. to noon nobles had the exclusive privilege of congregating here to hatch their plots. The ubiquitous pigeons on the Piazza di San Marco recall the time when the birds were officially protected by the republic; as legend has it, a flock of pigeons carrying little crosses guided the early Venetians, who were fleeing the Franks, to this site on the island of Rivo Alto, or Rialto, which thenceforth (A.D. 811) became the seat of the Venetian Republic.

**SAN LAZZARO,** *near the Lido on the lagoon in Venetia*
Between 1816 and 1819 the English poet Lord Byron resided at the 18th-century **Armenian Monastery** here, where he studied Armenian and wrote. Today the monastery houses a library with 30,000 volumes in Armenian, 40,000 books in European languages, 3,000 manuscripts, a picture gallery, and a printing shop.

**TORCELLO,** *10 kilometers northeast on the lagoon in Venetia*
In A.D. 452 the Illyrian tribe of the Veneti was driven from the northern Italian town of Altinum by Attila and his invading Huns and sought refuge on this island. Torcello became a flourishing center of life and commerce and was the seat of the first doge, who was elected in 697. As the island, or Rivo Alto or Rialto, grew in importance, becoming the seat of the Venetian government in 811, Torcello fell into decline. Facing the main piazza today is the **Cathedral of Santa Maria Assunto,** founded in 850, reconstructed in 1008, and containing fine Byzantine mosaics; adjacent are the 7th-century round **Baptistery** and the 12th-century octagonal Romanesque **Church of Santa Fosca.**

**VERONA,** *via N-11 and N-12 on the Adige River in Venetia*
A flourishing city of imperial Rome, Verona during the Middle Ages was considered the key to the conquest of northern Italy. The town was taken by the evil Ezzelino da Romano, vicar of Emperor Frederick II, in 1227 and was ruled by the Scaligers, the princes della Scala, from 1260 until 1387, when it reached the zenith of its fortunes. It was at Verona that the tragic love story of Romeo and Juliet, immortalized by Shakespeare, unfolded: in 1302, when all northern Italy was torn by strife between factions of Guelphs and Ghibellines, the powerful rival families of Romeo Montecchi (Montague), Guelph partisans, and Juliet Cappelletti (Capulet), Ghibelline supporters, were waging a bitter feud; the lovers' marriage, before their suicide, took place in a little **church** adjoining the Capuchin cloisters, where the **Tomb of Juliet** is now situated. The 13th-century **Palazzo Cappelletti** still stands at 23 Via Cappello. Verona subsequently passed to the Visconti of Milan (*see*), and from 1405 to 1801 it was part of the Venetian Republic. In 1822 the city was the scene of the Congress of Verona, which was attended by members of the Holy Alliance. The historic heart of town is the **Piazza delle Erbe,** the former site of the Roman forum, where chariot races and gladiatorial combats were held. Now surrounded by medieval and Renaissance edifices, the square has in its center the **Capitello,** a marble rostrum erected in 1207, from which public decrees and death sentences were proclaimed. The **Piazza dei Signori** was where the Scaliger family lived and governed. Structures here include the **Palazzo del Consiglio,** completed in 1493; the battlemented **Prefettura** (governors' palace), erected in 1272 as a private palace for Mastino I della Scala and later occupied by his descendants and by Venetian governors—Dante during his exile was a guest here for several months; the **Palazzo del Capitano,** begun in the 12th century and now serving as the law courts; and the **Palazzo Comunale** (town hall), raised in 1193 and boasting a 272-foot-tall tower. The opulent Gothic **tombs** of the Scaligers are in the nearby churchyard of Santa Maria Antica. Principal churches include that of **San Zeno Maggiore,** originally erected in the fifth century over the tomb of the first bishop of Verona and rebuilt from 900 to 1138, and the Romanesque-Gothic **Cathedral,** constructed from 1139 to 1514 on the site of a Roman temple to Minerva. Other

sights include the fortresslike **Castelvecchio** (old castle), built in 1354 by Cane Grande II della Scala, which later served as a Venetian stronghold and a barracks under Napoleon and now contains the **Municipal Museum of Art;** the **Castello San Pietro,** on the hilltop site of the former palace of Theodoric, king of the Ostrogoths, in the fifth century, and of Alboin, king of the Lombards, in the sixth century; and the immense Roman **amphitheater,** begun at the end of the first century A.D., which accommodated 25,000 spectators.

**VICENZA AND VICINITY,** *via N-46, N-11, and N-53 in Venetia*
This ancient Roman town became an independent republic during the Middle Ages and in 1405 fell to the Venetians. Vicenza is renowned as the birthplace of Andrea Palladio (1518–80), the last great architect of the Renaissance, who effected a revival of ancient Roman forms and rebuilt much of the town. Dominating the **Piazza dei Signori,** the site of the ancient forum, is the **Basilica Palladiana,** built from 1549 to 1614 and one of Palladio's masterpieces, which was used as a meeting place by Vicenza's notables. The **Loggia del Capitano,** seat of the Venetian governor, was begun by Palladio in 1571 and left unfinished. Other parts of Vicenza transformed by Palladio include many of the palaces along the **Corso Andrea Palladio,** the **Teatro Olympico,** modeled after ancient Greek theaters, which opened in 1585, and the **Palazzo Chiericati,** which now houses the **Municipal Museum.** Two kilometers southeast of town is the **Villa Capra,** one of Palladio's most original buildings.

**VINCI,** *25 kilometers south of Pistoia via A-11 in Tuscany*
Two kilometers north of this town on the slopes of Monte Albano is a **house** that was the birthplace of the great artist Leonardo da Vinci (1452–1519). The 11th-century **Castle** at Vinci houses a museum and the Leonardo Library.

**VITERBO,** *81 kilometers northwest of Rome in Latium*
From the 11th century until 1281 this medieval town flourished as the seat of the papal court. The celebrated conclave preceding the election of Pope Gregory X here in 1271 lasted nearly three years; it was concluded only when the captain of the people imprisoned the cardinals in the palace, had the roof of their meeting room removed, and cut off their food supplies. Ten years later, after two cardinals had been imprisoned by the townspeople, the papal court left Viterbo. Erected in 1192, the Romanesque **Cathedral** on the Piazza San Lorenzo was the scene of the 1271 murder of Henry of Cornwall, nephew of King Henry III of England, by Guy de Montfort, viceroy in Tuscany for Charles of Anjou. Henry's heart was returned to England in a golden cup. Other notable buildings include the Gothic **Palace of the Popes,** built in 1266, and the **Allesandri, Marzatosti,** and **Farnese Palaces.**

**VOLTERRA,** *via A-11 in Tuscany*
One of the 12 confederate city-states of Etruria, Volterra was subsequently ruled by the Romans and in the Middle Ages became a free town. In 1361 Volterra was annexed to Florence. Preserved here are an **Estruscan Tower,** the **Piazza dei Priori,** faced by grim 13th-century palaces, the **Fortrezza,** a foreboding example of military architecture, raised in 1472 with a keep and four corner towers and now used as a prison, and the Pisan-Romanesque **Cathedral** and octagonal **Baptistery.** Established in 1781, the **Museo Guarnacci** contains Etruscan antiquities.

# VATICAN CITY

**PIAZZA SAN PIETRO (SAINT PETER'S SQUARE)**, *in westcentral Rome*
Created between 1656 and 1667 by the renowned sculptor-architect
Giovanni Lorenzo Bernini, this monumental baroque square,
bounded by a semicircular colonnade, is a masterpiece of town
planning. At the center of the square stands an 83-foot-high **Obelisk**,
which was brought to Rome from Heliopolis, Egypt, during the
reign of Caligula about A.D. 40. Pope Sixtus V had the obelisk set
upon its present pedestal—a job that took 4 months, 600 men, and
150 horses—in 1586. A bronze door off the right colonnade leads
to the Vatican Palace (*see*).

**SAINT PETER'S BASILICA,** *in westcentral Rome*
Situated on the former site of Nero's Circus, where thousands of
early Christians suffered martyrdom, and on the spot where Saint
Peter, prince of the Apostles, was executed in A.D. 67 and buried,
this magnificent basilica is the largest church in Christendom—
with a capacity of 70,000 persons—and one of the wonders of the
world. In A.D. 90 the bishop Anacletus founded an oratory here to
mark Saint Peter's tomb; this was succeeded by a basilica, containing a nave and four aisles, established in 326 by Emperor Constantine. Over the centuries the basilica was lavishly decorated, but it
suffered frequent fires and was in ruins by 1452, the year Pope
Nicholas V decided to build a larger, more magnificent structure,
work that was interrupted by his death in 1455. In 1506 the project
was resumed under Pope Julius II, who commissioned Bramante
to design the building. Subsequently the work was directed by the
leading artists of the age, including Raphael, Michelangelo, who
began the majestic 390-foot-high dome in 1546, and Giacomo della
Porta and Carlo Maderna, who completed the 377-foot-long baroque
façade in 1614. Pope Urban VIII dedicated the basilica on Novem-

*Left: the interior of Saint Peter's, with Bernini's Baldaquin and the papal altar.*
*Right: Saint Peter's Basilica and Square, with its famed colonnade and obelisk.*
*Below: the Governor's Palace in Vatican City*

ber 18, 1626. The **Loggia,** or balcony, in the center of the façade is where the pope bestows his famous benediction "Urbi et Orbi" (to the city and the world). The immense interior is filled with masterpieces of statuary, mosaics, monuments, altars, and chapels, the most famous of which are Michelangelo's white marble **Pietà,** executed in 1500, and Bernini's 95-foot-high **Baldaquin** (grand canopy) on twisted columns, made in 1633 from bronze taken from the Pantheon (*see*). A disc of red porphyry near the door marks the spot where Charlemagne was crowned Holy Roman Emperor on Christmas Day in 800, and the right transept was the scene of the famous Ecumenical Council of the Vatican in 1869–70. Beneath the floor of Saint Peter's are the **Vatican Grottoes,** or crypt, entered to the left of the basilica beyond the Arch of the Bells. Pagan and Christian necropolises of the second and third centuries are contained in the lower grottoes; here Saint Peter was interred. The upper grottoes contain tombs of later popes, including the splendid **Mausoleum of Sixtus IV** by Antonio Pollaiuolo.

**VATICAN PALACE,** *in westcentral Rome*
The largest palace in the world was founded near the antecourt of the old church of Saint Peter (*see Saint Peter's Basilica*) in A.D. 498 by Pope Symmachus to serve as a papal residence. Enlarged over the centuries, the building housed Charlemagne on the occasion of his coronation in 800. Although a new building was begun in 1150 and extended in 1278, the Vatican was used primarily to shelter foreign dignitaries visiting Rome, and the Lateran Palace (*see Basilica of Saint John Lateran*) remained the papal residence. After the return of Pope Gregory XI from Avignon in 1377, the Vatican became the official papal domicile, and over the next several centuries it was expanded into the vast complex of edifices that stand today. In 1450 Pope Nicholas V decided to make the Vatican the most imposing palace in the world, and he commenced what are known as the **Borgia Apartments;** Pope Sixtus IV in 1473 added the **Sistine Chapel;** and early in the 1500s Pope Julius II added a **Loggia** and laid the foundations of the **Vatican Museums.** Subsequent popes vied with one another in the size and magnificence of their additions, and the greatest architects and artists of the day were employed to work on the Vatican. Today the Vatican Palace contains 80 grand staircases, 200 smaller staircases, 200 courts, and 11,000 halls, chapels, rooms, and apartments. Only a small section of the palace is used by the papal court, and the major portion is occupied by the museums—the oldest and most splendid public museums in the world—which include the collections of the **Pio-Clementine Museum** of Greco-Roman antiquities, the **Picture Gallery,** the **Chiaramonte Museum,** the **Library,** with its 500,000 volumes and 60,000 ancient manuscripts, and the Borgia Apartments, sumptuously adorned with paintings done by Pinturicchio between 1492 and 1495. Among the most interesting groups of rooms are the **Stanze,** which Pope Julius II entrusted to the 25-year-old Raphael to paint in 1508; the resulting frescoes of biblical, mythological, and historical scenes are among the world's masterpieces. The remarkable Sistine Chapel, a private papal chapel used for solemn ceremonies of the Holy See and conclaves for the election of popes, reflects Michelangelo's genius. Michelangelo's ceiling frescoes, executed between 1508 and 1512, depict scenes from Genesis; his *Last Judgment*, painted on the altar wall and completed in 1541, measures 66 feet by 33 feet, the largest, most comprehensive painting in the world.

SAN MARINO

Situated in the Apennines near the Adriatic coast, southwest of Rimini, Italy, the world's smallest republic—23 square miles—as well as the oldest state in Europe was founded, according to tradition, by Saint Marinus of Dalmatia. This devout stonemason at the time of Emperor Diocletian's persecutions of Christians in A.D. 300 fled from Rimini (*see*), where he was working, and found refuge on the thickly wooded slopes of **Mount Titano.** Here Marinus practiced his religion with a few followers and cured the sick sons of a Roman woman, who in appreciation bequeathed him Mount Titano. Upon his death, Saint Marinus left the mountain to the community on the condition that liberty and religion be protected there for all time. In 441 a hermitage was erected on the mountain, around which the tiny capital city of San Marino grew up. While other European states have changed rulers and forms of government many times over the centuries, San Marino, with only a few short interruptions, has remained a sovereign territory for 1,400 years. The earliest document recording the state's independence dates from 885, and San Marino's political history dates from 1000, when its democratic republic form of government, based on the rule of two captains regent and still in use today, was instituted: every April and October in an elaborate ceremony a new captain regent, elected by the 60-member Grand Council, in which every family is represented, is installed for a six-month term of office. During the Renaissance, in 1441, San Marino was allied to the Montefeltros of Urbino (*see*), participated in that family's struggles against the Malatestas of Rimini, and as a result extended its lands. The republic was dominated briefly early in the 1500s by Cesare Borgia. In 1549 Pope Paul III recognized the independence of the little state, which subsequently enjoyed peace and prosperity until the 18th century. In 1739 Cardinal Giulio Alberoni gained control and ruled as a despot, but the republic regained its freedom the next year. When Napoleon III in 1849 offered San Marino additional territory in return for its allegiance, the republic rejected the offer and instead gave asylum to the Italian patriot Giuseppe Garibaldi. In 1897 San Marino signed a friendship treaty with the kingdom of Italy. During World War II San Marino provided asylum within its restricted borders to 100,000 refugees. Although professing neutrality during the war, San Marino was bombarded and heavily damaged by the Allies in June, 1944, occupied by German troops in August, 1944, and taken by the British the following month. From 1945 until 1947 San Marino was governed by Communists. Since 1949 the republic has struck its own coins, and beginning in 1954 it has issued postage stamps. San Marino now boasts a population of 12,000 and a standing army of 120. Principal sights in the medieval-appearing city include the **ramparts;** the **Rocche**—three peaks crowned with three fortified towers, linked by sentry walks; the **Basilica of San Marinus,** which contains the tomb of the republic's patron saint; the adjacent **Church of San Pietro,** whose sacristan exhibits two niches hewn in rock, which Saint Marinus and his friend Saint Leo used as beds; and the 14th-century **Church of San Francesco.** The Gothic-style **Palazzo del Governo** was built in 1894 of stone quarried on Mount Titano; its collection includes a **Bust of Abraham Lincoln,** who accepted honorary citizenship of San Marino in 1861. The **Palazzo dei Valloni** houses a museum, national library, and picture gallery. A few miles from town in the village of **Verucchio** is the massive old **Castle of Saint Leo,** the birthplace of the Malatestas, which later served as a prison.

*Top: vista of the republic on Mount Titano. Below left: marchers in traditional costumes worn on ceremonial occasions. Right: Liberty Square*

# MALTA

Throughout their long history, the strategically situated Maltese Islands (Malta, Gozo, and Comino) have been a prize in the struggles of larger powers. The prehistoric inhabitants of the island of **Malta** erected such temple complexes as the one at **Tarxien** as early as the third millennium B.C. Malta's earliest known occupants were the Phoenicians—the inhabitants today claim Phoenician descent and speak a Semitic dialect—who found a natural shelter for their ships there. The island subsequently was colonized by the Carthaginians. During the Second Punic War (218–201 B.C.) the Romans took possession of Malta and ushered in an era of prosperity, which saw the construction of temples, villas, and baths. In A.D. 60 Saint Paul and Saint Luke were en route to Rome as prisoners when they were providentially shipwrecked on Malta; during their sojourn there they succeeded in converting the Roman governor to Christianity. As Luke reported, "And when we escaped, then we knew that the island was called Melita, but the barbarians shewed us no small courtesy...." Malta later passed to the Byzantines and was conquered in 870 by Arabs, who were finally expelled in 1091 by Roger of Normandy; he restored Christianity to the island

*Top left: the Hypogeum in the town of Mosta on Malta. Right: an aerial view of Mdina on Malta. Below left: the harbor of the island of Gozo. Right: the Inn of Castile in Valletta on Malta*

and to the neighboring islands of the Maltese archipelago. The Swabians, Angevins, Aragonese, and Castilians successively ruled Malta until in 1530 the king of Spain and Holy Roman Emperor, Charles V, gave the island to the Knights of Saint John of Jerusalem, who had recently been forced by the Muslims to abandon Rhodes. The order, which soon became known as the Knights of Malta, made the island a bastion of Christendom in the Mediterranean. The knights, who along with the rest of the Maltese population comprised a total of 9,000 defenders, in 1565 heroically withstood a four-month siege by 40,000 Turks under Suleiman the Magnificent, who had hoped to establish a steppingstone for the conquest of southern Europe. By the time the siege was lifted only 600 of the original defenders survived, but only 10,000 Turks returned to Constantinople. After this bloody struggle Jean Parisot de La Vallette, the 70-year-old grand master of the knights, directed the creation of the beautiful new city of **Valletta,** which boasted grand palaces and fortifications that Napoleon and Lord Admiral Nelson, more than two centuries later, considered to be the greatest stronghold in Europe. After a brief resistance the knights surrendered to Napoleon in 1798. The French so ravaged the island that the Maltese revolted and helped the British take possession of Malta in 1800. The 1814 Treaty of Paris confirmed the British occupation of Malta, which for most of the 19th century was ruled by a military governor and developed into an important British naval base. Malta was granted dominion status and limited self rule in 1921. During World War II Malta suffered heavy aerial bombardments by the Italians and Germans, and the loss of property and life was extensive; England's King George VI awarded its entire population the George Cross for heroism in 1942. Malta became an independent nation in the British Commonwealth in 1964. In 1971 NATO's naval headquarters were removed from Malta at the request of the Dominic Mintoff government. Overlooking Grand Harbour, the city of Valletta, Malta's capital, today preserves such historic monuments as the **Place of the Grand Masters,** completed in 1574 on the main square; its Council Chamber and Hall of Saint Michael and Saint George compete with one another in sheer magnificence, and its armory—only a portion of the original—now houses a museum with remarkable art treasures. The **Cathedral of Saint John** was erected in the 16th century by the famous Maltese architect Girolamo Cassar; this was the official place of worship of the knights and contains chapels for the knights of various nationalities. In the **Inns,** or **Auberges**—the finest of which are **Castile** and **Leon**—young knights from different countries were trained and their men-of-arms and servants lived. The **Manoel Theater,** which was raised in 1731, is one of the oldest theaters in Europe. Across Grand Harbour are the small towns of Vittoriosa, Cospicua, and Senglea. The last, situated near the dockyard, suffered great damage during World War II. In the middle of the island is the medieval fortified town of **Mdina,** the former capital, which contains a fine **Cathedral** and notable Roman antiquities, and the nearby town of **Mosta,** whose 19th-century **Church** boasts the third largest dome in the world and whose prehistoric remains include a labyrinthine sanctuary known as a **Hypogeum.** The island of **Gozo,** 4 miles off Malta, was the celebrated isle in Homer's *Odyssey* where the hero Ulysses spent seven years with the nymph Calypso; it contains vast prehistoric temples and the medieval fortified town of **Victoria** (formerly **Rabat**) in its center. Between Malta and Gozo is the island of **Comino,** which has a small ancient palace.

**PORTUGAL**

**ALCOBAÇA,** *on Routes N8, N8-6, and N8-4 in Estremadura*
    The vast Cistercian **Monastery of Santa Maria** was founded about 1152 by King Alfonso I in gratitude for his victory over the Moors at Santarém in 1147. The present building is the result of a reconstruction in the 13th century, additions in the 14th and 16th centuries, and renovations in the 17th and 18th centuries. In its prime the monastery was the most powerful in Portugal. Its church is 348 feet long, 75 feet wide, and 66 feet high, making it the largest in the country. In opposite transepts lie the marvelously carved Flamboyant Gothic 14th-century tombs of King Pedro I and his mistress and later wife, Inés de Castro (d. 1355). King Alfonso IV had Inés assassinated when he discovered his son Prince Pedro's liaison with her. When he became king in 1357, Pedro put her assassins to death and moved her body from Coimbra to the monastery church of Alcobaça. The enormous and severe **Claustro do Silencio** was built early in the 14th century, while the kitchen was restored in the 18th. The latter is 59 feet high and has a fireplace capable of holding half a dozen spitted cows. Running water is supplied by a tributary of the Alcoa River diverted through the kitchen.

**AVEIRO,** *on Routes N16-109, N230, N335, and N235 in Beira Litoral*
    This fishing port built on salt marshes in an impressively flat landscape faces a large saltwater lagoon. During the 15th and 16th centuries its fishermen ventured to the cod banks off Newfoundland. Then in 1575 a violent storm sealed the lagoon from the sea. Despite several attempts a passage was not successfully opened to the sea again until 1808. The harbor is protected from silting by breakwaters made from the town walls. Two distinctive types of boats are native to Aveiro: the sickle-shaped *esguichos,* which fish in the Atlantic, and the attenuated *moliceiros,* with high prows like swan's necks, which scour the lagoon for seaweed to be used as fertilizer and harvest the many salt pans there. The **Regional Museum** is installed in the former convent of Jesus, which was built between the 15th and 17th centuries. Here Saint Joanna, daughter of King Alfonso V, lived from 1472 until she died in 1489. The museum is notable for its works by 15th- and 16th-century Portuguese primitive painters, as well as for sculpture from the 16th-century Coimbra school. The interior of the 15th-century convent church is richly carved and gilded wood, chiefly of the 17th and 18th centuries, while the choir has an important coffered ceiling.

**AZORES,** *three groups of islands lying 900–1,200 miles west of Lisbon*
    This midatlantic archipelago of nine volcanic islands lies in a northwesterly-southeasterly line some 300 miles long. In the fourth century B.C. the islands were probably visited by the Carthaginians, as evidenced by coins found on Corvo Island. The existence of the archipelago was not noted, however, until late in the 14th century, when it appeared on an Italian map. The islands were found and claimed by Portugal in the next century, during the voyages of discovery sent out by Prince Henry the Navigator. Colonization of the deserted islands was rapid both by Portuguese and by Flemings, the latter immigrating by virtue of the fact that Isabella, duchess of Burgundy, was the sister of Henry the Navigator. In 1591 a famous sea battle took place off the Azores when English sea captain Sir Richard Grenville in the *Revenge* fought 15 Spanish treasure ships homeward bound from the New World. Alfred, Lord Tennyson, celebrated the exploit in "The Revenge."

*Top: the Royal Palace at Queluz. Center left: Church of Bom Jesus do Monte near Braga. Right: the old clock tower at the University of Coimbra. Below: the medieval castle of Almourol on the Tagus River near Constância*

SANTA MARIA ISLAND, *in the southeast group of islands*
This was the first of the Azores to be discovered by Prince Henry the Navigator's captain Diogo de Sevilla about 1427. It was also the first to be colonized by Gonçalo Velho Cabral, another of Prince Henry's captains, who arrived in 1432 and brought in domestic animals in succeeding years and the first settlers in 1439. Columbus is said to have stopped here in 1493 on his return from his first voyage of discovery. The principal town is **Vila do Pôrto.**

SÃO MIGUEL ISLAND, *in the southeast group of islands*
The largest, richest, and most populated of the Azores was settled about the same time as Santa Maria. The warm, damp climate contributes to substantial harvests, particularly of pineapples. In addition to settlers from the Algarve, along Portugal's southern coast, there are said to have been some black slaves and Moors, as well as in the 16th century a group of Bretons. The latter's blond hair and blue eyes are to be found in the northwest of the island, a region appropriately known as Bretanha. The chief town and also capital of the archipelago is **Ponta Delgada,** where on the fifth Sunday after Easter a 15th-century statue of Christ, *Santo Cristo dos Milagres*, loaded with jewels, is paraded through streets thronged by Azorians from as far away as Canada, Brazil, and California. The statue is kept on other days in the **Esperança Convent,** founded in the 16th century. Also to be seen in Ponta Delgada are the **Matriz Church,** built between 1533 and 1700, which has a handsome Manueline portal; the convent of Santo André (1567), now the **Carlos Machado Museum;** and the 16th-17th–century **São José Church.**

TERCEIRA ISLAND, *in the central group of islands*
This was the third of the Azores to be settled (about 1450), hence its name, which simply means third. The coasts are fertile, while the interior is a Dantesque vision of a volcanic landscape. Its chief town, **Angra do Heroísmo** (Bay of Heroism), was the capital of the archipelago from 1766 until 1832. Founded in 1534, it is the most ancient city in the Azores and still preserves the evidence of its past prosperity, when it was a stop for Portuguese merchantmen returning from India. When King Philip II of Spain took control of Portugal in 1580, the islanders resisted for three years. During the civil war (1828–34) the islanders supported the constitutionalist pretender Pedro IV, emperor of Brazil as Pedro I, whose daughter was finally named Queen Maria II. Among the sights in Angra do Heroísmo are the **Church of the Colégio,** a large 17th-century structure with a baroque interior; the former **Convent of São Francisco,** a 15th-century building rebuilt in the middle of the 17th century, which now houses an excellent museum of sculptures, coins, maritime affairs, and objects of anthropological interest; the 16th-century **Cathedral,** with a fine coffered ceiling of cedar; and the splendid **Fortress of São João Baptista.** This last was called the castle of Saint Philip when the Spanish built it early in the 17th century during the time they made Angra the center of their government of the Azores. It was here that King Alfonso VI was imprisoned from 1669 to 1674, after he had been dethroned and exiled by his brother, who became regent and later King Pedro II. The **Church of São João Baptista,** within the fortress grounds, was the first monument to be built on Portuguese soil to celebrate the country's liberation from Spanish domination in 1640. It was placed here in recognition of the island's resistance to the Spaniards in the 1580s and is a fine example of transitional Renaissance-baroque architecture. At **São**

Sebastião, 12 kilometers east of Angra, there is a Gothic church of 1455 with a handsome portal and interesting 16th-century frescoes.

**BATALHA,** *on Routes N1 and N356 in Beira Litoral*
The **Monastery of Santa Maria da Vitória** (known as Batalha, or battle) was begun in 1388 and along with the monastery at Alcobaça (*see*) is the finest example of Gothic architecture in Portugal. It was built to fulfill a vow made by King John I when he won the Battle of Aljubarrota on August 14, 1385. Grand master of the military order of Aviz (*see*) and the bastard son of King Pedro I, he defeated the Castilian army against overwhelming odds. The battle freed Portugal from Castilian domination and led to two centuries of expansion and prosperity for the country under the Aviz dynasty. The porch of the Gothic church leads to the octagonal **Capelas Imperfeitas** (unfinished chapels), intended to be the royal pantheon but never completed despite work by Kings Alfonso V (1438–81) and Manuel I (1495–1521). Adjoining the church is the **Founder's Chapel,** with an extraordinarily rich assembly of royal tombs. In the center is the sarcophagus of John I and his English wife, Philippa of Lancaster (d. 1415), daughter of John of Gaunt. Along the walls are the tombs of the couple's sons, including Prince Henry the Navigator, who did so much to further Portugal's overseas empire. The 62-foot-square **Chapter House,** with its architecturally remarkable unsupported vault, contains the tomb of Portugal's unknown soldier. In the **Royal Cloister,** the elaborate Manueline tracery does not overpower the simplicity of the Gothic design.

**BRAGA AND VICINITY,** *on Routes N101, N103, N309, N14, and N201 in Minho*
Five important military roads radiated from the Roman settlement of Bracara Augusta. This ancient city came under Moorish domination from 730 until it was retaken for the Christians by King Ferdinand I of Castile in 1040 and was made an archbishopric. In the 16th century, under Archbishop Dom Diogo de Sousa, there was much building in the Italian manner, but subsequent renovations have largely obliterated the architectural importance of the city. Although only fragments of the original Romanesque **Cathedral** remain in a building that has been much altered since, the rich interior is still worth visiting, especially the treasury. The former **Episcopal Palace,** of the 14th, 17th, and 18th centuries, contains a very rich library that includes the city's archives from the ninth century on. Six kilometers east of the city is the baroque pilgrimage **Church of Bom Jesus do Monte,** built between 1784 and 1811. Pilgrims mount to the hilltop church along the 18th-century **Via Sacra,** bordered by chapels in which realistic, life-size figures represent the stations of the cross. The Via Sacra leads into the **Escadorio dos Cinco Sentidos** (stair of the five senses), with its many allegorical fountains, and that in turn leads into the **Escadorio das Virtudes** (stair of the virtues), with statues illustrating the theological virtues. **Monte Sameiro,** a few kilometers farther along the Bom Jesus road, is crowned with a **Sanctuary to the Virgin** dating from the late 19th and early 20th centuries. Still farther along the same road is **Citánia de Briteiros,** a prehistoric hill fort occupied from the Bronze to the Iron ages (eighth to fourth centuries B.C.). Excavations begun in 1874 have revealed remains of a triple perimeter of walls and the foundations of more than 150 huts, two of which have been reconstructed. About 3 kilometers northwest of Braga on Route N201 are the remains of the seventh-century **Chapel of São Frutuoso,** now incorporated into the 18th-century church of Saint Francis.

**BRAGANÇA,** *on Routes N218, N217, N15, N103, N308.3, and N103-7 in Trás-os-Montes e Alto Douro*

A fief of the house of Bragança, which ruled Portugal from 1640 to 1910, the walled old town contains the remains of a **Castle** built in 1187 by King Sancho I, a Gothic **pillory**, the 16th-century **Church of Saint Mary,** and the 12th-century **Domus Municipalis,** the oldest city hall in Portugal.

**BUÇACO FOREST,** *just north of Luso off Route N234 in Beira Litoral*

This remarkable preserve of giant and exotic trees was walled by the Carmelites in the 17th century after they built a monastery here in 1628. In 1622 Pope Gregory XV had forbidden women to enter the forest on pain of excommunication, and in 1643 Pope Urban VIII decreed the same punishment for anyone who damaged a tree in the forest. Among other species the Carmelites introduced were Mexican cedars, which still flourish here but are now extinct in Mexico. In September, 1810, during the Peninsular War, the duke of Wellington won a daylong battle here against Napoleon's troops under Marshal André Masséna. The luxurious hotel in the forest was built as a **Royal Hunting Lodge** between 1888 and 1907.

**COIMBRA,** *on Routes N1-E50, N110, N1-E3, N17, and N111-1 in Beira Litoral*

The site of Portugal's first **University** was also the country's first capital, which it remained from the time of its reconquest from the Moors in the 11th century until the 13th century, when the kings of Portugal moved to Lisbon. King Diniz I transferred the university he had founded in Lisbon in 1307 to Coimbra in 1308. It was moved back to Lisbon subsequently and only permanently established in Coimbra in 1537 by King John III. The university's Manueline **Chapel** (1517–22) is decorated with 17th-century *azulejos,* or decorative tiles, while the **Library** (1716–23) is all carved and gilded wood. Around the old university the students live communally in groups of 10 to 15 in what are known as *repúblicas,* sharing a cook and electing a president. The **Sé Velha,** or old cathedral, was built between 1140 and 1175 by two French craftsmen, Bernard and Robert, in the style of the one at Santiago de Compostela, in northern Spain. The Flamboyant Gothic altarpiece of 1503–8 in gilded wood is particularly striking. The former episcopal palace (renovated in the 16th century) is now the **Machado de Castro Museum,** which contains good Renaissance sculptures, a fine archaeological section, and a very rich collection of Portuguese faience, as well as jewelry and paintings. The **Monastery of Santa Cruz** (Holy Cross), founded by King Alfonso I (1128–85), was rebuilt at the beginning of the 16th century by King Manuel I. The splendid tombs of Alfonso I and his son King Sancho I and the simple and elegant **Claustro do Silencio** (cloister of silence) are excellent examples of Manueline building. The former **Santa Clara-a-Velha** (convent of Santa Clara), of the late 13th century, was the residence of Saint Isabel, queen of Portugal, who caused it to be built between 1286 and 1292 and spent the last decade of her life there. It was also the resting place of the body of Inés de Castro after her assassination in 1355 and before its transfer to the monastery of Santa Maria at Alcobaça (*see*). The very large baroque church in the new convent of Santa Clara (1649–77) contains the tomb of Saint Isabel.

**CONIMBRIGA,** *near Condeixa off Route N1-E3 in Beira Litoral*

The ruins of this prosperous Roman town, founded in the first century, comprise **ramparts** built against the approaching barbarians in the third century, an **aqueduct** some two miles long, **baths** and **houses,** and **mosaics**. The **Museu Mongráfico** on the site contains many of the objects excavated.

## CONSTÂNCIA VICINITY
CASTLE OF ALMOUROL, *5 kilometers southwest off Route N3 on an island in the Tagus River*
The partially ruined castle on a romantically wooded island was built by the Romans; in 1171 it was rebuilt by Gualdim Pais, then Grand Master of the Knights Templars. Many legendary events have taken place in the castle, which today can be either reached or circled by boat.

**ELVAS,** *on Routes N246, N4-E4, N373, and N372 in Alentejo*
This border town was occupied by the Moors until recovered in 1226 by King Sancho II. It then resisted many Spanish attacks until the troops of King Philip II of Spain occupied it in 1580. In 1801 branches from the orange trees at the foot of its formidable 17th-century **ramparts** gave the fleeting War of the Oranges its name. The branches were plucked by Manuel de Godoy, the leader of the Spanish invaders, and sent to Madrid to his mistress, Queen María Louisa Teresa, wife of King Charles IV of Spain. Godoy had come to Portugal to force it—successfully—to close its ports to its ancient ally, England. The Gothic **Cathedral** with a handsome interior was rebuilt almost completely in the Manueline style by Francisco de Arruda about 1517. The **aqueduct,** which is still used, was built on Roman foundations between 1498 and 1622. The octagonal 16th-century **Church of Nossa Senhora da Consolação** (Our Lady of Consolation) has a lovely interior entirely covered with polychrome decorative tiles of the mid-17th century and a cupola supported on painted and gilded 18th-century columns. A 16th-century marble **pillory** stands in Santa Clara Square.

**ÉVORA,** *on Routes N18, N254, N380, and N114 in Alta Alentejo*
Architecturally one of the most interesting towns in Portugal, this was the Roman colony of Liberalitas Julia. A bishopric under the Visigoths, it remained in the hands of the Moors from 715 until it was retaken by Geraldo Sempavor (Gerald the Fearless) in 1165 and given to King Alfonso I. From the end of the 12th century the town was favored by the kings of Portugal. Its **Jesuit University,** founded in 1559, was suppressed by King Joseph Emanuel in 1759, ending the cultural importance of Évora. The granite **Sé** (cathedral), in the Romanesque-Gothic style, was begun in 1186 and finished in the middle of the 13th century except for spires of the towers, which were added in the 16th century. The second-century **Roman Temple,** probably dedicated to Diana, is one of the best preserved Roman architectural remains on the Iberian peninsula, largely because its columns were closed by a crenelated wall in the Middle Ages, when it served as a fortress. It then became a slaughterhouse before being excavated in 1870. The **Museu Regional,** in the former episcopal palace of the 16th and 17th centuries, has an interesting collection of sculptures from Roman times to the 16th century and good paintings of the Flemish and 16th-century Portuguese schools. Other notable buildings are the **Paço dos Duques de Cadaval,** whose façade was remodeled in the 17th century; the **House of the Counts of Portalegre,** in the Gothic and Manueline styles; the 16th-century **Garcia de Resende House;** the 15th-century **Soure House,** with its Manueline façade; the **Church of the Convento dos Lóios,**

its nave lined with beautiful 17th-century *azulejos;* the strange 16th-century **Church of Nossa Senhora da Graça** (Our Lady of Grace), with its baroque granite façade, classical pilasters, and portico with Tuscan columns; the early-16th-century **Church of São Francisco** (Saint Francis), with its Manueline portal and curious Gothic-Moorish porch, and its **Casa dos Ossos** (ossuary chapel), papered with human bones and skulls in the 16th century to induce meditation. Remnants of the three concentric **walls** that protected the town are visible: the innermost are the Roman walls reinforced by the Visigoths, then the 14th-century medieval walls, and finally the outer walls of the 17th century.

**ÉVORA MONTE,** *on Route N18 in Alentejo*
This small fortified town was the setting for the signing on May 26, 1834, of the convention that ended the Portuguese Civil War. The treaty forced King Miguel to abdicate and go into exile in favor of his niece Queen Maria II. The **Castle,** originally a Roman construction modified by the Moors and again in 1306 by King Diniz I, was partly ruined by an earthquake in 1531. It was restored by King John III but retains its primarily Gothic style. The view from the summit is splendid.

**GUIMARÃIS,** *on Routes N207.4, N101, N101.2, N105, and N206 in Minho*
The town was founded in the tenth century by a Countess Mumadona, a native of Leon, who erected the defensive tower that was converted into a **Castle** by Henry of Burgundy. There Henry received the county of Portucale from his father-in-law, King Alfonso VI of Leon and Castile. In 1112 the son of Henry and his wife, Teresa, Affonso Henriques, was born in the castle and in 1128 seized power from his mother, who had misruled the county as regent since his father's death in 1112. In 1139 he was proclaimed King Alfonso I of Portugal. Gil Vicente, (1470?–1536), the father of Portuguese theater, was also born in Guimarãis. The **Church of São Francisco,** a remodeled 15th-century building, has fine 18th-century decorative tiles depicting the life of Saint Anthony, and a richly decorated sacristy. The **Museu Alberto Sampaio** is notable particularly for the treasure from the 14th-century **Church of Nossa Senhora da Oliveira** (Our Lady of the Olive Tree), whose cloister and chapter house it occupies. The original building on the site, probably a monastery erected in the tenth century by the Countess Mumadona, has vanished. The **Paço dos Duques,** where the dukes of Bragança lived during the 15th century, has recently been restored. In the garden in front of it is the 12th-century **Church of São Miguel do Castelo,** containing the font in which Affonso Henriques is said to have been baptized.

**LAMEGO,** *on Routes N2 and N226 in Trás-os-Montes e Alto Duoro*
Here in 1143 the first Portuguese Cortes, or parliament, was held uniting representatives of the nobility, clergy, and towns and recognizing Affonso Henriques as king of Portugal (*see Guimarãis*). Only the square tower of the **Cathedral** still dates from the 12th century, when the church was first built. The interior was entirely redone in the 18th century. The **Regional Museum,** installed in the former episcopal palace, has a rich collection of 16th-century tapestries from the Low Countries; an interesting display of *azulejos,* showing the evolution of the characteristically Portuguese art of decorative tiles; and two 18th-century chapels of carved and gilded wood. The painted, coffered ceiling in the 17th-century **Church of Desterro**

(the Exile) is outstanding, while the **Sanctuary of Nossa Senhora dos Remédios** (Our Lady the Redeemer), built between 1750 and 1761, is reached by a marvelous 600-step **staircase** ornamented with *azulejos*, statues, and fountains.

**LEIRIA,** on *Routes E3-N1, N109, N242, and N356-2 in Beira Litoral*
When King Alfonso I (1128–85) built a fortified **Castle** here in 1135 it formed part of his southern line of defense, for Santarém and Lisbon were in Moorish hands until 1147. After that date the castle lost its strategic importance and fell into ruins until the reign of King Diniz I (1279–1325), who rebuilt it and lived there with his wife, Queen Isabel (*see also Coimbra*). The present buildings, most of which date from the 16th century, have recently been restored and constitute one of the handsomest specimens of Portuguese military architecture.

**LISBON,** on *Routes E3, N10, N8, N250.2, N249, N117, N6.3, N6, and E4 in Estremadura*
Ulysses, it is said, founded what has become the capital of Portugal. It is built on a number of hills commanding Lisbon Bay (Mar da Palha, or Straw Sea), a widening in the estuary of the Tagus River. The Phoenicians, Carthaginians, Romans, Visigoths, and finally the Moors occupied the city before it was taken for the Christians in 1147 by Affonso Henriques, then King Alfonso I, with the aid of ships on their way to the Second Crusade. But not until 1255, a century later, did King Alfonso III choose the city as his capital. Portugal's age of discovery in the 15th and 16th centuries made Lisbon one of the richest towns in the West. The devastating earthquake of November 1, 1755, however, destroyed almost all its important buildings and at least 30,000 of its citizens. Much of the swift re-building of the city along spacious and utilitarian lines is due to the marquês de Pombal, the influential minister of King Joseph Emanuel (1750–77). The Praça de Dom Pedro IV, better known as the **Rossio**, is the real heart of Lisbon. In the center of its black and white mosaic pavement is a **Statue of King Pedro IV.** Extending southward from that square toward the Tagus is the **Rua Augusta,** ending in a triumphal arch which in turn announces the enormous **Praça do Comércio,** known as the Terreiro do Paço. It measures 580 feet by 637 feet and is closed by the Tagus on the south and by arcaded buildings on the other three sides. In the center stands an equestrian **Statue of King Joseph Emanuel** designed in 1775 by Machado de Castro, Portugal's greatest 18th-century sculptor. Extending north from the Rossio, the 300-foot-wide **Avenida da Liberdade** leads to the **Praça Marquês de Pombal** and immediately after it to the elegant **Parque Eduardo VII,** named for the king of England in 1902 to commemorate the Anglo-Portuguese alliance that had persisted since the Treaty of Windsor in 1386. The Roman-esque **Sé,** or cathedral, east of the Rua Augusta, begun in 1150, was severely damaged in earthquakes of 1344 and 1755 and has been much restored. The **Castelo São Jorge** (castle of Saint George) nearby occupies a splendid height from which to view the river and the city. Visigothic and Moorish walls of the fifth and ninth centuries respectively remain. Within the castle grounds is the **Paço da Alcáçova,** a royal residence that was occupied from the time of King Diniz I (1279–1325) to that of King Manuel I (1495–1521). The view from the terrace is magnificent. The **Church of São Vicente de Fora,** rebuilt between 1582 and 1627 by Filippo Terzi, an Italian archi-tect, is one of the finest Renaissance buildings in Lisbon. Since the

*From left to right in Lisbon: the square called the Rossio, with its mosaic pavement and statue of King Pedro IV; a view from the Parque Eduardo VII*

time of King John IV (1640–56) the refectory of the **former convent** adjoining the church has been the royal pantheon for the house of Bragança. The 18th-century **Arsenal do Exercito** houses a military museum in which there is a most interesting collection of arms of all periods. The **Church of Madre de Deus,** rebuilt after the earthquake of 1755, is richly ornamented inside with *azulejos* and has a coffered vault with painted panels. The picturesque **Alfama Quarter,** the city's oldest and poorest, to the east of the Castelo São Jorge, is a maze of narrow streets and tall houses with overhanging second stories. Inhabited before the Visigothic occupation, it became the home of the Moorish nobility. The **Church of Conceição Velha** should be seen for the southern façade of the transept, all that remains of the grand building that King Manuel I erected on the site of a synagogue. The rest was destroyed in the earthquake of 1755. The most sumptuous survival of Manueline Lisbon is the **Monastery of Jerónimos,** begun in 1502 after designs by the French architect Boytac, who did so much to make the Manueline Gothic style rich but not vulgar. His work was continued by other talented architects throughout the 16th century. The city's other great Manueline monument is the **Church of Santa Maria,** whose south portal, vast interior, and richly carved cloister were designed and decorated by Boytac and his successor João de Castilho. Just west of the church is the **Museu Nacional de Arqueologia e Etnografia,** which has an outstanding collection of Iberian antiquities. Dating from 1515 to 1521 but uncharacteristically plain for Manueline building is the **Torré de Belém,** a tower built by Francisco de Arruda in which Romanesque and Gothic proportions are combined with Moorish decoration. Originally located in the middle of the Tagus, this fortress is now at the water's edge on the north bank because the river changed its course. The **Museu Nacional de Arte Antiga** has an excellent collection of works by Portuguese primitive painters of the 15th and 16th centuries, while the **Museu Nacional dos Coches,** in the former riding school in Belém Palace, has one of Europe's most important collections of coaches dating from the 16th to the 19th centuries. An archaeological museum is installed in the

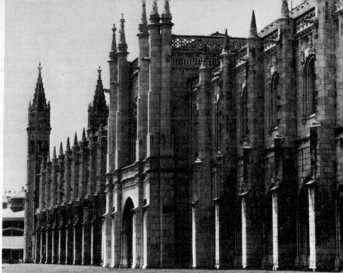

*of the Tagus River, showing the Castelo São Jorge on the hill at far left; the Monastery of Jerónimos*

ruined **Carmo Church** of the late 14th century, which collapsed in the earthquake of 1755. The **Padrão dos Descobrimentos** (Monument to the Discoveries), which represents the prow of a ship jutting into the Tagus, was erected in 1960 to commemorate the 500th anniversary of the death of Prince Henry the Navigator. The **Museum of Popular Art,** dating from 1940, attractively and thoroughly documents the folkways of Portugal. The **Gulbenkian Museum,** on the grounds of the Calouste Gulbenkian Foundation, has since 1969 housed the large, important, and eclectic collections of the late Armenian-born oilman of that name.

**MAFRA,** *on Routes N116 and N9 in Estremadura*

The enormous white marble **basilica-palace-monastery** here covers some ten acres of ground. It was designed by Friedrich Ludwig of Regensburg and built by King John V (1706–50) in gratitude for the birth of a daughter and heir. An imitation of Spain's Escorial, it has 4,500 doors and windows and took 50,000 workmen 13 years to build. It was here that Portugal's last king, Manuel II, took refuge from the revolution in Lisbon on October 4, 1910, and from here on October 6 that he went into exile.

**ÓBIDOS,** *on Route N8 in Estremadura*

After this town had been freed from the Moors by King Alfonso I in 1148, it was quickly rebuilt. It was so admired by Queen Isabella, the wife of King Diniz I (1279–1325), that she gave it to her, a practice followed by the kings of Portugal until 1833. With its well-preserved medieval **Castle,** and its **perimeter wall** built by the Moors and restored later, it is one of the most picturesque towns in Portugal today. The interior of the Renaissance **Church of Santa Maria** should be visited for its painted ceiling and the 18th-century *azulejos.* Just outside the town is a 15th-century **aqueduct.**

**OPORTO,** *on Routes E50-N1, N108, N15, N14, E50-N13, and N105-2 in Douro Litoral*

The second city of Portugal rises on granite hills chiefly on the north side of the Douro River not far from its junction with the Atlantic. The westward-flowing river proved a barrier to the Moorish conquest of the region known as Portucale, a rectangle extending from the Douro to the Minho River, which marks the present northern boundary with Spain. It was this county that Teresa, daughter of King Alfonso VI of Leon and Castile, brought as a dowry when she married Henry of Burgundy in 1095 (*see also Guimarãis*). In the 14th and 15th centuries the boatyards here contributed to the fleets that helped Portugal achieve maritime pre-eminence. Oporto equipped the ships that in July, 1415, helped take Ceuta, Morocco, and so secure the coasts and ports of Portugal from pirates. In 1628 and 1661 the citizens rose against what they considered unjust taxes, while in 1756 they revolted against the monopoly controlling the manufacture of wines from the upper Douro. The monopoly was established in the 18th century by the marquês de Pombal, the minister of King Joseph Emanuel, to combat the increasing English control of the wine trade in Oporto. The French held the city in 1805 and 1809, during the Peninsular War, until it was freed by the English. In 1820 the citizens revolted against the English occupation, establishing a reputation for rebellion that persisted well into the present century. The fortresslike **Cathedral** of the 12th and 13th centuries was much changed in the 17th and 18th centuries. Although the rose window dates from the 13th century, the interior is baroque. The Gothic **Church of São Francisco** was begun in 1233 but has elements of all succeeding centuries until the 18th, from which its astonishingly elaborate baroque interior dates. The 18th-century **Tower of the Church of Clérigos** is the highest bell tower in Portugal (245 feet). From the top there is a splendid view of the city including the **Vila Nova de Gaia Quarter**, on the opposite bank of the Douro, where the wine from the upper Douro is transformed into port. The **Church of Santa Clara**, of the 15th and 16th centuries, is richly decorated inside with gilded wood carvings. The **Museu Soares dos Reis** contains good collections of archaeological artifacts, paintings, sculptures, ceramics, and jewelry in addition to works by the 19th-century Portuguese sculptor for whom the museum is named. Three bridges span the Douro at Oporto: the **Dona Maria Pia**, an all-metal railway bridge completed by the French engineer Alexandre Gustave Eiffel in 1877; the **Dom Luís I**, a two-level, all-metal road bridge completed by a Belgian firm in 1886; and the **Arrábida Road Bridge**, whose single 886-foot-long reinforced concrete span is the longest in the world. It was built by a Portuguese engineer in 1953. On the south bank, in addition to the port wine quarter, is the former **Convent of Nossa Senhora da Serra do Pilar**, erected in the 16th century in the form of a rotunda.

**PORTÁLEGRE,** *on Routes N119, N18, N246, N359, and N246.2 in Alto Alentejo*
The handsome houses in this town date from the 16th century, when it was the center of the Portuguese tapestry industry, and the 17th century, when its silk mills added to its prosperity. The **tapestry workshops**, located in a former Jesuit monastery, may still be visited. The 16th-century **Cathedral** was restored in 1795. The **Palácio Amarelo** has remarkable 17th-century window grilles.

**QUELUZ,** *on Route N117 in Estremadura*
The **Royal Palace** was built here between 1758 and 1794 by the French architect J.-B. Robillon and the Portuguese Mateus Vicente, who took their inspiration from Versailles. It was the residence of Queen Maria I, who went mad when her husband, who was also

her uncle, died in 1786. The most spectacular room in the palace is the very ornate mirrored throne room. The splendid formal **gardens** surrounding the palace were designed in 1762 by Robillon in the manner of the 17th-century French landscape architect André Lenôtre. The **Lion Stair** leads from the palace to the canal garden.

**SAGRES POINT,** *on Routes N125 and N268 in the Algarve*
It was at this desolate world's end that Prince Henry the Navigator, third son of King John I, set up his school of navigation in 1418, and from here that he sent out voyages of discovery along the western coast of Africa. His former residence and school in Sagres, in which he died (1460), is now a youth hostel. **Cabo de São Vicente** (Cape Saint Vincent), 6 kilometers to the northwest, is the most southwesterly point in Europe, the Promontorium Sacrum of the ancients, where they watched, and, it is said, heard the sun sink into the sea with a great hiss. Several notable naval battles have been fought off the cape, including that of February 14, 1797, in which the British admiral John Jervis, assisted by Horatio Nelson, routed a Franco-Spanish fleet nearly twice as large.

**SANTARÉM,** *on Routes N3, N365, N114, and N368 in Ribatejo*
This town was a Roman and later Moorish stronghold because of its strategic situation along the approaches to Lisbon. The **Graça Church,** built between 1380 and the beginning of the 15th century, has a fine Flamboyant Gothic façade reminiscent in part of the one at Batalha (*see*). The rose window is particularly notable. The nave has been very well restored and contains the tomb of explorer Pedro Álvares Cabral (1460?–1526), who claimed Brazil for Portugal, as well as those of other notables. The former **Basilica of São João de Alporão,** now an archaeological museum, houses the sumptuous mausoleum of Duarte de Meneses, count of Viana—who was martyred by the Moors in 1464—which is one of the triumphs of the 15th-century Flamboyant Gothic style. The **Church of Marvila** was rebuilt under King Manuel I (1495–1521) and is lined with tiles.

**SETÚBAL AND VICINITY,** *on Routes N10 and N252 in Estremadura*
Portugal's third largest port has a sardine fleet of some 2,000 boats as well as excellent oyster beds. The **Church of Jesus** was built in 1491 by Boytac, the French architect who perfected the Manueline style. It is a splendid combination of the late Gothic mode and the nautically inspired Manueline decoration (in its twisted pillars and the spiral ribs of its vault). In the Gothic cloister is the **Museu da Cidade** (municipal museum), displaying a large group of paintings by Portuguese artists of the 15th and 16th centuries. Seven kilometers north, at Palmela, is a **Castle** that is one of the handsomest surviving specimens of Portuguese military architecture. The dungeon, keep, and parade ground date from the 14th century, but there are also the ruins of a **Mosque** (destroyed in the 1755 earthquake), attesting to Moorish occupation of the castle, which was not finally recaptured by the Christians until 1166. In 1186 the knights of Santiago de Compostela installed themselves in the castle and in the 14th century erected the **Church and Monastery of Saint James,** which are being transformed into a *pousada,* a first-class, government-run hotel. From the top of the castle keep one can see Setúbal and Lisbon and the Tagus and Sado rivers. Twelve kilometers west of Setúbal on Route N10 is the **Quinta de Bacalhoa** (Bacalhoa domain), a 15th- and 16th-century private house whose fine gardens are open to visitors when the owners are away.

**SINTRA AND VICINITY,** on Routes N249, N247, N9, N375, and N247.3 in Estremadura

In what was then the Dutch ambassador's residence (now a hotel), the Convention of Sintra was signed on August 30, 1808, during the Peninsular War. Under its terms the invading French, defeated by the British, were allowed to return home with all their equipment. The agreement so distressed the Portuguese that they called the ambassador's residence the **Palácio de Seteais** (palace of the seven sighs). The **Paço Real de Sintra** (royal palace) was begun in the 14th century by King John I on the foundations of a 13th-century palace. King Manuel I added new pavilions in the 16th century, changed the ogival windows to windows in the Manueline style, tiled the walls in splendid *azulejos*, and installed Mudéjar wooden ceilings and mosaic pavements, all of which gave the palace a distinctly Moorish look. Alterations in succeeding centuries have not been as happy. Not far from the palace, in the same misty and mountainous landscape, is the **Palácio da Pena,** a mid-19th-century pastiche of Moorish, Gothic, Manueline, Renaissance, and baroque styles situated on top of one of the highest peaks in the Serra de Sintra, or Sintra Mountains. It was built around a 16th-century monastery as his summer house by the husband of Queen Maria II (1826–53), Ferdinand of Coburg. The view from the top of the tower is splendid. To Richard Strauss the 300-acre park in which the palace stands was "the most beautiful thing I have seen in the world." Just north of the Pena Palace is the **Castelo dos Mouros,** also constructed on a 128-foot-high pinnacle. It originally dates from the seventh and eighth centuries but has been modified several times since and now consists of a perimeter wall guarded by four towers. A few kilometers northwest of the castle is the charming **Monserrate Park,** full of splendid trees and exotic vegetation planted around an 18th-century palace in the Oriental style. At the western end of the Sintra range is **Cape Roca,** the Promontorium Magnum of the Romans and the most westerly point of Europe, situated at the top of a 550-foot sheer drop into the Atlantic.

**TOMAR,** on Routes N238, N113, N3493, and N110 in Ribatejo

Here in 1160 the Grand Master of the Knights Templar began building what is the largest monastery in Portugal, the **Convento do Cristo,** whose round church and cloisters were not completed until the 17th century. The Knights Templars were suppressed in 1312, but eight years later King Diniz I founded the order of Christ, which was first established at Castro Marim and moved to the Convento do Cristo in 1356. Just as the Templars had played an important role in retaking Portugal from the Moors, so the knights of the order of Christ assisted Prince Henry the Navigator's voyages of discovery. King Manuel I was generous to the monastery, and the Manueline style of decorating, which drew heavily on seafaring motifs, is much in evidence. The **Charola,** or Templars' round church, dates from the 12th century; the nave from the 16th in the Manueline style. Of the seven cloisters, the charming Gothic **Cemitério** cloister and the **Lavagem** cloister were built in the time of Henry the Navigator. From the Renaissance cloister of **Santa Barbara** can be seen a window carved by Diogo de Arruda in 1510, which is the most elaborate example of the Manueline style in Portugal. The principal cloister of 1557 is commonly called the **Claustro dos Felipes** because according to tradition it was here in 1580 that King Philip II of Spain proclaimed himself also king of Portugal. The **Chapel of Nossa Senhora da Conceição,** with its three naves and delicately carved Corinthian capitals, is one of the purest Renaissance buildings in Portugal. The **Church of São João Baptista,** dating from the end of the 15th century, has a fine Flamboyant Gothic portal and a curious Manueline bell tower. An interesting 15th-century **Synagogue,** now a museum, is found at 73 Rua Dr. Joaquim Jacinto.

**VILA DO CONDE,** *on Route E50-N13 in Douro Litoral*
The vast **Monastery of Santa Clara** was founded in 1318 by Affonso Sanches, bastard son of King Diniz I, and Affonso's wife, Teresa Martins. The façade of the building was rebuilt at the end of the 18th century, but the church, with its single aisle, is of the 14th century. It is roofed with an ornate painted coffered ceiling of the 18th century. Not to be missed are the richly carved Renaissance tombs of the founders in one of the side chapels.

**VILA REAL VICINITY**
SOLAR DE MATEUS (MATEUS MANOR), *3 kilometers east off Route N15 in Trás-os-Montes e Alto Douro*
This superb 18th-century house belongs to the counts of Vila Real, but it is open to the public. The entrance on the first floor, and the double stair leading up to it, are at the far end of an oblong courtyard formed by two long wings. Every corner of the roof line is topped with outsize stone ornaments. The interior is also richly furnished. The manor is depicted on the label of the rosé wine for which the estate is justly renowned.

**VILA VIÇOSA,** *on Routes N255 and N254 in Alentejo*
In the 15th century the second duke of Bragança moved his court here. However, the fortunes of the Braganças, the future kings of Portugal, were much depressed when King John II had the third duke (his own brother-in-law) executed in 1483 on the charge of plotting against the monarchy. The present **Paço Ducal,** or ducal palace, was begun by the fourth duke of Bragança, Jaime I, in 1501 and not completed until a century later. It was here that Duke Jaime assassinated his wife in 1512 for an alleged adultery. The interior, richly but not uniquely furnished, is now a museum. The 5,000-acre **park** near the town was formerly the Braganças' hunting grounds. The **castle** and **ramparts** erected by King Diniz I in the 14th century were reinforced during the 17th century. A handsome granite **pillory** of the 16th century stands before the stout walls. To the north of the palace is the curious 16th-century **Porta dos Nós** (knot gate), all that remains of the perimeter wall.

**VISEU,** *on Routes N16-E51, N2, N231, N337-7, and N229 in Beira Alta*
Narrow streets of granite cobbles wind among fine **town houses** of the 16th through the 18th centuries. The 13th-century **Cathedral,** remodeled in the 16th, combines elements from both centuries in the elegant interior: 13th-century columns support a Manueline vault with ropelike liernes characteristic of that early-16th-century style. The 17th-century chancel houses a monumental gilded wooden altarpiece. The treasury and the gray granite 16th-century cloister should also be visited. Next to the cathedral is the **Museu Grão Vasco,** which occupies a late-16th-century palace modified in the 18th century. The museum has a superb collection of paintings by Vasco Fernandes (1480–1543), who was known as Grão Vasco (Great Vasco), and other painters of the 16th-century Viseu school.

# ANDORRA

This autonomous principality in the Pyrenees is jointly ruled by the president of France and the bishop of the Spanish town of Seo de Urgel (*see*). Polybius, the Greek historian, infers that the mountainous region had already been settled in the third century B.C., and Iberian and Roman coins have been found at **Santa Julià**. Tradition has it that Charlemagne and his son Louis I recovered Barcelona from the Moors in 803 and assigned that part of its territory now comprising Andorra to the bishop of Urgel. The region was contested by the French counts of Foix until 1278, when by arbitration Andorra became independent under a popularly elected council with the bishop and the count as joint princes. The count's rights descended to the house of Bearn and thence by marriage to the French Crown with the accession of King Henry IV in 1589. In 1793 the leaders of the French Revolution renounced that country's feudal rights in Andorra, but Napoleon reasserted them on the petition of the Andorrans themselves in 1806. Partial suzerainty has since devolved onto the president of the French republic. A feudal anachronism, Andorra pays annual tribute of 960 francs to the French president and 460 pesetas to the bishop of Urgel. Customs duties rather than taxes constitute the country's official income, although smuggling from France to Spain is said to contribute generously to the gross national product. There are some Moorish ruins in **Ordino**, and a 16th-century building in the capital, **Andorra la Vella**, is the administrative center for the tiny state.

*Left: a Romanesque chapel and Moorish ruins near the village of Bons. Right: the bridge of Sant' Antoni (top), north of Andorra la Vella, and the Church of Santa Coloma (below), south of the capital*

# GIBRALTAR

This limestone promontory at the southern tip of Spain is 1,396 feet high and measures 4.8 by 1.2 kilometers in area. In ancient times it was the northern Pillar of Hercules, the southern one being Mount Acho, on the North African coast. Tunneling into the great rock in 1944 revealed **Gorham's Cave**, which was dug out more thoroughly in 1948 to reveal four levels of occupation from Neanderthal to Roman times. Since 1704 the Rock has been a British possession. When the Moor Tariq ibn-Ziyad landed in 711 he renamed the place, until then called Calpe, Jebel-al-Tarik. Except between 1309 and 1333 the Moors remained in control until 1462, when the Spanish captured the Rock. Charles V had the fortifications strengthened in 1552 to guard against the attacks of the Turkish pirate Barbarossa. The British captured the Rock of Gibraltar during the War of the Spanish Succession (1701–14), ostensibly on behalf of Archduke Charles of Austria, whom they then recognized as king of Spain. But in fact the British took it for themselves, and it has remained British territory to this day despite sieges in 1704, 1727, and 1779–83 (the last particularly damaging **Gibraltar,** the chief town on the Rock). The Rock is home to a colony of Barbary apes, imported perhaps by the Moors from the apes' native habitat in North Africa. A 16th-century Franciscan **Monastery** is the present governor's residence, and nearby is the splendid **Alameda,** a tropical garden laid out in 1814 by Governor Sir George Don. Not far from the artillery barracks on the heights is an eighth-century Moorish **Castle.**

*Top: a view of the Rock of Gibraltar from the Mediterranean Sea. Below: the changing of the guard in front of the governor's residence*

# SPAIN

**ALBA DE TORMES,** *on Route C510 in Leon*
The **Tomb of Saint Theresa of Ávila,** who died in 1582, lies above the altar of the **Carmelite Convent,** which she founded here in 1570. Looming over the town is a tower that is the only extant portion of the **Palace of the Duke of Alba,** the cruel Spanish governor of the Netherlands in the 1570s. The palace itself was destroyed in 1809.

**ALCALÁ DE HENARES,** *on Routes N11, C100, and C300 in New Castile*
Known as Complutum in Roman times, the town became a Visigothic bishopric and a Moorish fortress. With the Christian Reconquest in 1118 the town was given to the archbishops of Toledo. In 1508 Cardinal Francisco Jiménez de Cisneros of Toledo founded a university in Alcalá, which soon thrived in the **Colegio Mayor de San Ildefonso,** a splendid Renaissance building whose magnificent plateresque façade of 1543 bears Cisneros's arms. The transfer of the university to Madrid in 1836 brought on the decline of Alcalá. Among the natives of the town were Miguel de Cervantes (1547–1616) and Catherine of Aragon, wife of Henry VIII of England.

**ALCÁNTARA,** *on Route C523 in Estremadura*
The town's name is derived from the Arabic *el kantara,* "the bridge," which aptly describes the chief feature of the town, a 617-foot-long **bridge** built for Trajan in A.D. 105. Its six granite arches span the Tagus River without the help of mortar. Partially destroyed by the Moors in 1213, it was rebuilt in 1543 by the emperor Charles V. In 1218 the defense of the town against the Moors was given to the knightly order of Alcántara. This and the 13th-century orders of Calatrava, Santiago, and Montesa were military-religious organizations whose members lived under the monastic rule of the Cistercians. These orders played an important role in the Reconquest of Spain from the Moors. The **Monastery of San Benito,** built between 1505 and 1576 and now in ruins, belonged to the knights of Alcántara.

**ALMERÍA,** *on Route N340 in Andalusia*
Probably founded in Phoenician times, the town was called Portus Magnus by the Romans. It received its present name from the Moors, who called it Al-Mariyat, "the mirror." The **Moorish Alcazaba,** or fortress, erected in the eighth century, was much damaged by an earthquake in 1522. During the 11th century Almería was the capital of an important Moorish kingdom. After 1091, under the Almoravides, it became the headquarters of a powerful band of pirates whose raids extended as far north as Galicia. King Alfonso VII of Leon and Castile captured the city for the Christians in 1147, but it was lost to the Moors again a decade later and remained under their control until taken by King Ferdinand II of Aragon in 1489. Its fortified **Cathedral,** never completed, was begun in 1524 according to plans by Diego de Siloé.

**ALTAMIRA CAVE,** *near Santillana off Route C6316 in Old Castile*
The celebrated prehistoric paintings were not discovered until 1879, although the caves had been found accidentally in 1868. The paintings were so fresh that their authenticity was disputed until the similar Lascaux cave paintings were found in the Dordogne region of France nearly two decades later. Some of the polychrome paintings at Altamira were made about 25,000 B.C., but the best of them were done toward the end of the Magdalenian period (about

*Top left: the Royal Palace at Madrid. Right: the cathedral at Santiago de Compostela. Center: Barcelona's busy port. Below left: the Lion Court of the Alhambra at Granada. Right: the walled city of Ávila*

15,000–12,000 B.C.). The number of visitors allowed into the caves is limited by the need to maintain exact levels of temperature and humidity.

**ARANJUEZ,** *on Route NIV in New Castile*

King Ferdinand II of Aragon and his queen, Isabella, liked the 14th-century hunting lodge built on the site of the present **palace** by the Grand Master of the knightly order of Santiago. Emperor Charles V hunted from it, but it was his son, King Philip II, who in 1561 employed Juan Bautista de Toledo and Juan de Herrera— who later designed the Escorial for him—to enlarge the palace. Fires in 1660 and 1665 did great damage, subsequently repaired. The present palace was reconstructed by King Philip V in 1727 in the style of Louis XIV. The charming and luxurious **Casa del Labrador,** a sort of Petit Trianon, was built at the end of the 18th century by King Charles IV. The late 17th- and 18th-century **gardens** are particularly splendid. In March, 1808, a popular revolt at Aranjuez overthrew King Charles IV's influential minister Manuel de Godoy, forcing Charles IV to abdicate in favor of his son, King Ferdinand VII. But Napoleon, whose troops Godoy had allowed into Spain, summoned both Charles and Ferdinand to Bayonne, forced both of them to abdicate in his favor, and named his brother Joseph to the throne of Spain, where he remained until 1814. These negotiations with Napoleon and the French occupation of Madrid led to an uprising there on May 2, which marked the beginning of the Peninsular War.

**ÁVILA,** *on Routes N501, N110, C502, and N403 in Old Castile*

Legend has it that the city was the Abula founded by Hercules. The Romans called it Avela. After Toledo fell to the Moors in 1085, Ávila became one of the Christians' bastions, and its nobility distinguished itself in the Reconquest. Although the town flourished in the 16th century—it is the birthplace of Saint Theresa (1515–82)— the expulsion of the Moriscos (Moors converted to Christianity) in 1609 deprived Ávila of its most active artisans and tradesmen, and the town gradually became the austere provincial capital it is today. The city is encircled by **medieval walls,** which are among the most complete in Europe. Punctuated by 88 towers and 8 gates, the walls date largely from the 11th century with 14th-century modifications. The apse of the impressive late Romanesque–early Gothic **Cathedral** forms a bastion in the wall. It was begun in 1157 and finished during the 14th century. The Romanesque **Church of San Vicente** was built between 1307 and 1440 on the presumed site of Saint Vincent's martyrdom in the fourth century. The **Convent of Santo Tomás** was built by King Ferdinand II of Aragon and his queen, Isabella I, between 1482 and 1493. It contains a masterfully carved marble tomb (1512) of their only son, Don Juan (1478–97), by the Florentine sculptor Domenico Fancelli and a plain slab marking the tomb of Grand Inquisitor Tomás de Torquemada (1420–98).

**BALEARIC ISLANDS,** *50–190 miles off the coast of Spain in the Mediterranean Sea*

The 16 inhabited islands and the uninhabited rocky islets near them form a province of Spain. The three chief islands are Majorca, Minorca, and Ibiza. Numerous vestiges attest to the occupation of the islands before recorded history. The earliest of these civilizations is known as that of the *talayoti* for the rough stone towers they built, particularly in Minorca. Although opinion is by no means unanimous, one theory is that this civilization began during the Bronze Age. The Carthaginians, the Romans (who founded Palma), the Vandals, and the Visigoths occupied the islands before the Moors (798–1229). King James I of Aragon (1213–76) took Majorca for the Christians and made it part of a separate kingdom, which he gave to his son, James I of Majorca (1276–1311). This was the beginning of a period of commercial and artistic prosperity for Majorca, which persisted through its annexation to the kingdom of Aragon in 1343 until the 18th century.

## IBIZA

Ebusus, which is to say the town of Ibiza on the island of the same name, was founded in the seventh century B.C. by the Carthaginians, whose necropolis dug out of the **Puig des Molins** (hill of the mills) a short distance from the city is the principal archaeological attraction of the island today. The objects found in some of the 3,000 tombs in the necropolis are housed in a small museum at the site. Also worth a visit are the varied collections of the **Archaeological Museum** in the city of Ibiza.

## MAJORCA

As befits a place that has always profited from the sea, the handsomest reminders of **Palma's** prosperity as a mercantile capital and the island's chief city are ranged along the harbor front. The **Almudaina,** the former palace of the kings of Majorca, was begun in 1309 by King James II of Aragon on the site of the citadel built by the city's Moorish rulers. Next to it is the beautiful Gothic **Cathedral,** founded in 1229 by King James I of Aragon, who retook the island from the Moors in that year. The sanctuary dates mainly from the 14th century, but the cathedral was not finished until 1601. Then, dangerously weakened by an earthquake in 1851, the western façade was rebuilt in the Gothic style. The small museum in the chapter house of the cathedral is notable for its Gothic paintings. Not far from the cathedral, also on the harbor front, is the **Lonja** (merchants' exchange), built between 1426 and 1456, which now houses a good collection of pictures by Balearic and Catalan painters of the 14th to the 16th centuries. The **Church of San Francisco,** built between 1281 and 1390, has a magnificent Gothic cloister and the incomplete tomb of Raymond Lully (1235?–1315), the theologian and philosopher, who was born in Palma. Of the houses of the nobility that attest to the former great prosperity of Palma the following are representative: the 18th-century **Casa Vivot** and the 17th-century **Casa Oleza,** both with charming interior courtyards, and the 16th-century **Casa Palmer,** with a splendid Renaissance façade. The **Castillo de Bellver** was begun in the reign of King James I of Majorca (1276–1311) and finished soon after his death as a royal palace, although it was soon turned into a prison, which it remained until 1915. Faithful to its curious circular shape are the double moat and circular patio. The **Cartuja de Valldemosa,** about 18 kilometers north of Palma, was a Carthusian monastery from 1399 until the monks were expelled in 1834, but most of the present buildings date from the 18th century. After 1834 the cells were rented to transients, among them, for the winter of 1838–39, George Sand, the French novelist, and Frédéric Chopin, the composer. **Petra,** 11 kilometers off Route C715 near Manacor, is the **Birthplace of Fra Junípero Serra** (1713–84), the Franciscan missionary who did so much to establish the mission churches of California. His house is now a museum.

MINORCA

The island was contested by the English and the French during the 18th century for the splendidly protected harbor at **Mahón,** the capital. The English occupied it from 1708 to 1756; the French from 1756 to 1763; the English again until 1782. Vestiges of the English occupation are a taste for rocking chairs; small clean houses, some with lace curtains, many with white trim; a few bay windows; and a drive from Mahón to San Luis, San Clemente, and back to Mahón that is still known as *la vuelta de milord* because it was a favorite with the English. The remains of the prehistoric civilization that peopled the Balearic Islands are particularly notable in Minorca, which abounds in stone *talayoti,* or towers; *taulas,* or large stone T-shaped constructions; and *navetas,* or mounds of stone shaped like upside-down boats. The greatest concentration of these are to be found near **Ciudadela,** in the northwest corner of the island.

**BARCELONA,** *on Routes N11, A17, N152, C246, and A2 in Catalonia*

The Carthaginian Barcino was founded by Hamilcar Barca about 230 B.C. on the low hill where the cathedral is now. Near the same site are the remains of the capital of the Roman province of Laye-tania, known as Julia Faventia Augusta Pia Barcino. The Visigoths succeeded the Romans, remaining until the Moors took the city in 713 for less than a century. In 801 Charlemagne's son Louis I ("the Debonair") drove the Moors from Catalonia and had the province administered by a vassal. But toward the end of the century the reigning count, Wilfred the Hairy (865–98), achieved a de facto independence for Catalonia—an attitude of mind that has persisted ever since and still distinguishes Catalonians from other Spaniards. In 1137 the count of Barcelona, Ramón Berenguer IV, married Petronilla, the two-year-old daughter of King Ramiro II of Aragon, who had inherited the kingdom of Aragon. The combined realm was not subject to centralized Spanish rule until the marriage of Ferdinand II of Aragon and Isabella I of Castile in 1474. Until then the power of Catalonia-Aragon grew both on and off the mainland. The city was occupied by the French from 1808 to 1814, the dura-tion of the Peninsular War, and throughout the rest of the 19th cen-tury the city resisted the authority of the Spanish government. In 1931 a Catalan republic was proclaimed, perpetuating the tradition of independence, and during the Spanish Civil War (1936–39) Bar-celona was solidly Republican until it fell to the Nationalists in January, 1939. The façade of the **Cathedral,** a splendid Catalan Gothic building, was not completed until 1892, but it is built ac-cording to a 15th-century design. The rest of the church dates from 1298 to 1438. It occupies the site of a Visigothic basilica destroyed by the Franks in the ninth century. The **Barrio Gótico** (Gothic quar-ter), of which the cathedral is a major ornament, is rich in 13th-to-15th-century buildings and in the remains of the Roman city. The **Palacio de la Diputación Provincial** is a 15th-century building with a 16th-century façade and was the seat of the ancient parliament of Catalonia. The stairs and Gothic inner courtyard are particularly fine. The **Ayuntamiento,** or city hall, was built in the last century but preserves the façade of its Gothic predecessor of 1399–1402 by Arnau Bargués. A much more recent but equally singular facet of Barcelona's architecture is the work done there by Antonio Gaudí (1852–1926), one of the most remarkable practitioners of the art nouveau style. His unfinished masterpiece, the **Church of the Sagrada Familia,** has been under construction since 1882 and is still far from completed. Other works by Gaudí are the **Parque Güell,** where Gaudí's house, now a museum, is located; two apartment houses known as **Battló** and **Milá,** at Numbers 43 and 92 Paseo de la Gracia; and the **Palacio Güell,** with its remarkable wrought-iron grilles, in the Via Conde del Asalto, which runs off the wide, tree-shaded **Rambla,** where all Barcelona buys flowers or has a coffee at outdoor stands and cafés. The city is also well endowed with museums, the most remarkable of which is the **Museo de Arte de Cataluña,** the world's most important collection of Romanesque painting. The **Museo Maritimo,** near the harbor, is installed in the town's remarkable medieval covered shipyards and contains many ship models and other reminders of Barcelona's long recognized and enduring importance as a port. Moored in the harbor there is a replica of Columbus's *Santa María.* The **Federico Marés Museum** has one of the richest collections in Spain of medieval sculpture; in the **Museo Arqueológico** the megalithic and Greco-Roman artifacts are well presented, while the **Museo Picasso** has recently been enlarged in order to house the gift of chiefly early paintings and drawings that the artist presented to the city before his death in 1973.

**BURGOS AND VICINITY,** *on Routes N623, E3-N1, N120, NI-E25, and E3-N620 in Old Castile*

The city was founded in 884 by Diego Rodriguez, count of Castile, and in 1037 became the capital of the kingdoms of Castile, Leon, and Asturias under the rule of King Ferdinand I. In 1937, during the Spanish Civil War, the city regained some of its past glory by temporarily becoming the capital of Nationalist Spain. The city's most famous son was Rodrigo Díaz de Bivar (1040?–99), known as the Cid, a soldier of fortune whose unscrupulous career was much purified in the epic poem of which he is the hero. In reality Rodrigo served Sancho II (1065–72) and then Sancho's brother Alfonso I (1072–1109), both Christian kings of Castile, until he was banished by the latter. Rodrigo then fought for the Moorish king of Saragossa before capturing Valencia in 1094 and making it his own principality. His ashes are interred in the **Cathedral** at Burgos, built between the 13th and the 15th centuries, which is one of the finest Gothic churches in Spain and contains many splendid works of art. Other vestiges of the city's importance are the **Arco de Santa María,** a gateway in the 11th-century fortifications that was much embellished between 1534 and 1536 in honor of the emperor Charles V; the 15th-century **Casa del Cordón,** in which King Ferdinand II and his queen, Isabella I, received Christopher Columbus in 1496 on his return from his second expedition to the Indies; the **Convent of Las Huelgas,** built by King Alfonso VIII in 1175 at the request of his wife, Eleanor, daughter of Henry II of England. Richly endowed by the king, the convent accepted only the noblest nuns in Spain. Many of the kings of Castile were crowned and chose to be buried here. Four kilometers east of Burgos is another royal pantheon, the **Cartuja de Milaflores,** founded in 1441 by King John II of Castile. In front of the altar is an exceptionally fine and elaborate funeral monument to the king and his second wife, Isabella of Portugal.

**CÁDIZ,** *on Route NIV in Andalusia*

The Phoenicians are said to have settled here as early as 1100 B.C., attracted by the tin and other mineral resources of Andalusia. There is archaeological evidence of Phoenician settlement on this rocky peninsula from the ninth century B.C. The Carthaginians and then the Romans succeeded to the town, which in Roman times was called Gades. Greek and Roman scholars would visit this western-most city of the Mediterranean to study the tides and sunsets; Pliny felt that it was part of the lost continent of Atlantis. In Roman times the city grew rich because of its monopoly of the trade in salt fish with Rome. After the fall of Rome Cádiz went into a period of decline, which did not end until the discovery of America. Then renewed prosperity made it the subject of sieges by Barbary coast pirates and by the English, who sacked and nearly destroyed the town in 1596. It was from Cádiz that Columbus set sail on his second voyage in September of 1493. The **Battle of Trafalgar,** in which Horatio Nelson lost his life in 1805, took place off the cape of that name near Cádiz, and the Franco-Spanish fleet that he defeated set sail from Cádiz's splendidly protected harbor. During the Peninsular War the Spanish Cortes took refuge here and in 1812 drew up a liberal constitution, which King Ferdinand VII revoked in 1814. The **Monument of the Cortes** on the Plaza de España commemorates the event. The city remained a center of liberalism and in 1820 again proclaimed the liberal constitution of 1812. As a result the king, always in opposition, was brought to the city by force in 1823. However, the French besieged the city the same year and forced the citizens to release the king. Among the landmarks in the city are the 13th-century **Catedral Vieja,** which was nearly destroyed in the siege of 1596 and rebuilt thereafter; the baroque **Catedral Nueva,** begun in 1722; the **Chapel of Los Capuchinos,** with the last work of Murillo at the high altar; and the city's landmark, the **Torre de Vigía.**

**CIUDAD REAL AND VICINITY,** *on Routes N420, N401, N430, and C415 in New Castile*

This was one of the first Spanish towns to form a *hermandad,* or brotherhood of bourgeois, which first resisted the excessive demands of the nobility and then protected the roads against thieves. King Ferdinand II (1474–1516) and his queen, Isabella I (1474–1504), expanded and consolidated these associations into a general police force, the Santa Hermandad. Some 17 kilometers southeast of the city is the **Castle** (now in ruins) of the knights of Calatrava, a Spanish military order. Founded in 1164 to defend the environs against the Moors of Andalusia, the order was suppressed by King Ferdinand and Queen Isabella. West of Ciudad Real is the **Alarcos Shrine,** commemorating the Battle of Alarcos, where in 1195 the Christians suffered a major setback in their extended fight to drive the Moors from Spain when King Alfonso VIII of Castile was roundly defeated by the Almohades. The tide did not turn in favor of the Christians again until the Battle of Las Navas de Tolosa in 1212.

**COCA,** *on Routes C606 and C605 in Old Castile*

The brick **Fortress** at the outskirts of this village was built by Moors at the end of the 15th century and is one of the most important examples of Mudejar architecture in Spain.

**CÓRDOBA,** *on Routes N432, E25-NIV, and C431 in Andalusia*

The Romans dedicated a temple to Janus on the site of the great **Cathedral-Mosque,** and the Visigoths built a church to Saint Vincent. In 785, 74 years after the Moors took the town, Abd-er-Rahman I (756–88)—who made Córdoba the capital of the caliphate of Córdoba, which for a time ruled all of Moorish Spain—began to build a mosque to rival the one in Damascus. One of his aims was to save

*Details of the interior arches and façade of the great mosque at Córdoba*

his subjects the need to make the long pilgrimage to Mecca. Additions continued to be made in the intervening centuries into the reign of Hisham II (976–1009), during which time Córdoba was the most populous city in the Western world and comparable in splendor only to Constantinople in the East. Córdoba was taken for the Christians in 1236 by Ferdinand the Saint, king of Castile, who renamed the mosque the church of the Virgin of the Assumption and had chapels constructed against the interior walls. A few years later the first of the approximately 850 columns in the interior of the mosque were removed for the construction of a Christian chapel. In 1523, against the advice of the city council but with the approval of Emperor Charles V, who had never seen the mosque, about 60 more of the columns were removed, and a cruciform Renaissance church was built over the course of a century inside the center of the mosque. When in 1526 he saw what had been done, Charles V much regretted having consented to it, saying, "You have built here what you or anyone might have built anywhere else, but you have destroyed what was unique in the world." Other notable sights are the **Museo Arqueológico Provincial**, installed in the 16th-century palace of Jerónimo Páez, which has an important collection of prehistoric, Roman, Visigothic, and Moorish antiquities; the first-century **Roman Bridge** over the Guadalquivir; and 9 kilometers west of the town, the ruined **Medina az Zahara**. This was once an immense palace, a city really, begun in 936 by Abd-er-Rahman III (912–61) for his favorite wife, Zahra (meaning flower). For 25 years 10,000 men and 400 camels labored on the city, and when it was completed it had a garrison of 12,000 and 2,000 horses in the palace stables. The whole complex was razed by discontented Berbers in 1010 and is being restored today. In the **Barrio de la Judería**, Jewish quarter, is a **Statue of Maimonides**, the famous 12th-century philosopher who was a native of Córdoba.

**COVARRUBIAS AND VICINITY,** *on Route C110 in Old Castile*

In the fine 14th- and 15th-century **Collegiate Church,** among some 20 medieval tombs, are those of Fernán González, count of Castile (923 or 932–970), and his wife. Fernán succeeded in carving out a viable province of Castile free from the domination of Leon, and he contributed much toward driving back the Moors from what are today the provinces of Santander, Álava, Logroño, Burgos, and Palencia. His exploits became the subject of an epic poem in the 13th century. Eighteen kilometers southeast of the town is the **Monastery of Santo Domingo de Silos,** a way station on the pilgrimage route to Santiago de Compostela (*see*) originally established by Fernán González. That building was sacked by al-Mansur, however, and the present monastery, with a beautiful, two-story Romanesque cloister, dates from the 11th century. The capitals and bas-reliefs on the first floor of the cloister are splendid. There is also an interesting pharmacy in the monastery, as well as a small museum.

**ESCORIAL,** *on Route C600 in New Castile*

The complex called the Escorial comprises a monastery, a church, a royal palace, a royal mausoleum, and a library. It was built by 1,500 laborers between 1563 and 1584 and designed by the architects Juan Bautista de Toledo (d. 1567) and his pupil Juan de Herrera. The Escorial is dedicated to Saint Lawrence, on whose day in 1557 King Philip II, the builder, won the Battle of Saint Quentin. The building was constructed in gratitude for that victory over the French and in obedience to the wish of his father, Emperor Charles V, to build a royal pantheon. The forbidding gray granite building covers 400,000 square feet and is said to contain a hundred miles of corridors and cloisters. Here Philip lived for 14 years, until his death in 1598, in a small, plain room with a clear view, through removable shutters in one wall, of the high altar of the enormous and ornate **Church.** In Philip's time the **Royal Pantheon** was a simple chamber; it received its rich embellishment of gilt bronze and marble under Philip III (1598–1621) and Philip IV (1621–65). Part way down the stairs to the pantheon is the *pudridero,* where royal corpses were placed for ten years before being consigned to one of the labeled black marble sarcophagi in the pantheon itself. The interior walls of the palace are covered by more than 300 Spanish and Flemish tapestries, while the famous **Library,** built around a nucleus of 10,000 books donated by Philip II, now contains more than 40,000 books and 4,000 manuscripts dating from the 5th to the 18th centuries, including many rarities. The excellent museum is devoted partly to the construction of the Escorial and partly to a centralized display of paintings that were formerly scattered throughout the building.

**ESTELLA,** *on Routes NIII, C132, and C123 in Navarre*

This Roman town was revived as a way station on the pilgrimage road to Santiago de Compostela (*see*) in the 11th century, and in the 12th was chosen as their residence by the kings of Navarre, whose **Palace** of that century—one of the oldest nonreligious buildings in Spain—remains. During the royal wars of the 19th century (1833–39 and 1872–76) Estella was the headquarters for the Carlist cause. The **Church of San Pedro de la Rúa** has a splendid Romanesque portal.

**GERONA,** *on Routes NII, N141, C250, and C255 in Catalonia*

The Gerunda of the Ausetani claims to have been the first city in Spain to be visited by Saint Paul and Saint James. From about 712 to 1015 it was in Moorish hands. The most famous of the many sieges to which it has been subjected took place in 1809, when the defenders under General Álvarez de Castro withstood 35,000 partisans of Napoleon for seven months before capitulating. The **Cathedral** is one of the most noteworthy Gothic buildings in Catalonia. The first church on the site was founded by Charlemagne in 786 and was rebuilt between 1016 and 1038, when the so-called **Torre de Carlomagno** was constructed. The bulk of the present church dates from 1312 to 1598. One of the treasures in the chapter house is a magnificent 12th-century **Embroidery of the Creation.** The **Museo Diocesano** has a noteworthy collection of Romanesque and Gothic paintings.

## GRANADA (ANDALUSIA)
### ALHAMBRA

This is both the name of one of three hills on which the city stands and the name of the **Palace** built during the Moorish occupation principally by the Nasrite rulers Yusuf I (1334–54) and his son Mohammed V (1354–91). After the reconquest of Granada in 1492, which completed the Christian Reconquest of Spain after 781 years of Moorish rule, King Ferdinand II and Queen Isabella I repaired the palace. But in 1526 Emperor Charles V pulled down part of Yusuf I's building and began his own Renaissance palace on the site. Although building continued for a century, Charles V's palace was never finished, and in the ensuing centuries the whole Alhambra deteriorated; restoration was begun in 1828. The American author Washington Irving was inspired by a visit to Granada to write *Tales from the Alhambra*, published in 1832. The palace of the Alhambra is the ultimate expression of Moorish art in Spain, with its profusion of lacy, airy decoration in wood, plaster, and brick and its graceful patios behind the severe exterior characteristic of Moslem architecture.

### CATHEDRAL

Work on this Gothic and Renaissance structure continued from 1523 to 1703. Its first architect, Enrique de Egas, also built the adjoining **Capilla Real,** or royal chapel (1506–21), one of the most richly decorated in Europe. The chapel was ordered built by King Ferdinand II and his queen, Isabella I, who are buried here. The magnificent recumbent marble effigies of the royal pair were completed in Genoa in 1517 by the Florentine sculptor Domenico Fancelli. Also buried in the chapel are Philip the Handsome, duke of Burgundy (1478–1506), and his wife, Juána the Mad (1479–1555), the parents of Emperor Charles V. Their marble effigies were designed by Bartolomé Ordóñez in 1519–20. In the sacristy is a small display of excellent Flemish, Spanish, and Italian paintings mainly from the collection of Queen Isabella.

### GENERALIFE

The buildings of this small 14th-century palace of the sultans of Granada have been much altered, but the terraced Moorish gardens with pools, cascades, and water jets still evoke most marvelously an entirely non-European aspect of Spain.

## GUERNICA, *on Route C6315 in the Basque Provinces*

During the Middle Ages the Basque parliament met under an **oak** in the center of the city. There too newly created nobles would swear not to infringe the *fueros*, or liberties, of the Basques (until the *fueros* were abolished in 1876). The present oak grew from an acorn of the original tree, the remains of which are enshrined beside it. On April 26, 1937, during the Spanish Civil War, Nazi planes bombed the town to support Nationalist ground forces. Some 2,000 people were killed and hundreds wounded. Pablo Picasso's celebrated painting of this unprecedented air raid hangs in the Museum of Modern Art in New York.

## HUELVA VICINITY (ANDALUSIA)

### MONASTERY OF LA RÁBIDA, *about 5 kilometers south*

Legend has it that in 1484 Christopher Columbus collapsed here after fruitlessly begging the backing of Queen Isabella I for the exploration of the Indies he sought to make. The prior, Juan Pérez de Marchena, received and revived the explorer and then persuaded the queen to reverse her decision. Just south of the convent is a **Statue of Columbus** erected in 1892, the date of the restoration of the convent. Columbus set sail in August, 1492, on his first voyage of discovery from the nearby village of **Palos de la Frontera**, where in 1528 Hernando Cortes landed after the conquest of Mexico. The port at Palos is now silted up.

## ITALICA, *near Seville on Route N433 in Andalusia*

The present ruins are of a town founded in 206 B.C. by Scipio Africanus for the veterans of the Spanish war against Carthage. It is said that three emperors were born here—Trajan (52?–117), Hadrian (76–138), and Theodosius (346?–75). The **Amphitheater** once accommodated 40,000. There are also remains of mosaic floors and houses.

## LA CORUÑA, *on Routes C552, E50-N550, and E50-NVI in Galicia*

The importance of the town in Roman times is exemplified by the so-called **Tower of Hercules**, in reality a second-century Roman lighthouse restored in the 18th century and still in use today. After a relatively short occupation by the Moors of about two centuries the town became Christian in 1002. King Philip II embarked from this fortified port in 1554 on his way to marry Mary Tudor, and it was from here that on July 26, 1588, the "Invincible Armada" of 130 ships sailed for England and its destruction in a storm. The following year, in reprisal, Sir Francis Drake burned the town. During the Peninsular War England was the ally of La Coruña in its vain attempt to resist Napoleon's troops. The city capitulated in January, 1809, after the British were beaten in the Battle of Elvina at the gates of the city. In 1820 the city rose in support of a liberal insurrection in Cádiz, but three years later the authority of King Ferdinand VII was re-established when French troops supporting him occupied the town.

## LEON, *on Routes N630, N621, N601, N622, N120, and C623 in Leon*

The city derives its name from the Roman seventh legion (*legio septima*), which camped here to defend the plains from Asturian highlanders in the first century. The Moors and Visigoths disputed Leon until it was taken by King Ordoño I of Asturias and Leon (850–66). King Ordoño II (914–23) made it the capital of the kingdom of the Asturias. King Ferdinand I of Castile and Leon (1037–65) was crowned in the cathedral. The city is fortunate in having some of the finest examples of Romanesque, Gothic, and Renaissance architecture in Spain. The collegiate **Church of San Isidoro el Real** was begun in 1054 by King Ferdinand I and was consecrated in 1149 in the presence of King Alfonso VII of Leon, who was also Alfonso II of Castile. The royal pantheon within the church contains the tombs of the early kings of Leon and Castile and is one of the first manifestations of the Romanesque style in Spain. It was splendidly frescoed in. the 12th century. The **Cathedral,** built in the purest Gothic style, ranks with those of Toledo and Burgos as the greatest churches in Spain. Building began in 1205 and was more or less completed by the beginning of the 14th century. The building was thoroughly restored in the second half of the 19th century. The principal façade and the stained glass (the oldest dating from the 13th century) are particularly spectacular. Finally, the **Convent of San Marcos,** founded in the 12th century for the knights of Santiago, was rebuilt in the plateresque style between 1513 and 1549. The façade is a masterpiece of Spanish Renaissance design.

**LUGO,** on Routes NVI, C547, and N640 in Galicia

In the reign of the emperor Augustus (27 B.C.–A.D. 14) the city, under the name Lucus Augusti, was the capital of Roman Galicia. The Moorish occupation began in 713 and ended with the reconquest of the city by King Alfonso I of Asturias and Leon in 755. The **Roman Wall,** more than two kilometers long, that surrounds Lugo is the most remarkable vestige of Roman military architecture in Spain. It is built chiefly of slate and is some 20 feet thick and between 30 and 40 feet high.

**MADRID,** on Routes E25-N1, A2, A3, NIV, N401, E4-NV, and NVI in New Castile

Situated some 2,130 feet above sea level on a plateau in the midst of an arid plain, Madrid is the highest capital in Europe. Yet compared to the other great cities of Spain it is hardly venerable. Before its reconquest by King Alfonso VI of Asturias and Leon in 1083, the Moorish Madjrit, or Magerit, was only a fortified outpost of Toledo. The Castilian Cortes met sporadically in Madrid during the 14th century, and King Francis I of France was briefly held there after his defeat at the Battle of Pavia (February, 1525); but it was King Philip II who first made Madrid the capital of Spain in 1561. Except for the years 1601–7, when King Philip III transferred the capital back to Valladolid, it has remained the capital city. The great period of building in Madrid dates from the end of the 18th and the 19th centuries. The most striking remains of the old city are to be found around the **Plaza Mayor,** completed in 1619 by Diego Sillero and Juan Gómez de Mora on the order of Philip III, whose equestrian statue stands in the center of the vast square. The plaza was the scene of executions, autos-da-fé, bullfights, and theatrical performances. The Peninsular War (1808–14) began in the city with the insurrection of May 2, when the citizens rose against the occupying French and were brutally put down. Francisco Goya's two paintings of the event, entitled El Dos de Mayo and El Tres de Mayo, hang in the **Prado.** One of the greatest museums in the world, the building was erected between 1785 and 1819 and upon completion was made the Spanish royal museum by King Ferdinand VII, who brought together paintings and sculpture collected by Emperor Charles V and subsequent kings of Spain. The museum's collection of about 2,500 paintings is particularly rich in the works of Goya and Velázquez, but also in paintings of the Flemish school, owing to Spain's long association with the Low Countries. During the Spanish Civil War Madrid resisted Nationalist attempts to seize it until the final Nationalist victory. The **Convent of las Descalzas Reales** was founded in 1559 by a daughter of Charles V in a former palace of the kings of Castile, which was remodeled in the 1550s. Since then the convent has benefited from a succession of rich and noble inmates. Particularly notable are 17th-century tapestries showing the triumphs of the Catholic Church after cartoons by Peter Paul Rubens, a number of sumptuous reliquaries, and good paintings and sculptures. The 353-acre **Parque del Retiro,** which provides welcome shade for present-day Madrilenians, is also a relic of the city's early days. It was created in the 15th century as the grounds to a palace that has now almost completely vanished. The present park was laid out between 1636 and 1639 by King Philip IV. During the 18th century the kings of Spain abandoned the palace in the Retiro for the present **Royal Palace,** begun for King Philip V in 1738 and completed under King Charles III in 1764 on the site of the palace of the early kings of Castile, which in turn succeeded the Moorish alcazar. In the **Real Armería** (royal armory), which occupies the west wing, is an exceptional collection of arms and armor, the nucleus of which was the private collection of Emperor Charles V. The cupola of the **Church of San Antonio de la Florida** was frescoed in a singularly secular way by Goya in 1798. The painter was reburied there in 1919, and the church became a monument to him. Among the many museums in Madrid the following may be singled out: the **Instituto Valencia de Don Juan** for its comprehensive collection of Spanish ceramics, especially Hispano-Moresque wares of 1450–1500; the **Museo Lázaro Galdiano** for its paintings and above all for its splendid enamels and ivories; the **Museo Arqueológico Nacional,** which is being remodeled but whose collections are admirably represented in the present exhibition rooms; and the **Real Academia de Bellas Artes de San Fernando** for its Goyas.

**MÉRIDA,** *on Routes E4-NV, C537, and N630 in Estremadura*
As the Roman capital of Lusitania, the city was called Emerita Augusta, and even today it has more Roman remains than any other city in Spain. It was founded in 25 B.C. for veterans of Roman campaigns in Iberia. It was important largely because of its strategic situation at the intersection of the roads from Salamanca to Seville and from Toledo to Lisbon. Saint Eulalia (291?–304) was burned alive here, and in the earliest Christian times it became the site of

*Left: the monastery of the Escorial, north of Madrid (see page 112). Right: the Prado in Madrid, which houses one of the world's greatest art collections*

a bishopric and then an archbishopric. But by the time of the Moorish conquest in 715 it was already in decline. A **Roman Bridge** more than half a mile long still spans the Guadiana River. It was probably built during the first century A.D. but has been restored many times since. An impressive **Roman Aqueduct,** now called Los Milagros, led the waters of the artificial lake of Proserpina, 5 kilometers away, to the town. The splendid 6,000-seat **Roman Theater,** begun in 24 B.C., was first rediscovered in 1794, was not properly excavated until 1910–33, and is still not entirely restored. Also of the first century A.D. is the adjacent **Amphitheater,** with a capacity of 14,000 people. It was the scene of gladiatorial and animal contests, chariot races, and naval battles (when the arena was flooded). A **Hippodrome** on the edge of town was partially excavated in 1920, and its shape at least is still evident.

**MONTSERRAT,** *on Route C1411 in Catalonia*

Anchorites are said to have taken refuge in this remarkable sawtoothed mountain during the Moorish domination in the eighth century. Early in the 11th century, with the expulsion of the Moors from this part of Spain, Benedictine monks from Ripoll created on the mountain a **Romanesque Abbey,** which was rebuilt during the 13th century. From 1499 it possessed a printing press, and during the 16th and 17th centuries it was an active center of theological studies. Pope Julius II (1503–13), who had once been abbot of Montserrat, was active in fostering its activities. In 1522 Saint Ignatius of Loyola, the founder of the Jesuit order, dedicated himself to the Virgin in the monastery church, which was completely rebuilt by King Philip II (1556–98). In 1811, during the Peninsular War, the monastery was sacked by the French. Thus the present sober buildings date largely from the last century. The monastery was suppressed in 1835 and then reinstated in 1874 by the bishop of Barcelona and is today most prosperous.

**MURCIA,** *on Routes N301 and N340 in Murcia*

The city was founded in 831 during the reign of the Moorish ruler Abd-er-Rahman II (822–52) and in 1243 was annexed to the Christian kingdom of Castile. During the War of the Spanish Succession (1701–14) the residents stopped the advance of Archduke Charles of Austria, and during the Peninsular War, in 1810, it was sacked by the French. Earthquakes and floods damaged the city in 1829 and 1879, while in 1936, during the Civil War, Murcia's art treasures were considerably damaged. The late-14th-century Gothic **Cathedral** has a remarkable 18th-century baroque façade by Jaime Bort. On the north side is an imposing **tower** begun in 1521 and not finished until 1792; the view from the top is spectacular. The **Museo Salzillo** in the Ermita de Jesús, which adjoins the church of San Andrés, houses the splendid *pasos* (carved figures carried in Holy Week processions) made by Francisco Salzillo (1707–83) and others of the best works by this wood sculptor.

**OLITE,** *on Route N121 in Navarre*

The **Castle** (built about 1400–1419) was the principal residence of the kings of Navarre during the 15th century. It has been much restored but still appears to be the three-dimensional incarnation of a castle in a medieval miniature. **Santa María la Real** is the former royal chapel and has a fine 14th-century portal. The **Church of San Pedro,** built at the end of the 12th and the beginning of the 13th centuries, has a handsome Romanesque portal and a Gothic spire.

**SPAIN**

**OVIEDO,** *on Routes N630, C635, N634-E50, and C634 in Asturias*

King Fruela I, the king of the Asturias, founded the town in 757, but in 789 it was destroyed by the Moors. The Asturian king Alfonso II, "the Chaste," rebuilt Oviedo, transferring the capital of his kingdom there from Pravia in 810. Among the few vestiges of his day is a casket of relics rescued from the Moors by Alfonso II and now in the Camera Santa, part of which also dates from his time, of the Flamboyant Gothic **Cathedral**, built between 1388 and 1528 on the site of a basilica erected by King Fruela I in the eighth century. In the antechamber to the Camera Santa are six pilasters, each bearing the statues of two Apostles, which are among the triumphs of 12th-century Spanish sculpture. King Ramiro I (842–50), who succeeded Alfonso II, built a palace on the slope of Mount Naranco, about 4 kilometers from the center of town. In the tenth century this was transformed into the **Church of Santa María de Naranco**, which can be visited today. In 1037 the kingdom of Asturias was absorbed by Castile, and Oviedo's importance waned. In 1934 the Camera Santa, university, and cathedral were damaged by fire during a violent insurrection by the miners of Asturias, which was put down with equal violence by the army. During the Spanish Civil War the city was occupied by the Nationalists and besieged by the Republicans.

**PALENCIA,** *on Routes N611, N610, E3-N620, C615, C613, and C617 in Leon*

The town was the site of the first university in Spain, founded in 1208 by King Alfonso VIII of Castile and transferred to Salamanca in 1239. The unfinished **Cathedral**, built between 1321 and 1516, lacks its west façade but inside has many interesting statues and paintings. The church incorporates a chapel built in 1034 by King Sancho I, "the Great," of Castile and Navarre on the spot where, boar hunting one day, he is said to have found a statue of the second-century martyr Saint Antoninus.

**PAMPLONA,** *on Routes N111, N121, N240, and C135 in Navarre*

The city is said to have been founded by Pompey (106–48 B.C.). It fell to Euric the Goth in 466 and to the Frankish king Childebert in 542. The Moors took the town in 738 but were driven out in 750 by the Navarrese with the aid of Charlemagne. The latter sacked the city, and in retaliation the Navarrese wiped out his rear guard at Roncesvalles (*see*) in 778. The city became the capital of the kingdom of Navarre during the tenth century and is today the capital of the province. When King Sancho VII (1194–1234) died without issue he bequeathed Navarre to the count of Champagne. French rule continued until 1512, when King Ferdinand of Aragon regained control of the part of the province extending south of the Pyrenees, while the territory north of the Pyrenees passed to the house of Albret. It was during a siege of Pamplona by Jean d'Albret in 1521 that Captain Íñigo de Oñez y Loyola, later Saint Ignatius of Loyola, was severely wounded. The spot where he fell is marked by a **tile** in the sidewalk of the Avenida de San Ignacio opposite a **Basilica** commemorating the event. Behind its 18th-century façade is a 14th- and 15th-century Gothic **Cathedral**, of which the cloister is particularly noteworthy. The **Museo de Navarra** has excellent collections of Roman mosaics, Romanesque capitals from Pamplona's 12th-century **Cathedral**, and Navarrese paintings from the 14th through the 16th centuries. A famous event in Pamplona today is the running of the bulls through the streets at 7 A.M. each July 7, the feast day of Saint Fermín. The event was described by Ernest Hemingway in *The Sun Also Rises.*

118

**PEÑÍSCOLA,** *near Vinaroz off Route N340 in Valencia*

The site, on a rocky peninsula rather like Gibraltar, was settled by the Iberians before being taken by the Phoenicians, who called it Tyriche because it so resembled Tyre. The Greeks renamed it Chersonesos, and it was here, when the city became Carthaginian, that Hannibal is said to have sworn his eternal hatred of the Romans. When King James I of Aragon retook the town from the Moors in 1234 he gave it to the Templars, the ruins of whose **Castle** can still be visited. In 1319 Peñíscola was taken over by the knights of Montesa, who completed the Templars' castle. Benedict XIII (the Aragonese cardinal Pedro Martinez de Luna, who had been named pope by the French cardinals sitting at Avignon) moved into the castle in 1417 when he was deposed by the Council of Constance, and he died there in 1423 still so convinced that he was the rightful pope that he named a successor. The 16th-century **city walls** date from the time of King Philip II.

**POBLET,** *about 5 kilometers from Espluga de Francolí off Route N240 in Catalonia*

Although it was badly damaged by mobs at various times during the 19th century, this now-restored 12th-century **Monastery** is still a rare example of medieval monastic architecture. It was founded in 1149 by Ramón Berenguer IV, count of Barcelona, who populated it with Cistercians from the abbey of Fontfroide, near Narbonne. The kings of Aragon consistently favored Poblet and chose to be buried there.

**RONCESVALLES PASS,** *on Routes C135 and C127 in Navarre*

In 778 Charlemagne's retreating rear guard, commanded by Roland and the 12 peers of France, was decimated by Basques at this famous pass in the Pyrenees. It is said that the spot where Roland fell is marked by the crypt in the **Chapel of Espiritu Santo** in the town of Roncesvalles, opposite the Augustinian **Monastery,** which has been one of the principal stopping places for pilgrims on their way to Santiago de Compostela (*see*) since the 12th century.

**RONDA,** *on Routes C344, C341, and C339 in Andalusia*

The city's almost impregnable situation on a bluff facing an amphitheater of mountains allowed the Moors to hold it until it was successfully besieged by Ferdinand II of Aragon in 1485. Through the middle of the town runs the 300-foot-deep *tajo,* or gorge, of the Guadiaro River, which separates the modern city from the walled Moorish town. In the latter is **Santa María la Mayor,** a 16th-century church, formerly a mosque, whose bell tower was originally the minaret. Also not to be missed is the **Casa del Rey Moro,** built in 1042 by a Moorish king who is said to have quaffed his wine from the jewel-studded skulls of enemies he himself had decapitated. Francisco Romero, who was born in Ronda about 1700, established rules for the previously unruly sport of bullfighting and invented the matador's cape and muleta.

**SAGUNTO,** *on Routes N234 and N340 in Valencia*

The town nestles at the foot of a hill by the Palancia River. The sprawling hilltop **fortifications** have been defended by Iberians, Romans, Moors, and Christians. The most famous siege began in 219–18 B.C. when Hannibal tried to take the town. After eight months of fruitlessly waiting for help from Rome the citizens fired the city and died in the flames rather than surrender. The fortifications even include some built early in the 19th century, when Sagunto vainly resisted a French siege in 1811.

## SALAMANCA (LEON)

### CASA DE LAS CONCHAS (HOUSE OF THE SHELLS), *Rua Mayor*
Finished in 1483, this is one of the most complete surviving mansions of the Spanish nobility. The shells that decorate the façade are echoed in the grillwork and are the emblem of Saint James. The patio inside is particularly graceful.

### CATEDRAL NUEVA, *Plaza Anaya*
This grand church was begun in 1513 on the plans of Juan Gil de Hontañón, and the first service was celebrated in 1560. His son Rodrigo and Rodrigo's assistant Juan de Álava continued the work. The tower at the southwest corner was designed by Rodrigo on the model of the cathedral tower at Toledo. The central cupola, begun in 1705 by José and Joaquin de Churriguera, was not finished until 1733. The Puerta de la Palmas has remarkable bas-reliefs representing Christ's entry into Jerusalem; the west front is a good example of exuberant late-Gothic decoration.

### CATEDRAL VIEJA, *Rua Mayor*
This 12th-century church exemplifies the transitional Romanesque-Gothic style. Not to be missed are the unusual dome, the curiously carved capitals of the columns in the cloister, the 14th-century organ in the **Chapel of San Bartolomé**, the tomb of Diego de Anaya, archbishop of Seville (d. 1437), and the 16th-century grille in front of it.

### CLERECÍA (SEMINARY), *Calle Compañia*
The patio of this Jesuit establishment is one of the finest extant examples of Spanish baroque architecture. The seminary was built between 1617 and 1755 at the instigation of King Philip III. The huge domed church is the work of the architect Juan Gómez de Mora, who also had a major hand in designing the Plaza Mayor in Madrid (*see*).

### PLAZA MAYOR
The scene of bullfights until 1863, this is one of the largest and is considered one of the finest arcaded city squares in Spain. It was begun in 1729 on the plans of Albert de Churriguera (1676–1759), one of the three brothers of that name, all natives of Salamanca, after whom the baroque Churrigueresque style is named.

### UNIVERSIDAD, *Rua Mayor*
Its elaborately carved gateway (1534) is a splendid example of the plateresque style and dates from this 13th-century university's zenith, when it had more than 6,700 students and dared to teach the Copernican theory, which was elsewhere considered heretical. The university was founded by King Alfonso IX of Leon in 1218 and received the protection and encouragement of the kings of Castile, Ferdinand III (1217–52) and Alfonso X (1252–84). During the 13th century Salamanca ranked with the universities at Paris, Oxford, and Bologna. In the 15th and 16th centuries it had 25 colleges divided into **Escuelas Mayores,** reserved for the aristocracy, and **Escuelas Menores.** The latter group is entered by plateresque portals. Notable also are the former library and chapel of the Escuelas Menores.

**SAN CUGAT DEL VALLÉS,** *13 kilometers northwest of Barcelona off Route C1413 in Catalonia*

The **Benedictine Abbey** here is one of the oldest in Spain, its most ancient part, the clock tower, dating from the 11th century. The façade of the abbey church and the remarkable rose window were constructed about 1350. The ground level of the large cloister was built at the beginning of the 13th century, the second story in the 16th.

**MONASTERY OF SAN JUAN DE LA PEÑA,** *near Jaca 12 kilometers off Route N330 in Aragon*

A strongpoint from which the Christians of Aragon resisted the Moors, the monastery was founded in the ninth century on this remote and beautiful site beneath a cliff. Surviving are a fine Romanesque church, its 12th-century cloister with splendidly carved capitals, its crypt, and the pantheon, in which are buried the first kings of Aragon and perhaps also Ximena, wife of the Cid. The pantheon was remodeled in 1770 by King Charles III.

**MONASTERY OF SAN SALVADOR DE LEYRE,** *at Yesa 4 kilometers off Route N240 in Navarre*

The existence of this great spiritual center of Navarre is recorded in the 9th century, but not until the end of the 11th century, when King García Sánchez took refuge here from the Moors, did it become the seat of the royal court. His successor, King García Sánchez III, "the Great" (1000–1035), continued to rule the province from here. Leyre was also the royal pantheon of Navarre until that role was taken over by the monastery of San Juan de la Peña (*see*) in the 12th century. To house the tombs a solid crypt was built, and over it rose one of the earliest Romanesque churches in Spain (consecrated in 1057). The church was altered in the 13th and 14th centuries in the Cistercian Gothic style.

**SANTA MARÍA DE HUERTA,** *on Route NII in Old Castile*

The great **Cistercian Monastery,** one of the most beautiful in Spain, was begun in 1179 thanks to the donation of King Alfonso VIII of Castile. Building continued throughout the 13th century and sporadically later. The plateresque upper cloister is a splendid Renaissance addition, while the refectory of 1215 is a marvelous evocation of the Burgundian Gothic style.

**MONASTERY OF SANTES CREUS,** *near Valls 7 kilometers off Route C246 in Catalonia*

Ramón Berenguer IV, count of Barcelona, founded the monastery in 1158, and it was favored by rich Catalans thereafter. Its great cloister (1303–41) is the purest Gothic, while in the Romanesque-Gothic church (1174–1221) is an admirable pantheon of the kings of Aragon.

**SANTIAGO DE COMPOSTELA,** *on Routes E50-N550, C547, N525, C541, C543, and C545 in Galicia*

According to tradition this much venerated place of pilgrimage is built over the burial place of Saint James the Apostle, who is said to have preached the gospel in Spain for seven years. After his martyrdom by Herod Agrippa I in 44, legend has it that his body, encased in a stone coffin, floated up at Padrón, 20 kilometers to the southwest, and was buried at a location not known until in the ninth century a bright star guided an anchorite to it (hence the name of the town, called in Latin Campus Stellae). A chapel built over the spot by King Alfonso II of Asturias and Leon (791–842) was enlarged to a cathedral between 874 and 899. This was destroyed by the Moor al-Mansur in 997, although Saint James's tomb was spared. A new **Cathedral** was built between 1074 and 1211 and became the object of pilgrims from all over Europe and as far away as England. Those who came overland proceeded over the renowned pilgrimage route from France and along the north coast of Spain. The cathedral has been added to constantly, and its exterior dates from the 17th and 18th centuries. Its principal façade, called the **Obradoiro,** is a masterpiece of Churrigueresque architecture built by Fernando Casas y Novoa between 1738 and 1750. Inside the cathedral, directly behind this façade, is the triple **Pórtico de la Gloria,** one of the most important surviving works of 12th-century sculpture. It was done by Mateo, who was master of the building of the cathedral from 1168 to 1217. The sculptured **Puerta de la Platerías** is an excellent example of early-12th-century carving, while the interior of the church is admirably restrained Romanesque work. Pilgrims to Santiago in the 16th century stayed in the vast **Hospital Real,** built by Enrique de Egas between 1501 and 1511 at the command of King Ferdinand II and Queen Isabella I. The splendid plateresque façade, however, dates from late in the 17th century. The hospital receives today's pilgrims too, for it is now a vast and luxurious hotel.

**SARAGOSSA,** *on Routes N123, NII, N330, and N232 in Aragon*

The Iberian city of Salduba became the Roman colony of Caesaraugusta in honor of the emperor Augustus in 25 B.C. On what tradition maintains was January 2, 40, Saint James the Apostle saw the Virgin descending from heaven on a pillar and vowed to build her a church on that spot. The chapel he erected was replaced by a church in the 13th century, but most of the present **Basilica of Nuestra Señora del Pilar** dates from the 17th and 18th centuries; it has murals by Goya. The city's first cathedral, **La Seo,** was begun early in the 12th century and not finished until 1550. Facing the square is a 17th-century façade, while facing the archbishop's palace is a most interesting brick and tile Mudejar façade. A tapestry museum inside La Seo has one of the most beautiful collections of 14th- and 15th-century tapestries in existence. The city was an important Moorish outpost called Sarakusta from 713 until it was retaken for the Christians in 1118 by King Alfonso I of Aragon. The 11th-century Moorish palace called **La Aljafería** was greatly enlarged by King Ferdinand II and Queen Isabella I. In 1808 and 1809, during the Peninsular War, the city was besieged by the French, only capitulating house by house after two months of heroic resistance. About half the inhabitants died during the siege.

**SEGOVIA,** *on Routes N603, N110, C603, and C605 in Old Castile*

Taken from the Celtiberians in 80 B.C. by the Romans, Segovia became a city of considerable importance in Roman Spain. The 889-yard-long **Aqueduct,** probably built during the reign of Trajan (98–117), is one of the largest Roman structures in Spain and still brings the waters of the Riofrío to the city. It is built of granite in two tiers of arcades entirely without mortar. The Moors, who were driven out in 1085, are said to have introduced the cloth industry for which the town was once famous. Alfonso the Learned and other kings of Castile made Segovia their capital in the 13th, 14th, and 15th centuries, and here Isabella I was proclaimed queen in 1474. Between about 1586 and 1730 Segovia was the seat of the Spanish mint. The **Cathedral** was begun in 1525 by Juan Gil de Hontañón and completed in the 1570s by his son Rodrigo, the two architects who also built the Catedral Nueva in Salamanca (*see*). The Segovia cathedral is a remarkable survival of the Gothic style in the 16th century. The **Alcazar,** high on the western extremity of the ridge on which the walled town is built, was much enlarged between 1352 and 1358 by the man who later ruled Castile as Henry II. Henry, in turn, built on the remains of 11th-century Moorish, and perhaps even Roman, foundations. A further remodeling took place in the 15th century, but the whole castle was much damaged by a fire in the 19th century, when it was used as an artillery school. What is now visible, apart from the towers, dates from a restoration of 1882.

**SEO DE URGEL,** *on Routes C145 and C1313 in Catalonia*
Since 1278 the bishops of Urgel have shared sovereignty over Andorra, first with the counts of Foix and now with the president of France. This makes the bishop of Urgel the only ecclesiastic in the Roman Catholic Church besides the pope with a temporal jurisdiction. The **Cathedral,** which was in the process of construction throughout the 12th century, owes its Lombard appearance to Maestro Ramón, a Lombard, who was master of the works between 1175 and 1183. The cloister is particularly fine.

**SEVILLE,** *on Routes N433, C431, E25-NIV, N334, C432, and N431 in Andalusia*
The important Roman city of Hispalis was built on the Phoenician, Greek, and Carthaginian settlements that preceded it, and perhaps even on the constructions of Hercules, who is said to have founded the town. It did not lose its standing in Visigothic times (fifth to eighth centuries), while under the Moors, to whom it fell in 712, it rivaled Córdoba, the capital of the caliphate to which it belonged. From the mid-12th to the mid-13th centuries the Almohades rulers built most of the surviving Moorish buildings in the city. In 1248 the Castilian king Ferdinand III, "the Saint," took the city for the Christians; from then on it was favored by the kings of Castile. The discovery of America in 1492 brought great prosperity to Seville,

*Left: a Moorish patio in Seville's Alcazar. Right: the Roman aqueduct at Segovia*

which in 1503 was granted by Queen Isabella I of Castile the monopoly of trade with America. From Seville the Portuguese navigator Ferdinand Magellan set out in 1519 to sail around the world. The city's decline began in 1649, when the plague wiped out a third of its population. By 1717 the Guadalquivir River, on whose banks Seville is situated, had so silted up that the city lost its monopoly of the American trade to Cádiz. Dredging in modern times has restored Seville's importance as a port. The most conspicuous monument to the Moorish occupation is the **Giralda,** a 309-foot-tall bell tower to the cathedral that was formerly the minaret to a vanished mosque. It was built in the 12th century to a height of 230 feet, while the remaining five-story bell tower was built in 1568 by Hernán Ruiz. A gentle ramp leads to the top of the Moorish tower. The other relic of the ancient mosque is the **Patio de los Naranjos,** a courtyard at whose fountain the Moslem faithful performed their ablutions. The court parallels the immense, quadrilateral **Cathedral,** which is built on the plan and site of the mosque for which the Giralda served as the minaret. The largest Gothic cathedral in the world, it was built between 1402 and 1506 by architects who were evidently well acquainted with French Gothic as well as Aragonese and Castilian architecture. The original brick floor of the grand and solemn interior was replaced with the present splendid marble one at the end of the 18th century. In the right arm of the transept is the colossal (19th-century) **Tomb of Christopher Columbus.** The chapels, sacristy, treasury, and sanctuary should all be visited for their rich sculptures, paintings, religious relics, and architectural details. Some 165 feet from the cathedral stands the **Alcazar,** founded by the Moors in 712 as a fortress and royal residence, in which capacities it also served the Christian kings of Spain for nearly 700 years. The present building is largely a Mudejar palace constructed between 1364 and 1366 by King Pedro the Cruel and much altered since then. Built by Moorish architects in Pedro's employ, it is perhaps the best expression in Spain of the ambiguous Christian-Moorish tradition of Andalusian architecture. Here Queen Isabella greeted Columbus on his return from his second voyage of discovery. Particularly notable are the tiled **Patio de las Doncellas** (maids of honor), the **Patio de las Muñecas** (dolls), and the **Salón de Embajadores,** the most beautiful room in the Alcazar, where Emperor Charles V was married in 1526 to Isabella of Portugal. The perfumed **Garden of the Alcazar** should not be missed. The 16th-century **Casa Lonja,** or exchange, houses the **Archivo de Indias,** an enormous collection of documents relating both to the discovery of America and to Spanish rule in North and South America. The **Casa de Pilatos** of the end of the 15th and the beginning of the 16th centuries is one of the most sumptuous noble houses in Seville. The **Museo Provincial de Bellas Artes,** installed in a former convent completed at the beginning of the 17th century, contains a number of paintings by Francisco de Zurbarán, Bartolomé Esteban Murillo, and Juan de Valdés Leal; but there is only one painting by Seville's most famous artist, Diego Velázquez.

**SORIA AND VICINITY,** *on Routes N122, N234, N111, and C115 in Old Castile*
This cold plains city is on one of the five great *canadas,* or 90-yard-wide sheep runs, maintained between Estremadura and Old Castile by the powerful sheep owners' group known as the Mesta, which was organized in the 16th century and did not go out of existence until 1836. The **Church of Santo Domingo** of the late 12th and early 13th centuries has one of the finest Romanesque façades and portals

in Spain. The long **Palace of the Counts of Gómara** was finished in 1592. The ruined **Monastery of San Juan del Duero** and what is left of its interesting cloister (the latter probably by a Mudejar craftsman) date from the 12th and 13th centuries respectively. The **Museo Numantino** contains 17,000 artifacts excavated at **Numantia,** 8 kilometers to the northeast. At Numantia one can see only the regular plan of the Roman town built during the second century B.C. The pre-existing Iberian city resisted five assaults by Roman legions until, in 134 B.C., Scipio Africanus himself came to direct the siege. After eight months the inhabitants burned the town and died in the flames rather than submit.

**TARRAGONA,** *on Routes N340, N240, and N420 in Catalonia*
 The earliest of the many archaeological remains in this ancient city are the **Cyclopean Walls** left by an Aegean people in the third century B.C. The Romans took the town in 218 B.C., and it came to be one of their most important outposts in Spain. Augustus made it the capital of the province of Tarraconensis. The **Paseo Arqueológico,** or archaeological walk, takes one past the cyclopean walls, which formed the foundation for the Roman wall. Besides the remains of a **Roman Amphitheater** and the **Praetorium,** the excellent **Museo Arqueológico** houses other relics. The interesting **Cathedral** (built between 1120 and 1331) is on the site of a mosque, which itself covered a Roman temple to Jupiter. Because the cathedral was begun before the Christian Reconquest of Spain was certain, the Romanesque apse has the look of a fortification. Construction continued for so long that all aspects of Gothic design were incorporated. The cloister is one of the most beautiful in Catalonia.

**TERUEL,** *on Routes N420, N234, and N330-N234 in Aragon*
 This was an important Moorish city, and many Moors stayed on after the Christian Reconquest in 1171 by King Alfonso II of Aragon. Jews too were an important element of the population until a massacre in 1486. Because the Moors lingered here for so long, Teruel is one of the best places in Spain to study the Mudejar style. The best examples of this style are four **towers** built between the 12th and 16th centuries; the finest of these serves as a bell tower for the **Church of San Martín.** The nave of the much-altered 13th-century **Cathedral** has a remarkable artesonado ceiling (a wooden ceiling paneled in the Moorish fashion). In this case the ceiling incorporates painted panels of Western inspiration: they depict human figures (which is not permitted to Moslem artists). Next to the Gothic **Church of San Pedro,** which also has a Mudejar tower, is the modern **tomb** of the legendary 13th-century lovers Diego Garcés de Marcilla and Isabel de Seruga, whose unhappy deaths have inspired a number of Spanish writers. On December 4, 1937, during the Spanish Civil War, the city was taken and sacked by the Republicans, but the Nationalists, under General Francisco Franco, retook it two weeks later.

**TOLEDO (NEW CASTILE)**
 ALCAZAR, *Cuesta del Alcázar*
  Rodrigo Díaz de Bivar, better known as the Cid, was the first governor of the fort that King Alfonso VI of Asturias and Leon erected on the site of a third-century Roman camp shortly after he liberated the city from the Moors in 1085. However, in the 16th century Emperor Charles V had the citadel almost entirely rebuilt by Alonso de Covarrubias. Charles's son, King Philip II, added the chief

*From left to right in Toledo: the Flamboyant Gothic cloisters of San Juan de los Reyes; the 16th-century Alcazar, atop the 13th-century Puente de Alcántara;*

façade, designed by Juan de Herrera. The building suffered three major fires: in 1710, during the War of the Spanish Succession; in 1810, during the Peninsular War; and accidentally in 1887. From July 21 to September 28, 1936, during the Spanish Civil War, it successfully resisted assaults by the Republicans, who carried out their threat to shoot the commandant's son when he refused to yield the Alcazar. Much of the destruction wrought by this siege has been preserved as a memorial to the Civil War. Inside the alcazar a small museum of relics from the siege helps immeasurably to explain that ferocious fratricidal war to non-Spaniards.

## CASA DEL GRECO, *Calle de Samuel Levi*

In 1585 Kyriakos Theotokopoulos, the Crete-born painter known as El Greco, rented lodgings in property belonging to the marquis de Villena and remained in them until he died. It is possible that this little house, admirably restored in the 16th-century style, is the one El Greco occupied. Next door is a small but choice museum of his paintings.

## CATHEDRAL, *Plaza Mayor*

Although legend has it that the first church on this site was built to honor the Virgin while she was still alive, the first known to history was a sixth-century Visigothic church, since Toledo was the Visigoths' capital. That church was used as a mosque during the Moorish occupation (711–1085) and demolished by King Ferdinand III of Castile, who laid the first stone of the present magnificent French-style Gothic building in 1227. The building was substantially completed by 1493. As the seat of the archbishop of Toledo, who is the primate of all Spain, the interior of the cathedral is enormously rich in religious art and should be explored at length.

## HOSPITAL DE SAN JUAN BAUTISTA, *Carretera Madrid*

Built between 1541 and 1599 by Juan de Bustamente for Cardinal Juan de Tavera, this edifice is now an orphanage, which also houses the private **Museo Tavera**, organized by the duchess of Lerma. This museum, which is open to the public, is a successful and evocative

*the interior of the Sinagoga del Tránsito, with Hebrew inscriptions on Mudejar plasterwork; the rococo Altar del Transparente in the cathedral*

re-creation of a noble's house of the 17th century. The pharmacy of the hospital is exactly as it would have been in the 16th century, while in the church is the marble tomb of Cardinal Tavera (d. 1545), the last sculpture made by Alonso Berruguete, who himself died at the hospital in 1561.

MUSEO DE SANTA CRUZ, *Calle Cervantes*
One of the most remarkable Renaissance buildings in Spain, this former hospital is now a splendid museum. It was built between 1514 and 1544 by Enrique de Egas for the archbishop of Toledo, Cardinal Pedro González de Mendoza. The museum is particularly rich in 16th-century works of art, including 22 paintings by El Greco.

CHURCH OF SAN JUAN DE LOS REYES, *Reyes Católicos*
Erected between 1477 and 1494 by King Ferdinand II and Queen Isabella I as the intended site of their tombs—which are actually in the royal chapel in Granada (*see*)—the combination of Flamboyant Gothic and Mudejar styles of architecture attests to the tolerance toward the Moors that was characteristic of Toledo after the Christian reconquest of 1085. The cloisters, much restored after they were damaged by the French in 1808 during the Peninsular War, are still among the best examples of Flamboyant Gothic art in Spain.

CHURCH OF SANTO TOMÉ, *Santo Tomé*
El Greco's greatest painting, *The Burial of the Count of Orgaz*, hangs in the southwest chapel of this 14th-century church, built in a mixture of the Gothic and Mudejar styles. The bystanders in the painting, which hangs where it was first installed, are distinguished citizens of Toledo at the time the painting was made (1584–88).

SINAGOGA DEL TRÁNSITO, *Paseo del Tránsito*
This former synagogue was built in the Mudejar style in 1366 by Meïr Abdeli for Samuel Levi, the Jewish treasurer of King Pedro the Cruel of Castile. After the expulsion of the Jews from Spain in

1492 the synagogue was given by King Ferdinand II and Queen Isabella I to the knightly order of Alcántara, which made it into a church. Adjoining it is a museum devoted to the history of the Jews in Spain.

### SINAGOGA DE SANTA MARIA LA BLANCA, *Reyes Católicos*

The oldest synagogue in the city was founded about 1180, when Toledo had more than 12,000 Jews and was the most important Jewish center in Spain. Religious toleration of the Jews, which had been practiced by the Moors, was continued by the Christian rulers of Toledo until 1391, when, goaded by Saint Vincent Ferrer, the Christians massacred the faithful gathered in this synagogue. The building was seized by the Christians in 1405 and given its present name.

### TORDESILLAS, *on Routes C611, E3-N620, NVI, and N122 in Leon*

Emperor Charles V's mother, Juana, spent the last 49 years of her life in a windowless cell in the **Convent of Santa Clara** here, having been driven mad by the premature death of her husband, Philip the Handsome, duke of Burgundy, in 1506. The convent, in the Mudejar style, was first a palace built by King Alfonso XI of Castile in the 14th century and was then occupied by King Pedro the Cruel, his successor. Pedro made it into a convent, where he kept Maria de Padilla, who some say was his mistress and others say he secretly, and bigamously, married.

### TORTOSA, *on Route C235 in Catalonia*

The strategic importance of the city's situation at the delta of the Ebro, Spain's greatest river, attracted the Iberians, the Romans, and the Moors (who held it from the eighth century until 1148). It was finally retaken for the Christians by Ramón Berenguer, count of Barcelona, with the help of the Knights Templar and a Genoese fleet, for by that time the city was a nest of pirates. A Moorish counterattack in 1149 was beaten off largely by the efforts of the women of Tortosa, who "manned" the battlements. For their heroism Berenguer allowed them to import dresses duty free and gave them precedence over their bridegrooms when they married. During the Spanish Civil War the Ebro at Tortosa was contested for nine months in 1938 and 1939, leaving 150,000 dead and the town much damaged. A **Monument** to the eventual victory of the Nationalists stands in the middle of the Ebro.

### TRALFALGAR, BATTLE OF. *See* CÁDIZ

### VALENCIA, *on Routes N234, C234, NIII-E101, N340, and N332 in Valencia*

The early Greek settlement passed successively into the hands of the Carthaginians, Romans, Visigoths, and in 714 the Moors. In 1094 the city was taken by Rodrigo Díaz de Bivar, known as the Cid, a soldier of fortune whose exploits were the basis for the 12th-century epic poem of the same name. The Cid ruled the city until his death in 1099. His widow, Ximena, continued to resist the Moors until 1101, when she was expelled by them. The Christian Reconquest was accomplished in 1238 by James I, "the Conqueror," king of Aragon. The prosperous city was the site of the first printing press in Spain (1474), and in the 18th century was the first city to have the night watchmen known as *serenos*, common today in all Spanish towns. In 1808, during the Peninsular War, the citizens rose against the French occupiers, and the city was ruled by the rebels until 1812, when the French retook it for another year. The ancient monuments suffered greatly during the Spanish Civil War, during which Valencia was for two periods the Republicans' capital. In March, 1939, the last of the Republican troops took refuge in Valencia, which did not capitulate to the Nationalists until Madrid fell on March 28. The fertile land around Valencia, whose irrigation system was instigated by the Romans and improved by the Moors, is called the *huerta* and is renowned for its orange groves. The 14th- and 15th-century **Cathedral,** much restored at the end of the 18th century, stands on the site of a Roman temple to Diana, which was transformed into a church by the Visigoths and into a mosque by the Moors. Next to the cathedral is the octagonal tower built between 1381 and 1429 and called the **Miguelete,** after its great bell named for Saint Michael. Noteworthy for their examples of paintings by Valencian artists of the 16th century are the interior rooms of the **Palacio de la Generalidad,** built between 1481 and 1510. Here the Cortes of Valencia met until 1707, when King Philip V abolished the *fueros,* or special rights, enjoyed by these local legislators. The **Lonja de la Seda,** or silk exchange, was built between 1483 and 1498 in the Flamboyant Gothic style, and its exterior is no less impressive than the Salón de Contrataciones, or room where the silk merchants gathered. A large and noteworthy ceramic museum, whose chief exhibits are from the region, is installed in the former **Palace of the Marqués de Dos Aguas.** The important Valencian artists of the 15th to 17th centuries can best be studied in the museum of the **Colegio del Patriarca** and the **Museo Provincial de Bellas Artes.** The **Puerta de Serranos** of 1238, flanked by late-14th-century towers, and the 15th-century **Puerta de Quart** are interesting examples of Gothic and late medieval military architecture.

**VALLADOLID,** *on Routes N601, N403, E3-N620, and N122 in Leon*
The Arabic name for the city, Belad-Ulid (land of the governor), dates from the Moorish occupation, which ended in 1074. Subsequently the city was much favored by the kings of Castile. Here in 1469 King Ferdinand II of Aragon married Isabella I of Castile, thus accomplishing the unification of Spain. Here, too, Columbus died in 1506. In 1561 King Philip II moved the capital to Madrid, but between 1601 and 1606 King Philip III transferred the capital back to Valladolid. The city's treasures suffered badly during the Peninsular War (1808–14). The most distinguished surviving monument is the **Colegio de San Gregorio,** completed in 1496. Its façade and two courtyards are richly decorated. The *colegio* now houses the **Museo Nacional de Escultura Religiosa,** a remarkable collection of Castilian religious sculpture from the 13th to the 18th centuries. It is particularly rich in works by Alonso Berruguete, master of the Spanish Renaissance style.

**VALLE DE LOS CAIDOS (VALLEY OF THE FALLEN),** *off Route C600 in New Castile*
This astonishing **Monument** to those who died in the Spanish Civil War was begun in 1940 and inaugurated in 1959. It consists of a reinforced concrete cross 413 feet tall, which towers over a hollow mountain in the Sierra de Guadarrama. The mountain has been tunneled to form an underground basilica, whose nave is 853 feet long. (Saint Peter's nave is 610 feet long.) It is hung with eight 16th-century Flemish tapestries representing the Apocalypse. Ossuaries at both ends of the transept contain the bones of those who fell in the Civil War, regardless of their political affiliation.

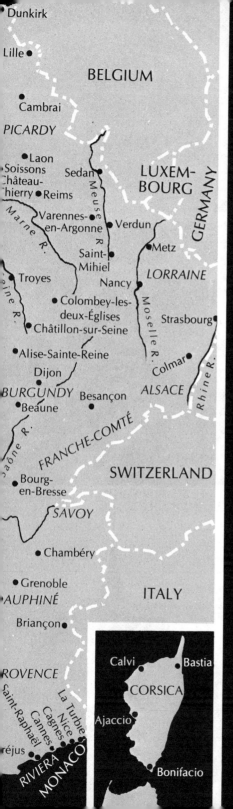

# FRANCE
## & MONACO

# FRANCE

**AGINCOURT,** *18 kilometers northwest of Saint-Pol via N-16 in Picardy*
During the Hundred Years' War, on October 25, 1415, the English
king Henry V, with an army of 10,000 English longbowmen and his
Burgundian allies, won a decisive victory at Agincourt over three
times as many knights of King Charles VI of France. At the time
France was torn by civil war, and the dukes of Burgundy had joined
the English side. The English subsequently reconquered most of
northern France, and in 1420 Charles VI, who was given to fits of
insanity, recognized Henry V as his heir in the Treaty of Troyes.

**AIGUES-MORTES,** *via N-579 in Provence*
In 1240 Saint Louis established the kingdom of France's first Mediterranean seaport and military base on this site. To defend the
Rhone River delta town, he undertook the construction of the
ramparts and **Tower of Constance,** which in subsequent centuries
was used to confine prisoners. From Aigues-Mortes Saint Louis
embarked on the Seventh Crusade in 1248, and on the Eighth
Crusade in 1270 to Tunis, where he died. Philip the Bold completed the massive **ramparts**—today well preserved—which are 30
feet high and 20 feet thick in places and contain 20 towers and 10
gates. The **Tower of the Burgundians** was so called during the
Hundred Years' War, when Burgundians captured the town and
were in turn massacred in their sleep; their mutilated corpses,
awaiting burial, were thrown in this tower. Aigues-Mortes remained
prosperous until the 14th century, when the sea receded, and
channels linking it with the town filled with sand.

**AIX-EN-PROVENCE,** *via N-96, N-7, and N-8 in Provence*
Founded in 123 B.C. on the site of a Gallic settlement dating from
the fourth century B.C. by the Roman consul Sextius, this town was
called Aquae Sextiae because of its thermal springs renowned for
their curative powers. In 102 B.C. the town was the scene of a bloody
battle between the Teutons, who were about to invade Italy, and
the Roman army under Marius; to commemorate the great Latin
victory here, Provençal parents have traditionally named one of
their sons Marius. Aix became an archbishopric in the fourth century A.D. and from the 12th century until 1486 was the capital of the
counts of Provence; the most famous count was King René I (1409–
80), who patronized the arts, worked his own vineyards, and introduced the muscat grape to Provence. In 1486 Aix was reunited with
France, and a parliament was created here in 1501. During the 17th
and 18th centuries the town was almost entirely rebuilt, and today
many of the splendid structures erected at that time survive. A **Statue
of King René I** holding a bunch of grapes stands on the Cours
Mirabeau; the **Hôtel de Ville** was erected from 1655 to 1670; the
**Archbishop's Palace** and the **Cathedral and Cloister of Saint Sauveur**
reflect architectural styles from the 5th to the 16th centuries; and
the **Pavillon Paul Cézanne** was the artist's former studio.

**ALENÇON,** *via N-12, N-138, and N-155 on the Upper Sarthe in Normandy*
This town is celebrated for its lace industry, which was introduced
in 1655 to compete with the current vogue for Venetian lace. By
1700 Alençon's needleworkers and lacemakers had developed a distinctive stitch of their own that was highly prized in fashionable
circles. During World War II Alençon was a key city in the Mortain-
Falaise (*see*) gap battle of August 6–12, 1944, at the end of which the
Allies forced the German Seventh Army to retreat east. Monuments include the Flamboyant Gothic **Church of Our Lady,** com-

*Top left: the Petit Trianon at Versailles. Right: the Roman amphitheater at
Nîmes. Center: the Arc de Triomphe in the middle of the Place de l'Étoile in
Paris. Below left: the Hôtel Dieu in Beaune. Right: Mont-Saint-Michel*

pleted in 1444, a restored 14th- and 15th-century **Castle** erected by Jean Le Beau, first duke of Alençon, and the **Saint Teresa Chapel** at the site where Saint Thérèse Martin was born on January 2, 1873.

**ALISE-SAINTE-REINE,** *via D-103 in Burgundy*
This town was the site of the famous camp of Alesia, where in 52 B.C. the army of Gaul under Vercingetorix heroically resisted a siege by the legions of Julius Caesar. Some 40,000 of Caesar's soldiers erected military works around the camp to prevent the Gauls inside from escaping and those outside from bringing relief. After a six-week siege, Vercingetorix surrendered to Caesar. Excavations on the **Cimetière Saint Père** plateau here have unearthed military works, objects left by Caesar's legions, and the later ruins of a Gallo-Roman town. The **Fountain of Saint Reina** stands on the spot where, it is said, a Christian maiden named Reina was beheaded in the third century after refusing to marry the Roman governor Olibrius.

**AMBOISE,** *via N-751, D-31, and D-61 in the Loire Valley*
Begun under King Charles VIII in 1492, the **Chateau of Amboise** was one of the largest and most magnificent of the royal residences. In the reign of Francis I (1515–47) the chateau became the center of a brilliant court life. Leonardo da Vinci, one of the many Italian artists imported to Amboise, spent the last years of his life at the chateau, where he died in 1519. During the wars of religion in 1560, the chateau was the scene of the Amboise Conspiracy, in which Huguenot reformers, plotting to force King Francis II to recognize their religion, were apprehended and mercilessly executed. However, in the 1563 Edict of Amboise members of the Protestant nobility were granted freedom of worship by Catherine de Médicis. French kings subsequently abandoned the castle. In 1631 its outer fortifications were razed, and after the French Revolution much of the castle was demolished. At Amboise today are the **Chapelle Saint-Hubert,** where Leonardo da Vinci is buried, the **Logis du Roi** (Royal Apartments), from whose balcony the insurgents of 1560 were thrown, the **Tour des Minimes,** with its famous ramp, and the **Clos Luce,** a 15th-century manor house containing mementos of Leonardo da Vinci.

**AMIENS,** *via N-35, N-16, N-319, N-29, and N-33 on the Somme River in Picardy*
Situated close to the national boundary of France, this ancient capital of the Celtic tribe of Ambiani has witnessed a turbulent history. In the first century B.C. Julius Caesar subjected the town. In the ninth century the Normans caused widespread devastation. The independent countship of Amiens was reunited to France late in the 12th century by Philip Augustus. The 1802 Treaty of Amiens, which brought peace for only a year during the Napoleonic Wars, was concluded here. Amiens was occupied by the Prussians in 1870 and was taken again in 1914. During World Wars I and II Amiens suffered heavy bombardment. Escaping destruction, the **Cathedral of Notre Dame,** begun in 1220 on the site of an earlier church that had burned down and essentially completed by 1269, is the largest and one of the finest Gothic edifices in France; the interior is an architectural masterpiece.

**ANGERS,** *via N-23, N-161, and N-152 on the Maine River in the Loire Valley*
This one-time capital of Anjou flourished between the 10th and 12th centuries as the seat of the famous Foulques family, counts of Anjou. In 1129 Geoffrey Foulque—who wore a sprig of broom in his

*The castle at Angers behind its curtain walls studded with seventeen towers*

cap, hence the epithet "Plantagenet"—married Matilda, granddaughter of William the Conqueror; their son, Henry Plantagenet, added most of southwestern France to his northern dominions by marrying Eleanor of Aquitaine in 1154. Two years later he also became King Henry II of England and thus held more territory than the reigning French monarch. Anjou became a province of France in 1205 under King Philip Augustus and for the next two centuries was governed by the dukes of Anjou, who beautified Angers and founded a prosperous university there. The most interesting landmark in Angers today is the **Chateau,** the former Foulque castle, rebuilt by Saint Louis between 1228 and 1238 of slate on a white stone foundation; it contains a magnificent collection of tapestries, the most famous being the 500-foot **Apocalypse Tapestry,** woven between 1375 and 1380. Preserved also is the **Cathedral of Saint Maurice,** erected in the 12th and 13th centuries.

**ANGOULÊME,** *via N-10, N-141, N-139, N-674, and N-737 in Angoumois*
This town was part of the province of Aquitaine under the Romans and later suffered successive invasions by the Visigoths, Franks, Saracens, Normans, and kings of England. Angoulême became part of France in 1303. In 1360 Angoulême was ceded to England by the Treaty of Brétigny; its inhabitants forced the English garrison to leave in 1373, and as a reward the town became an appanage of a son of the king. Margaret of Valois, queen of Navarre and sister of King Francis I, an accomplished author and poet, was born here in 1492. Francis I made Angoulême a grand duchy ruled by his mother, Louise of Savoy; the city was returned to the crown in 1545. During the wars of religion Angoulême changed hands between the Protestants and Catholics several times. Preserved today is the 12th-century **Cathedral of Saint Pierre,** one of the outstanding Romanesque churches in France, which was damaged by Calvinists in 1562 and later restored; the adjoining 15th-century **Bishops' Palace** now houses a museum. Two towers of the former **Chateau of the Counts of Angoulême** survive.

**ARGONNE FOREST.** *See* VARENNES-EN-ARGONNE

**ARLES,** *via N-570 and N-113 in Provence*

Founded in the sixth century B.C. by Greek colonists from Marseilles, Arles became a center of trade and navigation in the second century B.C., when the Roman consul Marius constructed a canal linking the Rhone River with the sea. Possessing the most southerly bridge on the Rhone, Arles was on the direct road from Italy to Spain and was also connected by roads to northern Gaul. An early center of Christianity, Arles was the scene of the first church council of the Western empire, held in A.D. 314, and of 18 subsequent councils. By A.D. 329 Arles was the third largest city in the Roman Empire, boasting fortified walls pierced with gates and a 47-mile-long aqueduct that provided the city with fresh water. Extant Roman ruins include the **Arena,** one of the most ancient in the Roman world, constructed about 46 B.C. and able to accommodate more than 20,000 spectators; the **Ancient Theater,** built late in the first century B.C.; a 50-foot-high **Obelisk,** part of the local Roman circus; and the **Palace of Constantine,** the former municipal baths erected in the fourth century A.D. After the fall of Rome, Arles suffered from Berber and Saracen invasions and declined in prestige and wealth. With the partition of Charlemagne's empire in the ninth century, Arles became capital of the kingdom of Arles, comprising Burgundy and part of Provence. In 1239 the city was placed under the rule of the counts of Provence, and in 1481, along with Provence, it became part of France. The **Alyscamps,** originally a Roman necropolis, became a renowned burial place during the Middle Ages, and bodies were brought from all over Europe to be interred here. The **Church of Saint Trophime,** the former cathedral, was established in 606 and rebuilt between the 11th and 15th centuries in the Romanesque style.

**ARQUES-LA-BATAILLE,** *8 kilometers southeast of Dieppe via D-1 and D-56 in Normandy*

This town is named in honor of Henry of Navarre, who in 1589, before becoming King Henry IV of France, defeated 30,000 members of the Catholic League with a force of only 7,000 men. The **Battle of Arques Monument,** an obelisk, commemorates the battle site in a field outside of town. Arques-la-Bataille also boasts the ruins of a feudal **Castle,** whose keep is perched high on a promontory.

**ARROMANCHES-LES-BAINS,** *via N-814 on the English Channel in Normandy*

During the Allied invasion of Europe in June, 1944, an artificial harbor known as **Mulberry B** was constructed by the British at this seaside resort. The port was used to land 9,000 tons of war supplies each day. The **Invasion Museum** contains dioramas, models, and a film of the D-day landing. (*See also Normandy Invasion Beaches.*)

**AURAY,** *off N-165 on the River Loch near the Gulf of Morbihan in Brittany*

This town was the scene of the famous battle of 1364 that ended the war of succession over the duchy of Brittany. It was fought between the troops of Charles de Blois, who was backed by the renowned warrior Bertrand Du Guesclin, and the forces of Jean de Montfort, aided by the English under Sir John Chandos. Charles was killed in battle, and the duchy secured for Montfort. Preserved here is the picturesque **Saint Goustan Quarter,** with its 15th-century houses, and a quay named in honor of Benjamin Franklin, who landed here in 1778 after headwinds prevented his reaching Nantes (*see*) on the

Loire to sign a treaty with France. In 1795, during the Breton Royalist revolt, Republicans massacred a force of 800 Royalists at the **Champ des Martyrs.** A leader of this revolt, Georges Cadoudal— who also tried unsuccessfully to kidnap Napoleon in 1804—is entombed near the gates of Auray.

**AUTUN,** *via N-78, N-73, N-80, and N-494 on the Arroux River in Burgundy*
Originally called Augustodunum and situated on Agrippa's Way, the great road extending from Boulogne to Lyons, this town was founded by the Roman emperor Augustus. Autun soon became a flourishing Gallo-Roman city, famed for its schools and monuments, and was referred to as the "sister and rival of Rome." Reduced to ruins by barbarian attacks during the Dark Ages, Autun regained much of its former prosperity in the 15th century, primarily as a result of the patronage of the great attorney Nicolas Rolin, born here in 1380, who became chancellor to the duke of Burgundy. Rolin's son, Cardinal Rolin, became bishop of Autun and helped make the city a religious center. In 1779 Napoleon and his two brothers attended the Jesuit college here. Today principal sights include the **Cathedral of Saint Lazare,** raised between 1120 and 1140, whose portals are among the masterpieces of Romanesque sculpture. The **Porte Saint André** and **Porte d'Arroux,** along with the **Roman Theater**—the largest in Roman Gaul, boasting a seating capacity of 33,000—are all that remain of the ancient fortifications, which included 4 gates and 62 towers and surrounded the town. Extant also are the ruins of the so-called **Temple of Janus,** a square building 80 feet high, of unknown purpose.

**AUXERRE,** *via N-6, N-77, and N-65 overlooking the Yonne River in Burgundy*
Established by the Roman conquerors of Gaul, this town, like Autun (*see*), was situated on the great road linking Boulogne with Lyons. Early in the fifth century a wealthy lawyer named Germain defended Auxerre from barbarians and eventually became bishop of the city. When Charlemagne's empire was partitioned in the 843 Treaty of Verdun (*see*), Auxerre became part of western Burgundy. In 1429 Joan of Arc passed through Auxerre while accompanying Charles VII to his coronation at Reims (*see*). And in 1815, upon his return from Elba, Napoleon marched to Auxerre, where his meager troops were reinforced by the army of Marshal Michel Ney. Today sights of interest include the Gothic **Cathedral of Saint Étienne,** erected between 1215 and 1560, and the former abbey **Church of Saint Germain,** the remains of a celebrated Benedictine abbey founded in the sixth century that by Charlemagne's time boasted 600 monks and more than 2,000 students.

**AVALLON,** *via N-444 and N-6 in the valley of the Cousin River in Burgundy*
Avallon was one of the principal fortified towns of Burgundy during the Middle Ages. In 1432, when Philip the Good, duke of Burgundy, was in Flanders, an adventurer named Jacques d'Espailly, better known as Fortépice, seized and pillaged the town. Philip returned, laid siege to Avallon, breached the ramparts, and eventually forced Fortépice to flee. After peaceful times were restored, Louis XIV sold the ramparts to the citizens of Avallon. Today the ancient **ramparts** may be seen, as well as the **Church of Saint Lazare,** consecrated in 1106 and added to over the centuries.

**AVIGNON,** *via N-7, N-542, N-100, N-573, N-570, and N-580 in Provence*
A town of secondary importance under the Romans, Avignon in the

12th and 13th centuries became a communal republic, and in the 14th century it achieved its greatest importance and prosperity when partisan quarrels in Rome drove the popes to Avignon in 1309. From this time until 1377—a period known as the Babylonian captivity—seven French popes were appointed in succession. Many Italians, including the author Petrarch, felt that the exile was too long and implored the popes to return to Rome; Gregory XI obliged in 1377, but he died a year later. His Italian successor displaced the cardinals of the Sacred College, who brought on the Great Schism by appointing a second pope, who returned to Avignon and became known as the antipope. The last antipope left Avignon in 1411. Avignon remained a fief of the papacy, administered by papal legates, until 1791, when it was reunited with France. For a short time in 1808 Napoleon imprisoned Pope Pius VII here. Dominating the town is the **Palais des Papes**, constructed between 1335 and 1367, which consists of myriad apartments, wings, corridors, reception halls, and common rooms. Surviving today at Avignon are the **ramparts** with their 8 gates and 39 towers, erected between 1350 and 1368. Another outstanding feature of the town is the 12th-century **Pont Saint Bénézet**, the "pont d'Avignon" of the celebrated nursery rhyme, of which only four arches remain. Across the Rhone is the village of **Villeneuve-lès-Avignon**, founded as a frontier town by Philip the Fair in 1292, which became the summer residence of the popes. The **Fort Saint André**, a stronghold erected between 1325 and 1350, and the 17th- and 18th-century palatial homes of nobles and cardinals are still extant.

**AVRANCHES,** *via N-173, N-176, and D-5 on Saint-Michel Bay in Normandy*
This medieval town was the scene of King Henry (II of England) Plantagenet's public penance of May 22, 1172, for his role in the murder of Thomas à Becket, archbishop of Canterbury, in 1170. Robert of Torigni, abbot of nearby Mont-Saint-Michel (*see*), held a council at Avranches, which decided that the excommunicated monarch should be absolved. Today the **Platform** where Henry knelt in his bare feet, clad only in a shirt, is preserved in a small square where the former cathedral stood. A **Monument** honors General George S. Patton, who left Avranches on July 31, 1944, to begin the offensive that smashed the German panzer counter-offensive from Mortain.

*The Palais des Papes (left) and the Pont Saint Bénézet at Avignon*

**BAYEUX,** *via N-814, N-172, and N-13 on the Bessin coast in Normandy*
This town was the site of the famous Oath of Bayeux of 1066, in which the future King Harold II of England pledged fealty to William the Bastard, duke of Normandy, whom Harold believed would succeed Edward the Confessor to the English throne. Upon his deathbed, however, the Confessor made Harold his heir, and Harold foreswore his pledge and seized the crown. This act paved the way for William's conquest of England that year at the Battle of Hastings. The **Bayeux Tapestry,** probably commissioned shortly after the conquest by William's comrade in arms the bishop of Bayeux, consists of colored wool embroidered on linen and chronicles in 58 dramatic scenes the epic of William the Conqueror. The tapestry is housed in a former bishops' residence near the Norman Gothic **Cathedral of Our Lady,** completed in 1077. On June 7, 1944, Bayeux became one of the first towns in France to be liberated.

**BEAUGENCY,** *via N-825 and N-152 in the Loire Valley*
Strategically situated at the only bridge that crossed the Loire between Blois and Orléans, this formerly fortified town was an object of much contention between the French and the English. In 1152 the council of Beaugency—held at the abbey **Church of Notre Dame**—annulled the marriage of Eleanor of Aquitaine to King Louis VII of France and paved the way for her marriage two years later to Henry Plantagenet, the future King Henry II of England. The English captured Beaugency four times during the Hundred Years' War (1337–1453). In 1429 the town was restored to France by Joan of Arc. During the wars of religion late in the 1500s, Beaugency passed back and forth between members of the Catholic League and the Huguenots, who burned the abbey in 1567. Interesting sights include the abbey, rebuilt in the 1700s, and an 11th-century castle **Keep,** with an adjoining 15th-century **Chateau** in the Place Dunois.

**BEAUNE,** *via N-74, N-73, and N-470 in Burgundy*
Originally a Gallic village and later an outpost of Rome, this town was the residence of the dukes of Burgundy from the early Middle Ages until they moved to Dijon (*see*). Here in 1203 Duke Eudes granted a charter of communal liberties, which is now preserved in the town archives. After the death of Charles the Bold, last duke of Burgundy, in 1477, Beaune stubbornly resisted efforts of Louis XI to annex it; it finally surrendered to the king after a five-week siege. Perfectly preserved today is the **Hôtel Dieu,** a still-functioning hospital erected between 1443 and 1451; its elegant roof covered with colored slates in intricate patterns is a marvel of Burgundian-Flemish art. Other sights include medieval **ramparts and towers,** the **Town House of the Dukes of Burgundy,** the **Hospice de la Charité,** and the Romanesque **Church of Notre Dame.**

**BEAUVAIS,** *via N-31, N-181, N-1, and N-327 in Île-de-France*
Strategically situated at the meeting place of routes linking Paris with the coast, Beauvais, over the ages, has been ravaged by the Normans, English, Germans, and Burgundians. During the Hundred Years' War with England, the townspeople supported the king of France, although Bishop Pierre Cauchon supported the English; he was driven from the town in 1429 and went to Rouen (*see*), where he condemned Joan of Arc to death in 1431. In 1472, when Beauvais was besieged by Charles the Bold, duke of Burgundy, Jeanne Leûne, daughter of a peasant, cut down an invader with a hatchet and inspired courage in her fellow defenders. Her name is com-

memorated in the **Place Jeanne Hatchette.** The most prominent edifice in Beauvais is the **Cathedral of Saint Pierre,** begun in 1227 and completed in the 16th century, which boasts, at 158 feet in height, the loftiest vault in the world. The famed 17th-century Beauvais **Tapestry Works** were partially destroyed during World War II.

**BELLEAU WOOD.** *See* CHÂTEAU-THIERRY

**BELLE-ÎLE,** *near Quiberon in the Bay of Biscay off the Brittany coast*
An outlying citadel of the French coast, this island sustained a 38-day siege by the British in 1761. Landing at **Port-Andros,** some 20,000 British forced the capitulation of fewer than 4,000 French defenders and held the island for two years before it was returned to the French under the 1763 Treaty of Paris. Surviving today are the 17th-century **ramparts,** erected by Superintendent Nicolas Fouquet, a wealthy minister of Louis XIV's who eventually fell from the king's favor. Traces of Roman entrenchments may be seen at **Vieux-Château Point.**

**BESANÇON,** *via N-57, N-486, N-73, N-67, and N-83 in Franche-Comté*
In the first century B.C. Julius Caesar realized the strategic importance of this Celtic settlement built around a fortified rock on the Doubs River. Under the Romans the town became the capital of the district of Sequania Maxima. A center of Christianity since the second century, Besançon became the seat of an archbishopric in the fourth century. During the Dark Ages the town was recurrently despoiled by barbarians; in 1031 Archbishop Hugues de Salins, the spiritual and temporal administrator of the diocese, undertook the reconstruction of Besançon. The German emperor, Rudolf I of Hapsburg—the nominal ruler of Besançon—granted the inhabitants communal liberty in 1290, and the town became, in effect, a small republic. Between 1534 and 1540 the seigneur de Granvelle, chancellor to Holy Roman Emperor Charles V, erected a grand Spanish Renaissance **Palace,** which stands today. During the 17th century Besançon was attacked by France because it harbored enemies of Cardinal Richelieu. Besançon was annexed to France in the 1678 Treaty of Nijmegen; Louis XIV subsequently made it the capital of a county and had Vauban erect **fortifications,** some of which remain. In 1890 the count of Chardonnet, who invented rayon, opened the world's first factory to turn out synthetic fibers here. Other sights include the **Birthplace of Victor Hugo,** France's outstanding literary figure, the **Porte Noire,** a Roman triumphal arch erected in A.D. 167 during the reign of Marcus Aurelius, and the 12th-century **Cathedral of Saint Jean.**

**BÉZIERS,** *via N-609, N-113, and N-112 in Languedoc*
A military colony under the Romans, Béziers was the seat of an archbishopric from the fourth century until 1802. During the Middle Ages the town was a center of the Albigenses, people who adhered to a heretical Christian doctrine. In 1209, under the order of Pope Innocent III, Simon de Montfort and an army of crusaders besieged the town, burned the buildings, and massacred the 60,000 inhabitants. The Crusade ended in 1229 with the Treaty of Meaux, terminating the independence of Languedoc. Béziers was subsequently rebuilt. In the 17th century the town was the birthplace of Pierre Paul de Riquet, who from 1666 to 1680 built the **Midi Canal,** linking the Mediterranean with the Atlantic Ocean. A **Statue of Riquet** stands today in central Béziers. The former **Cathedral of Saint**

Nazaire was erected late in the 13th century on the ruins of an edifice burned by Simon de Montfort. Preserved also are the **Basilica of Saint Aphrodise,** possessing a third-century Gallo-Roman sarcophagus, and the **Church of the Madeleine,** one of the principal sites of the 1209 massacre.

**BLOIS,** *via N-766, N-157, N-824, N-156, N-751, and N-152 in the Loire Valley*
Situated on an important bridgehead and dominated by its famous **Chateau,** Blois was the center of a powerful county during the Middle Ages. It was from Blois in 1429 that Joan of Arc set out to raise the siege of Orléans (*see*). In the mid-1400s Charles d' Orléans, father of King Louis XII, remodeled castle Blois's dour feudal castle into a more habitable mansion. Subsequently during the Renaissance, the chateau became a royal residence, with wings, terraces, and gardens added by Louis XII (who was born here) between 1498 and 1503, and by Francis I between 1515 and 1524. Mary queen of Scots and Queen Catherine de Médicis also resided here. In 1576 and 1588 Henry III had the States-General convene in the chateau's 13th-century **Salle des États,** a council hall. It was at the latter session that Henry's archrival, the duc de Guise, was assassinated in the king's second-floor apartments. In 1626 Gaston d'Orléans, the brother of Louis XIII, employed the architect François Mansart to erect another wing in the classical style. Today the various buildings of the chateau, reflecting different periods, are grouped around a central courtyard.

**BORDEAUX,** *via A-62, N-89, N-136, N-113, N-10, and N-650 in Aquitaine*
As capital of the province of Aquitaine, this town, with its splendid palaces and temples, was one of the show places of the Roman Empire. In A.D. 276 Germans overran Bordeaux, which was subsequently rebuilt and fortified; attracted by its wealth, Visigoths, Saracens, and Normans in turn attacked the city over the centuries. When in 1152 Eleanor, last heiress of the dukes of Aquitaine, married Henry Plantagenet, who became King Henry II of England in 1154, Bordeaux became an English possession and remained thus until 1453. During this period the city expanded and prospered by shipping its famous clarets and other exports to England. In the 14th century the Black Prince, son of Edward III, established his headquarters and court at Bordeaux, and later his son, the future Richard II of England, was born here. After Bordeaux was restored to France, its citizens periodically revolted against French rule until the reign of Louis XIV. In the 1700s Bordeaux became a modern port city. During the Revolution the Girondist party was formed here. Preserved today are the ruins of the **Palais Gallien,** a third-century Roman **Amphitheater,** the 11th-century **Cathedral of Saint André,** the 374-foot-high Gothic **Tour Saint Michel,** the highest tower in France, the **Grosse Cloche,** or Great Bell, a 15th-century gate tower that formerly tolled the signal for the grape harvest, and the 18th-century **Grand Theater.**

**BOURG-EN-BRESSE,** *via N-75, N-396, N-83, N-79, N-78, and N-436 in Burgundy*
This town is renowned for its **Church and Monastery of Brou,** built early in the 1500s in fulfillment of a vow. In 1480, when Philip, count of Bresse, had a hunting accident, his wife, Margaret of Bourbon, vowed to transform the humble priory of Brou into a monastery if he recovered. She died before undertaking her task, and twenty years later her son, Philibert, died suddenly. His wife, Margaret of

Austria, took this to be divine vengeance and in 1506 began work on the monastery to insure her husband heavenly repose. The magnificent Flamboyant Gothic-Renaissance church, erected from 1513 to 1532, contains the elaborately carved tombs of both Margarets and Philibert.

**BOURGES,** *via N-76, N-151, N-153, and N-140 in the Loire Valley*

Known to the ancient Gauls, this town, with its 40,000 inhabitants, bravely resisted Caesar's legions in the first century B.C. but was finally defeated and became the Roman Avaricum. By 250 Bourges had an archbishop; succeeding archbishops ruled the town until it passed to a line of counts who sold it to Philip I in 1101. In the 14th century Jean de France, first duke of Berry and third son of King John the Good, made Bourges the capital of his duchy and a flourishing center of the arts. In the 15th century, when much of France was occupied by the English, King Charles VII made Bourges the capital of his dominions. Louis XI founded a university here in 1463, which became a center of legal learning and was attended by John Calvin and other harbingers of the Reformation. Bourges became a principal battlefield during the wars of religion late in the 1500s, thus ending its prosperity. Sights today include the **Cathedral of Saint Étienne,** consecrated in 1224; the magnificent Gothic **Palais Jacques Coeur,** commissioned in 1443 by Charles VII's famous master of the mint, who was one of the richest merchants of his time; and the Renaissance-style **Hôtel de Cujas,** erected in 1515, the residence of the prominent jurist Jacques Cujas.

**BREST,** *via N-789 or N-12 on the Penfeld River on the Goulet Sound in Brittany*

Situated on one of the finest natural harbors in Europe, Brest preserves relics of a fascinating naval history. English invasions of the seaport began in 1342 during the war of succession, when troops of Edward III landed at Brest to aid Jean de Montfort, a contender for the duchy of Brittany. After becoming the duke of Brittany, Montfort, aided by the French king, was unable to expel his former allies; the English finally evacuated Brest in 1397 when King Charles VI of France persuaded his son-in-law Richard II to restore the town to the duke of Brittany. England subsequently invaded Brest late in the 1400s and in 1513. In the 17th century Cardinal Richelieu founded the Brest dockyard, which was expanded and completed by Jean Colbert, minister of the French Navy, who created a formidable fleet and made Brest the maritime capital of France. During the Napoleonic Wars the French were defeated here by a British fleet. During World War II the Germans used this strategic port as a submarine base to attack Allied shipping. Heavily bombed by the Allies, Brest was in ruins when it was liberated in 1944. Sights today include the restored **Castle,** erected between the 15th and 17th centuries on a site that had been fortified since Roman times, the **Cours Dajot,** a promenade built on the ramparts by convicts from the naval prison in 1769, and the **Naval Dockyard,** which contains the **"Consulaire" Column,** made from the barrel of a cannon through which the French consul to Algiers was shot in 1683, when Algiers was being bombarded by a French squadron.

**BRIANÇON,** *via N-91, N-94, and N-202 in Dauphiné*

Often referred to as the highest town in Europe, Briançon, in Roman times, served as a camp on the road from Milan to Vienna. In 1692 the town was burned by Sardinian invaders, and Louis XIV subsequently employed the engineer Vauban to reconstruct its fortifications. In 1815, at the very end of the Napoleonic Wars, the ramparts proved strong enough to enable General Eberlé, with a garrison of 70 gunners and 500 infantrymen, to withstand a siege by 20 times as many men of the Austro-Sardinian army from August to November. In June, 1940, Briançon repulsed an attack by the nearby Italian fort of Chaberton. Today the old section of town is contained within the extant **ramparts.** Here is Vauban's **Church of Notre Dame,** erected between 1703 and 1718. An inscription on the **Porte Pignerol** recalls the siege of 1815.

**CAEN,** *via N-13, N-175, N-162, N-158, N-815, or N-813 on the Orne River in Normandy*

Caen was the favorite town of William the Conqueror and his wife, Matilda. Although William was temporarily excommunicated for marrying a distant cousin, he was absolved for his sin in 1059. As penance, William and Matilda donated two abbeys—the **Abbaye aux Hommes** and the **Abbaye aux Dames**—and four hospitals to the city. In the mid-1800s Caen became a major seaport when a nine-mile canal connected it with the coast. During the Allied invasion of Europe a century later, the battle for Caen raged for more than two months between June and August, 1944. Much of the city was reduced to rubble, but some of the famous Norman buildings were spared war damage. Added to and reconstructed over the centuries are the Abbaye aux Hommes, whose **Church of Saint Stephen** contains the sarcophagus of William, and the Abbaye aux Dames, whose **Church of the Holy Trinity** houses Matilda's tomb. Other striking reminders of Caen's proud past include **Saint Peter's Parish Church,** with its famous belfry, completed in 1308, and the ruins of the **Castle,** erected by William.

**CAGNES-SUR-MER,** *via D-36, D-18, and D-136 on the Riviera*

The **Chateau** here was originally erected as a castle-fortress in 1309 by Raynier Grimaldi, lord of Monaco and admiral of France, at the time that he became lord of Cagnes. A descendant, Henri Grimaldi, converted the structure in 1620 into a finely decorated chateau. Loyal to the kings of France, he negotiated the 1641 Treaty of Péronne, in which his cousin Honoré II of Monaco renounced Spanish protection and placed himself under French rule. Louis XIII and Richelieu rewarded Henri with riches and honors. At the time of the Revolution the Grimaldis were driven from Cagnes and forced to take refuge in Nice. Today the chateau has been restored.

**CAHORS,** *via N-20, N-653, and N-111 in the Pyrenees*

The Romans built a large town here on the site of a sacred spring. The Visigoths captured the town in A.D. 471. When Eleanor of Aquitaine married Henry Plantagenet, the future King Henry II of England, in 1152, the town passed with the rest of the province under English rule. Cahors entered its golden age in the 13th century, when Lombard merchants and bankers, and later Templars, made the city the chief banking center of Europe. In 1331 the Avignon (*see*) pope John XXII, who was born at Cahors, established a university here that flourished for 500 years. When, during the Hundred Years' War, England seized the other towns of Quercy, Cahors alone remained impregnable; the 1360 Treaty of Brétigny ceded Cahors to the English, who held the city until 1450 and left it in ruins. A Catholic stronghold during the wars of religion, Cahors in 1580 was besieged and sacked by the Huguenot leader Henry of Navarre, the future King Henry IV. Today the town's principal sight is the **Pont Valentré**, begun in 1308, and according to local tradition, built over the next 50 years with the aid of the devil; the fortified Gothic bridge, with its six arches and three towers, is considered to be one of the most beautiful in the world. Other features include the **Cathedral of Saint Étienne**, begun in 1119, the **Maison de Roaldès**, where Henry IV resided in 1580, and a **Statue of Léon Gambetta**, the native statesman who defied the Prussians in 1870.

**CALAIS**, *via N-43, N-40, and N-1 on the English Channel in Picardy*
Situated only 21 miles from Dover, Calais has been involved in virtually all the conflicts between England and France. When English barons enlisted the aid of Dauphin Louis VIII against King John (Lackland) early in the 1200s, it was here that the fleet assembled. After his 1346 victory at Crécy (*see*), Edward III of England took Calais the following year after a long siege. He saved the town, but he made six of its leading citizens his servants and spared their lives only at the request of his wife, Philippa. Today Rodin's famous statue, *The Burghers of Calais*, in the **Place du Soldat-Inconnu**, commemorates the event. Calais was restored to the French in 1558 by François de Guise. During World War I Calais served as an English base; the older part of town was nearly razed. Surviving are the 13th-century **Tour du Guet** and the **Cathedral of Notre Dame**, built during the English occupation of Calais in the 14th and 15th centuries. In the vicinity of Calais is the site of the famous **Field of the Cloth of Gold**, where England's King Henry VIII met France's King Francis I amid much pageantry on June 7, 1520.

**CAMBRAI**, *via N-17, N-29, and N-39 in Picardy*
The memorable battle fought in the vicinity of this town on November 20, 1917, saw the first use of tanks in World War I, encouraging the Allies in their effort to end the stalemate on the Western front and ushering in a new age in warfare. The attack was conducted mainly by the British, who intended to pierce a 13,000-yard-long segment of the **Hindenburg Line**, capture Cambrai, and seize all Germans between the Saint-Quentin and Nord canals. The Germans were taken by surprise, and within one day of unprecedented success the British tank brigades and infantry divisions managed to advance some 10,000 yards, taking 8,000 German prisoners and capturing their guns. The Germans regained most of the lost ground ten days later. Cambrai suffered damage during the German withdrawal in 1918, was rebuilt, had damage inflicted again during World War II, and since has been restored.

**CANNES**, *via N-559, N-7, and N-567 on the Riviera*
On a small island (Îles de Lérins) off the present city of Cannes, Saint Honoratus settled about 410 and founded the influential **Monastery of Lérins**, a center of learning that lasted some 1,400 years and gave to Europe and Africa 20 saints and 600 bishops. From the tenth century, the fishing village of Cannes grew up as a dependency of Lérins. After Napoleon escaped from Elba and landed in France, he spent the night of March 2, 1815, bivouacked with his small army of 800 men on the outskirts of town; a tablet in the present **Church of Notre Dame-du-Bon-Voyage** marks the approximate site. The fashionable resort of Cannes originated in 1834 when Lord Brougham, lord chancellor of England, built a villa here. Preserved in the Old Town today are the 17th-century **Church of Notre Dame de l'Espérance**, traces of the **Chateau** built by the abbots of Lérins, and the 72-foot-high **Tour du Mont Chevalier**, raised

*Carcassonne's triple ring of fortifications in close-up and aerial view*

in the 14th century. Offshore, the Cistercian monastery is preserved at **Île Saint Honorat;** the island of **Sainte Marguerite** contains a **Fortress** built by Richelieu and strengthened by Vauban that contains the bare room in which the still anonymous "Man in the Iron Mask" —he actually wore a velvet hood—was imprisoned from 1687 to 1698 upon the order of Louis XIV.

**CARCASSONNE,** *via N-113, N-118, and N-119 in Languedoc*

Situated on an escarpment commanding communications between the Mediterranean and Toulouse, Carcassonne, with its triple ring of fortifications, is Europe's greatest extant example of a fortified medieval town. The Romans in the first century A.D. had an entrenched camp at the site, which in the fifth century was seized and refortified by the Visigoths, who used the outpost as a base for their conquest of southern France. In the eighth century the city fell to the Franks, and by the 12th century it had become the capital of a viscounty, ruled by the Transevals, viscounts of Toulouse, under whom Carcassonne rose to power and prominence. In 1209 Carcassonne, a seat of religious heretics known as the Albigenses, was besieged and captured during a Crusade by a royal army under Simon de Montfort (*see also Béziers*). In 1240 Raymond II, the last viscount, was expelled. King Louis IX subsequently allowed the lower town to be built in 1247, and from 1260 to 1270 he added the outer ring of fortifications to Carcassonne. The citadel was then considered to be impregnable, and during the Hundred Years' War it was not even attacked by the Black Prince, son of England's Edward III, who burned the lower town. By the time Carcassonne and its surrounding region were annexed to France in 1659, its military role had declined and it was no longer needed to fight off invaders. Today Carcassonne has been restored. Principal features in the Cité include the 12th-century **Castle,** the Romanesque and Gothic **Basilica of Saint Nazaire,** and the rows of **ramparts** punctuated by 54 towers.

**CARNAC,** *via N-781 and N-168 on the Quiberon Peninsula in Brittany*

This town is renowned for the more than 3,000 prehistoric megaliths, gigantic stones weighing up to 350 tons each, discovered in the vicinity. Erected from about 3500 B.C. to 1800 B.C. by precursors of the Gauls, the megaliths were probably associated with funerary rites and astronomical calculations. Specimens include menhirs, great upright stones either isolated or in rows, dolmens, burial chambers formed of upright stones supporting flat slabs, and tumuli, earthen mounds enclosing a tomb chamber. The most interesting monuments include the **Saint Michel Tumulus,** crowned by a chapel dedicated to Saint Michael, and the ¾-mile-long **Menac Lines,** comprising 1,009 menhirs up to 12 feet tall. At **Locmariaquer,** about 26 kilometers away, are the **Great Menhir,** broken into 5 pieces and weighing a total of 347 tons, and the **Merchants' Table,** a 40-yard-long dolmen.

**CHAMBÉRY,** *via N-491, N-512, N-6, and N-201 in Savoy*

Built near the site of a former Roman settlement, Chambéry served as the capital of the mountain duchy of Savoy until the 16th century. In 1232 Count Thomas I founded a castle here, around which the present town grew up. Savoy was ruled by counts from 1232 to 1416, dukes from 1416 to 1713, and kings of Sicily, Sardinia, and Italy from 1713 to 1860. The French occupied Savoy several times in the 15th and 16th centuries, but Emmanuel Philibert, a captain of Holy Roman Emperor Charles V, restored her sovereignty. In 1562 Turin replaced Chambéry as capital of Savoy, because the former was too close to the French border. Savoy and Chambéry became part of France in 1860. Preserved today are the ancient ducal **Castle,** which was reconstructed in the 14th and 15th centuries, and the **Church of Sainte Chapelle,** begun in 1408 as a shrine for the Holy Shroud and added to over the years.

**CHAMBORD (CHÂTEAU DE),** *via D-112 on the Cosson River in the Loire Valley*

Situated in a forested park more than 20 square miles in area and encircled by the longest wall in France, this 440-room castle is the largest of the Loire chateaux and one of the finest Renaissance edifices in the world. Chambord was begun in 1519 by Francis I, who lavished great sums on its construction; 1,800 laborers worked on the building for 15 years. Over the years Kings Henry II, Louis XIII, and Louis XIV added to and altered the chateau. For the Sun King, the playwright Molière presented two comedies at Chambord in 1669. In the 1700s Chambord was the residence of Stanislas Leszczyński, deposed king of Poland, and later was given by Louis XV to Marshal Saxe. Highlights of the chateau include the inner terrace, which presents a fantastic skyline of windows, spires, chimneys, gables, turrets, and pinnacles. The outstanding architectural feature of the interior is a staircase of two superimposed spirals.

**CHANTILLY (CHÂTEAU DE),** *via N-309, N-16, and N-324 in Île-de-France*

This famous chateau belonged to the Condé family from 1643 until 1830. A fortified castle had occupied this site in the Gallo-Roman era and was replaced by a feudal chateau in the Middle Ages. The Montmorency family acquired the property in 1450 and subsequently added the French Renaissance-style **Grand Château** in 1526 and the **Petit Château** in 1560. Charlotte de Montmorency and her husband, Henry I of Bourbon-Condé, inherited the palace in 1643. Under their son, the Grand Condé, the park and forest were landscaped by André Lenôtre, and the chateau was visited by such prominent personalities as Molière, and by King Louis XIV, who arrived in 1671 with 5,000 courtiers. The Grand Château was destroyed during the Revolution and a replica housing an art museum stands today. The Petit Château has been restored. During World War I the French general headquarters was located here.

**CHARTRES,** *via N-839, N-154, N-10, and N-821 in the Loire Valley*
This town, an important religious center since ancient times, is dominated by the **Cathedral of Notre Dame,** which with its harmonious proportions and beautiful stained-glass windows is one of the most celebrated buildings in the world. In the Gallo-Roman period this area was occupied by the Gallic tribe of Carnutes—whence the name Chartres—and was a center of druidism. Later, a Roman temple on the site contained a statue of the Mother Goddess that early Christians took to be a prefiguration of the Virgin; referred to as Our Lady Underground, the statue stood in each successive edifice and was the object of pilgrimages from afar. In 876 Charles the Bold gave the church a second important relic, the veil of the Virgin Mary. The crypt, tower, and portions of the façades are all that survive of the fifth building constructed at this site in the 11th century, which was destroyed by fire in 1194. The present building was erected between 1195 and 1228 and consecrated in 1260. In 1360 King Edward III of England was besieging the town when a hailstorm suddenly hit his camp. Edward lifted his arms toward Chartres and prayed that if the storm would stop, he would make peace with the king of France. The storm abated and a treaty was signed. In 1594 Henry IV was crowned king in the cathedral. Because of its spiritual and aesthetic significance, Chartres was spared the devastations of the wars in the following centuries.

**CHÂTEAU-THIERRY,** *via N-373, N-369, N-3, and N-37 in Île-de-France*
Throughout its long history, this town on the banks of the Marne has frequently been the scene of invasion and destruction. In 1814 Napoleon fought the Russo-Prussian army beneath the town walls. During the First Battle of the Marne in World War I, the Germans briefly held the town in September, 1914. From May to July, 1918, Château-Thierry witnessed fierce fighting as French and American troops resisted a German offensive to take the 50-mile-long road between that town and Paris. **Belleau Wood,** 11 kilometers northwest of town, was where the German drive was halted in June, 1918, by the American Second Division with the aid of the famous Marine Brigade. Today Belleau Wood has been dedicated as a permanent memorial to the American war dead. A **Chapel** commemorates the heroic sacrifices of the Allies, and the **Aisne-Marne American Cemetery** contains 2,288 graves.

**CHÂTILLON-SUR-SEINE,** *via N-65, N-71, N-80, and N-428 in Burgundy*
This community was the scene of a congress in February, 1814, between France and the allied powers—Prussia, Austria, Russia, and England—fighting her; Napoleon rejected the harsh terms laid down, and fighting continued until the collapse of the empire. In 1914 General Joseph Joffre, commander in chief of the French armies, made his headquarters here. During World War II Châtillon was the scene of several clashes between the resistance fighters of the region and the Nazis, and much of the town was destroyed. The town is famous for its **Museum,** which exhibits jewelry and other items from the sixth-century B.C. tomb of a Gallic princess excavated at nearby **Vix.** Among the objects is a five-foot-high vase decorated with a frieze of Greek and Etruscan origin.

**CHAUMONT-SUR-LOIRE (CHÂTEAU DE),** *via N-152, N-76, and N-751 in the Loire Valley*

Overlooking the Loire and surrounded by a park, this chateau was erected between 1465 and 1510 by Pierre d'Amboise and his son and grandson. In 1560 Catherine de Médicis, widow of King Henry II, acquired the Gothic and Renaissance-style castle and installed her Italian astrologer, Ruggieri, in a room connected by a staircase to the top of a tower used as an observatory. Later, in an act of revenge, the queen exchanged grim Chaumont for graceful Chenonceaux (*see*), the favorite retreat of Diane de Poitiers, mistress of the late king. In 1809 the famous writer Mme. de Staël was banished from Paris to Chaumont by Napoleon. Today Chaumont contains fine tapestries and furnishings and a collection of 18th-century glass and medallions engraved by the Italian artist Nini.

**CHENONCEAUX (CHÂTEAU DE),** *via N-76 in the Loire Valley*

This magnificent chateau, a rectangular mansion with turreted corners, was built between 1513 and 1521 on the site of an earlier chateau by Thomas Bohier, royal tax collector. Six women played a prominent role in Chenonceaux's 400-year history. Catherine Briçonnet, wife of Bohier, oversaw the construction of the mansion and was responsible for the arrangement of rooms on either side of a central vestibule. After Bohier's death the chateau passed to Francis I and then to Henry II, who in 1547 installed his mistress, the beautiful and charming Diane de Poitiers, on the premises. She added a splendid Italian garden and a bridge between the chateau and the bank of the Cher. In 1560 Henry's widow, Catherine de Médicis, forced Diane to relinquish Chenonceaux in return for Chaumont (*see*), although Diane never resided at the latter. Catherine employed the architect Philibert Delorme to build the two-storied classical gallery over the bridge and furnished the chateau lavishly for the festivals that she held frequently. After the assassination of Henry III the chateau was occupied by his widow, Louise of Lorraine. In the 1700s Mme. Dupin, a woman of letters and wife of the farmer-general, presided over a salon at Chenonceaux that was attended by such luminaries as Jean Jacques Rousseau. Chenonceaux emerged from the Revolution unharmed. In 1864 Mme. Pelouze purchased the estate and set to work restoring it to its original appearance under Bohier.

**CHERBOURG,** *via N-13, D-3, and N-801 on the Cotentin Peninsula in Normandy*

Liberated by the Americans on June 26–27, 1944, this port and naval base played a vital role in the battle for Normandy by serving as the port of supply for the Allied armies. In the 17th century the great military engineer Vauban first realized Cherbourg's potential as a transatlantic port. However, it was not until 1853 that the port opened and a naval base was established by Napoleon III. When the Americans captured Cherbourg during World War II, they quickly cleared the harbor of mines and rubble and prepared for the landing of heavy war materiel. During the Ardennes offensive, Cherbourg handled twice the tonnage every month that New York handled in 1939. Cherbourg was also the terminus for an undersea pipeline extending from the Isle of Wight, which supplied the Allies with oil. Reminders of the war may be seen on **Roule Hill,** the main point of German resistance, and at the **War and Liberation Museum,** whose Map Room illustrates the course of the war from the Allied landings (*see Normandy Invasion Beaches*) on June 6, 1944, until the final German surrender on May 7, 1945.

**CHINON (CHÂTEAU DE),** *via N-751 on the Vienne River in the Loire Valley*
Situated on a spur that had been fortified since Roman times, the present chateau of Chinon passed to the counts of Anjou in 1044. Kings Henry II (Plantagenet) and Richard the Lion-Hearted of England further fortified the castle late in the 12th century. In 1205 King Philip Augustus of France besieged Chinon and finally captured the fortress from the English. During the Hundred Years' War the court of the beleaguered dauphin Charles VII moved to Chinon in 1427. Joan of Arc had her first meeting with the dauphin here two years later, convinced him of her divine mission, and persuaded him to go to the relief of Orléans (*see*). The French court remained at Chinon until 1450. Later in the century, in 1498, King Louis XII received at Chinon the papal legate Caesar Borgia, who brought him a bull pronouncing his divorce. From 1631 until 1789 Chinon was a fief of the Richelieu family, during which time it fell into decay. Today the chateau consists of three distinct fortresses that include the ruins of **Fort Saint George**, erected by Henry II, who died there in 1189, the **Château de Milieu**, containing the great hall where Joan of Arc was received, and the **Château du Coudray**, where Joan lived during her stay in Chinon. In one of the houses (now a bakery) of the Old Town, Richard the Lion-Hearted died of wounds inflicted at a nearby siege in 1199.

**CLERMONT-FERRAND,** *via N-9, N-89, and N-141 in Auvergne*
Situated on an extinct volcano, the original Gallic village of Clermont-Ferrand subsequently became a trading center under the Romans. Christianity flourished here from the third century, when Saint Austremoine established its first church. During the Middle Ages the town was pillaged in turn by the Visigoths, Vandals, Goths, Franks, Normans, and Danes, but it managed to survive. At a council here in 1095, Pope Urban II preached the First Crusade to an assembly of churchmen and noblemen on what is now the **Place Delille**. All present attached a cross of red cloth to their shoulders, which became the emblem of the Crusades. Clermont was the birthplace of the famous scientist and philosopher Blaise Pascal in 1632. In 1665 Louis XIV sent a commission to Clermont to investigate the corruption of the local gentry; offenders were executed. During the 18th century the ramparts were demolished and the town embellished. The town's principal sight is the **Cathedral**, which was built between 1248 and 1298 of black volcanic rock and is one of France's great Gothic churches; just outside is a **Crusades Monument** with a statue of Urban II. In the old part of Clermont-Ferrand are many fine fountains and the Romanesque **Basilica of Notre Dame du Port**, dating from the 11th and 12th centuries.

**CLUNY,** *via N-80 and N-481 in Burgundy*
This abbey at Cluny was an important center of religious, intellectual, political, and artistic life during the Middle Ages and gave its name to the Cluniac order, which extended its influence throughout Christendom. Founded in 909 by William the Pious, duke of Aquitaine, the abbey was directly attached to the Holy See in Rome and was exempt from all temporal jurisdiction. Cluny developed rapidly under a succession of talented abbots and at the height of its prosperity, early in the 1100s, had 10,000 monks under its authority and boasted some 1,450 dependencies throughout Europe. By the 14th century the enormous wealth and power of the abbey had brought about a gradual decline; the abbots preferred their magnificent Paris town house (*see Hôtel de Cluny*) to their abbey. Cluny

*The Château de Chenonceaux and its reflection in the Cher River*

was desecrated during the wars of religion and nearly destroyed in the turmoil of the Revolution. The Romanesque abbey **Church of Saint Peter and Saint Paul,** completed in 1130, was the largest church in the West until the construction of Saint Peter's in Rome; all that remains are the south arms of the two transepts and the bases of the towers flanking the narthex. The former 13th-century abbey buildings, with their Gothic façades, house the **National School of Arts and Crafts.**

**COGNAC,** *via N-731 and N-141 in Angoumois*

This town was the birthplace in 1494 of Francis of Angoulême (*see*), who became King Francis I of France in 1515. The king, after returning from Spain in 1526, held a council of notables here to ratify the Treaty of Madrid. During the wars of religion, Cognac became a Protestant place of refuge. The town resisted an attack by Condé's army in 1651. Cognac later became the center of the brandy trade in France. The former 15th- and 16th-century **Chateau of the Valois,** where Francis I spent part of his childhood, has been used since 1795 as the storage cellers of Otard's, a brandy firm.

**COLMAR,** *via N-83, N-415, N-422, and N-417 in Alsace*

This Frankish town was the site of one of Charlemagne's imperial residences. During the Middle Ages Colmar became the chief trading town in upper Alsace and a center for the development of arts and crafts. The period of the Reformation and the Thirty Years' War was a troubled time for Colmar; peace was finally restored with Colmar's unification with France in 1635. In 1698 Colmar became the judicial capital of Alsace and the seat of the Supreme Council. Occupied for 47 years, from 1870 until 1918, by the Germans, Colmar always remained loyal to France. Principal sights include the 13th-century **Cathedral of Saint Martin,** and the former Dominican **Convent of Unterlinden,** an influential center of medieval mysticism, whose 13th-century chapel is now one of the finest provincial museums in France and contains the Issenheim altarpiece, painter Matthias Grünewald's masterpiece.

**COLOMBEY-LES-DEUX-ÉGLISES,** *12 kilometers east of Bar-sur-Aube via N-19 in Champagne*

General Charles de Gaulle, France's former president, who died in 1971, lies buried in the village churchyard. A simple cross marks his grave. Nearby is **La Boisseril,** his country estate.

**COMPIÈGNE,** *via N-35, N-31, and N-32 in Île-de-France*

This historic town was where Joan of Arc's military career ended in 1430. While she was covering the rear guard of the French army as it entered Compiègne, she was captured by the Burgundians and subsequently ransomed to the English (*see Rouen*). Compiègne, with its vast forest, was a favorite resort of French kings beginning in the Merovingian era. In 1374 Charles V erected a **Chateau** here that was the basis of the present palace. Compiègne was enlarged under Louis XIV, reconstructed under Louis XV, and completed by Louis XVI. After serving as a barracks and school of art during the Revolution, the castle was restored by Napoleon I. Compiègne was the favorite residence of Napoleon III and Empress Eugénie, who held lavish entertainments there. The **Clairière de l'Armistice** (Armistice Clearing) in the nearby **Forest of Compiègne** was the scene of the signing of the armistice of November 11, 1918, which ended World War I. Twenty-one years later, on June 21, 1940, Hitler came to the same clearing, entered Marshal Ferdinand Foch's railway car, which had been preserved as a shrine, and dictated humiliating terms to the capitulating French. The Germans destroyed the car when they retreated from Paris in 1944, and a marker now stands in its place.

**CORSICA**

AJACCIO, *via N-196, N-199, and N-193 on the west coast*

Established by the Genoese in 1492, this town has many historical associations with Napoleon. In 1811, to please his mother, the emperor made Ajaccio the capital of the island. With the fall of the empire, Corsica became part of France in 1815. Points of interest include the **Maison Bonaparte,** where Napoleon was born in 1769; the **Palais Fesch,** where Napoleon's mother, her stepbrother, Cardinal Joseph Fesch, and other members of the family are buried; and the **Hôtel de Ville,** which houses a Napoleonic museum.

BASTIA, *via N-198 and N-193 on the northeast coast*

Founded in 1380 by the Genoese, who erected a fortified castle here for defensive purposes, this town served as the capital of Corsica until it was replaced by Ajaccio (*see*). Although it sustained heavy bombing during World War II, some historic places are preserved —the **Old Port** and the 16th-century **Citadel,** built on the site of the original Genoese castle.

BONIFACIO, *via N-196 and N-198 on the southern tip*

Strategically situated on a promontory 330 feet above the sea, Bonifacio, Corsica's oldest town, was founded as a fortification in the ninth century by Boniface I, count of Tuscany. Principal features include the **Old Citadel,** where Napoleon served in 1792; here the

**Stairway of the King of Aragon**—a flight of 187 steps leading to the sea—was so called because it was supposedly hewn out of rock in one night when King Alfonso of Aragon was attempting to assault the town in 1420.

CALVI, *via N-199 on the northwest coast*
Founded in 1268, Calvi served for a time in the Middle Ages as the capital of the Genoese Republic. During the Napoleonic Wars, in 1793–94, Calvi was severely bombarded by the British; Lord Admiral Nelson lost his right eye in the struggle. Sights include the 16th-century **Church of Saint Jean** and the **Citadel**, which contains a house alleged to be the birthplace of Christopher Columbus.

CRECY, *about 18 kilometers north of Abbeville via N-1 in Picardy*
On August 26, 1346, this village was the scene of the first decisive battle of the Hundred Years' War between France and England. Here England's King Edward III, with a highly trained professional army of foot soldiers armed with longbows, soundly defeated the French knights of King Philip VI of Valois. England was thereafter established as a military power.

DIEPPE, *via N-25, D-1, N-15, and D-154 on the English Channel in Normandy*
This historic town is the oldest seaside resort in France. Early in the 16th century Jean Ango, shipbuilder and maritime counseler to King Francis I, joined the renowned mariners of Dieppe in constructing a fleet of privateers "such as would make a king tremble" in order to punish the Portuguese who were seizing French ships off the coast of Africa. Among the participating sailors was the Florentine explorer Giovanni da Verrazano, who in 1522 discovered the site of New York. By 1530 Ango's fleet had captured more than 300 Portuguese vessels, and the king of Portugal was compelled to negotiate a truce. Jean Ango is buried in the chapel he donated to **Saint James Church.** Ango's former **Manor House** is situated about 9 kilometers from Dieppe near **Varenseville.** During World War II, on August 19, 1942, a Canadian force of 7,000 men made the first Allied reconnaissance on the coast of Europe in the vicinity of Dieppe. During the commando raid, the battery near **Ailly Lighthouse,** outside Dieppe, was the only German stronghold to be taken; 5,000 Canadians were either killed or imprisoned. Today a plaque in the **Square du Canada** commemorates the so-called Operation Jubilee. Dieppe was finally liberated by the Canadian First Army in the summer of 1944.

DIJON, *via N-71, N-74, N-70, N-5, and N-396 in Burgundy*
A former Roman camp on the great military highway linking Lyons with Mainz, Dijon began its important role in history in 1015 when Robert I, duke of Burgundy, made the city the capital of his duchy. After a devastating fire in 1137, Duke Hugues II had Dijon rebuilt and encircled with ramparts and gateways. In 1364 Philip the Bold, son of King John II of France, inherited Burgundy, and thus began the century-long reign of the house of Valois. After his 1369 marriage to Margaret of Flanders, Philip became the most powerful prince in Europe. Among the monuments erected at this time was a Carthusian monastery intended by Philip to be a fitting burial place for himself and his family; the monastery was destroyed during the Revolution. His successor, John the Fearless (1404–19), was involved in the civil strife that divided France; he was brutally mur-

dered while waiting to make peace with the dauphin, Charles VII. In revenge his son, Philip the Good (1419–67), allied himself with the English, to whom he ransomed Joan of Arc when she was captured at Compiègne (*see*). He later made peace with Charles in the Treaty of Arras and greatly extended his domains. The last of the Valois, Charles the Bold (1467–77), waged war against King Louis XI and was killed besieging Nancy (*see*). Louis subsequently reunited the duchy with the crown of France, and Dijon became the seat of government of Burgundy, where the States-General, or regional assemblies, convened in the still-extant **Palace of Justice.** Preserved today is the **Ducal Palace,** which was converted into a parliament by Jules Hardouin-Mansart between 1686 and 1701; the east wing contains the **Museum of Fine Arts,** one of the oldest and richest in France. Other monuments include the **Cathedral of Saint Bénigne,** raised late in the 1200s, the 13th-century **Church of Notre Dame** in the Gothic-Burgundian style, with its gargoyles and statue of the Black Virgin, and the Flamboyant Gothic **Church of Saint Michael.**

**DINAN,** *30 kilometers south of Saint Malo via N-166 and N-176 on the north coast of Brittany*

In 1359 the duke of Lancaster laid siege to Dinan. France's renowned warrior Bertrand Du Guesclin and his brother Olivier defended the town, but the English forces were superior and the brothers agreed to a truce. In violation of the truce Olivier was taken prisoner by the knight of Canterbury, but he won his freedom when Bertrand defeated the Englishman in single combat at a spot now known as **Champ Clos.** After Du Guesclin's death in 1380, his heart was returned to Dinan; it is now buried in the Romanesque and Gothic **Basilica of Saint Saveur.** Other interesting sights include the **Castle,** with its enormous 14th-century tower known as the **Dungeon of Saint Anne,** and the **Old Town,** with its 15th- and 16th-century houses.

**DUNKIRK,** *via N-40 and N-16 in Picardy*

Settled around a church in the shelter of a dune about A.D. 800, this town has many historical associations with England. Situated on an invasion route by sea or land, Dunkirk was occupied at various times by the counts of Flanders, duke of Normandy, kings of England, and kings of Spain. The town was returned to France permanently in 1662, when Louis XIV purchased it for 5 million francs from Charles II of England; he later turned it into a defensive stronghold. The town was razed following the Treaties of Utrecht (1713) and Aix-la-Chapelle (1748) and rebuilt each time. Besieged by the duke of York in 1793, Dunkirk was relieved by the French general Houdart; a **Statue of Victory** commemorates the raising of this siege. A **Chapel** on the Rue Carnot, erected in 1405, served as a place of pilgrimage to seamen; destroyed in an explosion in 1793, it was reconstructed in 1818. By the 20th century Dunkirk was one of the most important ports in France and the site of a memorable human event in history. The so-called Miracle of Dunkirk occurred in the spring of 1940 when General Gerd von Rundstedt's German army broke through to the French channel ports and cut off land retreat for a third of a million men. The dramatic evacuation from the beaches of Dunkirk of 233,000 trapped British and 112,500 Allied troops was effected by an oddly assorted flotilla between May 26 and June 3.

ÉVREUX, *via N-13, N-154, and N-830 on the Iton River in the Eure Valley in Normandy*

War and devastation have characterized much of this city's history. Dating back to the Gauls and fortified by the Romans, Old Évreux was sacked by the Vandals in the fifth century A.D. The Normans invaded the town in the ninth century. In 1119 King Henry I of England, who was fighting the count of Évreux, set fire to the town, and at the end of the century, in 1193, Évreux was burned again by King Philip Augustus, who was betrayed here by King John of England. The town was besieged and burned in 1356 by King John the Good, who was struggling with the house of Navarre, and was besieged by Charles V in 1379. During World War II Évreux suffered damage from air raids. Remarkably, the town was rebuilt after each disaster. Reconstructed over the centuries, the **Cathedral of Our Lady** is Évreux's most interesting sight. Standing also are the former bishops' residence and former **Abbey Church,** dedicated to Saint Taurinus, first bishop of Évreux, which contains a 13th-century silver gilt reliquary.

FALAISE, *via N-811, N-158, D-243, and N-809 in the Ante Valley in Normandy*

This medieval village is dominated by its fortresslike **Castle,** which was the birthplace of William the Conqueror in 1027. William—the bastard son of Arlette, a comely peasant, and Robert, son of King Richard II—is commemorated with an **Equestrian Statue** in the **Place Guillaume-le-Conquérant.** Centuries later the castle served as a Nazi observation post during the Normandy campaign of 1944. After the Allies landed in June (*see Normandy Invasion Beaches*) and deepened the beachhead, they had to crack the German defensive ring and drive toward the Seine to liberate Paris. In July the United States Third Army broke through at Saint-Lô and Avranches (*see*); the British and Canadian units could not quite close a trap in the Falaise-Mortain-Alençon (*see*) pocket. Finally, after a fierce battle August 6–12, the Germans retreated eastward. Paris was finally liberated on August 25; the French Second Armored Division was the first to enter the city.

FONTAINEBLEAU (PALAIS DE), *via N-5, N-7, N-837, and N-51 in Île-de-France*

Surrounded by a 40,000-acre forest, this palace long served French royalty; two kings were born here—Philip IV in 1268 and Louis XIII in 1601. In the 16th century King Francis I replaced the 12th-century manor house with French Renaissance edifices in honor of his mistress, the duchess of Étampes. A galaxy of artists—forming the first Fontainebleau School—was brought in to decorate the new palace and to create, according to the king's wish, "a new Rome." Kings Henry II and Henry IV further embellished Fontainebleau for their respective mistresses. Louis XIV came to hunt every year and in 1685 signed the revocation of the Edict of Nantes here. Louis XV and Louis XVI enlarged and redecorated the apartments, which were emptied of furniture during the Revolution. Napoleon restored the palace, which he preferred to Versailles (*see*) because the latter evoked the memory of Louis XIV. Pope Pius VII was imprisoned here in 1812–14. On April 5, 1814, on a balcony overlooking the Cour de Cheval Blanc, the emperor signed his abdication and departed for Elba. Fontainebleau was further restored by Louis Philippe and Napoleon III. In the modern era, **NATO Headquarters** and the **American School of Fine Arts** have been housed at Fontainebleau. Spectacular examples of interior decoration may be seen in the **Great Apartments** of the first floor. The nearby village of **Barbizon** in the **Forest of Fontainebleau** gave its name to a school of French painters in the mid-19th century that included Jean François Millet, Théodore Rousseau, and Jean Baptiste Camille Corot.

**FONTEVRAULT-L'ABBAYE,** *via N-147 in the Loire Valley*
Founded by Robert d'Arbrissel in 1099, this Benedictine abbey provided separate facilities for monks, nuns, lepers, the sick, and noblewomen who wished to withdraw from the world. From 1100 until 1792 the community was governed by 37 consecutive abbesses. The abbey soon took on an aristocratic character, and the Plantagenet family chose the abbey church as their place of burial. The abbey was desecrated by the Huguenots in 1562. Early in the 1600s Jeanne Baptiste de Bourbon, daughter of Henry IV and referred to as the "Queen of the Abbesses," made the abbey into an important spiritual and cultural center. During the Revolution the monastery was destroyed, and Napoleon subsequently converted the remaining buildings into a national prison. Preserved today are the domed Romanesque **Abbey Church,** which contains the tombs of Henry II, his wife, Eleanor of Aquitaine, and Richard the Lion-Hearted, and the octagonal stone kitchen—88 feet high—known as the **Évraud Tower.**

**FOUGÈRES,** *at the junction of N-798, N-12, and N-155 on the Nançon River in Brittany*
Situated on the former frontier between Brittany and France, Fougères and its feudal **Castle** were of great military importance during the Middle Ages. In 1166 Henry II Plantagenet, king of England and duke of Normandy, besieged the castle and destroyed it. The powerful baron Raoul II immediately began to rebuild the structure, which was completed, with 13 towers in its massive walls, over the next few centuries. After Brittany was unified with France in 1532, the castle was used mainly as a prison. During the Revolution Fougères was a center of Breton Royalists. In the 1820s and 1830s Victor Hugo and Honoré de Balzac wrote of Fougères's turbulent history. The town contains two Gothic churches—**Saint Sulpice** and **Saint Léonard.**

**FRÉJUS,** *via N-7, N-98b, and N-98c on the Riviera*
Originally called the Forum Julii, this town was established by Julius Caesar in 49 B.C. as a trading post and stopping place on the great coastal highway that later became known as the Aurelian Way. Under Octavian, the future Emperor Augustus, the town became an important Roman naval base, with a 54-acre port and more than a mile of quays, where the fast and light galleys were built that were later to win the Battle of Actium against Antony and Cleopatra in 31 B.C. Augustus subsequently set up a colony of his veterans at Fréjus, which grew until it had a population of 25,000. The military port lost much of its importance during the long Pax Romana, and at the end of the second century A.D. the war fleet was moved away, and the harbor and canal began to silt up. Among Roman remains today are the **Amphitheater,** raised about A.D. 210, the **Theater, Aqueduct,** and the **Porte des Gaules,** an ancient gate in the Roman ramparts. Fréjus was destroyed by Saracens in 915 and rebuilt by Bishop Riculphe. During the Allied invasion (Operation Anvil-Dragoon) of the south of France in August, 1944, Fréjus was liberated on the second day.

**GRENOBLE,** *via N-75, N-512, N-90, N-523, and N-531 in Dauphiné*

This town, inhabited in pre-Roman times by the Allobroges, became an archbishopric in A.D. 375 and in 379 was enlarged and surrounded with ramparts by Emperor Gratian, after whom Grenoble (originally Gratianopolis) is named. The Burgundians occupied the town in the fifth century, and in 1023 it was incorporated into the German Empire. In the 12th century Grenoble and its surrounding territory were ruled by counts, who called themselves dauphins after the dolphins depicted on their coats of arms. The last of these dauphins, Humbert II, who founded the **University of Grenoble** in 1339, sold the region to the kingdom of France in 1349; the transaction stipulated that the territory should become the appanage of the oldest son of the king of France, who would assume the title of dauphin. Grenoble subsequently became a provincial capital with parliaments and law courts. In 1815 Napoleon I was enthusiastically received here on his return from Elba. Historic sites include the **Church of Saint André,** completed in 1236, whose crypt contains the tomb of the famous 15th-century knight the Chevalier Bayard; the **Palais de Justice,** where the former states of Dauphiné convened; the 11th-century **Church of Saint Laurent,** whose sixth-century crypt is one of the two oldest in France; and the **Cathedral of Notre Dame,** whose early portions date from the tenth century. About 19 kilometers northeast in the Dauphiné Alps is the famous Carthusian monastery of **La Grande Chartreuse,** where the liqueur of the same name is made.

**HONFLEUR,** *via N-813, N-179, and N-180 on the Seine estuary in Normandy*

This seaport is famous for its mariners, who during the 1600s made important voyages of discovery in the New World. In 1608 Samuel de Champlain sailed from Honfleur to found Quebec. During the reign of Louis XIV Canada was colonized with Norman peasants and soldiers, one of whom was the sieur de La Salle, Robert Cavelier, who explored Louisiana in 1682. In the second half of the 19th century Honfleur was a popular artists' and writers' colony. Preserved today are the picturesque **Old Dock,** remains of the **Governor's House,** and **Saint Catherine's Church,** a rare European example of a church constructed entirely of wood.

**LA ROCHELLE,** *via N-22, N-137, D-9, and D-21 in Aunis*

This seaport town was ruled by the English from 1152 to 1224 and from 1360 to 1372. After the discovery of America La Rochelle prospered as a center of trade with Canada. During the wars of religion La Rochelle was a Protestant stronghold known as the French Geneva. The city was besieged unsuccessfully by the royal army in 1573. In 1627–28, despite aid from its English allies, La Rochelle was blockaded by the Catholic forces of Cardinal Richelieu and Louis XIII, reduced to famine, and forced to surrender. When in 1685 Louis XIV revoked the Edict of Nantes, Protestant refugees from here founded New Rochelle in New York. Today principal sights include the Renaissance **Hôtel de Ville,** medieval arcades and half-timbered houses, and the **Old Port,** with its fortresslike **Tour Saint Nicolas,** one of three towers built to guard the harbor; a chain from the **Tour de la Chaine** was connected to the **Tour de la Lanterne** by Richelieu to close off the harbor during his 1627 siege. The chain is now in the **Musée d'Orbigny.**

**LA TURBIE,** *via N-7 and D-37 on the Riviera*

This village contains the only surviving trophy of the Roman world

*Left: the Old Port at La Rochelle. Right: Chapelle Saint-Michel at Le Puy*

in France. When Caesar died in 44 B.C., some 44 unconquered tribes remained in the Alps. Augustus eventually subdued them, and in 6 B.C. the Roman senate and people decided to commemorate his victories with a suitable monument, which was set up at the point where the main roads, constructed during the operation, crossed the Alps. Originally an imposing 164 feet high and 125 feet wide, the **Trophée des Alpes** has been ravaged over the centuries; all that remains is a ruined tower emerging from a cone of rubble.

**LAON,** *via N-367, N-44, N-2, D-181, and D-7 in Picardy*
Settled since Celtic times, Laon is famous for its **Cathedral of Notre Dame,** built between the 12th and 14th centuries. This early Gothic building served as a model for other French cathedrals.

**LASCAUX, GROTTE DE.** *See* MONTIGNAC

**LE HAVRE,** *via N-182, N-13b, N-25, and N-40 at the mouth of the Seine in Normandy*
Founded in 1517 by King Francis I to replace the silted-up port of **Harfleur,** Le Havre was laid out on a checkerboard plan in 1541 by the Italian architect Belarmato. Over the years the port was repeatedly modernized and enlarged. During the American Revolution Le Havre assumed its present importance as a commercial and transatlantic port by serving as the supplier for the patriots. In 1784 the Exchange was established, which became a powerful organization of international finance and commerce. The 19th century saw the arrival of American passenger ships. During World War II Le Havre was the scene of 146 air raids; when the town was liberated on September 13, 1946, it was the most severely damaged port in Europe Sights today include the modern **Port,** the façade of the 16th-century **Notre Dame Chapel,** and the old port of Harfleur.

**LE PUY,** *via N-102, N-88, and N-590 in Auvergne*
Situated on a plain studded with volcanic peaks, this town was a popular place of pilgrimage in the Middle Ages. Travelers en route to Saint James of Compostela in Spain would regularly stop at the Romanesque **Cathedral of Notre Dame de Puy,** erected in the 12th century on the site of a Roman temple, to venerate its famous statue of a Black Virgin. Besides the cathedral, sights of interest include

157

the 11th-century **Chapelle Saint-Michel-d'Aiguilhe,** which rests high on a giant needle of black lava, and a colossal **Statue of the Virgin,** situated atop the 2,477-foot-high volcanic peak known as the **Rocher Corneille,** which was cast in 1860 from the metal of 200 Russian cannon captured in the Crimea.

## LES ANDELYS

**CHÂTEAU DE GAILLARD,** *via D-1, N-313, and N-316 overlooking the Seine in Normandy*

Situated on a cliff, this fortresslike structure was erected in 1197 by Richard I (the Lion-Hearted), king of England and duke of Normandy, to prevent King Philip Augustus of France from passing through the Seine Valley on his way to Rouen (*see*). After Richard's death in 1199 and the accession of King John Lackland, Philip Augustus laid siege to the stronghold, which finally surrendered on March 6, 1204. Today ruins of the redoubt and of the main fort remain.

**LILLE,** *via N-17, N-350, N-41, A-1, N-25, and N-42 in Picardy*

This town has had a long history of warfare. During the Middle Ages Lille served as an important stronghold of the counts of Flanders. In 1667 Louis XIV commissioned Vauban to refortify the town. Extant today, Vauban's **Citadel** consists of a regular pentagon protected by outworks. The town was besieged in 1708 and 1792; a column commemorates the latter event. The **Palace of Fine Arts** houses one of France's most important art collections. Lille was the birthplace of Charles de Gaulle in 1890.

**LIMOGES,** *via N-147, N-20, and N-141 in Limousin*

This Gallo-Roman town became an episcopal see about A.D. 250, when Saint Martial converted the inhabitants of the region to Christianity. An abbey grew up here with the saint's relics, and the monastery at Limoges became an important pilgrimage center. Wealth and eventually world fame came to Limoges for its fine enamels, which were produced from the 5th to the 17th centuries. The porcelain industry, established here in 1768, is still in operation; the **Musée National Adrien Dubouché** displays 10,000 items of porcelain and enamel. Preserved here are the Gothic **Cathedral of Saint Étienne,** begun in 1273, the 14th-century **Church of Saint Michel-de-Lions,** which contains the relics of Saint Martial, and the 13th-century **Bridges of Saint Étienne and Saint Martial.**

**LOCHES,** *via N-143 and N-760 on the Indre River in the Loire Valley*

From the sixth century on, a fortified **Castle** has stood at Loches. In the ninth century the counts of Anjou established an entrenched camp at the castle. The defenses were augmented by a descendant, King Henry II (Plantagenet) of England. In 1205 Philip Augustus converted it into a royal residence. Subsequently a state prison was established here. In the mid-1400s Agnès Sorel, mistress of King Charles VII, lived at Loches; she is entombed in the castle. Later in the century King Louis XI devised wooden cages in which he confined prisoners in the castle's dank dungeons. Covering an area the size of a small town today, the castle includes the **Royal Dwelling,** where Kings Charles VII and VIII and Louis XI and XII resided; Joan of Arc was received here on June 3 and 5, 1429, by Charles VII, whom she persuaded to be crowned at Reims (*see*). The ancient fortress and keep include the 15th-century **Round** and **Martelet Towers** containing torture chambers and dungeons.

## LOURDES, *via N-21, N-637, and N-640 in the Pyrenees*

This is one of the world's most famous religious shrines. In the eighth century a castle crowning the Rock of Lourdes was occupied by Saracen invaders, who finally surrendered to Charlemagne and were converted to Christianity. From 1360, when the Treaty of Brétigny was signed, until 1404, when it was retaken by Charles VI, Lourdes belonged to the English. In 1858 a 14-year-old peasant girl named Bernadette Soubirous said that in the **Grotto of Massabielle** the Virgin had appeared to her in a vision, the first of 18 similar apparitions. In 1866 church authorities accepted the miracle as authentic and made February 11, the anniversary of the first apparition, a feast day. Devotion to Our Lady of Lourdes spread throughout the Christian world, and in 1872 the first national pilgrimage took place. Bernadette died in 1879 and was canonized in 1933 *(see also Nevers)*. Today nearly two million pilgrims visit Lourdes each year. Principal sights include the grotto, the **Basilique de Rosaire**, completed in 1888, two hospitals, the **Breton Calvary**, a 40-foot-high granite crucifix, and the former **Castle,** which houses a museum.

## LYONS, *via N-6, N-7, N-433, N-83, N-84, N-517, and N-518 in the Rhone Valley*

Strategically situated at the confluence of the Saône and Rhone rivers, Lyons was the site of a Gallic settlement and subsequently of the colony known as Lugdunum, founded by the Romans in 42 B.C. From 1033 until the 14th century, when Lyons became part of France, the city was part of the German Empire. The Jacobins were expelled from this center of Royalist sympathy during the Revolution, and in retaliation the Convention ordered the destruction of the city; some 6,000 citizens were executed, and the principal buildings were demolished. Today Lyons is the third largest French city. Preserved in the older part of town between the Rhone and Saône are the **Church of Saint Martin d'Alnay,** the oldest in Lyons, erected in the 11th century on the site of a former Roman temple, and the **Hôtel Dieu,** a hospital established in 1542 that currently houses a museum. The **Place Terreaux** was where citizens of Lyons were guillotined during the Revolution. Two **Roman theaters** have been excavated.

## MALMAISON (CHÂTEAU DE), *16 kilometers west of Paris via N-13 in Île-de-France*

Purchased in 1799 by Josephine Bonaparte, wife of Napoleon, this chateau was the First Consul's favorite retreat from 1800 to 1803. After becoming emperor in 1804, Napoleon was forced to live in his official residences, and visits to Malmaison were infrequent. Josephine resided here from the time of her divorce in 1809 until her death in 1814. She is buried in the nearby **Church of Rueil.** Today Malmaison contains a museum of the art and history of the Napoleonic era and is rich in memorabilia connected with Josephine.

## MARSEILLES, *via N-8, A-7, A-52, and N-559 in Provence*

The oldest town in France was founded about 600 B.C. by Greeks from Asia Minor and called Massalia. A prosperous commercial city under the Greeks, renowned for the wisdom of its laws, Marseilles became a republic allied to Rome in 122 B.C. In 49 B.C. Julius Caesar made the city a Roman colony because it had supported his rival Pompey. Although there flourished here a university that was the last vestige of the Greek spirit in the Occident, Marseilles had begun to decline by the third century A.D. In 1249 Marseilles supplied Saint Louis with galleys to transport his army on the Seventh Crusade, and in 1481 it was reunited with the crown of France. The town was devastated by plague in 1720: some 50,000 inhabitants perished. Marseilles received the Revolution with enthusiasm, and 500 volunteers marched into Paris chanting a hymn written by an Alsatian, Claude Rouget de Lisle, which became known as "The Marseillaise" and today is France's national anthem. The citizens of Marseilles eventually revolted against the Convention; a guillotine established on the famous artery **La Canebière** became the scene of frightful atrocities. Under the empire, Marseilles sympathized with the Royalists, and during the Second Empire the city had Republican sympathies. In the 19th century the port expanded to handle the traffic from the French colony in Algeria and the Suez Canal, opened in 1869. During World War II Marseilles was bombarded by Germans in 1940 and by the Allies in 1943–44. Today principal sights include the **Old Port,** situated between two forts, where the Greeks disembarked in 600 B.C. and where until the 19th century all maritime activity took place (the quays were constructed under Louis XII and Louis XIII); the **Basilica of Saint Victor,** the last remnant of a fifth-century abbey destroyed by the Saracens about 1040 and rebuilt and fortified in succeeding centuries; the former 12th-century **Ancienne Cathédrale de la Major;** and the **Château d'If,** a castle erected in 1529 on an island in the Bay of Marseilles, once used to hold political prisoners.

## MELUN VICINITY

VAUX-LE-VICOMTE (CHÂTEAU DE), *6 kilometers northeast via N-36 and N-5 in Île-de-France*
This sumptuous chateau was erected between 1656 and 1661 by Nicolas Fouquet, the ambitious Superintendent of Finance under Louis XIV whose motto was "Whither shall I not ascend?" Louis Le Vau, the architect, Charles Le Brun, the decorator, and André Lenôtre, the landscape gardener, as well as 18,000 other workers, were hired to create this monument to his success. On August 17, 1661, Fouquet gave a reception of unrivaled splendor at his newly completed chateau for Louis XIV, who was not amused by his host's ostentatious display of wealth. Fouquet was imprisoned shortly thereafter and his property confiscated. The building served as a prototype for Louis XIV's Versailles *(see).*

**METZ,** *via N-53, A-31, N-3, N-55, N-413, and N-57 in Lorraine*
Strategically situated at the confluence of the Seille and Moselle rivers, this town, known to the Romans, was an early center of Christianity. Metz was also a seat of Merovingian kings in the 500s and later was a favorite town of Charlemagne's; the remains of his wife and two small children were buried in the former **Abbey of Saint Arnoult.** In the 12th century Metz was a free city and the capital of a small republic. Metz was annexed to France by Henry II in 1552, after François de Guise raised a two-month siege of the city by Holy Roman Emperor Charles V. In 1870, during the Franco-Prussian War, a French army of 180,000 men capitulated after a two-month siege, and for the next 47 years Metz was a part of Germany. French troops liberated the city on November 19, 1918. During World War II Metz was encircled by German fortresses. The 2½-month-long Battle of Metz ended on November 19, 1944, when American troops under General George S. Patton entered the town. The principal feature of Metz today is the **Cathedral of Saint Étienne,** erected between 1250 and 1380 and one

of the finest extant examples of the Gothic style. Its stained glass was inserted between 1521 and 1529; the choir contains a Merovingian throne.

## MONTIGNAC VICINITY
GROTTE DE LASCAUX, *off N-704 east of Dordogne River in Aquitaine*
One of the most famous Paleolithic caves in the world contains hundreds of perfectly preserved paintings created by artists during the Magdalenian period about 12,000 B.C., and the preceding Aurignacian period. Discovered accidentally by schoolboys in 1940, the cave's four chambers contain drawings, some of which have been outlined in flint, of the various animals hunted by prehistoric man; these include oxen, cows, horses, deer, bison, and ibex. The lack of tools and utensils on the site suggests that the cave was used as a temple rather than as a dwelling. Most of the animals represented are female and pregnant, symbolic of fertility. Others are shown struck by arrows; their creators perhaps hoped that such illustrations would make game easier to catch.

## MONTPELLIER, *via N-113, D-24, N-109, and N-586 in Languedoc*
This town was established in the eighth and ninth centuries by merchants who imported spices from the Near East. A medical school was founded here in 1221, and the University of Montpellier, which became a renowned intellectual center, was chartered in 1289. During the wars of religion late in the 16th century, the Huguenots eventually made Montpellier a fortified stronghold; in 1622 royal troops of Louis XIII besieged the rebel town, which capitulated after three months. Louis XIV made Montpellier the administrative capital of Languedoc, and the town prospered late in the 1600s and 1700s. During these years the town received such embellishments, surviving today, as the **Promenade du Peyrou,** begun in 1688, the **Esplanade,** laid out in 1724, and many beautiful mansions. The fortresslike **Cathedral of Saint Pierre,** founded in 1364, was the only church in Montpellier not totally destroyed during the wars of religion.

## MONT-SAINT-MICHEL, *on N-776 near Avranches in the north of Normandy*
Rising steeply—260 feet—above its island of granite, this mighty abbey, with its buttresses, high walls, and spire, is known as the Wonder of the Western World. Mont-Saint-Michel's origins date back to A.D. 708, when according to legend the Archangel Michael appeared before Aubert, bishop of Avranches, and persuaded him to build an oratory on what was then known as Mont Tombe. Subsequently a Carolingian abbey was built on the island, renamed Mont-Saint-Michel, and this building was eventually superseded by Romanesque and Gothic structures. Benedictine monks established themselves in the abbey in 966, and in the 12th century Kings Henry I and Henry II of England held court there. Saint Louis stayed at Mont-Saint-Michel in 1254 and contributed to the fortifications then under construction. Although attacked over the centuries, the abbey was never captured. The mont became a popular shrine, and pilgrims flocked here even during the Hundred Years' War, when the English, who held the surrounding countryside, granted them safe conduct. The monastery declined in the 17th and 18th centuries and was abolished in 1790; the buildings were used afterward to hold prisoners. The restoration of Mont-Saint-Michel began in 1874. The island is entered through the **Porte de l'Avancée,** the only break in the ramparts. The steep ascent to the abbey is

made along the **Grande Rue,** lined with old houses. After entering the abbey via a fortified gateway, the **Escalier du Gouffre** (stairway of the pit) ascends to a **Guardroom,** La Porterie, a 13th-century hall that was the focal point of the abbey. From here the 90-step **Abbey Staircase** leads to a terrace known as **Gautier's Leap.** Adjoining the terrace is the **Church,** with a Romanesque nave and Gothic chancel. The **Monastery** itself, referred to as the "Merveille" (marvel) and built between 1211 and 1228, is an outstanding example of Norman Gothic architecture and consists of an almshouse, guests' hall, refectory, storeroom, knights' hall, and cloister.

### NANCY, *via N-57, N-74, and N-4 in Lorraine*

Founded in the 11th century, Nancy changed hands several times in the course of its history. In 1476 Charles the Bold of Burgundy invaded the duchy of Lorraine and drove Duke René II out of Nancy. A year later René retook Nancy, and Charles the Bold was killed in flight. Following the War of the Polish Succession (1733–35), the Treaty of Vienna granted Stanislas I Leszczynski, deposed king of Poland and father-in-law of Louis XV, the duchy of Lorraine as compensation. Installed at Nancy, Stanislas assembled the leading artists of the time to embellish his capital. The result is a masterpiece of 18th-century baroque town planning. The **Place Stanislas,** laid out between 1752 and 1760, with its gilded grilles, fountains, and balconies, reflects the elegance of the era. The square is surrounded by five pavilions, of which the largest is the **Hôtel de Ville;** the **Triumphal Arch of Louis XV** faces one side. Lorraine passed to the French crown in 1766. Nancy was attacked by Germans during World War I, and during World War II it was liberated by American forces on September 5, 1944.

### NANTES, *via N-165, N-23, and N-137 on the Loire River in Brittany*

Nantes, the one-time Gallic capital of Namnetes, fought for its independence from the Romans, Franks, Normans, English, and French successively over the centuries. During the Middle Ages Nantes was the capital of Brittany several times, achieving the pinnacle of its wealth and prestige in the 15th century under Francis II, duke of Brittany, and his daughter, Anne. A great historic event occurred on August 13, 1598, when King Henry IV of France signed the Edict of Nantes, granting religious freedom to Protestants as well as equal political rights with Roman Catholics. Notable sights include the massive **Ducal Castle,** erected on its present plan in 1466 and surrounded by a moat—the edict was signed on the premises; and the **Cathedral of Saint Peter and Saint Paul,** begun in 1434 and completed in 1893, which contains the tomb of Francis II.

### NEVERS, *via N-7, N-77, and N-78 in Burgundy*

In 52 B.C. Julius Caesar made this settlement a food and forage depot for his army. When Caesar's advance on nearby Gergovie was checked, the Edouen tribe burned Nevers and imperiled the Roman position in Gaul. In 1565 Luigi di Gonzaga, third son of the duke of Mantua, became duke of Nivernais. He brought Italian artists and craftsmen to Nevers; these artisans established glassmaking, enamel, and chinamaking industries that flourished until the Revolution. Dominating the town is the **Cathedral of Saint Cyr and Saint Juliette,** a vast basilica embodying all the architectural styles from the 10th to the 16th centuries. Also of interest are the **Bishop's Palace,** now the Municipal Museum, the Renaissance-style **Ducal Palace,** and the **Porte de Croux,** a square tower built from 1394 to

1398. The **Convent of Saint-Gildard** contains the remains of Saint Bernadette, who resided here 1860–79 (*see also Lourdes*).

**NICE,** *via N-7, N-204, N-564, and N-559 on the Riviera*

Founded in 350 B.C. by Greek traders from Marseilles (*see*), Nice became a modest market town. Later the Romans colonized the quarter known as **Cimiez,** in which are extant ruins of a **Roman Arena.** An early center of Christianity, Nice had a bishop in the fourth century. In 1388, after being fought over by various factions from Provence, Nice seceded from Provence and joined Savoy, under Count Amadeus VII. In 1543 Francis I of France and his Turkish allies, who were at war with Charles V of Austria, allies of the house of Savoy, laid siege to Nice, which capitulated after 20 days. The town changed hands several times until the 1748 Treaty of Aix-la-Chapelle returned it to Savoy. French troops occupied Nice in 1792, and Napoleon—then a general of the artillery—resided here in 1794. Nice was returned to the house of Savoy with the fall of the empire in 1814. The Treaty of Turin of 1860 between Napoleon III and Victor Emmanuel II, king of Sardinia, gave Nice back to France. A noted personality born at Nice was Giuseppe Garibaldi (1807–82), a principal author of the Italian revolution of 1860. The **Old Harbor,** begun in 1750, former **Governor's Palace,** erected in 1611 and now restored, and the hilltop site of the former fortress, demolished by the duke of Berwick in 1706, may be visited.

**NÎMES AND VICINITY,** *via N-579, N-86, N-99, and N-113 in Provence*

Founded about 121 B.C. on the site of a native village, the Roman colony of Nemausus was situated on the route between Italy and Spain and became one of the most important cities of Gaul. After his victory in Egypt over Antony and Cleopatra, Emperor Augustus gave the lands around Nîmes to his legionaires, who erected in the years before the Christian era many of the splendid edifices that stand today. The area was overrun by Visigoths about 470 and subsequently by Saracens, who were expelled from the region in 737

*Left: the Pont du Gard at Nimes. Right: a gilded grille from the Place Stanislas at Nancy*

by Charles Martel. After belonging to the kingdom of Aquitaine and the countship of Toulouse, Nîmes became part of France in 1227. In the 16th century Nîmes was the center of Protestantism in southern France; Huguenots fled from the city after the revocation of the Edict of Nantes in 1685, and in the repressions that followed, the town suffered much damage. The chief sights today include the **Roman Amphitheater,** built just before the Christian era, which holds 21,000 spectators, and the **Maison Carrée,** of the first century B.C.—an outstanding example of a Roman temple in France—which later served as a Visigoth fort, private house, church, and is now a museum of antiquities; it was here in 1787 that Thomas Jefferson had drawings made that would serve as a model for the Virginia state capitol. Other Roman remains include the **Tour Magne,** a 100-foot-high monument, the **Porte d'Arles,** a gate of 16 B.C., and the **Castellum Divisiorum,** built to hold town water sent by the great aqueduct called the **Pont du Gard,** which is situated over the Gard River about 19 kilometers northeast of Nîmes. Constructed about 19 B.C. out of colossal blocks, the aqueduct consists of three tiers of arches (160 feet high and some 600 yards long) and is nearly perfectly preserved today.

**NORMANDY INVASION BEACHES,** *along N-814 on the Gulf of Saint-Malo between the Orne and Vire rivers*
This expanse of Normandy coast was the setting of the D-day landings of June 6, 1944. On the night of June 5, 4,266 barges, landing craft, accompanying warships, and naval escorts preceded by mine sweepers left England to begin the Allied invasion of Europe. British and American airborne detachments landed at either end of the invasion front at the **Bénouville-Ranville Bridge**—now Pegasus Bridge—and Sainte-Mère-Église (*see*) respectively. Although failing to destroy Hitler's Atlantic wall completely, the Allied bombing and shelling succeeded in disorganizing the German defense. British, Canadian, and French ground forces landed at **Sword, Juno,** and **Gold beaches,** while the Americans landed at **Omaha Beach** and **Utah Beach** on the adjacent Cotentin Peninsula. Despite fierce counterattacks by German coastal batteries, the Allies had linked up with each other by June 12 and had established a solid beachhead. Late in July the defensive ring was cracked at **Saint-Lô,** and General George S. Patton's Third Army (*see Avranches*) swung into Brittany, then left to encircle the German armies in Normandy. Commemorating the American combatants at Omaha Beach are the **American Military Cemetery,** with 9,385 Carrara marble crosses, the **Fifth Engineer Special Brigade Memorial,** built on the remains of a German blockhouse, and the **Monument to the D-Day Landing** at Les Moulins. Many other monuments stand along the coast. (*See also Arromanches-les-Bains and Cherbourg.*)

**ORANGE,** *via N-7, N-575, and N-576 on the Meyne River in Provence*
Orange enjoyed great prosperity in Roman times with its own theater, amphitheater, circus, gymnasium, temples, and baths. Surviving today are the **Antique Theater,** with a seating capacity of 7,000, and a Roman **Triumphal Arch.** In the 13th century A.D. Orange became a small principality that eventually passed by marriage and inheritance to the Germanic house of Nassau, a branch of the house of Baux at Les Baux. When, in the 16th century, William of Nassau, prince of Orange, created the Republic of the United Provinces in the Netherlands, the town of Orange passed into his possession. In 1622 Maurice of Nassau fortified the town

and built a chateau there, which was destroyed later in the century by Louis XIV in the course of a war against Holland. Orange became part of France by the 1713 Treaty of Utrecht.

ORLÉANS, *via N-751, N-152, N-51, N-155, and N-20 in the Loire Valley*

This town has witnessed a long and bloody history. Captured by Julius Caęsar in 52 B.C., Orléans withstood an attack by Attila and his Huns in A.D. 451, was captured by Clovis, king of the Franks, in 499, and in 1428–29 was the scene of the famous siege by the English. After months of fighting, the morale of the French defenders was low. On April 29, 1429, Joan of Arc entered the city, and after engaging in several fierce skirmishes, finally forced the English to surrender on May 7. During the wars of religion, in the 17th century, Orléans was the principal Protestant stronghold and was besieged. Orléans was ransacked during the Revolution and was occupied for several months by the Prussians in 1870. The town suffered bomb damage in World War II. Preserved today is a **Monument to Joan of Arc** on the Place du Martroi, and the **Cathedral of Saint Croix,** begun in 1278, damaged by Protestants in 1567, and rebuilt by Henry IV in 1601.

## PARIS

### ARC DE TRIOMPHE, *Place de l'Étoile*

The largest triumphal arch in the world was conceived by Napoleon in 1806 to honor the imperial armies. Designed by Jean Chalgrin, who was inspired by the sculpture of ancient Rome, the arch was half built by 1810 when the new empress Marie Louise made her entry into Paris. The 160-foot-high arch was completed in 1836. The frieze depicts the successful campaigns of France's armies between 1790 and 1815. Today the **Tomb of the Unknown Soldier** —brought from Verdun in 1920—is beneath the monument. Twelve avenues radiate from the arch.

### BOIS DE BOULOGNE, *via Avenue Foch*

This forest received its name in 1308, when its inhabitants made a pilgrimage to Notre-Dame de Boulogne-sur-Mer on the English Channel and returned to erect a church called Notre-Dame de Boulogne-le-Petit. The forest became a royal hunting ground, which Colbert landscaped in the 17th century, and in the 1700s it was a fashionable meeting place. In 1815 British and Russian troops occupied the forest, which was completely devastated. The *bois* was subsequently replanted. In 1852 Napoleon III gave the forest to the city, and the *bois*, under Baron Georges Haussmann's direction, was transformed into a park, modeled after London's Hyde Park.

### CATHEDRAL OF NOTRE DAME, *on the eastern end of the Île de la Cité*

Begun in 1163 by Maurice of Sully, bishop of Paris, on the site of earlier religious structures that included a Gallo-Roman temple, Christian basilica, and Romanesque church, Notre Dame was completed in 1345. This cathedral, an outstanding example of Gothic architecture, was the scene of many important historic events. In 1423 Henry VI of England was crowned king of France at Notre Dame; he was driven from Paris six years later by Joan of Arc and Charles VII, who in 1529 was officially crowned at Reims (*see*). During the Revolution the cathedral was turned into the Temple of Reason and was sacked by a mob. Napoleon restored order, returned the church to the Roman Catholics in 1802, and in 1804 crowned himself emperor here in the presence of the pope. Viollet-le-Duc restored the cathedral between 1845 and 1865. On August 26, 1944, General Charles de Gaulle celebrated the liberation of Paris in a ceremony at Notre Dame.

**CHAMPS-ÉLYSÉES,** *bounded by the Place de la Concorde and the Place de l'Étoile*
This former marshland was first developed in 1616 by Marie de Médicis, who created the fashionable Cours la Reine along the Seine. The wooded plain between the Cours la Reine and the Grand Cours of the Tuileries (*see*) became known, from 1709 on, as the Champs-Élysées. In 1724 the Grand Cours was extended as far as the present Place de l'Étoile (*see Arc de Triomphe*). Over the years the Champs-Élysées was filled with fountains, drives, parks, statues, and edifices; today the tree-lined promenade is the finest in Paris.

**CHURCH OF THE MADELEINE,** *on the Boulevard de la Madeleine, the western terminus of the Grands Boulevards*
Situated where the former fortifications, or "bulwarks," of Paris once lay, this Grecian-style structure, with its 52 Corinthian pillars, was commissioned by Napoleon in 1805 in honor of his armies. In 1814 Louis XVIII converted the Madeleine into a church, which was nearly turned into Paris's first railway station before its consecration in 1842. The front pediment depicts the Last Judgment.

**HÔTEL DE CLUNY,** *Boulevard Saint-Germain, Latin Quarter*
This ancient town residence of the abbots of Cluny is a magnificent example of the Flamboyant Gothic style and is one of the two large examples of 15th-century domestic architecture extant in Paris (the other is the Hôtel de Sens). The site was occupied in Gallo-Roman times by the **Palais des Thermes,** baths built about A.D. 200 and destroyed by barbarians late in the century. Ruins of the Palais des Thermes include a vault, unique in France, and a pillar—the oldest sculptured work in Paris—dedicated to the Roman emperor Tiberius by Parisian boatmen. About 1330 Pierre de Châlus, abbot of Cluny, purchased these Roman ruins and erected a town house, which was later demolished. The present edifice was constructed between 1485 and 1510 for the abbot's servants and staff. From 1600 to 1681 the building housed papal nuncios, of whom the best known was Jules Mazarin. After the Revolution the structure fell into disrepair. A museum opened in 1844 now occupies 34 rooms of the building and contains more than 20,000 works of art of the Middle Ages.

**HÔTEL DE VILLE,** *Place de l'Hôtel de Ville, opposite the Pont d'Arcole*
Situated at what, until 1830, was known as the Place de Grève because unemployed workers had gathered here during the Middle Ages, this imposing structure stands on the site of earlier town halls. In 1260 Saint Louis created the first town council, which for many years consisted of representatives of various guilds who met at a pillared house on the square. In the 16th century Francis I built a magnificent town hall on the square, which was also the scene of Paris's festivals, and during the old monarchy, of public executions: aristocrats were killed with the sword or axe, heretics and witches by burning, murderers were broken on the wheel, and traitors quartered. In 1800 Napoleon reorganized the municipal government, appointing a mayor, two deputy mayors, and 24 councilors to run the city. During the Commune riots of 1871 the town hall was burned; it was rebuilt and enlarged between 1874 and 1882.

**LES INVALIDES,** *via the Pont Alexander III and the Avenue du Marechal Gallieni on the Left Bank of the Seine*

Founded by Louis XIV in 1670 to house up to 7,000 disabled soldiers, this vast edifice, completed in 1676, is considered one of the masterpieces of French classical architecture and symbolizes the grandeur of the Sun King's reign. On July 14, 1789, mobs invaded the Invalides and seized its store of weapons, which they used to attack the Bastille (*see Place de la Bastille*) later that day. The building is dominated by the superbly balanced **Church of the Dome,** erected between 1679 and 1706 by Jules Hardouin-Mansart; the sumptuous interior contains the tombs of Napoleon and other prominent French soldiers. The remains of Napoleon were brought to Paris in 1840, 19 years after his death, given a state funeral, and eventually buried, in 1861, in a tomb of red porphry in the Church of the Dome. The adjoining **Church of Saint-Louis** contains the death mask and other relics of the emperor. Today the secular buildings of Les Invalides house military agencies and the **Musée de l'Armee,** an important military museum. Leading to the Seine, the tree-lined **Esplanade des Invalides** provides panoramic vistas.

**L'OPÉRA,** *on the north side of the Place de l'Opéra off the Boulevard des Capucines*

Encompassing three acres, this imposing structure is the largest theater in the world. The Opéra was designed by Charles Garnier in the Second Empire style between 1861 and 1875 and was built of marble from every quarry in France. The building soon earned renown for its operatic productions, ballet, and magnificent costumes and décor.

**LOUVRE,** *bounded by the Seine, the Rue du Louvre, the Rue de Rivoli, and the Avenue Général Lemonnier*

This former palace of the kings of France is the largest in the world and houses one of its greatest museums. In the 16th century Francis I built a palace on the site of an old fortified castle that had been erected by Philip Augustus in 1200. Francis displayed casts of Greek and Roman sculpture as well as a few paintings here, and thus began the Louvre's collection. After Catherine de Médicis had a palace built at the nearby Tuileries (*see*), the **Petite and Grand Galeries** were constructed along the Seine to connect the two structures. The buildings of the **Cour Carrée** were erected under Louis XIII and XIV; its eastern façade, a classical colonnade designed by Claude Perrault, faces the venerable **Church of Saint Germain-l'Auxerrois,** begun in the 12th century. Jean Baptiste Colbert, Louis XIV's finance minister, added some 2,500 paintings to the Louvre and Versailles Palace (*see*). The Louvre fell into disrepair in the 18th century, and a vast slum sprawled all the way to the Tuileries. After the Revolution Napoleon I restored the buildings, began a new wing along the Rue de Rivoli, and added works of art from the nations he conquered. Work on the Louvre was completed by Napoleon III. During the Commune riots of 1871 the Tuileries Palace and linking buildings were destroyed. The latter were rebuilt during the Third Republic. Today the museum contains more than 200,000 works of art, including an unrivaled collection of paintings.

**LUXEMBOURG PALACE AND GARDEN,** *on the Rue de Médicis and Rue de Vaugirard*

Situated on the site of a former Carthusian monastery with a garden that flourished during the Middle Ages, this palace is the show place of the Left Bank. In 1612 Marie de Médicis, widow of Henry IV and mother of Louis XIII, decided to have a palace built here in the style of her native Tuscany. The palace was designed by Salomon de Brosse and occupied by the queen mother from 1625 until 1631, when she was exiled by her son. The palace remained royal property until the Revolution, after which time it housed several parliaments. Since 1946 the Luxembourg Palace has served as the meeting place of the Conseil de la Republique, the upper house of the French parliament

### MONTMARTRE, *in the ninth arrondissement*

Known in ancient times as the Mont de Mercure because a temple of Mercury stood on its summit, this steep hill in the eighth century became known as the Mont des Martyrs; tradition then had it that Saint Denis, first bishop of Paris, and his two prelates were beheaded here in 272. A **Chapel** on the Rue Antoinette stands on the site where the saints were martyred, and where, in 1534, Saint Ignatius Loyola and six companions vowed to fight the enemies of Catholicism and thus founded the Jesuit order. In the 19th century the picturesque district of Montmartre became a favorite haunt of artists and writers, many of whom are buried in its **Cemetery**, opened in 1795. Such dance halls in the vicinity as the Moulin Rouge and the Moulin de la Galette were made famous in the paintings of Henri de Toulouse-Lautrec and Auguste Renoir respectively. During the Commune riots of 1871 Montmartre was a center of popular uprisings against the government. In 1876, as an expression of love and contrition, French Catholics undertook the building of the **Basilica of Sacré Coeur,** the high domed white building crowning Montmartre that was consecrated in 1919 and rivals the Tour Eiffel (*see*) as a celebrated Paris landmark.

### PALAIS DE CHAILLOT, *Place du Trocadéro*

The present palace stands on the site of a former country home of Catherine de Médicis that was replaced in the 17th century by the convent of the Visitation of Our Lady. Napoleon planned to build a palace on this hill for his son and designated heir, the king of Rome. However, the fall of the empire halted the project. In 1827 the site was named Trocadéro to commemorate the French seizure of a fortress of that name in Cádiz in 1823. A pseudo-Moorish building stood here from 1878 until 1936, when it was demolished and replaced by the Palais de Chaillot, erected for the Exhibition of 1937. Consisting of two main buildings with curved wings, the palace houses ethnological, folklore, and historical museums.

### PALAIS DE JUSTICE, *on the northwest part of the Île de la Cité*

These law courts are built on the site of a former palace used by Roman prefects and subsequently by Capetian kings. In the 13th century Saint Louis erected a new royal palace, highlighted by the exquisite Gothic **Church of Saint-Chapelle,** which, boasting magnificent stained-glass windows, was consecrated in 1248. The buildings received additions, including the famous prison known as the **Conciergerie** and the four towers of the **Quai de l'Horloge,** in the 14th century, and the royal family inhabited the premises until the reign of Charles V (1364–80), after which they left the Île de la Cité. The royal palace was subsequently used by Parliament. After the Revolution courts of justice were established in the building, which was renamed the Palais de Justice. During the Reign of

Terror 1,200 inmates—among them Queen Marie Antoinette—were held at the Conciergerie. Most of them were guillotined. Nearby is the **Pont Neuf**, or new bridge, built between 1578 and 1604. Paved before any street in Paris was, the Pont Neuf is the oldest of Paris's surviving bridges and still serves modern traffic needs.

**PALAIS-ROYAL,** *Place du Palais Royal off the Rue de Rivoli*
Erected in 1632 as the residence for Cardinal Richelieu, this palace was left to Louis XIII upon the cardinal's death in 1642 and was thenceforth known as the Palais-Royal. The palace was occupied briefly by the young Louis XIV and in 1680 by Louis Philippe d'Orléans, later nicknamed Philippe-Égalité, who was the first cousin of King Louis XVI. Between 1781 and 1786 Louis Philippe had a row of houses that contained shops and arcades erected around the palace and built the nearby **Théâtre-Français,** a structure that from 1792 housed the Comédie-Française. During the Revolution Louis Philippe, a member of the Revolutionary Parliament, voted for the king's execution, only to be executed himself shortly thereafter. The Palais-Royal was burned during the Commune riots of 1871 and later rebuilt.

**PANTHÉON,** *on Saint Geneviève's Hill in the Latin Quarter*
This splendid monument was dedicated to Saint Geneviève, patron saint of Paris, who in the fifth century saved the city from Attila and converted Clovis, the first Christian king of France. When he was ill in 1744, Louis XV vowed that if he were cured, he would raise a fine church in honor of the saint. In 1764 work on the building began under Jacques Soufflot, who had seen the Pantheon of Agrippa in Rome. Completed in 1789, the structure, two years later, was turned into the Temple of Reason, in which leaders of the French revolutionary epoch would be buried. The comte de Mirabeau was the first to be entombed here and was soon followed by Voltaire and Jean Jacques Rousseau. During this period the edifice came to be called the Panthéon, a temple dedicated to all gods. Napoleon reconverted the building into a church in 1806, and after 1885, upon the death of Victor Hugo, who was buried in its crypt, it became the Panthéon again.

**PLACE DE LA BASTILLE,** *via Boulevard Henri IV, Rue Saint-Antoine, and Boulevard Beaumarchais*
This huge square was the site of the 14th-century fortress known as the Bastille, which witnessed a momentous event in French history. After its completion in 1382, the Bastille was soon full of prisoners detained by *lettres de cachet,* royal acts that allowed people to be imprisoned for indefinite periods without benefit of trial. Over the years Parisians came to see the Bastille as a symbol of tyranny and injustice, and on July 14, 1789, it was stormed by revolutionary mobs (*see also Les Invalides*), even though *lettres de cachet* had been abolished and only seven prisoners remained to be liberated. The storming of the Bastille has come to have great symbolic significance, and July 14 is celebrated as French independence day. The building was systematically razed in 1780, and the **Colonne de Juillet** in the center of the square today commemorates Parisians killed in the revolutions of 1830 and 1848.

**PLACE DE LA CONCORDE,** *via Rue Royale, Avenue Gabriel, Rue de Rivoli, Pont de la Concorde, and the Champs-Élysées*
Laid out by Jacques Ange Gabriel in 1754, during the reign of Louis

*Some of the famous landmarks of Paris, from left to right: Sacré Coeur on Montmartre; a view of the Seine River, with the Pont Neuf in the foreground and the*

XV, this square—the largest in Paris—was subsequently the scene of Louis XVI's execution on January 21, 1793. A guillotine was set up where the **Statue of Brest** now stands. Here the king uttered his last words: "My people, I die innocent of the crimes of which I am accused; may my blood consolidate the happiness of France." A few moments later his head was held up before the public. Later that year Marie Antoinette was also executed at the Place de la Concorde; before 1795 that guillotine near the Tuileries (*see*) saw 1,343 victims, including the revolutionary leaders Georges Danton and Maximilien de Robespierre, who had fallen into disfavor. In 1836, during the reign of Louis Philippe, the 150-ton **Obelisk of Luxor**, a gift from the Egyptian viceroy, was erected in the center of the square; the fountains and eight statues representing the French cities were raised during the reign of Napoleon III. The Louis XV-style buildings on the northeast side of the square include the **Admiralty**, the **Hôtel Crillon**, where a treaty was signed in 1778 by which France recognized American independence, the **Hôtel de la Vrillère**, where Talleyrand died in 1838, and the **United States Embassy**.

PLACE VENDÔME, *off the Rue Saint-Honoré*

Laid out by Jules Hardouin-Mansart in 1698 and also known as the Place Louis-le-Grand in honor of Louis XIV, this square evokes the splendor of the "Grand Siècle." A statue of Louis XIV originally stood in the center, but it was torn down during the Revolution; between 1806 and 1810 Napoleon had a **Column** built in the style of Trajan's column in Rome to commemorate his victory at Austerlitz. Encircled by a spiral band of bronze made from 1,200 cannon captured at Austerlitz, on which are bas-reliefs depicting military scenes, the column is surmounted by a statue of the emperor as Caesar.

PLACE DES VOSGES, *via Rue des Tournelles*

The oldest large square in Paris was begun by Henry IV in 1605 and completed in 1612, two years after the king was assassinated by

*dome of Les Invalides and the Eiffel Tower at left; a side view of Notre Dame Cathedral showing its flying buttresses and spire*

François Ravaillac, a Catholic fanatic. The square was built on the site of the former Hôtel des Tournelles, where Louis XII died in 1515; it was abolished by Catherine de Médicis after her husband, Henry II, was killed in a tournament on the nearby Rue Saint-Antoine in 1559. At first called the Place Royal, the square was planned with similar houses to provide a harmonious appearance and with walks for pedestrians—novelties for the time—and immediately became a fashionable meeting place. It was renamed the Place des Vosges in 1800. Victor Hugo lived on the second floor of No. 6 from 1832 until 1848. Today the **Musée Victor Hugo** houses the poet's memorabilia.

SAINT GERMAIN-DES-PRÈS, *Boulevard Saint-Germain on the Left Bank of the Seine*

This structure is the oldest church in Paris. The original abbey church was raised between 542 and 558 at the request of Saint Germain, bishop of Paris, who was later buried there and supposedly effected a number of miracles and cures soon after. In the eighth century Saint Germain-des-Prés became one of the wealthiest and most important of the Benedictine abbeys. The church was damaged by the Normans and rebuilt, in the Romanesque style, between 990 and 1021; the nave, transept, and steeple erected at that time stand today. The choir, rebuilt in the 12th century, is one of the earliest examples of the Gothic style. The abbey was closed at the time of the Revolution. The former **Abbot's Residence** is situated in back of the apse.

SORBONNE, *on the Rue des Écoles and the Rue Saint Jacques*

One of the oldest colleges of the University of Paris, the Sorbonne was founded in 1253 by Robert de Sorbon, a canon of Paris, to enable poor students to study theology. Until the time of the Revolution the Sorbonne served as the seat of the university and of its chancellor. The first printing press in France was set up here in 1470. Between 1624 and 1642 Cardinal Richelieu erected Jesuit-style edifices that stand today, as well as the **Church of the Sor-**

171

bonne, where he is buried in a white marble tomb sculpted by François Girardon in 1694. The Sorbonne was closed during the Revolution and reopened by Napoleon in 1806. The buildings were rebuilt and extended between 1885 and 1901. Today the Sorbonne contains parts of the School of Arts and Sciences and is the principal center of higher education in France.

TOUR EIFFEL, *on the Champ de Mars on the Left Bank of the Seine*
This steel tower, Paris's best-known landmark, was erected for the Universal Exposition of 1889. Containing three platforms and rising to a height of nearly a thousand feet, the structure was the tallest edifice in the world until New York's Chrysler Building was built in 1929. The tower was dedicated by Edward VII, Prince of Wales, and was a huge success due to its boldness and extraordinary novelty. Today the tower is used as a radio station. The Eiffel Tower is situated on the **Champ de Mars,** a former parade ground laid out by the architect Jacques Ange Gabriel between 1765 and 1767. The **École Militaire,** at the end of the Champ de Mars, was also designed by Gabriel under the auspices of Mme. de Pompadour, Louis XV's favorite mistress, for the training of young officers. Napoleon attended the military academy at the age of 15 in 1784.

TUILERIES, *bounded by the Seine, Rue de Rivoli, Place de la Concorde, and Avenue Général Lemonnier*
These gardens were originally laid out in the Italian style for Catherine de Médicis, who had a palace erected at this site—in earlier centuries, the Paris city dump—in 1563. Open to the public, the Tuileries soon became a fashionable meeting place. During the reign of Louis XIV the landscape architect André Lenôtre redesigned the gardens, adding terraces, fountains, and providing magnificent vistas. Here one of the earliest balloon ascents was made in 1783. And on August 10, 1792, an angry mob drove King Louis XVI and the royal family from the Tuileries Palace, massacring some 600 members of the Royal Guard in the gardens. Although the Tuileries Palace was destroyed during the Commune riots in 1871 and never rebuilt, the gardens remain much as they did when Lenôtre planned them. Panoramic views are afforded on the terrace—once the haunt of royal princes—by the river. At one corner of the garden stands the **Musée du Jeu de Paume,** a former tennis court, which now houses a famous collection of impressionist paintings.

PAU, *via N-117, N-134, and N-637 in the Pyrenees*
In the 11th century the viscounts of Béarn built a **Castle** at this site, around which a town grew up. During the 14th century Gaston Phoebus, the most famous of the counts of Foix, erected around the town a fortified wall, which was demolished, restored, and altered by various successors. In 1527 Henri d'Albret, king of Navarre and lord of Béarn and Bigorre, married Margaret of Angoulême, sister of King Francis I, who renovated the castle in the Renaissance style and made it one of the cultural centers of Europe. Her daughter, Jeanne d'Albret, married Antoine de Bourbon, a descendant of Saint Louis's, so that their son would inherit the throne after the last of the Valois monarchs died out with Henry III. She gave birth to Henry of Navarre, the future King Henry IV, at the castle on December 13, 1553. Henry proclaimed himself king of France and Navarre in 1589. Béarn and Pau were reunited with France in 1620 after Louis XIII came to Pau, a Protestant center, and re-established the

Catholic church there. Preserved in the chateau, which has been altered over the centuries, is the room in which Henry IV was born. The **Musée Bernadotte** is the birthplace of Jean Bernadotte (1763–1844), who became King Charles XIV of Sweden, founder of the present Swedish dynasty.

**PÉRIGUEUX,** *via N-21, N-89, and N-139 in Aquitaine*
Center of a distinctive cuisine and inhabited since prehistoric times, the Gallic settlement at this site capitulated to the Romans after it had sided with Vercingetorix against Caesar. During the Pax Romana one of the finest cities of Aquitaine, Vesuna, grew up here, with temples, basilicas, an arena, and an aqueduct. From the third century the town suffered the successive depredations of Alamanni, Visigoths, Franks, and Normans and was reduced to the status of a humble village, eclipsed by the neighboring town of Puy-Saint-Front. Bitter rivalry between the two towns ended in 1251 when they were united by the threat of an English invasion. Under the 1360 Treaty of Brétigny, Périgueux was ceded to England; the town was the first to rally to King Charles V's call to take up arms against England; from here the warrior Bertrand Du Guesclin planned the famous campaigns that expelled the invaders from the area. From 1575 to 1581 the city was held by the Huguenots, who wrought great damage. Between 1649 and 1653 Périgueux was besieged by the Frondeurs, who were revolting against royal authority; but it was retaken by the king's men. There are two distinct old districts: in the medieval **Puy-Saint-Front** is the white-domed **Cathedral of Saint Front,** erected from 1125 to 1150 and now restored; the Roman section contains ruins of the **Arena,** which once held 20,000 spectators, and the 80-foot-high **Tour de Vésone,** the only extant part of a second-century A.D. temple.

**PERPIGNAN,** *via N-9, N-617, N-114, N-612A, and N-116 in Roussillon*
This fortress-town, for much of its history, belonged to Spain. In 1172 the district of Roussillon, in which Perpignan is situated, passed to the house of Aragon. During the 13th century James I, king of Aragon, formed the kingdom of Majorca by combining Roussillon and the Balearic Islands and made Perpignan its capital; the kingdom ended in 1344 when Peter IV of Aragon captured these territories and incorporated them into the principality of Catalonia. Louis XI of France occupied the area in 1463 and captured Perpignan in 1475, but his successor Charles VIII, who sought Spanish friendship, ceded it to Ferdinand and Isabella in 1493. The French under Louis XIII besieged and took the town in 1642. Perpignan was permanently returned to the French crown by the Treaty of the Pyrenees in 1659. Principal sights include the 14th-century battlemented **Castillet,** which formed part of the city's defenses, the **Loge de Mer,** a merchants' exchange erected in 1397, the **Cathedral of Saint Jean,** begun in 1324, the 13th-century **Palace of the Kings of Majorca,** and the **Church of Sainte-Marie-de-la-Réal,** where in 1408 the Spanish antipope, Benedict XIII, excommunicated Gregory XII, the official pope.

**POITIERS,** *via N-10, N-147, and N-151 in Poitou*
This Roman town became the seat of a bishopric in A.D. 350, when Saint Hilary was appointed to the office. Visigoths conquered Poitiers in 409 and made the city the residence of their kings. During the famous **First Battle of Poitiers** in 732, Charles Martel repulsed a Moorish invasion from Spain and thereby secured the

future of Christianity in Europe. Poitou and Poitiers passed under English rule in the 12th century with the marriage of Henry Plantagenet—the future King Henry II of England—to Eleanor of Aquitaine, who had often resided in the town. King Philip Augustus restored the town to France 52 years later. Poitiers was recaptured by the English in 1356 in the **Second Battle of Poitiers,** when Edward, the Black Prince, routed and captured King John II on a battlefield outside town. The warrior Bertrand Du Guesclin returned Poitiers to France in 1372. The town subsequently flourished under Jean, duc de Berry and Auvergne, count of Poitou, who assembled the leading artists of the time at his court. Charles VII, who favored Poitiers, brought the Parliament here from Paris and established a **University** in 1431. During the wars of religion the town suffered at the hands of both Protestants and Catholics and was twice besieged. Preserved today are the **Palais de Justice,** where Charles VII was proclaimed king in 1422 and where Joan of Arc was interrogated before the court and acquitted in 1429; the 12th-century Romanesque **Church of Notre Dame la Grande;** and the **Baptistery of Saint Jean,** which was erected between 356 and 368 on Roman foundations and is probably the oldest extant Christian edifice in France.

**RAMBOUILLET (CHÂTEAU DE),** *via N-836, N-306, and N-10 in Île-de-France*
Erected in the 14th century, this chateau with its splendid park has been a favorite retreat of French monarchs. Francis I died in the **Round Tower** here in 1547. In 1706 the domain passed to the comte de Toulouse, son of Louis XIV and Mme. de Montespan, who built many of the apartments and wings of the present structure. Louis XVI acquired Rambouillet in 1783 and on the premises built the **Queen's Dairy,** where Marie Antoinette could play at being a milk-maid. Napoleon spent a night here in 1815 before departing for exile in Saint Helena, and in 1830 Charles X signed his abdication at Rambouillet. Since 1897 Rambouillet has served as the summer residence of presidents of the republic.

**REIMS,** *via N-51, N-38, N-44, and N-380 in Picardy*
One of the principal towns of ancient Gaul, this home of the Celtic tribe of the Remi became the seat of a bishopric in the third century. In 496, when Saint Remi, archbishop and patron of the city, crowned Clovis, the first Christian king of France, he thus established a long tradition: to be crowned at Reims was to be undisputed king of France. Erected between 1211 and 1294 on the site where Clovis was baptized, the **Notre Dame of Reims Cathedral,** a masterpiece of Gothic architecture and statuary, has become a sacred symbol to the French. A **Statue** in the square outside the cathedral commemorates Joan of Arc, who attended the coronation of Charles VII here on July 17, 1429. Reims suffered great damage from shelling during the Franco-Prussian War and World Wars I and II. It was at Reims on May 7, 1945, that the German forces in France signed their surrender. Other historic monuments include the **Porte de Mars,** a Roman triumphal arch of the second century A.D., and the Romanesque **Basilica of Saint Remi,** the oldest church in the city, erected from 1005 to 1049, which contains Saint Remi's tomb.

**ROUEN,** *via N-13b, N-14, N-28, N-30, N-138, and N-182 on the Seine in upper Normandy*
Dating back to Roman times, this Norman capital was the scene of Joan of Arc's famous trial and execution. During the Hundred Years'

War, in 1418, Rouen fell to the English forces of Henry V. Insurrections soon broke out against the "Goddams" (as the English were known because of their partiality to profanity), and terror reigned until the victories of Joan of Arc in the 1420s and the coronation of Charles VII at Reims (*see*) in 1429 gave the French new hope. Captured by the Burgundians at Compiègne (*see*) in May, 1430, Joan was subsequently ransomed to the English at Rouen, where she was charged with witchcraft and tried by a tribunal of French ecclesiastics. After a humiliating six-month-long trial, Joan was found guilty and burned at the stake on May 30, 1431, in the **Place du Vieux Marché,** where a plaque now stands to commemorate the event. Joan was officially rehabilitated in 1456 and became patron saint of France in 1920. After the Hundred Years' War Rouen prospered as a center of trade and textile manufacturing, and many sumptuous edifices were erected by its citizens. The **Old Quarter,** on the right bank of the Seine, was severely damaged during World War II but has since been repaired and restored. Notable monuments include the 13th-century **Cathedral,** which boasts an impressive façade with all its variety and openwork pinnacles, the exquisite abbey **Church of Saint Ouen,** begun in 1318 and completed in the 15th century, the Renaissance-style **Bourgtheroulde Mansion,** raised early in the 1600s, and the **Law Courts,** originally erected under Louis XII as the Normandy Exchequer but converted into a parliament by Francis I.

**SAINT-DENIS,** *via N-1 and N-86 in Île-de-France*

The kings and queens of France were buried here in the venerable early Gothic **Basilica.** Tradition has it that after Saint Denis, first bishop of Paris, was beheaded at Montmartre (*see*) in 272, he carried his severed head to this site. A chapel was soon founded to house his relics, and it became a popular pilgrims' shrine. In the seventh century King Dagobert founded a Benedictine abbey here that became the wealthiest, most powerful abbey in France. The present abbey church was constructed between 1136 and 1147 under the

*Detail (left) from the great portal and the façade of Reims Cathedral*

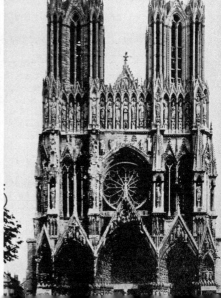

direction of Abbot Suger and enlarged and embellished in the 1200s; this church was the first major building in the Gothic style and served as a prototype for Chartres (*see*). As the royal necropolis, Saint-Denis housed the tombs of kings, queens, royal children, and such famous servants of the crown as the 14th-century warrior Bertrand Du Guesclin. During the Revolution mobs desecrated the tombs and scattered their remains. The church was restored in the 19th century by Viollet-le-Duc.

### SAINTE-MÈRE-ÉGLISE, *via N-13 and D-15 in Normandy*

On the night of June 5–6, 1944, American paratroops from the 82nd Airborne Division descended on this town to assist those soldiers arriving by sea at Utah Beach (*see Normandy Invasion Beaches*) during the D-day invasion of Normandy. Thus, Sainte-Mère-Église became the first town in France to be liberated. A **Monument** in the square and an **Airborne Troops Museum** commemorate the parachutists. The 13th-century **Church** suffered damage when American gunfire dislodged German snipers from the belfry.

### SAINT-GERMAIN-EN-LAYE (CHÂTEAU DE), *via N-184, N-190, N-13, and N-186 in Île-de-France*

From the 12th century onward the kings of France made their summer residence here. In the 1500s Francis I incorporated a Gothic chapel, built by Saint Louis between 1230 and 1238, and a keep, erected by Charles V in 1368, into the present battlemented Renaissance chateau. His son, Henry II, thought the edifice too foreboding and erected the New Chateau, where Louis XIV was born in 1638; it was demolished in 1780. Louis XIV had five pavilions constructed and a park and terrace laid out by André Lenôtre; his court would come and stay at either chateau for enjoyment and for refuge during times of trouble in Paris. Saint-Germain also had many English associations: Mary Stuart (later queen of Scots) occupied the premises before her marriage in 1558 to the dauphin, Francis II, as did the wife of Charles I during the Civil War between 1645 and 1648, and James II lived here after he was deposed in 1689. During the Revolution the chateau was stripped of its furnishings and was used as a military prison until Napoleon III had it restored and converted into the **French Museum of National Antiquities.**

### SAINT-LÔ. *See* AVRANCHES *and* FALAISE

### SAINT-MALO, *via N-155 or N-137 on the English Channel in Brittany*

This town was an important seaport that flourished from the Middle Ages to modern times. Saint-Malo became the seat of a bishopric in 1144. At that time the bishops undertook the construction of the town's massive **ramparts,** which were altered until the 18th century and which give Saint-Malo the appearance of a medieval fortress. Privateers sailed from Saint-Malo to pillage English, Dutch, and Spanish ships. In 1534 Jacques Cartier sailed from this port and discovered Canada and the mouth of the Saint Lawrence River, which he claimed for the king of France. Saint-Malo was occupied by the Germans during World War II and was left in ruins after being bombarded in 1944. The town has been restored. Preserved are the former **Cathedral,** the **Castle,** built as part of the town ramparts, the **Hôtel de Ville,** the poet François de Chateaubriand's birthplace in 1768, and **Chateaubriand's Tomb** of flagstone surmounted by a heavy granite cross, on the desolate island of **Grand Bé,** which can be reached by a short causeway.

**SAINT-MIHIEL,** *via N-401, N-64, and N-407 in Lorraine*

Founded as a Benedictine abbey in 709, this ancient town on the Meuse River was the scene of an important Allied victory in World War I. In September, 1914, the Germans captured Saint-Mihiel and installed a bridgehead, thus establishing the tip of their famous "salient," or outward projection of their line of defense. For the next four years the salient prevented the French army at Verdun (*see also*) from using the vital rail link from Nancy across the valley of the Meuse; instead all reinforcements and materiel had to be sent to Verdun by convoy on the route, beginning at Bar-le-Duc, known as **La Voie Sacrée.** On September 12, 1918, the United States First Army, commanded by General John J. Pershing, along with French forces—some 665,000 soldiers in all—launched a brilliant offensive against the Germans under General Fuchs, and by the next day succeeded in eliminating the salient. Today an **American Memorial** stands atop nearby Montsec, commemorating 7,000 American casualties. Twenty-four kilometers northeast is the **Saint-Mihiel American Cemetery.**

**SAINT-RAPHAËL,** *via N-98 on the Riviera*

A fashionable holiday resort in Gallo-Roman times, Saint-Raphaël was placed under the protection of the Knights Templars in the 12th century. In 1308 the Knights of Malta took over the defense of Saint-Raphaël. On October 9, 1799, Napoleon and his army, returning victorious from Egypt, disembarked here amidst great fanfare. A **Pyramid** on the Avenue Commandant Guilbaud commemorates the event. Napoleon again visited the town on April 28, 1814, when, escorted by English, Prussian, Austrian, and Russian generals, the defeated emperor was put on a frigate bound for Elba. Preserved today is the 12th-century Romanesque **Church of the Templars,** which, with its watch tower, was erected to serve also as a fortress and place of refuge in case of attack by pirates; in front, a **Milestone of the Aurelian Way** stands where it had been placed in the time of Emperor Augustus.

**SEDAN,** *via N-64 and N-77 in Alsace*

Situated at the foot of the Ardennes on the River Meuse, this town was the scene of the decisive battle of the Franco-Prussian War; here on September 2, 1870, the French army under Napoleon III capitulated to the numerically superior German forces. Sedan was occupied by Germans during World War I and was retaken by the A.E.F. on the very morning of Armistice Day (*see also Compiègne*). In May, 1940, Sedan gave its name to the sad World War II battle in which the German advance once more broke through and entered France. Damaged during the war, much of Sedan has been rebuilt. The 15th-century **Chateau-Fort** still stands. A **Memorial** in nearby Bazeilles honors those killed in the Franco-Prussian War.

**SENS,** *via N-5, N-439, and N-60 in Burgundy*

This town was named after the Senones, one of the most powerful tribes of Gaul, who in 390 B.C. invaded Italy and captured Rome. An important religious center since early Christian times, Sens was the scene of the church council that condemned the theologian Peter Abelard for heresy in 1140; it was the residence of Pope Alexander III from 1163 to 1164. Standing in the center of town is the imposing **Cathedral of Saint Étienne,** begun in 1140, which is one of the first of France's great Gothic cathedrals and served as the model for England's Canterbury Cathedral. It contains the relics of

*The great Cathedral of Notre Dame soaring over the rooftops of Strasbourg*

Saint Thomas à Becket, a native of the region, and a treasury filled with liturgical vestments, ivories, tapestries, enamels, and gold.

**SOISSONS,** *via N-31, N-37, and N-2 on the River Aisne in Île-de-France*

This town was the ancient capital of the Celtic tribe of Suessiones, who were conquered by Caesar in the first century B.C. In A.D. 486 Clovis defeated the Romans at Soissons, which subsequently became the capital of the west Franks. At Soissons in 752 Frankish magnates elected Pepin the Short, mayor of Neustria, king. In 923 Charles the Simple ceded his west Frankish kingdom to the house of France and the future Capetian dynasty. Over the centuries Soissons served as an outpost on the invasion route to Paris and was frequently attacked. Near the front lines throughout World War I, Soissons was twice occupied by the Germans (it was the south end of the Hindenberg Line), who destroyed many of its monuments, since restored. Still standing are the **Cathedral of Saint Gervais and Saint Protais,** an outstanding example of Gothic architecture, and the **Abbey of Saint Jean-des-Vignes,** where Thomas à Becket lived for several years.

**STRASBOURG,** *via N-63, N-68, N-4, and N-392 at the confluence of the Rhine and Ill rivers in Alsace*

Situated at the ancient crossroads where the route along the Rhine Valley crossed the route from southern Germany to Gaul, this settlement, dating from pre-Celtic times, has over the centuries been destroyed, burned, sacked, and rebuilt. By the sixth century the town was called Strateburgum, the city of roads. In 1003 Strasbourg became the seat of a bishopric; by 1262 it had won the status of a free city within the German Empire and subsequently became a center of literary activity. Here Johann Gutenberg developed the printing press between 1436 and 1444. In 1681 Louis XIV was recognized as sovereign and protector by the Strasbourgians. In 1771 Goethe received his doctorate at **Strasbourg University.** After the Revolution Strasbourg became increasingly French. Here in 1867 a chef named Close invented the goose-liver paté that became world famous. In 1870 Strasbourg capitulated to the Germans after a 50-day siege; the city was restored to France in 1918. During World War II Strasbourg was occupied by German troops from 1940 to 1944. Today the most celebrated structure in the city is the **Cathedral of Notre Dame,** begun in 1176 and completed in the 14th century, a masterpiece of Gothic architecture.

**TARASCON,** *via N-570 in Provence*

Originally a commercial outpost of Massalia (*see Marseilles*), this settlement was taken over by the Romans, who erected a fortress here. Tradition has it that about A.D. 40 Saint Martha, the sister of Mary Magdalene, came here from Saintes-Maries-de-la-Mer and subdued a monster known as the Tarasque, which would periodically emerge from the Rhone and devour the inhabitants. Martha's body was allegedly unearthed here in 1187, and ten years later the **Church of Saint Martha** was consecrated. Saint Martha's tomb is now in the crypt. In the 15th century, to commemorate the saint's conquest of the monster, King René of Provence instituted a festival, which is still celebrated. Dominating Tarascon is its **Chateau,** begun in the 14th century on the remains of a Roman edifice and completed by King René; it served as a prison for several centuries.

**TOULON,** *via N-97, D-42, N-8, and A-52 on the Riviera*

Known in Roman times for its manufacture of imperial purple dye from conch shells, this town assumed its great naval importance in 1589, when the **Vieille Darse** (Old Port) was begun by the governor of Provence. In the 17th century Richelieu had an arsenal constructed, and from 1680 to 1700 Vauban fortified the town and had the **Darse Neuve** (New Port) built. Galleys, which were manned by criminals and political and religious prisoners in the 17th and early 18th centuries, were abolished in 1748 and replaced by naval prisons. After the Revolution, in 1793, the Royalists handed Toulon over to an English-Spanish fleet; after a prolonged blockade in which a young battalion commander, Napoleon Bonaparte, took part, Toulon surrendered to the French republican army. During World War II Toulon suffered damage from aerial bombardments; the French navy scuttled 60 ships in the harbor in 1942 to keep them from the Nazis. In 1944, when the Allies invaded southern France, Toulon was taken within a week, and today it is France's foremost naval base. The Old Town contains the **Cathedral of Sainte Marie Majeure,** begun in the 11th century, and the **Poissonnerie** (fish market), erected in 1549.

**TOULOUSE,** *via N-20, N-88, N-621, N-113, N-632, and N-124 in the Pyrenees*

Founded before Rome, this town under the Romans became the cultural center of the Narbonne district. Christianity was introduced here by Saint Sernin, who became first bishop of Toulouse and in 257 was martyred by being tied to the tail of a wild bull. In the fifth century the city became a Visigoth capital. Between the 9th and 13th centuries Toulouse reached the height of its influence and glory under the dynasty of the Counts Raymond. In the 12th century Toulouse—a center of the Albigenses, a heretical sect—was captured by northern armies under Simon de Montfort (*see also Béziers*). Peace was restored to the area with the 1229 Treaty of Paris; the same year Count Raymond founded a university at Toulouse that became a stronghold of orthodoxy, and upon the death of his daughter in 1271, the county became the royal province of Languedoc and a center for troubadours and southern French literature. In 1632 Henri II de Montmorency, governor of Languedoc, instigated a rebellion against Louis XIII and was defeated and executed. And in 1814 the duke of Wellington fought his last battle here on April 10 and forced the French to abandon the town. Principal sights today include the **Basilica of Saint Sernin,** which, begun about 1075 and completed about 1096, is the largest and most perfect example of the Romanesque style in France; the 18th-century **Capitole,** where the duc de Montmorency was guillotined; and the **Cathedral of Saint Étienne,** built from the 11th to the 17th centuries.

**TOURS,** *via N-158, N-10, N-152, and N-751 in the Loire Valley*
An early center of Christianity, Tours is the town associated with Saint Martin, who became bishop in 370 and whose missionary activities made him famous throughout Europe. After his death in 397, the saint's tomb became a popular pilgrims' shrine, and in 470 a basilica was erected above the sarcophagus. Gregory of Tours, France's first historian, added an abbey, which grew up around the basilica in 573. At Tours in 732 Charles Martel won a great victory over the Moslems, which stopped their advance in the West (*see also Poitiers*). Between the 9th and 14th centuries Tours was torn by Norman invasions and was fought over by the rival counts of Blois and Anjou. A descendant of the latter, Henry II (Plantagenet) of England, made the town an English fief in the 12th century. Tours again became part of France in 1204, and it entered its peak period of prosperity in the 15th and 16th centuries after King Louis XI introduced silk manufacturing. The city was again a center of strife during the wars of religion late in the 1500s. Today all that remains of the **Ancienne Basilique Saint-Martin** is the ruins of the **Tour Charlemagne.** The body of the saint is buried in the **New Basilica.** Other sights include the picturesque **Old Town** and the **Cathédrale Saint Gatien,** built between 1220 and 1547, which contains magnificent stained-glass windows.

**TROYES,** *via N-60, N-77, N-19, and N-71 on the Seine in Burgundy*
This former Gallic capital and Roman stronghold was an important center of Christianity from the fourth century on. In 451 its illustrious bishop, Saint Lupus, to save Troyes from the Huns, offered himself as hostage to Attila; the chieftain was so impressed that he spared the town. In the tenth century Troyes became the capital of the counts of Champagne, under whom the city was enriched and embellished. The fairs of Troyes, founded by Count Thibaut IV, became famous throughout Europe. During the Hundred Years' War, in 1420, Isabella of Bavaria, wife of the mad king Charles VI, sided with the Burgundians and English and signed the Treaty of Troyes, disinheriting the dauphin, Charles VII, and handing France over to the English king, Henry V. The English occupied Troyes until 1429, when the town surrendered to Joan of Arc, who passed through there on the way to Charles VII's coronation at Reims (*see*). During the wars of religion late in the 1500s, Troyes was held by the Catholic League. Preserved today are the **Cathedral of Saint Peter and Saint Paul,** begun in 1208 and completed in 1638, the **Church of Saint Urbain,** built from 1262 to 1286 and one of the masterpieces of the Champagne region, and the 13th-century **Church of Saint Jean,** where the marriage of Isabella of Bavaria's

daughter, Catherine of France, to Henry V of England took place in 1420.

**VALENCE,** *via A-7, N-7, N-92, N-538a, and N-533 in the Rhone Valley*
Established by the Romans in 123 B.C. and called Valentia Julia, this ancient town in 1493 became the capital of the duchy of Valentinois, founded by Louis XII. The famous French satirist François Rabelais attended the university here, which opened in 1542 and was closed in 1793. Napoleon studied at the local school of artillery at Valence from 1785 to 1791 and lived at **No. 48 Grand Rue.** The town was damaged by bombs in 1944. Sights of interest include the 11th-century **Cathedral of Saint Apollinaire,** which contains a marble monument of Pope Pius VI, who died in exile here in 1700; the former **Bishop's Palace,** now a museum; and the **Pendentif,** an unusual square structure built in 1548 to commemorate a local family.

**VANNES,** *via N-165 or N-167 at the head of the Gulf of Morbihan in Brittany*
At a historic meeting held at Vannes in 1532, the duchy of Brittany was permanently united with the kingdom of France. Earlier in the ninth century the duchy of Brittany had been established by Nominoe, the count of Vannes. Preserved today are the **Place Henri IV,** with its 16th-century houses, **Saint Peter's Cathedral,** and the **ramparts,** erected between the 13th and 17th centuries.

**VARENNES-EN-ARGONNE,** *via D-38 in Lorraine*
This little village on the banks of the Aire River was the scene of the arrest of Louis XVI on June 22, 1791. The king and his family, who were attempting to escape from France in disguise, were recognized on June 21 at Sainte-Menehould by Jean Drouet, who crossed the **Forest of Argonne** and warned the townspeople of Varennes. Assisted by four National Guards and a few others, Drouet stopped the coach near the site of the present **Tour de l'Horloge** and took the royal family into custody. The king's hopes of deliverance by loyalist troops were shattered by the energetic vigilance of the citizens of Varennes and the National Guard. The following day orders came from Paris to arrest the king. Today the Tour de l'Horloge contains a Louis XVI museum, with documents pertaining to his flight. Here also is the **Pennsylvania Monument,** erected in 1927 to commemorate American soldiers who recaptured the town from the Germans on September 26, 1918, the first day of the Meuse-Argonne offensive, which ended on Armistice Day.

**VERDUN,** *via N-64, N-18, and N-3 in Lorraine*
Situated at a strategic point on the Meuse River, Verdun was the site of successive fortresses under the Gauls and Romans. In 843 the Treaty of Verdun was concluded here, which divided Charlemagne's empire between his three grandsons into France, Germany, and Lorraine; Verdun formed part of the last until it was annexed to France in 1648. After the Franco-Prussian War, it became France's most powerful fortress. In 1916 Verdun was the scene of World War I's longest (February 21–December 18) and bloodiest battle: France lost half a million men, and Germany upward of 400,000. The heroic defenders, led by Generals Henri Pétain and Robert Nivelle, withstood massive German artillery barrages. Fierce fighting raged around **Forts Douaumont and Vaux, Hill 304,** and **Le Mort Homme.** Today these battlefield sites among others—**La Voie Sacrée** (the supply route from Bar-le-Duc), the

vast **French Military Cemetery,** and the **Victory Monument** (erected in 1929)—are visited as national shrines. Although much of the town was left in ruins, surviving today are the Romanesque **Cathedral of Notre Dame,** consecrated in 1147, the **Porte Chaussée,** the old town gate, and the 17th-century **Citadel** built by Vauban.

**VERSAILLES (PALAIS DE),** *via N-10, N-184, N-838, and A-13 in Île-de-France*
This palace is a monument to the French monarchy at the height of its power and prestige. In 1661 Louis XIV engaged the leading architects, designers, and engineers of the time—including the creators of Vaux-le-Vicomte (*see Melun*)—to build a magnificent chateau on the site of a former hunting lodge of Louis XIII's. Over he next 50 years the king closely supervised the draining of the marshes, laying out of gardens, and construction of buildings. In 1682 his court of 20,000 persons moved into Versailles, where the social life was soon ordered by a rigorous code of etiquette. Louis XV and Louis XVI also resided at Versailles. On October 5, 1789, a Paris mob removed the latter from the palace. During the Revolution Versailles was stripped of furniture and threatened with demolition. Louis Philippe spent 23 million francs of his own fortune to restore the palace and convert it into a museum dedicated to "all the glories of France." The **Hall of Mirrors,** on January 18, 1877, witnessed the proclamation of the German Empire, and on June 28, 1919, was the scene of the signing of the Treaty of Versailles, ending World War I. Principal exterior sights include the **Royal Stables, Marble Court,** 744-yard-long park façade, and 250 acres of symmetrical gardens. Interior features include the **Opera, Chapel, State Apartments,** and **Royal Suites.** Other structures on the premises are the **Grand Trianon,** erected in 1687 for Louis XIV's mistress, Mme. de Maintenon, and the **Petit Trianon,** raised in 1766 for Louis XV, who frequented the place with Mme. du Barry.

**VÉZELAY,** *via N-157 in Burgundy*
Founded on a hilltop in the mid-ninth century by Girart de Rous-

*At Verdun, the grim trench of bayonets at Fort Douaumont*

sillon, count of Burgundy and legendary hero of medieval epic, the Abbey of Vézelay was consecrated in 878 by Pope John VIII. The abbey was at the peak of its prestige in 1146 when Saint Bernard, abbot of Clairvaux, preached the Second Crusade before King Louis VII, arousing widespread enthusiasm. In 1190 King Philip Augustus of France met King Richard the Lion-Hearted of England at Vézelay before departing on the Third Crusade. During the 13th century King Louis IX (Saint Louis) made several pilgrimages to Vézelay, and Saint Francis of Assisi established the first of his Minorite monasteries in France here. The present Basilica of Saint Madeleine, erected between 1120 and 1215 on the site of an earlier Carolingian church, was restored by Viollet-le-Duc in the 19th century.

### VICHY, via N-106, N-493, and N-9a in Auvergne

This famous health resort, with its thermal alkaline springs, was known to the Romans, who came here to cure liver, stomach, and other internal maladies. Vichy's modern prosperity as a spa dates from the time of Henry IV. From 1940 to 1944, after France concluded an armistice with Germany, Vichy was the seat of the German-controlled French government, headed first by Marshal Henri Pétain, the World War I hero of Verdun (see), and later by Pierre Laval.

### VIENNE, via A-7, N-7, N-502, N-538, and N-86 in the Rhone Valley

First conquered by the Romans in 122 B.C., this site became the capital of a province under Emperor Constantine. Vienne had a church by A.D. 177 and had become a bishopric by 250. The town served as capital of Burgundy from 413 to 534 and from 879 to 933. Pope Clement V presided over a great council at Vienne in 1311–12, which suppressed the Knights Templars. Vienne became part of France in 1450. Today Roman remains include the Temple of Augustus and Livia, erected in A.D. 25, an Arch, Theater, section of a road, and the Aiguille, a 52-foot-high obelisk that was part of a Roman circus. Other sites include the 13th–16th-century Church of Saint Maurice and the Church of Saint Pierre, raised between the sixth and tenth centuries, which now houses a museum.

### VINCENNES (CHÂTEAU DE), via N-4 and N-34 in Île-de-France

This fortified castle, built by the Valois monarchs on the site of a manor erected by Saint Louis in the 1200s, contains one of the most forbidding dungeons in France. Henry V of England, the victor at Agincourt (see), died here in 1422. In 1652 the architect Louis Le Vau added pavilions on either side of a court of honor for Jules Mazarin, governor of Vincennes. After the time of Louis XIV the castle served as a prison and an arsenal. A column at the foot of the keep commemorates the duke of Enghien, who was accused of plotting against Napoleon and executed here in 1804.

### VITRÉ, via N-157 or N-178, overlooking the valley of the Vilaine in Brittany

Flourishing from the 16th to the 18th centuries as a renowned center for textile manufacturing, Vitré is today the best preserved ancient town in Brittany. Sights include the restored Castle, the ramparts, the Flamboyant Gothic Church of Our Lady, and the Faubourg du Rachapt, a suburb occupied by the English during the Hundred Years' War and repurchased from the invaders by the citizens of Vitré. The nearby chateau of Les Rochers was the home of the 17th-century author Mme. de Sevigné.

MONACO

Situated on a headland overlooking the Mediterranean that was familiar to the ancient Phoenicians, Greeks, and Romans, this sovereign state of 8 square miles and its turbulent history are inextricably linked to the fortunes of the Grimaldi dynasty. Some conjecture that the Grimaldis trace their ancestry to a nephew of Charles Martel in the eighth century, while others believe that the family originated in Genoa. Genoese sailors settled in Monaco in the 13th century and sold their domain in 1408 to a Grimaldi, who established a line of rulers that still reign and whose name has been carried on the Monaco coat of arms ever since. From 1524 until 1641 Monaco passed under the protection of Spain, whose king bestowed the title of prince on the ruling Grimaldi. During this period Prince Jean I was assassinated by his brother, who was in turn murdered by his nephew; and in 1604 Prince Honoré I was thrown into the sea by his subjects. The principality remained under French guardianship from 1641 to 1814. During the Revolution, in 1793, Monaco, then known as Fort Hercule, was united with the county of Nice to form the French department of Alpes-Maritimes, but in 1814 after Napoleon's defeat the Allies placed Monaco under the protection of the kingdom of Sardinia—which lasted until 1861—and restored Honoré V as prince. In the last century three of Monaco's princes have served in the French military: Albert was an officer in the navy in 1870; Louis was a colonel in the First Regiment of the Foreign Legion in 1914; and the current ruler, Rainier, was a captain in World War II. Today the principality consists of three adjacent towns. **Monaco,** the old town and capital, occupies the summit of a sheer-sided, 200-foot-high rock jutting half a mile into the sea. The **Place du Palais** in the center of town boasts 16 bronze cannon donated to the prince by Louis XIV. Facing the square is the imposing **Palais du Prince,** whose oldest portions—including a crenelated Moorish tower—date from the 13th century and which contains a wing in the Italian Renaissance style. Inside are arcaded galleries enclosing a court of honor, a 17th-century palatine chapel, a throne room, and apartments. Erected between 1876 and 1893, the Romanesque-style **Cathedral** houses the tombs of Monaco's princes and bishops in its crypts. **Condamine,** the commercial town in the area of the harbor, is the site of the **Church of Devoté,** which was restored on its ancient foundations in the 19th century. According to local tradition, in the third century Saint Devoté was martyred in Corsica; the ship transporting his body to Africa was caught in a tremendous storm and was guided by a dove to this point on the French coast. During the Middle Ages the relics of Monaco's patron saint were stolen and spirited away in a ship, but the thieves were caught and the ship burned. This event is commemorated in a ceremony every January 26, when a ship is burned in front of the church. A **Statue of Prince Albert I** (1889–1922), who gained fame as an oceanographer, stands next to the marine museum that he founded. The new town of **Monte Carlo,** at the northern end of the principality, is famous for its **Casino.** In 1856 the prince of Monaco authorized the opening of a gambling house to raise revenues, and in 1862 a building for that purpose was opened on an isolated strip at Monte Carlo. Under the able management of M. Blanc, former director of the casino at Bad Homburg, Monte Carlo became a resort of the fashionable and rich, studded with sumptuous dwellings. The present casino, erected in 1878 by Charles Garnier, designer of the Paris Opéra (*see*), and completed in 1910, contains a fine opera house in addition to its gaming tables.

*Top: aerial view of the Principality of Monaco. Left: statue of Prince Albert I. Right: the casino at Monte Carlo. Below: the Palais du Prince*

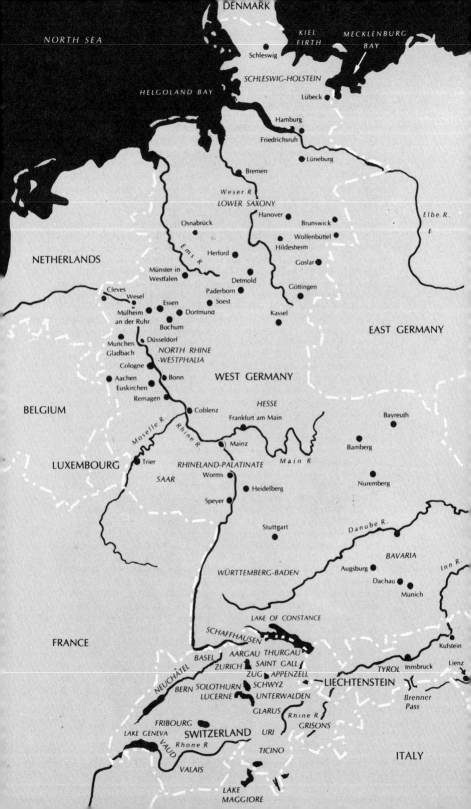

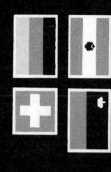

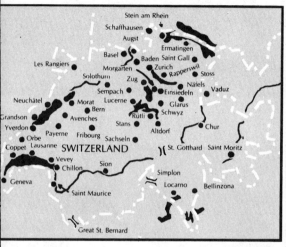

# *along the* RHINE & DANUBE

## AUSTRIA
## GERMANY
## LIECHTENSTEIN
## SWITZERLAND

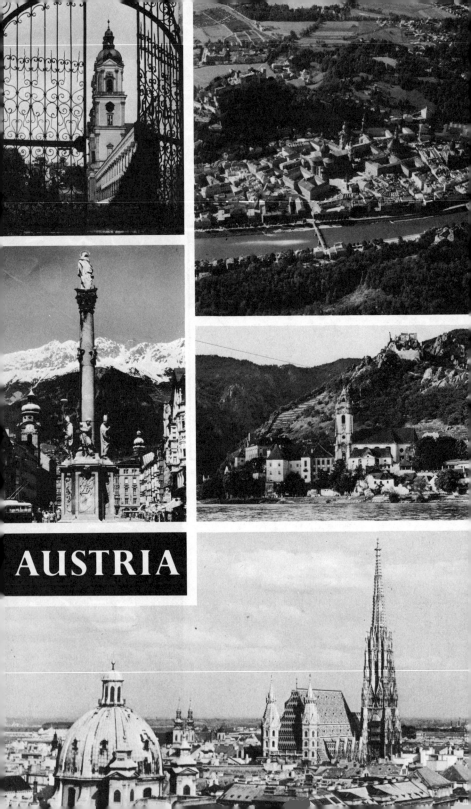

AUSTRIA

**BAD ISCHL,** *on Route 145 on the Traun River in Upper Austria*
One of the most fashionable watering places on the Continent during the long reign (1848–1916) of Emperor Francis Joseph I, Bad Ischl has been known since about 1820 for its curative sulfur and saline springs. The emperor's summer residence, the **Kaiservilla**, is situated in the **Kaiserpark**, a magnificent landscaped garden north of town. The Biedermeier-style villa was given to Francis Joseph and his wife, Empress Elizabeth, as a wedding gift by the emperor's mother, Archduchess Sophia. Elizabeth's **Gray Salon** remains exactly as she left it on July 16, 1898, on the eve of her departure for Geneva, where she was assassinated. The empress used **Marmorschlössel** ( now the Cottage Café), a small marble chateau located in the park, as a retreat. Among the nobility and intellectuals who frequented Bad Ischl during Francis Joseph's day were the composers Anton Bruckner, Johann Strauss, and Franz Lehár, whose villa is now a museum. The **Seeauer House** (now the Hotel Austria) on the **Esplanade** was the birthplace in 1832 of the ill-fated Maximilian, emperor of Mexico.

**BRAUNAU,** *on Routes 141 and 157 on the Inn River in Upper Austria*
This frontier town, which still has a quaint medieval **Old Quarter**, was the birthplace in 1889 of Adolf Hitler. A bridge over the Inn connects Braunau with the German town of Simbach am Inn.

**DEUTSCH WAGRAM,** *on Route 8 in Lower Austria*
The Battle of Wagram, fought here on July 5–6, 1809, resulted in Napoleon's decisive victory over the Austrians. Six days later Austria was forced to sue for peace, and by the humiliating Treaty of Schönbrunn, signed October 14, 1809, it lost 32,000 square miles.

**DÜRNSTEIN,** *on Route 29 on the north bank of the Danube in Lower Austria*
In 1192–93 Richard the Lion-Hearted, king of England, was imprisoned in the 12th-century **Castle of Dürnstein,** now in ruins. Richard was returning from the Third Crusade to the Holy Land when he was captured at Erdberg, once a village near Vienna, by Duke Leopold VI (the Glorious) of Austria, his bitter enemy on the crusade. It was here that his faithful minstrel Blondel de Nesle is said to have discovered him in the spring of 1193. But Richard was turned over to Holy Roman Emperor Henry VI and imprisoned in the imperial castle of Trifels in the Rhineland palatinate, where he remained for nearly a year before his liberty was secured for a huge ransom. On the **Hauptstrasse** is the early-17th-century **Schloss** of Count von Starhemberg. The **Pfarrkirche** (parish church) was once part of a 15th-century Augustinian monastery rebuilt in the 18th century in the baroque style. A museum of local history is housed in the mid-14th-century **Church of the Poor Clares.**

**EISENSTADT,** *on Route 50 in Burgenland*
Eisenstadt was a favorite residence of the Esterházys, a great Hungarian family who claimed to be descended from Attila and played a major role in establishing the Hapsburgs' rule in Hungary. The **Schloss Esterházy,** originally built in the 17th century on the site of an old fortress by Prince Pál Esterházy, was modified in the classical style between 1797 and 1805. Eisenstadt is also inseparably linked with the name of Joseph Haydn (1732–1809), who first came here in 1761. For the next thirty years he lived at Eisenstadt and sometimes at another Esterházy palace near Neusiedler Lake. Today the Schloss Esterházy is partly occupied by admini-

*Top left: the abbey in Markt Sankt Florian. Right: aerial view of Salzburg. Center left: Saint Anne's Column in Innsbruck. Right: Castle of Dürnstein on the Danube. Below: Saint Stephen's Cathedral in Vienna*

strative offices, but one can visit its famous **Haydn-Saal** (Haydn Room), where nearly every evening Haydn conducted the orchestra of the princely court, often performing his own work. On the far side of the palace park are the former **Royal Stables**, dating from 1743 and now containing valuable old carriages. On the **Haydn-gasse** is the modest house where Haydn lived from 1766 to 1778; a small **Museum** contains mementos of the great composer. The early-18th-century **Church of the Calvary** contains Haydn's tomb, and the **Franciscan Monastery** houses the Esterházy family vault.

**ENNS,** *on Route 1 on the Enns River in Upper Austria*
Enns was the site of the Roman camp of Laureacum, established by Marcus Aurelius in the second century. Here Saint Florian, the patron saint of Upper Austria, suffered martyrdom under Diocletian about A.D. 304. The municipal charter granted Enns in 1212 by Duke Leopold the Glorious is the oldest in Austria. Visitors can see the early Gothic **Parish Church**, remains of the medieval town walls, and the **Stadtturm** (city tower), which stands in the **Main Square,** surrounded by old arcaded houses. The former **Rathaus** contains the **Municipal Museum.**

**FELDBACH VICINITY**
 **RIEGERSBURG,** *northeast of Route 50 in Styria*
Proudly situated nearly 650 feet above the Grazbach Valley, Riegersburg has since Celtic and Roman times been a stronghold guarding Austria's eastern frontiers. The 13th-century **Castle,** reinforced in the 17th century, has successfully withstood attacks by the Hungarians and the Turks. In 1945 Riegersburg was the site of violent fighting between the Russians and the Germans. On an esplanade below the castle is a **War Memorial** to the numerous men from the district who fell in the desperate fighting.

**GRAZ,** *on Routes 67, E-93, 65, and 70 on the Mur River in Styria*
The capital of Styria, Graz developed from a small medieval fishing village. From late in the 15th century until 1683, when the Turkish threat hung over the whole province, a large arsenal of weapons was built up here. In 1642 the **Zeughaus** (arsenal) was constructed next to the Renaissance-style **Landhaus** (diet), built 1557–65. The four-story Zeughaus still contains more than 15,000 weapons, including several sets of 16th-century armor. The **Schloss-berg,** a hill overlooking the town, was a heavily fortified area until the Napoleonic Wars. During the campaign of 1809 Graz was occupied by French troops, and the redoubts and fortifications on the hill were dismantled. During the 19th century Archduke John decided to make his home at Graz, and in 1811 he established here the **Joanneum Landesmuseum,** Austria's first provincial museum. The **Styrian Folklore Museum** is housed in a former Capuchin monastery. The **Cathedral,** built in the 15th century by Emperor Frederick III, contains the tomb of Emperor Ferdinand II.

**HALLSTATT,** *on Route 166 on the west shore of the Lake of Hallstatt in Upper Austria*
Nestled on a steep slope of a foothill of the Dachstein, this village takes its name from the lake into which the slope dips. From about 1000 to 500 B.C. a prehistoric civilization of Celtic origin, characterized by the use of bronze and iron, flourished here. This epoch of the Iron Age has been named the Hallstatt Period because of archaeological discoveries made here. Salt has been mined in the

mountains around Hallstatt since Neolithic times, and numerous traces of early human activity have been unearthed, notably in the **Hallstätter Salzberg,** a salt mine where more than 1,000 Celtic tombs have been explored. Many of the finds are on view at the local museum in Hallstatt, at Linz (*see*), and at Vienna's Natural History Museum. The 15th-century **Parish Church** is romantically situated on the lake shore, and next to it is the **Chapel of Saint Michael,** a two-story Gothic structure dating from about 1300 and still used as the parish charnel house.

**INNSBRUCK,** *on Routes E-17, 1, E-6, and 185 on the Inn River in the Tyrol*
The cultural and tourist capital of the Tyrol, Innsbruck first gained significance in the 15th century when it became the seat of the dukes of Tyrol and later of Emperors Maximilian I and Ferdinand I. In 1494 Maximilian was married to his second wife, Bíanca Maria Sforza, in the parish church of Saint James, which since its rebuilding in the 18th century has been **Saint James's Cathedral.** Soon after his wedding, Maximilian built onto **Fürstenburg Castle** the famous **Goldenes Dachl** (little golden roof) of gilded copper, a cover for the spectators' balcony where members of the court watched tournaments and other amusements. During the reign of Maria Theresa Innsbruck experienced another brilliant period. In 1765, while the imperial family was celebrating the marriage of Leopold, grand duke of Tuscany, and Maria Ludovica, the infanta of Spain, Emperor Francis I, Maria Theresa's husband, died suddenly. The **Triumphal Arch,** erected at this time, commemorates both the royal marriage and the royal death. Francis died at the **Hofburg,** a baroque palace built by Maria Theresa on the site of an earlier Hapsburg residence. The decorations of the **State Rooms,** which may be visited, are devoted to the glories of the Tyrol and of the Hapsburg monarchy. The **Hofkirche,** originally a Gothic structure, is masked in part by Renaissance and baroque additions. It contains the ornate **Mausoleum** of Maximilian I, who planned to be buried here but was actually interred at Wiener Neustadt (*see*). The Hofkirche's **Silver Chapel** was built by Archduke Ferdinand (1529–95), regent of the Tyrol, so that he might rest with his beloved first wife, Philippine Welser, who was a commoner. **Annasäule** (Saint Anne's Column) was erected in 1706 to commemorate the retreat of Bavarian invaders on July 26 (the birthday of Saint Anne), 1703, during the War of the Spanish Succession. The **Bergisel,** a wooded hill (now laid out as a park) on the outskirts of town, was the site of several major battles during the Tyrolean war of liberation in 1809, when the French, allied with Bavaria and Saxony, attacked Innsbruck. The park contains a **Memorial to Andreas Hofer,** who defended Innsbruck against the invaders and is buried in the Hofkirche.

**KLAGENFURT,** *on Routes E-7, 17, 70, and E-94 in Carinthia*
The capital of Carinthia since 1518, Klagenfurt was a fortified town until 1809, when its walls were destroyed by the French during the Napoleonic Wars. The center of the old town is dominated by the **Alter Platz,** a square and wide street with many 16th-century baroque mansions. From here one can approach the **Landhaus,** completed in 1590 and originally used as an arsenal. Subsequently it served as the main government building of Carinthia, and today it houses the departments and assemblies of the regional government. The **Grosser Wappensaal,** a state hall on the first floor of the Landhaus, is decorated with 665 coats of arms of noblemen who sat

*Left: Geroldseck fortress in Kufstein. Right: Triumphal Arch in Innsbruck*

in the Parliament between 1590 and 1848. The **Landesmuseum** contains important 15th- and 16th-century religious art and exhibits of Celtic and Roman artifacts, some from the Roman town of Virunum, near Maria Saal (*see*).

**KUFSTEIN,** *on Route 175, off E-86, on the Inn River in the Tyrol*

The fortress of Kufstein, called **Geroldseck,** stands on a rocky height and with its massive round tower bears witness to the many centuries of enmity between Austria and Bavaria. Built about 1200 as a small medieval castle, Geroldseck was turned into a mighty stronghold early in the 16th century by Maximilian I. In 1703, during the War of the Spanish Succession, the fortress was taken by the Bavarians, and in 1809, during the Tyrolean war of liberation, in which the Tyrol was pitted against Bavaria and France, the Tyrolese unsuccessfully laid siege to it. Its **Bürgerturm** (burghers' tower) contains the **Heldenorgel,** a heroes' organ built to commemorate the German and Austrian dead of World War I; it was first played in 1931. Also in the castle are the local museum; the colossal **Kaiserturm** (emperor's tower), completed in 1522; as well as prison cells, bastions, and cellars. **Brunnen,** on the **Heldenhügel,** a former cavalry hill, is a memorial to Andreas Hofer, hero of the Tyrolean war of liberation.

**LEOBEN,** *on Routes 17 and E-7 on the Mur River in Styria*

A market town since medieval times, Leoben is famous as the site where Napoleon signed a peace treaty in 1797. After his victorious campaign through Italy in 1796, Bonaparte marched on Vienna through Carinthia and Styria. The French army arrived at Leoben on April 7, 1797, and was met by ambassadors of the Austrian emperor, who asked for an armistice. Napoleon, aware of his military strength, obtained the Low Countries and a frontier on the Rhine from Austria. Austria also gave up Lombardy, but it received Venezia, Illyria, and Istria. This agreement between France and Austria was formalized by the Treaty of Campo Formio, signed October 16, 1797.

**LIENZ,** *on Routes 100, 108, and 107A in the Tyrol*

The chief town in the eastern Tyrol, Lienz is dominated by **Schloss Bruck,** a fortified castle that was the seat of the counts of Gorizia until 1500, when it passed to the Hapsburgs. The *schloss* now contains the **Regional Museum of the East Tyrol.** About 4 kilometers east of town is **Aguntum,** originally an Illyrian settlement of the Hallstatt Period (*see Hallstatt*), later a thriving Roman agricultural and trading town, and still later a Christian settlement. Visitors can see the ancient town walls with gateways, houses with Roman heating installations, and many other Roman finds of the second and third centuries A.D.; there is also a cemetery with an early Christian burial church.

**LINZ,** *on Routes E-14, E-5, 129, and 125 on the Danube in Upper Austria*

As the Lentia of the Romans, Linz was an important transshipping point on the salt route between Hallstatt and Bohemia. In early medieval times the **Altstadt** (old town), on the south bank of the Danube, was the heart of Linz. The oldest section here is around the **Schloss** (15th and 16th centuries), now a museum devoted to the history and culture of Upper Austria. Above it is the **Martinkirche,** one the oldest churches in Austria, dating from the eighth century and reputed to have been built on Roman foundations by order of Charlemagne. The Altstadt bears the imprint of Renaissance architecture; a fine example is the **Landhaus,** a government building whose inner court is lined with arcades and contains a fountain commemorating the astronomer Johannes Kepler's residence at Linz from 1612 to 1626. The principal architectural style of the Altstadt, however, is baroque, visible in many of the town's churches and ecclesiastical buildings. Of particular note is the **Alter Dom,** also known as the Jesuit church, built in the second half of the 17th century, where Anton Bruckner served as organist for 12 years. The **Church of the Minorite Brothers** is a Gothic church founded by the Franciscans in the 13th century and remodeled in the rococo style in the 18th century. The baroque **Dreifaltigkeitsäule** (trinity column) was erected at the center of the **Hauptplatz** in 1723 to commemorate the town's escape from plague, fire, and invasion by the Turks. A magnificent view of Linz may be enjoyed from the **Pöstlingberg,** a hill on the north bank of the Danube.

**MARIA SAAL,** *on Route 17 in Carinthia*

One of the loveliest churches in Austria, the Gothic **Pilgrims' Church of Maria Saal** was constructed in the mid-15th century largely of ancient Roman stones; it stands on a hill in the middle of a fortified cemetery. The church complex, which includes several chapels, is the building nearest to the Roman city of **Virunum,** whose ruins are scattered over the Zollfeld, a plain between Klagenfurt and Sankt Veit (*see*) on which many Roman antiquities have been unearthed. Virunum, originally a Celtic settlement, was the capital of the Roman province of Noricum and later the seat of a Christian bishopric. Close to the excavations is the famous **Herzogstuhl,** a stone seat where until 1597 each new duke of Carinthia was awarded his fief. The objects found by archaeologists are on exhibit in the **Landesmuseum** at Klagenfurt (*see*).

**MARIAZELL AND VICINITY,** *on Route 23 in Styria*

The most frequented pilgrimage shrine in Austria, Mariazell was founded in 1157 by a small group of Benedictine monks from the Styrian abbey of Saint Lambrecht on land donated by the dukes of

Carinthia. About 1200 the Benedictines set up a holy statue of the Virgin Mary, carved out of limewood. In 1377 Louis I of Anjou, king of Hungary, won a victory over the Turks and attributed it to the Virgin of Mariazell. Subsequently the worship of the Madonna of Mariazell came to symbolize the spiritual force that guaranteed the solidity of the Austrian Empire. The Hapsburgs in particular venerated the shrine. The **Gnadenkirche**, as the present pilgrimage church is called, stands in a slightly elevated position on the **Hauptplatz**. It is a 14th-century Gothic church that was enlarged and altered in the baroque style in the 17th century. The miraculous Virgin is in the marble **Gnadenkapelle** (Chapel of Miracles). The town of Mariazell was severely damaged in World War II.

**MARKT SANKT FLORIAN,** *west of Enns off Route E-5 in Upper Austria*
This small market town is dominated by the **Abbey of Saint Florian,** built over the grave of Saint Florian, the administrator of the Roman province of Noricum, who was martyred at Enns (*see*) about A.D. 303 for refusing to sacrifice to the pagan gods. The abbey, which has been occupied since the 11th century by the Augustinians, was completely rebuilt in the baroque style in the 17th and 18th centuries. It is the largest abbey in Upper Austria and has long been an eminent cultural center. The **Stiftskirche,** completed in 1715, contains the tomb of Anton Bruckner, the composer of sacred music who was the abbey organist from 1848 to 1858 and who created some of his masterpieces while at Sankt Florian. The abbey tour also includes the **Kaiserzimmer,** the imperial apartments; the **Altdorfer Galerie,** containing works by Albrecht Altdorfer (1480–1538), a master of the Danubian school; the **Marmorsaal,** a marble hall honoring Prince Eugene of Savoy for the part he played in defending the Austrian Empire against the Turks (*see Vienna, Belvedere*); and the famous **Library,** with valuable early manuscripts and more than 125,000 books.

**MAUTHAUSEN,** *on Route 123 in Upper Austria*
Originally known for its granite quarries, which supplied most of the paving stones for Vienna, Mauthausen was the site of the Nazis' **Mauthausen Concentration Camp,** set up in one of the stone quarries after the incorporation of Austria into the German Reich in 1938. In 1949 the Austrian government declared the former camp a historic monument, and visitors may see the **Staircase of Death** and the huts and rooms where nearly 200,000 prisoners suffered and died between 1938 and 1945.

**MAYERLING,** *on Route 223 on the Schwechat River in Lower Austria*
Now a Carmelite convent of atonement, Mayerling was the hunting lodge of Crown Prince Rudolf, heir to the Austro-Hungarian Empire. On the night of January 30, 1889, the lodge was the scene of the death of Rudolf and his mistress, Baroness Marie Vetsera. The exact circumstances of the double death have never been explained, but it is thought that the lovers chose suicide rather than separation. Marie died first, and after writing letters to his mother and his wife, the young crown prince shot himself. The room in which he died has been turned into a chapel.

**MELK,** *on Route E-5 on the right bank of the Danube in Lower Austria*
Above the town of Melk, on top of a rocky bluff overlooking the Danube, stands the Benedictine **Abbey of Melk,** which is one of the finest baroque edifices in the world. Originally a Roman stronghold

and reputed to be the Medelike of the *Nibelungenlied,* Melk became the seat of the princely Babenberg family in the tenth century. Late in the 11th century Leopold III von Babenberg handed his castle at Melk over to the Benedictines, who converted it into a fortified abbey; it was gutted in the wake of the Turkish invasion of 1683 and was entirely rebuilt from 1702 onward. During his successful campaign against Austria in 1805–9, Napoleon established headquarters here. The **Emperors' Gallery, Marble Hall, Library, Terrace,** and **Abbey Church** should be visited.

**MILLSTATT,** *on Route 98 on the north shore of the Millstättersee in Carinthia*
The **Abbey** in the center of this summer resort town was successively a Benedictine monastery (1080–1469), a priory of the military order of Saint George (1469–1598), and a house of the Jesuits (1598–1773). The elegant 16th-century **Stiftshof,** or abbey courtyard, bears witness to the riches of the Knights of Saint George, whose order was founded by Emperor Frederick III to assist in the defense of Christendom against the heathen Turks. The main doorway and cloisters of the abbey church are among the glories of Romanesque art in Austria. Today most of the monastery buildings are occupied by the **Lindenhof,** a hotel belonging to the Austrian state.

**PERSENBEUG,** *on Route 123 on the Danube River in Upper Austria*
**Schloss Persenbeug** was the birthplace in 1887 of the last emperor of Austria, Charles I, who died in 1922.

**SALZBURG,** *on Routes 1, E-11, and E-14 on the Salzach River in Salzburg Province*
After its early beginnings as a Celtic and then a Roman settlement, Salzburg was made a church see shortly after A.D. 700 by Saint Rupert, and in the following century it was raised to an archbishopric. In the 13th century the bishops became princes of the Holy Roman Empire, with temporal power that extended into Italy. It was these rich prince-archbishops who over the centuries converted their little town of Salzburg into an Italianate city, with the luxurious palaces, churches, open squares, and maze of streets that characterize it today. The **Old Town** is clustered between the Salzach River and the **Hohensalzburg,** the former stronghold of the prince-archbishops, built on a rock some 400 feet above the river. The fortress, begun in the 11th century, was frequently enlarged and remodeled in later centuries. The **State Rooms** have been preserved, and the **Burgmuseum,** devoted to the history of the Salzburg archbishopric, has been installed in the castle. Below the Hohensalzburg in the **Petersfriedhof** (Saint Peter's Churchyard) are chapels containing the tombs of several generations of the patrician families of Salzburg. **Sankt Peterskirche** is a former triple-aisled Romanesque basilica, drastically remodeled in the 17th and 18th centuries in the baroque style. Romanesque arches (uncovered in 1957) on either side of the west door are the only traces of the 12th-century church. At the center of the Old Town is the huge **Dom**— a cathedral built early in the 17th century containing elements of both Italian Renaissance and baroque architecture—whose marble façade forms one end of the **Domplatz,** a fine square of great architectural beauty. In its center is the **Virgin's Column** (1771). The **Residenz,** which also abuts the Domplatz, is a complex of buildings begun in 1598 and enlarged in the ensuing centuries. It was a residence of the prince-archbishops and was the site of many historic meetings. In this palace Emperor Francis Joseph I received

Napoleon III in 1867 and the German emperor, Kaiser William I, in 1871. It was also here that Salzburg's most illustrious native son, young Mozart, gave many concerts for the guests of the prince-archbishops in the **Conference Hall.** On the east side of the square stands the famous **Glockenspiel,** a carillon of 35 bells cast in Antwerp and set up in Salzburg in 1705. The **Mozarts-Geburtshaus,** at 9 Getreidegasse, is the house where Wolfgang Amadeus Mozart was born on January 27, 1756. In the third-floor flat where he lived as a child, one can see the prodigy's violins, his spinet, and other memorabilia. One may also visit **No. 8 Marketplatz,** where the Mozart family lived from 1773 to 1787. Salzburg is filled with memorials to Mozart; in 1842 a statue was erected in his honor, and later a musical academy named the **Mozarteum** was established. In 1922 the first Mozart Festival was held, and since then each year during the month of August, about 30 lyric and dramatic performances and about 50 concerts have been held in Salzburg's various halls: the **Festspielhaus** (Festival Hall), the **Mozarteum,** the **Landestheater,** the **Mirabell Castle,** and the **Marionnette Theater.** Other highlights of historical Salzburg include the Romanesque and Gothic **Franciscans' Church,** consecrated in 1221; the baroque **Collegiate Church;** the **Rathaus;** the **Mirabell Gardens,** laid out early in the 18th century; the **Natural History Museum;** the **Saint Sebastian Cemetery,** with the tomb of the Renaissance alchemist Paracelsus, who died at Salzburg in 1541, as well as the tombs of Mozart's wife and father; and the **Nonnberg Convent,** a Benedictine nunnery founded by Saint Rupert.

**SANKT VEIT AN DER GLAN AND VICINITY,** *on Routes 17 and 94 in Carinthia*

Sankt Veit was the seat of the dukes of Carinthia until 1518, when Klagenfurt (*see*) became the regional capital. The nucleus of the town, clustered about the **Oberer Platz,** still retains much of its medieval character. The square contains several interesting structures: a traditional memorial column to the plague, erected in 1517; a fountain known as the **Schlüsselbrunnen,** whose basin is believed to have come from the forum of the Roman town of Virunum (*see Maria Saal*); the classical **Bezirkshauptmannschaft,** military headquarters, dating from 1780; and the **Rathaus,** a graceful municipal building with a baroque façade, a fine assembly hall, and the double-headed eagle of the Holy Roman Empire embossed on its pediment. The hills around Sankt Veit are rich in castles and ancient monasteries. These include **Hochosterwitz Castle,** with its 14 fortified gate-towers; **Schloss Fraunenstein,** a 16th-century fortified castle; and **Sankt Georgen,** once a Benedictine abbey for noble ladies. About 30 kilometers southeast of Sankt Veit is the **Magdalensberg,** a 3,471-foot-high mountain topped by a Gothic pilgrims' chapel. Near the base of the mountain are the **Ausgrabungen Excavations** of a Celto-Roman town inhabited during the first century B.C. by men who came to the area as traders. The so-called **House of Assembly** has been adapted as a museum.

**SPITTAL AN DER DRAU AND VICINITY,** *on Routes E-14 and 100 on the Drau River in Carinthia*

One of the main attractions of this pleasant tourist town is **Porcia Castle,** a cube-shaped structure built in the 16th century in the Italian Renaissance style; the **Regional Museum** is housed on its second floor. About 5 kilometers northwest of town are the **Teurnia Excavations,** the remains of the ancient Roman city of Teurnia,

which was Christianized in the fifth century A.D. and destroyed by
the Slavs about A.D. 590. Excavations have uncovered a Christian
cemetery church, whose south chancel contains a large mosaic done
about A.D. 500 with some designs representing animals, possibly
pagan or early Christian symbols.

## VIENNA AND VICINITY
### AM HOF, *off the Graben*

In the mid-12th century Henry II Jasomirgott, a Babenberg and the
first duke of Austria, moved his residence to Vienna and built a
castle, called Am Hof, on this site. On the southeast side of this huge
square is the **Jesuit Church** dedicated to the Nine Choirs of Angels,
built in the Gothic style by the Hapsburgs in the 14th century and
given an imposing baroque façade in the 17th century. In March,
1782, during a visit to Vienna, Pope Pius VI bestowed the apostolic
blessing on the people from the terrace of this church. In August,
1806, from this same balcony, the imperial commissioner an-
nounced the dissolution of the Germanic Constitution and the
renunciation by Francis II of Austria of the title of Holy Roman
Emperor. (Francis became Emperor Francis I of Austria.) In the
Am Hof students began the Revolution of 1848, which led to the
overthrow of Prince Metternich, and here in the same year a mob
hanged Count Latour, the minister of war.

### ASPERN AND ESSLING, *Grossenzersdorf district, on the north bank of the Danube*

These towns, now suburbs of Vienna, were the site of the Battle of
Aspern and Essling, fought May 21–22, 1809, in which the Austrians defeated the French and forced them to recross the Danube.
Earlier that month Napoleon had taken Vienna (May 13) and had
then crossed the island of Lobau, in the Danube (where traces of
Napoleon's encampments may still be seen). The French were subsequently routed at Aspern and Essling, but finally they defeated
the exhausted Austrians at Wagram (*see Deutsch Wagram*).

### AUGUSTINERKIRCHE, *on the Augustinerstrasse in Hofburg*

Built during the first half of the 14th century in the Gothic style,
this was the church of the Hapsburg court. Many marriages were
celebrated here, among the more famous that of Maria Theresa to
Francis of Lorraine (1736), and the marriages by proxy of the archduchess Marie Antoinette to the future Louis XVI of France, of
Marie Louise to Napoleon I (1810), and of Francis Joseph I to Elizabeth of Bavaria (1854). The church also contains the white marble
mausoleum of Maria Christina, the favorite daughter of Maria
Theresa. In the **Chapel of Saint George** are 54 urns containing
hearts of members of the Hapsburg family.

### BELVEDERE, *Rennweg 6a (Lower Belvedere) and Prinz-Eugen-Strasse 27 (Upper Belvedere)*

This magnificent baroque *schloss*, consisting of two separate structures with a large park between them, was built in the first quarter
of the 18th century as a summer residence for the great general
Prince Eugene of Savoy, a hero in the victory over the Turks of 1683.
From July to September of that year, Vienna was besieged by the
Turks. Finally, on September 10 Duke Charles of Lorraine arrived
with a relief force of some 80,000 Austrians, Poles, Saxons, Bavarians, Swabians, and Franconians. He camped on the **Kahlen-
berg,** a hill northwest of town, and the next day deployed his army

*In Vienna, from left to right: one of the gates of the Hofburg; Schloss Schön-*

in the **Vienna Woods.** On September 12 the Turks, caught between two fires, fled in panic; a long period of prosperity for the Austrian Empire ensued. It was from the Belvedere that Francis Ferdinand, heir to the Austrian throne, and his morganatic wife, Countess Sophie Chotek, set out in July, 1914, for their tour of the southern part of the Austrian Empire—the journey that was to end in their assassination at Sarajevo and the start of World War I. Today the **Lower Belvedere** is occupied by the **Museum of Austrian Medieval Art** and by the **Museum of Baroque Art.** The **Upper Belvedere,** which the prince used for his festivities, has been the Austrian Gallery for 19th and 20th century art since 1954. On May 15, 1955, the state treaty ending the Allied occupation of Austria was signed in its red marble hall.

DIANABAD, *Obere Donaustrasse 93*
    The Dianabad is the largest spa and bathing establishment in Austria. During the 19th century the interior was transformed into a ballroom during the winter, and here in 1867 the famous "Blue Danube Waltz" was played for the first time. The waltz, which was introduced to Vienna in the 1820s by Josef Lanner and Johann Strauss, Sr., reached its greatest popularity under Johann Strauss, Jr. (1825–99), who was known as the king of the waltz. A plaque on the wall of **No. 54 Praterstrasse** recalls the fact that the younger Strauss composed the "Blue Danube" while living here in 1867.

HAYDN-MUSEUM, *19 Haydngasse*
    The house where composer Joseph Haydn wrote some of his greatest works, notably *The Creation* and *The Seasons,* and where he died in 1809 has been turned into a Haydn memorial.

HEILIGENSTADT
    This district of Vienna is filled with memories of Ludwig van Beethoven (1770–1827). He wrote the *Pastoral Symphony* at **No. 2 on the Pfarrplatz,** a little 17th-century house (now a wine tavern); the *Eroica* at **92 Döblinger Hauptstrasse;** and in 1802 he wrote the famous letter entitled *The Testament of Heiligenstadt,* in which he laments his deafness, at **No. 6 Probusgasse.** There is a marble bust of the composer in the **Heiligenstadt Park.**

HOFBURG, *between Burgring and Michaelerplatz*
    A town within a town, the Hofburg was the imperial palace and

*brunn; the Johann Strauss Memorial in the Stadtpark; the Town Hall*

favorite residence of the Hapsburgs, who ruled Austria from 1273 to 1918. The huge, sprawling complex of buildings, which now house museums and government offices, was begun in the 13th century and continued to the early 20th century—the Hofburg is thus a compendium of architectural styles. The nucleus of the complex is the **Swiss Court,** bordered by the **Schatzkammer** (imperial treasury), which now houses the secular and liturgical treasures amassed by the Hapsburg dynasty, such as the solid silver cradle of the king of Rome. The **Burgkapelle** (castle chapel), also on the Swiss Court, was erected in the mid-15th century. Visitors should also see the **In der Burg,** a huge square with a monument to Emperor Francis II; the **Imperial Apartments,** which occupy parts of the **Chancellery** and the **Amalienhof;** the **Collection of Court Porcelain and Silver;** the **Spanish Riding School,** where the Lippizaner horses have been performing feats of *haute école* since the 18th century; the **Austrian National Library;** and the **Albertina,** one of the world's greatest collections of graphic art. The 17th-century baroque **Kapuzinerkirche,** with the **Capuchin Monastery** behind it, has been restored in the 19th and 20th centuries; at the left of the entrance is a **Statue of Marco d'Aviano,** the preacher who roused the people against the Turks in September, 1683 *(see Belvedere).* Beneath the church is the **Kaisergruft** (capuchins' crypt), the burial place of the Hapsburgs. The bare underground chambers contain the coffins of 12 emperors, 16 empresses, and more than 100 archdukes. Here one finds the double sarcophagus of Maria Theresa and her husband, Francis I, as well as the tombs of Marie Louise and of Francis Joseph, Empress Elizabeth, and their son Archduke Rudolf, who died at Mayerling *(see).* The Italian Renaissance **Neue Hofburg** (new castle), constructed between 1881 and 1908, contains numerous collections, including the **Ethnographic Museum** with Montezuma's treasure, which according to tradition was given to Cortes by the Aztec emperor himself.

## HOHER MARKT

The oldest square in Vienna stands on the site of the Roman camp, or *praetorium,* of Vindobona, built in the first century B.C. as an outpost against the barbarians. Vindobona began as a Celtic settlement in the fifth century B.C. This Celtic kingdom later allied itself with the Romans under Julius Caesar, and in 16 B.C. it was occupied by Emperor Augustus, who declared himself successor to the Celtic kings. In A.D. 180 Emperor Marcus Aurelius died at Vindobona, in a house on what is now **Marc Aurel-Strasse.** The Romans held the town until about 400, when a period of decline began. In the center of the Hoher Markt is the **Joseph Fountain,** in the late baroque style.

LEOPOLDSTADT, *between the Danube Canal and the Danube River*
This thickly populated quarter, whose main thoroughfares are the **Taborstrasse** and the **Praterstrasse,** was allotted to the Jews of Vienna in 1622. As early as Roman times Jewish merchants probably inhabited what is now Austria. In 1244 Duke Frederick II, the last of the Babenbergs, granted them protection of person, property, and religion and guaranteed them the right to practice usury. Subsequently the Jews played a major role in Austria's conversion from a barter to a monetary economy. During World War II the large Jewish population of Vienna (115,000 in 1938) was reduced to 6,000.

MOZART-ERINNERUNGSRAUM, *Domgasse 5*
This Mozart Memorial House contains souvenirs of the composer, who spent much of his life in Vienna *(see also Salzburg).*

PESTSÄULE, *in the Graben*
This 69-foot-high trinity column stands in the middle of the **Graben,** a street that is one of Vienna's most fashionable shopping areas. The Pestsäule was erected in 1682 to fulfill a vow made by Emperor Leopold II during the plague of 1768–69; it commemorates the city's deliverance from the pestilence.

SANKT MARXER FRIEDHOF (SAINT MARK'S CEMETERY), *off the Simmeringer Hauptstrasse*
On December 5, 1791, a pauper's hearse carried Mozart's remains to a common grave in this cemetery. Today a statue of the composer marks the probable site of his grave.

SCHLOSS SCHÖNBRUNN
Named for a spring *(Schöner Brunnen)* discovered on the property early in the 17th century, the palace of Schönbrunn was begun late in the 17th century when the Turkish peril was over. The magnificent baroque structure was completed in the mid-18th century under Maria Theresa, and during her reign it became the summer residence of the Hapsburg court. Maria Theresa's children, including Marie Antoinette, the future queen of France, spent their childhood here; the young Mozart played in the palace **Concert Room;** in 1805'and again in 1809 Napoleon I made his headquarters here; and in 1815 during the Congress of Vienna Schönbrunn's **Great Gallery** was the scene of many of the glittering receptions that were so much a part of the Congress. After the fall of the French Empire, Napoleon's only son, the king of Rome, lived at Schönbrunn, under the guardianship of his grandfather Emperor Francis II. The child was given the title of duke of Reichstadt. Here, too, Emperor Francis Joseph I was born in 1830 and died in 1916. In the **Blue Room** of this castle Charles I, last of the Hapsburgs, signed the Act of Abdication on November 11, 1918. The palace contains more than 1,000 rooms, 45 of which are open to the public. Among the most interesting are the **Apartments of Emperor Francis Joseph** and his empress, Elizabeth, and the **Napoleon Room,** which Napoleon used as a study and where his son died on July 22, 1832, at the age of 21. **Wagenburg,** the carriage collection, contains an interesting array of coaches used by the Hapsburgs. The 500-acre **Schönbrunn Park** was laid out in the 18th century in a mixture of rococo and antique

styles. Shaded walks lead to a fountain called the **Neptunbrunnen;** Roman ruins reconstructed by order of Maria Theresa; the **Tierpark,** zoological gardens; and finally to the elegant **Gloriette,** an arcaded gallery crowned by a stone canopy surmounted by the imperial eagle.

SCHUBERT-MUSEUM, *54 Nussdorferstrasse*
The birthplace of Franz Schubert in 1797, this house is now a museum devoted to Schubert memorabilia. The house at **9 Speigelgasse,** just off the Graben, where Schubert composed the "Unfinished Symphony," is now occupied by a small bar.

STAATSOPER (THE OPERA), *off the Karntner Ring Strasse*
This magnificent temple of art so beloved by the Viennese was originally constructed in the French Renaissance style between 1861 and 1869. Containing a foyer embellished with operatic scenes and busts of famous composers and seating 2,263, the opera opened amid grand fanfare in 1869 with a performance of Mozart's *Don Juan.* During World War II the building was destroyed; it was subsequently rebuilt and reopened in 1955 to the joy of all Viennese and music lovers everywhere.

STEPHANSDOM (SAINT STEPHEN'S CATHEDRAL), *Stephansplatz*
Located in the heart of medieval Vienna, this cathedral was originally a 13th-century Romanesque basilica, but in the next two centuries it was rebuilt to become the finest Gothic structure in Austria. It was damaged during the Turkish siege of 1683 (*see Belvedere*), and it fared even worse in 1945, when it was nearly destroyed by German and Russian bombardments. (Complete restoration has given the Stephansdom its former appearance.) The church contains the red marble **Tomb of Emperor Frederick III,** who died in 1493, and in the **Catacombs** are urns containing the entrails of many emperors of Austria. The famous **Steffel,** a steeple that is one of Vienna's best-known landmarks, may be ascended from the **Sacristy** and affords a fine view.

ZENTRALFRIEDHOF (CENTRAL CEMETERY), *on the Simmeringer Hauptstrasse*
Laid out in 1873–74, the Zentralfriedhof is Vienna's principal cemetery. It contains the tombs of many historical personalities, artists, poets, writers, and composers, including Christoph Willibald Gluck (1714–87), Ludwig van Beethoven (1770–1827), Franz Schubert (1797–1828), Johann Strauss (1804–49), and Johannes Brahms (1833–97). A section of the graveyard is devoted to soldiers who fell in World War I.

WIENER NEUSTADT, *on Routes E-7, 17, 53, and 54 in Lower Austria*
Founded by Duke Leopold VI in 1194 as a bulwark against the Magyars, this town was the imperial residence from 1440 to 1493, during the reign of Frederick III, duke of Styria, who inaugurated the Hapsburg policy of intermarriage and political succession. The **Neuklosterkirche** (new convent church), contains the tomb of Empress Eleanor of Portugal, wife of Frederick III. Maximilian I, Frederick III's son, was born at Wiener Neustadt in 1459. (He became king of Germany in 1486 and Holy Roman Emperor in 1493.) Maximilian is buried under a simple slab of red marble beneath the high altar of the Gothic **Georgskirche in der Burg,** far from his ornate mausoleum at Innsbruck (*see*).

# GERMANY

## AACHEN (NORTH RHINE-WESTPHALIA)

### DOM (CATHEDRAL), *via the Annastrasse*

Like virtually everything historic in this famous medieval city, the great church in the center of its oldest section is linked with Charlemagne, who made Aachen his northern capital. The Dom was founded by him; some of the original parts remain in the present building, to which additions were made through the 15th century. The **Karlsschrein** is the site of Charlemagne's tomb, and in the Dom's upper part is displayed his marble throne. The church and its **Domschatzkammer** (treasury), adjoining the main structure, contain a whole catalogue of medieval art objects.

### RATHAUS (TOWN HALL), *just north of the Dom*

The 14th-century building is on the site of Charlemagne's palace, and the original palace's **Granusturm** (Granus tower) has been retained. The **Coronation Chamber** of the Rathaus was in active service for almost six centuries during which Aachen was where German kings, many of whom were also Holy Roman Emperors, were crowned; from the accession of Otto I in 936 until 1531 the city was the coronation site. The treaty of 1748 that ended the War of the Austrian Succession was signed in another part of the Rathaus. The structure was heavily damaged during the fall of 1944, when Aachen became the first important German city to fall to United States troops.

## AUGSBURG (BAVARIA), *55 kilometers northwest of Munich via the Munich Autobahn (E11)*

Emperor Augustus founded Augsburg in 15 B.C. as a Roman colony. By the sixth century it had become an episcopal see, which gave impetus to the construction of many noteworthy churches in the following centuries. The **Dom** (cathedral), reached via the Frauentorstrasse in the northern part of the old district, was begun in the tenth century, and its art treasures include altar paintings by a famous native son, Hans Holbein the Elder. A short distance to the west is the **Heilig-Kreuz Kirche** (church of the Holy Cross), from the 12th century; a short distance south of the Dom is the 14th-century **Sankt Anna Kirche**. Farther south is **Sankt Ulrich Kirche**, reached via one of Germany's most famous thoroughfares, the Maximilianstrasse. Here a 15th-century structure houses both Catholic and Protestant churches and is therefore symbolic of the Peace of Augsburg, an outgrowth of the city's diet of 1555, which established the historic first permanent legal basis for the co-existence of Roman Catholicism and Protestantism (Lutheranism) in Germany. The **Rotes Tor** (Red Gate), south of Sankt Ulrich Kirche, is the principal remaining landmark of the fortifications of medieval Augsburg. Located approximately in the center of the old district of the city, east of the Maximilianstrasse, is the **Fuggerei**, established early in the 16th century as a pioneer housing project for the city's poor. It was one of the projects of Jakob Fugger II, whose family, together with the Welsers, made Augsburg a financial and commercial stronghold in the 15th and 16th centuries. It was heavily damaged, as were many other historic sites, in 1944–45.

## BAMBERG (BAVARIA), *50 kilometers northwest of Nuremberg via Route 4*

The magnificent Romanesque and early Gothic **Kaiserdom** (cathedral), on the Domplatz, was completed in the 13th century and contains the tombs of Henry II, king of Germany and Holy Roman Emperor (1002–24), and Pope Clement II (1046–47). Adjoining the

---

*Top left: Schloss Nymphenburg in Munich. Right: the Cathedral at Cologne. Center: Berchtesgaden, in the Bavarian Alps. Below left: terraced slopes and a castle on the Rhine. Right: Gutenberg statue and the cathedral in Mainz*

cathedral is the **Alte Hofhaltung,** a Renaissance palace, and adjoining the latter is the **Neue Residenz,** an episcopal palace completed early in the 18th century, which now houses a picture gallery.

**BAYREUTH (BAVARIA),** *66 kilometers northeast of Nuremberg via Route E6*
Although this Franconian town traces its history to the 12th century, its present fame dates from 1876, when the annual festival of operas by Richard Wagner was started. The productions are staged in the **Festspielhaus,** a theater designed by Wagner, north of the city center via the Bürgerreutherstrasse. The composer spent his last years in **Haus Wahnfried,** located near the Neues Schloss, and was buried in the garden of that house. Wagner's father-in-law, the composer Franz Liszt, is buried in the cemetery **Stadtfriedhof.**

**BERCHTESGADEN AND VICINITY (BAVARIA),** *13 kilometers southeast of Bad Reichenhall via Route 20*
The main square of this resort town, the Schlossplatz, is the site of its principal historic building: the **Schloss** (castle), originally an Augustinian priory and then, beginning in 1810, a royal residence of the Wittelsbach rulers of Bavaria. Just east of the town limits, in **Obersalzberg,** are a few traces of the **Berghof,** the elaborate chalet where Adolf Hitler, Martin Bormann, and other Nazi officials held court at the height of their power. Just south, in **Kehlstein,** was the site of Hitler's mountaintop retreat, "**Eagle's Nest.**" An Allied air raid in April, 1945, destroyed these buildings.

**BERLIN (WEST)**
CHARLOTTENBURGER SCHLOSS (CHARLOTTENBURG PALACE), *on the Schloss Strasse near the intersection with the Spandauer Damm*
Between them, two factors have taken a heavy toll of Berlin sites: wartime destruction attendant on the end of Hitler's Third Reich and peacetime division of the city following the war, which has put many localities off limits to American and West European visitors, or at least made them less accessible than before. A landmark that remains, with a rich collection of historic associations, is this late-17th-century palace named for Sophia Charlotte, queen of Prussia (1701–5) and wife of King Frederick I. A famous patron of the arts, she selected the site about 1695, the year in which construction was begun. Like many old palaces, this one is now a museum. The apartments of Sophia Charlotte and Frederick I contain period furnishings, and there are mementos of the Prussian royal house, together with collections of art objects, antiques, and old musical instruments. Standing in front of the palace is a landmark in its own right: the **Equestrian Statue of Frederick William,** Elector of Brandenburg ("the Great Elector"), executed between 1696 and 1703 by Andreas Schlüter, the chief architect of the royal palace itself. Behind the main structure is the **Schlosspark,** containing the tombs of a later and equally famous queen of Prussia, Louise of Mecklenburg-Strelitz (1797–1810); her husband, Frederick William III (1797–1840); and others of the Hohenzollern dynasty.

CITADEL, *about 15 kilometers west of the city center in Spandau*
The outlying Berlin district named Spandau became German about the middle of the 13th century, prior to which it had been settled by the Slavic people known as Wends. A tower of the citadel dates from about 1160, but the main structure was erected in the 16th century. It is one of the oldest of Berlin's buildings and formerly was employed as a political prison.

## GEDÄCHTNISKIRCHE (KAISER WILHELM MEMORIAL CHURCH), *at the eastern terminus of the Kurfürstendamm near the entrance to the Tiergarten*

Among the restored landmarks is this memorial to William I (Kaiser Wilhelm I), originally constructed in 1895 and reconstructed in a very modern style in 1961. The original tower, however, has been preserved in shattered condition (a legacy of World War II) as a sobering reminder of the devastation of that conflict. Skillfully incorporated in the restored upper portion of the church, the tower is one of the most striking sights along the Kurfürstendamm, West Berlin's central thoroughfare.

## GRUNEWALD JAGDSCHLOSS, *in Forst Grunewald*

The large park called Grunewald, located near the western terminus of the Kurfürstendamm, contains a Renaissance-style hunting lodge (*jagdschloss*) built in 1542. On view here are collections of hunting trophies and art objects. In summer the courtyard of the lodge is the scene of concerts.

## PLÖTZENSEE, *just north of the Goerdelerdamm in Wedding*

This was a political prison during the time of Adolf Hitler's Third Reich; now it serves as a memorial to all victims of that regime. Plötzensee, located in the northcentral Berlin district Wedding, gained special notice during the summer of 1944, when the tide of war was running against Germany sufficiently to stir thoughts of revolt at home as a way of averting complete disaster. On July 20 an officer of the reserve army attempted to assassinate Hitler by means of a concealed bomb. The plot misfired; its immediate consequence was the execution at Plötzensee of many of the plotters or suspects. The **Gedenkstätte von Plötzensee** (Plötzensee Memorial), in the form of a monument, was dedicated in 1952. Also in Wedding, due west on the Heckerdamm, is **Maria Regina Martyrum** (church of Mary, queen of martyrs), dedicated to victims of oppression.

## POTSDAMER PLATZ, *at the southeast edge of the Tiergarten*

This old square has acquired a whole new history since the end of World War II. It marks the convergence of the American, British, and Russian sectors of the divided city. For a time the visitor was not made aware of the physical division of Berlin into eastern and western sections, though the small army of officials at this strategic square made the fact of divided authority obvious from the outset of military government (July, 1945). Now, however, the presence of the **Berlin Wall** in this vicinity gives more tangible proof of Berlin's postwar fate. Nearby, at the corner of the Friedrichstrasse and the Zimmerstrasse, is the official point of entry for persons going from West Berlin to East Berlin, under strict supervision—the point that became famous by the name **"Checkpoint Charley"** (or Charlie). The present wall follows the exact boundary of the Soviet zone, and though the boundary was always recognized, not until May, 1952, was the frontier separating the two parts of the city sealed. Before 1952 passage from one part to the other was relatively easy. Thereafter it became more difficult, but not sufficiently difficult to prevent thousands of persons from fleeing westward from the Soviet zone. On the night of August 12, 1961, East German officials erected a barrier of barbed wire along the frontier to halt all unauthorized travel between the zones. Five nights later the Communists transformed this into a wall of concrete surmounted by barbed wire. A short distance northeast of the entry point through the wall, in an

*From left to right in Berlin: East Berlin stretching beyond the Brandenburg Gate and the Berlin Wall. The equestrian statue of Frederick William in front of*

area that once was part of the grounds of the Reich Chancellery, is a locality that still attracts the interest of visitors, despite its present desolate nature. A mound marks the site of the **Chancellery Bunker**, where Adolf Hitler died on April 30, 1945.

RATHAUS (CITY HALL), *on the John F. Kennedy Platz (formerly the Rudolph Wilde Platz) in Schöneberg*
Though its history as a government building dates only from 1948, when the split between the Soviet Union and the other occupying powers in Berlin became official, this structure has special associations for Americans. Its **Freedom Bell** is modeled on America's Liberty Bell; in the document collection is a **Freedom Scroll** containing the signatures of 17 million Americans. And from a platform erected on the steps of the Rathaus, President John F. Kennedy delivered one of his most memorable addresses, June 26, 1963, on the indivisibility of freedom even in a divided city. His concluding words touched off an ovation from West Berliners: "All free men, wherever they may live, are citizens of Berlin, and, therefore, as a free man, I take pride in the words *'Ich bin ein Berliner.'*" The words were prophetic; shortly after the speech, the Rathaus square was renamed in his memory.

REICHSTAG, *on the Platz der Republik*
This restored structure rose originally between 1884 and 1894 and first served as the home of the Prussian parliament in the latter year. Throughout the period of the Weimar Republic (1919–33) it was again the seat of the German legislature. On the night of February 27, 1933, the Reichstag was destroyed by fire—an event that, in retrospect, stands as a landmark in the formation of the Third Reich. Hitler had become chancellor, as head of a coalition, a month earlier; parliamentary elections were scheduled for early March. The spectacular fire, coming a week before the voting, served the Nazis well. By attributing it to a Communist plot, Hitler was able to proclaim a national emergency. And though the elections did not

*Charlottenburg Palace. The concrete memorial on the Platz der Luftbrücke commemorating the Allied airlift of 1948–49*

provide him with a clear majority in parliament, he was on his way to a succession of coups designed to cut the ground from beneath one opposition party or group after another, beginning with the Communists. Allied bombing during World War II further reduced the Reichstag building to a wreck. Now restored, it stands just north of another landmark, the Brandenburger Tor *(see next entry).* It also stands just outside the Berlin Wall, a reminder of Germany's postwar division. To the east is a separate country; the Federal Republic (West Germany) has its seat of government in Bonn.

SIEGESSÄULE (VICTORY COLUMN), *at the Grosser Stern on the Strasse des 17. Juni*
From the center of the circle known as Grosser Stern (great star) rises this tower, some 200 feet in height. It was completed in 1873 to mark Germany's triumph over France in the Franco-Prussian War. From its top the visitor can see the **Tiergarten,** the park that surrounds the monument, and parts of the city much farther off— including landmarks now in East Berlin. One such famous locality is the **Brandenburger Tor** (Brandenburg Gate), directly east on the Strasse des 17. Juni at the extremity of the Tiergarten and now cut off from the west by the Berlin Wall. The gate, once Berlin's arch of triumph, dates from 1791; despite damage suffered in World War II, it remains one of the great sites, even when viewed from long range. Beyond it, stretching farther into East Berlin, is the famous avenue **Unter den Linden.** The arterial street through the Tiergarten, on which both the Siegessäule and Brandenburger Tor stand, has historic significance of its own. The **Strasse des 17. Juni** takes its name from the insurrection that occurred in East Berlin in 1953. On June 17 of that year, East Berlin workers called a general strike in protest against the increasing severity of their lot. For almost a month martial law prevailed as the strike spread throughout East Germany, and Soviet tanks finally were brought into East Berlin to restore order. The thoroughfare now honors those killed in the uprising.

**TEMPELHOF ZENTRALFLUGHAFEN (CENTRAL AIRPORT),** *near the intersection of the Tempelhofer Damm and the Columbiadamm*

The visitor arriving at Tempelhof, just 6 kilometers south of the center of the city, can begin his or her tour of historic places on the airport grounds. The **Platz der Luftbrücke,** adjoining the intersection noted, is the site of a concrete monument commemorating the Allied airlift that enabled the embattled western part of the city to withstand the Russian blockade of 1948–49. Following the collapse of Nazi resistance, divided Berlin was governed through a Kommandatur with American, British, French, and Soviet representation. The difficulty of maintaining an effective presence by America, Britain, and France in a city located well within the boundaries of East Germany was entirely foreseeable; soon Berlin was split into two distinct administrations. Beginning early in April, 1948, there was increasing Russian pressure on West Berlin, culminating in restrictions on water, rail, and highway traffic into the city from the west. By the following June 24, after the Russians had quit the Kommandatur, all such traffic was halted. They had isolated West Berlin by land and water in an attempt to gain control of the entire city, but American and British authorities rose to the challenge by flying in almost 2.3 million tons of food, medical supplies, and other necessities between June 26, 1948, and October 6, 1949. Tempelhof, enlarged during this time of crisis, was the principal point of arrival for the airlift. The monument is a tribute also to pilots and other crewmen who lost their lives in this convincing demonstration of air power as a constructive force in a country that had been hard hit by aerial warfare. The blockade came to an official end on May 4, 1949, but the airlift was continued until early fall of that year.

## BOCHUM (NORTH RHINE-WESTPHALIA)

This mining center in the Ruhr has a unique attraction in the **Bergbaumuseum,** at Vödestrasse 28, which is devoted to mining.

**BONN (NORTH RHINE-WESTPHALIA),** *29 kilometers southeast of Cologne via Route E9*

In 1948 a constitutional assembly for West Germany met here, and a year later Bonn was made the capital of the Federal Republic. Thus Bonn has become a city with two aspects. Southeast of the city center, between the Rhine River and the Koblenzerstrasse, are modern government buildings, notably the **Bundeshaus** (home of the West German parliament). They contrast sharply with the atmosphere of the old city, a center of culture. Near the hub of the old quarter is the **Münster** (cathedral), on the Münsterstrasse, dating from the 13th century. Directly east of it is the seat of the famous **University of Bonn,** housed in an early-18th-century electoral palace. Just north, on the Marktplatz (market square), is the **Rathaus,** which became a center of German revolutionary activity in 1848. Directly east, overlooking the Rhine, is the **Alter Zoll,** a tower remaining from early fortifications. North of the Rathaus is the **Beethovenhaus,** at Bonngasse 20, birthplace of the composer (in 1770) and now a museum devoted to him. To the west is the **Rheinisches Landesmuseum,** off the Colmanstrasse, whose collections include Roman and Frankish relics together with the famous skull of a Neanderthal man *(see Düsseldorf).* And to the south is the 18th-century **Poppelsdorfer Schloss** (castle), now occupied by the university and linked to its central building by a spacious avenue, the Poppelsdorfer Allee.

## BREMEN (LOWER SAXONY)

BÖTTCHERSTRASSE, *between the Marktplatz and the Weser River*
Most of the treasures of historic Bremen are concentrated in the **Old Town**, on the right bank of the Weser. Böttcherstrasse, a narrow street, was created between 1923 and 1932 by the Bremen coffee merchant and industrialist Ludwig Roselius and rebuilt by him after World War II. Lining it are reproductions of medieval houses, shops, and taverns characteristic of early Bremen. On it is **Roselius Haus**, an authentic 16th-century merchant's home, now a museum. Adjoining this is the **Becker-Modersohn Haus**, containing a collection of the paintings of the late-19th-century artist for whom it is named.

DOM SANKT PETRI (CATHEDRAL OF SAINT PETER), *on the Marktplatz*
The present Romanesque-Gothic structure rose in the 11th century on the site of a wooden chapel erected in 787. It was rebuilt in the 16th century and again in the 19th century. Another famous church in the old quarter is the 13th-century **Liebfrauenkirche** (church of Our Lady), on the Sögestrasse behind the Rathaus.

RATHAUS, *on the Marktplatz*
Constructed between 1405 and 1409, the Gothic Rathaus (town hall) has long since yielded its governmental function to a new building, but it serves an equally valuable function as a museum devoted to Bremen's early history. In the Marktplatz itself is another authentic landmark, the huge **Statue of Roland,** which was erected in 1404 as a sign of the city's independence. Bremen, including the port of Bremerhaven, then was officially known as the Freie Hansestadt Bremen (Free Hansa City of Bremen); with Hamburg and Lübeck, it was a major port of the Hanseatic League. Later, as the Republic and Free Hansa City of Bremen, it became a member of the empire.

SCHÜTTING, *on the Marktplatz opposite the Rathaus*
Another site from Bremen's early period as a commercial center is this one-time headquarters of the city's guild of merchants. It dates from the 16th century. Other medieval commercial buildings were destroyed by heavy bombing during World War II.

WALLANLAGEN (RAMPART WALK), *encircling the old city*
Medieval Bremen was bounded by the Weser River and a semicircular moat alongside which were fortifications. In 1815 the old bastions were razed to permit expansion of the city, but the long arc that marked the placement of the fortified walls has been preserved as a landscaped parkway. A windmill along the parkway is one of the distinctive sights of the preserved old city.

## BRUNSWICK or BRAUNSCHWEIG (LOWER SAXONY), *63 kilometers east of Hanover via Routes E8 and 4*

When American troops neared it in 1945, this old ducal city was already heavily damaged. Fortunately, two of the remaining sites are intimately connected with Brunswick's long history. On the Burgplatz are the **Löwendenkmal** (lion monument), a statue in bronze (1166) symbolizing Henry the Lion, duke of Saxony and Bavaria, who granted the city its charter in the 12th century, and the **Dom** (cathedral of Saint Blasius), a 12th-century structure containing the tombs of Henry and his wife Matilda, daughter of Henry II of England. Many of the timbered houses that characterized the old city were destroyed during World War II; other churches in this section were badly damaged; a 12th-century castle and a 14th-century town hall were gutted. The **Altstadtmarkt** (old city market), a short distance east of the Burgplatz, suggests some of the architectural style of old Brunswick. Farther east, on the outskirts of the city, is the **Grave of Gotthold Ephraim Lessing,** the 18th-century dramatist and critic, in **Magni Cemetery.**

## CLEVES (NORTH RHINE-WESTPHALIA), *on Route 9 near the Netherlands border*

Beginning in the 11th century, this town was the residence of the counts of Cleves. In 1417 it became the seat of a duchy, and a number of the dukes of Cleves are buried in the **Collegiate Church** (completed 1402) in the old section. Another attraction is the 11th-century **Schwanenburg** (swans' castle), associated with the legend of Lohengrin, the medieval German knight who was transported in a boat drawn by a swan. Wagner's opera derives from this source. The castle now houses a court of law. Anne of Cleves (1515–57) was the fourth wife of Henry VIII of England for a short time in 1540; this alliance of the daughter of Duke John of Cleves, leader of West German Protestants, and Henry was a marriage of political convenience for the latter. Cleves was French during the Revolutionary and Napoleonic periods and became part of the empire in 1871.

## COBLENZ (RHINELAND-PALATINATE), *83 kilometers southeast of Cologne via Route 9*

The city, originally founded by the Romans in 9 B.C., is at the confluence of the Rhine and Moselle rivers, and the northeast corner of the old section, at the point of the meeting of the streams, is known as the **Deutsches Eck.** The spot is still a tourist attraction, though it is now marked only by the base of a large statue of Emperor William I that formerly stood here. Directly across the Rhine is **Festung Ehrenbreitstein,** an imposing fortress developed early in the 19th century by the Prussians (though the site has been fortified since the 10th century). Of historic interest on the west side of the Rhine are two structures dating from the time of the Electors of the Holy Roman Empire: the **Schloss** (electoral palace), on the Rhine bank near the crossing of the Pfaffendorter Brücke, and the 13th-century **Alte Burg** (electoral fortress), now the city library, on the Moselle at the crossing of the Balduinbrücke. Historic churches include the **Kastorkirche,** on the site of a 9th-century basilica near the Deutsches Eck, and the 12th-century **Liebfrauenkirche,** reached via the Görgenstrasse.

## COLOGNE (NORTH RHINE-WESTPHALIA)

DOM (CATHEDRAL), *adjoining the Haupt Bahnhof on the left bank of the Rhine River at the crossing of the Hohenzollern Brücke*

The largest Gothic church in northern Europe was one of the very few sites in Cologne's inner city that escaped severe damage in World War II. It is on the locale of an original 9th-century cathedral; the present structure was begun in the 13th century and finally completed in 1880. Among the Dom's many treasures are relics, in the high altar, said to be the belongings of the Magi. Housed near the south side of the Dom is the famous **Dionysos Mosaik,** the second-century Roman mosaic floor of a house whose plan was uncovered in 1941. Along with the plan, workmen excavating for an air-raid shelter found the precious flooring, which has been preserved at the site of the discovery. Other famous medieval churches of the inner city include, from north to south: **Sankt Andreas,** just west of the Dom on the Komodienstrasse, with the tomb of Saint Albertus Magnus, teacher of Thomas Aquinas in Cologne; **Sankt Gereon,** off the Christophstrasse; **Sankt Ursula,** just northwest of the Haupt Bahnhof, with a famous Goldene Kammer (golden chamber, or treasury); **Sankt Maria im Kapitol,** off the Pipinstrasse near the Rhine; **Sankt Aposteln,** west of the Neumarkt; **Sankt Pantaleon,** off the Waisenhausgasse, with the tomb of Theophano, influential wife of the tenth-century Holy Roman Emperor Otto II; and **Sankt Severinus,** on the Severinstrasse.

**HAHNENTOR,** *at the junction of the Hohenzollernring and the Hohenstaufenring*
> This is one of three remaining gates of the medieval fortified wall that surrounded the old part of Cologne, the inner city or semicircular area along the Rhine, dating from the days when the city was a prosperous member of the Hanseatic League. Hahnentor is the western extremity of the semicircle. At corresponding points along the site of the former wall are **Eigelsteintor,** near the northern extremity, and **Severintor,** near the southern one. A short distance east of the Severinstor on the Rhine bank is a medieval tower, or **Bayenturm.** A **Römerturm** (Roman tower), via the Friesenstrasse, dates from about the second century. A famous medieval site, now restored, is the **Festhaus Gürzenich,** a 15th-century banquet and reception hall of the town council, which is located just south of the old **Rathaus** (town hall) in the inner city.

**DACHAU (BAVARIA),** *17 kilometers northwest of Munich*
> Though its recorded history dates from 805, this town was little known outside Germany until 1933, when the Nazis established a concentration camp here on the site of a former ammunition factory. Between that date and 1945, more than 200,000 prisoners passed through its gates. More than 40,000 of them are known to have been put to death; of that number between 85 and 90 per cent were Jews. The still-inconclusive total accounts only for deaths certified by the Allied Powers and does not include prisoners sent elsewhere for assignment and probable execution. The site now contains a modern museum and memorial to the victims.

**DETMOLD AND VICINITY (NORTH RHINE-WESTPHALIA),** *26 kilometers southeast of Bielefeld via Route 239*
> Located within the city limits, near the Marktplatz, is the 16th-century **Schloss** (castle), a former royal residence of the princes of Lippe, subsequently rebuilt in Renaissance style. A short distance to the south is the **Palais Musikakademie** (North West German Academy of Music), housed in a palace erected between 1708 and 1717. Just south of the palace, and adjoining it, is an elaborate garden. Detmold is located on the north slope of the Teutoburger Wald (Teutoburg Forest), an area rich in relics of the Stone, Bronze, and Iron ages; a collection of these artifacts is on view in the city's **Lippisches Landesmuseum.** Of historical interest is the **Hermannsdenkmal,** a monument in the form of a statue of Arminius, or Hermann, the German national hero, located on the summit of the Grotenberg about 5 kilometers southwest of the city limits. It was probably at this site that Arminius, upon returning to his homeland, led his countrymen in a rebellion against occupying Roman legions and defeated the Romans in A.D. 9. As a result the Roman frontier was pushed back to the Rhine.

## DÜSSELDORF AND VICINITY (NORTH RHINE-WESTPHALIA)

### HEINE BIRTHPLACE, *53 Bolkerstrasse in the Altstadt*

Famous as a center of heavy industry, Düsseldorf also has important cultural associations. Robert Schumann and Felix Mendelssohn contributed to its musical life, and Goethe and Heinrich Heine to its literary background. The poet Heine was born in 1797 in a house, now reconstructed, on the Bolkerstrasse, one of the most famous streets of the **Altstadt** (old city), near the bank of the Rhine.

### KÖNIGSALLE, *running north from Graf-Adolf Platz to Corneliusplatz*

The Königsalle has become one of Europe's most fashionable streets; along "KÖ," as it is known, are many of the city's most modern attractions. Yet it has a historic association since it is constructed along part of a moat that used to surround the Altstadt, which lies just west of the Corneliusplatz in the direction of the Rhine.

### LAMBERTIKIRCHE (CHURCH OF SAINT LAMBERTUS), *north of the Marktplatz (market square) in the Altstadt*

This 14th-century church, with its distinctively twisted belfry, is one of the genuine landmarks of old Düsseldorf, which grew up along the right bank of the Rhine. The church contains a late Gothic tabernacle. Nearby and directly south is another familiar sight, the **Schlossturm** (castle tower), all that remains of the city castle dating from the 13th century. In the immediate vicinity also are the old **Rathaus**, from the 16th century, and alongside it, a **Statue of Johann Wilhelm II**, or Jan Wellem, Elector of the Palatinate. The monument was erected in 1711 in recognition of his support of the city.

### NEANDERTHAL, *11 kilometers east via Route 3*

In 1856, in a gorge not far from the city limits, the skeletal remains of Neanderthal man were discovered here, and the locality has given its name to this long-extinct species. The site of the discovery is marked, and there is a museum of prehistoric life nearby (though the famous Neanderthal skull is in a Bonn [*see*] museum).

### SCHLOSS BENRATH, *10 kilometers from the city center on the right bank of the Rhine River*

This elaborate rococo castle, built by Nicolas de Pigage in 1768, is

*The elegant Schloss Benrath, on the Rhine River beyond Düsseldorf*

one of the centers of interest in the outlying sections of the city along the Rhine. The Benrath district was incorporated into Düssel- dorf in 1929.

SCHLOSS JÄGERHOF, *on the Jägerhofstrasse at the northwest extremity of the Hofgarten*
Düsseldorf is also famous for its parks, foremost among which is the Hofgarten. Jägerhof Castle is an old hunting lodge used by the German princes (Electors) who were charged with selecting the emperor during the period of the Holy Roman Empire. It was built between 1752 and 1763 and is now a museum containing exhibits of porcelain and carpeting, as well as modern paintings. East of the castle on the Jägerhofstrasse, near the intersection with the Kaiser- strasse, is the **Goethe Museum,** containing manuscripts, first editions, and other material relating to the noted poet and drama- tist, who resided in Düsseldorf for a time.

## ESSEN (NORTH RHINE-WESTPHALIA)
MÜNSTER (CATHEDRAL), *on the Burgplatz*
In the center of a city heavily bombed during World War II stands this church founded in the middle of the 9th century and completed in the 15th century. It was extensively restored after 1945. Its particular treasure is the Goldene Madonna (gold Madonna), dating from 980, reputedly the oldest statue of the Virgin in the West. The church treasury also contains other notable items, among which are three crosses of the Abbess Mathilde; these are on display in a museum just to the south. Still farther south the **Folkwang Museum,** Bismarckstrasse 66, contains important modern paintings.

VILLA HÜGEL, *south of the city center near the Baldeneysee, entrance via the Haraldstrasse*
Essen's rapid development as an industrial center stemmed from the founding here, about 1810, of the vast ironworks of the Krupp family. Friedrich Krupp was the first of the line, and the family name was to become synonymous with German armament. In part as a consequence of this, Essen was a major target of Allied airmen during World War II. Villa Hügel was the estate of the Krupps near the lake known as Baldeneysee, a body of water formed by the dam- ming of the Ruhr River. Since 1953 it has been used for cultural events. The former residence is open to the inspection of visitors, and there is also a museum, **Historische Sammlung Krupp,** devoted to the long history of the Krupp enterprises, which now concentrate on peacetime pursuits.

WERDEN KIRCHE, *6 kilometers south of the city center via Route 224*
Werden, formerly a suburb but now a district of Essen, was the site of an abbey founded in 796. The convent and monastery were abolished in 1803, but the remaining church, begun in the ninth century, retains some of the flavor of the original Benedictine abbey.

## FRANKFURT AM MAIN (HESSE)
DOM (CATHEDRAL OF SAINT BARTHOLOMEW), *near the bank of the Main River just west of the Alte Brücke (old bridge)*
One of the genuinely historic churches of Germany, Saint Barthol- omew's was the site of the coronation of Holy Roman Emperors from 1562 until the end of that confederation. It retains the **Wahl- kapelle** (election chapel), where the seven Electors met to choose the emperors. The 13th-century structure, with a notable 15th-

century Gothic tower, is on the foundations of a 9th-century church. It overlooks the **Altstadt** (old city), the historic semicircular area on the north bank of the Main that was almost demolished in March, 1944, by Allied bombers. Just south is the **Leinwandhaus** (drapers' hall), on the Weckmarkt, originally a 14th-century cloth market, which recalls the city's famous medieval trade fairs. Two noted churches just west of this are the **Nikolaikirche** (13th century) and **Leonhardskirche** (15th century). **Katharinenkirche** (17th century) is on the square An der Hauptwache.

GOETHEHAUS, *Grosser Hirschgraben 23 near the Berlinerstrasse*
The poet Johann Wolfgang von Goethe was born at this site in 1749 and spent much of his youth here. The interior furnishings have been preserved; the exterior was rebuilt with care after World War II destruction of the Altstadt. An adjoining museum is devoted largely to Goethe and his world.

GRÜNEBURG, *northwest of the Altstadt and east of the Palmengarten*
This public park was once the estate of the Rothschild family of financiers, whose founder, Meyer Amschel Rothschild (1743–1812), pursued a career in business and government service in Frankfurt am Main. The family mansion formerly on this site was the victim of World War II bombing.

PAULSKIRCHE, *on the Paulsplatz between the Dom and the Goethehaus*
Constructed between 1789 and 1833, this church was the site of an unsuccessful attempt (1848–49) to unify the German states under a constitution—one of the outgrowths of the revolutionary uprisings of 1848. A preliminary gathering of representatives of the states in Frankfurt led to the election in 1848 of a national assembly, the Frankfurt Parliament. Meeting in the Paulskirche, that body drafted a constitution and chose Frederick William IV, king of Prussia, to receive the imperial crown of the proposed federation. His refusal of the offer torpedoed the project. In 1866 Frankfurt was incorporated into Prussia.

RÖMER, *on Römerberg Platz (square) just west of the Dom*
The group of 15th-century buildings collectively known as the Römer has been restored. Its central structure, the Haus zum Römer, contains the elaborate **Kaisersaal** (imperial hall), once the site of coronation festivities. The palace of the Holy Roman Emperors was in this immediate area; in the square on which these buildings face is a fountain, **Justitia** (1543), which Goethe celebrated as a coronation landmark. The old Rathaus was in the Römer.

GOSLAR (**LOWER SAXONY**), *southwest of Brunswick via Routes 490 and 6*
In a section of West Germany that is notable for its medieval and Renaissance sites, Goslar is outstanding. The city has managed to retain much of its earlier appearance despite World War II. The visitor can see all the old quarter, moreover, with a minimum of effort, for it is arranged compactly around the **Marktplatz** (market square). The focal point in the arrangement is the Gothic **Rathaus** (town hall), on the square. It dates from the 15th century and contains the **Huldigungssaal** (chamber of homage), brilliantly painted with historical scenes and originally used as a meeting room by the city elders, and the adjoining **Huldigungszimmer** (chapel). Also on the Marktplatz is the **Marktkirche** (market church); it is one of a group of surviving old churches and is of particular interest because

its manuscript collection dates back to the time of Martin Luther. Reminiscent of the days when Goslar was a prosperous member of the Hanseatic League are a number of former guildhalls; one of them, the **Kaiserworth** (1494), just south of the Rathaus, has been converted into a hotel. A short distance south of the Marktplatz stands the Romanesque **Kaiserpfalz** (imperial palace) as a reminder of the time when German emperors made frequent stays in Goslar. The Kaiserpfalz was built by Henry III about 1050 and was rebuilt in 1879. Its special attraction is a large **Reichssaal** (imperial hall). Half-timbered houses that remain include the **Brusttuch** (1526), just off the Marktplatz, and **Siemenshaus** (1693), on the Bergstrasse, originally the home of Hans Siemens, one of the city's most prominent residents. Along the **Wallanlagen** (rampart walk) are remains of early fortifications. One of the most striking of these is the **Zwinger**, southeast of the Marktplatz, a 16th-century round tower.

**GÖTTINGEN (LOWER SAXONY),** *39 kilometers northeast of Kassel*

Located near the center of the inner city is the 14th-century **Rathaus,** on the Marktplatz. Standing before it, and looking in every direction, the visitor can see the six 14th- and 15th-century churches that surround the Rathaus. The same area is famous for its half-timbered houses, dating from the 16th century, relics of the time when Göttingen was a member of the Hanseatic League. Because the city was spared major damage during World War II, much of its old flavor has been retained. **Göttingen University**, founded in 1737 by the future King George II of England, was a famous German intellectual center in the 19th century—the brothers Grimm taught here—and continues to be so today.

**HAMBURG AND VICINITY (HAMBURG STATE),** *on the Elbe River on Routes E3 and E4*

In 1842 a disastrous fire wiped out about a third of Hamburg's inner city. A century later an equally destructive war rained down tons of bombs. Consequently, though it is rich in history, Germany's second city has rather few remaining sites to relate to that past, apart from museums. The earliest recorded structure, the fortress Hammaburg, was captured by Charlemagne early in the ninth century. An early milestone in the city's emergence as one of the world's great trade centers was the commercial treaty with Lübeck in 1241, which soon led to the formation of the Hanseatic League. In 1510 Hamburg became a free imperial city, and in 1558 it was the site of the first German exchange. The 19th century, following the Napoleonic Wars, saw a resurgence of commercial development; at the same time the city, the birthplace of the composers Johannes Brahms and Felix Mendelssohn, took its place with Germany's cultural leaders. Modern Hamburg is a mecca for lovers of night life, but its oldest surviving structures are churches. Notable among these is the **Hauptkirche Sankt Michaelis** (Saint Michael's Church), near the intersection of the Ost-West Strasse and the Martin Luther Strasse, first built in the mid-17th century and rebuilt in present form a century later. The tower is all that remains of **Sankt Nikolai Kirche,** also on the Ost-West Strasse; it dates from about 1200. Nearby is 14th-century **Sankt Katherinen Kirche,** off the Zollkanal at the Brandstwiete Strasse. **Sankt Petrikirche** (Saint Peter's Church), between the Monckebergstrasse and the Speersort, is from the 12th century. Behind it and due east is **Sankt Jakobikirche** (Saint James's Church), completed in the 15th century and still the possessor of a famous 17th-century organ.

**FRIEDRICHSRUH,** *22 kilometers east of central Hamburg*

This was the estate of Otto von Bismarck, first chancellor of the German Empire and one of the dominant European statesmen of the last half of the 19th century. Emperor William I, an advocate of Bismarck and the latter's Prussian generals, presented the site and surrounding territory in the woods known as the Sachsenwald to Bismarck early in his reign. When Bismarck broke with William II and went into retirement in 1890, he settled at Friedrichsruh and remained here until his death on July 30, 1898. His mausoleum is on the grounds. It was here that the famous "Iron Chancellor" wrote his *Gedanken und Erinnerungen* (Reflections and Reminiscences), published the year of his death.

**HANOVER or HANNOVER (LOWER SAXONY),** *on Routes 3, 6, E8*

Historic Hanover is largely concentrated in a relatively small area, the **Altstadt,** on the right bank of the Leine River. Since Hanover suffered major damage during World War II, particularly in this section, the number of remaining sites is limited. The **Marktplatz** is the locality of the **Altes Rathaus** (old city hall), dating from the 15th century and now restored, and the **Marktkirche** (market church), a 14th-century building whose art treasures include a 15th-century altarpiece of carved wood. Among the surviving half-timbered structures in the immediate vicinity is the 17th-century **Ballhof.** Since 1945 Hanover has been the capital of Lower Saxony, whose parliament meets in another of the old buildings, the **Leineschloss,** on the bank of the Leine. Just across the river is restored **Neustädter Kirche** (1666–70), which contains the tomb of Gottfried Wilhelm von Leibnitz, the philosopher and mathematician. From 1676 until his death here in 1716, Leibnitz made Hanover his headquarters and had general charge of the ducal library. The house in the Altstadt where he spent his last years was one of the sites that was damaged beyond repair. Along with some famous gardens, Hanover has several noted museums to compensate for the loss of many of its historic places.

**HEIDELBERG AND VICINITY (WÜRTTEMBERG-BADEN),** *18 kilometers southeast of Mannheim via the Autobahn (E4)*

The ruins of the Renaissance **Schloss** (castle) tower over this city and help to make it a great tourist attraction. Built principally between the 15th and 17th centuries, the castle was despoiled by the French in the 17th century and later struck by lightning. Among its many points of interest is a cellar containing a gigantic wine cask (49,000 gallons). Buildings of the equally famous **University of Heidelberg,** founded in 1386, lie below, as does the 15th-century **Heiliggeistkirche** (church of the Holy Spirit), with the tomb of Emperor Rupert, just south of the **Alte Brücke** (old bridge). Near the village of **Mauer,** 10 kilometers southeast, is the site where the jawbone of the prehistoric Heidelberg man was found in 1907.

**HILDESHEIM (LOWER SAXONY),** *27 kilometers southeast of Hanover via Route 6*

There is a familiar pattern here: a group of sites in a central medieval quarter arranged around the **Dom** (cathedral), which was begun about 850 and contains important art treasures. In the cloister at the east end of the cathedral is a famous rose bush that is said to be a thousand years old. Just south of the cloister is the **Antoniuskapelle** (Saint Anthony's Chapel), which can be reached from Hückedahl Street. Just northeast of the cathedral are **Sankt Andreaskirche**

*Left: the Rathaus in Hanover. Right: the castle and old bridge in Heidelberg*

(church of Saint Andrew), from the 14th century, and the **Tempel-haus** (Templars' House), a 15th-century residence adjoining the Marktplatz. A short distance northwest of the cathedral is **Sankt Michaelis Kirche** (church of Saint Michael), which rose in the 11th century and was rebuilt after suffering destruction in World War II. **Sankt Godehardkirche** (church of Saint Godehard), south of the cathedral, dates from the 12th century. The residential quarter known as the **Brühl**, adjoining the cathedral, contains late-Gothic and Renaissance timbered houses.

**KOBLENZ.** *See* COBLENZ

**KÖLN.** *See* COLOGNE

## LÜBECK (SCHLESWIG-HOLSTEIN)

HOLSTENTOR (HOLSTEIN GATE), *at the intersection of the Holsten Strasse and the Possehl Strasse*

The famous gate with two towers, formerly fortified, is among the most characteristic sights of Lübeck, one of the great commercial centers of all Europe in the Middle Ages. The gate now houses a museum devoted to the city's history. Formerly it guarded the western approach to the inner city, just as the **Burgtor,** also still standing, defended the isthmus that afforded the only land approach from the north. Both date from the mid-15th century, when Lübeck was head of the Hanseatic League. The inner city's other fortifications are now gone, but a medieval character still pervades the area. Among the secular buildings of note is the large **Rathaus,** located centrally on the Marktplatz. It was built originally about 1250, but the process of adding and altering continued for three centuries.

MARIENKIRCHE (SAINT MARY'S CHURCH), *near the intersection of the Meng Strasse and the Breite Strasse*

Of the surviving medieval churches, this one, completed in 1330, is most famous. Dietrich Buxtehude, who did much to make the city a point of interest musically, was organist-composer here from 1668 until his death in 1707. Two somewhat older structures are also worthy of mention: the 12th-century **Domkirche** (cathedral), founded by Henry the Lion, duke of Saxony and Bavaria, and located on Pferdemarkt Parade; and the 13th- and 14th-century **Jakobikirche** (Saint James's Church), at the intersection of the Königstrasse and the Breite Strasse.

**LÜNEBURG (LOWER SAXONY),** *56 kilometers southeast of Hamburg via Route 209*

The **Rathaus,** on the Marktplatz, is the principal attraction, built between the 12th and 18th centuries. Notable features of this town hall are the **Grosse Ratsstube** (great council chamber), with elaborate wood sculptures; the **Fürstensaal** (princes' apartment); and the **Laube** (hall of justice), containing paintings by Hans Memling. Many old homes remain in the old part of the town, together with three medieval churches: **Johanniskirche** (Saint John's), on the Altenbrückertor Strasse; **Michaeliskirche** (Saint Michael's), off the J. S. Bach Platz; and **Nikolaikirche** (Saint Nicolas's), on the Bardowickerstrasse.

**MAINZ (RHINELAND-PALATINATE),** *35 kilometers southwest of Frankfurt via Route 455*

Originally a Celtic settlement, Mainz became the site of a fortified Roman camp, Maguntiacum, in the first century B.C. A period of Frankish rule followed, and in the eighth century the city was the center of an archbishopric, whose clerical rulers were entitled to crown the Holy Roman Emperors. The former **Electors' Palace,** built between the 15th and 17th centuries and located near the bank of the Rhine, just north of the Heuss Brücke (bridge), now houses the **Römisch-Germanisches Zentralmuseum** (Roman German Museum). The **Dom** (cathedral), consecrated in 1009, is just south of the Marktplatz and easily the center of interest in this city. As a historic place of worship and residence of many art treasures, it has survived three major fires; restored in the 19th century, the Romanesque structure was again heavily damaged during World War II. Just west of it is the Gutenbergplatz, with a **Statue of Johann Gutenberg,** German inventor of printing from movable type and a native of Mainz. The **Gutenbergmuseum,** just northeast of the Dom, contains his hand press and the famous 15th-century Gutenberg Bible.

**MÜLHEIM AN DER RUHR (NORTH RHINE-WESTPHALIA),** *north of Düsseldorf on Route 1*

Adjoining Essen (to the east), Duisburg (to the west), and Oberhausen (to the north), Mülheim retains a historic landmark in **Schloss Broich,** on the Schloszstrasse, which towers over this industrial city to the west of the oldest section. The former citadel of the counts von Broich dates from the 11th century and was once one of the great strongholds of the lower Rhine. East of it, off the Teinerstrasse, is the 11th-century **Petrikirche** (Saint Peter's Church), now restored after heavy damage in World War II. In the vicinity are many half-timbered houses characteristic of medieval Germany. A 13th-century **Convent Church** has survived on the grounds of a former Cistercian nunnery in the city's Saarn district.

**MÜNCHEN GLADBACH AND VICINITY (NORTH RHINE-WESTPHALIA),** *26 kilometers west of Düsseldorf on Route 57*

This textile center developed around a Benedictine abbey founded late in the tenth century. The brick building now on that site, in the old section of the city, dates from the 14th century and serves as the **Rathaus** (town hall). Adjacent to this is the 13th-century Romanesque **Münster** (cathedral), with a notable early Gothic Münsterchor (choir), attributed to the Cologne cathedral architect Gerhard von Riehl. A crypt in the church is estimated to be as old as the tenth century. A building that housed a 12th-century **Benedictine Convent** is in the Neuwerk quarter. Just south of the city limits, via Route 57, is **Rheydt,** twin city of München Gladbach, with which it was formerly joined. On the northeastern edge of Rheydt stands a 16th-century **Renaissance Castle,** now the home of a museum.

## MUNICH (BAVARIA)

### ALTES RATHAUS (OLD CITY HALL), *on the Marienplatz*

The Marienplatz is at the center of Munich's old inner-city district, which, like those of most of Germany's industrial capitals, suffered major damage from World War II air raids. The Altes Rathaus, older of Munich's two city halls, dates from 1470; now rebuilt, it retains some of the prewar structure (principally external portions). Typically, the inner city was once walled, and three of the 14th-century gates of this original perimeter remain: **Karlstor,** on the Karlsplatz; **Sendlinger Tor,** at the end of the Sendlingerstrasse; and **Isartor,** on the Isartorplatz. Though few of the old residences of the inner city remain, there is an abundance of the old beer halls that have been a Munich tradition for centuries. One that has a claim to history, the **Hofbräuhaus,** was the scene of the Nazi meetings leading to Adolf Hitler's first bid for power: the Munich "beer-hall putsch" of November, 1923, which landed its leader in prison. By then Hitler had been active in Munich for 11 years. On September 30, 1938, the Bavarian capital was the scene of his historic meeting (in the Führerhaus) with Neville Chamberlain and others; the resulting Munich Pact sanctioned the partition of Czechoslovakia and made Munich a symbol of appeasement.

### FRAUENKIRCHE (CHURCH OF OUR LADY), *just off the Kaufingerstrasse*

Munich's cathedral, built between 1468 and 1488, is another authentic landmark of the old quarter. Beside its south tower is the **Tomb of Louis IV,** king of Germany and Holy Roman Emperor, who died in Munich in 1347. Just west is the Renaissance **Michaelskirche** (16th century), on the Neuhauserstrasse, containing the tombs of 25 Wittelsbach rulers; a short distance south of both are **Peterskirche** (12th century), off the Marienplatz, and **Johannes Nepomuk Kirche,** also called **Asamkirche** (18th century), on the Sendlingerstrasse.

### RESIDENZ, *via the Hofgartenstrasse*

Just north of the old quarter's center is this one-time royal residence of the Wittelsbach family, whose members ruled Bavaria from the 12th century to the outset of World War I. The palace is a complex of buildings, some of which date from the 15th century. Its **Schatzkammer** (treasury) contains the family crown jewels. The complex also houses one of the many outstanding museums of Munich, the **Residenzmuseum;** the **Altes Residenztheater;** and the **Bayerisches Nationaltheater,** one of the strongholds of German opera.

### SCHLOSS NYMPHENBURG, *in Nymphenburg on the city's western border*

The baroque castle here was begun in the 17th century and served as the summer residence of the Wittelsbachs. On the grounds are a famous park and a hunting lodge, **Amalienburg.**

## MÜNSTER IN WESTFALEN (NORTH RHINE-WESTPHALIA)

### DOM (CATHEDRAL), *on the Domplatz (cathedral square)*

Romanesque and Gothic statuary and sculpture adorn the interior of this 13th-century structure, located in the center of the city's oldest section. There is an **Astronomische Uhr** (astronomical clock) with a glockenspiel, and in the choir chapel is the tomb of Christoph Bernhard von Galen, 17th-century prince-bishop of Münster. Like all buildings in this section, the cathedral was heavily damaged during World War II. Other notable churches, restored after the fighting, are **Lambertikirche** (church of Saint Lambert), just east of the cathedral, and **Überwasserkirche** (church of Our Lady), just west of the cathedral. Both are from the 14th century.

### RATHAUS (TOWN HALL), *on the Prinzipalmarkt just southeast of the Dom*

The series of religious conflicts known as the Thirty Years' War (1618–48) was terminated by the Treaty of Westphalia, and Münster, like Osnabrück (*see*), was a key city in the negotiations. While representatives of the German emperor were meeting with the Protestant diet and Swedish negotiators in Osnabrück during the period 1643–48, the emperor and officials of the Catholic states of France and Spain were at work in Münster during the same period, laying the foundation for the peace proclaimed here and in nearby Osnabrück on October 25, 1648. The town halls of both cities were the scene of the negotiations. Münster's Rathaus, which first rose in the 14th century, retains the **Friedenssaal** (peace chamber), where the negotiators met. Originally this was the Ratsstube, or council chamber devoted to the administration of Münster. Paintings in the chamber are of Catholic officials who participated in framing the Treaty of Westphalia.

### RESIDENZSCHLOSS, *west of the Dom off the Hindenburgplatz*

Of many old castles in the vicinity of Münster, this one is probably the best known. It is within the city proper and is now part of Wilhelms Universität (university). Formerly it was the residence of the prince-bishops who ruled the area until it was secularized early in the 19th century.

## NUREMBERG or NÜRNBERG (BAVARIA)

### DÜRERHAUS, *on the Bergstrasse*

The painter and engraver Albrecht Dürer was one of the natives of the city who gave it international standing as a cultural center. His last years (1509–28) were spent in this house in the northwest part of the old inner city. The building's interiors have been largely preserved, and there are many examples of his work on display.

### FEMBOHAUS, *Burgstrasse 15*

This preserved burgher's home (1591) is now the site of a museum devoted to the city's history of some 400 years, beginning in the 15th century. Just south of it, on the Marktplatz, via the Burgstrasse, is perhaps the old section's most familiar landmark, **Schöner Brunnen** (beautiful fountain). A short distance farther south is **Heiliggeistspital** (hospital of the Holy Spirit), spanning the Pegnitz River east of the Königstrasse; it was founded in 1331. Still farther south on the Königstrasse is the **Mauthalle**, a 15th-century granary.

KAISERBURG, *via the Burgstrasse*

Standing on the northern edge of the Altstadt is Kaiserburg fortress, parts of which date from the 11th century. Nuremberg's medieval fortifications also included a wall, from which remain four principal gates marking its extremities: **Frauentor** (southeast), **Laufertor** (northeast), **Neutor** (northwest), and **Spittlertor** (southwest). Within these boundaries grew a prosperous trade center, which in the 15th and 16th centuries also became a stronghold of the arts. An industrial boom came in the 19th century. Under the Third Reich the city was the site of Nazi congresses. In 1945 it was the seat of the international tribunal on war crimes, held in the **Palace of Justice.**

LORENZKIRCHE, *on the Königstrasse*

Among the art treasures of this church, which was begun in the 13th century, are works by Veit Stoss, the noted wood carver, and Adam Kraft, the stone sculptor. Two of the inner city's famous churches are just to the south, on the Königstrasse: **Klarakirche**, whose earliest parts date from the 13th century, and **Marthakirche**, a 14th-century site known as a gathering place of Nuremberg's Meistersinger, following a tradition set by Hans Sachs. **Frauenkirche**, to the north on the Marktplatz via the Königstrasse, is from the 14th century. A short distance to the west, on the Burgstrasse, the 13th-century **Sebalduskirche** has creations by Stoss, the painter and engraver Michel Wohlgemuth, and the Vischer family of sculptors and brass founders.

LUITPOLDHAIN, *southeast of the city center via the Munchnerstrasse*

From 1933 to 1938 this arena and a nearby stadium provided the impressive setting for Nazi party rallies each September. Hitler and the principal organizer of the *Sturmabteilung* (storm troopers, or S.A.), Ernst Röhm, presided over the first; a year later Röhm was the victim of an assassination plot directed by Hitler. At the 1935 party congress here, the severely repressive Nuremberg Laws, aimed expressly at German Jews, were proclaimed. Nuremberg's reputation as a center of anti-Semitism traced also to the activity of Julius Streicher, the Nazi editor and politician who was hanged in this city as a war criminal in 1946.

OSNABRÜCK (LOWER SAXONY), *north of Münster via Route E3*

The city's particular treasure is the old **Rathaus** (town hall), on the Marktplatz, originally constructed early in the 16th century and restored after 1945. In the **Friedenssaal** (peace chamber) of this building, Protestant negotiators convened between 1643 and 1648; their work formed part of the basis of the Treaty of Westphalia, which ended the Thirty Years' War and was proclaimed from the steps of the Rathaus on October 25, 1648. Opposite the Rathaus is the **Marienkirche** (Saint Mary's Church), a 14th-century Gothic structure also damaged in World War II. Just beyond it is the **Dom** (Saint Peter's Cathedral), originally founded in 785 and rebuilt in late Romanesque style following a fire in 1254. Another notable church, **Johanniskirche** (Saint John's), on nearby Johannisstrasse, is a 13th-century Gothic building.

PADERBORN (NORTH RHINE-WESTPHALIA), *37 kilometers south of Bielefeld via Route 68*

This town is famous as the meeting place of Charlemagne and Pope Leo III in 799, the year before Leo crowned Charlemagne emperor of the West. About the same time Charlemagne created a bishopric at Paderborn; the town was the residence of prince-bishops of the Holy Roman Empire until 1803. Charlemagne also built the original **Dom** (cathedral), on the Domplatz (cathedral square), in the eighth century. The present Romanesque-Gothic structure on the site was completed in the 13th century. An early-17th-century **Rathaus** also stands nearby, though, like the cathedral, it was the victim of extensive damage during World War II.

**REMAGEN (RHINELAND-PALATINATE),** *19 kilometers southeast of Bonn via Route 9*

A Rhine crossing point since the days of the Roman Empire, the town served that function again in March of 1945 when American troops made their first passage over the river in a decisive action.

**SCHLESWIG (SCHLESWIG-HOLSTEIN)**

SANKT PETRI DOM (SAINT PETER'S CATHEDRAL), *in the Altstadt*
One of the most visited cathedrals in Germany, Sankt Petri contains sections dating from the 11th century. The particular attraction is an altarpiece, the **Bordesholm Altar,** with 392 wooden figures carved by Hans Brüggemann in 1521.

SCHLOSS GOTTORP (GOTTORP CASTLE), *off Friedrichsberg on an island in the estuarine inlet Schlei*
The original castle on this site dated from the 12th century; the present-day restoration is that of a 16th-century structure, once the residence of the dukes of Schleswig-Holstein. The present West German state, Schleswig-Holstein, comprises the territory of two former duchies, Schleswig, long allied with Denmark, and Holstein, a member of the Holy Roman Empire and then of the German Confederation. Danish-German rivalry for control of these areas, spanning four centuries, culminated in war in 1864, after Denmark

*The Albrecht Dürer house and statue in Nuremberg*

sought to annex both. Prussia and Austria united to defeat Denmark, which lost both duchies. Schloss Gottorp houses two of the principal museums of present-day Schleswig-Holstein. Of special historical interest are relics ranging in time from the Stone and Bronze ages to the Viking era, when Scandinavian mariners established an important center of trade near the present city of Schleswig. The remains of a Viking defense entrenchment are visible at **Haddeby**, on the outskirts of Schleswig via Route 76, together with other Viking relics. In a building just west of the castle is the **Nydam-Boot** (Nydam ship), a fourth-century Anglo-Saxon craft with a hull 75 feet long and 10 feet wide. It was discovered in 1863 in the Nydam marshes of Denmark.

### SOEST (NORTH RHINE-WESTPHALIA), *48 kilometers east of Dortmund via Route 1*

At the center of the old section of the town is the **Patroklusdom** (Saint Patroclus Cathedral), a Romanesque structure from the 11th and 12th centuries. North of it is the **Wiesenkirche** (church of Our Lady of the Pastures), from the 14th century, which contains a famous 1520 stained-glass window representing the Last Supper, complete with Westphalian ham, beer, and dark rye bread. There are remains of medieval fortifications, including the **Osthofentor** (east of the cathedral on the Osthofenstrasse), a 16th-century fortified gate dating from the days when Soest was a prosperous member of the Hanseatic League.

### SPEYER (RHINELAND-PALATINATE), *80 kilometers southeast of Mainz via Route 9*

DOM, *overlooking the old section*

The cathedral was founded in 1030 by Conrad II, Holy Roman Emperor and one of eight German emperors buried in its crypt. Speyer is famous in religious history as the site of the diet of 1529, at which the declarations of the Edict of Worms (1521), asserting the authority of Rome, were confirmed (*see Worms*). Martin Luther's followers, gathered at Speyer, protested strongly, giving rise to the term "Protestant." Their protest is commemorated by a late-19th-century church, the **Gedächtniskirche**, on the Bartholomäus-Weltz Platz in southwestern Speyer.

HISTORISCHES MUSEUM DER PFALZ (PALATINATE MUSEUM), *south of the Dom*

This ancient town's history, which goes back about 3,000 years, is traced in collections concentrating on pre-Roman, Roman, and medieval times. About 400 B.C. Speyer (then Noviomagus) was the principal Celtic settlement in the Palatinate. It became a leading Roman site before being sacked by the Huns about 450. After five centuries under Roman control, Speyer, like Trier, became a Frankish center. The **Wine Museum** in the cellar of this structure contains a bottle of wine said to date from the third century.

### STUTTGART (WÜRTTEMBERG-BADEN), *on Routes E70, 14, and E11*

Though the prevailing atmosphere is that of postwar modernism, there are some reconstructed remains of old Stuttgart, the capital of the duchy of Württemberg from late medieval times. The most striking of these are concentrated just north of the Marktplatz (market square) in the historic city center, which was almost wiped out in World War II. The **Altes Schloss** (old castle), originally a 13th-century fortress and remodeled in the 16th century, now houses the

Württembergisches Landesmuseum. On its north side is the 18th-century baroque **Neues Schloss** (new castle), also once the residence of Württemberg royalty. The city's most historic church, the **Stiftskirche** (Collegiate Church), on the Schillerplatz just west of the Altes Schloss, is a 15th-century building on the foundation of a 12th-century place of worship. West of the old section, on the western outskirts of the city, is **Schloss Solitude,** reached via the Böblingerstrasse. Like the foregoing sites, this 17th-century rococo castle contrasts with Stuttgart's gleaming industrial plants and its impressive television tower.

## TRIER AND VICINITY (RHINELAND-PALATINATE)

### AMPHITHEATER, *east of the Kaiserthermen off the Olewigerstrasse*

For its size, Trier has a striking abundance of historic places; in Roman sites, it takes second place to no other German city. The emperor Augustus founded Trier about 15 B.C. It was the capital of the Roman province Belgica and then of the Roman prefecture of Gaul before its capture by the Franks early in the fifth century. It was a wine center under the Roman Empire, as it is today, and though it was heavily damaged during the American drive into Germany early in 1945, the Roman sites were largely spared. The amphitheater, oldest of these, dates from about 100 and has a capacity of more than 20,000.

### DOM (CATHEDRAL), *on the Windstrasse*

Part of a fourth-century Roman basilica is incorporated in this famous church, most of which is of 11th-century Romanesque design with baroque additions. The treasury contains many precious items, including a seamless robe said to have been worn by Christ. It is displayed only rarely, and those times have been the occasions of major pilgrimages.

### HAUPTMARKT (MARKET SQUARE), *via the Simeonstrasse from the north*

This place is marked by a cross (958) symbolizing the city's right to conduct a market. Just south is **Sankt Gangolfskirche** (15th century), one of Trier's many historic churches. Bordering the square on the west are medieval burghers' homes, including the reconstructed **Steipe** (15th century).

### IGEL, *8 kilometers southwest of the city limits on the Moselle River*

This village is remarkable for a sandstone **obelisk** rising more than 70 feet and dating from ancient Roman times. It is thought to be a family monument.

### KAISERTHERMEN (IMPERIAL BATHS), *south of the Palastgarten off the Östallee*

These Roman ruins, dating from the fourth century, are in the southeast section of the city's most historic area. Directly west are the **Barbarathermen** (Saint Barbara's Baths), off the Südallee near the bank of the Moselle River. The substructures here are from the second century. A short distance to the north is the **Römer Brücke** (Roman bridge), which spans the river.

### KARL MARX HAUS, *Brückenstrasse 10*

The house in which the political theorist was born, in 1818, is not far from most of the city's other historic landmarks. It contains manuscripts related to his work.

LIEBFRAUENKIRCHE (CHURCH OF OUR LADY), *adjoining the Dom on the south*

The Gothic (13th-century) church is one of Trier's architectural gems. Just south, on the Constantinplatz, is the 18th-century **Kurfürstlicher Palast** (electoral palace) with its garden. On the same square stands the **Basilika,** a brick structure rebuilt since World War II and now a Protestant church; formerly it was a civil basilica that served Roman emperors probably as far back as the fourth-century period of Constantine I ("the Great"). In this immediate area are two museums rich in Roman antiquities: the **Bischöflichesmuseum,** directly south of the Liebfrauenkirche, containing fourth-century frescoes from Constantine's palace excavated beneath the Dom, and the **Rheinischeslandesmuseum,** in the Palastgarten.

MATTHIASKIRCHE (CHURCH OF SAINT MATTHEW), *south of the old section via the Saarstrasse*

The remains of Saint Matthew are in this 12th-century structure— the only tomb of an Apostle north of the Alps and consequently a magnet for religious tourists.

PAULINUSKIRCHE (CHURCH OF SAINT PAULINUS), *north of the Porta Nigra via the Paulinstrasse*

Consecrated in 1754, the church was designed by the baroque master Balthasar Neumann.

PORTA NIGRA, *via the Simeonstrasse*

Overlooking historic Trier is this fortified north gate, the proudest relic of Roman times, dating from the fourth century—when it was, in effect, also the north gate of the Roman Empire. In 1035 the massive structure was converted into a two-level church, the Simeonskirche. Early in the 19th century it was restored to its original form.

WOLFENBÜTTEL (LOWER SAXONY), *12 kilometers south of Brunswick via Route 4*

Like Brunswick, Wolfenbüttel was a ducal residence. In the 17th century in particular, the town gained a reputation as a cultural center and the home of an outstanding library. From 1770 Gotthold Ephraim Lessing was librarian of this ducal library; during this period he wrote *Nathan der Weise* (Nathan the Wise), among other works. Wolfenbüttel was, in fact, Lessing's last place of residence, and his last home, **Lessing Haus,** is at the north end of the esplanade. Also surviving are a **Castle,** reached via the Krambuden Strasse, rebuilt from a 12th-century structure once captured by Henry the Lion; and the Gothic **Hauptkirche** (church of Saint Mary), east of the castle, dating from 1608.

WORMS (HESSE), *46 kilometers southeast of Mainz via Route 9*

The **Dom,** reached via the Kämmererstrasse, is principally from the 12th century. Just north of it is the **Lutherdenkmal,** a monument dedicated to Martin Luther and commemorating his history-making appearance here at the diet of 1521, when he refused to recant (following his excommunication a year earlier) and was consequently put under the ban of the empire. Another famous monument, the **Hagendenkmal,** on the Rhine bank, is a representation of one of the principal figures of the *Nibelungenlied.* Worms is a center of action in that epic. The ancient city was originally a Celtic settlement and then a Roman possession beginning in 14 B.C. The **Museum der Stadt Worms** has Roman and pre-Roman relics from the area.

# LIECHTENSTEIN

One of the smallest sovereign states in Europe, the Principality of Liechtenstein covers an area of about 62 square miles. The country was originally the northern outpost of the Roman province of Rhaetia, part of which evolved into the Swiss canton of Grisons. In 15 B.C., when the Romans annexed Rhaetia, they built a main road through Liechtenstein—the present highway follows its course—and in A.D. 261 the Alemanni used this road to chase the armies of Roman Emperor Gallienus out of Rhaetia. For a time the Alemanni established settlements at the present-day towns of Vaduz and Balzers. During the Middle Ages the area that would eventually become Liechtenstein consisted of the county of Vaduz and the barony of Schellenberg, both of which passed through many hands before 1613, when they were purchased by Count Kaspar of Hohenems. Like previous rulers of what is now Liechtenstein, the count found himself in serious financial difficulties, and in 1696 Vaduz and

*Top left: Vaduz Castle, residence of the reigning prince of Liechtenstein. Below: the Parliament Building and Parish Church in Vaduz. Right: Castle of Gutenberg near Balzers*

Schellenberg were seized by the Austrian emperor. Schellenberg was sold to Prince Hans Adam of Liechtenstein-Nickolsburg, an enormously wealthy Austrian landowner who in 1712 purchased Vaduz as well. Finally in 1719 Emperor Charles VI united Vaduz and Schellenberg as the Principality of Liechtenstein, to be ruled by the Liechtenstein family as an independent state within the Holy Roman Empire. During the Napoleonic Wars French troops invaded Liechtenstein, and from 1806 until 1815 it was a member of the Confederation of the Rhine; from 1815 until 1866 the principality was a member of the German Confederation. Since 1719 the hereditary monarchy has passed through the male line according to the Salic law. In the 18th and early 19th centuries the Liechtenstein princes remained on their huge estates in Austria and Czechoslovakia and rarely, if ever, visited their principality on the Rhine. Alois II was the first prince to visit Liechtenstein (sovereigns had previously appointed resident commissioners to act as bailiffs). John the Good, Alois's son, who ruled from 1858 to 1929, visited the principality several times and greatly improved conditions there; he gave much of his vast personal fortune to the country, which was in dire financial straits after World War I. Prince John had prevented his nation from participating in that conflagration, but nevertheless his people suffered great hardships. Until 1919 the principality was closely allied with Austria, but in 1921 it adopted Swiss currency, and in 1924 it became part of the Swiss customs union. Liechtenstein emerged unscathed but impoverished from World War II, and since then the economy has steadily improved. Today the tiny principality is a center of tourism and industry and a tax-free haven for many international corporations. Most of Liechtenstein's settlements and towns may be reached via Route E-77, the main road, which passes through Liechtenstein between Maienfeld and Feldkirch, Austria. Going north from Maienfeld, the first major Liechtenstein town one encounters is **Balzers,** the site of the nearby medieval **Castle of Gutenberg,** which stands on a hill east of town. In 1499, when the Swiss invaded the area and defeated Swabian troops near Triesen, the castle was the only stronghold to remain in Swiss hands. Continuing north, one comes to the town of **Triesen,** near which is the historic little **Saint Mamerten Chapel,** dedicated to the missionary who first introduced Christianity to this part of the world. After 2 kilometers the road reaches **Vaduz,** the capital and seat of government. The town is dominated by **Vaduz Castle,** now the residence of Francis Joseph II, who has ruled since 1938 and is the first prince to have taken up permanent residence in Liechtenstein. A hilltop fortress whose traditions go back to Roman times, Vaduz Castle was built in the 13th century, but it fell into decay and has been reconstructed several times. At the foot of the castle stands the Gothic **Parish Church,** and almost adjacent to it, a fine Renaissance **Parliament Building,** where the principal government and legal offices are housed. The **Englanderbau** (English building or national tourist office) contains a fine postal museum and the **Liechtenstein Museum,** with paintings from the prince's collection, one of the finest privately owned collections in the world. Farther along the main street are the modern **Town Hall** and the **Natural History Museum.** Continuing northward out of Vaduz via the main road one passes the **Rathaus,** one of the oldest buildings in the area. It was once the residence of 15th- and 16th-century bailiffs of a Benedictine monastery in Switzerland and later of the prince's commissioners. Farther north is **Schaan,** whose church dates back to the 11th century.

# SWITZERLAND

**ALTDORF,** *on Route 25 in Uri Canton*

Altdorf is famous for its associations with Switzerland's legendary folk hero, William Tell. The German poet Friedrich von Schiller immortalized the tale in his drama *Wilhelm Tell,* which is enacted summers at Altdorf's **William Tell Theater.** The background of the Tell saga is historically accurate, for in 1291 Swiss representatives from three central cantons met at Rütli (*see*) and vowed to oust their Hapsburg overlords. According to the legend, at this time William Tell defied the authority of Gessler, the Hapsburg bailiff of Uri. In reprisal Gessler forced the archer to shoot at an apple placed on his son's head. The wily Tell escaped capture by leaping out of his prison-bound boat at **Tellenplatte,** on the shore of the Lake of Uri. Tell subsequently ambushed and killed Gessler in the **Hohle Gasse,** or Sunken Road, near Küssnacht, a deed that inaugurated an era of Swiss liberty. All the sites associated with the Tell legend are now tourist attractions. In the Rathausplatz of Altdorf is the **Town Hall** (1805), and in front of a medieval tower with a baroque cupola is the famous **Tellsdenkmal** (William Tell Monument). The neoclassic **Saint Martin's Church,** the local **Historical Museum,** and the **Capuchin Monastery** are also of interest.

**AUGST,** *10 kilometers southeast of Basel on Route 3*

This town, which is divided into Baselaugst (in the canton of Basel) and Kaiseraugst (in the canton of Aargau), is near the site of a pre-Roman settlement. The Roman colony of Augusta Raurica was founded here about 44 B.C., and excavation has uncovered the remains of a huge amphitheater, temples, and other structures. There is also a museum and a reconstruction of a Roman villa.

**AVENCHES,** *on Route 1 in Vaud Canton*

This small town stands on the site of the old Celtic capital of the Helvetii, later the Roman Aventicum, which was sacked by the Alemanni in the middle of the third century A.D. The modern city of Avenches, which is much smaller than the ancient one, is perched on the hill that served the Romans as their capitol. The excavated ruins, which are east of the modern town, include an **Amphitheater** that could seat more than 10,000 spectators, as well as walls and towers that were part of Aventicum's vast fortifications. A **Roman Museum** is installed in a large square tower whose lower portion dates from the Roman era. Avenches also boasts a Renaissance-style castle and an 18th-century **Town Hall,** which incorporates a 15th-century tower.

**BADEN,** *on Route 35 in Aargau Canton*

Picturesquely situated on the banks of the Limmat River, Baden has played host to the diverse peoples that have occupied the region. Originally Celtic, as Aquae Helveticae of the Romans it was famous for its hot springs. The town was destroyed by barbarians, but in the 13th century it was revitalized by the Austrians as a fortified town. Baden fell to the Swiss Confederates in 1415 and was the site of a Confederate Diet in 1712. The **Old Town** is dominated by the ruins of the **Castle of Stein,** an imposing fortress used by the Hapsburgs as an arsenal and haven during the campaign that ended in their defeat in the 14th-century battles of Morgarten and Sempach (*see both*). Burned and rebuilt several times, the castle was finally destroyed by the Protestants during the religious war in 1712. Interesting sites in the Old Town are the **Stadkirche,** a late-Gothic parish church; the **Stadtturm,** a 15th-century city tower; the **Stadthaus,**

*Top left: the Roman theater in Avenches. Right: Reformation Monument in Geneva. Center: the Castle of Chillon. Below left: the Santa Maria della Grazie Church in Bellinzona. Right: a guildhouse and Saint Peter's Church in Zurich*

or town hall, where the Confederation held its meetings from 1424 to 1712; and the **Landvogteischloss,** a medieval castle that served as a residence for the bailiffs of Baden from 1487 until 1798 and now houses a historical museum.

**BASEL,** *on the Autobahn in Basel Canton*

Switzerland's second largest city and a major industrial center, Basel has kept much of the character of an old Rhenish city built primarily of sandstone. It takes its name from the Roman Basilia, meaning "royal residence," a stronghold erected probably in A.D. 374 to house the Roman emperor Valentinian after the Alemanni had invaded and destroyed an earlier Roman camp at Augusta Raurica, near Augst (*see*). Later Basel came under the rule of a prince-bishop, and in 912 it passed to Burgundy and was thus incorporated into the Holy Roman Empire in 1032. By 1225, when the first bridge was built over the Rhine River, Basel was already a major seat of learning. Its famous university was founded by Pope Pius II in 1460, and under Erasmus of Rotterdam, who taught there 1521–29 and 1535–36, it became the principal center of humanism. Chief things to see in Old Basel are the **Kunstmuseum** (Fine Arts Museum) and the twin-towered **Münster,** a Romanesque-Gothic ed sandstone cathedral that was consecrated in 1019 and largely rebuilt over the years. The cathedral contains the tombs of Erasmus and of Anna, wife of Rudolf of Hapsburg. This church was also the site, in 1431–49, of the Basel Ecumenical Council. Other places of interest are the **Martinskirche,** Basel's oldest parish church, consecrated in 1398; the **Historisches Museum** (Historical Museum), housed in a former 14th-century Franciscan church; the **Rathaus,** an imposing 16th-century sandstone Burgundian city hall; the **Stadthaus,** seat of the municipal council, a rococo building dating from 1771; and the **Kirschgarten Mansion,** a fine 18th-century structure that houses a museum of period furnishings. About three kilometers southwest of Basel, located on the great esplanade of the Battery, is the **Battery Tower,** which commemorates the redouts built here by the Swiss Confederates in 1815, during the last campaign of the allies against Napoleon I.

**BELLINZONA,** *on Route 21 in Ticino Canton*

A place of strategic military importance since Roman times, Bellinzona was already enclosed by walls in the sixth century. Between the 13th and 16th centuries a network of fortifications consisting of three imposing castles (**Saint Michele, Montebello,** and **Corbaro**) connected by walls was built; much of the complex is still extant. In 1503, having been captured from France by the Swiss Confederates, Bellinzona was ceded to the forest cantons of Uri, Schwyz, and Unterwalden, which ruled harshly until 1803, when Bellinzona became part of the newly created canton of Ticino. Places of interest in Bellinzona are the **Collegiate Church,** with a 1565 Renaissance façade; the old **Franciscan Monastery;** the **Church of Santa Maria delle Grazie,** consecrated in 1505; and the old **Ursuline Convent,** now the seat of the cantonal government.

**BERN,** *on the Autobahn in Bern Canton*

The capital of the Swiss Confederation, Bern was founded on an easily defensible site in 1191 by Duke Berchtold V of Zähringen. In 1218, after the extinction of the Zähringen family, Emperor Frederick II granted self-government to the city. Bern joined the Confederation in 1353 and by the end of the 16th century dominated all the country between the lower Reuss and Lake Geneva. It had accepted the Reformation in 1528. During the French Revolution and its aftermath, Bern lost a huge slice of territory, but it later regained some land and since 1848 has been the seat of the Swiss federal government. The oldest part of this beautiful town is traversed by one main thoroughfare with various names. It begins as the **Spitalgasse,** at the end of which is the famous **Käfigturm,** or Prison Tower, marking the boundary of the town in the 13th century. Then begins the **Marktgasse,** with 17th- and 18th-century houses; it ends in the **Zeitglocken** (clock tower), dating from 1530. The **Kramgasse** and the **Gerechtigkeitgasse** lead to the **Nydeggbrücke,** the bridge that crosses the Aar River and leads to the popular **Bear Pit,** where the bears, the heraldic symbol of Bern, are kept. Other major attractions include the **Münster** (Cathedral of Saint Vincent), built in the 15th and 16th centuries, with a 328-foot-high tower that was not finished until 1893; the 15th-century **Rathaus** (city hall), now the seat of the Bern municipal council; and the **Parlamentsgebäude** (Federal Parliament Building), a 19th-century structure in the Florentine Renaissance style. There are many museums in Bern, notably the **Natural History Museum,** the **Bernese Historical Museum,** the **Fine Arts Museum,** the **Swiss Alpine Museum,** and the **Swiss Postal Museum.**

**CHILLON,** *off Route 9 in Vaud Canton*
Built on a rocky islet close to the southeast shore of Lake Geneva (Lac Léman), the **Castle of Chillon** is a famous Swiss monument. The fortress on the site, incorporating Roman fortifications, was constructed in the ninth century to guard the road over the Great Saint Bernard Pass (*see*) into Italy. The castle took on its present appearance in the 12th and 13th centuries, when it was reconstructed by the dukes of Savoy. In 1536 it was conquered by the invading Bernese, and in 1798 it was retaken by Vaudois patriots; it has belonged to the canton of Vaud since 1803. In 1816 Lord Byron visited the castle and was inspired to write "The Prisoner of Chillon," a lyrical poem that commemorates the captivity of a 16th-century humanist, François de Bonnivard, who was imprisoned at Chillon for six years by the duke of Savoy, an ardent Catholic who resented Bonnivard's attempts to introduce the Reformation in Geneva.

**CHUR (COIRE),** *on Route 3 in Grisons Canton*
Chur is one of the oldest towns in Switzerland, having been settled by the Celts about 2000 B.C. In 15 B.C. the Romans took possession of the site and built a large fort, which they called Curia Rhaetorum. In the **Old Town** the **Church of Saint Martin** and the nearby **Rathaus** both date from the 15th century. The **Rhaetian Museum,** containing antiques, furniture, arms, and armor, is housed in the 17th-century **Buol Mansion.** On a hill above the Old Town is the **Cathedral of Saint Lucius,** a Romanesque and Gothic structure of the 12th and 13th centuries. Near it the **Bishop's Court,** an extensive group of buildings around a courtyard, recalls the period when the bishops of Chur were princes of the Holy Roman Empire. The **Kunstmuseum** (Fine Arts Museum) features works of Grisons artists.

**COPPET,** *on Route 1 in Vaud Canton*
This scenic little town on the north shore of Lake Geneva is traversed by a main street lined with arcaded houses built after the invasion of Bernese troops in the 16th century. Coppet's main attraction, however, is the large chateau beautifully situated in a park

above the town. The chateau, which dates from the 12th century, was rebuilt in its present, rather sober style in the 1770s. In 1784 it was acquired by Jacques Necker, the Genevese banker who was for a time finance minister to Louis XVI. Later Necker's daughter, the author Germaine de Staël, lived in the chateau after Napoleon ousted her from France as an "undesirable." At Coppet Mme. de Staël presided over an intellectual court whose literary salons were frequented by many famous 19th-century romantics. The chateau's interior, elegantly furnished in Louis XVI and Directoire styles, remains as it was in Mme. de Staël's lifetime. A historical museum devoted to the Swiss in Service Abroad has been installed in the castle's north wing.

**EINSIEDELN,** *off Route 8 in Schwyz Canton*
A famous pilgrimage center in Switzerland, this little resort town is dominated by its Benedictine abbey, situated at one end of a large square. The church and monastery buildings are lavish baroque edifices rebuilt in the 18th century on the site of a monastery founded in 934 above the cell of Saint Meinrad, a hermit who was murdered in 861. The **Abbey Church,** called Our Lady of Einsiedeln or Our Lady of the Hermits, is dedicated to Saint Maurice of Agaune and Saint Sigismund, the king of Burgundy, both of whom were patrons of Einsiedeln. The attraction for pilgrims is the **Gnaden-kapelle** (Holy Chapel), located in the basilica and made of black marble. It contains the miracle-working Black Madonna of Einsiedeln, a lavishly carved wooden statue of the Virgin dating from the 15th century. (Seen from a distance, the Madonna appears to be a rich bronze color, not black.) In front of the abbey church is a great square; in the center is a statue of the Virgin. In this square Don Pedro Calderón's religious play *The Great World Theater* is performed every five years (the next performance will be in 1975).

**ERMATINGEN VICINITY**
ARENENBERG CASTLE, *about 2 kilometers west on Route 16 in Thurgau Canton*
This small castle, sometimes called the Swiss Malmaison, is beautifully situated in a park overlooking the Untersee, the western basin of the Lake of Constance (Bodensee). Originally built in the 16th century, the castle was acquired in 1817 by Queen Hortense, the daughter of Josephine de Beauharnais and the wife of the former king of Holland, Louis Bonaparte. Hortense and her son, the future Napoleon III, summered at Arenenberg until Hortense died here in 1837. After the fall of Napoleon III's Second Empire in 1870, his wife, the empress Eugénie, and their only son, the prince imperial, spent much time at this castle. In 1906 Eugénie presented Arenenberg to the canton for use as a **Napoleonic Museum.**

**FLÜELI-RANFT.** *See* SACHSELN

**FRIBOURG,** *on Route 12 in Fribourg Canton*
The center of Catholicism in Switzerland, Fribourg was founded late in the 12th century by Berchtold IV of Zähringen as a stronghold on the Saane River. The town subsequently passed to the Kyburgs, Hapsburgs, and the dukes of Savoy, among others, before joining the Confederation in 1481. The Reformation had no decisive influence here; the inhabitants remained staunchly Catholic because the town had long been the site of Dominican, Jesuit, and other communities. Its internationally renowned **Catholic Uni-**

versity was established in 1899. In the middle of the **Old Town** is the **Hôtel de Ville,** built in 1522 with a clock tower added in 1642. Nearby are the **Cathedral of Saint Nicholas,** a Gothic structure begun in the 13th century and completed in the 17th century, and the 12th-century **Church of Notre Dame,** the oldest in the city. The adjacent **Convent des Cordeliers,** a Franciscan friary, has a 13th-century church and valuable works of art.

#### GENEVA, *on Route 1 in Geneva Canton*

Geneva, situated where the Rhone River emerges from Lake Geneva, is the Rome of the Protestants and a truly international city. The Celtic Allobroges settled here more than 4,000 years ago. They were overrun in 120 B.C. by the Romans, who named the settlement Geneva. In A.D. 443 the Romans were ousted by the Burgundians, who in turn were replaced by the Franks from 536 to 888, when the Burgundians regained control. Christianity came to Geneva in the fifth century, and in 1034 the town became a prince-bishop's see and a free city of the Holy Roman Empire. In 1536, under the influence of the French theologian John Calvin, Geneva adopted the Reformation; it subsequently became a center for Protestant refugees, notably Huguenots. From the 11th century until the 17th century Geneva was frequently at war with the people of neighboring Savoy, and on the night of December 12, 1602, the duke of Savoy launched a surprise attack against the city. Thanks to the courage of the people of Geneva the duke's "escalade" (attempt to scale the walls) was repulsed, an event that is celebrated each year. Annexed by France in 1798 following the Revolution, Geneva finally threw off foreign rule and in 1815 became the last Swiss canton to join the Confederation. The **Old Town** is dominated by the part-Romanesque, part-Gothic **Saint Peter's Cathedral,** dating from the 10th and 13th centuries; here one can see Calvin's Chair, among other treasures. Nearby are the 13th-century **Church of Notre-Dame-la-Neuve,** where Calvin expounded his dogmas; the **Palais de Justice** (1709); the 16th- and 17th-century **Hôtel de Ville** (town hall); and the **Monument de la Reformation,** with statues of John Calvin, Guillaume Farel, Théodore de Bèze, and John Knox, among others. At Geneva are the headquarters of many international organizations, including the Red Cross, founded in 1863 by Geneva-born Henri Dunant. On the lake shore is the **Palais des Nations** (Palace of Nations), headquarters of the League of Nations until 1939 and now the European headquarters of the United Nations. Geneva boasts many museums, notably the **Musée d'Art et d'Histoire** (art and history), the **Musée d'Histoire Naturelle** (natural history), and the **Bibliothèque** (library). Within the Bibliothèque are the **Ami Lullin Room,** which contains manuscripts, books, and archives concerned with the history of the Reformation, and the **Jean Jacques Rousseau Room,** which features mementos of this native-born writer. The **Institut et Musée Voltaire** (Voltaire Institute and Museum) is housed in **Les Délices,** where Voltaire lived from 1755 to 1763; the structure is now a research center devoted to the works of its famous guest.

#### GLARUS, *on Route 17 in Glarus Canton*

Glarus is famous as the site of the Landsgemeinde, the canton's great open-air assembly, which takes place annually on the first Sunday in May in the main town square. At this highly ceremonious and democratic meeting, which goes back to 1387, all Glarus men aged 20 or older vote on questions affecting the community.

**GRANDSON,** *on Route 5 on south shore of Lake of Neuchâtel in Vaud Canton*
On March 2, 1476, the Swiss Confederates won their first victory over Charles the Bold, duke of Burgundy, at Grandson. After the battle the duke abandoned all his artillery and much treasure to the victors. Of particular interest is the 13th-century **Castle,** built on the site of an 11th-century stronghold. The castle was rebuilt in the 15th century, when the domain of Grandson became the property of the towns of Bern and Fribourg (*see both*), and was used as the bailiffs' residence. The half-Romanesque, half-Gothic **Église Saint Jean-Baptiste** dates from the 12th century.

**GREAT SAINT BERNARD PASS,** *on Route 114 in Valais Canton*
This historic alpine pass connects the Rhone Valley of Switzerland with the Val d'Aosta in Italy. The route through the Great Saint Bernard was used by the Celts, by the Romans after 105 B.C., by the Lombards in A.D. 547, and by numerous Holy Roman Emperors on their way to Italy (Charlemagne in 773, Henry IV in 1077 on his way to Canossa, Frederick Barbarossa in 1175). In May, 1800, Napoleon I with 40,000 men crossed the pass to Aosta on his way to defeat the Austrians at Marengo and drive them out of Lombardy. Scenically, the road from Martigny is very impressive as it climbs to the top of the Great Saint Bernard (8,114 feet) with its famous **Hospice,** which was founded about 1045 by Saint Bernard of Menthon, bishop of Aosta. For centuries its monks gave refuge without charge and when necessary rescued pilgrims and weary travelers. Today tourists are directed to a hotel within the hospice. The **Hospice Museum** illustrates the long history of the pass, which was already a holy place in Roman times, when it was known as the Mount of Jupiter. In the kennels behind the hotel one may see the Saint Bernard dogs that accompany the monks on errands of mercy.

**LAUSANNE,** *on Route 1 in Vaud Canton*
Situated on the north shore of Lake Geneva, Lausanne was the site of thriving communities in the Bronze and Iron ages and had a population of several thousand when the Romans took it from the Celts in 47 B.C., calling the place Lausonium. In A.D. 379 the Roman town was sacked by the Alemanni, and its inhabitants fled to the hills until the plunderers departed. Here, several hundred feet above the lake, where the **Cathedral of Notre-Dame** now stands, they established another settlement. At the end of the sixth century the first bishop, Saint Marius, came to Lausanne, and the first cathedral was built two centuries later. The Cathedral of Notre-Dame was consecrated in 1275 by Pope Gregory X in a ceremony that was one of the greatest events in Lausanne's history. The Reformation was preached at Lausanne as early as 1529 by Guillaume Farel, and it scored a sweeping success there. In 1536, when the Bernese, who had already been converted, conquered the town, all the churches except the cathedral and the **Church of Saint Francis** disappeared. Lausanne did not attain political autonomy until 1803, when it joined the Confederation. During the 18th century, when Lausanne came under French influence, especially that of the Encyclopedists, the town was an important cultural center. The **Old Town** of Lausanne clusters around the Cathedral of Notre-Dame, considered by many to be the finest Gothic building in Switzerland; the **Place de la Palud** contains the **Town Hall,** with a Renaissance façade, and the **Fountain of Justice** (16th–18th centuries). Just above the cathedral is the **Château Saint Maire** (Bishops' Castle), built in brick and stone between the 13th and 15th cen-

turies. It housed the bishops of Lausanne before it was taken over by the Bernese bailiffs, and today the cantonal government meets there; the **Palais de Rumine** complex houses the **University**, the **Library**, the **Fine Arts Museum**, the **Natural History Museum**, the **Archaeological and Historical Museum**, and the **Museum of Decorative Arts.**

**LES RANGIERS,** *on Route 6 in Bern Canton*
At the tiny village of Les Rangiers, near the summit (2,400 feet) of the ridge of Mont Terri, stands **La Sentinelle des Rangiers,** a monument erected in 1924 to commemorate the Swiss army's mobilization on the Swiss frontier during World War I. It was sculpted by Charles L'Eplattenier.

**LOCARNO,** *on Route 21 in Ticino Canton*
Situated at the northeast end of Lake Maggiore, this town became internationally famous when the World Disarmament Conference of 1925 was held here in the **Palazzo Pretorio** (Courts of Justice); the actual table on which the resultant Locarno Pact was signed is preserved. The chief historical feature of the town is **Castello Visconti,** a 15th-century castle of the dukes of Milan, which was partly destroyed in 1518 and is now a small archaeological museum. West of the castello is the former monastic **Church of San Francesco,** which dates back to the 13th century and has a 16th-century Renaissance façade. North of the castello are the **Church of Santa Maria dell' Assunta,** with a baroque façade, and **Sant' Antonio Abate,** dating from late in the 17th century. Locarno has long attracted pilgrims, who come to visit the **Church of the Madonna del Sasso,** situated on a rock dominating the town. Here in 1480 the Virgin appeared in a vision to the monk Bartolomeo da Ivrea, and the church was erected on the site six or seven years later; in 1520 it became a Capuchin monastery.

**LUCERNE,** *on Route 4 on northwest end of Lake of Lucerne in Lucerne Canton*
Little is known about Lucerne's history prior to the establishment early in the eighth century of the small Benedictine monastery of

*Left: view of the Old Town of Lausanne with the Cathedral of Notre-Dame in the center. Right: Church of the Madonna del Sasso in Locarno*

Saint Leodegar. With the opening of the Saint Gotthard (*see*) route in the 13th century, the town became the major trading center between the upper Rhine and Lombardy and joined the Confederates in 1332. During the Reformation Lucerne assumed leadership of the Catholic resistance, and in 1574 the Jesuits opened a college here, their first in German Switzerland. From 1601 to 1873 Lucerne was the seat of the Apostolic Nuncio for Switzerland, Rhaetia (the Grisons), and upper Germany. The River Reuss, which flows through the town, is spanned by seven bridges; the most famous are the 14th-century **Kapellbrücke** (Chapel Bridge) and the smaller 15th-century **Spreuerbrücke** (Mills Bridge), both of which are covered and decorated with interesting paintings. The **Old Town,** on the right bank of the Reuss, still has many 16th- and 17th-century houses. Above it, to the north, are the remains of the town walls, with nine towers dating from the 14th and 15th centuries. Notable sights include the **Kornmarkt** (corn market); the handsome **Rathaus** (town hall), built between 1599 and 1606 and containing the **Historical Museum;** the **Hofkirche** (Cathedral of Saint Leodegar), a collegiate church dedicated to Lucerne's patron saint, which was rebuilt in the 17th century in late Renaissance style. The **Jesuitenkirche** (Jesuits' Church of Saint Francis Xavier), a 17th-century baroque structure, and the **Fine Arts Museum** are of interest, as is the **Government Building,** a 16th-century Renaissance palace with a Tuscan inner courtyard. On Denkmalstrasse toward the outskirts of town is the famous **Löwendenkmal** (Lion of Lucerne Monument), one of the trademarks of the city. It was hewn out of natural sandstone rock in 1821 by sculptor Lukas Ahorn after a. model by the Danish sculptor Bertel Thorvaldsen. The dying lion commemorates the heroism of the Swiss Guards who fought to the death while attempting to protect King Louis XVI of France during the storming of the Tuileries in Paris on August 10, 1792, during the French Revolution. About a kilometer toward Tribschen, the **Richard Wagner Museum** is the house where the German composer lived from 1866 to 1872.

**MORAT (MURTEN),** *on Route 10 in Fribourg Canton*

Overlooking the east shore of the lake that bears its name, Morat is the site of a Swiss victory over the duke of Burgundy, Charles the Bold, during his wars with the Confederacy (1474–77). Defeated at the Battle of Grandson (*see*) in March of 1476, Charles marched north and laid siege to Morat. On June 22, after a fierce struggle, the Swiss Confederate army, under Adrian von Bubenberg, won a decisive victory. The duke fled, and 8,000 of his soldiers perished, many of them drowned in the lake. An obelisk (2.4 kilometers from the center of town) erected in 1823 commemorates the battle. Morat still retains most of its medieval architecture, including a 15th-century Gothic church and town hall. At the northern end of the Hauptgasse is the 18th-century **Berntor** (Bern Gate), surmounted by a graceful belfry. From the **Stadtmauer** (ramparts) near the gate there is a fine view of the Old Town and the lake. At the other end of the Hauptgasse is a grim, 13th-century castle built by the duke of Burgundy.

**MORGARTEN,** *on Route 30 in Zug Canton*

On November 15, 1315, a battle took place on the mountain slope of Morgarten in which the Confederates won their first victory over the Austrian Hapsburgs. On the summit of the pass is a **Memorial Chapel** (1603), built where the Swiss mountaineers are thought to have had their post. The **Morgarten Monument** (1908) is beside Lake Ägeri.

**MOUDON,** *on Route 1 in Vaud Canton*
Originally a Celtic settlement, this town was fortified by the Romans, who called it Minnodunum. In the fifth century A.D. the Alemanni razed most of the Roman fortifications, and Moudon did not prosper again until the 14th century, when it was ruled by the counts of Savoy. From the bridge over the Broye River one can see the Bourg quarter, with its 15th-, 16th-, and 17th-century houses, as well as the old **Rochefort** and **Carrouge castles** and the **Tour de Broye,** part of a 12th-century tower that was destroyed by fire. The Castle of Rochefort (1595) houses collections of local costumes and wrought-iron signs in the **Musée du Vieux Moudon.** The 11th-13th–century **Église Saint Étienne** is flanked by a fortified belfry that was once part of the town walls; in its chancel are richly carved choir stalls of 1502. The **Musée Eugène Burnand** contains a collection of the 19th-century artist's paintings.

**NÄFELS,** *on Route 17 in Glarus Canton*
A monument here recalls the Battle of Näfels in 1388, in which the three original cantons of the Swiss Confederation (Uri, Schwyz, and Unterwalden) successfully defended themselves against the Austrians. An annual commemorative ceremony is held here on the first Thursday in April. The **Freulerpalast,** a luxurious mansion built in the 1640s by Caspar Freuler, a colonel in the Swiss Guard at the French court, houses the regional **Glarus Museum.** Näfels also has a baroque **Parish Church** of 1781 and a **Chapel** (near the church) built late in the 14th century and rebuilt in 1612.

**NEUCHÂTEL,** *on Route 5 on northwest shore of Lake of Neuchâtel in Neu-châtel Canton*
This town takes its name from a tower (new castle) built in the fifth century near a former lake settlement. Neuchâtel was attached to the Holy Roman Empire from the 11th century until 1504, when it passed to the French dukes of Orléans-Longueville. In 1707, after the extinction of that house, it became the personal property of the king of Prussia; the Hohenzollerns held Neuchâtel until 1848, when it was fully incorporated into the Swiss Confederation. In the Old Town the 12th-13th–century **Collégiale** (Collegiate Church of Notre-Dame), with Romanesque cloisters, and the 15th-16th–century **Château,** once the residence of the counts and princes of Neuchâtel, form an imposing complex. The classical **Hôtel de Ville** (1788) and **Les Halles,** formerly an enclosed marketplace and an elegant Renaissance structure built in 1570, are of architectural interest. **La Tène,** a lakeside site about 6 kilometers northeast of Neuchâtel where archaeological finds have been made, has given its name to a period late in the Iron Age (about 500 B.C. to 50 B.C.).

**ORBE,** *on Routes 79 and 85 in Vaud Canton*
Built on a hill spur above the Orbe River, Orbe was the Urba of the Romans. From the 7th to the 15th centuries it was the fortified capital of the Burgundian possessions beyond the Jura. In the tenth century it shared with Payerne (*see*) the honor of being the chief residence of the kings of New Burgundy. Places of interest are the **Place du Marché,** with its 17th-century fountain, the nearby **Church of Notre-Dame** (15th–16th century), and the **Town Hall** (1786).

About 2 kilometers north of town on the road to Yverdon are the **Urba Mosaics,** Roman mosaics of the first and second centuries A.D. depicting laurel leaves and Roman deities.

**PAYERNE,** *on Route 79 in Vaud Canton*
Situated in the rich Broye Valley, Payerne was—especially in the tenth century—a frequent residence of the kings of Upper, or Trans-jurane, Burgundy. A Benedictine abbey was founded here in the tenth century by Empress Adelaide, consort of Otto I (the Great), often regarded as the founder of the Holy Roman Empire. The **Église Abbatiale,** all that remains of the large abbey, was built in the 11th and 12th centuries and is one of the most important examples of Romanesque architecture in Switzerland. Adjacent to the abbey church is the austere 16th-century Protestant **Parish Church,** which since 1864 has contained the tombs of the Burgundian kings.

**RAPPERSWIL,** *on Route 117 in Saint Gall Canton*
Prettily situated on a small peninsula jutting into the Lake of Zurich, Rapperswil was founded in 1229. From 1415 to 1464 it was a free city of the Holy Roman Empire. The upper town, which has kept its medieval appearance, is dominated by an imposing castle begun in 1229 by the ruling counts of Rapperswil. A massive structure flanked by three grim-looking towers, the **Schloss** became a Hapsburg stronghold in the 14th century. From 1870 to 1939 it was a repository for Poland's national relics during that country's long fight for freedom, and in the courtyard there is still a memorial to Polish heroes. At present the castle is the headquarters of the International Institute for Research into Historical Castles; it also contains the **Swiss Castles Museum.**

**RÜTLI,** *off Route 129 on west shore of Lake of Uri in Uri Canton*
This field is one of the most sacred spots in the Confederation. In 1291, when Rudolf of Hapsburg died, the Swiss resolved to liberate themselves from feudal obligations before another emperor could be elected. On August 1 of that year, representatives of the three central cantons of Uri, Schwyz, and Unterwalden met in the clearing at Rütli to create a perpetual pact. After making this pact, which marks the foundation of the Swiss Confederation, they returned to their homes to organize their resistance to the Hapsburgs. In 1940 Rütli once again witnessed a resolution to withstand outside force—Swiss military leaders met here to consolidate opposition to Nazi attempts to violate Swiss neutrality.

**SACHSELN AND VICINITY,** *on Route 4 on east shore of Lake of Sarnen in Unterwalden Canton*
A place of pilgrimage for Swiss Catholics, Sachseln is the site of the tomb of Saint Nicholas of Flüe, Switzerland's patron saint. Born in 1417 in the hamlet of Flüeli, this remarkable man had fathered ten children before he abandoned his family to live in a tiny cell on the Ranft Gorge. In 1481, when the Swiss Confederates were on the verge of war over the admission of Fribourg and Solothurn to the league, Nicholas intervened. In a dramatic appeal to the Diet at Stans (*see*) he persuaded the Confederates to settle their differences by compromise rather than by war. Saint Nicholas' relics and tomb are preserved in the great baroque church (1672–82) at Sachseln. In **Flüeli,** about 3 kilometers northeast of Sachseln, visitors can see the house where he was born and the chalet in which he lived with his family. On leaving Flüeli one can visit **Ranft,**

which is reached via a steep descent toward the floor of the Melch-
Aa Valley. The pilgrimage chapel here dates from the 17th century;
it is decorated with painted panels illustrating the life of the recluse.
Nearby is the hermit's cell, where he lived for 19 years.

**SAINT GALL (SAINT GALLEN),** *on Route 7 in Saint Gall Canton*
Saint Gall is the site of an abbey founded about A.D. 612 by Gallus,
an Irish missionary. By the eighth century the abbey was an important Benedictine monastery, and by the tenth century it was an
outstanding intellectual center of medieval Europe. The **Abbey of
Saint Gall** flourished until 1524, when humanist Joachim von Watt
(better known under the scholastic name of Vadianus) introduced
the Reformation to Saint Gall. The monastery buildings fell into disrepair, and the abbey church was eventually destroyed. The monastery was largely rebuilt in the 17th and 18th centuries and today
houses several schools, the cantonal government, and residences of
Protestant bishops and church dignitaries. In the collections of the
famous **Stiftsbibliotech,** or abbey library, are some 100,000 volumes
and illuminated manuscripts. The **Vadiana Library** on the Notker-
strasse houses Vadianus' personal collection. His statue stands on
the Marktplatz.

**SAINT GOTTHARD PASS AND ROAD,** *in Uri and Ticino cantons*
The famous Saint Gotthard Road leads through the Saint Gotthard
mountains, a group in the Lepontine Alps, joining Göschenen and
Airolo. Most of the present road dates from 1830, but it has been
greatly improved since then. Not until a road was built through the
Schöllenen Gorge of the Reuss Valley in the 13th century could
the Saint Gotthard be used. After that time it became a vital com-
munication link among the central cantons and adjoining lands as
they consolidated their efforts to win independence from the
Hapsburgs. The Saint Gotthard Pass is in a mournful setting of
bleak rocks and scattered lakes at an altitude of 6,929 feet. It owes
its name to a chapel erected about 1300 in honor of Saint Gotthard,
bishop of Hildesheim, Germany. The **Saint Gotthard Hospice,**
founded in the 14th century and frequently rebuilt, and a meteoro-
logical station are in the pass. The **Saint Gotthard Tunnel** (more
than nine miles long) is the second longest Alpine tunnel (*see also
Simplon*).

**SAINT-MAURICE,** *on Route 37 on left bank of the Rhone River in Valais
Canton*
This small town is the site of Switzerland's oldest monastery, parts
of which date back to the fourth century. As the Celtic town of
Agaunum, this was the principal village of the Nantuates tribe.
Later, under Emperor Augustus, it became the capital of what is
now Valais. About A.D. 302 the Theban legion, recruited in Africa
and commanded by the Primicerius Maurice, was massacred near
here because Maurice and his soldiers refused to worship the gods
of Rome. It is thought that between 350 and 370 a monastery was
built on the site. In 515 King Sigismund of Burgundy founded here
an **Augustinian Abbey,** which during the Middle Ages became one
of the holiest places in Christendom. Each year on September 22
Saint-Maurice holds a great celebration in honor of the martyrs of
the Theban legion. The **Église Abbatiale** was rebuilt early in the
17th century, although its belfry dates from the 11th century and
its stone spire from the 13th. It is possible to visit the catacombs,
narrow underground passages leading to the crypt and Saint

*Left: the Cathedral of Saint Ursus in Solothurn. Right: view of the village of Sachseln and the Lake of Sarnen*

Maurice's tomb. The church treasure, one of the richest ecclesiastical treasures in the Christian world, comprises notable works of the Merovingian and Carolingian periods.

**SCHAFFHAUSEN,** *on Routes 4, 13, and 15 in Schaffhausen Canton*

Built on terraces on the right bank of the Rhine near the scenic Rhine Falls, Schaffhausen became an early commercial center. By late in the 12th century Schaffhausen was a free city of the Holy Roman Empire, and in 1501, when it was liberated from Austrian domination, it entered the Swiss Confederation. East of the town are the remains of the massive 16th-century **Munot Castle,** whose battlements provide an excellent vista of the Rhine Valley. West of the Munot lies the **Old Town,** which has preserved its medieval character. In the center of this district is the **Fronwagplatz,** with the **Moor's Fountain** (1520) and the **Butcher's Fountain** (1524). On the Vordergasse the **Haus zum Ritter** (Knight's House) displays a frescoed façade painted about 1570 by the Schaffhausen master Tobias Stimmer. Nearby are the 15th-century **Rathaus** and the **Münster,** a Romanesque abbey church (late 11th and early 12th centuries) that was once part of the Benedictine monastery of All Saints. The abbey church was accidentally bombed by the Americans during a tragic raid of Schaffhausen in 1944, but it was restored in 1958. Unfortunately the damage to the interior was beyond repair. In front of one of three small chapels is the famous **Hosanna Bell** (which inspired Friedrich von Schiller's "Ballad of the Bell"), cast in 1486. The former monastery buildings now house the **Museum zu Allerheiligen** (All Saints' Museum), with ecclesiastical art, manuscripts, and early printed books, and a remarkable onyx taken from Charles the Bold's treasure after the Battle of Grandson.

**SCHWYZ,** *on Routes 2 and 8 in Schwyz Canton*

Schwyz lies in the heart of the region that gave birth to modern Switzerland, for the town gave its name and its red flag with a white cross to the Swiss Confederation. By the 16th century the town was famous as a supplier of soldiers to the courts of Europe, especially French legions. Many men of Schwyz distinguished themselves with their bravery, returned home with large fortunes, and built sumptuous houses, some of which are still occupied by their descendants. The oldest, called **Bethlehem House,** was occupied for a while by King Sigismund, Holy Roman Emperor, in 1417. The main square contains the 16th-century **Rathaus** and opposite, the ornate baroque parish **Church of Saint Martin** (1774). On the Bahnhofstrasse stands the renowned **Bundesbriefarchiv** (Archives of the Federal Charter), a modern building housing many historical documents, notably the **Bundesbrief** (Pact of 1291), which marks the establishment of the Swiss Confederation. Also on exhibit here is the **Morgartenbrief** (Pact of Brunnen of 1315), in which the Confederates, after the Battle of Morgarten (*see*), renewed their alliance.

**SEMPACH,** *on east bank of Lake of Sempach in Lucerne Canton*
At the Battle of Sempach, on July 9, 1386, an army of 1,500 Swiss Confederates led by Arnold von Winkelried won a great victory over the 6,000 Austrians under Hapsburg Duke Leopold III. The battlefield itself is about 2 kilometers east of town on the road to Hildisrieden. According to tradition, the Swiss victory was due to the bravery of von Winkelried, who in order to open a breach in the Austrian formation, which was bristling with pikes, spurred his horse forward and embraced and fell upon as many pikes as he could hold. A chapel and a monument on the hillside perpetuate his heroic deed. The main street of Sempach has an old-fashioned air, with its **Witches' Tower,** its handsome timber-framed **Rathaus** (1737), its flower-decked fountain, and houses with wide brown tile roofs. On Church Square is 13th-century **Saint Martin's Church** and a victory memorial erected in 1886.

**SIMPLON PASS AND ROAD,** *in Valais Canton*
Rising to an altitude of 6,589 feet, the Simplon Pass forms a divide between the Pennine Alps and the Lepontine Alps. The Simplon Road, which connects Brig and Domodossola, Italy, was built by Napoleon (1800–1806) as an artillery road. However, as early as the 17th century Kaspar Jodok von Stockalper, a wealthy merchant of Brig, adapted the Simplon road from Brig to Italy for commercial mule trains. At the pass today, one can see the **Alter Spittel,** a former hostel built by Stockalper. The present hospice, built by Napoleon, is kept by the monks of the Great Saint Bernard Pass (*see*). A stone eagle commemorates the watch kept on the frontier during World War II. The great **Simplon Tunnel,** at more than 12 miles the longest in the world, connects Brig and Iselle, Italy.

**SION,** *on Route 9 in Valais Canton*
This 2,000-year-old town occupies a majestic site in the Valais plain, for it is dominated by the two rocky peaks of Valère and Tourbillon, each crowned with the ruins of an episcopal fortress. The town, originally settled by the Celts, was called Sedunum when occupied by the Romans; later it seems to have been the first Helvetic town to adopt Christianity. In the 17th-century **Town Hall** a Christian inscription dates back to A.D. 377, one of the oldest of its type in Europe. The bishopric of Sion, founded in the fourth century, played a vital role in religion and politics in the Middle Ages. Early in the 11th century Sion became even more important when Rudolf III, the last king of Transjurane Burgundy, made the bishop a temporal lord and a real sovereign prince with full royal prerogatives. On the way to the Hill of Valère one passes the 14th-century **All Saints' Chapel,** and at the summit of the hill are the ruins of the fortress-church of **Notre-Dame-de-Valère** (11th–15th centuries), once the residence of the chapter of Sion. The **Musée de Valère,** in an adja-

cent building, contains fine works of art that once belonged to the bishops of Sion; in an annex are prehistoric and Roman objects. On the other peak are the ruins of the **Castle of Tourbillon,** built at the end of the 13th century and destroyed by fire in 1788. On the way back to town one passes a former episcopal residence called the **Castle of Majorie,** now housing the Fine Arts Museum.

## SOLOTHURN (SOLEURE), *on Route 5 in Solothurn Canton*

Solothurn, more than 2,000 years old, was first a Celtic settlement, then a Roman camp known as Salodurum before it was taken over by the Alemanni in the fifth century and subsequently by the Franks in the sixth century. The town became a free city of the Holy Roman Empire in 1250 and joined the Confederation in 1481. However, its golden age coincided with the residence there, from 1530 to 1792, of the French ambassadors to the Swiss Diet. The **Old Town,** on the left bank of the Aar River, is enclosed by 17th-century walls and contains many fine Renaissance and baroque buildings. One of the most striking features here is the **Crooked Tower** (1462). In the center of Old Town is the Marktplatz, with a 16th-century fountain and the famous **Zeitglockenturm,** a 12th-century clock tower whose astronomical clock face is surmounted by the figures of Death, a king, and Saint Ursus, the patron saint of the town. Nearby is the **Jesuit Church** (1680–89), a remarkable example of south German baroque architecture. By the Basel Gate is the famous Italian baroque **Cathedral of Saint Ursus** (1763–73), many of whose valuable possessions are on view in the treasure, at the foot of the tall tower. The **Altes Zeughaus** (Old Arsenal, 1610–14) is now a military museum with arms and armor of the 16th and 17th centuries.

## STANS, *on Route 130 in Unterwalden Canton*

This market town was the site of the Diet of Stans (1481), at which Nicholas of Flüe (*see Sachseln*) intervened to save the fragile Swiss Confederation from civil war. The main town square is adorned with a stately early baroque parish church, rebuilt in 1641–47 but still retaining its large four-tiered Romanesque belfry. Near the church is a 16th-century chapel with a monument commemorating the heroism of Arnold von Winkelried at the Battle of Sempach.

## STOSS, *on Route 150 in Appenzell Canton*

On July 14, 1405, Stoss Pass was the site of a battle that effected the liberation of the Appenzell district from the Austrian Hapsburgs. A chapel and a memorial commemorate the victory of 400 Appenzellers over 3,000 Austrians.

## VEVEY, *on Route 9 on west shore of Lake Geneva in Vaud Canton*

Vevey is a well-known resort and the capital of the famous Lavaux vineyards. (About every 25 years—the next time will be 1980—the town holds a lavish feast of the vine growers, which ends in a display honoring Bacchus, god of wine.) The town has a long history. As the Roman Viviscus, it was the chief harbor on the lake. After 1720 Vevey was very popular with English tourists, and many men of letters lived here, including Percy Bysshe Shelley, Leigh Hunt, Lord Byron, and Edward Gibbon. In 1730 Jean Jacques Rousseau lived here in the **Auberge de la Clèf.** The 12th-century **Église Saint-Martin** contains the tombs of Edmund Ludlow and Andrew Broughton, two of the judges who condemned English king Charles I to death. They fled to the Continent after the Restoration and ended their days at Vevey.

**YVERDON,** *on Route 5 in Vaud Canton*

A mineral-water spa at the south end of the Lake of Neuchâtel, Yverdon was the Eburodunum of the Romans. It is also where the famous Swiss educator Johann Heinrich Pestalozzi founded a school in 1805. There is a fine statue of this reformer in front of Yverdon's lovely **Town Hall,** with its Louis XV façade. Also of interest here is the **Chateau,** which in its present appearance dates from the 13th century.

**ZUG,** *on Route 4 on northeast end of Lake of Zug (Zugersee) in Zug Canton*

This charming little town was an important settlement as long ago as 2000 B.C. (there are remains of this period in the **Prehistoric Museum** on the Ägeristrasse). Centuries later the town belonged to the Hapsburg family before joining the Confederation in 1352. The **Old Town,** with its narrow streets and ruined fortifications, preserves 15th- and 16th-century architecture, such as the **Zytturm** (Clock Tower), the chief tower of the fortifications; the Gothic **Saint Oswald's Church;** and the **Rathaus.** Kolinplatz is adorned with a flower-decked fountain and a statue of the standard-bearer Wolfgang Kolin, a local hero who gave his life to save his banner in the Battle of Arbedo (1422), in which the Confederates were outnumbered and defeated by the forces of the duke of Milan.

**ZURICH,** *on north end of Lake of Zurich in Zurich Canton*

The most important industrial and commercial center in Switzerland, Zurich is a very ancient city, having been founded about 3000 B.C. on the site of an even earlier lake settlement. This in turn became a Celtic settlement some 2,000 years later, and in 58 B.C. the Romans occupied the site, calling it Turicum. They built a large fortress that in the ninth century became an imperial palace, remaining so until the end of the Middle Ages, when the palace fell into ruins. Zurich became a free city of the Holy Roman Empire in 1218 and a member of the Confederation in 1351. About 1519 Ulrich Zwingli, pastor of the Grossmünster (cathedral) began to denounce traffic in indulgences, declaring that the Bible was the sole authority in matters of faith. By 1526 his ideas were widely accepted, and the Reformation was in full swing in Zurich. Zwingli's authority alarmed the Catholic cantons of Lucerne, Uri, Schwyz, Unterwalden, and Zug, which allied themselves against Zurich. War erupted in 1531, and on October 11 of that year Zwingli fell in the Battle of Kappel. However, his religious ideas eventually spread throughout German Switzerland. Although there is no one quarter of Zurich that has kept its antique appearance, the area between the **Bahnhofstrasse** and the Limmat River is worth exploring. Here one finds the **Lindenhof,** a shady esplanade with a fountain marking the summit of a hill, where the Celtic and Roman settlements were. Also in this quarter is the **Fraumünster,** a church dating from the 12th and 15th centuries, with the remains of Romanesque cloisters on its south side. Nearby is the **Zufthaus zur Meise,** which contains the ceramic collections of the Swiss National Museum. On the other side of the Limmat there are some fine old houses; the **Rathaus;** the **Wasserkirche,** a 15th-century chapel; and dominating the whole with its two towers is the **Grossmünster,** erected between the 11th and 13th centuries. Other places of interest are the **Schweizerisches Landesmuseum** (Swiss National Museum), with exhibits illustrating the full range of Swiss history from prehistoric times to the present, the **Fine Arts Museum,** and the **Museum of Decorative Arts.**

# BENELUX

## BELGIUM
## NETHERLANDS
## LUXEMBOURG

**ANTWERP,** *via N-14 and E-3 on the east bank of the Scheldt River in Antwerp*
Antwerp's recorded history dates back to the eighth century, and by 1031 the town was known as a seaport. In 1313 the city became a member of the Hanseatic League, a mercantile organization. Antwerp superseded Bruges (*see*), whose port had silted up, as the center of the textile trade at the end of the 15th century; by the mid-1500s, under the protection of Charles V of Spain, it was the wealthiest and busiest trading port in Europe. Under the rule of Charles's son, Philip II, an intolerant Catholic and promoter of the Inquisition, Antwerp's prosperity declined. The duke of Alba's subsequent rule was even more repressive; in 1576 the Spaniards sacked the city, massacring 7,000 and forcing thousands of Protestants to flee. In 1585 Duke Alessandro Farnese, Philip II's nephew, took Antwerp and hastened its ruin. In the 1600s Antwerp was the center of an important school of painting headed by Peter Paul Rubens, who resided there from 1608 until his death in 1640. The Dutch took over the city's declining trade, and the Scheldt River was closed to Antwerp's ships by the 1648 Treaty of Westphalia. Antwerp's industry and commerce revived in 1803, when Napoleon began developing the port, and continued after 1815 under Dutch rule through trade with Dutch colonies. In 1830 and 1832, during the Belgian Revolution, the city suffered damage by bombardment. The city was strongly fortified in 1859 and by 1863 had become one of the world's leading seaports. During World War I Antwerp was held by the Germans from 1914 to 1918. During World War II the Germans occupied Antwerp from 1940 to 1944, when it was liberated by the British. Antwerp's principal churches include the **Cathedral of Notre Dame,** erected from 1352 to 1584 and the largest Gothic structure in the Low Countries, which contains three masterpieces by Rubens; the Flamboyant Gothic **Church of Saint James,** where Antwerp's leading families, as well as the artist Rubens, were buried; and the Jesuit **Church of Saint Charles Borromeo,** erected between 1615 and 1621. Other vestiges of Old Antwerp include the **Plantin-Moretus Museum,** the Flemish-Renaissance home of the famous 16th-century printer Christophe Plantin; the **Rubens House,** built for the artist shortly after 1610; the **Exchange,** constructed on the site of one raised in 1531; the **Groote Markt** (great marketplace), which is surrounded by **guildhouses;** and the **Stadhuis** (town hall) of 1564. Reminiscent of Antwerp's maritime role are the **Steen National Museum of Shipping,** housed in a 13th-century castle, and the **port,** whose oldest part consists of the **Bonaparte and Willem Docks** (1804–13).

**BASTOGNE,** *via E-40, N-4, N-15, and E-9 in Luxembourg*
Fortified since the 14th century, this town became famous as one of the centers of fighting in the German Ardennes tank offensive of December, 1944. Here American troops heroically resisted the Germans under Field Marshal Gerd von Rundstedt, who besieged and encircled them from December 22 to 26, until the United States Third Army brought relief. When ordered to surrender, General Anthony McAuliffe's succinct reply was "Nuts!" Today the star-shaped **Mardasson Monument** commemorates the 77,000 American soldiers who perished in the Battle of the Bulge. Other sights include the **Nuts Museum,** which reconstructs the historic encounter of December 22, 1944; the 14th-century gate known as the **Porte de Trêves,** a relic of Bastogne's defenses that were demolished in 1688; a nearby **church** dating from the 12th century; and huge **Allied Cemeteries** on the outskirts of town.

*Page 245. Top: guildhouses on the Groote Markt in Antwerp. Center left: Bruges canal scene. Right: Cinquantenaire Park in Brussels. Center below: Saint Martin's Cathedral in Ypres. Bottom: Chateau of the Counts of Flanders in Ghent*

**BRUGES,** *via N-10, N-71, N-67, and N-64 on the Reye River in West Flanders*
This well-preserved medieval town grew up around a castle erected near a bridge—the Flemish *brugge*—in the ninth century by Margrave Baldwin, the "Iron Arm," founder of the powerful dynasty of the counts of Flanders. Advantageously connected to the Zwyn estuary of the North Sea by means of the Reye River, the town soon became a flourishing trading port. Bruges took part in the establishment of the Hanseatic League, a mercantile organization composed of various European cities, and became head of the Flemish "Hansa" in London, nearly monopolizing trade with England, whose wool was so vital to the Flemish cloth workers. In 1302 the burghers of Bruges revolted against King Philip of France's appointed stadholder of Flanders. That year Bruges' citizens massacred the French garrison in what is known as the Bruges Matins and defeated French knights at the Battle of the Golden Spurs near Courtrai (*see*), thus insuring the independence and future prosperity of Flemish cities. In the 15th century under the dukes of Burgundy, who ruled as counts of Flanders, Bruges was a center of brilliant artistic activity. The religious wars of the late 1500s and a decline in commercial activity hastened Bruges' demise, and the invasion of the French in 1794 destroyed many important monuments. The town recovered some of its prosperity after a canal opened in 1907, linking Bruges with the North Sea port of Zeebrugge. Preserved around the **Groote Markt** are the city's foremost landmark, the Gothic **Market Hall,** with its belfry and carillon, begun in the 13th century, and the **Cranenburg,** where King Maximilian was imprisoned by the burghers of Bruges and Ghent for 11 weeks in 1488 until he agreed to remove foreign troops from Flanders. The **Place du Burg,** on the site of the earliest castle of the dukes of Burgundy, is surrounded by the **Town Hall,** raised from 1376 to 1420; the 16th-century **Court of Justices of the Peace;** the 18th-century **Palace of Justice;** and the **Basilica of the Holy Blood.** Nearby are the brick **Gruuthuse Mansion,** where England's exiled Edward IV found asylum in 1471, which now houses a museum of archaeology and applied art, and the **Church of Notre Dame,** raised in the 12th and 13th centuries with an imposing 400-foot tower and containing the tombs of Duke Charles the Bold of Burgundy (d. 1477) and his daughter Mary. Other sights include the **Cathedral of Saint Saviour,** the city's oldest church, the earliest part of which dates from 961; the **Béguinage,** a retreat for lay sisters founded by the countess of Flanders in 1245; the 13th-century harbor basin known as **Minnewater** (Lake of Love); and **Saint John's Hospital,** founded in the 12th century.

## BRUSSELS AND VICINITY (BRABANT)

ANDERLECHT, *southwest via the Boulevard du Prince de Liège*
This suburb is famous for its **House of Erasmus** (1466?–1536), where the great humanist and leader of the Renaissance in northern Europe and his entourage, which included Thomas More, lived in 1521. The various rooms contain a museum displaying Erasmus's papers, library, and first editions of his works. Nearby are the **Vieux Béguinage,** a retreat for religious women established in 1252, and the 14th-15th–century **Collegiale Church of Saints Pierre and Guidon.**

CATHEDRAL OF SAINTS GUDULE AND MICHAEL, *off the Rue Royale*
Tradition has it that this church was founded by Saint Gudule, a

*From left to right in Brussels: the Gothic Town Hall with its 320-foot-high belfry on the Grand-Place; the Royal Palace with its Louis XVI-style façade; the sym-*

12th-century maiden of Brussels whose piety triumphed over the Devil. Dedicated also to the Archangel Michael, Brussels' other patron saint, the present Gothic building was begun about 1220 and completed in the 17th century. Emperor Charles V was crowned here in 1516. The cathedral contains tombs of the dukes of Brabant, whose ancestors settled on the site of Brussels in the 11th century.

CHURCH OF NOTRE-DAME DE LA CHAPELLE, *on the Place de la Chapelle*

Begun about 1250 and completed in the 15th century, this Romanesque-Gothic church houses the tomb of the painter Pieter Brueghel the Elder (1520?–1569), placed here by his son Jan.

COLONNE DU CONGRÈS, *on a terrace off the Rue Royale*

This column was raised in 1859 to commemorate the promulgation of the Belgian constitution by the National Congress, following the Revolution of 1830 against Dutch rule. Surmounting the column is a bronze statue of Leopold I, prince of Coburg, who was chosen king of Belgium in 1831 by the National Congress. In front of the column's entrance is the **Tomb of the Unknown Belgian Soldier.**

GARE DU NORD, *off l'Alée Verte*

This was the scene of the opening of the first railway in continental Europe in 1835. Three locomotives, the last of which was named Stephenson after the English inventor (1781–1848) of the steam engine, followed one another from Brussels to Mechlin (*see*).

GRAND-PLACE, *via the Rue de l'Etuve*

Admired by Victor Hugo and celebrated by Jean Cocteau, this monumental medieval marketplace, with its blend of Gothic and baroque, is one of the finest squares in the world. Facing the southwest side of the square is the **Town Hall**, begun in the Flamboyant

bol of Brussels—the Manneken Pis; the Maison du Roi, or bread market, also on the Grand-Place, rebuilt 1873–95 in the Neo-Gothic style

Gothic style in the 15th century when Charles the Bold, duke of Burgundy, who held his court in Brussels, laid the first stone and made it the seat of government in the Low Countries. In 1568 the Grand-Place was the scene of the execution of Counts Egmont and Hoorn, Flemish leaders who opposed the oppressive rule of the duke of Alba and instigated the revolt of the Netherlands against Spain. In 1695, during the War of the League of Augsburg, France's King Louis XIV sent Marshal Villeroi to seize Brussels, a Spanish possession; during the ensuing bombardment most of the Grand-Place was destroyed. Surrounding the square are various guildhouses begun in the 16th century and later restored: the **Maison du Roi,** opposite the Town Hall, was formerly the Guildhouse of Bakers and now houses a museum of city history; other guildhouses include the **Grocers',** the **Boatmen's,** the **Archers',** the **Joiners' and Coopers',** the **Grease Merchants',** the **Painters',** where Victor Hugo lived in 1852, and the **Brewers',** surmounted with an equestrian figure of Duke Charles of Lower Lorraine.

LAKEN, *north of the docks via the Boulevard du Jubilé*
The Belgian royal family made this suburb their favorite residence. Kings Leopold I (1831–1865) and Leopold II (1865–1909) died here, and they are buried in the royal vault of the Neo-Gothic **Church of Notre Dame.** The nearby **cemetery** contains the tombs of important Belgian families. Facing the **Park of Laken,** with its **Monument to Leopold I** in the form of an obelisk, is the **Royal Palace,** erected in 1784 for the stadholder Duke Albert of Saxe-Teschen.

MANNEKEN PIS, *southwest of the Town Hall at the intersection of the Rue de l'Etuve and the Rue de Chêne*
Erected in 1619 by Duquesnoy to replace an earlier figure of the same type, this fountain with a bronze statue of a nude boy, known

249

variously as Little Julien and the oldest citizen of Brussels, performing a bodily function, is the mascot of the city. On feast days the statue, since the time of Louis XV, has been attired in a military uniform; many of the costumes are displayed in the Maison du Roi (*see Grand-Place*).

PALAIS DE JUSTICE, *on the Place Poelaert*
Constructed from 1866 to 1883 by the architect Joseph Poelaert, this hilltop structure housing the law courts is the largest European edifice raised in the 19th century; the enormous domed building covers an area of 280,000 square feet.

PLACE DU PETIT-SABLON, *via the Boulevard de Waterloo on the Rue de la Regence*
This square is surrounded by a wrought-iron railing decorated with 42 columns bearing bronze statuettes that represent various 16th-century guilds. A **Monument to Counts Egmont and Hoorn,** Flemish patriots who rebelled against Spanish rule during the religious wars of the 1560s and were executed in 1568, stands here. Among the aristocratic mansions around the square is the **Palais d'Egmont,** a 19th-century building on the site of the count's former residence.

PLACE ROYALE, *off the Rue Royale*
This square, with its classical ensemble of buildings built between 1773 and 1780, is situated on the Coudenberg (cold hill), seat of rulers since the 11th century. The Place Royale looks out toward the **Royal Palace,** erected in 1829 on the site of the former ducal palace that burned down in 1731, and the **Park of Brussels,** originally laid out as a ducal hunting ground in the 14th century. In the center of the square is an equestrian **Statue of Godfrey of Bouillon,** duke of Lower Lorraine, who led the First Crusade in 1097. The court **Church of Saint Jacques sur Coudenberg** is on the southeast side of the square. On the west side are the **Museum of Ancient Art,** with Belgian sculptures and paintings by Flemish and Dutch old masters, and the **Museum of Modern Art,** housed along with the state archives in the **Palace of Industry,** raised in 1830. Just north of the square is the **Hôtel Ravenstein,** constructed late in the 1400s and the only extant example of a nobleman's palace of the Burgundian period in Brussels.

PLACE SAINT GÉRY, *off the Rue du Borgval*
This square, with its market hall, marks the site where Brussels was founded; about 580, tradition has it, Saint Géry, bishop of Cambrai and apostle of Belgium, established a chapel on an island of the Senne River around which a settlement grew up. The river's course has since shifted, and the site is no longer an island.

**CHARLEROI AND VICINITY,** *via N-21, E-41, and N-5 on the Sambre River in Hainaut*
This town was founded by the Spanish in 1666 for military purposes and named in honor of their king, Charles II. King Louis XIV of France subsequently occupied Charleroi and had the architect Vauban construct its fortifications. Fierce fighting occurred here in the late 1700s and early 1800s, when the town served as a base for the armies of the French republic and later of Napoleon during their Belgian and Rhine campaigns. The ramparts were transformed into boulevards in 1868. During World War I Charleroi was the scene of a battle in which the Allies bravely but vainly defended

the approaches to the Sambre, capitulating to the Germans on August 23, 1914. Today Charleroi is a modern industrial city in the heart of an iron- and coal-mining region. The old part of town is enclosed in the **Lower City.** A short distance from Charleroi are the ruins of the **Abbey of Aulne,** founded in the seventh century by Augustinians, occupied after 1147 by Cistercians, and burned by French revolutionaries in 1794; and the picturesque towns of **Lobbes,** with vestiges of an 18th-century **Abbey,** and **Thuin,** which belonged after the ninth century to the prince-bishops of Liège (*see*), who built its **fortifications.**

**COURTRAI,** *via E-3, N-9, N-71, and N-14 on the Lys River in West Flanders*
Founded by the Romans, this town was the scene of the famous Battle of the Golden Spurs, fought on the **Groeninghe Veld** outside its walls on July 11, 1302. Flemish burghers and guild craftsmen routed the French, led by the count of Artois, and later retrieved 700 golden spurs from the bodies of the fallen French knights, which they hung as an offering in the **Church of Notre Dame** (1191). In reprisal, France's King Charles VI burned Courtrai to the ground in 1382 and recovered the spurs. Courtrai reached its zenith in the 14th century with the expansion of the cloth-making industry. In the **Groote Markt** in the center of town stand the 14th-century **Belfry**—originally surmounted with statues that were stolen late in the 1300s by Duke Philip the Bold of Burgundy and later reproduced—the **Town Hall,** raised from 1418 to 1420, and the Gothic **Church of Saint Martin.** Nearby is the **Béguinage,** a retreat for lay sisters established in 1241.

**FURNES,** *via N-65 in West Flanders*
An ancient stronghold destroyed by Norman invaders in the ninth century, Furnes was rebuilt by Margrave Baldwin, the "Iron Arm," in 870 and subsequently became the capital of a lordship of the counts of Flanders. During the years of Spanish occupation, the town's architecture and decoration took on a foreign flavor. Since the plague year of 1644 Furnes has been the scene of the annual Procession of the Penitents, in which the Passion of Christ is enacted on the last Sunday of July. Early in World War I, from 1914 to 1915, Furnes was the headquarters of the Belgian army. Today the old **Marketplace** is lined with the former **Meat Market,** raised in 1615; the so-called **Spanish Pavilion,** erected in the 1400s and used to house Spanish officers in the 17th century; the **Town Hall,** built from 1596 to 1612, which contains rooms upholstered in Cordovan leather; the 17th-century **Palais de Justice;** and many Renaissance homes. Nearby is 13th-century **Saint Walpurga's Church.**

**GHENT,** *via N-10, N-66, N-14, E-3, N-56, and N-58 in East Flanders*
This town at the confluence of the Scheldt and Lys rivers was settled about the mid-seventh century, when Saint Amand, apostle of Flanders, evangelized the area—one of the last strongholds of paganism in Gaul—and founded two abbeys. The present town was begun by Baldwin, the Iron Arm, founder of the dynasty of the counts of Flanders, in 870, following the destruction of the original settlement by Norman invaders. Ghent became a nearly independent commune in 1126, and its famous cloth-making industry emerged at the end of the century. By 1297 the citizens were so powerful that they repulsed an invasion of 24,000 soldiers of England's King Edward I. Early in the 1300s the citizens revolted against the

count of Flanders, who took France's side at the outbreak of the Hundred Years' War, and chose as their leader Jacob van Artevelde (1290?–1345), a local patrician who allied himself with England. In 1453, after a bloody battle at Gavere on the Scheldt, Ghent came under the domination of the dukes of Burgundy and subsequently saw a flowering of culture and the arts. During the 16th century Ghent became a Spanish possession under Emperor Charles V, who was born there and later developed the shipping industry. Torn by the religious wars of the late 1500s, the town was the scene of an uprising by Calvinist iconoclasts in 1566, which was quelled by the duke of Alba, and of the signing of the Pacification of Ghent in 1576, which united the provinces of the Low Countries against Spain. Ghent finally surrendered to Duke Alessandro Farnese, Philip II's nephew, in 1584. After a century of decline the advent of the cotton industry sparked a commercial revival. On December 24, 1814, Ghent's former Carthusian monastery was the scene of the signing of the Treaty of Ghent, ending the War of 1812 between England and the United States. Ghent was occupied by Germans during both world wars. In the heart of the picturesque old town is the **Cathedral of Saint Bavon**, which was begun in the 12th century and completed in the 16th and contains the colossal altarpiece entitled *The Adoration of the Lamb*, painted by Hubert and Jan van Eyck between 1420 and 1432 and considered the greatest extant medieval altarpiece. Nearby stand the 15th-century **Cloth Hall**, in back of which rises the 312-foot-high **Belfry**, built from 1320 to 1339 and containing a 6-ton Roeland bell, a 52-bell carillon, and a museum; and the Gothic-Renaissance **Town Hall**, erected from the 16th to the 17th centuries. Lining the **Graslei Quay** are old gabled guildhouses constructed from the 12th to the 16th centuries: the **Skippers' House** of 1531 is considered the finest Gothic guildhouse in Belgium. Across the Lys is the **Church of Saint Michael**, which was built from 1440 to 1648 and houses paintings by old masters, and farther north is the **Square of Saint Veerleplein**, where many executions were carried out—including the autos-da-fé of Lutheran heretics during the Inquisition (1545–76). Nearby is the impressive moated **Chateau of the Counts of Flanders**, constructed from 1180 to 1200 by Philip of Alsace; the chateau, with its massive halls and dungeon, contains a museum displaying, among other things, ancient instruments of torture. Other sights include the **Friday Market**, the former political center of town, with its **Statue of Jacob van Artevelde**, and the **Prinsenhof**, incorporating the remains of the palace that was occupied by the counts of Flanders after 1350 and that was the birthplace of Emperor Charles V in 1500. The **Byloke Abbey**, raised from the 13th to the 17th centuries, houses a museum of municipal antiquities, and the **Church of Saint Peter** is built on the site of the abbey founded by Saint Amand in 630. **Saint Bavon's Abbey**, also founded by Amand, was the birthplace of John of Gaunt (1340–99), fourth son of England's King Edward III. The **Great Béguinage** of Saint Elizabeth and the **Little Béguinage** were founded in 1232 and 1242 respectively as retreats for religious women.

**HASSELT,** *via N-2, N-25, N-15, N-24, and N-22 on the Demer River in Limburg*
Receiving its charter in 1232, this town was a dependency of the bishopric of Liège (*see*) from the 14th through the 18th centuries. During the religious wars of the late 1500s Hasselt's Protestants participated in uprisings against the prince-bishops. Hasselt was the scene of a battle on August 6, 1831, in which the Dutch, who had

ruled Belgium since 1815, defeated the Belgian nationalists. Notable sights include the **Groote Markt** in the center of town, faced by a structure of 1639 known as the **House of the Iron Arm**; the parish **Church of Saint Quentin,** with its 13th-century clock tower; the 1675 **Stadhuis** (town hall); the 18th-century **Béguinage Church,** which houses a local museum; and the ancient fortified **Refuge of the Abbey of Harkenrode.** Every seven years the town is the site of an Assumption Day (August 15) fete and is thronged with pilgrims.

**HUY,** *via N-23, N-48, N-632, N-618, E-41, N-17, N-41, and N-43 in Liège*
A town stood at this site as early as A.D. 148, when Roman Emperor Antonius fortified its immense rock towering over the Meuse. Due to its strategic location, Huy over the centuries was subjected to many sieges and suffered much damage by invaders. Huy is dominated by its **Citadel,** known as Tschestia, which was erected on the heights above the Meuse in 1818 by the Dutch on the site of an ancient chateau and which, during World War II, served as a concentration camp for members of the anti-Nazi resistance. Preserved at Huy are the **Collegiate Church of Notre Dame,** completed in the 16th century and Belgium's best example of the Flamboyant Gothic style, and the **Grand-Place,** with its **Town Hall** of 1766 and Gothic **Church of Saint Mengold.** On the outskirts of town are the ruins of the **Monastery of Neufmoustier,** founded in 1101 by Peter the Hermit, whose preachings were responsible for launching the First Crusade; he is buried beneath his statue here.

**LIÈGE,** *via N-3, E-5, N-15, N-17B, E-9, N-43, and N-35 in Liège*
This town at the confluence of the Meuse and Ourthe rivers was founded in the seventh century on the spot where Saint Lambert, bishop of Maastricht, was assassinated; a chapel built on the site soon became a popular place of pilgrimage. By 721 Liège was a bishopric, and the town long kept its distinct ecclesiastical character. By the 14th century Liège had become the capital of an extensive principality, although the citizenry had to share power with the prince-bishops, who retained their temporal sovereignty until the French Revolution. During the 15th century the Liègeois bravely resisted the dukes of Burgundy, who had taken over the rest of Belgium, but finally succumbed to Charles the Bold, whose troops razed the fortifications in 1467 and burned the city the following year, sparing only churches and monasteries. Liège was subsequently rebuilt, and its independence was restored with Charles's death in 1477. In the 16th century, under Prince-Bishop Eberhard de la Marck, who reigned from 1505 to 1538, Liège prospered with the opening of its coal fields—the oldest in Europe —and the growth of its arms-manufacturing industry. Liège welcomed the French Revolution; it was ruled by the French and then the Dutch until the Belgian Revolution in 1830. Liège grew into an important industrial town in the 19th century—building Europe's first locomotive in 1835—and by 1891 was protected by a circle of fortifications that along with Namur (*see*) became a mainstay of the Meuse defenses. Liège was occupied by Germans during both world wars, and in the latter suffered damage by bombing, which has since been repaired. Churches preserved here include the **Cathedral of Saint Paul,** started in the 13th century, whose treasury contains a golden reliquary of Saint Lambert donated by Charles the Bold in 1471; the **Church of Saint Jean,** erected in 982 by Liège's first prince-bishop Notger; the **Church of Saint Croix,**

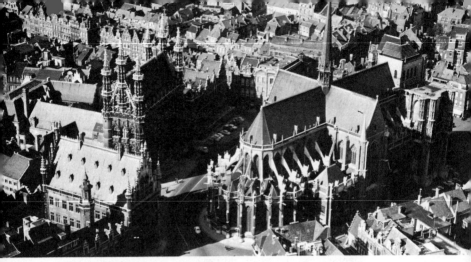

*An aerial view of Louvain showing the cruciform Church of Saint Peter (right)*

raised by Bishop Notger in 986 and later reconstructed; and the **Basilica of Saint Martin,** founded in the 1200s. Facing the **Place Saint Lambert**—built on the site of the former cathedral destroyed by French revolutionaries and their Liègeois comrades—is the **Palace of the Prince-Bishops,** established by Notger in the 11th century and rebuilt by Cardinal de la Marck in the 16th century, which contains the Palace of Justice. The baroque **Fountain du Perron** of 1696, in the nearby **Marketplace,** is regarded as the emblem of Liège, symbolizing municipal freedom. Other sights include the 19th-century **Academy of Fine Arts,** the **Arms Museum,** housed in the former 18th-century prefecture, the **Walloon Museum,** situated in the Court of Miners, a fragment of a 17th-century Franciscan monastery, and the 18th-century **Citadel.**

**LOUVAIN,** *via E-5, N-2, N-3, E-39, N-51, and N-53 in Brabant*

Situated on the trade route between Cologne and Bruges (*see*), Louvain developed into an important town after the 12th century, becoming the capital of Brabant and the center of the cloth-weaving industry. By the 14th century Louvain boasted more than 2,500 looms and had become one of the largest cities in Europe. In the 15th century Louvain came under Burgundian domination, and its celebrated university—attended by such personalities of the day as Emperor Charles V and the humanist Erasmus—was established in 1425; during the 1500s the university had some 6,000 students attending 52 colleges, and it was mandatory for public officials in the Austrian Netherlands to have studied there. Louvain experienced further growth in the 19th century under Belgian rule. The city was severely damaged in World Wars I and II, but has since been restored. Chief sights include the **Town Hall** in the **Groote Markt,** a fine example of the Flamboyant Gothic style begun in 1448 by Duke Philip the Good of Burgundy; and the **Church of Saint Peter,** raised in the 15th century, which houses many art treasures and whose crypt contains the tombs of the dukes of Brabant. The **University,** which occupied the Cloth Hall from 1432 until that building was burned out in World War I, is now situated in new buildings. Other relics of the old town include the **Grand Béguinage,** a retreat for religious women built around a church of 1235, the Benedictine **Abbey of Saint Gertrude,** with its

254

Gothic church, a **tower** from the earliest town walls preserved in Saint Donatus park, and the **Cesarberg,** or Mont Cesar, site of the former castle of the counts and dukes of Brabant, which is now surmounted by a Benedictine abbey. On the outskirts of Louvain is the **Premonstratensian Abbey,** founded in 1129, whose major part dates from the 17th and 18th centuries.

### MALMÉDY, *via N-32 in Liège*

This town grew up around a monastery that was established on this site by Saint Remacle, bishop of Maastricht, in 648. Subsequently Malmédy, along with Stavelot, constituted the seat of an ecclesiastical principality that was dependent on the Holy Roman Emperor until the time of the French Revolution. From 1815 until 1919 Malmédy was part of Prussia. By the 1919 Treaty of Versailles, following World War I, the town, along with neighboring Eupen, was annexed to Belgium. During World War II, on December 11, 1944, the town was the scene of the "Malmédy Massacre," in which 100 American prisoners were shot by the Germans. The old houses surrounding the **Grand-Place** in the center of town were destroyed at this time by aerial bombardments but have since been restored. The former **Benedictine Abbey Church,** constructed from 1775 to 1784, now houses administrative offices.

### MECHLIN, *via N-51, N-1, N-16, and E-10 on the Dyle River in Antwerp*

During the Middle Ages this fishing and shipping town belonged to the bishopric of Liège (*see*) from 915, and after 1213 it was nearly independent until it was sold to the count of Flanders in 1333. Mechlin became a Burgundian domain in 1369. In 1473 the town became the seat of the Great Council, the supreme law tribunal in the Low Countries. Under the enlightened rule of Margaret of Austria, who served as regent of the Netherlands and guardian of her nephew Charles V of Spain from 1507 to 1530, Mechlin developed into a center of arts and letters. The succeeding stadholder, Mary of Hungary, who served as regent from 1531 to 1552, moved her court to Brussels, and Mechlin was compensated for this loss in 1560 by becoming an archbishopric and the ecclesiastical capital of the Netherlands; the first archbishop, Antoine Perrenot de Granvelle, served as an adviser of Charles V and his son Philip II. During the religious turmoil late in the 16th century, Mechlin joined the Union of Utrecht in 1579 and was held by Protestants. During the 1600s and 1700s the city became a renowned manufacturer of lace. In the 20th century it suffered heavy damage during both world wars, which has since been repaired. Medieval aspects of Mechlin are preserved in the **Groote Markt:** surrounding the square are the present **Stadhuis,** or town hall, which was erected in 1326 as the Cloth Hall; the **Post Office,** which housed the town hall from the 14th to the 18th centuries; and the ancient **Schepenhuis** (bailiff's house), Mechlin's original town hall, which served as the seat of the Great Council from 1474 to 1616 and now contains the city library and archives. Erected between the 13th and 16th centuries, the **Cathedral,** or Metropolitan Church of Saint Rombaut, contains an unfinished 318-foot-high tower constructed from 1452 to 1520 and intended to be the highest in Christendom, as well as the tombs of many of the city's archbishops, including that of Cardinal Mercier (1851–1926), famous for his heroic stance against the Germans in World War I. Other sights include the 15th-century **Church of Saint Jans,** with Rubens's famous triptych *The Adoration of the Magi;* the **Gerechtshof,** or Palace of Justice, the residence of Margaret of Austria and later Cardinal Granvelle, which served as the seat of the Great Council from 1616 to 1794; and the **Ijzeren Leen,** a former market named for its 16th-century iron screens, which protected a now-covered canal leading to the three-arched **Groote Brug** (great bridge) over the Dyle. On the other side of the river are the **Salt Wharf,** the 16th-century **Fishmongers' Guildhouse**—the House of the Salmon—and the twin-towered **Brusselse Poort,** the sole survivor of the 12 city gates.

#### MONS, *via E-10, N-22, N-61, N-7, and E-41 in Hainaut*

Growing up around a convent established by Saint Waltrudis in 650 and a chateau built at the top of an eminence, Mons was recognized as the capital of Hainaut by Charlemagne in 804. During the Middle Ages and later under King Charles V of Spain, Mons prospered as the center of a cloth-making industry. On August 23–24, 1914, the first engagement of the British Expeditionary Force took place beneath the town walls; the British held the Germans back for 48 hours before making their heroic retreat. Principal sights include the **Town Hall,** built from 1459 to 1467, in the **Marketplace;** the 17th-century baroque **Belfry,** overlooking Mons near the remains of the former **Chateau;** and the imposing late-Gothic **Collegiate Church of Saint Waltrudis,** raised between 1450 and 1621 and containing many notable works of art.

#### NAMUR, *via E-40, N-4, E-41, N-22, N-51, and N-17 in Namur*

Strategically situated at the confluence of the Meuse and Sambre rivers, this town has been of military importance from the Roman epoch through World War II. From the tenth century Namur was the seat of a countship that submitted to Burgundy in 1420. Namur became a bishopric in 1559. The town was besieged and taken by the French military engineer Vauban before the eyes of France's King Louis XIV in 1692. After the Battle of Waterloo (*see*), the rear guard of the French army made its retreat from Namur toward the Meuse valley. The town's outlying forts, constructed from 1889 to 1902, became a strong point on the Belgian-Meuse line in both world wars and were the scene of heroic resistance, but they nevertheless fell to the Germans both times. High above the city on a rocky promontory overlooking the two rivers is the **Citadel,** begun in the 11th century but mainly constructed in the 1600s, which now houses a museum of arms and military history. Nearby are two medieval **towers** and the ancient **Chateau of the Counts of Namur.** Other sights include the neoclassic domed **Cathedral of Saint Aubain,** raised from 1751 to 1767, the **Church of Saint Loup,** erected by Jesuits from 1621 to 1653, and the old **Meat Hall** of 1588, which contains an archaeological museum.

#### NIEUPORT, *via N-57 and E-5 on the Yser River in West Flanders*

Dating from the ninth century, this town received its present name in 1160 when Count Philip of Flanders established a "new port" here, after the Yser had changed its course. In its turbulent history Nieuport suffered ten sieges, including the one of 1600 when Maurice of Nassau defeated the Spaniards under Archduke Albert. During World War I Nieuport was the scene of continual trench warfare and was almost completely destroyed; after the Germans invaded the town in 1914, its sluices were opened and the entire region flooded. Today the city has been restored in the Flemish style, and principal sights include the **Cloth Hall** of 1480, **Belfry,** and **Town Hall** on the **Marketplace.**

**OSTEND,** *via N-318, N-72, N-63, N-69, E-5, and N-10 in West Flanders*
During the Middle Ages Crusaders set sail from this North Sea port. A fortress was erected here in the 1400s, and late in the 16th century Ostend was the last stronghold of the Dutch in the southern Netherlands; the Spanish took the town in 1604 after a three-year siege in which 72,000 people were killed. Ostend's famous oyster beds were established in 1763. In the 1800s the town became one of Europe's most fashionable seaside resorts and also prospered from its mail and passenger steam service to and from England. Ostend served as a German U-boat base during World War I. Aerial and sea bombardments inflicted heavy damage during World War II. Chief sights include the early Gothic **Church of Saints Peter and Paul,** which contains the tomb of Belgium's Queen Louise, who died at Ostend in 1850; the **Salle de Fête,** on the site of the former Town Hall, which was destroyed in World War II; the 100-foot-wide **Zeedijk** (dike); and a **Monument** to H.M.S. *Vindictive,* sunk in an attempt to block the German exit from the harbor in 1918.

**OUDENAARDE,** *via N-9, N9bis, N-11, and N-59 on the Scheldt River in East Flanders*
A fortified castle was constructed at the site of this town by Baldwin of Lille in the 11th century. In 1460 France's dauphin, Louis XI, took refuge in the former chateau of Burgundy, which in the 1560s was the scene of the defenestration of four monks who were thrown into the Scheldt by Protestant fanatics. In the 1500s Emperor Charles V visited Oudenaarde to see Johanna Van der Gheenst: their daughter, Margaret of Parma (1522–86), who served as regent of the Low Countries from 1559 to 1567, was born here in the **Old Bishop's Residence.** Oudenaarde became a center of the tapestry industry in the 16th and 17th centuries. The town witnessed a siege in 1684 by the marshal of Humières, who commanded the armies of Louis XIV. During the War of the Spanish Succession, on July 11, 1708, Prince Eugene and the duke of Marlborough defeated the French led by the duke of Vendôme beneath the town walls. Occupied by Germans during World War I, Oudenaarde was liberated by American and French forces on November 1, 1918. Principal sights on the **Marketplace** include the late Gothic **Town Hall,** with its five-story belfry, erected from 1526 to 1530 and now housing a museum, and the **Church of Saint Walpurga,** raised from the 12th to the 16th centuries. To the north, the 13th-century **Cloth Hall** is where the first weavers of Gobelin tapestries were trained; it now contains a museum.

**SPA,** *via N-29 and N-32 in the valley of the Wayai Brook in Liège*
This famous watering spot developed around mineral springs discovered here in 1326. From the 16th century Spa became so popular that the town gave its name to the generic term for any natural curative waters. By the 18th century Spa had reached the zenith of its success as the most popular resort in Europe, frequented by Emperor Joseph II of Austria and Russia's Peter the Great, who gave his name *pouhan* to the oldest spring. Much of the town burned in 1807 and was subsequently rebuilt. During World War I, from March to November, 1918, Spa was the general headquarters of the German army and the scene of Kaiser William II's abdication in 1919. Sights include the **Place Royale,** around which are the **Casino,** raised from 1903 to 1908, with its **Theater,** dating from 1863, and **Baths;** the **Parc de Sept-Heures,** with its **monument** to the com-

poser Giacomo Meyerbeer (1791–1864) and the **Armistice Monument** of 1926; and the **Museum of the Ardennes.**

**TONGRES,** *via N-18 and E-5 on the Geer River in Limburg*

Claiming to be the oldest town in Belgium, Tongres was established as a campsite by two of Caesar's lieutenants, whose legions had been massacred on this spot in 59 B.C. during an insurrection of the Eburone tribe led by the chieftain Ambiorix, who temporarily freed part of Belgian Gaul from Roman occupation. Under the Romans the town developed rapidly and became an important fortified outpost on the great Roman road from Bavay to Cologne. Barbarian invasions at the end of the second century A.D. led to the construction of new fortifications and the town's decline. Tongres' bishopric was transferred to Maastricht, and then in the eighth century to Liège (*see*), and in 881 the town was destroyed by Norman invaders. Tongres revived in the 13th and 14th centuries, when it received a solid communal organization, as well as a third set of fortifications. Roman remains include huge **tumuli,** or mounds, where 8,000 legionaries killed by the Eburones were buried; part of a fourth-century **wall** with a **tower** on the west side of town; and a **Gallo-Roman Museum.** On the **Marketplace** are the Gothic **Basilica of Notre Dame,** with its Romanesque cloisters, a **statue of Ambiorix,** and the 18th-century **Town Hall.** Well-preserved medieval remains include the **Moerenpoort,** a 14th-century gate, and the **Béguinage,** a religious retreat for women.

**TOURNAI,** *via N-71, N-8, and N-60 on the Scheldt River in Hainaut*

Inhabited since Roman times, this city, along with Tongres (*see*), is the oldest in Belgium. In the fourth century Tournai became the seat of a bishop and the residence of Merovingian kings; Clovis, considered to be the father of the French monarchy, was born here about 466, and the town's coat of arms still carries a fleur-de-lis. Tournai subsequently fell to the counts of Flanders, and in 1188 it again came under French rule. During the Hundred Years' War, when most of Belgium espoused the English cause, Tournai was one of the few Belgian towns to remain faithful to France; Joan of Arc even enlisted its citizens to attend the coronation of Charles VII at Reims. From 1513 to 1519 Tournai was ruled by King Henry VIII of England, who added a portion of the **city walls** that were dominated by a dungeon now known as the **Tower of Henry VIII.** King Charles V of Spain reunited Tournai with the Low Countries. France's King Louis XIV gave to Tournai much of its splendid and sophisticated architecture in the 1600s, and the city was alternately governed by France and Austria in the following century. In 1940 Germans bombarded the town, inflicting heavy damage on many of its historic monuments. Dominating Tournai today is the Romanesque **Cathedral of Notre Dame,** built in the 11th and 12th centuries and one of the most important churches in Belgium, which has influenced church architecture throughout the Scheldt Valley. Other sights include the **Belfry,** begun in 1187 and Belgium's oldest, and the **Bridge of Holes,** raised in 1290. In the 12th and 13th centuries Romanesque houses rose in profusion, and many of the 700-year-old **houses** are still occupied.

**WATERLOO,** *18 kilometers south of Brussels via N-5 in Brabant*

Just beyond this village is the **battlefield** of the same name, where Napoleon's career was ended when his French army was decisively defeated by the allied British, Prussian, and Netherlands armies under Wellington and Blücher on June 18, 1815. On June 16 the allied armies were moving toward France when Napoleon advanced to meet them and attempted to crush them separately: at the village of **Ligny** the emperor won a costly battle over Blücher, while Marshal Ney's forces violently but unsuccessfully attacked Wellington at **Quatre Bras.** On June 17 Napoleon left to meet Wellington, but because of inclement weather he could not begin the battle on the plain of Mont Saint Jean until noon on June 18. The fighting was fierce, and Napoleon awaited 30,000 reinforcements. Meanwhile Blücher reorganized his troops and managed to penetrate the right French flank to rejoin the British army and win their victory. Today the vicinity is scattered with monuments of the battle. In the village itself is the house that served as **Wellington's Headquarters** from June 17 to 19, which now contains a museum. South along the Charleroi Road is a crossroads marked by **Belgian, Hanoverian, and British Monuments:** one road leads to the 130-foot-high **Lion Mound,** built from the earth and debris of the battle and surmounted with a great cast-iron lion, which looks arrogantly toward France. At the foot of the mound is a museum containing a panorama of the battle. At a crossroads south of the mound is the **Farm of Mont Saint Jean,** where Wellington stayed the morning of the battle. Farther south are the **crossroads** where the furious cavalry charges of Ney and Kellermann took place; the **Farm of La Haye Sainte,** situated in the center of the English lines, which was taken by the French after a heroic defense; the **Farm of Hougoumont,** which managed to hold out against the French; the **Farm of Belle-Alliance,** Napoleon's post during the battle, where Wellington and Blücher met afterward; the **Farm of Le Caillou,** where Napoleon spent the night before the battle, which now contains a museum of the emperor's personal mementos; and the village of **Plancenoit,** near which the remnants of the French "garde" protected the retreat that became a rout.

**YPRES,** *via N-65, N-69, and N-70 on the Yperlee River in West Flanders*

This town grew up in the tenth century around the castle of Count Baldwin of Flanders. Owing to the rise of the cloth-making industry Ypres by the 13th century, was, along with Ghent and Bruges, one of the three most important towns in Flanders. Taking the side of France during the Hundred Years' War, Ypres was besieged in 1383 by rival Ghent, which was allied to the English; the city withstood the siege, but the surrounding working-class districts were devastated and the weavers driven away, thus bringing on Ypres's decline. Ypres was despoiled during the religious wars of the late 1500s and was frequently besieged by the French in the 17th century. During World War I, from October 19, 1914, until May 25, 1918, Ypres, an important road center, was the middle of the British salient against the German army. In three major battles (1914, 1915, 1917) and during continual bloody fighting 300,000 Allies lost their lives. By the end of the war Ypres was reduced to rubble; its medieval monuments have since been reconstructed. Facing the **Groote Markt** are the imposing **Cloth Hall,** with its 230-foot belfry, symbolic of the wealth and power of 13th-14th–century Flanders; the **Meat Hall,** containing a museum; and the 13th-century **Cathedral of Saint Martin.** Erected by the townspeople from 1923 to 1927, the **Menin Gate** is inscribed with the names of 58,000 British soldiers who died in World War I and have no known graves. The countryside around Ypres is virtually a vast necropolis with **40 war cemeteries.**

# NETHERLANDS

## AMSTERDAM, *via E10, E9, and E35 in North Holland*

The constitutional and commercial capital of the Netherlands lies on the south side of the Ij, an inland arm of the North Sea. Amsterdam is something of an engineering marvel, having been built entirely on piles over swampland. (Erasmus once compared its citizens to rooks who lived in the tops of trees.) It consists today of some 70 islands linked by 50 miles of concentric and radial canals and 400 bridges. The city traces its origins to a small 13th-century fishing village that grew up around a dam across the Amstel River. The Amstel lords, its nominal owners, lost Amsterdam to Guy of Hainaut in 1296, and it was he who granted the town its first charter in 1300. City walls went up in the 15th century, when Amsterdam joined the Hanseatic League and became one of the chief trading centers in Europe. When the schism with Spain came, it was careful to avoid military confrontations, though it embraced the Reformation. A reputation for religious toleration brought waves of refugees, first from Flanders, then from Portugal and Spain, and then from France, to swell the middle class. (The diamond industry moved here in 1576.) Between 1585 and 1595 the city nearly doubled in size. The truce with Spain (1609), the commercial ruin of Antwerp and Ghent, and the founding of the East India Company in 1602 combined to propel Amsterdam to the forefront of European cities, a position it maintained until late in the 18th century, when war with England reduced its fortunes. French interference proved even more devastating, and Napoleon's continental blockade stopped all trade through Amsterdam for a time. Louis Bonaparte, however, made Amsterdam the capital of his new kingdom, and when the French departed the title was reaffirmed by the Dutch constitution—though The Hague (*see*) remained the seat of government. The city's commercial revival came later in the century: in order to keep the port open, the North Sea Canal was dredged in 1876, and the Merwede Canal to Utrecht was completed in 1892. World War II brought German occupation and the deportation of some 60,000 Jews, nearly 10 per cent of the population. A tour of Amsterdam should begin in the **Old Town,** which developed in a semicircle around the original dam. Three main canals were dug parallel to this core in the 17th century, with smaller canals crossing. A boat trip on the canals will reveal numerous historic buildings as well as miles of old brick and limestone residences with peaks that lean into the streets—to facilitate lifting goods to the upper stories. At the center is the Dam, a large plaza, fronted by the **Dam Palace.** This 17th-century neoclassic structure was originally designed as Amsterdam's town hall, but since 1808 it has been one of the residences of the royal family (who usually reside in Soestdijk). Also on the Dam is a **World War II Monument** to the fallen. Nearby is 1408 **Nieuwe Kerk,** where the sovereign is invested and many notable Dutchmen are buried. The Protestant **Oude Kerk,** a short distance east, dates from the 13th century, and the **Westerkerk** (1631), west of the Dam, is remarkable both for its commanding tower and for its tomb of Rembrandt (1606–69), who lived and worked in Amsterdam. **Rembrandt Huis,** where he lived for 20 years until expelled by his creditors, is to be seen in the old **Jewish Quarter** in the eastern part of the city. A number of other world-famous museums are to be found in Amsterdam, chief among them the **Rijksmuseum,** begun by Louis Bonaparte in 1808 and installed in its present quarters in 1885. Dominated by the works of Rembrandt, it exhibits principally Dutch art from the 15th through the 19th centuries, as well as collections relating to the minor arts,

*Top left: an Amsterdam landmark, the Mint Tower. Right: the Erasmus Statue in Rotterdam. Center left: old Leiden University. Below: the Begijnhof in Breda. Right: the Town Hall of Gouda*

crafts, and history. An important collection of modern works is to be found in the **Stedelijks,** or municipal, **Museum,** built in 1895. The **Tropen Museum** houses exhibitions from the Indies and Africa. And the **Anne Frank Huis,** a small 17th-century house in which the Franks hid from the Nazis from 1942 to 1944, has been opened as a museum, documenting both the experience of this Jewish family and of victims of persecution elsewhere. Any tour of the city should also include a walk on the **Prins-Hendrik-Kade** (along the docks, near the Dam), where a tablet marking the site of Henry Hudson's 1609 departure for the New World can be seen.

### ARNHEM AND VICINITY, *via N93 and E36 in Gelderland*

Arnhem owes its position as provincial capital to the counts, later dukes, of Guelders, who made it their residence from 1233 to 1538. The town prospered from that time on, becoming a center for the rich, particularly the nabobs who came home from the East Indies to retire here. The city proper was severely damaged on September 17, 1944, when 9,000 men of the British First Airborne Division parachuted on the city in an effort to seize crucial bridges and canals and hold them until the tank corps arrived. The plan failed. After nine days of fighting, the Allies had lost more than two thirds of their number, and the Germans continued to hold the prize until April, 1945. In the suburb of **Oosterbeek** a **British war memorial,** a **cemetery,** and a **museum,** housed in the rebuilt Doorwerth Castle, mark the event. In spite of massive bombings, a number of fine buildings, some of them reconstructed, remain. Besides the 15th-century Protestant **Groote Kerk,** the **Duivelshuis** is the most interesting. So called for the three devils on the entrance gate, this Renaissance building was originally the residence of Maartem van Rossem, general of the duke of Guelders. It was said that Van Rossem ordered the devils sculpted to annoy Arnhem's magistrates after they denied him permission to pave his entryway with gold. On the outskirts of the village is the **Openluchtmuseum,** which contains several working farms whose occupants dress in traditional costume and pursue a variety of traditional arts and crafts.

### ASSEN AND VICINITY, *via E35 in Drenthe*

This city owes its existence to a convent founded here in the 13th century. The order was dissolved during the Reformation, but portions of the buildings survive as Assen's **Town Hall.** Before the government moved indoors, custom had been for the legislators of Drenthe to hold their assemblies and dispense justice in the nearby woods, as was the ancient tradition of all Germanic peoples. Today Assen's most interesting sights lie in the surrounding countryside, particularly at **Borger,** 17½ kilometers southeast, where a number of megalithic tombs can be seen. Called by the Dutch *hunebedden,* these "giants' beds" are in fact the stone burial markers of the Funnel-Beaker people, who settled in the region about 2000 B.C.

### BREDA, *via E37, E10, E38, N93, and N97 in North Brabant*

Situated midway between Amsterdam and Brussels, Breda has played a key role in Low Countries history. The counts of Nassau-Orange made the town their home from the 12th century, commencing the building of their Kasteel in the 1100s and fortifying the city in 1534. In 1566 the castle was the scene of a conclave of nobility who came together to demand an end to the Inquisition. This Compromise of Breda is often cited as the opening gambit in the bloody 80-year revolt against Spain. Breda was taken by the enemy in 1581 but recaptured in 1590, when Maurice of Orange-Nassau, William I's successor and himself something of a military genius, smuggled 70 men into town in a barge and took the Spanish by surprise. Breda fell to the Spanish once again in 1625 (a battle immortalized on canvas by Velázquez) and was not returned to the Dutch until 1637. England's King Charles II, in exile during Oliver Cromwell's Civil War, came to Breda in 1660 to issue the declaration that won his restoration to the throne. Ironically, it was also in Breda only seven years later that William III of Orange-Nassau was forced to conclude the naval wars with England by ceding to his recent guest the New World colony of New Amsterdam. In 1793 and 1794 Breda was captured by the French, who remained until Napoleon's defeat in 1813. Breda still retains many old structures. The **Kasteel** has been occupied since 1828 by the Royal Military Academy. The **Begijnhof**, a semimonastic community of pious women who live and work together in an assemblage of cottages under church supervision, dates from 1531. The **Groote Kerk** was begun in 1290 and embellished through centuries. Among the many notable sights within its walls are the tombs of several counts of Orange-Nassau and in the choir stalls some delightful wood carvings satirizing the clergy.

**DELFT,** *via E10 in South Holland*

If it had done no more than share its famous sons with the larger world, Delft would have had reason enough for fame. Huig de Groot (Latinized as Hugo Grotius) was born here in 1583, studied law at Leiden (*see*), and went on to become Grand Pensionary of Rotterdam and eventually to write *De Jure Belli et Pacis,* the foundation work of international law. Jan Vermeer, born here in 1632, became Holland's consummate genre painter and colorist. Anton van Leeuwenhoek, also born in 1632, who used a simple microscope to observe and describe natural phenomena, is honored as a revolutionary scientist. Generations of Delft's craftsmen have contributed its world-famous earthenware, a trade that dates back to the first decades of the 17th century, when Chinese porcelain began to find its way to Europe via the Dutch East Indies trade. Delft faience was initially an imitation of blue and white Ming porcelain, though it was with the later Dutch-inspired genre scenes on tile that Delft won even greater fame. One of those factories, the **Porceleyne Fles,** founded in 1655, continues to produce the traditional wares. The city, whose name translates roughly as "ditch," was founded by Godefroi the Hunchback in 1074. In the 13th and 14th centuries linen manufactories and breweries provided the city's chief source of wealth. In the 15th century a defensive wall was thrown up around its margins. A fire in 1536 and an explosion in 1654 destroyed many of the older buildings, and the rebuilt city has today a remarkably homogeneous appearance. Among the older structures that survived are the **Nieuwe Kerk,** a Gothic edifice built early in the 15th century. Here are buried 37 members of the house of Orange-Nassau, most notably William the Silent, who was assassinated in 1584. His **Mausoleum,** designed by Hendrik de Keyser, is one of the finest examples of Dutch baroque sculpture to be found, combining statues of Justice, Liberty, Religion, and Valor, as well as a seated statue of the prince. William's **Prinsenhof,** the palace where he died, stands directly opposite the **Oude Kerk,** a church dating from 1250. As in so many Dutch cities, a network of canals lined with old houses gives the city much of its charm.

**DORDRECHT,** *22 kilometers south of Rotterdam in South Holland*

This city's name, like Utrecht, Maastricht, and numerous others, recalls its ancient function as a ferry crossing—in this case a ford for the Dordtse Kil, an arm of the Maas (Meuse) River. Owing to its commanding riverine position, Dordrecht was long the principal commercial town of the Low Countries. Chartered and fortified in the 13th century, it began to exact heavy tolls on all Rhine Valley shipping that flowed past its walls and was a wealthy enclave when disaster struck in the 15th century. First besieged by the forces of John, duke of Brabant, it was inundated in 1421 by the disastrous flood of Saint Elizabeth. This massive flood, which took more than 10,000 lives and washed over more than 72 towns, changed the landscape for miles around. Its effects can still be seen in nearby Biesbosch, or "Reed Forest," a 40-square-mile swamp that before the floods was covered with polders and towns. A rebuilt Dordrecht was razed by fire in 1457, but rose again to become in 1572 the "cradle of independence." In that year the first free assembly of the States of Holland—the future United Provinces—rejected the rule of Philip of Spain and elected William I of Orange to act as governor. Dordrecht also was the site of the Synod of Dort, which met from November, 1618, to May, 1619. The synod's purpose was to bring together the forces of liberal and conservative Protestantism, but it ended with the liberal Arminian view (so called after Jacobus Arminius) being rejected by the conservative Gomarists (after Franciscus Gomarus). In reality the struggle had been between the military landed aristocracy and the middle class, and its most immediate outcome was the beheading of Holland's great statesman Jan van Olden Barneveldt, who was an outspoken Arminian. Dordrecht began to lose its dominant position in the 17th century as Rotterdam grew, but it has remained a commercially active city. Handsome 16th- and 17th-century **residences,** a Gothic **Town Gate,** and a **Cathedral** dating from 1300 are among its present attractions.

**GOUDA,** *via E8 and E36 in South Holland*

The community of Gouda arose in the Middle Ages under the watchful eyes of the Ter Gouw lords, who built their castle at the mouth of the Gouw River. The town, which was soon a thriving center of the cloth industry, received its charter in 1272. This proud moment is re-enacted every half hour on one of the towers of Gouda's 15th-century **Town Hall,** as miniature clockwork figures go through the motions of receiving the formal documents. One hundred years after the grant, Gouda also boasted a major beer-brewing industry, which along with clothmaking brought the city great prosperity. In gratitude the citizenry embarked on the most ambitious church-building project in all the Netherlands. **Sint Janskerk,** measuring almost 400 feet in length, was founded in the 15th century and rebuilt twice after major fire damage. After the second disaster, some 70 stained-glass windows were commissioned, most of them the donations of princes, wealthy prelates, merchant groups, and other towns. Gouda's early manufacturing bases declined in the 16th century to be replaced by two others, which have largely supported the city ever since. When smoking "Nicot's herb," or tobacco, became a fashionable pastime, Gouda became the center of a sizable pipe-making industry. By 1720, 15,000 citizens of Gouda worked in the pipe factories. Gouda is also the home of Gouda cheeses, which are brought to market here every Thursday. Gouda's **Groote Markt** is the largest in the Netherlands, and its **Weighing House** is a handsomely decorated 17th-century structure.

**THE HAGUE,** *via E8, E10, and N99 in South Holland*

The Netherlands' seat of government carries the name of a small community that grew up in the hunting preserves of the counts of Holland. Its full name, s'Gravenhage, means "counts' hedge, or wood." Count William II built a castle here in 1248, the nucleus of an assemblage of buildings that would make up the **Binnenhof** (inner court) and the **Buitenhof** (outer court), which still dominate the central city. William's son Floris V enlarged the castle and about 1280 went on to build on the east side of the Binnenhof the **Ridderzaal** (knights' hall), which has since become the royal throne room. During the 15th-century reign of Philip the Good law courts were added; in 1697 the **Armistice, or Truce, Hall,** designed by Daniel Marot, was erected. The former chamber of the States of Holland, now the **Assembly Hall** of the 75-man Eerste Kamer (senate), was constructed in 1652. The **Ballroom,** built in 1790, has since become the meeting place of the Tweede Kamer, the 150-man chamber of deputies. (Both houses are in session from September 15 to March 31.) The Hague assumed the mantle of political capital in 1593, when the States-General were installed, and it was here, in the Binnenhof, that Jan van Olden Barneveldt was executed in 1649 for his Arminian, oligarchic views (*see Dordrecht*). Despite The Hague's national importance, it was denied municipal rights (much as the District of Columbia is) and thus prevented from direct participation on its own behalf until Louis Bonaparte, king of Holland, moved the capital to Amsterdam in 1795. The Hague then gained equal status with other cities and kept it when the government and court were reinstalled in 1814. (The constitutional capital continues to be Amsterdam.) Since then The Hague has grown in size and dignity. The first world peace conference—called by Nicholas II of Russia—was held here in 1899, at the 17th-century **Huis ten Bosch** (house in the woods), and in 1913 Andrew Carnegie funded $1½ million for the construction of the **Vredespaleis** (palace

*Landmarks in The Hague: the Ridderzaal (left) and the Vredespaleis (right)*

of peace); furnished and decorated by many nations, it was completed just as World War I broke out and has since become the home of the International Court of Justice, the Academy of International Law, and the Permanent Court of Arbitration. Among the many government buildings, parks, and museums worth visiting, the **Mauritshuis,** on the Buitenhof overlooking the Hofvijver (royal pond), is outstanding. Completed in 1644, it was the residence of Prince Joan Mauritz van Nassau-Siegen, governor of Brazil, and subsequently, in 1821, it became the repository of the art collections of the princes of the House of Orange. On exhibition are first-rate works by such masters as Frans Hals, Jan Vermeer, Jan Steen, Gerard Dou, Gerard Terborch, and Gabriel Metsu. Rembrandt is perhaps the best represented, with 15 canvases. The **Royal Library** contains more than one million volumes and manuscripts, as well as numismatic collections. The Hague's chief religious edifice is the **Groote Kerk** (Saint Jacob's), which was erected in the 15th and 16th centuries; aside from its architectural interest (a hexagonal tower, late Gothic choir, carved wooden pulpit), it contains the tombs of the poet and diplomat Constantijn Huygens (d. 1687) and of his son Christian, the mathematician, astronomer, and inventor, who died in 1695. The smaller **Nieuwe Kerk,** built between 1649 and 1656, is the burial place of the eminent philosopher Baruch Spinoza (1632–77) and of Jan and Cornelis De Witt, who were killed in 1672 by a mob in retribution for an alleged assassination plot against William III. Death came outside the **Gevangenpoort,** a prison built about 1400, where Cornelis was held. The prison is today a museum whose exhibits include a variety of old torture instruments. A museum of a very different sort is the **Gemeeente-museum,** or municipal museum, designed by the seminal modern architect H. P. Berlage, which houses collections of decorative arts, musical instruments, engravings, and most importantly, modern art.

**HAARLEM,** *via N99 in North Holland*

Less than 8 kilometers from the North Sea and the dunes and barely above sea level, this lovely garden city has been for much of its history a center of the flower-bulb industry and of linen manufacturing. It was first settled about the tenth century, when a community, perhaps seeking refuge from the West Frisians, set down roots here in the protection of a feudal castle. In the 12th century Haarlem became the residence of the counts of Holland, and in 1245 the town received a municipal charter. The city joined the revolt against Spain in 1572, for which the Spanish punished it with a seven-month siege. Haarlem finally fell to the ravages of starvation, but it was recaptured in 1577 by the forces of William of Orange and incorporated into a united Netherlands. Within the next century came great prosperity, much of it based upon Haarlem's horticultural industry. Though the export of bulbs was an established trade, it was the introduction and development of the tulip that turned Haarlem farmers into wealthy men almost overnight. This native Turkish flower had been brought to the West as something of a curiosity and had gained the particular fancy of the French court. As a result it became very fashionable all over Francophile Europe, and Haarlem, whose sandy soil and expert farmers made a productive combination, became the center of the industry. A chance plant disease that struck the area produced wild color mutations in the tulip. Soon a hundred variations were produced, and speculation in bulbs became a business in itself, with guilds neglecting their trades to deal in tulips. The bubble burst in 1637, leaving many Dutchmen ruined financially. Meanwhile Haarlem was also flowering artistically. Frans Hals had come to the city as a boy at the end of the 16th century. In 1616 he produced the first of his "Civil Guard" group portraits, a series that was to occupy him intermittently until his death. Eight of these canvases and a number of his other works may be seen in the city's **Frans Hals Museum,** installed in the former Hofje (home for the aged), where the impoverished master died in 1666. A tour of Haarlem should also include a stroll around the **Groote Markt,** with its handsome **Vleeshal,** or meat market, built in the style of the Dutch Renaissance; the 15th-century **Cathedral,** with its renowned organ (which Handel and the young Mozart are said to have played); and the **Stadhuis,** built in the 14th century and containing Renaissance embellishments. Recent centuries have seen Haarlem develop an ever larger industry as the sandy soil around the city has been drained. The region is at its most spectacular from mid-March to early May, when first the hyacinths and then the tulips flower.

**HOORN,** *19 kilometers southwest of Enkhuizen in North Holland*
In his *Chronicle and Truthful Description of Friesland after the Creation of the World,* Ockam Scharlensen told of Hoorn's beginnings: "In the year 726 a certain Hornus, that bastard son of King Radbode, built himself a homestead in a corner of West Friesland, which he surrounded with some small earthworks and a canal, and which he named *Horne* after himself." Hornus seems to have been dogged by bad luck, for just a year later the place burned to the ground. Evidently a community did continue to live there, however precariously, for in the 13th century Hoorn suddenly found itself a seaport, thanks to the storms that had broken through the natural defenses of the Zuider Zee and turned the freshwater lake into an arm of the North Sea. By the 14th century the population hovered at about 400, with an active trade along the British coast. In the following centuries Hoorn sailors sailed to some of the most exotic parts of the world, and returned not only with salt but with other rare commodities. Hoorn was one of the six original members of the United Netherlands East India Company, and it was a Hoorn ship that found the southernmost tip of South America in 1616 and named it Cape Horn. Hoorn was also the birthplace in 1587 of Jan Pieterszoon Coen, founder of the Dutch colonial empire in the East Indies. A **Statue to Coen** was erected late in the last century close by Hoorn's **Rode Steen.** This large red boulder, a relic of the glacial age, has been the traditional center of the town almost from its beginnings, recalling the place where trading was conducted and where public punishments were meted out. **Sint Jan's Gasthuis,** a 16th-century hospital, has an interesting sculptured façade. Hoorn has many distinguished blocks of 16th- and 17th-century residences, among them the so-called **Bossuhuizen,** which owing to their vantage of the harbor enjoyed a fine view of the 1573 naval battle in which Admiral Bossu and his Spanish fleet were defeated.

**LEEUWARDEN,** *via E10, N90, and N91 in Friesland*
Speaking a language of their own and going their own way politically, the people of Friesland have a reputation for independence and democratic government that goes back to ancient times. Although the territory of Frisia has diminished steadily over the centuries through the incursions of the sea and the machinations of princes, the heart of West Frisia remains intact, with its capital at Leeuwarden, or Ljouwart, as the natives call it. The Frisians were

partially converted to Christianity in the seventh century by Saint Willibrord and Saint Boniface, and they subsequently submitted to the Franks. Charlemagne nevertheless found it prudent to recognize them as a free people under their own body of laws, and he had the code recorded in the *Asegabuch* in their native language. After the 11th century the authority held by the original tribal families totally dissolved. Despite efforts to remain independent, Leeuwarden and the rest of Friesland came under the counts of Holland in the 14th century. The city received its charter in 1435 and became the capital and the residence of the stadholders of Friesland-Groningen after 1504. Though the stadholders continued to run provincial affairs, the Frisians were under nominal control of Albert of Saxony, then under Charles V in 1523, and then under the Union of Utrecht in 1579. However, Frisia did not fully participate in Dutch affairs until 1748, when its own William IV of Orange became sole stadholder of all the United Provinces. The Frisians are credited with being the first to recognize the United States of America in 1782, and they extended the struggling newcomer a $30 million loan. Leeuwarden was famous for clockmaking and gold- and silverwork from the 16th to the 18th centuries, but it is today best known as the center of the Frisian dairy industry, which predates Roman settlement. Its indoor cattle market, dealing chiefly in black and white Frisian stock, brings traders from all over Europe each Friday. Leeuwarden's **Fries Museum,** installed in an 18th-century mansion, offers an outstanding historical and cultural collection of the region.

**LEIDEN,** *via E10 and N99 in South Holland*

Of ancient origin, Leiden was raided by the Norsemen in 856, when it was known as Leithen. By the end of the 14th century it had become a leading textile center, due in part to the influx of displaced Flemish weavers (*see Ypres*). When the Netherlands revolted against Spanish rule, Leiden endured two bloody sieges, in which half the population succumbed to disease and famine without yielding. William the Silent, prince of Orange, finally came to its rescue in 1574, cutting the dikes in several places to flood the land and permit his ships to sail up to the city walls. When a grateful William offered Leiden a choice between the gift of a university or exemption from taxes for several years, civic leaders wisely chose the university. The **University** was founded in 1575 and installed shortly after in what had been a Jacobin nunnery. Soon Leiden was one of the major intellectual centers in Europe; here the great theological debate between the Arminians and the Gomarists was nurtured (*see Dordrecht*). Later Leiden was host to Hermann Boerhaave, who founded the university's great medical school. Still later, in the 18th century, Pieter van Musschenbroek invented the Leiden jar, a major discovery in the development of electrical condensers. The university also enjoyed a wide reputation for its botanical work. Its **Botanical Gardens** were first laid out in 1587, and perhaps it was while strolling among rows of greenery here that a 17th-century professor of medicine was inspired to flavor distilled alcohol with juniper berries. In any case, it was at the university that the Dutch gave birth to gin. The establishment of the university also brought the Elzevir family and printing to the city in 1580. The city's reputation for liberal Protestantism made it the temporary haven of the Pilgrims from 1608 to 1620. The Pilgrims sailed by canal boat from Leiden to Delfshaven to embark for England and the New World. Their pastor, John Robinson, is buried in a side chapel of the 16th-century **Sint Pieterskerk.** In the 17th century Leiden also gave birth to such great Dutch painters as Rembrandt, Jan Steen, Gerard Dou, Lucas van Leyden, and Gerard Metsu. A stroll around Leiden reveals a city still rich in Renaissance architecture, old mills **(de Valk),** markets **(Vismarkt),** gardens, bridges, and canals. Particularly attractive is the **Rapenburg Canal,** which loops around a section of the Old Rhine River.

### MAASTRICHT, *via E9 and N2 in Limburg*

The site of Maastricht has been settled since Neolithic times. The Romans named it Trajectum ad Mosam (Maas Passage) and made it a station on the east-west highway between Cologne and the French coast. As Roman power faded, the Salian Franks took over; the remains of their garrison city can be seen in the center of Maastricht. Soon after Frankish settlement, Christianity began to penetrate this area and according to legend Saint Servatius, the first bishop of Tongres (*see Belgium*), fled to Maastricht to seek refuge from the barbarians in 382. Though Servatius died there two years later, the town continued to be the seat of the bishopric until 721 A church, **Sint Servaaskerk,** was erected over his tomb in the sixth century and a magnificent reliquary executed for his remains by the master enamelist Godefroid de Claire in the 12th century. In 1579, nine years after the Netherlands had begun its 80-year war for independence from Spain, Maastricht was sacked by Alessandro Farnese, the duke of Parma. When the siege was over, a mere 400 people remained alive within the city. By 1632 Spain was nearing exhaustion, and Prince Frederick Henry brought the city into the newly formed United Provinces. Maastricht, which then became the nominal capital of the province of Limburg, prospered in peace for a time, but in 1672 Louis XIV sent 100,000 Frenchmen to appropriate a share of the wealth. Maastricht was taken the following year in a battle that left 8,000 dead. Twice again, in 1748 and 1794, the Maas River port was captured by the French, the second time in conjunction with France's annexation of Belgium; the city was not returned to the Dutch nation until 1830, following a local uprising. Maastricht escaped major devastation in the world wars and remains one of the richest cities, architecturally, in the region, with a variety of distinguished churches—the Romanesque **Vrouwekerk** and Gothic **Sint Janskerk**—government buildings, and fine squares.

### NIJMEGEN, *via N93, N95, and N9 in Gelderland*

Clustered on seven low hills, this ancient city overlooks the Waal River, the southern channel of the Lower Rhine; from this geographical position it has functioned through history as one of the "gates" of Holland. Nijmegen dates from the time of the Roman occupation in the first century A.D., when it was a frontier stronghold. The Roman fortress was to become the nucleus of Nijmegen. Under Charlemagne Nijmegen became an imperial residence. The **Valkhof Palace,** founded in 768, stood within the grounds of a park on one of the hills above the Waal. The town once again enjoyed favor in the reign of Frederick Barbarossa, who began the rebuilding of the palace in 1165. (The chapel consecrated by Pope Leo III in 799, and a Romanesque choir apse believed to have been built at Frederick's direction, are all that remain of the once splendid complex.) Nijmegen was chartered in 1184, and in 1230 it attained the status of a free city under the Holy Roman Empire, the only urban center in the Netherlands ever to enjoy this privilege. Nijmegen continued to prosper and joined the Hanseatic League in 1248.

Four centuries later it played host to delegations from France, Germany, Spain, and Holland during the signing of three peace treaties ending the Third Dutch War. During World War II it was held by the Germans and consequently sustained heavy American bombardment toward the end of the fighting. Among the buildings damaged was the **Stadhuis,** a fine 16th- and 17th-century edifice. Among other sights to be seen are the 13th-century Protestant **Groote Kerk,** otherwise known as Saint Stephen's, and the old **marketplace,** with its 17th-century public **Weigh House.**

### ROTTERDAM, *via E36, E10, and N96 in South Holland*

The Netherlands' second largest city and largest port straddles the New Maas River (one of the Rhine's distributaries) at a point about 30 kilometers from the North Sea. Rotterdam owes its beginnings to a dike built about 1240 along the north bank of the New Maas, at its juncture with the smaller Rotte River. The little community that settled here was granted municipal status in 1340 and given the right to dig a canal to the Scheur River, thereby linking Rotterdam to the larger towns of Delft, Leiden, and The Hague. With Dordrecht, the principal trading center at the time, just a few kilometers up river, Rotterdam began to prosper. The revolt against Spain temporarily halted growth, but as Philip II's influence lingered in the south, numbers of Antwerp citizens migrated here in search of greater freedom. In the last quarter of the 16th century the city council instituted a plan for enlarging the town by digging the harbor and building up the ground level around it. Rotterdam received another big boost with the rapid growth of the Ruhr Valley industries and the unification of Germany in the latter half of the 19th century. Construction was begun on the New Waterway in 1866 and completed in 1872, opening an 18-kilometer, 35-foot-deep shipping channel capable of carrying the largest oceangoing vessels to and from the port. In consequence of these and later shipping capabilities, Rotterdam was a prime target for Axis destruction in World War II. The devastation began with aerial bombardment on May 14, 1940, and continued sporadically throughout the war. The **City Hall,** completed in 1920, the **Central Post Office,** the 18th-century **Stock Exchange,** the 15th-century **Groote Kerk,** and a **Statue of Erasmus** (born here in 1467) survived intact, but 30,000 other structures were destroyed with a loss of at least 900 lives. Reconstruction began almost immediately after the war, with the revitalization of the port and the building of a new central core. Rotterdam is today one of the most exciting of modern cities; the works of many noted architects and sculptors can be seen here, among them Marcel Breuer's **De Bijenkorf Department Store** and Ossip Zadkine's semi-abstract figure entitled *The Dying City.* Among a variety of fine museums in Rotterdam, the **Boymans-van Beuningen Museum** is outstanding. It houses old and modern works of Netherlands painters as well as a wide variety of contemporary arts and crafts.

### s' HERTOGENBOSCH, *via E9 and N93 in North Brabant*

The name of this city translates "duke's woods," and it once belonged to the dukes of Brabant, who granted municipal rights to the community in 1185. **Sint Jans Cathedral** was begun sometime shortly afterward in the Romanesque style, was rebuilt after 1280, and was given its late Gothic appearance in the 15th and 16th centuries, when it became the seat of the bishopric; it is today one of the outstanding architectural sights of Holland. Particularly celebrated is its choir, with its chapels, choir stalls, and screen. Sint Jans is also richly ornamented on the outside with a number of grotesque figures atop the flying buttresses; some have conjectured that these were inspired by the fantasist painter Hieronymus Bosch, who was born here in 1450. Now the capital of the province, s' Hertogenbosch is situated at the confluence of the Aa and Dommel rivers and is the northeastern terminus of the 76-mile-long Zuid-Willems Canal, which runs to Maastricht and northern Belgium, a location that has contributed to the city's economic growth. The city was taken by the French in 1794 after 18 days of fighting and for a time was renamed Bois-le-Duc. During World War II it suffered heavy air bombardment and damage.

**UTRECHT,** *via E9, E8, and E36 in Utrecht*

The Romans first called the settlement Trajectum ad Rhenum, announcing that it stood at a ford of the Rhine River. Later the name was changed to Ultrajectum—"beyond the ford"—and finally to Utrecht. When the Franks succeeded the Romans in the area, they built a church here, dedicated to Saint Martin, on the site of the Roman fortifications. It was probably the first Christian church in the still barbaric north, and it set the enduring course for Utrecht as a religious capital. About 690 the Frankish king Pepin II permitted the Anglo-Saxon "apostle of the Frisians," Willibrord, to establish his see here, and Willibrord, who founded both a monastery and a school, is credited with having converted most of the northern Netherlands to the new faith. Fourteen years after Willibrord's death, the German Saint Boniface was named as successor. During Boniface's era Utrecht seems to have come increasingly under German influence, and after his death it lost its independent status and became subordinate to the bishopric of Cologne. German Emperor Henry V, who made it one of his residences, granted the town its charter in 1122; Utrecht was by then a prosperous center of trade and industry, particularly cloth weaving. Despite minor setbacks, it continued to thrive as the most important town in the northern Netherlands, passing under the influence of the Burgundian dukes and then to the Hapsburgs. The issue of whether temporal power properly belonged to the bishops or to the citizens was partially resolved in 1517, when Bishop Henry of Bavaria ceded that power to Emperor Charles V. Spain continued to control Utrecht's destiny unopposed until 1577, when Katrijn van Leemput led the women of Utrecht in a march on Charles's fortress, the Vredenburg. This dramatic event swung popular opinion over to the side of William of Orange, and Catholic Utrecht became predominantly Calvinist. On January 23, 1579, Gelderland, Holland, Zeeland, and Utrecht signed the Union of Utrecht, with the tacit approval of Friesland, Overijssel, and Drenthe. The union was an agreement to drive out the Spaniards, and it may be regarded as the beginning of the unification of the Netherlands. Utrecht was once again the stage for international diplomacy in 1713, when Louis XIV's ambitions to dominate all of Europe were quashed here. The Peace of Utrecht, ending the War of the Spanish Succession, involved virtually all the kingdoms of Europe. Utrecht was destined to play host to the French again in 1807, when Napoleon's brother chose it as his residence, but the rule of Louis Bonaparte, king of Holland, was short-lived, and the French evacuated in 1813. The years since have been less stormy as the city has settled down to being a university city, a Roman Catholic archbishopric, a provincial capital, and an economic hub of the Netherlands. Utrecht's numerous historic places include **Vredenburg Square,** a vast plaza that was formerly the site of Charles V's castle and now functions as a market and fair site; the **Domkerk,** dedicated to Saint Michael and begun in 1254; the **Domtoren** (cathedral tower), a 14th-century structure that at 367 feet remains the tallest tower in the Netherlands; and the **University,** founded in 1636. The university's **Chapter House** was host to the signers of the Union of Utrecht. Nearby is the **Paushuize,** or pope's house, built for the provost of Saint Salvador, Charles V's tutor and later Pope Adrian VI, the only Dutchman ever to become pope. Also of interest is the **Huis Oudaen** (home for the aged), east of the Vredenburg. This 14th-century mansion witnessed the signing of the Treaty of Utrecht in 1713.

### VLISSINGEN, *via N97 in Zeeland*

Now a popular seaside resort, Vlissingen was once a major naval base commanding one of the entrances of the Scheldt River, and as such it has figured in several decisive actions in Dutch history. When the Low Countries, led by the dissident "Sea Beggars," rose against Spanish rule in 1572, Vlissingen was the first Dutch town to go over to the revolution. One by one, other towns followed, proclaiming allegiance to William of Orange. But despite brave words and valiant actions, neither William nor the States-General could hold the provinces together against Spanish opposition. When in 1584 William was assassinated by a supporter of Philip of Spain, the Low Countries turned to England for protection. Queen Elizabeth agreed to send 6,000 men in return for possession of Vlissingen and Brielle. The English remained in what became known as Flushing until 1587. They returned in 1809 as part of an ill-fated attempt to break Napoleon's blockade of the Continent. Late in July of that year, 40,000 troops landed on the island of Walcheren. They took Vlissingen and nearby South Beveland, but were stopped from further advances by the French and Dutch; after a five-month stalemate they went home in shame. Vlissingen's life was once again disastrously upset in World War II. The Allies, in an effort to end German control of the Scheldt and to unblock the river route to Antwerp, breached the dikes holding back the sea in four places, flooding much of the former island, including Vlissingen. An 18th-century **Stadhuis** and remnants of the 16th-century **town gate** are extant.

### ZWOLLE, *via E35, N91, and N93 in Overijssel*

Already a thriving commercial town in the 13th century, Zwolle prospered for many centuries as an entrepôt for riverine traffic between North Germany and the rest of the Low Countries. The town, which is the capital of the province, lies on the Zwartewater, a small river that feeds into the Ijsselmeer 19 kilometers beyond. The town's Protestant **Groote Kerk** was begun in the lifetime of Thomas a Kempis, who spent 64 years of his life at nearby Mount Saint Agnes residing among the Brothers of the Common Life. Here he is said to have written in 1418 his *Imitatio Christi,* a devotional manual second only to the Bible in the number of languages in which it is translated. Anti-intellectual and pietistic, it is still considered a Christian classic. Zwolle's **Stadhuis** dates from the same period and contains a handsome **Trouwzaal** (marriage chamber) and a **Schepenzaal** (magistrates' hall), the latter curiously decorated with grotesque carvings on the ceiling. These little figures were meant, some say, as not so subtle caricatures of certain officials in the rival city of Kampen, 48 kilometers west.

# LUXEMBOURG

**BEAUFORT,** *southwest of Route 19*

The remains of the **Château de Beaufort,** a feudal fortress built in the 12th, 13th, and 16th centuries, stand beside a small lake. Behind the chateau is a 17th-century **manor house** built by the lord of Beaufort.

**BOURSCHEID,** *north of Ettelbruck via secondary road*

From atop a steep hill the ruins of **Bourscheid Castle,** a medieval stronghold destroyed in 1684, overlook the Sûre valley. General George S. Patton was a frequent visitor to this tiny Ardennes village when his general quarters were in Luxembourg.

**CLERVAUX,** *on Route 18 on the Clerf River*

Situated on a promontory formed by the Clerf, Clervaux is dominated by the feudal **Chateau** of the seigneurs de Lannoy, one of whom was an ancestor of President Franklin D. Roosevelt's. The chateau, flanked by fine towers, dates from the 12th to the 17th centuries and was restored after bombardments during World War II. It now contains a hotel, a youth hostel, and some museum rooms furnished in antique styles. Above the castle one finds the Rhenish-Romanesque **Parish Church,** built in 1910. Still higher is the Benedictine **Abbey of Saint Maurice and Saint Maur,** built 1909–12, with a fine church in the neo-Romanesque style; behind the church is an exhibition devoted to 20th-century monastic life. The graves of French soldiers killed in 1798 in a peasant revolt against conscription into the French revolutionary army, after the land had been ceded to France, are on the other side of the river, as is the **Chapel of Notre-Dame de Lorette** (1786).

*Left: General George Patton Jr.'s monument at Ettelbruck. Top right: a view of Luxembourg City with the spires of Notre-Dame Cathedral on the left. Below: Vianden Castle*

**DALHEIM,** *just north of Route 15*

A commemorative column erected in 1855 marks the site of the Gallo-Roman camp of Ricciacum, one of the most important Roman forts in the grand duchy.

**DIEKIRCH,** *on Routes 14, 15, 16, and 19 on the Sûre River*

Diekirch was an important station in Roman times, and in 1926 remains of Roman baths were uncovered here. Just north of town the museum in the **Brandenbourg Ruins** contains Roman mosaics of the third century A.D. Also in this area are the ruins of the 12th-century **Brandenbourg Castle,** destroyed by the French in 1668. The town of Diekirch possesses three fine churches: the parish **Church of Saint Nicholas** (10th–16th centuries), the former **Church of Saint Lawrence,** and the new **Church of Saint Lawrence,** built in neo-Romanesque style in 1868.

**ECHTERNACH,** *on Route 11 on the Sûre River at the German border*

The remains of its medieval walls with their five towers, and the ancient monastery, basilica, and town hall, give Echternach a medieval air. The town clusters around the former **Benedictine Abbey,** which now houses various public offices; it was founded in 698 by Saint Willibrord, who came from Northumberland to convert the Frisians to Christianity. Saint Willibrord died at Echternach in 732 and was buried in the former abbey church, the **Church of Saint Willibrord,** which was almost completely reconstructed after World War II. Each year on Whit Tuesday Echternach is the scene of the famous "Dancing Procession," instituted in the 13th century in honor of Saint Willibrord. Throughout the Middle Ages thousands of ailing pilgrims were reputedly cured of epilepsy and other ills after having venerated the saint's relics. The procession, which begins with the tolling of a huge bell given to the town in 1512 by Emperor Maximilian, ends at Saint Willibrord's tomb.

**EISCH VALLEY.** *See* MERSCH

**ETTELBRUCK,** *on Routes 15, 7A, and 19 at the confluence of the Wark, Alzette, and Sûre rivers*

A popular starting point for hikes into the Ardennes forests, this town has erected a **monument** to General George S. Patton, Jr., who liberated it from the Nazis early in 1945.

**LUXEMBOURG CITY AND VICINITY,** *on Routes 1, 5, 6, 7, 11, and E9*

Luxembourg City originated in 963 when a count of Sigefroi in the Moselle country built a fortress on the Bouc, a rocky plateau that descends steeply to the winding Alzette River. The town grew up around the citadel, which was reinforced and enlarged each time Luxembourg changed hands. This castle was at one time connected to nearly 60 outer forts by more than 14 miles of corridors, and the ramparts were fortified with casemates—armed compartments for artillery blasted out of the solid rock. The ancient **Bouc Casemates,** whose entrance is at the foot of the **Pont du Château,** may be visited. Today ruins of the towers are all that remain of Luxembourg City's once impregnable fortress. In the old section of Luxembourg City is the **Place de la Constitution,** which contains a **monument** to the Luxembourg volunteers who fought in World War I. The entrance to the **Pétrusse Casemates** is at the northeast corner of the square. Not far away stands the 17th-century **Cathedral of Notre-Dame,** which contains the tomb of Jean d'Aveugle (John the Blind), count of Luxembourg and king of Bohemia, who was killed while fighting the English at the Battle of Crécy (1346). Farther north in Old Luxembourg is the **Place Guillaume,** with an equestrian statue of William II, grand duke of Luxembourg and king of Holland. The **Town Hall** (1830–38) is at the south side of the square. To the east is the **Place du Marché aux Poissons,** the oldest square in the city and the site of the **National Museum,** with its exhibits of art and history. Old streets radiate in all directions from this square, one leading to the late-16th-century **Grand Ducal Palace,** which is partly occupied by the royal family and partly by the legislature. One of the most enjoyable walks in the old quarter is to take the **Promenade de la Corniche,** which begins at the Place du Saint Esprit and follows some of the old ramparts. It leads to the Montée de la Pétrusse, at the foot of which stands the ancient **Chapel of Saint Quirinus,** cut into the rock. The promenade ends at the Bouc. West of the old city is the **Parc Public,** laid out in 1872 on the site of the town's westerly fortifications. The **United States Army Cemetery,** in the suburb of Hamm, about 5 kilometers from Luxembourg City, contains the graves of more than 5,000 American soldiers killed in battles of the Ardennes in World War II. The grave of General George S. Patton is here.

**MERSCH AND VICINITY,** *on Routes A, 7, 8, and 9 on the Alzette River*
An old market town, Mersch is known for its onion-domed **church tower** (1707), its classical-style **church** (1884–50), and a former 17th-century **fortress** surrounded by moats and now used as a youth hostel. About a kilometer west of town is a wooded hill, called the **Helpert Knap,** where Roman objects have been discovered. Going southwest from Mersch, a road winds through the charming Eisch valley, known as the Valley of Seven Castles. One passes the **Castle of Hollenfels,** with a 13th-century keep and a newer portion dating from the 16th century, and **Ansembourg,** with a ruined castle and the 17th-century Chateau with formal gardens. Nearby are the ruins of the **Abbey of Marienthal,** founded in 1237, as well as a **monastery** built in the 1880s by the Pères Blancs d'Afrique, with a missionary school and a small **Congo Museum.** The next towns are **Septfontaines,** with an old church and a ruined manor house, and **Koerich,** with a church and a ruined castle.

**VIANDEN,** *on Route 15 on the west bank of the Our River*
This picturesque town nestling in the valley of the Our was founded in the ninth century and was granted a town charter in the 14th century by Philip of Vianden. Of particular interest in the ancestral home of the counts of Vianden are the **Byzantine and Gothic Rooms** and the **Knights' Hall,** which could accommodate 500 men-at-arms. The cloister of the 13th-century Gothic parish **Church of the Trinitarians** contains the tombs of two lords of Vianden. The house where Victor Hugo stayed in 1870–71, during his wandering exile, is now the **Victor Hugo Museum.**

**WILTZ,** *on Routes 25 and 29*
Oberwiltz, the upper town, is noted for a medieval **Castle,** which can be seen for miles around. The 12th-century **Parish Church** contains numerous tombstones of the feudal counts of Wiltz. The town, which saw action in the Battle of the Bulge (December, 1944–January, 1945), is filled with mementos of World War II, including a national **monument** in honor of the day in 1942 when local workers went on strike against occupying German forces.

# UNITED KINGDOM & IRELAND

ENGLAND
NORTHERN IRELAND
SCOTLAND
WALES

OUTER HEBRIDES
BENBECULA
Dunvegin
SOUTH UIST
SKYE
BARRA
INNER
HEBRIDES

Sea of the Hebrides

IONA

ATLANTIC OCEAN

NORTH
CHANNEL
Ballycastle

Bushmills
Carrickfergus
Londonderry Belfast
Donegal
NORTHERN
IRELAND Greyabbey
DONEGAL
Devenish Armagh Downpatrick
INISHMURRAY Island Dundrum
Sligo Monea
SLIGO
LOUTH
Carlingford
MAYO WEST Kells Drogheda
MEATH
Boyne R. Newgrange
ROSCOMMON Trim Tara
Athlone OFFALY
Galway Clonmacnoise Maynooth Dublin
Shannon R. KILDARE
Galway IRELAND CARLOW
Bay CLARE LAOIGHIS Carlow
Barrow
R.
Kilkenny
Limerick KILKENNY
Askeaton LIMERICK Cashel
Adare TIPPERARY Wexford
Kilmallock Waterford
KERRY Blarney WATERFORD SAINT
Cork GEORGE'S
Youghal CHANNEL
CORK

ATLANTIC OCEAN

# ENGLAND

**ARUNDEL CASTLE (SUSSEX),** *92 kilometers south of London off A29*
This ancient castle has for more than 500 years been the seat of the dukes of Norfolk, premier dukes and hereditary Earl Marshals of England. Begun in the reign of Edward the Confessor, it was besieged by Henry I in 1102 and by Stephen in 1139, and during the Civil War it was occupied by Parliamentarians after a 17-day bombardment. The castle was extensively rebuilt and restored in the 18th century and again late in the 19th. The 12th-century keep has been retained; inside the castle are fine period furniture and paintings.

**ASHBY-DE-LA-ZOUCH (LEICESTER),** *14 kilometers southeast of Burton-on-Trent on A50*
The ruined **Castle** is perhaps most famous for its role in Sir Walter Scott's *Ivanhoe*: the novel's chivalric pageant and tournament are set here and in a nearby field. The castle was begun late in the 15th century by Lord Hastings, to whom Edward IV had granted the property in appreciation for Hastings' support in the Wars of the Roses. In 1569 Mary queen of Scots stayed here for a short time as a prisoner of Hastings' grandson, the first earl of Huntingdon. James I visited the castle with his entire court in 1617; Charles I and Henrietta Maria were guests in 1634; and Charles I rested here before and after the Battle of Naseby. During the Civil War the castle was demolished.

**AVEBURY (WILTSHIRE),** *on A361*
The largest **Stone Circle** in Europe—with its bank and ditch it encloses 28 acres—surrounds Avebury village. Somewhat older than Stonehenge (it dates from about 2000 B.C.), its purpose also is unclear. Inside the 15-foot-high outer bank and 30-foot-deep ditch was a main circle of about 100 huge unhewn sarsen stones, and two smaller circles. Many of the stones, which weighed as much as 60 tons, have disappeared, having been broken up over the centuries for use as building materials. The mound of **Silbury Hill,** nearby, is the oldest prehistoric structure in Great Britain.

**BAKEWELL VICINITY (DERBY)**
CHATSWORTH HOUSE, *about 4 kilometers northeast on A623*
This mansion, notable for its lavishly decorated interior and its impressive grounds, is the seat of the dukes of Devonshire. The original home on this site was begun by Sir William Cavendish, second husband of Bess of Hardwick, in the 16th century. Mary queen of Scots visited there several times between 1570 and 1581, while she was in the custody of Bess's fourth husband, the earl of Shrewsbury. In 1687 William Cavendish, first duke of Devonshire, began the present house; only the **Hunting Tower** remains from the original buildings. George II died at Chatsworth and was laid out in the **State Bedroom.**

**BATH (SOMERSET),** *via A46, A4, A36, and A367*
Soon after the Romans invaded Britain they discovered the medicinal qualities of the hot springs here and established the town of Aquae Solis, which became a thriving spa until the fourth century. In the center of the town was an elaborate system of baths, the remains of which are remarkably well preserved. The **Great Bath** has its original pavements and lead floor and is still supplied with hot water through the original Roman pipes. Other remains include two smaller baths; a hypocaust, or hot room; and in the adjoining mu-

*Top left: the houses of Parliament in London. Right: the Royal Pavilion at Brighton. Center: Windsor Castle in Berkshire. Below left: the mysterious monument of Stonehenge on Salisbury Plain. Right: Magdalen Tower at Oxford*

seum, relics of the Temple of Minerva, which was attached to the baths. In the 18th century Bath once again emerged as England's most fashionable spa, in large part because Beau Nash (1674–1762) came to live here. Nash set Bath's social standards, and architects John Wood and his son began to build what was in effect a new Georgian city to accommodate the influx. Wood's harmonious designs included **Queen's Square** (1728) and the **Circus** (1754). His son John Wood the younger was responsible for the **Royal Crescent** (1775), a semi-ellipse of 30 houses. Bath today remains a Georgian showpiece.

**BATTLE (SUSSEX),** *9½ kilometers northwest of Hastings on B244*
The momentous Battle of Hastings, in which the forces of William, duke of Normandy, defeated the Saxon troops of Harold II and thereby brought England under Norman rule, actually took place here, on what in 1066 was moorland. Before the battle William vowed to build an abbey on the site if he was victorious. The fulfillment of that vow, **Battle Abbey,** was erected on the spot where Harold was killed. Parts of the abbey and the Benedictine monastery that grew around it were destroyed after the dissolution of the monasteries, but there are still remains on **Battle Hill,** where the famous battle was fought.

**BEDFORD (BEDFORD),** *via A428, A6, A603, and A418*
This county town is noted for its associations with John Bunyan (1628–88), Cromwellian soldier and later Nonconformist preacher, who was imprisoned for about 12 years for religious dissent and wrote part of *Pilgrim's Progress* while in jail. The **Bunyan Meeting House** was erected in 1850 as a memorial on the site of the barn where Bunyan used to preach; it contains a museum with many of Bunyan's personal possessions. Of the old churches here, **Saint Mary's** and **Saint John's** date from the 14th century, and **Saint Peter's** incorporates Saxon and Norman elements.

**BERKELEY CASTLE (GLOUCESTER),** *just west of A38*
Here, in 1327, Edward II was brutally murdered by henchmen of his wife, Queen Isabella, and Roger de Mortimer. The room where he was killed remains as it was at the time of his death. The imposing castle, a well-preserved moated stronghold, has been the home of the Berkeley family since it was begun in 1153.

**BLENHEIM PARK (OXFORD),** *12 kilometers north of Oxford via A34*
This seat of the dukes of Marlborough was given by a grateful Queen Anne to John Churchill, first duke of Marlborough, following his victory over Louis XIV's army at Blenheim (1704) in the War of the Spanish Succession. Parliament appropriated a huge sum of money to build **Blenheim Palace,** which was designed by Sir John Vanbrugh and erected between 1705 and 1722. The vast building, covering three acres, was decorated by the greatest artists and craftsmen of the day and filled with fine tapestries, furniture, and art. On the first floor is the small, simply furnished room where Sir Winston Churchill was born in 1874. The large park on the estate contains a lake created by damming the River Glyme.

**BOSTON (LINCOLN),** *on A16 and A52*
In 1607 William Brewster and other "Pilgrim Fathers" were imprisoned and eventually tried in Boston's **Guildhall** for trying to flee England; their cells can be seen. In 1633 John Cotton, Puritan vicar

of the **Church of Saint Botolph,** sailed with a group of Puritans to
Massachusetts Bay, which was renamed Boston. A chapel in Cotton's memory was restored at Saint Botolph's in 1857 by New England Bostonians, and a tablet on the church tower is inscribed with
the names of five governors of Massachusetts who came from
Lincoln-Boston.

## BRANDON VICINITY (SUFFOLK)
GRIME'S GRAVES, 5½ *kilometers northeast off B1108*
These Stone Age flint mines date back to about 2100 B.C. Some 400
shafts have been discovered, two of which can be explored.

## BRIGHTON (SUSSEX), *via A23, A27, and A259 on the Channel coast*
This seaside resort became fashionable in the 18th century, particularly after the Prince of Wales and his friends became frequent
visitors. In 1786 the prince began building his famous **Royal Pavilion,** built first in classical style and then, beginning in 1817, rebuilt by John Nash in its present Indian Mogul style, complete with
domes, spires, and minarets. The prince continued to come here
after he became George IV. William IV also stayed here; but Queen
Victoria closed the Pavilion in 1845 because it did not offer enough
privacy, and most of the lavish, Chinese-style furnishings were removed. In recent years the town of Brighton has restored the building. The **Dome,** formerly the royal stables, is now an assembly room.

## BUCKLAND MONACHORUM (DEVON), *about 6 kilometers south of Tavistock*
**Buckland Abbey,** dating from the 13th century, was converted to a
residence by the Grenville family after the dissolution of the monasteries and was bought by Sir Francis Drake in 1581. It is now a
museum containing Drake relics.

## BURY SAINT EDMUNDS (SUFFOLK), *at the junction of A134, A143, and A45*
James I granted this cathedral town its motto—"Shrine of a king,
cradle of the law"—in commemoration of two important events in
its history, both associated with its now-ruined **Abbey.** In 903 the
remains of the martyred King Edmund of East Anglia, who had been
slain 33 years earlier by the Danes, were removed to the monastery
founded here about 630. The burial place became a famous shrine,
and early in the 11th century the monastery was raised to the status
of abbey by Danish-born King Canute. Two centuries later, in November, 1214, King John's barons swore at the church high altar
that they would force the king to accept the Magna Charta—thus
the second part of the motto. In the 12th century the abbey flourished as a cultural center; today only fragments of the original abbey
remain. Henry VIII's sister, Mary Tudor, is buried in the 15th-century **Saint Mary's Church.**

## CAMBRIDGE UNIVERSITY (CAMBRIDGE), *via A604, A45, A603, and A10 on the River Cam*
Like Oxford (*see*), this great university had its beginnings in the
12th century, when groups of scholars began coming to the town to
study with the various religious orders that by then had settled
there. As early as 1231 Cambridge was recognized as an important
seat of learning in a writ by Henry III. The first college, **Peterhouse,**
was founded in 1284 by Hugh de Balsham, bishop of Ely. Cambridge's reputation spread throughout Europe, and with the arrival of Erasmus in 1510, the school became a center of the new

learning of the Renaissance. Cambridge has had many royal and ecclesiastical benefactors, who have been responsible for the establishment of several of the university's 23 colleges. Henry VI founded **King's College** in 1441; his queen, Margaret of Anjou (1448), and later Elizabeth Woodville (1465), wife of Edward IV, were responsible for **Queens' College**. In 1496 John Alcock, bishop of Ely, founded **Jesus College** on the site of a suppressed nunnery. Lady Margaret Beaufort, mother of Henry VII and one of Cambridge's great benefactors, was responsible for two colleges: **Christ College** (1505) and **Saint John's College** (1511), which was finished after her death by the renowned humanist bishop John Fisher. Cambridge's largest college, **Trinity**, was founded in 1546 by Henry VIII. The university's most famous medieval building is **King's College Chapel**, begun in 1446. It is notable for its dimensions—300 feet long, 80 feet high, and 40 feet wide—its fan vaulting, and its 25 stained-glass windows. The university's first classical building was the chapel designed by Christopher Wren in 1664 for **Pembroke College**. The **Fitzwilliam Museum** houses the valuable collections of Viscount Fitzwilliam of Merrion, which he bequeathed to the university in 1816.

## CANTERBURY (KENT), *via A2, A290, A28, and A257*

This town has for centuries been most famous for its **Cathedral**. Saint Augustine of Canterbury (d. 604) founded an abbey and the original cathedral shortly after his arrival here from Rome in 596. A few years later Canterbury became the metropolitan city of the English church, and Augustine became the first archbishop of Canterbury and primate of England. The cathedral itself was destroyed several times by the Danes; the present building was started in 1070 by Bishop Lanfranc. Until this point **Saint Augustine's Abbey**, now in ruins, eclipsed the cathedral in importance. Then in 1170 Archbishop Thomas à Becket was murdered in the cathedral after years of bitter quarreling with Henry II. England was horrified, Becket was canonized in 1172, Henry did public penance at the cathedral the next year, and suddenly Canterbury was the chief religious site in England. For the next several centuries pilgrims from all over Europe flocked to Becket's shrine, until Henry VIII destroyed it in 1538. The exact site of Becket's murder, in the northwest transept, is marked by a small plaque. Before its destruction the shrine was in Trinity Chapel, which contains the tombs of Henry IV (d. 1413) and his wife Joan of Navarre (d. 1437), and of Edward, the Black Prince (d. 1376). During the reign of Elizabeth I many Huguenot immigrants settled in Canterbury; in the chapel where they worshiped, off the huge Norman crypt, services still are held in French. Much of the **Benedictine Monastery** that adjoins the cathedral has survived, including a water tower that was part of an advanced water-supply and sanitation system. Other points of interest in Canterbury are **Saint Martin's Church**, parts of which may predate Saint Augustine; **Saint Dunstan's Church**, where a family vault contains the severed head of Sir Thomas More (d. 1535); and the 11th-century **Hospital of Saint Thomas**.

## CARLISLE (CUMBERLAND), *on A595, A6, A69, and A7*

From the time William Rufus (William II) began building a castle, a priory, and town walls here in 1092, Carlisle was an important border fortress that was repeatedly assaulted during the clashes between England and Scotland. During the Civil War the **Castle** was besieged and taken by Scottish Parliamentary forces under Gen-

*Left: Canterbury Cathedral. Right: Compton Wynyates Tudor mansion (see page 284)*

eral David Leslie; in 1745 it was again taken, this time by Bonnie Prince Charlie at the beginning of his unsuccessful uprising. Mary queen of Scots was kept here for two months in 1568, her first English prison after her flight from Scotland. The castle remains include **Queen Mary's Tower** and the central keep. Carlisle's 12th-century **Cathedral** was partly destroyed in 1645 by General Leslie, who used the stones to repair the town wall and the castle.

**CASTLE RISING (NORFOLK)**, *8 kilometers northeast of King's Lynn on A149*
The 12th-century Norman castle here is surrounded by defensive earthworks of spectacular proportions, which may date back to the Roman occupation. About 1330 the castle became the residence of Queen Isabella, widow of Edward II, whose death she helped arrange.

**CHAWTON (HAMPSHIRE)**, *1½ kilometers south of Alton off A31*
Jane Austen lived here from 1809 until just before her death in 1817, writing *Mansfield Park, Emma,* and *Persuasion* during those years. The house where she lived is now a museum.

**CHESTER (CHESHIRE)**, *via A41, A56, A54, A548, and A540*
Chester was a flourishing seaport under the Romans and again in the Middle Ages before its harbor silted up in the 15th century, and it is famous for its remains from these two periods. As the Roman city of Deva it was the headquarters of the Roman 20th Legion, one of the three Roman legions in Britain. Several stretches of the impressive **Roman Wall** remain intact; they can be seen on the north and east sides of the present city wall. Among other Roman remains are the **quay wall** from the Roman harbor (now on dry land), and the stone **amphitheater**, the largest yet discovered in Britain. Under the Normans Chester again thrived. The Roman walls were reconstructed, and several towers and gates were added; they remain unbroken today. From **King Charles's Tower** Charles I supposedly watched the defeat of his forces in the Battle of Rowton Moor in September, 1645. The tower now houses a Civil War exhibit, marking a period during which Chester suffered heavily

for its loyalty to the king. Among Chester's many notable buildings are the **Cathedral,** which before the dissolution of the monasteries was the abbey church of a rich and powerful Benedictine monastery; the **Castle,** begun in 1069 but heavily altered in the 18th century, where Richard II was held a prisoner and John Wesley found refuge; and the famous medieval **Rows,** a double tier of shops, each tier with its own walkway. The Chester mystery plays, begun in the 14th century, were presented in **Abbey Square,** then the outer court of Saint Werburgh Abbey.

**CHIPPING CAMPDEN (GLOUCESTER),** *about 38 kilometers southeast of Worcester north of A44*

This town, with its many stone houses built by wealthy wool merchants in the 14th and 15th centuries, is typical of the wool towns that flourished in the Cotswolds in the Middle Ages and have remained unchanged to the present. Like other rich market towns, Chipping Campden had a **Market Hall** and an impressive church, the 15th-century **Church of Saint James.**

**COLCHESTER (ESSEX),** *84 kilometers northeast of London via A12*

Great Britain's oldest recorded town traces its earliest settlement back to the Bronze Age, about 1100 B.C. In the first century A.D. Cunobelinus (Cymbeline) made it his capital. Claudius captured it in A.D. 44 and established a major Roman colony there, Camulodunum. Today substantial portions of the **Roman Walls** remain. After the Norman conquest, William I began a **Castle** here (about 1085), whose enormous keep—the largest in Europe—survives. The keep is now a museum containing Celtic and Roman relics. The 11th-century **Priory of Saint Botolph** is now in ruins.

**COMPTON WYNYATES (WARWICK),** *about 17 kilometers southeast of Stratford-on-Avon*

This beautiful Tudor mansion, made of pink brick, wood, and stone, was begun by Edmund de Compton in 1480 and completed by his son, Sir William, some 40 years later. Henry VIII, a friend of Sir William's, stayed here often, as did Elizabeth I, James I, and Charles I. In 1644 Parliamentary troops besieged and captured the house from the Comptons, who by then were the earls of Northampton and were staunch Royalists. Compton Wynyates was returned to the family only after they agreed to fill in the moat and pay a large fine. The house has almost 100 rooms and has remained virtually unchanged since its completion.

**CORFE CASTLE (DORSET),** *off A351 on the Isle of Purbeck*

This Norman castle, now a striking ruin, is on the site of the Saxon fortress where in 978 King Edward the Martyr was murdered by his stepmother to gain the throne for her son, Ethelred (the Unready). King John used the castle as his state prison. Edward II was kept here in 1326 before he was killed at Berkeley Castle (*see*). In the Civil War Lady Bankes, the widow of the castle's owner, held out against 600 Parliamentary troops for six weeks, until a member of the garrison opened the gates to the besiegers.

**COVENTRY (WARWICK),** *on A444, A423, and A45*

On the night of November 14, 1940, Coventry suffered through an 11-hour air raid. It was the longest single German air bombardment in the Battle of Britain, the titanic struggle between the German air force, which was trying to destroy British defenses as a prelude to a German invasion of England, and the badly outnumbered but gallant RAF, which eventually repulsed the Germans. The entire center of Coventry was destroyed, including many of the city's historic buildings. Chief among them was the 14th-century **Cathedral of Saint Michael**; only the outside walls and the tower survived the bombing. Between 1954 and 1962 a new cathedral, designed by Sir Basil Spense, was constructed on the north side of the ruins.

## DEAL AND VICINITY (KENT), *12½ kilometers north of Dover via A259 on the coast*

**Deal Castle**, built about 1540, was one of a chain of defensive forts erected by Henry VIII after his break with Rome to protect the Channel coast against possible French attack. Its design, like that of the others, is unusual: a central circular keep is surrounded by six inner and six outer semicircular bastions, with thick walls and a total of 145 gun embrasures. Not until the Civil War was the castle besieged, falling to Parliamentarians after several weeks.

WALMER CASTLE, *1½ kilometers south of Deal via A258*
Erected about 1540 by Henry VIII as one of a group of defensive forts along the southern coast (*see also Deal*), Walmer Castle became the residence of the Lord Warden of the Cinque Ports early in the 18th century. Among its residents were William Pitt (the **Pitt Room** contains personal items), and the duke of Wellington, who died here in 1852. The castle still is used by the present Lord Warden.

## DORCHESTER VICINITY (DORSET)
HIGHER BOCKHAMPTON, *4½ kilometers northeast of Dorchester*
Thomas Hardy, in whose novels Dorset and the surrounding counties play such an important role, was born in this hamlet in 1840; his **Birthplace** now belongs to the National Trust. Hardy's notebooks and letters are in the **County Museum** in Dorchester.

MAIDEN CASTLE, *about 3 kilometers southwest of Dorchester off A354*
This prehistoric fort, one of the finest in Britain, consists of rings of earth ramparts encircling a flat 100-acre hilltop. They probably were constructed in the first century B.C., although there is evidence of a Neolithic camp here as early as 2000 B.C. In A.D. 43 Vespasian's Roman legion reduced the fort.

## DOVER (KENT), *on A2 and A258 on the Channel coast*
Situated at one end of the shortest sea route between England and the Continent, Dover has always been of vital defensive importance. Its mighty medieval **Castle**, overlooking the Channel, is on a site that probably was fortified well before the Roman invasion. The Romans also built a fortress here; within the castle walls is a Roman *pharos*, or **Lighthouse** (about A.D. 50), the earliest in Britain. After the Roman occupation ended, the lighthouse became a part of the Saxon **Church of Saint Mary-in-Castra**. The present castle, begun shortly after the Conquest and referred to as the "key of England," was refortified several times: after an unsuccessful French attack in 1216; during the Napoleonic Wars, when an invasion was feared; and again during the Second World War, when Dover came under continual shellfire. Dover is the chief of the Cinque Ports (*see also Deal*), which during the Middle Ages furnished men and ships for the defense of England in return for special privileges.

## DURHAM (DURHAM)

### CASTLE, *off Saddler Street*

Situated, with Durham Cathedral (*see*), on a bluff nearly encircled by the River Wear, Durham Castle was begun by William I about 1072, after the Normans had ravaged the north to put an end to local rebellions. The castle became the seat of the bishops of Durham, who were given sovereign powers in return for defending the northern marches. The castle is now part of Durham University.

### CATHEDRAL, *off North Bailey*

This great Norman cathedral is on the site of a Saxon church built in 995 as a shrine for Saint Cuthbert, whose body had been carried from Lindisfarne (*see Holy Island*) by monks fleeing a Viking raid. The offerings of pilgrims who flocked to the shrine enabled Durham's prince-bishops to begin constructing, in 1093, one of England's finest Romanesque buildings. Saint Cuthbert and the Venerable Bede are among those entombed here. Also of interest are two Norman churches, **Saint Giles's** and **Saint Margaret's.**

## ELY (CAMBRIDGE), *25 kilometers northeast of Cambridge via A10*

Ely, in the heart of The Fens, is dominated by its **Cathedral,** a testament to the bishops of Ely, who once ruled here with the power of feudal monarchs. On the site of an abbey founded by Saint Etheldreda in 673, the present cathedral was begun in 1083. The vicarage of the nearby **Church of Saint Mary** was the home of Oliver Cromwell and his family from 1636 to 1647.

## ETON (BUCKINGHAM), *opposite Windsor on the Thames*

England's best-known public school was founded here in 1440 by Henry VI. Some of the original buildings, including the **Lower School,** are still in use.

## EVESHAM BATTLEFIELD (WORCESTER), *about 5 kilometers east of Evesham off A44*

Here in August, 1265, Henry III's son Edward (later Edward I) defeated Simon de Montfort, the rebel leader in the Barons' War. De Montfort, his son Henry, and some 4,000 soldiers died in the battle. An obelisk marks the site.

## FLODDEN FIELD (NORTHUMBERLAND), *south of Saint Paul's Church in Branxton*

Here in September, 1513, an English army under Thomas Howard, second duke of Norfolk, defeated a Scottish force led by James IV. James was killed in the battle; a marker stands on the spot where he fell.

## FOUNTAINS ABBEY (YORK, WEST RIDING), *5 kilometers southwest of Ripon off B6265*

This 12th-century Cistercian abbey is one of the best preserved in England. Most of the buildings of this land- and wool-rich monastery stand, giving a good picture of medieval monastic life.

## FRAMLINGHAM (SUFFOLK), *northeast of Ipswich on B1119*

**Framlingham Castle** was built by Roger Bigod, second earl of Norfolk, about 1190; it was of a very modern defensive design for the time, with a curtain wall and towers replacing the old keep-and-bailey plan. In the 16th century the castle passed to the Howard family, dukes of Norfolk, who in 1553 sheltered Mary Tudor here when her succession to the throne was threatened by Lady Jane Grey's supporters. In the 17th century the castle was bequeathed to Pembroke College, Cambridge, which converted the great hall into a poorhouse and pulled down all the rest except the walls.

**GEDDINGTON (NORTHAMPTON)**, *5 kilometers north of Kettering on A43*
In the village square is an **Eleanor Cross**, one of several crosses erected by Edward I to mark the funeral procession of his wife, Eleanor of Castile, on the long trip from Harby, where she died in 1290, to Westminster Abbey, where she was entombed.

**GLASTONBURY (SOMERSET)**, *on A39, A361, B233, and B391*
**Glastonbury Abbey** is associated with two legends: that Saint Joseph of Arimathea built the first Christian church in England here; and that the remains of King Arthur and Queen Guinevere are interred in the church. Founded by King Ine of Wessex in the eighth century, the abbey was rebuilt beginning in 1184, after a fire destroyed the old buildings. In the Middle Ages it was famous as a center of scholarship and as an object of pilgrimages.

**GLOUCESTER (GLOUCESTER)**, *on A430, A38, A40, and A417*
Gloucester's great **Cathedral** was begun as a Benedictine abbey church in 1089 and was rebuilt in the 14th century. Edward II was buried in the church after his murder in 1327; his son Edward III erected the stone-canopied tomb. Robert, duke of Normandy, eldest son of William I, also is buried here, his tomb decorated with a carved-oak effigy. There are other medieval structures in Gloucester—the **Church of Saint Mary-de-Crypt**, the **Abbot's House**, and **New Inn**.

**GOODRICH CASTLE (HEREFORD)**, *about 8 kilometers southwest of Ross off A40*
Overlooking the River Wye, this imposing ruin was an important Welsh border castle in the 12th and 13th centuries. William de Valance, a half brother of Henry III's, came into possession of the castle in 1245 and added the outer walls during Edward I's conquest of Wales. During the Civil War the castle fell to Parliamentarian forces.

**GRASMERE (WESTMORLAND)**, *off the Keswick road just north of Grasmere Lake*
William Wordsworth, his sister, Dorothy, and later his wife, Mary, lived in **Dove Cottage** from 1799 to 1808; during those years the house was a gathering place for such writers as Samuel Taylor Coleridge, Robert Southey, and Thomas De Quincey. The house is open to the public, and there is a **Wordsworth Museum** nearby. Wordsworth is buried in **Saint Oswald's Churchyard**. After he moved from Dove Cottage, De Quincey took it over until 1835.

**HADRIAN'S WALL (NORTHUMBERLAND, CUMBERLAND)**, *running from Wallsend to Bo'ness, at the head of Solway Firth*
Built on the order of Roman Emperor Hadrian beginning in A.D. 122, this great fortification was erected as a defense against barbarian invaders from the north, as well as a base for attack. The 74-mile-long wall was built of stone in the east part and turf in the west. Standing about 20 feet high, it had 15 large forts for permanent garrisons; smaller forts, or milecastles, at every Roman mile; and two signal towers between each pair of milecastles. To the north of

the wall was a ditch, 27 feet wide and 9 feet deep; to the south was a flat-bottomed trench. Garrisoned by infantry and cavalry from all over the empire, it remained important until well into the fourth century. Much of the wall was destroyed after 1715, when its stones were used to build a new road from Newcastle to Carlisle. Among the best preserved forts are those at **Housesteads** and **Chester**, near Chollerford.

**HAMPTON COURT PALACE (MIDDLESEX),** *3 kilometers west of Kingston-on-Thames on A308*

Cardinal Thomas Wolsey began this magnificent house in 1514, intending it to be the largest and richest private residence in England. By 1529 Wolsey had fallen from power, and Henry VIII had taken over Hampton Court. Henry added the great hall and the chapel, and the palace remained a royal residence until the death of George II in 1760. During the reign of William III, Sir Christopher Wren made further additions. Much of the historic palace is open to the public, including the **State Apartments,** with their great paintings, tapestries, and pieces of sculpture. There are extensive and beautifully maintained **gardens** that include a maze planted during the reign of Queen Anne.

**HASTINGS, BATTLE OF.** *See* BATTLE

**HATFIELD HOUSE (HERTFORD),** *32 kilometers north of London off A1*

The great Jacobean mansion was built in 1610–11 by Robert Cecil, first earl of Salisbury. It is on the grounds of the **Old Palace,** the 15th-century residence of the bishops of Ely, which Henry VIII seized at the Dissolution and where his children Mary and Elizabeth spent much of their time. Elizabeth was forced to live there during the reign of her half sister Mary; there, in 1558, she was told of her accession to the throne, under an oak tree whose remains are preserved. One wing of the palace still stands, including the hall where Elizabeth I held her first privy council.

*Left: a section of Hadrian's Wall in Northumberland. Right: Hampton Court Palace*

**HAWORTH (YORK, WEST RIDING)**, 6½ *kilometers southwest of Keighley on A6033*

> This bleak village on the moors became the home of clergyman Patrick Brontë and his family in 1820. Their house is now the **Brontë Parsonage Museum,** containing manuscripts, personal relics, and furnishings. Members of the family are buried in **Haworth Church.**

**HEVER CASTLE (KENT)**, *off B2027*

> Anne Boleyn (1507–36) spent her childhood in this moated 14th-century manor house, and here she supposedly met Henry VIII. Early in the 20th century the building was bought and restored by William Waldorf Astor.

**HIGH WYCOMBE VICINITY (BUCKINGHAM)**

> HUGHENDEN MANOR, 2½ *kilometers north off A4128*
>
> Benjamin Disraeli, earl of Beaconsfield and British prime minister, lived here from 1847 until his death in 1881 and was buried here. The house is now a Disraeli museum.

**HOLY ISLAND** or **LINDISFARNE (NORTHUMBERLAND)**, 4½ *kilometers off the coast of Beal, connected by a causeway*

> In A.D. 635 Saint Aidan came here from Iona, off the coast of Scotland, establishing a monastery and introducing Celtic Christianity to England. The famous Lindisfarne Gospels, an illuminated manuscript in the British Museum, date from before 700. In 875 the abbey was destroyed by Danes. The present ruins are of a priory built in the 11th century by Benedictines from Durham.

**HUNTINGDON (HUNTINGDON)**, 25 *kilometers northwest of Cambridge via A604*

> This county town has associations with Oliver Cromwell and his family. The Protector was born in **Cromwell House** on High Street in 1599. The former grammar school is now the **Cromwell Museum.** The **Falcon Inn** is thought to have been Cromwell's headquarters during the Civil War. Just outside Huntingdon, on the road to Brampton, is **Hinchinbrooke House,** a former nunnery that from 1538 to 1627 was the seat of the Cromwell family.

**JARROW (DURHAM)**, 11 *kilometers east of Newcastle-upon-Tyne via A185*

> The **Church of Saint Paul** is on the site of the seventh-century monastery where the Venerable Bede lived most of his life and where he died in 735. There are scanty remains of the monastery.

**KENILWORTH CASTLE (WARWICK)**, 1½ *kilometers west of Kenilworth off B4103*

> For centuries this imposing ruined castle was a mighty fortress, in the possession both of kings and nobles. Geoffrey de Clinton, treasurer to Henry I, founded the castle about 1122; his son added the keep, which still stands. Fortified with money provided by King John, the castle was for a time in royal hands, until in 1244 Henry III granted it to Simon de Montfort, his brother-in-law. Simon later became a leader in the Barons' Wars against Henry III, and in 1266, the year after Simon was killed at Evesham (*see*), Kenilworth Castle was besieged and after nine months fell to the king's forces. In the 14th century the fortress became the property of John of Gaunt, who transformed it into a grand palace by adding large living quarters, including the great hall. The castle again

became royal property from the time of John's son Henry IV until 1563, when Queen Elizabeth conferred it upon her favorite, Robert Dudley, later earl of Leicester. Leicester spent money lavishly on the castle, renovating and adding buildings and providing expensive entertainments for the queen, who was a frequent visitor there. Kenilworth's period of glory ended with Leicester's death. During the Civil War Cromwell ordered the castle destroyed. The ruins were never restored.

**KINGSTON-ON-THAMES (SURREY),** *London suburb across the Thames from Hampton Court Park*

Between 902 and 979 seven Saxon kings were crowned in this ancient town. The **Coronation Stone** stands in front of the modern guildhall.

**LANCASTER CASTLE (LANCASHIRE),** *on Castle Hill*

This castle, now a law court and prison, was begun about 1170 on the site of a Roman camp and was later extended by King John. Through his marriage to Blanche of Lancaster it passed to John of Gaunt, Shakespeare's "time-honour'd Lancaster." From one of its turrets, known as John of Gaunt's Chair, the approach of the Spanish Armada was signaled.

**LEOMINSTER VICINITY (HEREFORD)**

MORTIMER'S CROSS, *about 9 kilometers west of Leominster on A4110*

On this battlefield Edward, duke of York, defeated a Lancastrian force under Owen Tudor in 1461, in one of the bloody battles in the Wars of the Roses. After his victory Edward marched unopposed to London, where he was crowned Edward IV. A 1799 obelisk marks the battle site.

**LICHFIELD (STAFFORD),** *on A38 and A446*

Lichfield is famous as the town where Dr. Samuel Johnson (1709–84) spent his boyhood. **Dr. Johnson's Birthplace,** on the corner of Breadmarket Street in Market Square, is now a museum containing personal memorabilia. The **Cathedral,** the only church in England with three spires, was built between 1195 and 1325.

**LINBY (NOTTINGHAM),** *about 12 kilometers northwest of Nottingham*

This town is most famous for **Castle Mill,** a battlemented building east of the village where in 1785 James Watt set up his first steam engine for spinning cotton. In the nearby churchyard are the graves of 163 children who died as a result of working conditions in Watt's factory.

**LINCOLN (LINCOLN)**

CASTLE, *Castle Hill*

William the Conqueror began this immense, thick-walled castle in 1068. In 1141 King Stephen was captured while besieging the castle, during his struggles with Matilda, daughter of Henry I, for the English throne. The castle walls enclose a six-acre lawn on which is a fragment of an Eleanor Cross (*see Geddington*).

CATHEDRAL, *Castle Hill*

Exceeded in size only by York Minster and Saint Paul's in London, Lincoln Cathedral was begun in 1072, when William I ordered Bishop Remigius to build a cathedral comparable in importance to the vast area it would serve. Nearly destroyed by fire and then by an earthquake in 1185, it was restored by Bishop Hugh of Avalon (d. 1200), with additions made as late as the 17th century. From the central tower hangs the famous bell **Great Tom of Lincoln.** In the **Treasury** is one of four original copies of the Magna Charta.

## JEW'S HOUSE, *15 The Strait*

This 12th-century stone house, in addition to being an excellent example of Norman domestic architecture, attests to the economic success of Jewish moneylenders in medieval England. Its owner was a rich merchant, Aaron the Jew, who lent money to, among others, the king of Scotland and the archbishop of Canterbury.

## NEWPORT ARCH, *Bailgate*

In Roman times Lincoln was the important settlement of Lindum Colonia, and Newport Arch (which probably dates from the second century) was the northern gate of the walled city. The gateway has been in use since then.

# LONDON

## BANQUETING HOUSE, THE, *Whitehall*

This building, all that remains of the old Whitehall Palace, was designed by Inigo Jones in 1619 to replace an earlier banqueting hall that had burned down. Whitehall Palace had been a royal residence since 1529, when Henry VIII seized York House from Cardinal Wolsey, renamed it Whitehall, and enlarged it. Charles I envisioned the new Banqueting House as the first in a grandiose plan that would turn Whitehall into a royal estate. But in 1698 fire destroyed the rest of the palace. The Banqueting House, which has been restored, features a ceiling painted by Peter Paul Rubens for Charles I in 1629–34.

## BRITISH MUSEUM, *Great Russell Street*

This great museum was established by an act of Parliament in 1753, after the government purchased Sir Hans Sloane's collection of botanical specimens and scientific books and manuscripts. That same year it acquired Sir Robert Cotton's extensive collection of books, manuscripts, and coins, and the Harleian Library of Sir Robert Harley and his son Edward. Other bequests followed, including the royal libraries of George II and III. In 1847 the museum's present quarters were completed. Among its many treasures are the **Elgin Marbles,** sculptures that originally were on the Parthenon in Athens, Greece; the **Rosetta Stone,** an inscribed Egyptian slab from the time of Ptolemy V; and the **Codex Sinaiticus,** a fourth-century Greek illumination of the Bible.

## BUCKINGHAM PALACE, *The Mall*

This 600-room palace has been the London residence of Great Britain's monarch since the beginning of Queen Victoria's reign. Built in 1703 by the duke of Buckingham, it was bought in 1762 by George III and became a residence for Queen Charlotte. In 1825 John Nash began extensive alterations. Further changes were made for Queen Victoria and George V. The colorful ceremony of the changing of the guard attracts many spectators.

## CARLYLE'S HOUSE, *Cheyne Row*

The famous historian Thomas Carlyle and his wife, Jane, lived here from 1834 until his death in 1881. Now a museum, the house contains many personal possessions and pieces of furniture.

### DICKENS' HOUSE, *48 Doughty Street*

Although novelist Charles Dickens had several London residences, this is the only one to have survived. Dickens lived here from 1837 to 1839, during which time he completed the *Pickwick Papers.* The house has been reconstructed by the Dickens Fellowship and serves as a Dickens museum and library.

### GUILDHALL, *Gresham Street*

This hall, London's civic center, had its origins in the guilds that flourished in the Middle Ages. Begun in 1411, most of the building was destroyed in the Great Fire of 1666 and again in the 1940 blitz, and only a few fragments of the original building remain. The trial of Lady Jane Grey and her husband was held in 1553 in the **Great Hall,** now restored. The **Guildhall Museum** has a collection of objects from Roman and medieval London.

### HOUSES OF PARLIAMENT, *Parliament Square*

Known also as the Palace of Westminster, this huge Gothic-style structure was erected in the mid-19th century to replace the old palace buildings, which were destroyed by fire in 1834. The original palace, begun by Edward the Confessor, served as the royal residence until the 16th century, when Henry VIII moved to Whitehall Palace (*see Banqueting Hall*). Thereafter the houses of Commons and Lords met in Westminster Palace. Only two of the original buildings, **Westminster Hall** (added in 1097 by William II) and **Saint Stephen's Chapel,** survived the fire of 1834; they have been incorporated into the present two-chambered building. Westminster Hall was the chief law court of England until 1882 and the site of many famous trials, including those of Sir Thomas More (1535) and Charles I (1649).

### INNS OF COURT, *in the area between the City and Westminster*

In the Middle Ages the four Inns of Court (Inner Temple, Middle Temple, Lincoln's Inn, Grays Inn) were schools of law; today they are legal societies that control admission to the English bar. The Inner and Middle temples, located between Fleet Street and Victoria Embankment and known together as the Temple, are on land that originally was the property of the Knights Templar. That medieval order was dissolved in 1312, and in 1346 the property was leased to law students. Among the many famous members of Grays Inn was Francis Bacon, who lived there from 1597 until his death in 1626 and reputedly laid out the gardens.

### JOHNSON'S HOUSE, *17 Gough Square*

Dr. Samuel Johnson, the famous and eccentric author and critic, lived here from 1748 to 1758, compiling his *Dictionary* (1755) in the attic. The house contains many of his personal belongings.

### KEATS' HOUSE, *Keats Grove, Hampstead*

Keats lived here from 1818 to 1820, fell in love with Fanny Brawne (her family lived in the other half of the house), and wrote some of his best poems, including "Ode to a Nightingale" and the unfinished "Hyperion." The house contains many of the poet's personal relics, including letters, annotated books, and early editions of his poems.

### KENSINGTON PALACE, *Kensington Gardens*

In 1689 William III—who felt that the London air made his asthma worse—bought the earl of Nottingham's country home in Kensington village, renamed it Kensington Palace, and moved there from Whitehall. Sir Christopher Wren enlarged the palace for William and designed the orangery for Queen Anne. Kensington was the royal residence until 1760, when George III moved back to London, to Saint James's Palace (*see*). Queen Victoria was born in the palace and in a room in the State Apartments learned of her accession to the throne. Today the palace houses the **London Museum,** whose collection illustrates London's history from Roman times to the present.

LAMBETH PALACE, *Lambeth Palace Road*
This brick Tudor building on the Thames has for centuries been the residence of the archbishops of Canterbury. While most of the palace was built in the 15th century, the crypt dates from about 1200. The **Great Hall** houses a fine library that includes illuminated manuscripts, early printed books, William Gladstone's diaries, and Elizabeth I's prayer book.

THE MONUMENT, *Fish Street Hill*
Sir Christopher Wren erected this 202-foot-high fluted Doric column to commemorate the Great Fire of 1666, which began in a baker's shop in nearby **Pudding Lane** and in four days destroyed 13,200 houses, 84 churches, and Saint Paul's Cathedral (*see*). Wren played a major role in the rebuilding of the city; his works included 52 London churches, among them Saint Paul's.

ROYAL NAVAL COLLEGE, *Greenwich*
This was once the site of Greenwich Palace, a favorite residence of Tudor monarchs. Henry VIII and his daughters Mary I and Elizabeth I were born there; Edward VI died in the palace. In 1662 Charles II had the badly decayed buildings demolished, and John Webb, architect Inigo Jones's assistant, began rebuilding. Late in the 17th century Queen Mary commissioned Sir Christopher Wren to turn the palace into Greenwich Hospital for disabled naval veterans. Wren's grand design included four quadrangles, two of them colonnaded and domed. At the center is the **Queen's House,** a separate 29-room palace that Inigo Jones had started in 1616 for Queen Anne, wife of James I; it was completed in 1635 for Henrietta Maria, wife of Charles I. In 1873 the hospital was given to the Royal Naval College. The Queen's House is now part of the **National Maritime Museum.**

SAINT JAMES'S PALACE, *Pall Mall*
Henry VIII built this palace beginning in 1530 (the original gatehouse remains), and it became the official royal residence in 1698, after Whitehall Palace burned down. Although its use as a royal residence ended with Queen Victoria in 1861, the British court still is known as the Court of Saint James's. In 1649 Charles I spent his last night here before his execution outside Whitehall.

SAINT PAUL'S CATHEDRAL, *Ludgate Hill*
There has been a church on the site of Sir Christopher Wren's great cathedral since at least early in the seventh century, when King Ethelbert dedicated a wooden church to Saint Paul. Destroyed first by Vikings and then, in 1087, by fire, it was replaced in the 12th century by a Norman structure, which itself was completely destroyed in the Great Fire of 1666. Almost immediately Wren set

*From left to right in London: Nelson's Column in Trafalgar Square; the law courts on the left side of the Strand, which runs into Fleet Street beyond the*

to work on designs for a new cathedral, and in 1675 work on the present domed structure, with its long nave and choir, was begun; it was completed in 1708. The cathedral survived the 1940 blitz, although the high altar was destroyed and the crypt damaged. Among its many memorials is a striking statue of John Donne (d. 1631), poet and dean of Saint Paul's, who posed in a shroud shortly before his death. Among those buried in the large crypt are the duke of Wellington, Lord Nelson, and Wren himself, whose epitaph reads "*Si monumentum requiris, circumspice*" ("If you seek a memorial, look around you").

### TEMPLE CHURCH, *The Temple*

This church, which today serves the Inner and Middle temples (*see Inns of Court*), was consecrated in 1185 by the Knights Templar, who had their English headquarters on the site. As in most of the Templars' churches, the Romanesque nave is round. In the nave are 13th-century effigies of knights. Heavily damaged during World War II, the church has been restored.

### THEATRE ROYAL, *Drury Lane*

The first theater on this site was erected in 1663 under a charter from Charles II; the fourth and present building was built in 1812, each of the previous ones having been destroyed by fire. The Drury Lane, as it is known, is the oldest English theater still being used.

### TOWER OF LONDON, *Tower Hill*

An ancient fortress, palace, and prison, the Tower of London dates from the time of the Norman occupation and is London's oldest major edifice. Soon after the Conquest, William I began the White Tower, the massive keep at the fortress's heart, which he built to intimidate and control his new subjects. In the 13th century the

*monument; Buckingham Palace, the royal residence; and Westminster Abbey, the site of royal coronations and burials*

White Tower was surrounded by two walls containing in all 19 other towers. Used as a palace during the Middle Ages (the palace buildings were later destroyed by Oliver Cromwell), the Tower achieved its bloody reputation because of its subsequent use as a prison. Kings and commoners, political, religious, and criminal offenders, were imprisoned, tortured, and executed here. Among the most illustrious prisoners were Princess (later Queen) Elizabeth, imprisoned by Queen Mary for six months in the **Bell Tower;** Sir Walter Raleigh, who spent 13 years in the **Bloody Tower** after the accession of James I; Sir Thomas More, Lady Jane Grey, Archbishop Laud, Anne Boleyn, Catherine Howard, the second early of Essex, and James, duke of Monmouth. Many of the Tower's prisoners carved inscriptions on the wall. Many were ultimately executed, either within the Tower walls or on nearby **Tower Hill.** The execution axe and block as well as instruments of torture are on display in the **White Tower.** Political prisoners arrived at the Tower via the Thames and entered through the **Traitor's Gate.** Today the **Wakefield Tower** is the home of England's crown jewels; and in the **Armouries** is the national collection of medieval weaponry and armor, including Henry VIII's arsenal. The Tower of London is guarded by Yeoman Warders ("Beefeaters") dressed in Tudor uniforms.

## TRAFALGAR SQUARE

John Nash designed this square early in the 19th century to commemorate Admiral Horatio Nelson's great victory in 1805 over the combined French and Spanish fleets at Trafalgar, off the coast of Spain at Cádiz. Dominating the square is **Nelson's Column,** a colossal monument topped by a 17-foot-high statue of the hero.

## WESTMINSTER ABBEY, *Parliament Square*

Between 1050 and 1065 Edward the Confessor built an abbey

church on this site and a palace nearby. From that time, London was effectively divided into two major areas: the City became London's commercial center, while the court and government centered on Westminster. In 1245 Henry III began demolishing and rebuilding Edward's church. Henry intended his new church to serve as a monument to the sainted Edward, as well as a fitting coronation site and burial place for royalty. He did not finish the project in his lifetime, but subsequent builders remained faithful to Henry's French Gothic design. The culmination of the great work was the completion in 1519 of the remarkably beautiful, elaborately decorated **Chapel of King Henry VII.** Completed after Henry's death, it contains, in addition to the tombs of Henry VII and his wife, those of Queen Elizabeth I and Mary queen of Scots. Since Harold, every English monarch except Edward V and Edward VIII has been crowned in Westminster Abbey. In the **Chapel of Edward the Confessor**—which contains the saint's tomb—is the **Coronation Chair,** designed in 1300 by Edward I to hold the Stone of Scone, which he had taken from Scotland as evidence of Scotland's subservience to England. The chair has been used at every coronation since then. The abbey also is crowded with tombs of and monuments to the dead—monarchs, statesmen, and other distinguished British subjects. **Poets' Corner,** in the south transept, contains the tombs of, among others, Geoffrey Chaucer, Edmund Spenser, John Dryden, Robert Browning, and Alfred, Lord Tennyson.

## LUDLOW (SHROPSHIRE), *via A49, A4113, and A4117*

In 1085, a few decades after the Norman Conquest, Roger de Lacy began the **Castle** here both to help the Normans control their new subjects and to guard against marauding Welshmen from across the nearby border. By the 13th century the fortified town of Ludlow had grown beneath it, and the castle itself had been greatly enlarged with the addition of new defenses. In the 14th century Roger de Mortimer—who as Queen Isabella's lover helped her bring about the death of her husband, Edward II—transformed the fortress into a majestic palace, adding the **Great Hall** and extensive **State Apartments.** In the Wars of the Roses Richard, duke of York, made the castle his military headquarters. Richard's son Edward in 1461 became Edward IV, and Ludlow Castle became crown property. After Edward's death in 1483, the young Edward V and his brother were imprisoned in **Pendover Tower** during the power struggle between their two uncles that resulted in the transfer of the young boys to the Tower of London and their eventual murder. Under the Tudors the castle became seat of the president of the Council of Marches of Wales. Prince Arthur and Catherine of Aragon spent their honeymoon in **Prince Arthur's Apartments** in 1501, and in 1502 Arthur died in the castle. John Milton's masque *Comus* was given its first performance in the Great Hall in 1634. After the Council of Marches was abolished in 1689, Ludlow Castle fell into its present ruined state.

## MANSFIELD VICINITY (DERBY)

### HARDWICK HALL, *9½ kilometers west off B6093*

Rich, powerful, and eccentric, Elizabeth, countess of Shrewsbury (Bess of Hardwick), built this monument to herself after the death of her fourth and last husband, the earl of Shrewsbury. She began it in 1591 when she was 73, completed it in 1597, and spent the last ten years of her life there. Each of the house's four heavily glassed towers is topped with the large initials ES.

**MARSTON MOOR BATTLEFIELD (YORK, WEST RIDING)**, *12½ kilometers west of York south of A59*

Here, in July, 1644, in the first decisive battle of the Civil War, the Parliamentary forces of Oliver Cromwell and Lord Fairfax defeated Charles I's troops, led by Prince Rupert and the duke of Newcastle. Some 40,000 troops took part in the three-hour battle.

**NASEBY BATTLEFIELD (NORTHAMPTON)**, *outside Naseby 11 kilometers southwest of Market Harborough*

Here, in June, 1645, in the decisive battle of the Civil War, Charles I was defeated by the Parliamentarians under General Thomas Fairfax and Oliver Cromwell. A column marks the battle site.

**NEWARK CASTLE (NOTTINGHAM)**, *via A46, A616, A638, A1, and A17*

Now a ruin, Newark Castle was a Norman stronghold that figured in the struggles between King John, who stayed here often, and his barons, who seized the castle and briefly held it before the king recovered it. John died here in 1216. During the Civil War the castle withstood all the efforts of the Parliamentarians to take it and surrendered only at the king's command.

**NEWSTEAD ABBEY (NOTTINGHAM)**, *about 14 kilometers north of Nottingham off A60*

This ancestral home of Lord Byron was originally a priory founded by Henry II in 1170. At the dissolution of the monasteries it was purchased by Sir John Byron of Colwick. When Byron first came into possession of the property he and his mother were too poor to live there, but he did spend several intervals there between 1806 and 1816, after which his financial problems forced him to sell the house. Now publicly owned, the house contains the poet's possessions.

**NORWICH (NORFOLK)**, *at the junction of A140, A11, A47, A1067, A1151, and A146*

Norfolk's capital city still is dominated by its cathedral and its castle, which date from the Norman Conquest, when Norwich was the most important town in East Anglia. Settled by the Saxons more than 1,000 years ago, by the 11th century it was already a major commercial center; **Tombland** (off Wensum Street), now a Georgian square, once was the Saxon marketplace. The Norman **Castle**, begun soon after the Conquest, is today a museum of local history and art. At the end of the 11th century Bishop Herbert de Losinga moved the East Anglian see to Norwich and soon thereafter began the great **Cathedral**, razing a large part of the Anglo-Saxon town to do so. Norwich thereafter thrived as an ecclesiastical as well as a commercial center, as evidenced by its 32 surviving medieval churches.

**OXFORD UNIVERSITY (OXFORD)**, *in Oxford*

Europe's second oldest university—only the Sorbonne in Paris was established earlier—had its beginnings in the 12th century, during the reign of Henry II, when scholars began coming to Oxford to attend lectures. **University College**, the earliest of the present colleges, was founded in 1249. It was followed shortly by **Baliol** (1266) and **Merton** (1264), the latter being Oxford's first residential college. With Merton the system of autonomous colleges, each with its own rules, buildings, and customs, was established. By the end of the 13th century Oxford had become one of Europe's leading intellectual centers, attracting such scholars as Bishop Robert Grosseteste, Roger Bacon, and John Duns Scotus. As its fame spread, benefactors established additional colleges, most of them of interest architecturally as well as for the famous scholars associated with each one. **Christ Church,** Oxford's largest college, was founded by Cardinal Thomas Wolsey in 1525; its chapel is a cathedral. Other buildings of interest are the **Ashmolean Museum,** England's first public museum, which has great art and archaeological collections; **Bodleian Library** (founded 1450), with its priceless collection of rare books and manuscripts; the **Radcliffe Camera** (1749), a circular domed building that is the reading room of Bodleian Library; and Sir Christopher Wren's **Sheldonian Theatre** (1669). The **Church of Saint Mary the Virgin,** which dates mainly from the 15th century and is the university church, has associations with many of Britain's famous religious leaders. The reformer John Wycliffe preached here in the 14th century; in 1555 Archbishop Hugh Latimer was tried for heresy in the church and condemned to death; from 1828 to 1843 John Newman (later cardinal) was vicar.

**PETERBOROUGH (NORTHAMPTON),** *at the junction of A47, A15, and A605*
This town's best known structure is its Norman **Cathedral,** on the site of a Benedictine monastery founded in 655 by King Peada of Mercia. Destroyed by the Danes in 870, it was rebuilt in the following century by King Edgar, only to be destroyed again, this time by fire, in 1116. Two years later the present church was started; it was completed by 1238. Catherine of Aragon (d. 1536) is buried in the church; her tomb was damaged by the Puritans who sacked the cathedral during the Civil War. Mary queen of Scots was buried here from 1587 until 1612, when her son James I had her body transferred to Westminster Abbey; today a slab marks the site. The foundations of the early Saxon church are visible beneath the south transept. Another early monument is the Monks' Stone in the choir aisle, commemorating the monks slain by the Danes in 870. There is also a series of effigies of 12th-century Benedictine abbots.

**PEVENSEY CASTLE (SUSSEX),** *in Pevensey off A259*
This stronghold was originally the Roman fort of Anderida, one of the great Saxon Shore fortresses. Its strategic importance was recognized at once by William I, who landed at Pevensey Bay in 1066. Soon after the Conquest a Norman keep and bailey were built inside the Roman walls, and the castle became as important to the Norman coastal defenses as it had been to the Roman. Although its importance declined in the 15th century as the sea receded, it was refortified on several subsequent occasions: against the Spanish Armada in the 16th century and Napoleon in the 19th century, and again during World War II, when pillboxes were hidden in the ruins. About half the **Roman Walls** are standing, and parts of the castle are well preserved.

**PONTEFRACT (YORK, WEST RIDING),** *on A639 and A645*
Only sparse ruins remain of infamous **Pontefract Castle,** Shakespeare's "bloody Pomfret." Richard II died here, probably murdered, in 1400, a year after he was deposed and imprisoned. During the Wars of the Roses many executions were carried out in the castle. James I of Scotland was imprisoned here by Henry IV; and Charles d'Orléans was held here for many years after his capture at Agincourt (1415). The castle was dismantled in 1649.

**PORTCHESTER CASTLE (HAMPSHIRE),** *11½ kilometers northwest of Portsmouth off A27*

This castle is really two fortresses. The outer walls belonged to a fort erected by the Romans late in the third century as part of their Saxon Shore defenses and occupied by them until about A.D. 370. The 20-foot-high walls of its 14 bastions still stand. In the 12th century Henry II built a Norman castle in the northwest corner of the Roman fortress, and at the end of the 14th century Richard II added a small palace, now in ruins. Henry V assembled his Agincourt expedition here. Also within the Roman walls is the **Church of Saint Mary,** founded as an Augustinian priory by Henry I in 1133.

**PORTSMOUTH (HAMPSHIRE),** *reached via A3, A333, and A27*

This coastal city has been a major naval base since Henry VII established the first dry dock here in 1495. In the dockyard is H.M.S. *Victory,* Admiral Nelson's flagship at Trafalgar. Opposite the ship is the **Victory Museum,** which contains naval relics. Much of Portsmouth was heavily damaged during the Second World War. One building that survived is Charles Dickens's birthplace (393 Commercial Road), now the **Dickens Museum.**

**RICHBOROUGH CASTLE (KENT),** *2½ kilometers northwest of Sandwich off A257*

This "castle" actually is the ruins of an important third-century Roman fort, built at the site of the Roman landings in A.D. 43 and guarding the major east-coast port of Rutupiae. Inside the well-preserved walls are the remains of several buildings; outside are a series of defensive ditches. The fort stood at one end of **Watling Street,** one of the great highways the Romans built across England.

**RUFFORD ABBEY (NOTTINGHAM),** *3 kilometers from Ollerton via A614*

This Elizabethan and Jacobean house was built on the remains of a 12th-century Cistercian monastery, whose vaulted undercroft is part of the present house. It was the home of Arabella Stuart, daughter of the earl of Lennox and Elizabeth Cavendish, who died a prisoner in the Tower of London because as a cousin of James I's she was close in line to the succession.

**RUNNYMEDE (SURREY),** *outside Egham on the south bank of the Thames*

In these meadows King John met with his rebellious barons and on June 15, 1215, after several days of negotiating, signed the first draft of the Magna Charta. A memorial marking the possible location of the signing was erected in 1957 by the American Bar Association. Nearby is a **memorial** to United States President **John F. Kennedy.**

**SAINT ALBANS AND VICINITY (HERTFORD),** *33 kilometers northwest of London via A5*

Saint Albans is on the site of the Roman town of Verulamium, which was one of the most important Roman settlements in Britain. It was Britain's only *munucipium,* a status that granted its inhabitants the privileges of Roman citizenship. Destroyed by Boadicea in A.D. 61, Verulamium was rebuilt and flourished until early in the fifth century. Excavated remains include a portion of the **wall,** a **Roman theater,** a **temple,** and a mosaic floor. Many relics are displayed in a nearby museum. **Saint Albans Abbey** was founded in the eighth century on the site of the murder of the first British martyr, a Roman soldier who was beheaded in A.D. 303 for helping the priest who had converted him to Christianity. After the Norman Conquest the Benedictine abbey became wealthy and powerful. The **Norman Cathedral** was built largely from brick taken from Verulamium. It was restored in the 19th century. At the end of Abbey Mill Lane is the **Fighting Cocks Inn,** possibly the oldest inn in England. **Saint Michael's Church** is the burial place of Sir Francis Bacon (d. 1626), who was created Baron Verulam and Viscount Saint Albans by James I. **Gorhambury House** (3 kilometers north of Saint Albans), the 18th-century house of Bacon's descendant the earl of Verulam, is next to the ruins of Sir Francis's home. Gorhambury contains books and other possessions of Bacon's.

**SAINT MICHAEL'S MOUNT (CORNWALL),** *on an island off Marazion in Mounts Bay*

The monastery here dates from the mid-11th century, when the island came under the control of Benedictine monks from Mont Saint Michel, off the coast of Brittany. It was an important pilgrimage center until the 15th century, when the Crown ejected the monks and turned the island into a fortress. In the 17th century it was converted into a residence for the Saint Aubyn family.

**SANDRINGHAM HOUSE (NORFOLK),** *14½ kilometers northeast of King's Lynn on B1440*

This country home of the queen was bought by Edward, Prince of Wales (later Edward VII), in 1861. King George V (1936) and King George VI (1952) died here.

**SCARBOROUGH (YORK, NORTH RIDING),** *via A170, A171, A164, and A65*

The headland on which ruined **Scarborough Castle** is situated was an important defensive site before the Roman occupation. The castle dates mainly from the 12th century. The unpopular Piers Gaveston, Edward II's favorite, was captured by hostile barons here in 1312. During the Civil War the castle was twice besieged and taken by Parliamentarians.

**SEDGEMOOR MARSH (SOMERSET),** *4½ kilometers southeast of Sedgemoor*

Here on July 6, 1685, the forces of King James II routed the army of James, duke of Monmouth, illegitimate son of Charles II, who a few weeks earlier had landed on the Dorset coast and claimed the English throne. A stone marks the site of the Battle of Sedgemoor, the last fought on English soil.

**SEVENOAKS VICINITY (KENT)**

KNOLE, *38 kilometers southeast of London via A21*

This mansion, one of England's largest and finest, was built in 1456 by Thomas Bourchier, archbishop of Canterbury. Thomas Cranmer turned it over to Henry VIII, and in 1603 Elizabeth I granted it to Sir Thomas Sackville, to whose family Knole still belongs. Aside from the Elizabethan furniture, of particular interest are the portraits (painted by, among others, Philip van Dyck, Thomas Gainsborough, and Joshua Reynolds), the tapestries, and the solid silver furniture in the **King's Bedroom,** prepared for the use of James I.

**SHREWSBURY (SHROPSHIRE),** *at the junction of A49, A488, A5, A528, and A458*

Founded in the fifth century by Britons from the Roman city of Uriconium, or Wroxeter (8 kilometers to the southeast), Shrewsbury

*Anne Hathaway's Cottage at Shottery (see Stratford-on-Avon)*

was a Saxon and then a Norman stronghold, and it flourished despite frequent plundering by the Welsh. In 1070 Roger de Montgomery founded the **Castle,** which Edward I later enlarged and used as his headquarters during his subjugation of Wales (1277–83). Today it is a municipal building. In 1403, on a plain 5½ kilometers north of the city, rebel Henry Percy (Hotspur) was slain by Henry IV's army in the Battle of Shrewsbury; **Battlefield Church** was erected on the site in 1408 to commemorate the battle. **Rowley's Mansion** (on Bridge Street) houses the **Uriconium Museum,** which has relics from the Roman city.

## STAMFORD VICINITY (NORTHAMPTON)

BURGHLEY HOUSE, *2 kilometers south off Barnack Road*

Sir William Cecil, first Baron Burghley, began his great Elizabethan house in 1560, shortly after Elizabeth I ascended to the throne. By the time the house was finished in 1587, Cecil had become Elizabeth's Lord High Treasurer. The house has been in the Cecil family since then.

## STOKE POGES (BUCKINGHAM), *north of Slough*

The beautiful churchyard of **Saint Giles Church** was the inspiration for Thomas Gray's "Elegy Written in a Country Churchyard" (1751). Gray (1716–71) is buried here, and there is also a monument.

## STONEHENGE (WILTSHIRE), *about 13 kilometers north of Salisbury*

This great—and mysterious—prehistoric monument on the Salisbury Plain is awesome in its immensity and complexity. Actually it was constructed in three stages spanning many centuries. Phase I (about 1800 B.C.) saw the construction of the outer bank and ditch, inside which were 56 small holes that may have been used for cremations. In Phase II (about 1650–1500 B.C.) 60 to 80 huge bluestones were brought from Wales and erected in an unfinished double circle, whose entrance aligned with the sunrise of the summer solstice. At the beginning of Phase III (about 1500 B.C.) the bluestones were taken down, and the enormous sarsen stones (sandstone boulders) were brought from the Marlborough Downs and erected in an outer circle with lintels and an inner horseshoe. Between 1500 and 1400 B.C. some of the bluestones were dressed and set in an oval inside the sarsen horseshoe. Finally, about 1400 B.C., the bluestones were reset as they are arranged today, in a circle inside the sarsen circle and an innermost horseshoe.

## STRATFORD-ON-AVON (WARWICK), *at the junction of A34, A46, A422, and A439 on the west bank of the Avon*

Stratford was a thriving Midland market town long before its associations with William Shakespeare made it famous. In 1769, some 200 years after the playwright was born here, actor David Garrick organized the first Shakespeare festival in Stratford, and since then thousands of visitors have flocked to the town each year. **Shakespeare's Birthplace,** on Henley Street, where the playwright probably was born in 1564, was actually two adjoining buildings in his lifetime, one the family home and the other his father's warehouse. Today one part is furnished as a home might have been in Shakespeare's day, while the other is a museum. In 1597 Shakespeare bought **New Place,** then Stratford's largest house; he retired there in 1612 and remained until his death four years later. Today only the site and the foundations remain; they are reached through Nash's House. At Shottery, about 2 kilometers from the town, is **Anne Hathaway's Cottage,** the home of the woman Shakespeare married in 1582. At the end of Old Town is the **Church of Holy Trinity,** the imposing parish church where Shakespeare was baptized in 1564 and buried in 1616. The family properties are administered by the Shakespeare Birthplace Trust, which was formed for that purpose in 1847. Among the places in Stratford that are not associated with Shakespeare is **Harvard House,** on High Street, the childhood home of Katherine Harvard, whose son founded Harvard University in the United States. In 1909 the house was presented to the university.

## SULGRAVE MANOR (NORTHAMPTON), *11 kilometers northwest of Brackley on B4525*

This was the home of George Washington's ancestors for about a century beginning in 1539, when Laurence Washington purchased the house and rebuilt it. It was restored early in the 20th century and is now a Washington museum, containing portraits and some possessions of the first United States President.

## TEWKESBURY (GLOUCESTER), *17 kilometers north of Gloucester via A38*

This ancient town has one of England's finest Norman churches, **Tewkesbury Abbey.** The church was built early in the 12th century on the site of an earlier Benedictine monastery. The interior contains tombs of some of medieval England's most powerful families, all patrons of the rich and famous abbey. One of the largest abbeys to survive the Dissolution, the cathedral-sized building was bought shortly thereafter by the people of Tewkesbury as a parish church. About a kilometer south of Tewkesbury is the so-called **Bloody Meadow,** where in 1471 one of the bloodiest battles in the Wars of the Roses was fought, ending in a decisive victory for Edward IV over the Lancastrians under the duke of Somerset.

## WARWICK (WARWICK)

### LORD LEICESTER HOSPITAL, *High Street*

In 1571 Robert Dudley, earl of Leicester, transformed the buildings of three once-powerful religious guilds into a home for 12 old or disabled "brethren"—soldiers who had served the Crown. The buildings, rebuilt by Leicester and perfectly preserved, still are used; on special occasions the brethren wear traditional Elizabethan gowns. The guildhall is now a museum.

CHURCH OF SAINT MARY, *Church Street*
Like much of the rest of Warwick, Saint Mary's was rebuilt after a disastrous fire in 1694; only the 12th-century **crypt**, the 14th-century **chancel**, and the 15th-century **Beauchamp Chapel** survived the fire. In the center of the latter is the beautiful tomb of its founder, Richard de Beauchamp, earl of Warwick (d. 1439), who commanded Calais for Henry V. Among the Dudleys buried in the chapel are Robert Dudley, earl of Leicester (d. 1588), and his second wife, Lettice (d. 1634). In the center of the chancel are alabaster effigies of Thomas de Beauchamp (d. 1369) and his wife, depicted holding hands. The poet and statesman Fulke Greville, Lord Brooke (d. 1628), is buried in the former chapter house.

WARWICK CASTLE
This great medieval fortress was begun late in the 11th century, when Turchil, a Saxon earl of Warwick, acting on instructions from William the Conqueror, rebuilt a fortress erected about 915 by Ethelfleda, daughter of Alfred the Great. William promptly gave both the castle and title to Henry de Newburgh, a Norman follower. In the 15th century, after the walls had been heavily damaged in the Barons' Wars, the castle passed by marriage to the De Beauchamps. They rebuilt the fortifications, adding the 14th-century curtain wall and the massive tower defenses that stand today. In 1604 James I granted the castle, by then in poor condition, to Fulke Greville, Lord Brooke, who spent huge sums repairing it; Sir William Dugdale described the results as "the most princely seat within the midland parts of this realm." In 1642, during the Civil War, the castle was successfully defended against Royalists. Still inhabited by the earls of Warwick, it has a notable collection of armor, furniture, and paintings.

WELLS (SOMERSET), *on A371 and A39*
From its beginnings Wells was primarily an ecclesiastical city. It is still dominated by the medieval **Cathedral of Bath and Wells,** with its surrounding ecclesiastical buildings, all of which are particularly well preserved. The cathedral's west front serves as a screen for more than 300 13th-century sculptures, the most extensive collection of medieval sculpture in England. North of the cathedral are the **Chapter House,** the **Vicars' Close,** the **Deanery,** and the **Chancellor's House** (now a museum). The 15th-century **Cloisters** and the 13th-century **Bishop's Palace** are to the south.

WESTERHAM VICINITY (KENT)
CHARTWELL, *3½ kilometers south via B2026*
From 1922 until his death in 1965, this was Sir Winston Churchill's country home, It is now preserved as a memorial to him.

WHITE HORSE VALE (BERKSHIRE), *in the Berkshire Chalk Downs near Uffington*
Carved high up on the side of **White Horse Hill,** a huge white chalk horse (374 feet long and 130 feet high) probably dates from the late Iron Age, about 100 B.C. Nearby is **Dragon Hill,** where according to tradition Saint George slew the dragon.

**WHITTINGTON (DERBY),** *5 kilometers north of Chesterfield via A619*

Here, in **Revolution House** (formerly the Cock and Pynot Inn), the earl of Devonshire and other conspirators plotted the overthrow of James II in 1688. The house is now a museum.

**WIGHT, ISLE OF (HAMPSHIRE)**

CARISBROOKE CASTLE, *1½ kilometers southwest of Newport*

In November, 1647, Charles I sought refuge in this fortress, only to be kept a prisoner here until shortly before his execution in January, 1649. His daughter, Princess Elizabeth, died a prisoner here the following year. The castle's Norman keep was built by the earl of Hereford in the 12th century; the outer defenses were erected about 1588, when England was threatened by the Spanish Armada.

OSBORNE HOUSE, *about a kilometer southeast of Cowes*

This was the favorite home of Queen Victoria, who died here in 1901. Designed in the Palladian style by Thomas Cubitt and Prince Albert in 1846 and given to the nation in 1902 by King Edward VII as a memorial to his mother, the house remains a rich example of Victorian life and tastes.

**WINDSOR CASTLE (BERKSHIRE),** *in Windsor about 26 kilometers west of London via A4*

The largest inhabited castle in Europe, covering nearly 13 acres, Windsor has been a chief royal residence since it was begun by William the Conqueror in the 11th century. William's wooden buildings no longer exist, but his plan of two large baileys and a central mound has been preserved. Nearly every monarch who has lived there has renovated or added to the castle. Henry II built the first stone buildings, including the massive **Round Tower,** from the top of which it is possible to see 12 counties. Henry III added the castle's defenses, which remain substantially unchanged. Edward III, who was born here in 1312 and loved Windsor, enlarged the **State Apartments** and founded the Order of the Garter, for whose members in 1475 Edward IV began **Saint George's Chapel.** In this splendid Gothic church, with its richly carved stalls and delicate ironwork, many of England's monarchs are buried, including Henry VI, Edward IV, Henry VIII, Charles I, George III, George IV, William IV, and George VI. The castle's present skyline dates from the reign of George IV, who heightened the Round Tower and added or heightened other towers.

**WINCHESTER (HAMPSHIRE)**

CASTLE HALL, *off High Street near the Westgate*

This 13th-century Great Hall is all that remains of the castle built by William I, who after the Norman Conquest made Winchester and London his joint capitals. Winchester rivaled London in importance for many years, and several parliaments met in the castle. The Great Hall, added to the castle by Henry III, was the scene of many notable trials, including that of Sir Walter Raleigh in 1603. Hanging on one wall is the so-called **Round Table of King Arthur,** which dates from sometime before 1400.

CATHEDRAL, *off High Street*

When this cathedral was begun in 1079 over an earlier Saxon church, Winchester already was an important religious center, having been a bishopric since the seventh century. During the Middle Ages the cathedral was an important stopping place for pilgrims on their way to Canterbury, who came here first to pay homage at Saint Swithin's Shrine. As the richest see in England, Winchester was a plum for many powerful churchmen. Among its archbishops who wielded great political as well as ecclesiastical power were William of Wykeham, who served as chancellor under both Edward III and Richard II, and Cardinal Henry Beaufort (d. 1447), chancellor for Henry IV, Henry V, and Henry VI. Both are buried in the cathedral as are several early kings including Canute, and Jane Austen and Izaak Walton.

### WINCHESTER COLLEGE, *College Street*

Founded by William of Wykeham in 1379, this school became a model for England's great public schools. It is allied with New College at Oxford, which Wykeham also founded (1394).

### WOLVESEY CASTLE, *College Street*

Bishop Henry de Blois, King Stephen's brother, began this castle in 1129. Queen Mary I lived here in 1554. The castle was destroyed during the Civil War, and only ruins remain.

### WOBURN ABBEY (BEDFORD), *14 kilometers northwest of Dunstable on A50*

Henry VIII presented this property to John Russell at the Dissolution, but the Russell family, who became the dukes of Bedford, did not live here until the 17th century. Most of the present house dates from the 18th century. In addition to historical family relics, Woburn Abbey has notable collections of paintings and furniture. In the huge park are rare wild animals.

### WOLVERHAMPTON VICINITY (STAFFORD)

MOSELEY OLD HALL, *6½ kilometers north off A640*

In this Elizabethan house, owned at the time by the Whitgreave family, Charles II hid for two days after his defeat in the Battle of Worcester in 1651. The bed in which the king slept may be seen, as well as the cramped hiding place where he crouched while Cromwell's men searched for him.

*Left: deer grazing in the park at Woburn Abbey. Right: Winchester Cathedral*

## WORCESTER (WORCESTER)

### CATHEDRAL, *off College Street overlooking the Severn River*

Worcester is an ancient cathedral city, having become the seat of a bishopric about 680. The present cathedral was begun by Bishop Wulfstan about 1095, on the site of an earlier Saxon church and monastery. Wulfstan's Norman crypt remains unchanged, but most of the rest of the cathedral dates from the 14th century. In front of the high altar is the **Tomb of King John** (d. 1216), topped by the oldest marble royal effigy in England. Nearby is **Prince Arthur's Chantry**, tomb of Henry VII's eldest son, who died at 15 in 1502.

### COMMANDERY, THE, *adjoining 79 Sidbury*

This Tudor house was Royalist headquarters during the Battle of Worcester (1651), in which Oliver Cromwell's forces routed Charles II and his Scottish army, forcing Charles to flee to France.

## YORK (YORK)

### CASTLE MUSEUM, *off Tower Street*

Housed in the 18th-century Debtors' Prison and Female Prison, this folk museum has reconstructions of streets and houses to illustrate five centuries of English life.

### CITY WALLS

The Normans rebuilt and expanded the Roman city walls in the 11th century, after they had destroyed York during their rampage through the north in 1069 to quell local rebellions. these fortified Norman walls were in turn rebuilt beginning in the 13th century; the present well-preserved walls date mainly from the reign of Edward III (1327–77). The four fortified medieval bars, or gates, that commanded the main roads to the city still stand.

### CLIFFORD'S TOWER, *off Tower Street*

This 13th-century fortification was erected on the site of one of the two wooden castles William I put up in 1068. The original Norman keep was burned in 1190 during anti-Jewish riots.

### MULTANGULAR TOWER (ROMAN), *on Museum Street*

This fourth-century defensive tower was part of the legionary fortress established here by the Romans in A.D. 71. York (the Roman Erboracum) was an important military headquarters and the capital of Roman Britain. In 306 Constantius I died in York, and his son, Constantine I, was proclaimed emperor there. The city came under frequent attacks from the north; the Multangular was erected after one of these assaults.

### SAINT PETER'S SCHOOL, *on Clifton Street, an extension of Bootham*

Founded in the eighth century, this school was headed by Alcuin, the great Yorkshire scholar who helped make York a famous center of learning before he left to found Charlemagne's palace school at Aachen about 871.

### YORK MINSTER (CATHEDRAL OF SAINT PETER), *Minster Yard*

There has been a church on the site of this great cathedral since the seventh century, when Archbishop Paulinus erected a chapel for the baptism of King Edwin of Northumbria. Since then York has been the ecclesiastical center of northern England. The present building, England's largest medieval cathedral, was erected between 1220 and 1470. It is famous for its stained-glass windows.

# NORTHERN IRELAND

**ARBOE (TYRONE),** *on B73 on the west bank of Lough Neagh*

A ruined tenth-century church is all that remains of the abbey founded in the sixth century by Saint Colman. Next to the church is a fine **High Cross,** more than 18 feet high and sculptured with Biblical scenes.

**ARMAGH (ARMAGH),** *on A28, A29, A3, and A5*

Armagh has been Ireland's chief ecclesiastical city since the fifth century, when Saint Patrick founded his church on the site now occupied by the Protestant cathedral. Armagh rapidly became a center of Christian learning, but its fame also attracted marauding Norsemen, who repeatedly plundered the town. In the 16th and 17th centuries Armagh again suffered heavily, this time at the hands of the O'Neills during their struggles with the English Crown. As a result, little remains of the old town. Armagh today is dominated by its 18th-century **Protestant Cathedral** and 19th-century **Roman Catholic Cathedral.** In the yard of the Protestant cathedral is the reputed grave of Brian Boru, who drove the Danes from Ireland in the 11th century. Three kilometers west of Armagh is **Navan Fort,** or Emain Macha, a huge elliptical hill-fort, traditionally the palace of the kings of Ulster for about 600 years, until the fourth century A.D.

**BALLYCASTLE (ANTRIM),** *43 kilometers north of Ballymena on A44 and A2*

This town has associations with Sorley Boy MacDonnell, a celebrated Scots-Irish chief who struggled with Queen Elizabeth and with the O'Neills for control of Antrim. Ruined **Bunamargy Friary,** a Franciscan house founded in 1500, was burned in 1584 during a MacDonnell attack on English troops garrisoned there. The Mac-Donnells subsequently converted part of the church into a family mausoleum, where Sorley Boy and his descendants, the earls of Antrim, are buried. Near the town are the ruins of **Dunanynie Castle,** home of Sorley Boy from 1558 until his death in 1590.

**BELFAST (ANTRIM, DOWN),** *on A24, A2, A6, A52, A20, A501, A1, and A23 at the head of Belfast Lough*

Like so many other Irish towns, Belfast began with a castle erected on a strategic site—in this case a river ford. In 1177 John de Courcy, the Anglo-Norman conqueror of Ulster, built one of his many castles here, just south of what is now **Castle Place.** The fortress was the scene of many bloody battles between Anglo-Normans and Irish, and in 1315 it was destroyed by Edward Bruce, the Scottish nobleman who was briefly king of Ireland. Along with much of the rest of Ulster, the Belfast site was confiscated from its Irish owners and granted to an Englishman early in the 17th century: in 1603 Sir Arthur Chichester of Devonshire established a settlement, bringing over English colonists and erecting a new castle. Incorporated in 1613 by James I, the town did not really prosper until late in the century, when the monopoly on imports was purchased from the town of Carrickfergus, and an influx of French Huguenots sparked the linen trade. Late in the 18th century Belfast was a center for the movement for political reform, marked by cooperation between Protestants and Catholics who were united in opposing English rule. Here, in 1791, Wolfe Tone founded his revolutionary United Irishmen society. A century later, however, the political mood had shifted, partly as a result of the growing number of privileges Catholics had won. (**Queen's University,** for instance, was established by the British government in 1845 for the education of those who did not belong to the Church of Ireland.) Instead of being a

*Page 307. Top left: Belfast Castle. Right: the city walls of Londonderry. Center: Dunluce Castle near Bushmills in Antrim. Below left: the Roman Catholic Cathedral in Armagh. Right: the Round Tower on Devenish Island*

center of Irish republicanism, the city became a center of Protestant opposition to home rule. After Ireland was partitioned in 1920, Belfast became the capital of Northern Ireland, and the British government began the construction of **Parliament House** in the suburb of Stormont as the seat of local government; the building was opened in 1932. But partition did not alleviate Catholic-Protestant tensions. In 1935 religious riots broke out following a Protestant celebration of the Battle of the Boyne. And beginning late in the 1960s Belfast, with the rest of Northern Ireland, was torn by civil war.

### BUSHMILLS (ANTRIM)
DUNLUCE CASTLE, *4 kilometers northwest off A2*
Situated on a rocky precipice high above the sea, this impregnable fortress was probably erected by Richard de Burgo about 1300. Sorley Boy MacDonnell took it from the MacQuillans about 1560, after which the castle became the home of his descendants, the earls of Antrim, who reconstructed it. It underwent several sieges before being abandoned after the Restoration of Charles II. Part of the curtain wall, two of the original five towers, and the 16th-century gatehouse, great hall, and kitchen stand.

### CARRICKFERGUS (ANTRIM), *16 kilometers northeast of Belfast via A2*
This town is dominated by its fine **Norman Castle**, which was probably begun in the 12th century by John de Courcy, who overran eastern Ulster in 1177 after Ireland had submitted to England's Henry II. In 1210 King John besieged and took the castle during a visit to secure English authority in Ireland. In 1316 the castle fell after a yearlong siege to Scotland's Edward Bruce, who for a short time was king of Ireland. William of Orange landed beneath the castle wall in 1690 on his way to the Battle of the Boyne, where he defeated James II; a stone marks the spot. The castle has been restored. There is also a fine Elizabethan church, **Saint Nicholas**, in the town.

### DEVENISH ISLAND (FERMANAGH), *about 4 kilometers north of Enniskillen in Lough Erne*
There is a fine 12th-century 85-foot-high **Round Tower** here, associated, like other ecclesiastical remains on the island, with a monastery founded in the 6th century by Saint Molaise.

### DOWNPATRICK (DOWN), *on A25 and A22*
This ancient county town is famous as the alleged burial place of Saint Patrick; a boulder outside the **Cathedral** marks the supposed grave. It is unlikely that the saint is actually buried here, however: in the 12th century John de Courcy—who conquered this area after the Anglo-Norman invasion and made Downpatrick one of his seats (*see also Carrickfergus*)—pretended to bring Patrick's bones to his new cathedral, probably to conciliate the Irish clergy whom de Courcy had begun to supplant with English monks. The present cathedral, begun in 1790, retains fragments of the original building, including a Norman font. About 2½ kilometers east of Downpatrick are the **Wells of Struell,** beside which Saint Patrick is believed to have built a chapel. About 3 kilometers northeast are the scant remains of 12th-century **Saul Abbey,** near the spot where the saint first landed in Ireland in 432 and where he established his first church. Ruined **Inch Abbey,** about 4 kilometers northwest, was founded as a Cistercian house by de Courcy in 1180.

**DUNDRUM CASTLE (DOWN),** *3 kilometers southeast of Clough on A2*

This well-preserved fortress, which has a three-story circular keep and is surrounded by a moat cut into the rock, was begun by John de Courcy in the 13th century. An important Norman stronghold, its commanding situation made it the object of many fierce struggles until it was dismantled by Oliver Cromwell in 1652.

**GREYABBEY (DOWN),** *52 kilometers southeast of Belfast on A20*

Affrica, wife of John de Courcy, founded the Cistercian abbey from which this town takes its name in 1193. It was one of several established by the zealous de Courcys, and its well-preserved ruins give a good idea of an English-influenced monastery. Greyabbey was dissolved in 1537 and was burned by Sir Brian O'Neill in 1572 to keep it out of the hands of English colonists.

**LONDONDERRY (LONDONDERRY),** *on A2, A5, A6, and A40 on the River Foyle near Lough Foyle*

Derry, which began with a monastery established by Saint Columba in A.D. 546, received its modern name in 1609, when King James I granted the town to a London merchant company, the Irish Society. Derry was by then in ruins, having been destroyed during the ultimately successful efforts of the English to break the power of the O'Neills of Ulster. The Irish Society imported Protestant colonists and began immediately to rebuild the city and enclose it with walls, which were completed in 1618. The Protestant stronghold withstood three assaults in the 17th century: by Irish rebels in 1641, Royalists in 1649, and James II's army in the great siege of 1688–89. Beginning December 18, 1688, when 13 apprentices slammed closed Ferryquay Gate in the face of James II's approaching troops, Londonderry held out for 105 days against a Jacobean blockade, until finally relief troops arrived to break the siege. Toward the end, hundreds within the walls were dying of starvation daily. The well-preserved walls contain many monuments to the siege, including **Ferryquay Gate.** At **Bishop's Gate** a triumphal arch commemorating the siege was erected in 1789. The **Walker Monument,** in the Royal Bastion, is a 90-foot-high column commemorating the Reverend George Walker, the eloquent clergyman-commander who inspired Derry's 30,000 inhabitants to hold firm until relief arrived. In the Double Bastion is **"Roaring Meg,"** the largest gun used in the siege. There are other relics in the **Protestant Cathedral** on Bishop Street, erected by the Irish Society in 1633. In recent years Londonderry, with the rest of Northern Ireland, has again been embroiled in religious strife. The eruption of violence in 1968 was triggered by a Catholic civil rights march here. Since then Derry's Catholic area—called **Bogside** from the plantation days, when Catholics were forced to live outside the city walls, in the marshy "bog side" —has been a center of resistance. Here, in February, 1972, one of the worst episodes in the conflict took place when British troops sent to Northern Ireland to keep the peace opened fire on a crowd of 20,000 Catholic demonstrators, killing 13.

**MONEA (FERMANAGH),** *4½ kilometers northwest of Enniskillen off A46*

The area's best preserved **Plantation Castle** is here, built about 1620 by the Reverend Malcolm Hamilton, rector of Devenish. Early in the 17th century thousands of acres of Ulster land were granted to English and Scottish Protestants. The Jacobean plantation law required that every planter build a strong castle and bawn on his land; the ruins of these castles survive in Fermanagh and Tyrone.

# SCOTLAND

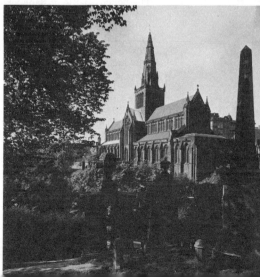

**ALLOWAY (AYR),** *just south of Ayr on B7024*

Robert Burns was born here on January 25, 1759, in **Burns's Cottage,** which is open to the public. There are personal relics in the adjoining museum. Farther down the street is the **Burns Monument,** which contains additional Burns memorabilia. In Ayr, just to the north, is the **Auld Kirk,** where Burns was baptized. Ayr's **Tam o'Shanter Inn,** a favorite of the poet's, is now a museum.

**WALL OF ANTONINUS (DUMBARTON, LANARK, STIRLING, WEST LOTHIAN),** *extending from the Firth of Forth just east of Bo'ness to Old Kilpatrick on the Firth of Clyde, a distance of about 57 kilometers*

This ancient Roman fortification consisted of a turf rampart paralleled by a ditch to the north and a military road to the south. Built beginning in A.D. 140, it marked the northern limits of Roman Britain. The wall, which was strengthened by some 15 forts—one about every 3 kilometers—was set up as a defense against invasions from the north. It was abandoned within 50 years, and only traces remain. The best preserved parts are near Falkirk (*see*).

**ARBROATH ABBEY (ANGUS),** 28 *kilometers northeast of Dundee via A92 on the North Sea*

This once-powerful monastery was founded in 1178 by William the Lion, who was buried in the church. In 1320 an assembly of the Estates of Scotland met in the abbey to reaffirm Scottish independence and acknowledge Robert I, "the Bruce," as king. Burned twice in the 13th century, the abbey was neglected after the Reformation and fell into its present ruined state. Today the **Abbey Church** and the **Abbot's House** remain; the latter has been restored and is a folk museum. In 1951 the Stone of Scone (Coronation Stone) was removed from Westminster Abbey and placed on the church altar for a short time before being returned to England.

**BALMORAL CASTLE (ABERDEEN),** 78 *kilometers west of Aberdeen on Route 93 on the River Dee*

The Scottish residence of the British sovereign, the present white granite building was begun in 1853 under the direction of Prince Albert on a site once occupied by the castle of the Farquharson clan. The gardens are open to the public.

**BANNOCKBURN (STIRLING),** *about 4 kilometers south of Stirling off A9*

The famous Battle of Bannockburn was fought about 12 kilometers to the north of this village in June, 1314, when 30,000 men led by Robert I (Robert the Bruce) routed an English force of 100,000 under Edward II. Robert, who in defiance of Edward had been crowned king of Scotland at Scone (*see*) in 1306, had slowly been retaking Scottish lands and castles from the English. In 1314 he besieged Stirling Castle (*see*), the last Scottish castle in English hands. Edward was trying to reach the castle with reinforcements before the English garrison there capitulated when Robert intercepted him at Bannockburn. Robert's overwhelming victory led to the surrender of the castle and in effect assured Scottish independence, although fighting continued for several more years. A memorial at the field includes the **Borestone,** where according to tradition Bruce planted the Scottish royal standard.

**BLAIR-ATHOLL (PERTH),** 56 *kilometers northwest of Perth via A9*

The seat of the duke of Atholl, **Blair Castle** dates from 1269, when the northeast tower, Cumming's Tower, was built. It was an important fortress in the Scottish civil wars: James Graham, marquis of Montrose, garrisoned it in 1644, and it was occupied by Oliver Cromwell in 1652 and by Bonnie Dundee (John Graham of Claverhouse) in 1689. Prince Charles Edward Stuart (Bonnie Prince Charlie) visited here in 1745 and again in 1746; but later in 1746 it was taken for the duke of Cumberland, whose defenders successfully withstood a 17-day siege. The castle also is the headquarters of the Atholl Highlanders, the duke of Atholl's private army; the duke is Great Britain's only private citizen allowed to maintain his own army. Behind the castle, in the ruined **Church of Saint Bride,** Bonnie Dundee was buried after Killiecrankie (*see*).

**BORTHWICK CASTLE·(MIDLOTHIAN),** *about 20 kilometers southeast of Edinburgh off A7*

This double-towered, restored 15th-century castle was the home of Mary queen of Scots and the earl of Bothwell for a few days shortly after their marriage in May, 1567. In June Bothwell, alarmed by the approach of hostile Scottish lords, fled to Dunbar (*see*); two days later Mary followed, disguised as a page.

**BOTHWELL (LANARK),** *15 kilometers from Glasgow via A721 and A74 on the River Clyde*

Here, on June 22, 1679, at the Battle of **Bothwell Bridge,** a force of Scottish Covenanters was routed and slaughtered by Royalist troops under the duke of Monmouth and John Graham of Claverhouse, Viscount Dundee. Northwest of town is **Bothwell Castle,** a ruined 13th-century stronghold that is one of the most impressive in Scotland. From 1361 it belonged to the Douglas family. In 1455 James, earl of Douglas, forfeited his lands after leading an abortive rebellion against James II. For a time the castle passed to the earl of Bothwell, who in 1492 gave it to Archibald, earl of Angus, another branch of the Douglases, in exchange for Hermitage Castle (*see Newcastleton*).

**CARBERRY HILL (MIDLOTHIAN),** *a few kilometers southeast of Musselburgh via A6124*

Here, on June 15, 1567, Mary queen of Scots surrendered to the rebellious Scottish lords after a bloodless confrontation. The rebellion had been sparked by Mary's marriage, a month earlier, to the earl of Bothwell, an act that had cost Mary the support of most of Protestant Scotland. After her surrender Mary was imprisoned at Lochleven Castle (*see*). Carberry Hill marked the end of Mary's freedom; she remained a virtual prisoner, first of the Scots and then of the English, for the rest of her life.

**CAWDOR (NAIRN),** *8 kilometers southwest of Nairn via B9090*

In Scottish tradition, **Cawdor Castle** is the place where Macbeth, thane of Cawdor, murdered King Duncan I in 1040 (*see also Glamis*). Actually, Duncan probably was killed in battle, and the oldest remaining part of the castle, a central tower, was built in 1454. Most of the picturesque castle dates from the 16th century. About 2 kilometers west of Cawdor is **Kilravock Castle,** built in 1460.

**CULLODEN MOOR (INVERNESS),** *8 kilometers east of Inverness via B9006*

At the Battle of Culloden Moor, fought on April 16, 1746, Prince Charles Edward Stuart's Highland army was crushed by an English army under the duke of Cumberland, bringing to an end the Jacobite uprising of 1745 and the hopes of the Stuarts to regain the English throne. For days after the battle, on the order of "Butcher" Cumberland, English cavalry hunted down and massacred wounded Highlanders who had escaped. A tall cairn marks the battle site, while the graves of fallen Highlanders are marked by stones bearing the names of the clans. Near the field is the **Cumberland Stone,** marking the spot from which the duke of Cumberland watched the battle. **Old Leanach** farmhouse, on the battlefield, purportedly was the Jacobite headquarters. Across the River Nairn are the **Stones of Clava,** Bronze Age burial cairns dating from 1800–1500 B.C.

**DOUNE CASTLE (PERTH),** *outside Doune between the River Teith and Ardoch Burn*

This restored 15th-century castle is one of the best preserved strongholds in Scotland. It was built by Robert, duke of Albany (d. 1419), regent for James I of Scotland. It was held for Prince Charles Edward in the uprising of 1745, and Royalist prisoners taken at the Battle of Falkirk (*see*) were confined here.

**DRUMCLOG MOOR (LANARK),** *23 kilometers from Kilmarnock on A71*

On June 1, 1679, 200 Covenanters routed a force of royal soldiers on their way to disperse an armed conventicle, an illegal religious meeting often held, as in this case, in an isolated outdoor spot. The defeated royal dragoons were led by Viscount Dundee, known as Bonnie Dundee, a controversial chieftain who was considered a monster by the Covenanters and a hero by Royalists. A marker on Drumclog Moor commemorates the confrontation.

**DUMBARTON (DUMBARTON),** *on A814, A812, and A82 near the mouth of the River Clyde*

Dumbarton, once capital of the medieval kingdom of Strathclyde, is best known for its **Castle.** Six-year-old Mary queen of Scots was secretly sent from the castle to France in 1584, thereby confounding English plans for a Scottish-English alliance. In 1571, with Mary a prisoner in England, the castle was captured from her followers. Today the castle consists of modern barracks, although a 12th-century archway and a sundial presented by Mary have been preserved.

**DUMFRIES (DUMFRIES),** *about 11 kilometers inland from Solway Firth at the junction of A710, A711, A75, A76, A701, and A709*

Dumfries was created a royal burgh in the 12th century. In 1306, after Edward had conquered a rebellious Scotland, Robert the Bruce killed guardian of the realm John Comyn (known as the Red Comyn), a supporter of Edward I, in the former **Greyfriars Monastery Church.** The murder led to a renewal of war with England that resulted ultimately in Scottish independence. A plaque on a wine store in **Castle Street** marks the site of the murder. Robert Burns came to Dumfries in 1791 and spent the last years of his life here. **Burns's House** on Burns Street, where the poet died, contains Burns memorabilia, as does one of his favorite taverns, the **Globe** (on High Street). In the churchyard of **Saint Michael's Church** is **Burns's Tomb,** where the poet, his wife, and several of their children are buried. About 3 kilometers northwest of the city, off A76, is **Terreglas Mansion,** where Mary queen of Scots, fleeing south after her defeat at Langside (*see Glasgow*), made her decision to seek refuge in England. On May 15, 1568, she embarked at Port Mary and crossed Solway Firth to England.

**DUNBAR (EAST LOTHIAN),** *45 kilometers from Edinburgh via A1 on the Firth of Forth*

The Battle of Dunbar, in which Oliver Cromwell in 1650 defeated the Covenanters who at that time were supporting Charles II, actually took place just southeast of the town at **Doon Hill,** off the Great North Road near Broxburn. Cromwell's victory established his authority over all Scotland south of the Forth. The ruined **Castle** overlooking the harbor of this old seaport once was a formidable stronghold. In 1339 the countess of Dunbar, known as Black Agnes because of her swarthy complexion, successfully withstood a six-week siege of the castle by the English. In 1566 Queen Mary fled to the castle with her husband Lord Darnley after the murder of her secretary, David Rizzio. Shortly thereafter Mary appointed the earl of Bothwell, a loyal supporter, governor of the castle. The following year, after Darnley himself was murdered (a murder for which Bothwell was widely believed to be responsible), Bothwell carried Mary off to the castle from Edinburgh. Three weeks later, on May 15, 1567, he married her. Following Mary's subsequent surrender to the enraged Scottish lords at Carberry Hill *(see)*, Dunbar Castle was destroyed by the earl of Moray, Mary's half brother, who became regent after her imprisonment at Lochleven Castle *(see)* in 1567.

**DUNFERMLINE (FIFE),** *26 kilometers northwest of Edinburgh via A90*

This royal burgh is famous as a birthplace and burying place of Scottish royalty. Its abbey was begun about 1070 by Malcolm III Canmore and his wife, Queen Margaret, shortly after Malcolm had made Dunfermline the royal residence. The magnificent **Abbey Church,** of which the original nave remains, was added in 1128 by their son, David I. Robert the Bruce (d. 1329) is buried in the church; his tomb is marked by a brass plate. Malcolm III and Margaret were buried here, as were several of their children and descendants. The ruined **Palace** was also built by Malcolm III. His children were born there; so was Charles I of England, son of James VI, in 1600. **Andrew Carnegie's Birthplace** is at 4 Moody Street; a memorial building adjoins the house.

**DUNNOTTAR CASTLE (KINCARDINE),** *south of Stonehaven off A92*

In 1652, during the Commonwealth wars, the Scottish regalia were kept here for eight months and then smuggled to safety just before the castle fell to Cromwell's troops. In 1685, 167 Covenanters were imprisoned in the dungeon. The castle was dismantled after the Jacobite rebellion of 1715; remains include a 14th-century tower and chapel and a gateway from about 1575.

**DUNSTAFFNAGE CASTLE (ARGYLL),** *off the Oban–Connel road (A85) overlooking Dunstaffnage Bay*

This ruined stronghold, dating in part from the 13th century, was given by Robert the Bruce to the Campbells. Flora MacDonald was imprisoned here for ten days in 1746 after helping Prince Charles Edward escape following the Battle of Culloden Moor *(see)*. Dunstaffnage was capital of the early Scottish kingdom of Dalriada, and the Coronation Stone was kept here before its removal to Scone.

**EDINBURGH (MIDLOTHIAN)**

CRAIGMILLAR CASTLE, *on the southeastern outskirts of town on the Old Dalkeith Road*

This notable ruined castle, which has a massive square keep dating from 1374, was a favorite residence of Mary queen of Scots. Mary came here in 1566 after her near-fatal illness at Jedburgh (*see*), and with Bothwell, Archibald, earl of Argyll, George Gordon, earl of Huntly, and William Maitland, she is said to have plotted the murder of her husband, Lord Darnley.

### EDINBURGH CASTLE, on Castle Rock at the west end of the Royal Mile

The castle actually is a collection of buildings dating from several periods. The earliest known building on the site was a castle-fort built about 617 by King Edwin of Northumbria, for whom Edinburgh was named. In the 11th century King Malcolm III made the castle his residence. His wife, the saintly Queen Margaret (d. 1093), built the **Chapel** that bears her name and that still stands today, the oldest surviving building in Edinburgh. The town that grew around the castle became capital of Scotland in 1437. Edinburgh frequently came under attack during the border wars, and the castle itself changed hands several times. Edward I of England captured it in 1296; the Scots recaptured it in 1313 and the following year destroyed all buildings but the chapel to keep them from English hands. Refortified by Edward III in 1337 after Edward de Baliol, pretender to the Scottish throne, turned the site over to the English in return for English support of his claims, it was again retaken by the Scots in 1341. James VI (later James I of England), son of Mary queen of Scots, was born in **Queen Mary's Apartments** in 1566. In **Old Parliament Hall**, an early-15th-century structure rebuilt by James IV in the 16th century, the Estates of the Realm met occasionally before the union with England in 1707. In the Crown Room of the **Old Palace**, another building dating from the 15th century, are the **Regalia** of Scotland, including the crown refashioned for James V in 1540. **Argyll's Tower** contains the dungeon where the marquis of Argyll, a Protestant leader who turned from Oliver Cromwell after initially supporting him, was imprisoned before his execution for treason in 1661, at the Restoration. The castle overlooks both the **Old Town** (*see Royal Mile*) and the **New Town**. The latter, constructed during the eighteenth century, has broad streets and squares lined with stately Georgian homes, many of them designed by the eminent 18th-century architect Robert Adam.

### GRASSMARKET, via King's Stables Road, West Port, Victoria Street, Candlemaker Row

Once an open market, this oblong area served, after 1660, as a place of execution. Many Covenanters—Presbyterians who refused to accept the episcopal edicts of Charles II and James II—were martyred here. The execution of a Scottish smuggler, Andrew Wilson, in 1736 led to the anti-English Porteous Riot. When a crowd sympathetic to Wilson became restless, Captain John Porteous, head of the town guard, ordered his men to fire into the crowd. Several people were killed; although Porteous was tried and sentenced to death, he was subsequently reprieved. An angry mob broke into the Old Tolbooth prison (*see Royal Mile*), where Porteous was being held, dragged him to the Grassmarket, and hanged him. The **White Hart Inn**, on the north side of the Grassmarket, was patronized by Robert Burns and William Wordsworth.

### GREYFRIARS CHURCH AND CHURCHYARD, at the top of Candlemaker Row

In 1638 Scotland's leading Protestant nobles signed the National Covenant in Greyfriars Churchyard; some signed their names in

*Left: changing of the guard at Edinburgh Castle. Right: Holyroodhouse Palace*

blood to this solemn pledge to defend the reformed religion from Archbishop William Laud's episcopal innovations. Today copies of the Covenanters' flags hang above the pillars of the church.

**HOLYROOD ABBEY,** *adjacent to the Holyroodhouse Palace*

Holyrood Abbey (abbey of the Holy Cross) was built for Augustinian canons in 1128 by David I, son of Saint Margaret. According to legend, David founded the abbey on the spot where he had been miraculously saved from being gored to death by an angry stag through the interposition of a cross. The first three Jameses preferred the abbey to the less comfortable castle as their royal residence. In 1430 James II was born here. He, James III, and James IV were married in the church, as were Queen Mary and Lord Darnley in 1565. Like the palace, the abbey was severely damaged in 1544 and 1547, during the English depredations of southern Scotland. The church was restored by Charles I and under Charles II became the Chapel Royal. Sacked by a Presbyterian mob after James II of England was deposed during the Revolution of 1688, the ruin of the chapel was completed in 1768 when a roof caved in. Today all that remains of the abbey is the nave of the Chapel Royal. Among those buried in the chapel are David II, James II, James V, Darnley, and David Rizzio, Queen Mary's secretary.

**HOLYROODHOUSE PALACE,** *off Canongate, at the east end of the Royal Mile*

The primary royal palace of Scotland is most famous for the six turbulent, romantic, ultimately tragic years spent there by Mary queen of Scots. The palace was begun about 1500 by James IV; construction was continued by James V, who built the northwest tower so that he could see up the Canongate. The palace was largely detroyed in 1544 by England's earl of Hertford (later duke of Somer-

317

set), who that year invaded Scotland to retaliate for Scotland's support of France and the Catholic interests against Henry VIII's religious policies. Somerset again inflicted heavy damage during his rampage through southern Scotland in 1547, after he defeated the Scots at Pinkie (*see*). In 1561, following the death of the regent Mary of Guise, young Queen Mary, recently widowed, returned from France and took up residence at Holyrood. Shortly after her arrival, the young Catholic queen received in her **Apartments** the fiery Presbyterian leader John Knox. In a famous confrontation, the two debated theology and the question of how much loyalty a subject owed his sovereign. In 1566, in these same apartments, Mary's favorite and secretary, David Rizzio, was murdered by a group of jealous nobles who broke into the palace with the help of Mary's husband, Lord Darnley. In May, 1567, after Darnley himself had been murdered, Mary married the earl of Bothwell in the hall that is now the **Picture Gallery.** Oliver Cromwell occupied the palace in 1650, after he defeated the supporters of Charles II at Dunbar (*see*). In 1745 Bonnie Prince Charlie, Stuart pretender to the throne, held a brief but gay court here during the ill-fated Jacobite uprising. Adjacent to the palace is a small 16th-century lodge known as **Queen Mary's Bath House,** through which Rizzio's murderers may have made their escape. During repairs to the bath house in 1852 an ornate dagger was found, possibly one of the murderers'.

ROYAL MILE, *from Edinburgh Castle along Castle Hill, the Lawnmarket, High Street, and Canongate to Holyroodhouse Palace*

Following the gently sloping ridge down the east side of **Castle Rock** is the succession of streets called the Royal Mile, so named because it was the route used by royalty traveling between Edinburgh Castle (*see*) and Holyroodhouse Palace (*see*). The Royal Mile was the heart of activity in Edinburgh's **Old Town,** and many of the buildings and sites on and around the Royal Mile are associated with famous people and important events. The philosopher David Hume and later biographer James Boswell lived in a flat on **James's Court,** off the **Lawnmarket.** On **High Street** a heart-shaped design in the causeway marks the site of the **Old Tolbooth,** or prison, which figured in Sir Walter Scott's famous romance *The Heart of Midlothian.* Behind the historic **Church of Saint Giles** (*see*) is the **Parliament House,** dating from 1632, where the Scottish parliament met until its dissolution in 1707. Farther on is the **John Knox House,** a 15th-century building, where the great Scottish religious reformer supposedly lived from 1561 until his death in 1572. Toward the bottom of the **Canongate** is one of the Old Town's most picturesque courtyards, the **White Horse Close,** with its restored **White Horse Inn,** a famous hostelry dating from about 1623, which figured in Sir Walter Scott's novel *Waverley.*

SAINT GILES CHURCH, *High Street on the Royal Mile*

Once the High Kirk of Scotland, Saint Giles was constructed in the 14th and 15th centuries, after an earlier structure had been destroyed by Richard II of England in 1385. The famous central tower with its "crown" steeple was added about 1495. At the Reformation the church's 44 altars and the statue of Saint Giles were removed. Between 1559 and 1572 John Knox was minister, preaching his fiery sermons to large congregations. For two short periods in the 17th century, the church became a cathedral: under Charles I in 1633, and again under Charles II until 1688, when the Presbyterian Church of Scotland was established in place of episcopacy.

**ELGIN (MORAY),** *at the intersection of A941 and A96 on the south bank of the River Lossie*

Elgin's ruined **Cathedral of Moray** once was one of Scotland's finest. In 1390 it was burned by the notorious Alexander Stewart, earl of Buchan and lord of Badenoch, who was known as the Wolf of Badenoch; Buchan's vengeful act came after he had been excommunicated following a quarrel with the bishop. In the 16th century the church was again heavily damaged during a bloody brawl between the Dunbar and the Innes families.

**FALKIRK (STIRLING),** *40 kilometers west of Edinburgh on A9*

Two significant battles took place here: in 1298, on the south side of Callendar Wood, Edward I of England defeated Scottish patriot Sir William Wallace. In 1746 Prince Charles Edward Stuart and his retreating army defeated pursuing English troops led by General Henry Hawley. Mary queen of Scots was a frequent guest at **Callender House,** on whose grounds are a well-preserved section of the Wall of Antoninus (*see*). **Rough Castle,** the best-preserved fort from the wall, lies just west of Falkirk.

**FALKLAND (FIFE),** *on A912 at the northern base of the East Lomond*

This town is famous for **Falkland Palace** of the Stuarts. Begun by James III before 1500, it was greatly improved by James V; it became one of his favorite royal residences, and he died here brokenhearted after his crushing defeat by the English at Solway Moss in 1542. As James lay dying, he was told of the birth of his daughter, the future Mary queen of Scots, at Linlithgow (*see*). He commented: "God's will be done; it cam wi' a lass and it'll gang wi' a lass."

**GLAMIS CASTLE (ANGUS),** *about 2 kilometers north of Glamis near A94*

This famous castle, seat of the earl of Strathmore, was Shakespeare's setting for the murder of King Duncan by Macbeth. Actually the feudal castle was built at a later date. In 1537 Lady Glamis was burned for witchcraft, and the castle was forfeited to James V; eventually it was restored to her son. The present appearance of the castle dates from the 17th century. Princess Margaret, granddaughter of the 14th earl of Strathmore, was born at Glamis in 1930.

**GLASGOW**

GLASGOW CATHEDRAL, *on Castle Street*

The original cathedral was begun in 1163 over the grave of Saint Kentigern (also known as Saint Mungo), the patron saint of Glasgow, who died in 603. Burned in 1192, the cathedral was immediately rebuilt; part of the new crypt, consecrated in 1197, remains. The crypt and choir were not completed until the mid-13th century; the nave dates from late in the 15th. The traditional tomb of Saint Mungo is in the center of the crypt. The cathedral is the only one of Scotland's great Gothic churches that has remained undamaged.

LANGSIDE MEMORIAL, *at the south gate of Queen's Park*

This memorial marks the site of the battle in which Mary queen of Scots was defeated after escaping from Lochleven Castle (*see*), thereby losing her last chance to regain control of Scotland. Mary and her followers were trying to reach Dumbarton, a stronghold held by Mary's supporters in a part of Scotland sympathetic to her cause. However, the regent James Stewart, earl of Moray, intercepted them at Langside and won a decisive victory that sent Mary fleeing south to England.

**PROVAND'S LORDSHIP,** *3 Castle Street*

Probably the oldest house in Glasgow, this building was erected in 1471 by Bishop Andrew Muirhead of Durisdeer, whose arms appear on the south gable. James II and James IV supposedly lived here, and Mary queen of Scots is said to have stayed here while visiting Darnley in 1567. The house today has 17th-century furnishings.

**GLENCOE (ARGYLL),** *near A82 south of Loch Leven in the valley of the Coe*

This famous glen was the site of the savage massacre of the MacDonalds of Glencoe by troops under John Campbell of Glen Lyon in February, 1692. The massacre took place because the MacDonald chieftain had been a few days late in taking the oath of allegiance to King William III. At dawn on February 13, government troops who had been living for some days with the inhabitants of Glencoe suddenly began their attack. Forty of the 200 inhabitants of the glen were slain, and many more died of exposure after fleeing. Because the order for the massacre is said to have been written on the nine of diamonds, that card has since been known as the curse of Scotland. A marker indicates the site of the massacre, and a **monument** to the murdered MacDonald chief is near the entrance to the glen.

**GLENFINNAN (INVERNESS),** *30 kilometers from Fort William on A830*

The Jacobite uprising of 1745 began here when on August 19 Prince Charles Edward, the young Stuart pretender to the English throne, raised his standard at a gathering of the clans. **Prince Charles's Monument,** erected in 1815, marks the spot where the prince unfurled his banner.

**HEBRIDES, INNER (INVERNESS, ARGYLL)**

IONA, ISLE OF (ARGYLL)

This three-mile-long island of the Inner Hebrides is famous as an early center of Celtic Christianity. In 563 Saint Columba came here from Ireland and remained until his death 34 years later. The oldest remaining building on the island is the restored **Saint Oran's Chapel,** thought to have been built by Queen Margaret in 1080. Iona was an early pilgrim resort and until the 11th century was the burial place of Scottish kings. **Saint Oran's Cemetery,** the oldest Christian burial ground in Scotland, contains the graves of 48 Scottish kings, the last of whom was Duncan (d. 1040). Several interesting old crosses, **MacLean's Cross** and **Saint Martin's Cross,** have been preserved on Iona.

SKYE, ISLE OF (INVERNESS)

This picturesque island, the largest and most northerly of the Inner Hebrides, is well known for its associations with Prince Charles Edward and Flora MacDonald, the Jacobite heroine who helped the fugitive prince escape his pursuers after his defeat at Culloden Moor (*see*) in 1746. Prince Charles had made his way from the Highlands to Benbecula, in the Outer Hebrides. From there, on June 29, 1746, Flora MacDonald smuggled him, disguised as Betty Burke, her maid, to Skye. They landed near **Monkstadt House** (north of Uig on the northwest coast) and spent the night at **Kingsburgh House,** a few miles to the south. The next day they traveled to Portree, where the prince left Flora and made his way back to the Highlands, and from there eventually to France. For her part in the escape Flora MacDonald spent a short time in the Tower of London. In 1750 she married Allan MacDonald, the laird of Kingsburgh, and thereafter was visited by many celebrities, including Dr. Johnson and Boswell in 1773. She is buried at **Kilmuir,** her grave marked by a tall Celtic cross inscribed with a tribute by Dr. Johnson. Famous **Dunvegan Castle** at Dunvegan, which dates from the 15th to the 19th centuries, has long been the seat of the Macleods. It has many family and other historical relics.

### HEBRIDES, OUTER (INVERNESS, ROSS AND CROMARTY)

The Outer Hebrides, like Scotland's other northern islands, have many prehistoric remains—cairns and broches—as well as remains from their early settlement by Norsemen. Most striking are the remarkable **Standing Stones of Callernish,** located about 25 kilometers west of Stornoway on the west coast of **Lewis.** These ancient monoliths, about 50 in all, are second in importance only to Stonehenge in Britain. In 1746 Prince Charles Edward, fleeing from pursuers in the Highlands, landed on Lewis at Ardvourlie Bay and walked 32 kilometers north to **Arnish Moor,** near Stornoway, where he spent the night at a farm. A cairn on the moor commemorates the event. A memorial cairn at **Milton,** on South Uist, marks the birthplace of Jacobite heroine Flora MacDonald. On an island in **Castle Bay,** Barra's harbor, is the 15th-century **Kisamul Castle,** restored seat of the powerful MacNeils of Barra.

### INVERARAY (ARGYLL), *on A83 and A819 on the northwestern bank of Loch Fyne*

This town is best known for **Inverary Castle,** the ancestral seat of the duke of Argyll, head of the powerful Campbells. The present castle, designed in 1780, replaced a 15th-century castle, some ruins of which remain. The castle contains historical relics.

### JEDBURGH (ROXBURGH), *17 kilometers north of the English border on A68*

Once an important border town, Jedburgh is the site of famous **Jedburgh Abbey,** founded about 1118 by David I. During the border

*Left: Abbotsford near Melrose (see page 323). Right: Inveraray Castle*

wars the English sacked the abbey repeatedly and it suffered heavily. **Queen Mary's House,** where for ten days in 1566 Mary lay seriously ill after a long ride to see Bothwell at Hermitage Castle (*see Newcastleton*), is now a museum containing relics from Mary's stay there.

**KELSO (ROXBURGH),** *via A698 and A699 on the north bank of the Tweed*
Kelso is the site of **Kelso Abbey,** founded in 1128 by David I and probably once the finest and most powerful of the border abbeys. In 1545 the garrisoned abbey, taken after a siege by the earl of Hertford, was almost entirely destroyed by the English. Only a small portion remains today. Immediately northwest of Kelso is **Floors Castle,** on whose grounds James II was killed by an exploding cannon in 1460 while he was besieging nearby Roxburgh Castle. A holly tree marks the spot.

**KILLIECRANKIE, PASS OF (PERTH),** *5 kilometers northwest of Pitlochry*
In the Battle of Killiecrankie, which took place at the upper end of this pass in July, 1689, a Highlander army under John Graham of Claverhouse, Viscount Dundee, won a resounding victory for James VII and II over Royalist troops led by General Hugh Mackay. "Bonnie Dundee," a fiery leader and Jacobite hero, was slain in the battle; a stone marks the spot where he fell (*see also Blair-Atholl*).

**LINLITHGOW (WEST LOTHIAN),** *27 kilometers west of Edinburgh on A9 on the south shore of Loch Linlithgow*
This ancient county town is notable for its fine church and its ruined palace. A royal burgh under David I, in 1301 Linlithgow was occupied by Edward I of England, who in 1302 built a tower that was made a part of the **Palace;** the tower still stands. Most of the present palace dates from late in the 15th century. In one of the turrets is **Queen Margaret's Bower,** where in 1513 the queen waited in vain for James IV to return from the Battle of Flodden. In 1542 Mary queen of Scots was born to Mary of Guise in a first-floor room, while her father lay dying at Falkland Palace (*see*). **Saint Michael's Church** dates from the twelfth century. Here, in one of the chapels, James IV received a vision warning him against fighting the English; soon after he died at Flodden. In 1570 the earl of Moray, regent of Scotland, was shot and killed by one of the Hamiltons as he rode through the town. A plaque outside the present **County Buildings** marks the spot.

**LOCHLEVEN CASTLE (KINROSS),** *on Castle Island in Loch Leven*
Mary queen of Scots was imprisoned in this 15th-century castle in June, 1567, after her surrender to the Scottish lords at Carberry Hill (*see*). The following month she abdicated in favor of her infant son, James VI, and appointed her half brother, the earl of Moray, regent. One year later, with the help of a friend of her jailer's son, Mary escaped from Lochleven. The queen's freedom was short-lived, however: 13 days later she was defeated by Moray at Langside (*see Glasgow*) and fled to England.

**MAYBOLE VICINITY (AYR)**
CULZEAN CASTLE, *about 1½ kilometers west of A719*
The top floor of this splendid 18th-century mansion—one of the finest designed by Robert Adam in Scotland—was given to Dwight D. Eisenhower as a Scottish residence in 1946. It is now a memorial to him.

## MELROSE AND VICINITY (ROXBURGH), *50 kilometers southeast of Edinburgh on A6091*

This town, in the heart of Sir Walter Scott country, is the "Kennaquhair" of Scott's *Abbot* and *Monastery*. Its beautiful ruined **Abbey**, dating from 1136, was perhaps the finest in Scotland. Like so many abbeys and castles near the border, it was repeatedly wrecked during English invasions and several times restored. Robert I bequeathed his heart to the abbey after restoring it in 1326; the heart supposedly lies beneath the east window of the chancel. Near the altar are tombs of the Douglases.

## ABBOTSFORD, *4 kilometers west off B6360 on the River Tweed*

Sir Walter Scott built this mansion beginning in 1817 (he designed it himself) and lived here until his death in 1832. The house, including the study where he wrote many of his novels, is preserved virtually as he left it. It contains, in addition to personal mementos, many historical relics that Scott collected. The author is buried in nearby **Dryburgh Abbey.**

## NEWCASTLETON VICINITY (ROXBURGH)

HERMITAGE CASTLE, *8 kilometers north off B6399*

This restored 13th-century fortress was the primary stronghold of the Douglases beginning in 1341. In 1492 the Douglases exchanged it for Bothwell Castle (*see*). In 1566 Mary queen of Scots and several members of her court rode here from Jedburgh to visit the earl of Bothwell, who had been wounded in a border foray. They returned the same day, since Hermitage was not prepared to receive her overnight. Although the journey—about 80 kilometers round trip—was not considered unusually difficult, the queen fell seriously ill on her return and nearly died.

## ORKNEY ISLANDS, *32 kilometers north of the mainland across Pentland Firth*

The islands have many prehistoric remains, some of the most notable of which are on **Pomona** (also called the Mainland), the largest of the Orkneys. **Maeshowe** (off A965 near Loch Stenness) is a huge Neolithic chambered burial mound dating from about 1500 B.C. The many runic inscriptions on the wall were added at a much later date. Between Lochs Stenness and Harray (on B9055) are the **Standing Stones of Stenness,** two incomplete circles of stones that date from about 2000 B.C. Nearby is the **Cairn of Unston,** containing the largest collection of Neolithic pottery in Scotland. **Skara Brae** (off B9056 near Aith) is a famous prehistoric Stone Age village. Dating from about 1500 B.C., it is remarkably well preserved. South of the Mainland is **Scapa Flow,** an area of water 15 miles long and 8 miles wide, which was the seat of British naval operations in World War I and World War II. In July, 1917, the British ship *Vanguard* was torpedoed here. In June, 1919, the German fleet was scuttled in Scapa Flow. In 1939 a German submarine penetrated British defenses and sank the battleship *Royal Oak*. The attack led to the construction the following year of the **Churchill Barrier,** a series of causeways linking Mainland with South Ronaldsay and thereby blocking sea access to the flow from the east.

## PERTH (PERTH), *at the head of the estuary of the River Tay*

Perth was capital of Scotland until 1437, when James I was assassinated by a group of nobles in the former Blackfriars Monastery. In 1559, in the **Church of Saint John,** John Knox preached his famous sermon against idolatry that inflamed Scotland and led to a widespread destruction of monasteries, including Perth's four. In 1644 the earl of Montrose, after defeating an army of Covenanters at **Tippermuir** to the south and seizing Perth, imprisoned 800 in the church. The **County Buildings** on South Street are on the site of the former Gowrie House, in 1600 the scene of the Gowrie conspiracy, an apparent attempt by John Ruthven, earl of Gowrie, and his brother Alexander Ruthven to lure James VI into the house, seize him, and use his captivity to political advantage. The plot failed when James got free and called for help; Gowrie and Ruthven were slain, and the name Ruthven was proscribed as a result.

### HUNTINGTOWER CASTLE, *5 kilometers northwest off A85*

This 15th-century castle, called Ruthven until 1600, was the scene of the "Ruthven Raid" of 1582. William Ruthven, earl of Gowrie, and a group of Protestant nobles invited 16-year-old James VI to Ruthven, then held him captive and demanded that he dismiss his favorites, the duke of Lennox and the earl of Arran. After several months James escaped, and in 1584 Gowrie was beheaded for his part in the conspiracy. The castle has been restored.

### PINKIE BATTLEFIELD (MIDLOTHIAN), *10 kilometers from Edinburgh on the eastern outskirts of Musselburgh off A1*

In 1547 Edward Seymour, duke of Somerset, led an English army into Scotland and on September 10, at Pinkie, routed a larger Scots army led by the earl of Arran, regent to the young Mary queen of Scots. Somerset, protector to the boy king Edward VI, had invaded Scotland to enforce a marriage treaty between Edward and the four-year-old Mary, which had been made by Edward's father, the late Henry VIII. Despite Somerset's victory, the savagery with which the English subsequently ravaged southern Scotland so enraged the Scots that they turned to France, arranging a marriage between Mary and the French dauphin and hastily sending Mary to France. Near the battlefield is **Pinkie House**, a magnificent Jacobean mansion where Prince Charles Edward, the Young Pretender to the English throne, spent the night after his victory over the English at Prestonpans (*see*) in September, 1745.

### PRESTONPANS (EAST LOTHIAN), *15 kilometers east of Edinburgh on A198 on the Firth of Forth*

Prestonpans was the scene of the first and only major victory of Prince Charles Edward Stuart ("Bonnie Prince Charlie"), leader of the unsuccessful Jacobite uprising of 1745. Since the deposition of England's James II in the Glorious Revolution of 1688, the Jacobites had launched several attempts to restore the Stuarts to the throne. In 1745 Prince Charles Edward, James II's grandson, landed in Scotland and rallied the Highlanders. "The '45," as the uprising became known, began auspiciously at Prestonpans: it took the popular Young Pretender and his forces only ten minutes to defeat an English force under Sir John Cope. However, after advancing into England as far as Derby, Charles was forced to retreat, and in 1746 his army was crushed at Culloden Moor (*see*).

### RUTHWELL (DUMFRIES), *about 16 kilometers southeast of Dumfries on B725*

The famous **Ruthwell Cross** is preserved inside the parish church. The 18-foot-high cross, which probably dates from the eighth century, contains the earliest extant specimen of written English, a poem in runic characters, in the Northumbrian dialect.

## SAINT ANDREWS (FIFE)

HOLY TRINITY (TOWN CHURCH), *off South Street in the square opposite Town Hall*

> Founded in 1412, Town Church has been altered many times, and the original structure is virtually unrecognizable, although the 16th-century tower remains. John Knox preached his first public sermon here in 1547.

SAINT ANDREWS CASTLE, *just northwest of the cathedral on a rock overlooking the sea*

> The ruined castle, which was begun in 1200, 40 years after the founding of the cathedral, served as the episcopal palace. Many early reformers were imprisoned here. In March, 1546, Roman Catholic Cardinal David Beaton watched from the castle as the reformer George Wishart, who had converted John Knox, was burned as a heretic. Two months later a Protestant mob seized the castle, killed Beaton in retaliation, and hung his body from the battlements. Protestant adherents, including John Knox, flocked to the castle and held it for over a year, despite a siege by French troops under Mary of Guise, the Catholic regent. In July, 1547, the castle finally fell, and Knox and many others were sent to serve in the French galleys. The **Sea Tower** contains a 25-foot-deep dungeon where reformers were confined. Near the courtyard is an underground passage that contains mine fragments from the siege of 1546.

SAINT ANDREWS CATHEDRAL, *facing the eastern end of South Street*

> Scotland's largest cathedral was founded in 1160 and consecrated in 1318, in the presence of King Robert I (Robert the Bruce). It witnessed many historical events: James V and Mary of Guise were married in the cathedral; George Wishart was tried for heresy within its walls. In 1559, after four sermons by John Knox, the cathedral's images and ornaments were destroyed; the building's present ruined condition, however, was largely a result of neglect after 1649. The adjacent cloister houses a **Museum,** which contains early Christian carved stones and a tenth-century sarcophagus.

SAINT ANDREWS UNIVERSITY

> The university, Scotland's oldest, was founded in 1411. The United College on North Street is on the site of the old college of Saint Salvator, which was founded in 1450 by Bishop James Kennedy. Of Kennedy's original buildings, only the **Church of Saint Salvator,** now the university chapel, survives. It contains the tomb of Bishop Kennedy and John Knox's pulpit from Town Church. **Saint Mary's College** on South Street was founded in 1537 by Cardinal Beaton. Its quadrangle contains a flourishing thorn tree that was planted by Mary queen of Scots.

## SCONE (PERTH), *5 kilometers northeast of Perth on the Blairgowrie Road*

> Old Scone, west of the modern village of New Scone, was the coronation place of Scottish kings from Kenneth Macalpine (ninth century) to James I. Charles II, who was crowned king of Scotland in 1651 during Oliver Cromwell's reign in England, was the last king to be crowned here. The Coronation Stone—traditionally identified with Jacob's pillow at Bethel and Ireland's stone of destiny —was here from about the ninth century until Edward I carried it off to England in 1297. The original abbey and palace were destroyed in 1559 by a mob from Perth that had been inspired by John Knox. The present palace dates from early in the 19th century.

**SHETLAND ISLANDS,** *about 96 kilometers northeast of the Orkneys in the North Sea*

These islands have many splendid prehistoric remains. On the island of Mousa is the 45-foot-high **Broch of Mousa,** the only extant Pictish broch (a prehistoric fort) that has survived in its original height. Near the southern tip of Mainland Island is **Jarlshof,** where excavations have revealed remains from different periods: Bronze Age huts, an Iron Age broch (first century A.D.), and Norse farmers' houses dating from the ninth century. **Scalloway Castle,** 10 kilometers west of Lerwick on Mainland, is a notable ruin. It was built by forced labor in 1600 for the notorious Patrick Stewart, earl of Orkney, who wielded virtually independent power over the islands and who eventually was executed for his tyrannous acts.

**STIRLING (STIRLING),** *44 kilometers from Glasgow via A803 on the River Forth*

The history of Stirling is closely connected with the history of mighty **Stirling Castle,** rising on a rock 240 feet above the Forth. The castle, begun in 1107 by Alexander I, overlooks two battlefields that were of great importance in the fight for Scottish independence: Bannockburn (*see*) and Stirling Bridge. At the battle of the latter, fought at a wooden bridge about a mile upstream from the present **Old Bridge** (which dates from about 1400), Sir William Wallace in September, 1297, routed an English army of more than 50,000 as the Englishmen tried to cross the bridge. The slaughter marked the beginning of Wallace's efforts to drive Edward I from Scotland and establish Scottish independence. Wallace's successes were short-lived, and by 1304 only Stirling was still holding out against Edward I. Besieged by the English king in person, the fortress finally capitulated. Ten years later it was returned to Scottish control. Kings James II, James III, and James IV were born there; James VI, son of Mary queen of Scots, was baptized in the **Chapel Royal** and spent part of his youth in the castle, which is now being restored. In the **Church of the Holy Rude** (begun about 1414), nine-month-old Mary queen of Scots was crowned in 1543; Mary of Guise, her mother, was appointed regent in 1544; and one-year-old James VI was crowned king in 1567, with John Knox preaching the sermon. Beyond Stirling Bridge to the north is **Causewayhead.** Here, atop the 362-foot-high Abbey Craig, is the **Wallace Monument,** erected in 1869. A tall, elaborate tower, it contains Wallace's sword.

**TRAQUAIR (PEEBLES),** *south of Innerleithen via B709 on the Quair Water*

**Traquair House,** possibly the oldest inhabited house in Scotland, has been unaltered since the 17th century, although it contains treasures dating back to the 12th century. William the Lion held court here in 1209, and in 1566 Mary queen of Scots and Lord Darnley stayed here.

**WHITHORN (WIGTOWN),** *on A746 near the tip of the Machers peninsula*

Both Whithorn and the Isle of Whithorn (just off the coast, about 5½ kilometers southeast of Whithorn) claim to be the site of the chapel of Saint Ninian, who introduced Christianity into Scotland. Built in 397, the chapel was a stone building covered with plaster. Whithorn's ruined 12th-century **Priory Church** may have been built on the site of the earlier building; excavations have in fact revealed the walls of an ancient plaster-covered building nearby. A museum has been set up at the priory gate; it has an outstanding collection of early Christian crosses.

**WALES**

**BEAUMARIS AND VICINITY (ANGLESEY),** *on A545 along the Menai Strait*
The island of Anglesey, once the chief seat of the druids, was a stronghold of the Welsh princes who were finally subjugated by England's Edward I in 1277. In 1293 Edward founded the **Castle** at Beaumaris, now an impressive ruin. In 1400 Henry IV gave lifetime ownership of the castle to Henry Percy, and in 1646 the fortress fell to the Parliamentarians, a political faction opposing King Charles I. Also of interest in town are a **timbered house** dating from 1400 and the **Old Bull Inn** and **County Hall,** each built in the 17th century. About 8 kilometers northeast is **Penmon Priory,** with its early Norman church.

**BRECKNOCK (BRECKNOCK),** *at the junction of A40, A438, and A470*
Originally built in the 12th century by a Norman lord and reconstructed during the reign of Edward I, **Brecknock Castle** is now a ruin on the grounds of a hotel. The red sandstone **Priory Church,** parts of which date back to the 12th century, has been restored and is used as a cathedral. About 2 kilometers northwest of Brecknock is the site of a Roman fort, **Y Gaer,** which the Romans used from about A.D. 75 to 140.

**BRIDGEND VICINITY (GLAMORGAN)**
EWENNY PRIORY, *2½ kilometers south near A48*
This fortified monastery was built in 1141 as an adjunct to the Benedictine abbey at Gloucester; the existing walls were probably erected in the 13th century. The vault of the chancel is regarded as an example of the finest Norman work.

**CAERLEON (MONMOUTH),** *on A472*
A **Norman Church,** largely rebuilt in the 15th century and again in the 19th century, stands in the center of the site of a 50-acre Roman fortress, **Isca,** founded about A.D. 75. Visible today are buildings and sections of walls built in stone about A.D. 100, as well as a completely excavated **Amphitheater** used as a drill square by the Roman legion. Isca has been identified by some Arthurian enthusiasts as the site of Camelot.

**CAERNARVON (CAERNARVON),** *at the junction of A4086, A4085, A487, A499, and A4087*
Although Edward I built six castles in Wales, **Caernarvon Castle,** constructed between 1285 and 1322, was the only one designed as a royal residence as well as a fortress. The future Edward II was born there in 1284; he was later given the title Prince of Wales, and since 1301 that title has been granted to the oldest son of every reigning sovereign. (Since 1911 every Prince of Wales has been invested here, including Prince Charles in 1969.) Richard II spent several nights here in 1399. Henry IV and the rebellious Welsh chieftain Owen Glendower each tried and failed to take the castle early in the 15th century. The interior of the castle is in ruins, but its walls and octagonal towers are impressive. The **town walls** of Caernarvon, dating from 1284, are in good condition. Nearby is the site of a Roman fort, **Segontium.**

**CAERPHILLY (GLAMORGAN),** *at the junction of A469 and A468*
Covering 30 acres, huge **Caerphilly Castle,** now mainly in ruins, is second only to Windsor Castle in area. Built about 1272 by Gilbert de Clare, earl of Gloucester and Hertford, the castle was long owned by the Despenser family, who virtually ruled England during the

*Page 327. Top: the North Wales town of Caernarvon with its imposing castle. Center left, above: the town of Llangollen. Center left, below: Cardiff Castle. Center right: Tintern Abbey. Below: the ruins of Caerphilly Castle*

reign of Edward II. The latter sought refuge here in 1326 when his wife led an invading force against him.

**CARDIFF (GLAMORGAN),** *via A48, A4119, A470, A469, or A4160*
The walls of a **Roman Fort,** built here about the end of the third century, have been restored and stand in dramatic contrast to the modern buildings that surround them. **Cardiff Castle** was erected about 1090 on the site of another Roman fortification; the stone keep was built late in the 12th century, and there have been innumerable additions subsequently. Robert II, duke of Normandy, was kept prisoner in the castle for 26 years by his brother, Henry I, after the latter defeated him at the Battle of Tenchebrai in 1106. The castle was partially destroyed in 1404 by Owen Glendower, leader of a Welsh revolt against the English. The **Welsh National Museum** was founded in 1907 "to teach the world about Wales and the Welsh people about their own fatherland."

**CHEPSTOW (MONMOUTH),** *on A466 just off A48*
On a hill above the River Wye, the Normans built a fort in 1067 to defend the road to South Wales. Rebuilt and enlarged in the 13th century, **Chepstow Castle,** now in ruins, was the site of fighting during the Civil War and was used by Parliament as a prison from 1648 to 1660. The 11th-century **Church** here once belonged to a Benedictine priory.

**CONWAY (CAERNARVON),** *at the junction of A55 and B5106*
**Conway Castle,** with its 15-foot-thick walls and 8 cylindrical towers, is the most picturesque of Edward I's Welsh castles. Of interest too are the **town walls,** the 13th-century **Saint Mary's Church,** and **Plas Mawr,** an Elizabethan mansion built between 1585 and 1595 that now houses an art academy.

**CORWEN (MERIONETH),** *on A5 just east of A494*
This market town was the headquarters of Owen Glendower, the Welsh prince who led a revolt against the Anglo-Saxons beginning in 1399. On the parish **Church,** parts of which date back to the 13th century, is a dagger mark said to have been made by Glendower. To the north is **Caer Drewyn,** a remarkably well preserved prehistoric stone rampart that may date from the Bronze Age.

**DENBIGH CASTLE (DENBIGH),** *at the junction of A525 and A543*
Erected by the earl of Lincoln in the 13th century, this impressive fortress was later sold by Queen Elizabeth to the earl of Leicester, who entertained her here. In 1645 Charles I sought refuge at Denbigh after the Battle of Rowton Moor; besieged by Oliver Cromwell's forces, the castle fell in 1646.

**FLINT CASTLE (FLINT),** *on A548*
Unlike the other castles built by Edward I in the 13th century, this one, now in ruins, had a detached circular keep surrounded by a moat. Here in 1399 Richard II yielded to Henry Bolingbroke, duke of Lancaster, who became Henry IV of England.

**HARLECH (MERIONETH),** *on A496*
Founded by Edward I in 1285, **Harlech Castle** was captured in 1404 by Owen Glendower during his rebellion against the English. Despite Glendower's brilliance as a guerrilla fighter, he lost Harlech to the king's forces again in 1409. Some 60 years later

Harlech was a Lancastrian stronghold that fell to Yorkist forces after a siege. In 1647 the castle was the last Royalist fortress in Wales to be captured by the Parliamentarians.

## KIDWELLY (CARMARTHEN), *on A484*

The 12th-century **Castle** here stands on the site of an early Norman fortress erected in 1094. Among the notable features of the ruined castle are the chapel, on the third story of a tower, and the great gatehouse. The nearby **Church,** with its 13th-century tower, was built for the Benedictines.

## LAUGHARNE (CARMARTHEN), *on A4066*

Dylan Thomas (1914–53), the famous Welsh poet, is buried in this small town, which contains many fine Georgian buildings and the ruins of a 12th-century **Castle.**

## LLANDILO VICINITY (CARMARTHEN), *at the junction of A40, A483, and A476*

A mile west of this small town is **Dynevor Castle,** a modern structure built on the site of a Norman castle, now in ruins, and of a fortress built in 870 by the Welsh prince Rhodri Mawr. Several miles to the southeast is **Carreg-Cennen Castle,** which stands in ruins on a rock high above a ravine. Built by a Welsh leader in the 13th century, it was later owned by John of Gaunt and Henry IV. According to legend Sir Urien, one of Arthur's knights of the Round Table, had a fortress on the site.

## LLANGOLLEN AND VICINITY (DENBIGH), *at the junction of A5 and A542*

The **Valle Crucis Abbey,** 2½ kilometers northwest of town, was founded about 1200 by Madoc ap Gruffyadd Maelor, prince of Powis. Key sections of the church and monastery still stand and have been called the most impressive monastic remains in North Wales. In a field north of the abbey is **Eliseg's Pillar,** the 6½-foot shaft of a cross erected in the ninth century in honor of a war hero. In Llangollen is **Plas Newydd,** home of the two eccentric "Ladies of Langollen"—Irish gentlewomen who lived there together from 1776 to 1829 and entertained many notables of the time. North of town is the ruined **Castell Dinas Bran,** occupied by Madoc ap Gruffyadd Maelor in the 13th century and described by Wordsworth as "relic of kings, wreck of forgotten wars."

## MACHYNLLETH (MONTGOMERY), *at the junction of A487 and A4084*

Owen Glendower was crowned Prince of Wales here in 1402. Among the many old buildings is one reputed to have been the Welsh hero's home and another where he allegedly convened a Welsh parliament in 1402.

## OFFA'S DYKE, *extending south from the mouth of the River Dee to the mouth of the River Wye at Chepstow*

This ancient earthwork, parts of which may still be seen, was built in the eighth century by Offa, king of Mercia, to keep the Welsh from impinging on his domain.

## PEMBROKE CASTLE (PEMBROKE), *at the junction of A4139 and A477*

The first castle on this site was probably built shortly after the Norman conquest; it withstood a Welsh siege in 1094. The existing ruins date back to the 13th century, when the castle was a key element in the English conquest of Wales. The earls palatine of

Pembroke ruled here until 1536, when Henry VIII stripped away their power. In 1648 the castle was besieged by Oliver Cromwell's forces. Visible today are a circular vaulted keep with 75-foot-high and 7-foot-thick walls, a fine gatehouse, and an adjoining tower, where the future Henry VII was born in 1457.

**RUTHIN (DENBIGH),** *at the junction of A494 and A525*
Of interest in this old town are the **Maen Huail,** a stone block on which the brother of Gildas the historian was reputedly beheaded by order of King Arthur; the **Church of Saint Peter,** with its carved timber roof dating from the 15th century; **Nantclwyd House,** a 13th-century mansion; and the **Lordship Court-House,** built in 1404.

**SAINT DAVID'S AND VICINITY (PEMBROKE),** *on A487*
This small cathedral city is built around the church erected between the 12th and 14th centuries to honor the patron saint of Wales. The **Cathedral,** constructed of purple sandstone, is noteworthy for its nave roof of Irish oak and its 125-foot tower. Nearby are the **Bishop's Palace,** featuring an arcaded parapet, and the ruins of **Saint Mary's College,** which was founded by John of Gaunt. Two miles north is **Saint David's Head,** where there is a prehistoric stone rampart shielding huts and rock shelters.

**STRATA FLORIDA ABBEY (CARDIGAN),** *off B4343*
In the 12th and 13th centuries the Cistercian abbey here was the cultural center of Wales and the burial place of many Welsh princes. An ornamental doorway and some medieval tiles remain.

**TENBY (PEMBROKE),** *at the junction of A4139 and A478*
An early Danish fishing station and in the 11th century a center for Flemish clothworkers, Tenby became an important medieval seaport. Henry VII came here after the Battle of Tewkesbury in 1471 and reputedly fled from here to France. During Elizabeth's reign the **town walls** of Tenby were strengthened in anticipation of the Spanish Armada. The **Church of Saint Mary,** dating from the 13th century, has a 15th-century chancel roof with bosses, and the ruins of a Norman castle are incorporated in the town museum. The 15th-century **Plantagenet House** and the **Tudor Merchant's House** (from about 1500) are of interest. Boat trips may be taken to **Caldy Island,** which has a 12th-century monastery.

**TINTERN ABBEY (MONMOUTH),** *6 kilometers north of Chepstow on A466*
Immortalized in poetry by William Wordsworth, this abbey in the beautiful Wye valley was founded in 1131 by Cistercian monks. The ruins visible today date from the 13th and 14th centuries.

**TOWYN (MERIONETH),** *on A493*
This old village contains a notable **Church** with an early Norman nave that may have been built in the 11th century. Of particular interest is **Saint Cadvan's Stone,** a long thin stone inscribed on all four sides with seventh- or eighth-century Welsh writing.

**WREXHAM (DENBIGH),** *at the junction of A483, A534, A525, and A541*
The **Church of Saint Giles,** famous for its beautiful 135-foot-high tower, was built in the 15th century; additions were incorporated later. The chancel gates and the 18th-century monuments inside the church are noteworthy. Buried here is Elihu Yale (1649–1721), founder of Yale University, whose family came from Denbighshire.

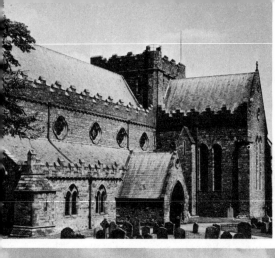

# IRELAND

**ADARE (LIMERICK),** *16 kilometers southwest of Limerick on T28*
Although little is known of this village's early history, there was already a strong O'Donovan **Castle** here when the Normans arrived in the 12th century. Later the castle became a stronghold of the Fitzgeralds, earls of Kildare, who drove the O'Donovans out of Limerick into Cork and Kerry. The ruins are on the grounds of **Adare Manor,** the seat of the earl of Dunraven, where there are also the remains of a 15th-century **Franciscan Friary** founded by Thomas Fitzgerald, seventh earl of Kildare. In the village are the remains of two other 14th-century religious houses: an **Augustinian Friary** and a **Trinitarian Friary** known as the White Abbey.

**ASKEATON (LIMERICK),** *25 kilometers southwest of Limerick on T68*
The Desmond branch of the Fitzgeralds, a powerful Anglo-Norman family, built one of their principal fortresses here. Gerald, 15th earl of Desmond (d. 1583), rebelled against the English Crown in the course of his struggles with the Butlers, earls of Ormonde, traditional enemies of the Fitzgeralds. In 1579 he took refuge in the **Castle,** but the following year the fortress surrendered in the face of a threatened artillery bombardment by English troops, and Gerald fled to the Kerry hills. The castle remained in English hands until 1652, when it was wrecked by Oliver Cromwell's soldiers. The ruins include a large banqueting hall.

**ATHLONE (WESTMEATH),** *on T31, T34, and T4*
This one-time bridgehead on the Shannon River has been of great strategic importance since ancient times. Under King John a **Castle** was erected here in 1210, which was considerably altered and strengthened by later monarchs, including Elizabeth I. In 1691 Athlone was taken by William of Orange's forces after a long, fierce battle.

**BLARNEY (CORK),** *5 kilometers northwest of Cork on L9*
**Blarney Castle,** a 15th-century McCarthy stronghold, is famous for the **Blarney Stone,** situated just below one of the battlements: according to tradition, it has the power of bestowing eloquence on whoever kisses it.

**CARLINGFORD (LOUTH),** *on T63 on the west shore of Carlingford Lough*
After the establishment of **King John's Castle** here early in the 13th century, Carlingford became an important medieval town and a border fortress of the Pale, the English-dominated area around Dublin. In the days of the Pale virtually every home in this outpost was fortified. Two that have survived, both from the 16th century, are **Taaffe's Castle** and **The Mint.**

**CARLOW (CARLOW),** *on T16, T51, L18, and L31*
Situated on the edge of the Pale, Carlow was an important Anglo-Norman and English stronghold and the scene of many battles. In 1798, during the anti-English uprising of the United Irishmen, Irish insurgents fought a bloody but losing battle in Carlow. Afterward some 400 rebels were buried in the **Graiguecullen Gravel Pits,** on the other side of the Barrow River; a monument marks the grave site. In addition to its ruined 13th-century **Castle,** Carlow is noted for **Saint Patrick's College.** Opened in 1793 for the education of priests, it was the first Catholic college that the English had allowed in Ireland in 250 years.

*Top left: Saint Canice's Cathedral in Kilkenny. Right: Trim Castle in Meath. Center: the Custom House in Dublin. Below left: Blarney Castle in Cork County. Below top: King John's Castle in Limerick. Below bottom: Saint Finbarr's Cathedral on the River Lee in Cork*

**CASHEL (TIPPERARY),** *at the junction of T36, T9, T49, T37, L111, and L185*
In early times this town was of great political and religious importance. A fort, built on the 200-foot-high **Cashel Rock,** was the seat of the kings of Munster from the fifth century to early in the 12th, when King Murtough O'Brien gave the site to the Church. In 1127 Cormac McCarthy, king of Desmond and bishop of Cashel, began to erect **Cormac's Chapel,** one of the great surviving examples of Irish Romanesque architecture. It is adjacent to the ruins of the 13th-century **Cathedral of Saint Patrick,** with the 15th-century **Bishop's Castle** at the west end and a fine 11th-century **Round Tower** adjoining the northern transept. The ancient **Cross of Cashel** is also here. The rock was the scene of a momentous gathering in 1172, when England's Henry II received the homage of the Irish princes, including Donal O'Brien, king of Thomond. In 1315 Edward Bruce summoned a parliament here.

**CLONMACNOISE (OFFALY),** *20 kilometers south of Athlone on the east bank of the Shannon River*
In A.D. 547 Saint Cieran founded a monastery here; the ecclesiastical community that grew around it was unrivaled in Ireland as a center of religion, learning, literature, and art. Despite repeated assaults by Vikings, Irish enemies, and after 1178 the English, the abbey flourished until 1552, when the English garrison at Athlone destroyed it. Among its remains are the ruins of seven churches, two round towers, three high crosses, and a remarkable collection of more than 400 early gravestones.

**CORK (CORK),** *on T11, T6, T65, T29, L128, L66, and L42*
Ireland's second largest city was a swamp when Saint Finbarr founded a famous monastery here in the seventh century. **Saint Finbarr's Cathedral** (Church of Ireland), a 19th-century structure in the French Gothic style, is on the site of the original church. Like so many rich monasteries, Finbarr's was plundered by the Danes, who stayed to trade until they were ousted by Dermot McCarthy, Irish lord of Desmond; McCarthy in turn lost it to the Anglo-Normans. In 1690 John Churchill, later duke of Marlborough, took the city for William of Orange; the **Red Abbey Tower** (off Mary Street), the remains of an Augustinian abbey, served as the duke's headquarters. Many public buildings were destroyed in the fighting between the Sinn Fein and the British government in 1920.

**DONEGAL (DONEGAL),** *on T72 and T18 on Donegal Bay*
This town was the seat of the O'Donnells, lords of Tyrconnel, whose ruined **Castle** dates from the 15th century. In 1610 Sir Basil Brooke turned the castle into a fortified manor house. (Brooke had been granted Donegal after Rory O'Donnell and Hugh O'Neill had fled the country in 1607—the "flight of the earls" that lead to the English plantation of Ulster.) In 1474 Hugh O'Donnell and his wife founded a **Franciscan Friary** here; part of the church and two cloister walls remain.

**DROGHEDA AND VICINITY (LOUTH),** *48 kilometers north of Dublin on T1, T26, L21, L6, L125, and L88*
This town on the Boyne River, a tenth-century Danish stronghold, became an important English settlement in the Middle Ages. The Anglo-Normans erected town walls and built a castle atop the **Mill Mount,** a large prehistoric mound. Of Drogheda's ten medieval gates, only the twin-towered **Saint Lawrence's Gate**—actually a

barbican that stood in front of the original gate—remains intact. The Dominican friary was the site of the submission, in 1395, of the princes of Leinster and Ulster to England's Richard II; of that friary, the 14th-century **Magdalene Tower** survives. Several medieval parliaments met in Drogheda, including the one that passed the infamous Poynings's Law, which deprived the Irish Parliament of its independence. In 1649 Oliver Cromwell stormed the town, massacred some 2,000 defenders, and sent many survivors to Barbados as slaves. About 5 kilometers west of Drogheda is the **Site of the Battle of the Boyne,** where in 1690 William of Orange defeated James II and thereby ended James's chance to regain the English throne. An obelisk marks the battle site.

MELLIFONT ABBEY, *about 7 kilometers west of Drogheda south of T75*
The founding of this monastery, the first Cistercian house in Ireland, was a milestone in Irish ecclesiastical history; thereafter the Cistercian order spread rapidly and supplanted the Celtic monastic system. Mellifont was founded about 1142 by Irish and French monks under the inspiration of Saint Malachy O'Morgair. The remains include the church foundations, the chapter house, and part of an unusual 12th-century octagonal lavabo, or washing place. Devorgilla (d. 1193), wife of Tiernan O'Rourke, king of Breffni, spent the last years of her life here. Her abduction by King Dermot McMurrough of Leinster was indirectly responsible for the Anglo-Norman invasion of Ireland (*see Wexford*).

MONASTERBOICE, *about 9 kilometers northwest of Drogheda off T1*
This ancient monastery, dating from the eighth or ninth century, is famous for its three **High Crosses.** Muiredach's Cross, dating from early in the tenth century, is perhaps the finest of Ireland's many early figured crosses, which told scriptural stories through carved pictures.

## DUBLIN (DUBLIN)
### ABBEY THEATRE, *Abbey Street*
This famous theatrical company was one of several literary and dramatic societies founded in the wake of Ireland's late-19th-century Gaelic renaissance, which centered in Dublin. The theatre grew out of the Irish National Dramatic Society, founded in 1902 by the great poet and dramatist W. B. Yeats. Yeats, with the help of the poet AE (George Russell) and Lady Gregory, purchased a building on Abbey Street and began presenting the plays of such Irish dramatists as Sean O'Casey, John Millington Synge, and Padraic Colum. In 1951 the theatre was gutted by fire. It reopened in 1966.

### BANK OF IRELAND (PARLIAMENT HOUSE), *College Green*
One of Dublin's many outstanding 18th-century buildings, this was begun in 1729 to house the Irish Parliament. James Gandon designed the Corinthian-columned east front in 1785 to harmonize with Trinity College (*see*). After the Act of Union with Britain in 1800, the government sold Parliament House to the Bank of Ireland. The building was remodeled, but the old House of Lords remains intact.

### CHRIST CHURCH CATHEDRAL (CHURCH OF IRELAND), *Christchurch Place and Winetavern Street*
Dublin's oldest church was founded about 1038 by Sitric, a Danish

king of Dublin. The Danes had founded a settlement here about 840, which soon became the center of the Norse holdings in Ireland. Although in 1014 High King Brian Boru crushed the Vikings at Clontarf, Dublin remained in Norse hands until 1170, when the Anglo-Normans under Richard Strongbow, second earl of Pembroke, took the town for Henry II. Strongbow almost at once built a new, and grander church on the site, and at his death (1176) was buried here; his tomb is in the nave. In 1394 Richard II received homage here from four kings: O'Neill of Ulster, McMurrough of Leinster, O'Brien of Munster, and O'Connor of Connaught. Pretender Lambert Simnel was crowned king of England in the cathedral in 1486 by Yorkists who believed he was Edward, earl of Warwick. Here James II assisted at a Mass before the Battle of the Boyne (*see Drogheda*)—the tabernacle and candlesticks from the Mass are in the crypt—and here William III offered thanksgiving after the battle. The cathedral was restored in the 19th century.

### CUSTOM HOUSE, *Abbey Street*

Perhaps Dublin's finest building, designed by James Gandon and completed in 1791, the Custom House dates from Dublin's golden era in architecture, when many of the city's great public buildings and private homes were constructed. Like many other buildings on the north bank of the Liffey, the Custom House was burned during the bloody skirmishing that preceded and followed the founding of the Irish Free State in 1922. The interior, which was completely destroyed, has been restored.

### DUBLIN CASTLE, *Cork Hill*

When this castle was built early in the 13th century, Dublin already was the chief English town in Ireland (it would remain so until the 20th century) and the center of the Pale, the English-controlled area that was subject to English laws and protected against assaults from rebel Irish lords by a ring of castles. Dublin Castle served primarily as a court of justice and a defensive fortification until the reign of Elizabeth I, when it became the residence of the lords lieutenant of Ireland; it remained the seat of the British administration until 1922. The **Record Tower,** with walls 16 feet thick, is one of the castle's four original towers; it is in the Upper Castle Yard. The Lower Castle Yard includes the **State Apartments,** as well as the 15th-century **Bermingham Tower,** the state prison. The tower's famous prisoners included Hugh Roe O'Donnell (1586), who after a daring escape from the castle led a rebellion against the English that nearly succeeded.

### FOUR COURTS, *Inns Quay*

Designed, like the Custom House, by James Gandon, this seat of the High Court of Justice of Ireland was completed in 1802. In 1922, when civil war broke out following the establishment of the Irish Free State, republicans who objected to the terms of the treaty with England seized the Four Courts, garrisoned it, and held it for two months, until government troops bombarded the building and forced the rebels to evacuate. The heavily damaged interior eventually was restored.

### GENERAL POST OFFICE, *O'Connell Street*

This 19th-century building was seized by the nationalist Irish Volunteers in the anti-British Easter Week Rebellion of 1916. The insurgents, led by Patrick Pearse and James Connolly, proclaimed an Irish republic, but their rebellion was soon put down by the British, whose gunboats in the Liffey shelled the Post Office, setting it on fire; Lower O'Connell Street and the streets surrounding it also were destroyed by fire during the uprising. The Post Office was rebuilt in 1929.

### LEINSTER HOUSE, *Kildare Street*
Now the house of the Irish Parliament, this imposing Georgian mansion was built in 1845 as the town house of the earls of Leinster. Among the Fitzgeralds who lived here was Lord Edward, a leader of the 1798 uprising against British rule.

### SAINT PATRICK'S CATHEDRAL, *Patrick Street*
The national cathedral of the Church of Ireland (Protestant) is probably best known for its associations with Jonathan Swift, who was dean from 1713 until his death in 1745. Among the many rich monuments in the cathedral are the tombs of Swift and Stella (Esther Johnson, d. 1728); Swift's pulpit and a bust of the satirist are nearby. The church was begun in 1191 by John Comyn, first Anglo-Norman archbishop of Dublin, on the site of an older church associated with Saint Patrick, as a rival to Strongbow's Christ Church (*see*). The archbishop erected strong walls around his ecclesiastical complex to protect against the raids of the O'Byrnes and the O'Tooles from the south. The original church was altered in the 13th and 14th centuries, and over the years parts fell into ruin and others were used as separate churches. The cathedral was restored in the 19th century. Perhaps its most striking monument is the immense **Boyle Monument,** erected by the earl of Cork (d. 1643). Its removal from its original location by the earl of Strafford, lord deputy of Ireland (1632–38), earned him Boyle's undying enmity, a factor in Strafford's subsequent execution.

### TRINITY COLLEGE, *College Green*
This famous university was founded in 1592 by Elizabeth I on the grounds of a monastery established in the 12th century by Dermot McMurrough. The present buildings date from 1759. Trinity's great library contains the *Book of Kells*, a magnificent ninth-century illuminated copy of the Gospels.

### GALWAY (GALWAY), *on T71, T40, T11, T4, and L100 on the north side of Galway Bay*
Galway emerged as an English citadel in the 13th century, shortly after Henry III granted Richard de Burgh the kingdom of Connaught in 1227. De Burgh subdued the O'Connors, fortified Galway, and colonized the surrounding country. Medieval Galway itself came to be ruled by 14 English merchant families. Dubbed, derogatorily, "the tribes of Galway" by Cromwell's soldiers, these close-knit families were ardent Royalists who shunned any contact with the native Irish, even ostracizing the de Burghs when the latter renounced their allegiance to England and changed their name to Burke. The virtually independent city-state thrived on foreign trade, especially with Spain; the Spanish influence is evident in the massive **Spanish Arch,** a fragment from the medieval town walls. Among many notable buildings constructed in the 16th and 17th centuries was **Lynch's Castle,** built for the Lynch family, the foremost of the 14 tribes; the building is now a bank. In a fragment of another house on Market Street is the **Lynch Stone,** which marks the spot where, supposedly, James FitzStephen Lynch, mayor of

the town in 1493, personally hanged his own son for murder when no one else would perform the execution. The **Church of Saint Nicholas,** founded in 1320, is one of the largest medieval parish churches in Ireland (*see also Youghal*). Galway was heavily damaged by Cromwell's army in 1652.

## KELLS (MEATH), *at the junction of T9, T35, L14, and L142*

Saint Columba founded a monastery here in the sixth century, after which Kells (officially Ceanannus Mór) became one of the great Celtic Christian centers of learning. The famous *Book of Kells,* an exquisitely illuminated copy of the Gospels, was produced in the monastery in the eighth century; it is now in Trinity College Library (*see*), Dublin. **Saint Columba's House,** an early stone-roofed church, was built in the ninth century by monks who fled here from Iona. Other remains of the monastery include a 100-foot-high **Round Tower,** located in the parish churchyard, and five tenth-century **High Crosses.**

## KILKENNY (KILKENNY), *on T19, T6, T51, T20, T14, L26, and L126a*

Kilkenny has long been one of Ireland's most important towns, having been the seat of the kings of Ossary before the Anglo-Norman invasion. Strongbow built a castle here in 1172, which was rebuilt by his son-in-law, William the Marshal. After the manor was purchased by James Butler, third earl of Ormonde, in 1391, Kilkenny became the principal seat of the Butlers, whose fierce conflicts with the Fitzgeralds, earls of Kildare and Desmond, dominated much of medieval Irish history. Kilkenny was a principal meeting place of the Anglo-Irish parliaments, one of which (1366) passed the Statutes of Kilkenny, an attempt to halt the Gaelicization of the Anglo-Normans by forbidding them to marry Irish women or to adopt Irish dress, names, or language. In the rebellion of 1641, which was sparked by the English plantation of Ulster and the threatened plantation of Connaught, the Old Irish allied with the Catholic lords of the Pale, whose Catholic Confederation sat in Kilkenny until 1648. Oliver Cromwell took the town in 1650, after a five-day siege. The **Castle,** which remains the seat of the marquess of Ormonde, was restored in the 19th century. The **Cathedral of Saint Canice,** begun in 1251, is on the site of the monastery established in the sixth century by Saint Canice. It has a notable collection of medieval monuments. Next to it is a Romanesque **Round Tower** from an earlier church on the site. Kilkenny has many notable late medieval buildings, including the **Rothe House** (1594), a large town house, and **Shee's Almshouse** (1581). The city also has many fine Georgian buildings. **Kilkenny College,** founded in 1666, had among its students Jonathan Swift, William Congreve, and Bishop Berkeley.

## KILMALLOCK (LIMERICK), *32 kilometers south of Limerick on T50a, T36, and L28*

Kilmallock followed the pattern of towns established by the Anglo-Normans, who provided each of their settlements with fortifications and a religious house. Kilmallock's benefactors were the powerful Fitzgeralds of Desmond, who from the 14th to the 16th centuries were the virtually unchallenged rulers of Munster; the town was the seat of the so-called White Knight branch of the family. Remains of Fitzgerald structures include the ruins of the 13th-century **Dominican Friary,** portions of the town wall, and **Blossom's Gate,** one of the original gateways. **King's Castle** (15th century) was used as a hospital by Cromwell, who razed Kilmallock's fortifications.

## LIMERICK (LIMERICK), *on T11, T68, T57, T13, and T5 near the head of the Shannon estuary*

Like many other Irish seaports, Limerick was settled in the ninth century by Vikings who came to plunder and settled down to trade. A century later it was taken by Brian Boru, king of Thomond, who made the town capital of Munster. The O'Brians lost the town briefly to the Anglo-Normans under Raymond le Gros in the 12th century, but King Donal O'Brien quickly regained possession, razed the town, and on the site of his former palace built the **Cathedral of Saint Mary,** which still stands, although much rebuilt and modified. With Donal's death the Anglo-Normans once more secured the city; by early in the 13th century it was English Crown property, and King John, during a visit in 1210, arranged for the building of **King John's Castle.** Defensive walls were erected, creating the first two of the three divisions of the modern city: the Normans lived in the original walled town, called **English Town,** on an island encircled by the Abbey River; to the south was **Irish Town,** at first outside the town walls but eventually enclosed within them; when the walls were abandoned late in the 18th century, the town spread farther south, and the area known as **Newtown Pery** (after Edmond Sexton Pery, who founded it) developed, a Georgian section laid out on a regular plan. Portions of the **walls** remain, including a section behind **Saint Munchin's Church** (seventh century) on Castle Street. Limerick's early loyalty to the English Crown brought it under repeated assault from the Irish. In 1316 it was held for several months by Edward Bruce, who had his court here during his brief period as king of Ireland. In 1641, at the beginning of the Eleven Years' War, it fell to forces of the Catholic Confederacy; but the Irish eventually were crushed by Cromwell, who in 1652 retook Limerick. In 1691 the city, James II's last Irish stronghold, was taken by William III's army, after a long siege marked by repeated acts of valor on the part of the defenders. The city surrendered with the signing of the Treaty of Limerick, which granted Irish and Catholics some of the rights taken from them by the Penal Laws. The treaty was soon violated, however, and in the 18th century Catholics were more harshly treated than ever. The **Treaty Stone,** on which the Treaty of Limerick was supposedly signed, is beside Thomond Bridge.

## MAYNOOTH (KILDARE), *west of Dublin on T3*

Now a massive ruin, this **Castle** was the medieval seat of the powerful Geraldine family, earls of Kildare and dukes of Leinster. Maurice Fitzgerald was granted the land by Richard de Clare, earl of Pembroke (known as Richard Strongbow), who with Fitzgerald had invaded Ireland in 1170 in response to a request for aid from King Dermot of Leinster. The castle remained a Fitzgerald stronghold until 1535, when English troops took it, after a siege, from rebel Lord Thomas Fitzgerald (known as Silken Thomas because of his dress). Returned to the Fitzgeralds in 1552, it was dismantled by Irish rebels under Owen Roe O'Neill in 1647, during the Eleven Years' War.

## NEWGRANGE (MEATH), *about 11 kilometers southwest of Drogheda off T26*

This prehistoric tumulus is the largest and most important of three similar burial places of the pagan kings of Tara, situated close to one another in the River Boyne valley. They date from the Bronze Age, about 2000 B.C. Newgrange consists of a 44-foot-high mound of stones, now covered over with grass. Beneath the mound is a passage grave, with a 62-foot-long entrance passage to a central cruciform chamber; many of the stones bear elaborate patterned carvings. The entire structure was surrounded by a ring of stones, of which several have survived. About 1½ kilometers northwest is the **Knowth** tumulus, while about the same distance from Newgrange to the northeast is the tumulus of **Dowth**. Both are passage graves, containing inscribed stones.

### ROSS CASTLE (KERRY), *south of Killarney off T65*
This 14th-century fortress, the principal stronghold of the O'Donoghues, was the last in Munster to surrender to Cromwell's forces (1652).

### SLIGO AND VICINITY (SLIGO)
CARROWMORE, *3 kilometers southwest off L132*
This area contains the largest collection of megalithic monuments in the British Isles, including many passage graves.

INISHMURRAY, *6½ kilometers off the Sligo coast*
This island is the site of one of the best preserved early monasteries in Ireland, founded in the sixth century by Saint Molaise. The large stone cashel encloses three small churches, three beehive cells, and three altars.

SLIGO ABBEY, *Abbey Street*
This Dominican friary was founded by Maurice Fitzgerald, earl of Kildare, in 1252, soon after he had been granted the area. The friary was burned in 1414 and was sacked by Parliamentarians in 1641. The remains contain many interesting tombs and monuments, including the tomb of Cormac O'Crean.

### TARA (MEATH), *10 kilometers southeast of Navan just west of T35*
This low hill is one of the most famous sites in Ireland, the seat of the ancient high kings of Tara, rulers of all Ireland. Its importance is both legendary and factual: Tara was a chief pagan center from as early as the Bronze Age until the mid-sixth century A.D., reaching its greatest glory under Cormac MacArt in the third century A.D. Many ancient earthworks remain, whose names are traditional rather than historical. The **Fort of the Kings** is a large oval hill-fort enclosing the crown of the hill. Within it are two adjoining mounds, the **Royal Seat** and **Cormac's House**. Atop the latter is a standing stone known as the **Lia Fáil**; it commemorates insurgents who died in a battle here in the rebellion of 1798. The original Lia Fáil, on which the kings of Tara were crowned, was on a tumulus known as the **Mound of the Hostages**. Other earthworks include the **Fort of the Synods**, where religious ceremonies were held in the second century A.D., and a long, rectangular earthwork known as the **Banqueting Hall**.

### TRIM (MEATH), *on T26, L3, L25, and L23*
**Trim Castle**, the largest Anglo-Norman fortress in Ireland, was founded in 1173 by Hugh de Lacy, who made Trim his capital after Henry II granted him the kingdom of Meath. Leveled by the Irish, it was rebuilt late in the century and thereafter figured significantly in the struggles between the Irish and the English. Richard II con-

fined Henry of Lancaster (later Henry V) and Humphrey of Gloucester here late in the 14th century. The ruins, especially the massive keep, are well preserved.

**WATERFORD (WATERFORD),** *on T7, T12, T13, T14, T63, and L157*
When Richard Strongbow, earl of Pembroke, took it in 1170, this city was already an important port, having been established by the Danes in the ninth century. Soon after his arrival Strongbow married Eva, daughter of King Dermot MacMurrough of Leinster (*see Wexford*); the wedding was celebrated in **Reginald's Tower,** which the Danish chieftain Reginald had erected in 1003. In 1171 Henry II landed at Waterford, intent on seeing that Strongbow did not usurp too much power for himself in Ireland. Henry declared Waterford a royal city, and for the next several centuries it remained unwaveringly loyal to the English Crown, a loyalty for which it was frequently rewarded and commended. In the 18th century Waterford became a famous glass-manufacturing center.

**WEXFORD (WEXFORD),** *on T8, T12, and L127*
The flourishing port that the Vikings established here in the ninth century was the first Irish town to fall to Henry II's invaders. Although Henry had for years aspired to annex Ireland, his opportunity did not come until 1166, when King Dermot MacMurrough of Leinster—who had been defeated and banished for various misdeeds by a coalition of his enemies, led by High King Rory O'Connor of Connaught—appealed to the English king for help. With Henry's approval, Dermot recruited volunteers among the Anglo-Normans in Wales, chief among them Richard de Clare, earl of Pembroke (known as Strongbow), to whom Dermot promised his daughter in marriage. In 1169, the year before Strongbow landed at Waterford, Dermot took Wexford with the help of two other Norman allies. In 1172 Henry II, on his way to Dublin to secure that city for the Crown, did penance at **Selsker Abbey** for the murder of Thomas à Becket. In 1649 Cromwell seized the town and massacred most of its inhabitants; the worst slaughter of noncombatants took place in the **Bull Ring.** In the uprising of the United Irishmen in 1798, Wexford was held by insurgents for a month; a **Monument** commemorates the rising. One of the medieval town's five fortified towers, **West Gate Tower,** survives.

**YOUGHAL (CORK),** *on T12 on the west side of Youghal harbor*
Beginning in the 13th century this settlement became an important town of the Fitzgeralds, earls of Desmond. In 1579 rebel earl Gerald Fitzgerald, who had been proclaimed a traitor by Queen Elizabeth, sacked and burned the town after the sympathetic mayor had allowed Desmond's men to breach the walls. Desmond was captured and killed in 1583, after which his lands were distributed by the queen among her loyal followers, chief among them Sir Walter Raleigh. Raleigh lived for a time in **Myrtle Grove,** an Elizabethan house; here, in the garden, he allegedly planted the first potato in Ireland. In 1604 Raleigh sold his Irish holdings to Richard Boyle, later earl of Cork, who for the next several decades kept Munster loyal to the Crown. In 1649 Cromwell was welcomed into the city. **Saint Mary's Collegiate Church** (Church of Ireland), built in the 15th century by Thomas, eighth earl of Desmond, is the largest parish church in Ireland. It contains many early English tombs, including that of the earl of Cork, which has effigies of him, his two wives, and nine of his children.

# SCANDINAVIA

DENMARK
FINLAND
ICELAND
NORWAY
SWEDEN

# DENMARK

## AALBORG VICINITY (JUTLAND)

### LINDHOLM HØJE, *near the Lim Fjord*

Recent excavations here have uncovered a sizable Viking burial ground, with graves enclosed by stones in the form of ships. The remains are on view in a public park.

## AARHUS (JUTLAND)

### CATHEDRAL, *on Saint Clemens Square*

The 13th-century church, built by Peder Vognsen, has been rebuilt and altered several times. **Vor Frue Kirke,** the former cathedral and oldest surviving structure in the city, is situated just west on the Vestergade. It dates from the start of the 12th century.

### DEN GAMLE BY, *in the Botanical Garden*

Like the Frilandsmuseet near Lyngby (*see*), this is an assemblage of buildings from towns in the vicinity, including Aalborg. Whereas the Frilandsmuseet re-creates rural Denmark, Den Gamle By preserves the atmosphere of the early Danish town.

## ASKOV VICINITY (JUTLAND)

### SKIBELUND KRAT, *about 3 kilometers south*

This thicket of shrubbery contains the **Magnus Stone** (1898), by Niels Skovgaard, celebrating the victory of Magnus the Good over the Wends (a slavic people of eastern Germany) on Lyrskov Heath in 1043. Also here are memorials to the Danes who resisted the Prussian conquest and annexation of northern Schleswig, which was effected in 1864–66.

## COPENHAGEN (ZEALAND)

### AMALIENBORG, *off the Amaliegade*

The octagonal area here is bordered by four imposing rococo palaces completed in 1760 and used as royal residences and as quarters for visiting officials. The first palace on the site arose in 1669. The present ones are identical in design and take their name from Sophie Amalie, wife of King Frederick III (1648–70). In recent times Amalienborg has been the actual royal residence, succeeding Christianborg (*see*). During the fall and winter, when the royal family is in Copenhagen, the changing of the Amalienborg guard at noon provides a colorful ceremony for spectators.

### BØRSEN (STOCK EXCHANGE), *northeast corner of Slotsholmen*

Among the claims of this handsome structure, built between 1619 and 1640, is that it is the oldest surviving commercial exchange in Europe. Four dragons with interlocked tails form the striking tower. A Bertel Thorvaldsen statue of Christian IV, in the principal hall, honors the king for whom the Børsen was created.

### CHARLOTTENBORG, *on the east side of Kongens Nytorv (square)*

Since 1754 this palace, in Dutch baroque style, has been the home of the Royal Academy of Arts. The building was erected between 1672 and 1683 for a natural son of Frederick III, Count Ulrik F. Gyldenløve. It took its present name from the dowager queen Charlotte Amalie, who acquired the property as a home in 1700. The noted Danish sculptor Bertel Thorvaldsen resided here for a time, following his return from Rome in 1838. A building behind the palace serves both as an exhibition hall and as the academy library. Charlottenborg is alongside **Nyhavn,** a canal in whose immediate vicinity are cafés popular with seamen, artists, and writers, and

*Top left: The Little Mermaid in Copenhagen Harbor. Right: Frederiksborg castle at Hillerod. Center: royal guard at Fredensborg Palace. Below left: Sankt Bendt's Church in Ringsted. Right: the Stock Exchange in Copenhagen*

colorful old houses. One of these **(No. 67)** served as a home for Hans Christian Andersen from 1848 to 1865.

## CHRISTIANBORG PALACE, *on the island of Slotsholmen*

The present structure, completed in 1916, is the home of the Rigsdag (Parliament), Supreme Court, and Foreign Office. The first castle on the site, built by Archbishop Absalon in 1167, in time gave way to a succession of buildings closely associated with Danish government; the name Christianborg derives from the palace completed here in 1745 by Christian VI. Until the end of the 18th century this site was also the Danish royal residence, and a number of rulers, beginning with Christian I, who was king from 1448 to 1481, were born here. It has been the seat of the parliament since 1849. The palace is adjoined by the **Slotskirke** (Royal Chapel).

## HELLIGAANDSKIRKEN (CHURCH OF THE HOLY GHOST), *on the Niels Hemmingsensgade*

The historical associations here begin with the first building on the site, a 14th-century convent church, which was rebuilt in 1732. The burial chapel of the Griffenfelds, family of Count Peder Griffenfeld (1635–99), is here, and there is a memorial to the Danish patriots who died during the German occupation, 1940–45. Since the war an annual memorial service has been held here on May 5.

## HOLMENS KIRKE, *on Holmens Kanal opposite Slotsholmen*

The tombs of two of Denmark's naval heroes, who distinguished themselves in action against Sweden, are in a chapel of this church: Niels Juel, active in the war of 1675–77, and Peder Tordenskjold, who lived early in the 18th century. Also here is the grave of the composer-conductor Niels Gade (1817–90). The building has undergone several alterations since it was converted from an anchor forge in 1619 by King Christian IV.

## KASTELLET (CITADELLET FREDERIKSHAVN), *north of the Esplanaden*

Surrounded by a moat, the citadel dates from 1661, when it was constructed to protect the entrance to the city's harbor. It still houses a small garrison and serves as the official residence of the army's commander in chief. Beyond it, across the dock railway, is a waterside promenade, **Langelinie.** Following its course, the visitor passes a landmark as familiar as Tivoli: the bronze sculpture *Den Lille Havfrue (The Little Mermaid),* by Edvard Eriksen, inspired by an Andersen tale.

## KØBENHAVN UNIVERSITET (UNIVERSITY OF COPENHAGEN), *facing the cathedral across Frue Plads*

King Christian I founded the university in 1479. A new building was erected in 1601, but it was destroyed in the great fire of 1728. Its successor, completed in 1732, was a victim of the British bombardment of 1807. The present main building was completed in 1836. Behind it, with an entrance in the Krystalgade, is the **Zoological Museum,** containing a valuable collection of Danish fossils.

## KONGELIGE BIBLIOTEK (ROYAL LIBRARY), *on the island of Slotsholmen*

Denmark's national library dates from the reign of King Frederick III (1648–70), but the present building arose about 1800. Among its treasures are manuscript pages from the history of Saxo Grammaticus; manuscripts and letters of Hans Christian Andersen, Henrik Ibsen, and Sören Kierkegaard; manuscript accounts of Norse voyages; and collections of Danish folklore.

**KONGELIGE TEATER (ROYAL THEATER),** *south side of Kongens Nytorv (square)*
The present quarters of the chief national theater of Denmark were opened in 1874, and an annex, inaugurated in 1931, now gives this famous building two stages, called old and new. An earlier theater on the site was opened in 1748. The Royal Theater, which functions under the Ministry for Cultural Affairs, is the home of drama, ballet, opera, and concerts of the Royal Orchestra. The Royal Theater also maintains the ballet school from which, for the most part, are recruited members of the house's internationally famous dance troupe, the Royal Danish Ballet.

**NATIONAL MUSEUM OF DENMARK,** *entry to adjoining buildings from Frederiksholms Kanal and the Ny Vestergade*
The panorama of Danish history, from about 10,000 B.C. to the present, stretches forth in this collection, which is one of the largest, and oldest, in Europe. An earlier Royal Museum was disbanded in 1821, and its collections were distributed among independent Copenhagen institutions. Gradually state-owned collections were merged administratively in 1892 to form the present museum; from 1920 this also has included the Danish Folk Museum, set up in 1885, and the Frilandsmuseet (Open-Air Museum) near Lyngby (*see*).

**ROSENBORG,** *westcentral part of Kongens Have (King's Garden)*
Kongens Have is the park created in 1606 by King Christian IV. Between 1608 and 1617 he built the palace, Rosenborg, as his country residence; at that time the park was not within the city's boundaries. After Christian IV died here in 1648, a number of his successors used it as a residence. Since 1858 Rosenborg has been a museum, little changed in an architectural sense since its earliest years. Its priceless collection includes the Danish crown jewels.

**RUNDETAARN (ROUND TOWER),** *in the Købmagergade*
Christian IV constructed this landmark as an observatory in 1642. Like most of Copenhagen's buildings, it was largely destroyed in the fire of 1728; not until 1930 was it restored for its original purpose. The top of the structure (118 feet) can be reached by a spiral ramp; it is said that Peter the Great and Catherine I of Russia rode up the ramp in a carriage in 1716. Adjoining the tower is **Trinitatis Kirke,** completed in 1657 and restored after the fire of 1728. Opposite the tower is **Regensen College,** founded by Christian IV in 1623 to provide free residence for its students.

**SANKT NIKOLAJ'S KIRKE,** *just east of Højbro Plads*
Hans Tausen, the 16th-century Danish religious reformer and student of Martin Luther, introduced the doctrines of the Reformation to his native land in churches in Copenhagen and Viborg, including this 13th-century structure. It lay in ruins from 1795, when it was swept by fire, until reconstruction was undertaken during World War I. On the upper level is the **Royal Navy Museum.**

**TIVOLI,** *principal entrance in the Vesterbrogade*
The park and amusement garden that is Copenhagen's most famous

attraction dates from 1843 and is located on part of the fortifications—ramparts and moats—that composed the southern boundary of the old city. Open from early May to mid-September, Tivoli offers concerts, ballet, pantomime, and variety entertainment.

## TØJHUSMUSEET (ROYAL ARMORY MUSEUM), 9 *Tøjhusgade, Slotsholmen*

About 1600 King Christian IV constructed the Lange Tøjhus (Long Arsenal), which is now the site of a military museum tracing the evolution of implements of warfare from about 1400. In the courtyard to the rear is a famous monument, **The Lion of Isted,** by the 19th-century Danish sculptor H. W. Bissen, originally created in memory of Danish forces who lost their lives in the war with Prussia (1848–50) and placed in a cemetery in Flensburg, near the Danish border. It was carried off þy Prussians in 1864, upon their occupation of Flensburg, but was reconstructed here in 1945.

## VOR FRUE KIRKE (OUR LADY'S CHURCH), *the Nørregade and the Studiestraede*

The present structure arose between 1811 and 1829 and has been designated the city's cathedral since 1924. The site, however, has been famous in Danish ecclesiastical history for a much longer period. Archbishop Absalon founded the first church here in the 12th century. After a fire in 1728, the building was enlarged. Then, during the Napoleonic Wars, the three-day British bombardment of 1807 almost completely destroyed the building and set the stage for construction of the present church. During the Middle Ages many Danish kings were crowned on the site, and bishops are still ordained here. Like many of Denmark's historic churches, Vor Frue Kirke has great interest for students of art and architecture.

## DALMOSE VICINITY (ZEALAND)

### BORREBY CASTLE, *about 11 kilometers northeast of Skaelskor*

The Renaissance castle built here in 1556 by Chancellor Johan Friis is in almost its original condition. A park on the grounds is open to visitors.

## FREDENSBORG (ZEALAND)

### PALACE, *in the town park*

Another of Denmark's royal residences is here, richly furnished and handsomely landscaped. Constructed about 1720 for King Frederick IV, it is still in active service. The town's name derives from the Danish word for "peace"; it was here, in 1720, that the peace treaty ending hostilities between Denmark and Sweden was signed.

## FREDERICIA (JUTLAND)

The town came into being in 1650 as a fortress, and visitors still can tour it by walking on the surviving ramparts. Every July 6 the Danes pay tribute to their military forces, which in 1849 broke a siege imposed by combined Prussian and Schleswig-Holstein regiments here. There are several monuments to this action, part of a long struggle between Denmark and her southern neighbors.

## FREDERIKSBERG (ZEALAND)

### FREDERIKSBERG SLOT (CASTLE), *on southern edge of Frederiksberg Have*

Early in the 18th century this chateau was built for King Frederick IV. Later it served as a home for Frederick VI, and now it is a military academy. Opposite the entrance to **Frederiksberg Have,** a large park that is one of the landmarks of this largest of Copenhagen's suburbs, is **Frederiksberg Kirke,** a church dating from 1734.

## GLAVENDRUP VICINITY (FYN), *north of Odense on the road to Bogense*
A rune stone dating from A.D. 900 is here, together with a Viking monument consisting of two rows of stones in the shape of a ship.

## HELLERUP VICINITY (ZEALAND)
RYVANGEN MINDELUNDEN, *.8 kilometers south, on Tuborgvej*
A memorial grove here honors Danes active in the resistance to the Nazi occupation, 1940–45. Located near their execution grounds, it contains the graves of the victims of the German conquerors.

## HELSINGOR (ELSINORE) (ZEALAND)
KARMELITERKLOSTRET (CARMELITE MONASTERY), *near the intersection of the Saint Annagade and the Sudergade*
King Eric VII of Pomerania established a monastery here in 1430. The well-preserved property contains much of artistic and architectural interest. One wing houses the **Church of Saint Mary,** where the 17th-century composer Dietrich Buxtehude was organist from 1660 to 1668.

KRONBORG, *on the harbor's edge overlooking the Oresund*
The Renaissance castle here achieved its status as an especially noted landmark in part through its association with one of the most famous works in dramatic literature. It is the setting of Shakespeare's *Hamlet*. It was built for King Frederick II about 1574–85, fell victim to fire and then to capture by the Swedes in the 17th century, and then for a century and a half, beginning about 1785, served as military barracks. In the course of restoring the old structure to its present condition, authorities uncovered some of the remains of the first fortress on the site, built by Eric of Pomerania early in the 15th century as an instrument for collecting tolls on foreign shipping passing through the Oresund. Just northwest of Kronborg is **Marienlyst,** a town museum housed in a 16th-century royal chateau, whose collection includes much material relating to *Hamlet*.

SANKT OLAI KIRKE, *on the Saint Annagade, just south of the Karmeliterklostret*
Helsingor's main church, dating from late in the 15th century, is on an original church foundation laid about 1200. The Renaissance furnishings are noteworthy, as are the town's historical memorials.

## HILLEROD (ZEALAND)
FREDERIKSBORG SLOT (CASTLE), *on three isles near the western side of the slotssø (lake)*
Until 1859, when it was swept by fire, this was a royal residence. Now, carefully restored, it houses the **Museum of National History.** About 1560 King Frederick II built a castle here, only a few outer portions of which remain. Christian IV, his son, who was born in the first structure, had it destroyed; on its site, between 1602 and 1620, Christian IV had the original of the present castle built. It was the coronation place of Danish rulers as well as their summer place of residence. Many of the art treasures depict or are associated with great events in the Danes' national story. The chapel, which largely escaped the fire, contains a 1610 organ. On the northeast portion of the grounds is the castle park, with a formal French garden.

**DENMARK**

## HOBRO VICINITY (JUTLAND)
### FYRKAT, *about 3 kilometers southwest*
Throughout the 1950s excavation and reconstruction of a Viking fortress took place here under supervision of the National Museum. The plan of the original structure parallels that of the remains uncovered at Trelleborg, near Slagelse (*see*), though it is somewhat less elaborate than the Trelleborg fortification. The basic design again is a circular rampart enclosing groups of barrackslike buildings. The plan bears resemblance to that of a Roman military camp. Fyrkat, like Trelleborg, dates from about A.D. 1000 and also contains a burial ground. The care with which these fortresses were laid out has done much to revise earlier ideas of the Vikings as warriors capable only of savage raids.

## JELLING (JUTLAND)
### JELLING HØJENE (JELLING HILLS), *near the town center*
The two hills, or mounds, are thought to mark the oldest royal monumental tombs in the country—the resting places of Gorm the Old (who died about 940 and was the first king of united Denmark) and his Queen Thyre (or Thyra). Of equal interest are two runic stones, the larger of which was erected about 980 by the son and successor of Gorm, Harald Bluetooth.

## KOGE (ZEALAND)
### SANKT NIKOLAJS KIRKE, *in the Nørregade*
From the tower windows of this 15th-century church, marauding Wends used to be hanged when caught and subdued. The tower commands a view of this old town, with its timbered houses, and of Koge Bay, where in 1677 a Danish force under Niels Juel defeated the Swedish fleet. King Christian V may have watched the action from this church.

## KOLDING (JUTLAND)
### KOLDINGHUS, *north of Axeltorv, the central square*
The ruins of this royal castle, constructed in the 13th century as a defense against encroachment from the south, now house a museum. King Christian III died here in 1559. The castle was often attacked and as often restored; in 1808 it was severely damaged by fire at the hands of Spanish forces during the Napoleonic Wars.

## LADBY (FYN)
### LADBYSKIBET (BOAT OF LADBY), *near Kerteminde Fjord, on route from Odense to Kerteminde*
A Viking burial ship dating from about 950 was located here in 1935 by the archaeologist P. Helweg Mikkelsen. Following excavation, a protective structure was built over this rare find, which has been preserved with great care. Visitors can descend to the exhibition area to view the craft, 72 feet in length and 9 feet in width, which originally served as the resting place of a tenth-century warrior. To provide a suitable entourage for the journey to Valhalla, he was buried with full arms, personal wealth, horses, and hunting dogs.

## LYNGBY VICINITY (ZEALAND)
### FRILANDSMUSEET (OPEN-AIR MUSEUM), *just north of the town*
The history of rural Denmark, with emphasis on the 18th and 19th centuries, is in a sense traced here in a museum, established in 1901 and now part of the National Museum based in Copenhagen (*see*). Typical rural buildings from Denmark and from the southern areas

of Sweden that once were Danish have been reconstructed and furnished in their original style. Nearby are the **Agricultural Museum** and a royal chateau, **Sorgenfri,** constructed in 1705. King Frederick IX was born at Sorgenfri in 1899.

## NYBORG (FYN)
### HOLCKENHAVN (NYBORG CASTLE)
The remains of this oldest royal castle in Scandinavia, dating from 1170, were restored shortly after World War I and now serve as a museum. For a period of some two hundred years, beginning about 1200, Nyborg was Denmark's center of national government; it was here, in a hall of the castle (still preserved), that the Danehof, or early parliament, met, and it was here that King Eric (Klipping) issued the constitution of 1282. The castle, constructed of brick, was designed as protection for the Store Baelt (or Great Belt, the strait connecting the Kattegat and the Baltic Sea) against Wendish marauders. It was heavily damaged in the Danish war with the Swedes, 1658–60; at this site a Swedish army surrendered in 1659. During the Napoleonic Wars early in the 19th century, a Spanish force occupied the castle for a time. Later it served as an armory and still later as a storage place for grain.

## ODENSE (FYN)
### HANS CHRISTIAN ANDERSEN BIRTHPLACE, *corner of the Hans Jensensstraede and Bangs Boder*
The one-story house where Odense's most famous native son is thought to have been born, in 1805, has been reconstructed as a museum to him, and the project also comprises some adjoining buildings. Here visitors can see first editions of his writings (including the *Fairy Tales,* which gave the world "The Ugly Duckling," "The Snow Queen," and "The Red Shoes"); specimens of his correspondence (with Charles Dickens and Jenny Lind, among others); and personal belongings, including the famous top hat and umbrella. At Munkemøllestraede 3 is the house in which the author spent his years between two and fourteen. Near Kongens Have (King's Garden) is the old **Church of Saint Hans,** at whose 12th-century font Andersen was baptized.

### SANKT KNUDS KIRKE, *near the west bank of the Odense River in the middle of the old section of the city*
A noteworthy example of Gothic church architecture, this brick structure is dedicated to Canute IV (or Knud IV, in Danish), king of Denmark for six years until his murder in 1086 and patron saint of Denmark. The first church on this site was begun by Canute IV (grandnephew of Canute II, "the Great") shortly before his death. After his canonization, his remains were placed in the first church, which burned in 1247. The crypt of the present cathedral, built about 1300, retains the shrine to Canute IV; the shrine is thought to contain his remains as well. Also in the crypt are the tombs of two later Danish kings, Hans (King John I, 1481–1513) and Christian II (1513–23). Bordering the cathedral on the north is Albani Torv (Saint Alban's Square), the probable site of the church before whose high altar Canute IV was slain by rebels.

## OXNEBJERG (FYN), *32 kilometers west of Odense on the road to Assens*
On this site in 1535 a combined army of Danes and Swedes defeated the forces of Lübeck, then the leading town of the old Hanseatic League and now West Germany's leading Baltic port.

## RIBE (JUTLAND)

### CATHEDRAL, *on the market square in the Skolegade*

The central building of this very old town was constructed early in the 12th century and stands on the site of a church built in 862 by the monk Anschar, who is credited with introducing Christianity to Denmark. The tomb of Hans Tausen, the disciple of Martin Luther's who was bishop of Ribe (1542), is here. The house nearby that he occupied is now a museum.

## RINGSTED (ZEALAND)

### SANKT BENDT KIRKE (CHURCH OF SAINT BENDT), *on Torvet, the central square*

The graves of more than 20 kings and princes are here, though none of the original tombs remain. Among the royal remains are those of Waldemar I (the Great), king of Denmark 1157–82; Waldemar II, king 1202–41; Waldemar III, coregent with his father, Waldemar II; Eric IV (Ploughpenny), king 1241–50; Eric Moendved, king 1286–1319; and Prince Canute Lavard (1094?–1131).

## ROSKILDE (ZEALAND)

### DOMKIRKE, *on the Kirkestraede*

The first church on the site dated from about 960. The present one, with an exterior of red brick, was begun a little more than two centuries later under Archbishop Absalon. Architecturally it is of great interest because of (and in spite of) the many styles it represents. The graves of most of the Danish kings and queens of the Oldenburg and Glücksburg dynasties are here; Queen Margaret's tomb is behind the altar. Just east of the cathedral, and connected to it by an arch, is the **Bishop's Palace,** constructed 1733–36. It was here that the constitution of 1849 was drafted—a liberal document that ended absolute monarchy and provided a wide suffrage.

### VIKING SHIP MUSEUM, *on the shore of Roskilde Fjord*

Since the summer of 1969 this modern building has been the home of five Viking ships that had lain underwater in the fjord for almost a thousand years. Apparently they were sunk about A.D. 1000 as part of a defensive strategy to protect Roskilde harbor from enemy vessels. Excavation was carried out in 1962 and 1963 with great care; from near Skuldelev, where the remains were located, more than 50,000 parts were taken to the National Museum for conservation. The timbers were treated at great length with preservatives before the reconstruction process. The ships represent both commercial vessels and warships. The largest, 90 feet in length with room for more than 50 warriors, is longer than any other known ship of the Viking era. A much smaller trading vessel (44 feet long) retains traces of the original cuts of the Viking axes.

## SANDVIG VICINITY (BORNHOLM)

### HAMMERSHUS SLOT (CASTLE), *about 3 kilometers southwest*

The ruins of a 13th-century castle, built by the archbishop of Lund, Jacob Erlandsen, are visible here. In 1525 the stronghold was captured by the forces of Lübeck, then head of the Hanseatic League. Regained by the Danes, it was used as a place of confinement for political prisoners until the garrison was transferred to other forts on the island. The castle was partially dismantled by 1822, when through the efforts of the National Museum work on its restoration was begun. The setting, between the sea and heather-covered hills, is one of the most picturesque in Denmark.

### SLAGELSE VICINITY (ZEALAND)
#### TRELLEBORG, 5 kilometers west
The Viking fortress and encampment here, dating from A.D. 990–1000, were uncovered through excavations that spanned the latter half of the 1930s. The remains are open to visitors and constitute one of the principal visible landmarks of the Viking era in Scandinavia. The fortress comprises inner and outer wards, circular in design, each with a rampart and moat. Within each ward were wooden structures serving as barracks and providing accommodations for more than 1,300 warriors in winter quarters. Though the buildings themselves have long since disappeared, the excavations have provided valuable clues to their shape (which was boatlike) and size (nearly 100 feet in length); on the basis of this information, one of the inner-ward buildings has been reconstructed. The outer ward encloses a burial ground of 150 graves.

### SONDERBORG AND VICINITY (JUTLAND)
#### DYBBOL (DÜPPEL) BANKE (DYBBOL MILL), about 3 kilometers west
This small town was the scene of action in the 1848–50 war between Denmark and Germany over Schleswig-Holstein. In 1864 the Prussians overpowered an outnumbered Danish force here and subsequently inflicted a defeat on Denmark. A Prussian victory memorial erected here was later destroyed by the Danes after 1945.

#### SONDERBORG SLOT (CASTLE), at the mouth of Als Sound
The royal castle here was probably erected in the 12th century. It was attacked by the Swedes in 1658 and shelled by the Prussians in 1864 (after which, until the 1920 plebiscite, Sonderborg was part of Germany). A military museum here traces the castle's history.

### SORO (ZEALAND)
#### ABBEY CHURCH, just beyond the Town Hall in the square
Established about 1160 as part of a Cistercian monastery, this beautiful place of worship houses the tombs of some notable Danes, including Archbishop Absalon, its founder, who died in Soro in 1201 after a remarkable career as soldier, statesman, and cleric. The church, restored after a fire in 1247, contains the marble sarcophagus of Ludvig Holberg (1684–1754), generally regarded as the founder of modern Danish literature, and those of the 14th-century kings Christopher II and Waldemar (or Valdemar) IV. Further restoration was undertaken in the mid-19th century. Adjoining the church is **Soro Academy**, dating back to 1584.

### VIBORG (JUTLAND)
#### CATHEDRAL, off the Saint Mogensgade
The principal church of this very old city was built in the first half of the 12th century on the site of earlier places of worship (dating back to the era of paganism). A great fire in 1726 and subsequent misfortunes caused it to be replaced in 1876 by the present granite structure, noteworthy for its artwork.

### VORDINGBORG (ZEALAND)
#### CASTLE, on the Algade, about 1 kilometer from the town station
King Waldemar (or Valdemar) I built this fortress as protection from the Wends and died here in 1182, as did his son and successor Waldemar II in 1241. The surviving ruins include an outer wall and tower (surmounted by a golden goose screaming defiance at Germany) added by the 14th-century ruler Waldemar IV (Atterdag).

# FINLAND

**BORGA.** *See* PORVOO

**HÄMEENLINNA (HÄME),** *96 kilometers northwest of Helsinki via Route 3*
Overlooking Lake Vanajavesi in the northern part of the city stands
**Häme Castle,** which commands interest through its link with
medieval Finland, even though the site has no historical associations
of great magnitude. The first mention of the castle in a historical
account occurred in 1308, but its oldest sections are believed to date
from about 1250. The northern section of the city also contains
**Sibelius Park,** named for the composer whose music drew on much
of Finland's ancient cultural heritage and in turn was closely
identified with the national aspirations of the Finns. Jean Sibelius
was born in Hämeenlinna in 1865.

**HAMINA (KYMI),** *16 kilometers northeast of Kotka on Route E3*
This town on the Gulf of Finland bears the name of a historic treaty
of 1809, under whose terms Sweden ceded all of Finland to Russia.
The pact meant that Finland no longer was the battleground for
Swedish and Russian armies that it had been during the preceding
century. Under the Treaty of Hamina the Finns, as a grand duchy of
Russia, also realized a considerable measure of domestic self-rule.
The **Tower of Peace,** on Market Square, commemorates that treaty.
Two other points of interest in Hamina are the **Town Hall,** constructed in 1798 on the square in the town's center, and a **Medieval
Church,** located west of this square, which was completed in 1396
and restored in the 19th century. The church is the principal remaining structure of the original town on this site (Vehkalahti), which
was destroyed during the period 1713–21, when Peter I of Russia
invaded Finland, then under Swedish control.

**HELSINKI (HELSINGFORS) AND VICINITY (UUSIMAA)**
HOUSE OF THE ESTATES, *off Senate Square on the Snellmaninkatu*
This was the home of the Finnish parliament during the period
1809–1917, when the country was under Russian control as a grand
duchy. The structure now houses scholastic societies.

HOUSE OF THE NOBILITY, *near Senate Square on the Aleksanterinkatu*
A collection of the arms of the noble families of Finland is on display here. In the rear of this building, on the Hallituskatu, is the
**Finnish Literary Society,** a center of documents relating to the
country's vast folklore.

KAUPPATORI (MARKET SQUARE), *on South Harbor near the quay for
passenger ships*
In or bordering this square, which is famous for its colorful commercial activity during morning hours, are several important sites.
**City Hall,** dating from 1832, was designed by Carl Ludwig Engel,
who was municipal architect during one of the greatest periods of
modern Helsinki's development. The **Supreme Court** building is
here, and so is the **President's Palace,** formerly the Russian Imperial
Palace but now the residence of Finland's president. Just beyond
the President's Palace, on a small island, Katajanokka, connected to
the mainland by a bridge, is the **Uspenskaia** (Russian Orthodox
cathedral), completed in 1868. In the center of the square an
obelisk, the **Empress Stone,** commemorates the first visit to the city
by Nicholas I in 1833, when Finland was under Russian rule.

*Top left: Uspenskaia, the Russian Orthodox cathedral in Helsinki. Right:*
*Lutheran cathedral in Turku. Center: Senate Square in Helsinki, showing the*
*cathedral and university. Below: Häme Castle in Hämeenlinna*

## MANNERHEIM MUSEUM, *Kalliolinnantie 22*

Baron Carl Gustaf Emil von Mannerheim had a distinguished career in the Russian army and then, from 1918, as a Finnish soldier and statesman. His former home, in the southern residential section Kaivopuisto, contains a collection of his many trophies. He is buried in the **Military Cemetery** off Lapinlahti Bay, near the city's Western Harbor.

## PARLIAMENT HOUSE, *on the Mannerheimintie, west of the main post office*

The parliament of the present republic has met here since 1931. The public is admitted to the gallery during sessions of the legislative body; between sessions there are tours of the building. Parliament meets from early September to mid-December and from early January to mid-June.

## SENATE SQUARE, *just north of City Hall in Kauppatori*

Also known as the Great Square, this area is in the heart of the old city. On the north side is **Helsinki Cathedral (Great Church)**, formerly known as Saint Nicholas's Cathedral; designed by C. L. Engel, it was completed in 1852. The **Government Palace** for administrative offices is on the east side. On the west side, on the Fabianinkatu, is the **University of Helsinki,** whose construction was begun under Engel's direction in 1828. Its library also serves as the national library of Finland. On the square's south side, on the Katariinankatu, is Helsinki's oldest surviving residence, **Sederholm House,** dating from 1757.

## SUOMENLINNA, *3 kilometers southeast of the city center, on islands in the Gulf of Finland*

Helsinki's historic fortress, protecting her harbor, was begun by Count Augustin Ehrensvärd in 1748, during the period when Finland was a duchy of Sweden (and when this site had the Swedish name Sveaborg). Ehrensvärd, who was both a military engineer and field marshal, is buried here, and the site is also noted for its museums, parks, and gardens. The fortress, formerly called the Gibraltar of the North, was surrendered to Russian forces in 1808, the year in which Finland passed from Swedish to Russian hands as an autonomous duchy favored by rule considerably more liberal than that of the Russian people themselves. In 1855 Suomenlinna was shelled by an Anglo-French fleet during the Crimean War. In 1918, during the period of Finnish civil war, nationalist forces in union with German troops wrested it from Finnish Bolsheviks.

# KAJAANI AND VICINITY (OULU)

## KAJAANI CASTLE, *below the bridge spanning the Kajaaninjoki River*

The ruins of this fortress, built originally between 1604 and 1619 and enlarged and improved 50 years later, bear witness to the struggle between Sweden and Russia for possession of Finland in the 18th century. Not until 1809 did control of all Finland pass from Sweden to Russia (*see Hamina*), but the forces of Peter I of Russia invaded Finland early in the 18th century and succeeded in capturing parts of it. Kajaani, in central Finland, was sacked in 1712; the castle, however, resisted capture until 1716, when it was largely destroyed by the Russians. It has now been partially restored. The Swedish historian and poet Johannes Messenius, who was accused of plotting with Roman Catholics, was imprisoned in the castle from 1616 until his death in 1636.

LÖNNROT HOUSE, *on the northwest side of Market Square*
For 20 years, beginning in 1833, Elias Lönnrot was a district
medical officer with headquarters in Kajaani. In the light of his
subsequent fame, the house that he occupied here has taken on
considerable importance. While pursuing a government career
early in his lifetime (1802–84), Lönnrot was active in two areas in
which he made a lasting mark. His study of ancient Finnish literature and folklore culminated in his compilation of the national
epic, *Kalevala,* for which he collected and edited component folk
and heroic songs of the Finns. The first edition appeared in 1835;
the second, 1849, gave the monumental work its present form. His
Finnish-Swedish lexicon (1874–80) represents the most tangible
result of his pursuit of historical linguistics. Visiting many segments
of the Finnish people, including Lapps and neighboring Estonians,
he helped to establish Finnish as an official language besides
Swedish in his country. That development, in turn, was the main
impetus for the rise of a modern literature in the Finnish language.

PALTAMO CHURCH, *8 kilometers northwest on Routes 5 and 77*
In the village of Paltamo are a church dating from 1726 and containing murals painted by Mikael Toppelius and a building next to
the church housing mementos of Czar Alexander I's visit here in
1819.

**KOKKOLA (VAASA),** *about 113 kilometers northeast of Vaasa on Route 8*
This seaport on the Gulf of Bothnia was founded in 1620. During
the Crimean War, in 1854, a British fleet sought to make a landing
here but failed. There is a monument to this action at the site of
Kokkola's old port. Near the north end of the main street, the
Isokatu, is a park with a building containing a British vessel captured during the war.

**LAPLAND.** *See* SODANKYLÄ

**LAPPEENRANTA (KYMI),** *96 kilometers northeast of Kotka via Route 61*
At the northern terminus of the Kauppakatu, a principal thoroughfare, near the shore of Lake Saimaa, are the ruins of 18th-century
fortifications. A park nearby has a memorial to the battle that took
place here in 1741, when invading Russian forces defeated a
Swedish-Finnish army and destroyed this fortified town near the
present U.S.S.R. frontier. From 1743 to 1812 Lappeenranta was in
Russian hands.

**NYKARLEBY.** *See* UUSIKAARLEPYY

**NYSTAD.** *See* UUSIKAUPUNKI

**PORVOO (UUSIMAA)**
CATHEDRAL, *in the center of the old town*
The Gothic cathedral, built between 1414 and 1418, dominates the
old section of one of Finland's oldest towns, incorporated about
1350. Porvoo is largely populated by Swedish-speaking people and
is still often called by the Swedish name Borga. The cathedral contains a bronze memorial commemorating the Finnish diet that met
here in 1809 to pledge allegiance to Alexander I of Russia at the time
that Finland became his duchy. Just south is the old **Town Hall**
(1764), now a historical museum, and next to it is the **Ville Vallgren
Museum,** whose collection is housed in 18th-century buildings.

**RUNEBERG HOUSE**, *at the intersection of the Runeberginkatu and the Aleksanterinkatu*

Known as a cultural center, Porvoo was the home of Finland's national poet, Johan Ludvig Runeberg. The house where he resided, and where he died in 1877, has been preserved as it was in his lifetime, as a mecca for Finns and foreigners alike.

**RISTIINA (MIKKELI)**, *21 kilometers south of Mikkeli on Route 72*

A fortified castle, **Brahelinna**, was completed here in 1649, during the administration of Count Per Brahe as Finland's governor general. Its remains still stand at the site of this village.

**SAVONLINNA (MIKKELI)**, *89 kilometers east of Mikkeli on Route 14*

Located in narrows between lakes of the Saimaa system, this resort town developed around the fortified castle known as **Olavinlinna**, on a small island in the Kyrönsalmi Strait. The castle, which dates from 1475, is still one of Finland's principal tourist attractions. It was built originally as a means of stopping invasion from the east, and its early history is something of a microcosm of Finnish history. Russia attacked it several times from the east, notably in 1714 and 1742. Almost to the time of the peace signed at Hamina (*see*) in 1809, the Swedes and the forces of their duchy, Finland, sought to regain possession, most notably during the futile war against Russia waged by Sweden's Gustavus III in 1788. The Hamina pact ended Olavinlinna's military importance, but the structure has been well maintained to the present.

**SODANKYLÄ (LAPI)**, *105 kilometers northeast of Rovaniemi on the Arctic Highway, Route 4 (Rovaniemi–Utsjoki)*

This Lapp trade center has a wooden church, dating from 1689, that is frequently visited by travelers in northern Finland. In ancient times the Lapps were not confined to the north; before the eighth century they were driven from the southern regions and retreated north to areas that were often penetrated by Finnish traders in the years that followed. Since Lapland is defined as the area lying above the Arctic Circle, Finnish Lapland comprises the territory north of Rovaniemi. Some of the oldest traces of human life in Finland have been found in this northern area, and the construction before World War II of the **Arctic Highway**, connecting Rovaniemi with the Arctic Ocean, stimulated travel to the north.

*A river view of Porvoo, one of Finland's oldest towns*

Unfortunately for travelers of the present day, Finnish Lapland suffered severe damage during the Russian invasion of 1939–40, and even greater loss during the expulsion of German troops from Finland in 1944. Having joined the Nazis in 1941 in a drive on the old enemy, Russia, Finland paid dearly; the peace that ended the war cost Finland still more territory, which went to the Soviet Union, and even before the fighting had ceased, the Finns were forced to drive out their former allies, the Germans, who systematically destroyed the northern areas they had occupied. Though Finnish Lapland has largely been rebuilt now, many historic sites were lost.

**SUOMUSSALMI (OULU),** *about 80 kilometers north of Kajaani on Route 5*
> Now principally visited because of its scenic qualities, this village near the U.S.S.R. border was in the center of the fighting during the Russo-Finnish war of 1939–40. The Finns had a major success here during that six-month struggle.

**TAMPERE (HÄME),** *160 kilometers northwest of Helsinki on Tammer Rapids*
> This modern industrial city was founded in 1779 by King Gustavus III of Sweden, but its development traces from 1821, when Alexander I of Russia, with an eye to expediting Tampere's industrial growth, made it a free city. That status remained unchanged until 1905, the year of the general strike stemming from the marked tightening of Russian control over all Finland. Meanwhile, in 1820, a Scot, James Finlayson, began to pioneer Tampere's industrial potential. More recently the city was the site of a decisive victory by nationalist troops under Baron Carl Gustaf Emil von Mannerheim over Finnish Bolsheviks in the country's war of independence (1917–18). The taking of Tampere by Mannerheim in April, 1918, was one of the last major steps in the suppression of the workers' republic. Among the city's architectural landmarks the most famous is the **Cathedral,** on the Rautatienkatu. It was built in 1907 and houses frescoes by Magnus Enckell and murals by Hugo Simberg. South of the cathedral, on the Keskutori (central square), is the **Town Hall** (1890). On the north side of this square is the wooden **Old Church** (1824), designed by Carl Ludvig Engel. In a small park adjoining the church is Wäinö Aaltonen's **Statue of Alexis Kivi,** one of the first and greatest of the literary figures to achieve fame through writings in the Finnish language.

## TURKU AND VICINITY (TURKU-PORI)
CATHEDRAL, *at the end of the Aninkaistenkatu*
> Completed in 1290 and frequently rebuilt and restored, this has long been the seat of the country's Lutheran archbishop. There are monuments and memorials to Finnish notables of the Thirty Years' War, and the cathedral's frescoes re-create much of Finland's early history. Two of the most celebrated scenes show heathen Finns being baptized by the English bishop Henry, and Michael Agricola offering his Finnish version (1548) of the New Testament to Gustavus I (Gustavus Vasa), king of Sweden, during whose reign Finland was a Swedish duchy and a royal appanage.

HANDICRAFT MUSEUM, *in the Luostarinmäki quarter*
> Pottery makers, weavers, and other artisans, all employing techniques dating back more than a century, work here in a group of old buildings that escaped both the fire of 1827, which wiped out most of the city, and the effects of World War II.

KULTARANTA, *13 kilometers west on Luonnonmaa Island*
The summer residence of the Finnish president was constructed in 1916. It faces Naantali (Swedish, Nådendal), a hamlet, now popular as a seaside resort, that housed a 15th-century monastery. The monastery church still serves the community here.

TURKU CASTLE, *at the mouth of the Aura River near Kanavaniemi*
During the period of Swedish control of Finland, this was the Finns' most important stronghold. The older part of the castle dates from late in the 13th century; the newer, from the 16th. Like much of Turku, which was heavily damaged in the Russo-Finnish war and by other action of World War II in this century, the castle was scarred by bombing in June, 1941. The castle is now a museum with exhibits dating back to the 16th century.

UUSIKAARLEPYY AND VICINITY (VAASA), *64 kilometers northeast of Vaasa on Route 8*
This town is in a predominantly Swedish-speaking region and is known also by the Swedish name Nykarleby. Its church dates from 1708. Just north of the town's borders, on the banks of the Lapua River, is the **Topelius Museum,** originally a house where the poet, dramatist, and novelist Zachris Topelius was born in 1818. The village of **Juuttaa,** 4 kilometers south, was the scene of a Finnish victory over the Russians during the war of 1808–9, which nevertheless ended with Russian conquest of all Finland (*see Hamina*). A memorial marks the battleground.

UUSIKAUPUNKI (TURKU-PORI), *66 kilometers northwest of Turku by rail*
This town on the Gulf of Bothnia has a 17th-century church that also functions as a museum. Uusikaupunki's place in history is better secured by a pact signed here in 1721 and known as the Treaty of Nystad (the Swedish name for Uusikaupunki). Finland was then ruled by Sweden, whose king Charles XII became alternately known as the Alexander of the North and Madman of the North during a succession of early triumphs over the Danes, Russians, Saxons, and Poles, which ended in disaster for him during a second invasion of Russia (1707–8). His armies were decisively defeated by Peter I (Peter the Great) at Poltava in 1709; the Nystad treaty of 1721 resulted in Sweden's loss of Vyborg (Viipuri) to Russia. Vyborg was in turn given to Finland in 1812, in whose possession it remained until ceded to the U.S.S.R. in 1940.

VAASA (VAASA)
OSTROBOTHNIAN HISTORICAL MUSEUM, *in Marianpuisto Park*
A room of the museum is given over to the Finnish war of independence, in which Vaasa played an important role. After nearly a century of Russian rule, during which Finland had a large measure of autonomy, the accession of Nicholas II as czar brought a period of repression resulting in Finland's general strike of 1905. Revolution in Russia led to a Finnish declaration of independence in 1917; that in turn led to civil war in Finland, which lasted until spring of 1918 and pitted nationalist (White) forces, reinforced by Germans, against Finnish Communists. During the struggle Vaasa became the capital of White Finland, Helsinki having been seized by the short-lived Workers' Republic. The museum collection gives prominence to Baron Mannerheim, who led nationalist troops to victory, and to Pehr Evind Svinhufvud, who headed the nationalist government during the critical period of 1917–18.

# ICELAND

**ICELAND**

### GEYSIR, *80 kilometers east of Reykjavik*

One of the world's most visited natural wonders, the hot spring called Geysir, or Great Geysir, was famous as early as the 13th century. In 1846 the German chemist Robert Wilhelm Bunsen conducted important pioneering experiments here, and the site has given the generic term "geyser" to the English language as the word for such springs. Geysir itself has been active only sporadically since about 1915, but there are some 50 active springs in the immediate vicinity, near the south foot of the Langjokull glacier.

### HEKLA, *about 112 kilometers east of Reykjavik*

Iceland's most famous volcano, Hekla, can be viewed from the air during a flight from Reykjavik that extends as far west as the western part of the glacier Vatnajokull (*see*). Or the more adventurous visitor may choose to climb to the volcano's summit (4,747 feet)—a trip requiring two days. Since the first recorded eruption in 1104, Hekla has poured forth lava more than 20 times; as recently as 1970 there was still another eruption. The eruption of 1766 resulted in widespread destruction and loss of life. The nearby lava-covered valley named Thjórsárdalur contains a village, **Stöng** (272 kilometers from Reykjavik), where a medieval farm has now been excavated. A large building of turf and stone, together with two smaller structures, is among the remains on view.

### REYKHOLT, *64 kilometers northeast of Reykjavik*

Even by Icelandic standards, Reykholt is little more than a dot on a map, but it has a solid claim to historic significance. It was the home of Snorri Sturluson (1178–1241), who not only recorded history but made history as well. Like his countryman Jón Sigurdsson in the 19th century, Snorri was both a literary and a political figure. He is credited with authorship of the *Heimskringla*, a verse chronicle of Norse mythology and history, which traces the lives of Norwegian kings from a mythological origin to near the close of the 12th century, and of the *Younger (Prose) Edda*, both a work on Norse mythology and a manual of poetry, which explains the elaborate language and the forms of ancient Scandinavian writers. He was prominent in public life as the head of Iceland's highest court and to a lesser extent, as a lawmaker. He flourished in the last years of Iceland's first republic. Though he sought, unsuccessfully, to bring his country under the rule of King Haakon IV of Norway, he incurred the enmity of that monarch, who had him assassinated in Reykholt. By 1262 Haakon had succeeded in bringing both Iceland and Greenland under Norwegian rule. There is a **Statue of Snorri** in Reykholt, and a bath frequented by him has been preserved.

### REYKJAVIK

#### ALTHING (PARLIAMENT), *in Austurvollur (square)*

Iceland's national parliament, the Althing, has met in this building since 1881. The legislative assembly itself dates from its first gathering at Thingvellir (*see*) in 930. The Althing was abolished in 1798 and re-established in 1843, and since the latter date it has met in Reykjavik. Sessions begin each year about October 1 and continue for six months. Visitors are able to view the proceedings from a gallery. Nearby, in the center of the important square named **Austurvollur**, stands a **Statue of Jón Sigurdsson**, a distinguished Icelandic man of letters who also had an important political career. An early president of the Althing, he was long active in promoting Icelandic home rule in the 19th century. The country

*Page 361. Top: Thingvellir, site of Iceland's first parliament. Left: a spring in the Geysir thermal area. Right and below: in Reykjavik, the Arnarson Memorial and Independence Day celebration in Austurvollur Square*

was ultimately governed from Copenhagen after 1380, but the constitution granted to Iceland by the Danes in 1874 made provision for home rule. Sigurdsson, who had a major role in the securing of the constitution, died five years after it was proclaimed. Iceland became a sovereign state in union with Denmark in 1918; complete separation from Denmark was effected through a referendum of 1944, when the present republic came into being.

### ARNARSON MEMORIAL, *overlooking the harbor*
The statue here, executed by one of the country's leading sculptors and painters, Einar Jónsson, honors Ingólfur Arnarson, who is credited with establishing the first permanent settlement in Iceland in 874. When Arnarson and his party from western Norway landed on the site of modern Reykjavik, the country was largely uninhabited. Irish religious hermits who had set foot on Icelandic soil not long before the Norwegians' arrival soon left the country to the pagan newcomers.

### SKALHOLT, *64 kilometers east of Reykjavik*
Especially important in Iceland's religious history, this locality became the site of a Catholic bishopric in 1056. Some 50 years earlier Christianity had been introduced in the country, and there has been a church in Skalholt for more than 900 years. (The present structure is the 11th in the series.) In the mid-16th century Lutheranism was introduced forcibly in Iceland: the arrival of the Reformation meant abolition of the religious see. Jón Arason, the last Catholic bishop in the country, resisted the official proscription of his church, and he was executed at Skalholt in 1550. The place of his beheading is marked by a plaque.

### THINGVELLIR, *40 kilometers northeast of Reykjavik*
This site on Lake Thingvallavatn, now a national park, is one of the country's most visited localities, and understandably so. The ancient republic of Iceland was established here in 930, the year in which the national legislature, the Althing (*see also Reykjavik*), a pioneer among democratic parliaments, first assembled. At the outset the Althing had both legislative and judicial functions. In addition to transacting affairs of state, its meetings provided an early forum for narrative poets and thus served as an important stimulus to the rise of Icelandic literature. The republic went out of existence midway in the 13th century, when Iceland and Greenland came under Norwegian control. But the Althing persisted. Its meeting place was Thingvellir until 1798; by that time, under Danish rule, the assembly had gradually lost its basic legislative function and ceased to exist for 45 years. When the modern independent republic was set up, it was proclaimed at Thingvellir on June 17, 1944. Even the site's spectacular scenic attractions have historical associations. The plain is surrounded by mountains including extinct volcanoes, and it is covered with solidified lava—a reminder of the devastating volcanic eruptions of the period 1793–95.

### VATNAJOKULL, *southeastern Iceland*
This huge area of ice is now often viewed by visitors during the course of airplane excursions from Reykjavik. Vatnajokull is Europe's largest glacier, 3,200 square miles in area, 90 miles long (measured from east to west), and 60 miles wide at its broadest point. The average elevation is about 2,000 feet; in the south it contains Iceland's highest peak, 6,952-foot **Hvannadalshnjukur**.

**NORWAY**

## BERGEN AND VICINITY (HORDALAND)

**BERGENHUS,** *on the north side of the harbor entrance*

Bergen was the principal residence of medieval Norwegian kings, and the fortress named Bergenhus was at the center of the city's early history. Some 30 years after Bergen's founding, in 1070, there was a castle on this site; about 1200 it was made into a fort. In the 13th century King Haakon IV built a sumptuously decorated hall, **Håkonshall** (Haakon's Hall), within its boundaries, and today the hall remains one of the principal attractions of Norway. Restored in the 19th century, this hub of the former royal residence was badly damaged in 1944 by the explosion of a German ship loaded with munitions. Now it has been restored anew, together with nearby **Rosenkrantz Tower,** which was constructed about 1565 on the site of a stone structure from the time of Haakon IV.

**HANSENLISKE MUSEET (HANSEATIC MUSEUM),** *in Finnegården on the quay Bryggen*

Especially in earlier years, Bergen was largely a trading center, and until the middle of the 16th century commerce was dominated by the old Hanseatic League, a German mercantile alliance, which had a major foreign establishment here. This museum, located in the old, formerly walled, quarter of the city, comprises several buildings on the quay and adjacent to nearby Mariakirken (*see*), itself identified with Hanseatic days. The museum seeks to re-create the milieu of a 15th-century trader: his office, wareroom, living quarters, and facilities for his employees. This immediate area contains many old wooden commercial buildings, some still in use, that date from early in the 18th century but are closely modeled on medieval structures that first stood on the site.

**LYSEKLOSTER,** *35 kilometers south*

Directly down the coast from Bergen are the ruins of a Cistercian monastery dating from 1146, when it was established by members of an abbey in England. Opposite the monastic grounds is **Lysøya,** site of the villa of the composer and violin virtuoso Ole Bull (1810–80), whose later years were spent in the United States.

**MARIAKIRKEN (MARIA, or SAINT MARY'S, CHURCH),** *just east of Bergenhus near the waterfront*

This early-12th-century structure is particularly associated with the period, from the 13th to 16th century, when German merchants and the Hanseatic League dominated the city's trade. The baroque pulpit was a contribution of Hanseatic merchants.

**TROLDHAUGEN,** *8 kilometers south*

Norway's most eminent composer, Edvard Grieg, who was born in Bergen in 1843, built this estate just outside the city in 1885. It has been maintained much as he left it; on the grounds is the studio where he worked. Grieg's ashes and those of his wife were sealed in urns placed in rocks overlooking the lake on the property. During the regularly held festivals in Bergen, Troldhaugen has been visited by thousands of music lovers. Just beyond it are **Fantoft Stave Church,** a well-preserved legacy of the late years of the Viking period, and **Fana Church,** another medieval structure.

*Top left: Borgund stave church near Laerdal. Right: the Oslo Town Hall, overlooking the harbor. Center: changing of the guard at the Royal Palace in Oslo. Below: the Hanseatic Wharf, Bryggen, in Bergen*

**NORWAY**

## EIDSVOLL VICINITY (AKERSHUS)
EIDSVOLD VERK, *5 kilometers from the railroad station on Road 50*
The main building of this 18th-century manor, now a national monument, was the scene of a national assembly in April, 1814, at which a Norwegian constitution was drafted. On May 17 of that year it was proclaimed. The occasion followed on the heels of the Treaty of Kiel, which ended the successful Swedish invasion of Denmark. By its terms Denmark ceded Norway to Sweden; Norway became a separate kingdom but was united to the Swedish crown. The new constitution was part of an unsuccessful attempt to establish an independent Norwegian kingdom. When the Norwegians persisted in their attempt, the Swedes under Crown Prince Charles John invaded Norway and quickly defeated his new subjects. But the treaty that followed (1815) recognized Norway as "a free, independent, and indivisible kingdom," governed by its own constitutional laws though "united with Sweden under one king." In the Middle Ages a regional Norwegian legislative assembly met at Eidsvoll. Even earlier, from the first century, it was the meeting place of the Eidsivalag, an ancient Norse confederacy.

## FREDRIKSTAD (OSTFOLD)
KONGSTEN, *just beyond the outer ramparts of the old town*
This fort, dating from 1630, was the key to the defense of Fredrikstad, located about 80 kilometers south of Oslo and founded in 1567 by Frederick II as a fortress town in the period (1563–70) when he was at war with Sweden. Within the ramparts of the old town, on the left bank of the Glomma River, are other surviving early structures. The road to nearby Halden takes the visitor through an area of grave mounds and carved rocks dating from prehistoric times. Jewels and ancient iron implements have been uncovered in the Fredrikstad vicinity in recent years.

## GRIMSTAD (AUST-AGDER)
IBSENMUSEET (IBSEN MUSEUM), *in the Østergate*
A museum in a building dating from 1750 and a house in the Storgaten where he lived are two remaining memorials to Norway's foremost literary figure, Henrik Ibsen, in this town on the Skagerrak, 42 kilometers up the coast from Kristiansand. During his Grimstad years, 1844–50, the youthful Ibsen was a chemist's assistant. Here he wrote his first play, the unsuccessful tragedy *Catilina.* Grimstad is recognizable in the later drama *Pillars of Society.*

## HALDEN (OSTFOLD)
FREDRIKSSTEN, *via Idd Road through Charles XII Park*
The fortress here overlooks a town, 97 kilometers east-southeast of Oslo, that withstood several Swedish invasion attempts. In the period 1716–18, Charles XII of Sweden besieged Halden (called Frederikshald until 1927) three times. The last attempt (1718) resulted in his death from cannon shot. A **monument** in the now-demilitarized fortress marks the place where he died. During World War II Halden was a center of resistance to the Nazi occupation.

## HAUGESUND VICINITY (ROGALAND)
AVALDSNES, *about 6 kilometers southeast*
King Olaf I (Olaf Tryggvesson) lived in the village of Avaldsnes in 998. An existing link with the Middle Ages is the **church** here, dating from about 1250, beside which is a large stone bearing a runic inscription.

366

HARALDSHAUGEN, *about 2 kilometers north on Route 14*
Of the relics of ancient and medieval times in the vicinity, the most impressive is the supposed burial ground of King Harold I here, near what was a royal residence. In 1872 a monument some 60 feet in height was dedicated at this site, to mark the thousandth anniversary of Harold's victory at Hafrs Fjord (*see Stavanger, Ullanhaug*). From that naval battle of 872 emerged a united Norway as Harold established his dominance over regional rulers. The monument's design symbolizes the unifying effect of the historic battle. Nearby are runic stones and at **Gard** a stone cross believed to date from the start of the Christian era in Norway.

KONGSBERG (BUSKERUD), *64 kilometers southwest of Oslo on Route E-76*
In 1623 deposits of silver were discovered in Kongsberg. Tourists can tour the old mines and visit the **Royal Norwegian Mint** situated here. A mining museum and a large and attractive church dating from 1741 are other leading attractions.

KRISTIANSAND AND VICINITY (VEST-AGDER)
CHRISTIANSHOLM, *in the southeast quarter*
This old fortress is one of the surviving features of one of Norway's southernmost cities, situated on an inlet of the Skagerrak. Kristiansand was founded (and named) by King Christian IV in 1641. Fires have destroyed many of the early landmarks, including the original cathedral, but the **Folk Museum** has preserved some of the sights of the area and the valley known as Setesdal (*see*). In the vicinity are a church, **Saint Olav's**, probably from the 11th century; **Gimle Castle,** to the north of the church and dating from about 1800; and **Kongsgård,** formerly a manor for royal officials and the clergy dating from 1637.

LAERDAL VICINITY (SOGN OG FJORDANE)
BORGUND STAVE CHURCH, *southeast on Route 52*
This medieval stave church is one of the best-preserved examples of a unique style of architecture that once flourished in Norway. Built of wood, the *stavkirke* retained elements—upturned dragonhead terminals of gables and elaborate wood carvings of the ancient sagas—of the pagan temples they replaced. The village of Borgund is situated down a steep zigzag road from the resort town of Laerdal, which is set amid towering mountains at the head of Sogne Fjord.

NARVIK (NORDLAND), *177 kilometers northeast of Bodo on Route E-6*
This important port and rail terminal was the scene of some of the fiercest fighting when Hitler's forces invaded Norway. Action on land and sea resulted in the fall of Narvik on April 9, 1940. On May 28 of that year a French and British expeditionary force joined remnants of the Norwegian army in retaking Narvik for a short time. On June 9 it returned to the invaders' hands at a heavy cost to them in naval forces. The city has since been largely rebuilt. Its cemetery contains the graves of many Allied dead. Nearby at **Lapphaugen** a monument honors the commander of the Norwegian forces in the Narvik sector, General Fleischer, in the 1940 action.

OSCARSBORG (AKERSHUS)
FORTRESS, *on Kaholmen Isle, north end of Oslo Fjord narrows*
Approaching Oslo by ship, the traveler will note this bastion, 29 kilometers south of the capital, whose guns sank the German cruiser *Blücher* during the Nazi invasion in April, 1940.

## OSLO (OSLO COUNTY)
### AKER CHURCH, *Akersbakken*
The oldest structure in Oslo, this church probably dates from the reign of Olaf II (Saint Olav), 1016–28, with additional existing parts from the reign of Olaf Kyrre, 1066–93. The church suffered greatly during the wars with Sweden and was finally restored about the middle of the 19th century.

### AKERSHUS, *on the harbor between Bjørvika and Pipervika*
Facing the modern town hall, but at another pole historically, is the medieval fortress named Akershus, built by King Haakon V about 1300. It was a royal residence for some 60 years, until 1380; more than 200 years later it was enlarged and restored by Christian IV. During the Nazi occupation it was the scene of the execution of Norwegian patriots—and eventually the place where Vidkun Quisling, the Nazi collaborator, was shot in 1945.

### CATHEDRAL, *at Stortorget, intersection of the Karl Johans Gate and the Kongensgate*
The original building arose between 1694 and 1699. Much of the impressive décor dates from the second restoration, of 1950.

### HISTORICAL MUSEUM, *Fredriksgate 2*
The University of Oslo's collection of antiquities is rich in Viking discoveries, including objects found near the craft now housed in Oslo's Vikingskiphuset (*see*).

### HOLMENKOLLBAKKEN (HOLMENKOLLEN HILL), *Holmenkollen Station*
This slope has been the scene of internationally famous skiing competitions since 1892; the hill also offers a splendid view of Oslo, its environs, and Oslo Fjord. It is the locale of a museum, established in 1925, that traces the history of skiing from the discovery of the oldest Norwegian skis, found in a marsh and dating from about 2,500 years ago. Also in the museum is equipment used by the noted Norwegian explorers Fridtjof Nansen, who pioneered the Greenland ice fields as early as 1888, and Roald Amundsen, discoverer of the South Pole (1911) and later explorer of the North Pole, in which vicinity he disappeared in 1928.

### NATIONAL THEATER, *off the Karl Johans Gate*
The theater has been in operation since 1899. Appropriately, the statuary around its entrance gives prominence to Henrik Ibsen, whose dramas have contributed immensely to its repertory. Ibsen was director of a predecessor of this theater, the Norwegian Theater of Oslo, from 1857 to 1862.

### NORWEGIAN FOLK MUSEUM, *Bygdoy Peninsula, on Oslo Fjord*
The varied collection here includes the reconstructed study of the dramatist Henrik Ibsen, examples of Norwegian arts and crafts and of ecclesiastical art, and a typical Scandinavian open-air display of more than a hundred old timber houses, each transported from an original site and carefully reassembled. These buildings in some cases have been arranged in a way that reproduces the layout of typical old towns; collectively they trace the development of Norwegian rural architecture and interiors from the Middle Ages to the more recent past. A famous 12th-century stave (wooden) church from Gol is one of the particular treasures.

RÅDHUS (TOWN HALL), *overlooking the harbor just south of the National Theater*

This modern city hall, comprising two large towers of red brick, was inaugurated in 1950 during the celebration of the 900th anniversary of Oslo's founding. Twenty years in the making, the structure represents the work of many of the country's best-known modern sculptors, painters, and tapestry weavers, whose subject matter is taken from Norway's long history.

ROYAL PALACE, *at the west end of the Karl Johans Gate*

Charles XIV (Karl Johan), king of Sweden and Norway 1818–44, originated construction of the building, which was finished in 1848. The royal family resides in the palace, but the park in which it is located is open to the public.

STORTING, *off the Karl Johans Gate, just east of the National Theater*

The home of Norway's parliament, which is open to the public during the legislative sessions (September through mid-June), was constructed in 1866. A new wing was built in 1956.

VIKINGSKIPHUSET (HALL OF VIKING SHIPS), *Bygdoy Peninsula, on Oslo Fjord*

Three Viking craft dating from about 800 are housed inland in a museum on Bygdoy, approximately 3 kilometers southwest of central Oslo (but within the city proper). They were found, in well-preserved condition, in a rural area near Fredrikstad (1867), in Gokstad (1880), and in Oseberg (1903–4). The three localities are in southeastern Norway. The largest ship, from Gokstad, is about 77 feet long and was intended for seagoing voyages. The Oseberg craft was the tomb of a queen, intended for her trip to Valhalla in the company of a servant, horses, dogs, and household utensils and furnishings, all richly ornamented. Near the ferry station on the shore of Bygdoy is the **Framhuset,** containing the *Fram,* the historic polar ship first employed in the North Pole expedition of 1893–96 by Fridtjof Nansen and Otto Neumann Sverdrup, and then used by Roald Amundsen in his pioneer exploration of the South Pole, 1910–12. Close by is a new building housing the *Kon-Tiki,* the balsawood raft (a replica of a prehistoric Inca craft) on which Thor Heyerdahl and his scientific party crossed the Pacific Ocean, from Peru to Polynesia, in 1947. Bygdoy's panorama of Norwegian navigation includes, in addition, the collection of the **Norwegian Maritime Museum.**

RJUKAN (TELEMARK)

VEMORK PLANT OF NORSK HYDRO, *in the Månedal*

Now principally known for its skiing facilities, Rjukan (on Route 37) is also the site of a hydroelectric plant that figured prominently in the underground movement of World War II. At that time the occupying German forces used it to produce heavy water in the race to perfect atomic weapons. In February, 1943, Norwegian paratroopers made a daring attack on Vemork, which was put out of commission by subsequent bombardment from the air.

SETESDAL VALLEY (AUST-AGDER), *on Route 12 extending northward from Byglandsfjord*

Long isolated from the surrounding areas of Norway, this valley still preserves the dress, customs, songs, dances, and architecture of earlier centuries. The lower valley's central town, **Bygland,** is

80 kilometers north of Kristiansand; **Valle,** 40 kilometers farther north, is especially noted for its charm and local color. And **Rygnestad,** about 10 kilometers north of Valle, contains the former headquarters of a notorious 16th-century outlaw, Vonde Åsmund, now preserved as a museum.

## SKIEN (TELEMARK)
### REGIONAL MUSEUM, *in Brekke Park*
Mementos of the career of Henrik Ibsen (1828–1906), Skien's most distinguished native son, are gathered here. The family home at 27 Snipetorget, and nearby **Venstøp Farm,** where he spent his early years, are two more centers of interest in this city 105 kilometers southwest of Oslo.

## STAVANGER AND VICINITY (ROGALAND)
### CATHEDRAL OF SAINT SWITHIN, *on the northeast shore of the Bredevann*
Apart from being one of the notable examples of medieval church architecture of northern Europe, the cathedral is the most impressive landmark of the old town, some of which dates from the ninth century and contrasts strikingly with the bustle of modern Stavanger. Construction of Saint Swithin's (or Saint Swithun's) was begun in 1130; a fire in 1272 caused subsequent alteration of the original Anglo-Norman style, for the choir was rebuilt along Gothic lines.

### KONGSGÅRD, *near the cathedral*
A 13th-century chapel here is the connecting link with the early history of the Kongsgård, originally the residence of the bishop of Stavanger. The bishop's chapel remains, but the building's main function now is to house the grammar school.

### LEDÅL, *west of the Bredevann*
The 18th-century mansion stands on the former estate of the Kielland family, where Alexander Kielland, a novelist and playwright, was born. Now public property, the residence is both a museum and the home of the royal family when its members are residing in Stavanger.

### MUSEUM, *on the Musegaten south of the Bredevann*
Among the high points of the archaeological section are early human skeletal remains and a representation of a dwelling of the Stone Age. An ethnological collection includes exhibits of Norwegian folklore, and a marine section traces the long history of Stavanger as a center of shipping and shipbuilding.

### ULLANHAUG, *just southwest of the city limits, overlooking the Hafrs Fjord*
From here the visitor can view the inlet of the North Sea where, in 872, King Harold I (the Fairhaired) won an important naval battle over the forces of Norwegian petty kings and earls. The victory climaxed the first real attempt to create a unified Norway and forced many of the defeated regional rulers to seek refuge outside the country. (*See also Haugesund, Haraldshaugen.*)

### UTSTEIN MONASTERY, *northern tip of Mosterøy Island in the fjord just north of Stavanger*
The monastery probably dates from the rule of Queen Margaret late

in the 14th century. Some 500 years earlier, according to medieval sagas, the site was a royal residence. King Harold I is said to have stayed here.

**STIKLESTAD (NORD-TRONDELAG),** *about 15 kilometers northeast of Levanger via Routes E-6 and 757*

This village was the scene of the death of Olaf II (Saint Olaf) in 1030. King of Norway from 1016 to 1028, he incurred the enmity of the country's petty rulers, who in league with Canute II, king of England and Denmark, forced Olaf II to flee to Sweden in 1028. Two years later Olaf's attempt to retake Norway from Canute, who was his successor, ended in the defeat of Olaf's forces and in his own death. A statue honors Olaf II, canonized in 1164 and still patron saint of Norway. The church here, dating from about 1200, is thought to be on the place where he fell; it was restored in 1930.

**SUNDE VICINITY (HORDALAND)**

ROSENDAL, *about 25 kilometers northeast on Route 13*

Rosendal, a hamlet situated amid the natural wonders of the coastal area bordering the Hardanger Fjord, between Haugesund and Bergen, is the site of a 17th-century baronial estate. The grounds originally were part of a medieval manor. The surviving main building, dating from 1663, contains furnishings from that period. A 12th-century **Gothic church** is nearby.

**TONSBERG (VESTFOLD)**

TUNSBERGHUS, *on the Slottsfjellet*

High on a hill are the ruins of a fortress, Tunsberghus, that enclosed a royal castle and an abbey. Located 72 kilometers south of Oslo on Route 18, Tonsberg lays claim to being the oldest city in Norway on the basis of historical mention in 871. Ancient royal burial mounds are in the vicinity; 5 kilometers northeast is **Oseberg,** site of the discovery of an ancient craft now in the Vikingskiphuset in Oslo (*see*).

**TROMSO (TROMS),** *153 kilometers northeast of Narvik on Route E-78*

This coastal town in the land of the midnight sun was the last seat of the Norwegian government during World War II (April–June, 1940) prior to its move to England. In 1944 the Royal Air Force sank the battleship *Tirpitz,* one of the Germans' principal warships, near Tromso's harbor.

**TRONDHEIM (SOR-TRONDELAG)**

NIDAROS CATHEDRAL, *in the old quarter, on the north bank of the Nid River*

The church here, one of the largest and finest in northern Europe, was built originally about 1075 on the site where King Olaf II (Saint Olaf) was buried after his death in 1030 in battle at Stiklestad (*see*). For many years it was a shrine visited by Norwegian pilgrims; it was subsequently rebuilt between the 12th and 14th centuries and restored during the last half of the 19th century. A medieval **Archbishop's Palace** still stands near the cathedral. Just southeast of them, across the Nid, is **Kristiansten,** Trondheim's 17th-century fortress.

STIFTSGÅRDEN, *on the Market Square*

This structure, dating from about 1770, is one of the largest wooden buildings in Europe. For many years it has served as the official residence for the royal family during stays in Trondheim.

# SWEDEN

**BASTAD AND VICINITY (KRISTIANSTAD)**, *13 kilometers south of Halmstad on Route E-6*

Though Bastad is now best known as a resort and sports center, its site has important historical associations. The town overlooks **Laholm Bay** of the Kattegat, and it was there that King Harold III of Norway defeated the Danes in 1062 during the course of his lengthy war with Denmark (1047–64). The town church dates from the 15th century. Just east of Bastad is another resort, **Malen**, with a burial mound from the 11th century B.C., now excavated and restored in the form of a Viking ship.

**DALBY (MALMOHUS)**, *11 kilometers southeast of Lund on Route 16*

A church originally constructed as the seat of a bishopric about 1065 and thought to be the oldest stone building in southern Sweden is still standing in this village.

**GOTEBORG or GOTHENBURG (GOTEBORG OCH BOHUS)**

DOMKYRKAN (CATHEDRAL), *Kungsgatan and Västra Hamngatan*

The history of Goteborg, on its present site, dates from 1619, and the cathedral was erected in 1633. Following a fire the cathedral was rebuilt between 1815 and 1825; it was restored during 1956 and 1957. Among the city's older surviving churches, **Kristine Kyrkan** (Christina Church), just north of the cathedral on the Norra Hamngatan, dates from 1648 and was rebuilt in the mid-18th century. It adjoins a chapel housing the remains of Marshal Rutger von Ascheberg, a major figure in the wars of King Charles XI (king 1660–97).

NYA ÄLVSBORG (NEW ALVSBORG), *at the port entrance*

Facing the sea, this imposing fortress was constructed about 1650 primarily as security against an attack from nearby Denmark. Until the 19th century Goteborg was protected by a surrounding moat, portions of which can still be seen. Nya Älvsborg is one of three remaining forts that were keys to the city's defenses. **Skansen Lejonet** (Lion Fortress), off the Kruthusgatan and northeast of Central Station, is east of the old part of the city. Southwest of that section, off the Linnegatan in Skans Parken, is **Skansen Kronan** (*see*), or Crown Fortress, also recently restored and now the site of a military museum.

RESIDENSETS (GOVERNOR'S RESIDENCE), *on the Södra Hamngatan just east of the harbor*

The residence of the governor of the county was built shortly before 1650. It was where King Charles X Gustavus died on February 13, 1660.

SKANSEN KRONAN (MILITARY MUSEUM), *off the Linnegatan in Skans Parken*

A fortress dating from the earliest years of Goteborg provides the setting for a collection of Swedish arms, uniforms, and military regalia. The city is noted for its wealth of museums. The **Sjöfartsmuseet** (Maritime Museum), in Gamla Varvsparken near the Gota River, contains ships' models from the Viking era to the present. Near it is a **Monument** commemorating the first Swedish emigration to North America (1638)—the colony of New Sweden at the present site of Wilmington, Delaware. The **Kulturhistoriska Museet** (Cultural History Museum), Norra Hamngatan and Västra Hamngatan, housed in a building constructed for the Swedish East India Com-

*Top: Drottningholm Castle and gardens just outside Stockholm. Center: the Old Town of Stockholm with Riddarholms Church at center right. Left: the 12th-century fortress at Kalmar. Right: a Lapp church in Kiruna*

pany in 1750, has valuable historical, archaeological, and ethno-graphical collections. An entire section is devoted to the history of Goteborg; another contains artifacts from the earlier settlements on the site now occupied by the city.

## GRIPSHOLM (SODERMANLAND), *48 kilometers southwest of Stockholm via Routes E-4 and 3*

The famous castle here on Lake Malar was built in the 16th century by Gustavus I (Gustavus Vasa) on the site of a 14th-century structure. It was the birthplace (1566) of Sigismund III, king of Poland and Sweden. Gustavus IV (Gustavus Adolphus) was confined here at the time of his dethronement in 1809.

## HALMSTAD (HALLAND), *about 113 kilometers southeast of Goteborg via Route E-6*

In the south part of this town on the Kattegat are a restored 14th-century **Church** and a 15th-century **Castle**. The latter, beside the Nissa River, is now the residence of the governor of this province. Halmstad, chartered in 1322, was the scene of regular meetings of Swedish and Danish leaders during the period of union between the countries. The **Norreport** (North Gate), in the north section of town, is the principal surviving remnant of the medieval defenses of Halmstad. **Halland Museum**, beyond the railroad station, houses antiquities from the region; north of the town limits, on the slopes of the Galgberget, is **Hallandsgården**, an open-air museum with a collection of rural buildings.

## HALSINGBORG AND VICINITY (MALMOHUS)

### BERNADOTTE MONUMENT, *near the Ferry Station at the harbor*

The site marks the approximate spot where Jean Baptiste Jules Bernadotte, founder of the current Swedish royal line, first set foot in Sweden in 1810. French-born, he had served in the Revolution and had risen from the ranks to become one of Napoleon's marshals. His wife, Desirée Clary, had once rejected Napoleon's marriage proposal. As Charles John he was elected crown prince of Sweden in 1810; three years later he led an allied army against Napoleon, and in 1818 he succeeded to the throne of Sweden and Norway as Charles XIV John.

### KÄRNAN (CITADEL TOWER), *off Stortorget*

Rising more than 100 feet, the tower is also the historical high point of Halsingborg, which was chartered in 1085. The Kärnan is all that remains of the 12th-century fortified castle on this site. From its summit the visitor can see Helsingor (Denmark) with its Kronborg castle, just three miles across the Oresund (sound). For years the Halsingborg fortress was coveted by both Danes and Swedes. In 1658 the city and its castle were ceded to Sweden by Denmark. In 1676 they were seized and pillaged by the Danes. Finally, in 1710, Count Magnus Gustafsson Stenbock, serving King Charles XII of Sweden, defeated the last Danish force to invade Swedish soil in a historic battle at Halsingborg. The Kärnan was rebuilt about 1400 and again in 1894.

### MARIAKYRKAN (SAINT MARY'S CHURCH), *on the Södra Storgatan*

Erected originally in the 13th century, this Gothic structure was restored in the 15th century and again in the mid-19th century. It contains a notable 15th-century German triptych and a 17th-century late Renaissance pulpit.

SOFIERO, 5 kilometers north via the Drottning Gatan
This royal summer residence, completed in 1876, is on the Oresund,
a half-hour's walk north from the suburban resort of Pålsjöbaden.
The gardens surrounding the castle are open to the public.

## JONKOPING AND VICINITY (JONKOPING)

BOTTNARYD CHURCH, 20 kilometers west on the Goteborg road
Here is the tomb of Johan Björnsson Printz, who was governor of
New Sweden, the Swedish colony on the Delaware River and now
part of Delaware, from 1643 to 1653. Upon his return to Sweden he
was governor of Jonkoping County.

TÄNDSTICKSFABRIKEN MUSEET, on the Västra Storgatan
Although Jonkoping was chartered in 1284, it is chiefly famous because it is the center (since 1844) of the match-manufacturing industry of Sweden. The museum here devoted to the history of the
safety match occupies the former plant of the Swedish Match Trust,
Tändsticksfabriken, whose new factories are in the western part of
the city. Also on the Västra Storgatan is a bust of the company's
founder, J. E. Lundström, who invented the safety match in 1853.

## KALMAR (KALMAR)

KALMAR CASTLE, on an island near the south end of Stadsparken
This huge fortress dates from late in the 12th century, and it was
rebuilt in the 16th century by Gustavus I (Gustavus Vasa). As the
structure known as the "key of Sweden," it withstood more than
20 sieges during the recurrent Danish-Swedish wars throughout
the 14th and 15th centuries. It contains a hall where the Kalmar
Union—under which the crowns of Sweden, Denmark, and Norway
were joined, with Eric of Pomerania nominally as sole ruler—is
thought to have been ratified in 1397. A shaky arrangement from the
outset, the union managed to preserve "eternal and unbroken
peace" for little more than a half century, after which Denmark and
Sweden renewed hostilities. The castle later served as a distillery,
granary, and prison. Since 1880 it has contained an important historical museum.

KIRUNA (NORRBOTTEN), 265 kilometers northwest of Lulea via Routes 97
and 98
Norrbotten includes areas of Swedish Lapland that offer much of interest to visitors in northern Sweden. Kiruna, a major iron-mining
center near the Norwegian border, has a 13th-century Lapp church
containing symbolic works of sculpture.

LANDSKRONA (MALMOHUS), 31 kilometers northwest of Malmo on Route
E-6
The remains of a citadel begun by King Christian III in the 16th
century include the moat and well-preserved ramparts. This historic town on the Oresund was chartered in 1413, burned by the
Hanseatic League in 1428, and overrun by warring Danish and
Swedish forces during the 16th and 17th centuries. It was the site
of a Swedish naval victory over the Danes in 1677. The novelist and
poet Selma Lagerlöf taught at a girls' school here from 1885 to 1895,
while writing her noted novel Gösta Berling.

## LIDKOPING VICINITY (SKARABORG)

LÄCKÖ CASTLE, 24 kilometers north on peninsula in Lake Vaner
This large granite structure, now a national monument, was built

late in the 13th century as a stronghold for the bishops of Skara. It belonged to the noble family of de la Gardie in the 17th century, when it was given its present form.

## LINKOPING (OSTERGOTLAND)

### DOMKYRKAN (CATHEDRAL), *on the Domkyrkogatan*

This large church was begun about 1120 but was not completed until late in the 15th century. Adjoining it on the west is a 13th-century castle, originally built as the bishop's palace and now used, after restoration, as the residence of the governor of the district.

### STORATORGET, *via the Storgatan*

The city's principal square, Storatorget, was the site of an event that is one of Linkoping's chief claims to historical importance. Here, in 1600, a number of the remaining followers of King Sigismund III (Sigismund Vasa) were beheaded in an execution commonly known as the Linkoping Massacre. Two years earlier, at Linkoping, Sigismund, king of Poland and Sweden, had been defeated in battle by Swedish Protestant forces when he attempted to reintroduce Roman Catholicism into Sweden. The victors were led by the duke of Södermanland, uncle of Sigismund and his successor (as Charles IX) on the Swedish throne. Though he never relinquished his claim to the crown, Sigismund was forced to retire to Poland permanently after the engagement here in 1598.

## LULEA (NORRBOTTEN)

### NORRBOTTENS LÄNS MUSEET, *south side of Hermelins Park*

The collection devoted to Lapp history and culture is the most extensive in all Sweden. It includes many examples of the primitive people's huts, tents, and reindeer sledges, together with Lapp clothing, utensils, and handicraft items.

## LUND (MALMOHUS)

### DOMKYRKAN (CATHEDRAL), *on the Kyrkogatan*

This is the principal surviving reminder of Lund's ecclesiastical eminence in the Middle Ages, when the city had, in addition to the cathedral, more than twenty churches and seven monasteries. From the start of the 12th century Lund was the seat of an archbishop; with the coming of the Reformation its position as a religious capital—and its importance in other respects—declined sharply. The cathedral was begun about 1080, and parts of the first structure survive in the present church, which was completed about 1160 and restored in the mid-19th century. One of the most striking possessions of this Romanesque church is an astronomical clock recording the positions of the heavenly bodies. The large crypt under the choir contains tombs and memorials dating from 1200. The remains of some of Scandinavia's leading medieval clerics are in the cathedral.

### HISTORICAL MUSEUM, *just east of the Domkyrkan*

Because Lund suffered heavily in the wars between Sweden and Denmark, much of its history must be sought here on the grounds of Lund University, founded in 1668. Besides an art collection, the Historical Museum contains remains from the earliest known times of the district, including Viking relics. Originally Danish, Lund probably dates from the reign of Canute the Great (1018–35), and it was the medieval capital of Denmark. Like Halsingborg (*see*), it was the object of both Danish and Swedish designs. In 1452 Lund was burned by Charles VIII of Sweden; from 1658 it was the permanent possession of the Swedes, but it was largely destroyed in 1676 when Charles XI defeated the Danes. Just north of the Historical Museum is the **Cultural History Museum**, housed in a collection of buildings including representative structures transported from throughout southern Sweden.

SANKT PETRI KLOSTER KYRKAN, *just southwest of the central railroad station*
> This 14th-century church is the sole remaining structure of a Benedictine monastery first erected here in the 12th century.

TEGNÉRHUSET, *on the Stora Gråbrödersgatan, just behind the Domkyrkan*
> From 1812 to 1824 Esaias Tegnér, one of Sweden's leading poets, was a professor of Greek at Lund University. The building in which he resided during that period is now a museum to his memory. His cycle *Frithjofs Saga* was written during the Lund years.

## MALMO (MALMOHUS)

MALMOHUS, *north side of Kungsparken*
> Originally a moated fortress and now a municipal museum, Malmohus is one of the principal links of this modern city to its past, which goes back to the 12th century. Both as fort and museum, the castle is a key to Malmo's history, which parallels that of neighboring Halsingborg and Lund. Malmohus was begun in 1434 by Eric of Pomerania, successively king of Norway, Denmark, and Sweden until a series of uprisings drove him into exile and a life devoted to piracy. The structure was destroyed in 1534 and rebuilt by Christian III of Denmark between 1537 and 1542. With the exception of two short periods in the 14th century, Malmo was a Danish possession until 1658 and long an object of rivalry between Denmark and Sweden. In 1524 Gustavus I (Gustavus Vasa) of Sweden and Frederick I of Denmark made peace in Malmo, but it was not a lasting one. Sweden finally gained the city in 1658 and retained it 20 years later despite a Danish siege. For many years Malmohus was a prison, and its most famous inmate was the earl of Bothwell, third husband of Mary, queen of Scots; he was held here from 1567 to 1573, after his forced departure from Scotland in the former year. (Bothwell was subsequently moved to Dragsholm Castle in Zealand, where he died an insane prisoner in 1578.) The castle was restored about 1870. Since 1937 it has been a city museum with important historical (military and maritime) and art collections.

RÅDHUSET (CITY HALL), *on the south side of Stortorget (square)*
> Erected in 1546, this structure has been rebuilt several times. Of particular interest is one of its chambers, Knutssalen (Saint Canute Hall), meeting place of the medieval merchants' Guild of Saint Canute, founded in the mid-14th century. A neighboring governmental building, the **Residenset** (Governor's Residence), on the north side of the same square, dates from the 18th century. Charles XV, king of Sweden and Norway, died here in 1872. The Residenset was the scene of a meeting of the kings of Sweden, Norway, and Denmark in 1914, at the outset of World War I.

SANKT PETRI KYRKAN (SAINT PETER'S CHURCH), *intersection of the Östergatan and the Kalendegatan*
> The large Gothic structure, one of the oldest surviving in southern Sweden, was completed in 1319. It has since been restored.

ULFELD HUSET (ULFELD HOUSE), *Adelgatan 4*

Among the remaining old private residences, this one, now converted into an inn, is noteworthy. It dates from 1519. Nearby are the **Flensburg Huset,** on the Södergatan, built for a 16th-century merchant, and **Jörgen Kocks Huset,** on the Suellsgatan, named for a 16th-century mayor of the city.

MARBACKA (VARMLAND), *48 kilometers northwest of Karlstad on east shore of Lake Fryk*

Selma Lagerlöf, the first woman to win the Nobel prize for literature (1909), was born in this village and died here in 1940; and here most of her novels and stories were written. Her manor house is now a museum; she is buried at nearby Östra Ämtervik Church.

MARSTRAND (GOTEBORG OCH BOHUS), *29 kilometers northwest of Goteborg via Route E-6*

This town, on a small island of the same name in Skagerrak, was founded by Norwegians about 1225. It became Swedish territory midway in the 17th century, and in 1689 arose **Karlsten Fortress,** originally a bastion and later a prison. Now it is an imposing ruin sharing the interest of tourists with a nearby church dating from the 14th century, when Marstrand was a trade center.

NYKOPING (SODERMANLAND)

NYKÖPINGSHUS, *via the Slottsgatan*

The fortress named for this city was built early in the 13th century. In the 18th century the northeast part was restored as the residence of the governor of the district. Other portions now house a museum. Before he became King Charles IX of Sweden, the duke of Sodermanland made his home here, and he died here in 1611. His grandson, Charles X Gustavus, was born at this site in 1622.

OLAND ISLAND (KALMAR)

BORGHOLM CASTLE, *.8 kilometer southwest of Borgholm*

On the outskirts of Borgholm, capital city of Oland, Sweden's second largest island, stand the ruins of a castle first recorded in 13th-century history, rebuilt in the 16th century, and largely destroyed by fire in 1806. About a kilometer southwest is **Solliden,** one of Sweden's royal summer residences, with gardens open to the public.

GRÅBORG FORTRESS, *30 kilometers northwest of Farjestaden*

This is the most imposing of the ancient strongholds on the island of Oland, which date from about the fifth century. The sole remains are stone walls rising almost 25 feet.

RONNEBY (BLEKINGE), *19 kilometers west of Karlskrona on Route 15*

The principal point of interest is the medieval church, almost as old as the town itself, which was founded in the 13th century. Originally the church was fortified, and some traces of the fortifications remain, together with evidence of the fierce combat that took place in the area during the period 1563–70, when King Eric XIV fought a long war with the Danes.

SKOKLOSTER (UPPSALA), *16 kilometers south of Uppsala on northeast arm of Lake Malar*

The castle completed in 1679 for Field Marshal Karl Gustav Wrangel, Swedish hero of the Thirty Years' War (1618–48), contains

*Skokloster Castle contains a valuable library, art, and arms collection.*

his famous collection of arms. Nearby is a restored 13th-century convent church.

## STOCKHOLM AND VICINITY (STOCKHOLM)

DROTTNINGHOLM, *on the island of Lovo in Lake Malar*
The chief summer residence of the Swedish royal family is one of the showplaces of all Scandinavia, complete with an 18th-century court theater built for Gustavus III, himself a poet and playwright. This beautiful French Renaissance palace, completed about 1700, replaced an earlier one here dating from 1581.

HAGA, *in Haga Park just beyond the city limits, via the Norrtullsgatan*
This summer pavilion was constructed for King Gustavus III (1771–92). Nearby, via the main road along the park, is Stockholm's principal cemetery, **Norra Kyrkgården,** containing the grave of Sweden's foremost playwright, August Strindberg.

KUNGLIGA OPERAN (ROYAL OPERA HOUSE), *on the east side of Gustav Adolfs Torg (square)*
The present building was completed in 1898. Its predecessor was the scene of the assassination of King Gustavus III during a midnight masked ball in 1792, when he was shot in the back by an army officer serving an aristocratic conspiracy. This event provides the basis of Verdi's opera, *A Masked Ball.*

KUNGLIGA SLOTTET (ROYAL PALACE), *on the north end of Staden Island via the Norrbro*
This huge landmark, completed in 1754, replaced a medieval royal palace that burned in 1697. Though the palace is the home of the royal family, the inner courtyard is always open to the public, as

are many other parts. Among the high points are a chapel, a museum, and the Rikssalen (Throne Room), used by the king at the opening of each Parliament and on other major occasions. King Gustavus (or Gustaf) VI (1950–73) was born here in 1882; his successor, Carl XVI Gustaf, was invested here in 1973.

### RIDDARHOLMS KYRKAN, *on Riddarholm Island near the canal bridge from Staden in the Old Town*

Transformed from a 13th-century Franciscan church, this is now the burial place of Sweden's monarchs from King Gustavus II Adolphus (1611–32) to the present era.

### RIDDARHUSET (HOUSE OF THE NOBILITY), *on Riddarhustorget, northwest corner of Staden*

Dating from the 17th century, this palace was the former meeting place of Swedish nobles, whose coats of arms still decorate the hall where they gathered before the reorganization of the Swedish parliament. Throughout much of the 18th century Sweden was torn by political intrigue, and royal power was low. Early in his reign, Gustavus III, who reasserted the position of the throne, proclaimed a new constitution here in 1772, after surrounding the Riddarhuset and subduing the nobility by force of arms.

### STATENS HISTORISKA MUSEET (NATIONAL HISTORICAL MUSEUM), *at the Storgatan and the Styrmansgatan*

Among Stockholm's many museums, this one is notable for its prehistoric and medieval collections. Located on the Djurgårdsvägen are **Nordiska Museet** (Northern Museum), which traces Swedish civilization from the 15th century and also contains the Royal Armory, and **Skansen,** a typical Scandinavian open-air collection of regional and rural structures transported from original sites. The last-named has a Lapp encampment with turf huts, storehouses, and accessory buildings. Nearby, on Djurgården, is the 17th-century man-of-war *Vasa*, which sank in Stockholm harbor in 1628 and was raised, in remarkably good condition, in 1961.

### STORKYRKAN (CATHEDRAL), *just southeast of Kungliga Slottet*

Known also as the Great Church and Church of Saint Nicholas, this has been the scene of many Swedish coronations from the 14th century to modern times. It was built about 1260 and was rebuilt in the 16th century and again in the 18th century.

### STORTORGET, *just south of the Storkyrkan*

The original marketplace of Stockholm was the site of the massacre of more than 100 Swedish noblemen, churchmen, and merchants, instigated by Christian II, in 1520. As king of Denmark and Norway he had conquered Sweden in that year and was crowned king of Sweden in Stockholm. The executions were designed to strengthen his control of his new possession; they led to the uprising of the Swedes under Gustavus I (Gustavus Vasa), who drove Christian II out of Sweden and succeeded him on the Swedish throne in 1523.

### STRANGNAS (SODERMANLAND), *56 kilometers west of Stockholm via Route E-3*

The town's principal attractions are its 13th-century **Cathedral,** near the harbor on Lake Malar, and just east of it the **Roggeborgen,** or former episcopal palace, where Gustavus I Vasa was elected king of Sweden in 1523.

## UPPSALA AND VICINITY (UPPSALA)

### DOMKYRKAN (CATHEDRAL), *via the Borjegatan*

This largest cathedral in Sweden was begun late in the 13th century. Formerly a coronation site, it is the burial place of Gustavus I Vasa (king 1523–60) and one of his sons and successors as king, John III. It is situated beside the lovely River Fyris (see page 383), which mirrors its tall spires.

### GAMLA UPPSALA, *3½ kilometers north on Route E-4*

Gamla Uppsala (Old Uppsala) is the site of the original settlement here. In the ninth-century pagan era it was the Swedish capital. Of interest now are stone monuments and burial mounds dating from as early as the fourth century.

### GUSTAVIANUM, *just west of the Domkyrkan*

Originally a medieval ecclesiastical structure, this was remodeled in the 17th century to house Uppsala University, the oldest in Sweden, dating from 1477. The Gustavianum, now a museum, is just east of the present main university building. The university library, nearby, contains a priceless collection, including the Codex Argenteus (Silver Bible).

## VADSTENA (OSTERGOTLAND), *40 kilometers west of Linkoping via Routes 36 and 50*

In the northeast quarter of this town is the abbey begun in 1368 by Saint Bridget (or Birgitta), a Roman Catholic nun and mystic and the patroness of Sweden. Its focal point is the **Klosterkyrkan** (Abbey Church), completed in 1430. Adjoining nuns' and monks' cloisters also stand. Near the town harbor used by Gota Canal traffic is a moated castle constructed by King Gustavus I (Gustavus Vasa) in 1545.

## VARBERG (HALLAND), *64 kilometers south of Goteborg via Route E-6*

Now a resort town, Varberg was the scene of much action during the wars between Sweden and Denmark, extending from the 15th to the 17th century. On a cliff overlooking the Kattegat is **Varberg Fortress**, containing remains of a castle begun by Danes in the 13th century. It has long since ceased to have a military function, but it houses an important museum of antiquities. Of special interest is a remarkably well preserved suit of 14th-century male clothing belonging to a corpse discovered in a nearby peat bog. It is said to be the only example of full male attire from the Middle Ages still surviving. On Stora Torget, the main square of Varberg, is **Gamleby Church,** an 18th-century structure.

## VISBY (GOTLAND)

### DOMKYRKAN (CATHEDRAL OF SAINT MARY), *on the Norra Kyrkogatan*

Of more than a dozen medieval churches within Visby, the cathedral is the only one still in actual use. It was founded in 1225, and there were additions up to the 18th century. Among church ruins are those of **Saint Katarina,** on the south side of Stora Torget; **Helgeandskyrkan** (Church of the Holy Ghost), on the Norra Kyrkogatan; and **Saint Nikolai,** originally part of a Dominican monastery, off the Nikolaigatan. All date from the 13th century, as do two of the most frequently visited churches just outside the city: **Barlingbro,** 13 kilometers southeast, and **Bro,** 11 kilometers northwest on the Tingestäde road.

**GOTLANDS FORNSAL (GOTLAND MUSEUM),** *on the Strandgatan*
Life on Gotland, the large island in the Baltic of which Visby is the capital, is traced from the Stone Age in the collections here. Visby originally was a pagan religious center. From the 11th to the 13th century it was a thriving commercial center, at first an independent republic and then a key part of the Hanseatic League. Among its great contributions was an international code of maritime law. Medieval Visby was almost completely enclosed by a wall, the present portions of which date from the 13th century. The wall's fortified towers are still visible. The Danes conquered Visby in 1361–62; until 1645, when Gotland became permanently Swedish, the city was largely under Danish control. From 1439 to 1449 Eric VII of Pomerania, having been driven from the thrones of Denmark, Sweden, and Norway, lived the life of a pirate with headquarters in Visby, where he built **Visborg Castle** in the southern part of the city. The museum contains a representation of this fortress, once one of Scandinavia's most powerful. Many remaining merchants' houses testify to the city's former importance as a commercial center.

## YSTAD (MALMOHUS)

**RÅDHUSET (TOWN HALL),** *on Stortorget*
Although the building itself dates from the 19th century, it rises over cellars in use from early in the 15th century. The timbered houses and narrow, serpentine streets of this Baltic seaport contribute much to its old-world atmosphere. Among other noteworthy secular buildings are the **Grammar School** and **Kemnerska Gården** (said to have been occupied by Charles XII of Sweden), both from the 16th century and reached via the Stora Västergaten; and the 15th-century home of Axel Brahe, a Danish nobleman, on the Stora Norregatan

**SANKT MARIA KYRKAN (CHURCH OF SAINT MARY),** *on Stortorget behind the Rådhuset*
One of the oldest surviving churches in Sweden, Saint Mary's has portions from about 1200. Additions were made in several succeeding centuries.

**SANKT PETRI KYRKAN,** *on the Klostergatan*
This 13th-century church stands amid the remains of the Franciscan monastery around which Ystad grew. In the immediate vicinity are the **Jens Jakobsen House** and the **Burgomaster's Residence.** All but the church now serve as a museum devoted to historic Ystad and its prehistoric site.

*The Uppsala cathedral and its reflection in the Fyris River*

# ACKNOWLEDGMENTS AND PICTURE CREDITS

*The editors wish to express their deep gratitude to the personnel of various European government tourist offices, consulates, international airlines, and steamship companies, and to the many other individuals whose generous help provided text information and pictorial material. Unless otherwise indicated, the picture credits are listed below in the order that the illustrations are described in the captions.*

1 Swedish National Tourist Office. 2–3 TWA. 4 Italian Government Tourist Office. 9 All: Greek National Tourist Office. 15 Greek National Tourist Office. 22 Greek National Tourist Office. 27 Top and center: Italian Government Travel Office. Alitalia Airlines. Pan American World Airways, Inc. Italian Government Travel Office. 34 Both: Italian Government Travel Office. 42 Both: Alitalia Airlines. 47 Alitalia Airlines. 52 Sara Krizmanich. Alitalia Airlines. 56 Italian Cultural Institute. Italian Government Travel Office. 60–61 Italian Government Travel Office. Alitalia Airlines. Italian Government Travel Office. Pan American World Airways, Inc. 65 Italian Cultural Institute. 75 Both: Italian Government Travel Office. 80 All: Italian Government Travel Office. 82 All: Italian Government Travel Office. 84 All: Malta Government Tourist Board. 88 Heyward Associates, Inc. TAP. Right and below: Heyward Associates, Inc. 96–97 TAP. Heyward Associates, Inc. TAP. 102 Rapho-Guillumette Pictures—Yan. Right top and below: Sindicat d'Iniciativa de Andorra. 103 Italian Line. Gibraltar Tourist Office. 104 Ministry of Information & Tourism of Spain, Madrid. Marshall B. Davidson. Spanish National Tourist Office, N.Y. TWA. Ministry of Information & Tourism of Spain, Madrid. 111 Both: Spanish National Tourist Office, N.Y. 116 Both: Ministry of Information & Tourism of Spain, Madrid. 123 Both: Ministry of Information & Tourism of Spain, Madrid. 126–27 Spanish National Tourist Office, N.Y. Ministry of Information & Tourism of Spain, Madrid. Spanish National Tourist Office, N.Y. Ministry of Information & Tourism of Spain, Madrid. 132 All: French Government Tourist Office. 135 French Government Tourist Office. 138 Both: French Government Tourist Office. 145 Both: French Government Tourist Office. 150 French Government Tourist Office. 157 Both: French Government Tourist Office. 163 French Government Tourist Office. Marshall B. Davidson. 170–71 All: French Government Tourist Office. 175 French Embassy Press & Information Division. French Government Tourist Office. 178 French Government Tourist Office. 182 French Embassy Press & Information Division. 184 All: Monaco Government Tourist Office. 188 Top left and right: Austrian Information Service. Center left, right, and below: Austrian National Tourist Office. 192 Both: Austrian National Tourist Office. 198–99 Austrian Information Service. All others: Austrian National Tourist Office. 202 Top left, right, and center: German National Tourist Office. German Information Center. German National Tourist Office. 206–7 All: German Information Center. 212 German National Tourist Office. 217 Both: German National Tourist Office. 222 German National Tourist Office. German Information Center. 226 All: Swiss National Tourist Office. 228 All: Swiss National Tourist Office. 235 Both: Swiss National Tourist Office. 240 Both: Swiss National Tourist Office. 245 All: Belgian Consulate General, N.Y.C. 248–49 Belgian National Tourist Office. All others: Belgian Consulate General, N.Y.C. 254 Belgian Consulate General, N.Y.C. 260 Top left, right, center left, and below left: Netherlands National Tourist Office. KLM. 265 KLM. Netherlands National Tourist Office. 273 All: Luxembourg Tourist Office. 278 All: British Tourist Authority. 283 Both: British Tourist Authority. 288 Both: British Tourist Authority. 294–95 All: British Tourist Authority. 301 British Tourist Authority. 305 Both: British Tourist Authority. 307 All: British Tourist Authority. 311 All: British Tourist Authority. 317 Both: British Tourist Authority. 321 Both: British Tourist Authority. 327 All: British Tourist Authority. 332 All: Irish Tourist Board. 344 Top left, right, center, and below left: Danish National Tourist Office, N.Y. Royal Danish Ministry for Foreign Affairs. 354 All: Finnish National Tourist Office. 358 Finnish National Tourist Office. 361 All: Icelandic Airlines. 364 All: Norwegian National Tourist Office. 372 Swedish Information Service. All others: Swedish National Tourist Office. 379 Swedish Information Service. 383 Swedish National Tourist Office.